The Aims of Argument
A Text and Reader

SIXTH EDITION

The Aims of Argument
A Text and Reader

Timothy W. Crusius
Southern Methodist University

Carolyn E. Channell
Southern Methodist University

McGraw-Hill
Higher Education

Boston   Burr Ridge, IL   Dubuque, IA   New York   San Francisco   St. Louis
Bangkok   Bogotá   Caracas   Kuala Lumpur   Lisbon   London   Madrid   Mexico City
Milan   Montreal   New Delhi   Santiago   Seoul   Singapore   Sydney   Taipei   Toronto

The **McGraw·Hill** Companies

Mc Graw Hill

McGraw-Hill
Higher Education

This book is printed on acid-free paper.

2 3 4 5 6 7 8 9 0 DOC/DOC 0 9

ISBN-13: 978-0-07-332617-7
ISBN-10: 0-07-332617-8

Vice president and Editor-in-chief: *Michael Ryan*
Publisher: *David S. Patterson*
Director of development: *Carla Kay Samodulski*
Sponsoring editor: *Christopher Bennem*
Developmental editor: *Joshua Feldman*
Marketing manager: *Allison Rauch*
Production editors: *April Wells-Hayes/Melissa Williams*
Lead production supervisor: *Randy Hurst*
Interior designer: *Maureen McCutcheon*
Cover designer: *Laurie Entringer*
Photo researcher: *Lou Ann Wilson*
Compositor: *Aptara, Inc.*
Typeface: 10.25/12 *Giovanni Book*
Printer and binder: *RR Donnelley & Sons*

Cover art © Tracy Melton

Text and photo credits appear on pages 723–726 at the back of the book and constitute an extension of the copyright page.

LIBRARY OF CONGRESS CATALOGING-IN-PUBLICATION DATA

Crusius, Timothy W.
  The aims of argument : a text and reader / Timothy W. Crusius,
Carolyn E. Channell.—6th ed.
    p. cm.
  Includes index.
  ISBN 0-07-332617-8; 928-0-07-332617-7
  1. English language—Rhetoric—Handbooks, manuals, etc. 2. Persuasion (Rhetoric)—
Handbooks, manuals, etc. 3. Report writing—Handbooks, manuals, etc. I. Channell,
Carolyn E. II. Title.

PE1431.C778 2009
808'.042—dc22   2008003452

www.mhhe.com

For W. Ross Winterowd

As its first five editions were, the sixth edition of *The Aims of Argument* is different from other argumentation texts because it remains the only one that focuses on the aims, or purposes, of argument. That this book's popularity increases from edition to edition tells us that our approach does in fact satisfy the previously unmet need that moved us to become textbook authors.

NOTES ON THIS TEXT'S ORIGINS

With more than sixty years of teaching experience between us, we had tried most argument books. Many of them were good, and we learned from them. However, we found ourselves adopting a text not so much out of genuine enthusiasm but because it had fewer liabilities. We wondered why we were so lukewarm about even the best argumentation textbooks. We boiled our dissatisfaction down to a few major criticisms:

- Most treatments were too formalistic and prescriptive.
- Most failed to integrate class discussion and individual inquiry with written argumentation.
- Apart from moving from simple concepts and assignments to more complicated ones, no book offered a learning sequence.
- Despite the fact that argument, like narrative, is clearly a mode or means of discourse, not a purpose for writing, no book offered a well-developed view of the aims or purposes of argument.

We thought that these shortcomings had undesirable consequences in the classroom, including the following:

- The overemphasis on form confused students with too much terminology, made them doubt their instincts, and drained away energy from inventing and discovering good arguments. Informal argumentation is not formal logic but open-ended and creative.

- The separation of class discussion from composing created a hiatus between oral and written argument. Students had difficulty seeing the relation between the two and using insights from each to improve the other.

- The lack of a learning sequence—of assignments that build on each other—meant that courses in argumentation were less coherent and meaningful than they could be. Students did not understand why they were doing what they were doing and could not envision what might come next.

- Finally, inattention to what people actually use argument to accomplish resulted in too narrow a view of argument and in unclear purposes for writing. Because instruction was mainly limited to what we call arguing to convince, students took argument only as monologues of advocacy. They ignored inquiry.

We set out to solve these problems. The result is a book different from any other argument text because it focuses on four aims of argument:

Arguing to inquire, questioning opinions

Arguing to convince, making cases

Arguing to persuade, appealing to the whole person

Arguing to mediate, finding common ground between conflicting positions

COMMON QUESTIONS ABOUT THE AIMS OF ARGUMENT

Instructors have certain questions about these aims, especially how they relate to one another. Here are some of the most frequently asked questions:

1. *What is the relative value of the four aims? Because mediation comes last, is it the best or most valued?* No aim is "better" than any other aim. Given needs for writing and certain audiences, one aim is more appropriate than another for the task at hand. Mediation comes last because it integrates inquiry, convincing, and persuading.

2. *Must inquiry be taught as a separate aim?* No. It *may* be taught as a separate aim, but we do not intend this "may" as a "must." Teaching inquiry as a distinct aim has certain advantages. Students need to learn how to engage in constructive dialogue, which is more disciplined and more focused than most class discussion. Once they see how it is done, students enjoy dialogue with one another and with texts. Dialogue helps students think through their arguments and imagine reader reaction to what they say, both of which are crucial to convincing and persuading. Finally, as with mediation, inquiry offers avenues for assignments other than the standard argumentative essay.

3. *Should inquiry come first?* For a number of reasons, inquiry has priority over the other aims. Most teachers are likely to approach inquiry as prewriting, preparatory to convincing or persuading. And commonly, we return to inquiry when we find something wrong with a case we are trying to construct, so the relationship between inquiry and the other aims is also recursive.

   Moreover, inquiry has psychological, moral, and practical claims to priority. When we are unfamiliar with an issue, inquiry comes first psychologically, as a felt need to explore existing opinion. Regardless of what happens in the "real world," convincing or persuading without an open, honest, and earnest search for the truth is, in our view, immoral. Finally, inquiry goes hand in hand with research, which requires questioning the opinions encountered.

4. *Isn't the difference between convincing and persuading more a matter "of degree than kind?* Sharp distinctions can be drawn between inquiry and mediation and between both of these aims and the monologues of advocacy, convincing and persuading. But convincing and persuading do shade into one another so that the difference is clearest at the extremes, with carefully chosen examples. Furthermore, the "purest" appeal to reason—a legal brief, a philosophical or scientific argument— appeals in ways beyond the sheer cogency of the case. Persuasive techniques are submerged but not absent in arguing to convince.

   Our motivation for separating convincing from persuading is not theoretical but pedagogical. Case-making is complex enough that attention to logical appeal by itself is justified. Making students conscious of the appeals to character, emotion, and style while they are learning to cope with case-making can overburden them to the point of paralysis.

   Regardless, then, of how sound the traditional distinction between convincing and persuading may be, we think it best to take up convincing first and then persuasion, especially because what students learn in the former can be carried over intact into the latter. And because one cannot make a case without unconscious appeal to character, emotional commitments (such as values), and style, teaching persuasion is a matter of exposing and developing what is already there in arguing to convince.

Here are the central tenets of an approach based on aims of argument:

- *Argumentation is a mode or means of discourse, not an aim or purpose for writing;* consequently, we need to teach the aims of argument.

- *The aims of argument are linked in a learning sequence so that convincing builds on inquiry, persuasion on convincing, and all three contribute to mediation;* consequently, we offer a learning sequence for conceiving a course or courses in argumentation.

We believe in the sequence as much as the aims. We think that many will come to prefer it over any other approach.

Of course, textbooks are used selectively, as teachers and programs need them in achieving their own goals. As with any other text, this one can be used selectively, ignoring some parts, playing up others, designing other sequences, and so on. If you want to work with our learning sequence, it's there for creative adaptation. If not, the text is flexible enough for almost any course structure or teaching method.

A NOTE ABOUT THE READINGS

Since the fourth edition, we have divided the readings into two sections: casebooks and readings chapters. The former may need some explanation. We introduced the casebook for two reasons: to allow deeper exploration of some topics and to provide enough readings to permit research assignments drawing on source material only from the textbook. Obviously, as teachers struggle more and more with plagiarism and with problems connected with skillful paraphrasing and summarizing of sources, the casebook offers significant advantages over less controlled outside research.

However, concerns regarding the book's length prompted us in this edition to reduce both the number and the length of the pieces chosen, while still retaining greater depth and the potential to evaluate more easily student use of sources.

We have avoided the "great authors, classic essays" approach (with the exception of Martin Luther King, Jr.'s "Letter from Birmingham Jail"). We tried instead to find bright, contemporary people arguing well from diverse viewpoints—articles and chapters similar to those that can be found in our better journals and trade books, the sort of publications students should read most in doing research. We have not presented any issue in simple pro-and-con fashion, as if there were only two sides.

Included in the range of perspectives are arguments made with both words and images. We include a full instructional chapter examining visual arguments such as editorial cartoons, advertisements, public sculpture, and photographs.

A FINAL WORD ABOUT THE APPROACH

Our approach is innovative. But is it better? Will students learn more? Will instructors find the book more satisfying and more helpful than what they currently use? Our experience—both in using the book ourselves and in listening to the responses of those who have read it or tested it in the classroom or used it for years—is that they will. Students complain less about having to read this book than about having to read others used in our program. They do seem to learn more. Teachers claim to find the text stimulating, something to work with rather than around. We hope your experience is as positive as ours has been. We invite your comments and will use them in the perpetual revision that constitutes the life of a text and our lives as writing teachers.

NEW TO THE SIXTH EDITION

The more important changes and additions to this edition are the following:

1. **A new chapter on plagiarism and ethical writing** To have all of the advantages of computers and online research, we have paid a price—more intentional and unintentional plagiarism because students can so easily copy and paste from their research sources. This new chapter offers a focused and comprehensive explanation of the ethical and unethical use of sources and advice on the ethics of receiving help on papers.

2. **A new appendix on fallacies and critical thinking** Instead of a list of items often called fallacies, we've defined "fallacy" as the misuse of legitimate kinds of persuasive appeal. We think our treatment leads students to distinguish sound from unsound thinking better than traditional approaches based on formal logic.

3. **Increased emphasis on visual persuasion** This edition expands our already extensive coverage of visual arguments. Chapter 4, "Reading and Writing about Visual Arguments," has been significantly revised. Just as important, we have added new visual material to all parts of the book, so that arguments made through photographs, cartoons, graphics, and so on are integrated throughout.

4. **A new casebook: "The Consumer Society"** Like it or not, we are a consumer society, and we define ourselves in part by what we buy—hence the importance of understanding consumerism. We have taught this topic for many years and find it engaging to students and a nearly inexhaustible source of interesting paper topics.

5. **Casebook overhaul: "Romantic Relationships"** This revised casebook now focuses on essential questions of love and sexuality in modern culture.

6. **Four new reading chapters, all new selections** The new reading chapters cover global warming, twenty-something, immigration, and an updated examination of the War on Terror. Twenty-something deals with the difficult situation facing young adults today, rooted in economics but branching into other concerns, especially beliefs and values.

In addition to these major additions and changes, those familiar with the fifth edition will detect many more: for instance, several new student essays, more process coverage in the persuasion chapter, and a much-needed updating of the research chapter. We think the year's work that went into this new edition of *Aims* was worth the effort and hope you will, too.

Revised Online Learning Center

In addition to the many changes the sixth edition offers in the text itself, this edition of *Aims* is accompanied by a newly revised Online Learning Center, accessible at www.mhhe.com/crusius. The site features all the tools of Catalyst 2.0, McGraw-Hill's award-winning writing and research Web site. You will find integrated references throughout the text, pointing you to additional online coverage of the topic at hand.

Online Course Delivery and Distance Learning

In addition to the Web site, McGraw-Hill offers the following technology products for composition classes. The online content of *The Aims of Argument* is supported by WebCT, Blackboard, eCollege.com, and most other course systems. Additionally, McGraw-Hill's PageOut service is available to get you and your course up and running online in a matter of hours—at no cost! To find out more, contact your local McGraw-Hill representative or visit <http://www.pageout.net>.

PageOut

McGraw-Hill's widely used click-and-build Web site program offers a series of templates and many design options, requires no knowledge of HTML, and is intuitive and easy to use. With PageOut, anyone can produce a professionally designed course Web site in very little time.

AllWrite! 2.1

Available online or on CD-ROM, *AllWrite!* 2.1 offers more than 3,000 exercises for practice in basic grammar, usage, punctuation, context spelling, and techniques for effective writing. The popular program is richly illustrated with graphics, animations, video, and Help screens.

Teaching Composition Faculty Listserv at <www.mhhe.com/tcomp>

Moderated by Chris Anson at North Carolina State University and offered by McGraw-Hill as a service to the composition community, this listserv brings together senior members of the college composition community with newer members—junior faculty, adjuncts, and teaching assistants—in an online newsletter and accompanying discussion group to address issues of pedagogy in both theory and practice.

ACKNOWLEDGMENTS

We have learned a great deal from the comments of both teachers and students who have used this book, so please continue to share your thoughts with us.

We wish to acknowledge the work of the following reviewers who guided our work on the first, second, third, fourth, and fifth editions: Linda Bensel-Meyers, University of Tennessee, Knoxville; Elizabeth Howard Borczon, University of Kansas; Joel R. Brouwer, Montcalm Community College; Lisa Canella, DePaul University; Mary F. Chen-Johnson, Tacoma Community College; Matilda Cox, University of Maryland–College Park; Margaret Cullen, Ohio Northern University; Dr. Charles Watterson Davis, Kansas State University;

Amy Cashulette Flagg, Colorado State University; Richard Fulkerson, Texas A&M University–Commerce; Lynee Lewis Gaillet, Georgia State University; Cynthia Haynes, University of Texas at Dallas; Matthew Hearn, Valdosta State University; Peggy B. Jolly, University of Alabama at Birmingham; James L. Kastely, University of Houston; William Keith, Oregon State University; Lisa J. McClure, Southern Illinois University, Carbondale; Rolf Norgaard, University of Colorado at Boulder; Julie Robinson, Colorado State University; Gardner Rogers, University of Illinois, Urbana-Champaign; Judith Gold Stitzel, West Virginia University; Cara-Lynn Ungar, Portland Community College; N. Renuka Uthappa, Eastern Michigan University; and Anne Williams, Indiana University-Purdue University Indianapolis; John F. Barber, University of Texas, Dallas; Claudia Becker, Loyola University; Kathleen Bell, University of Central Florida; Richard Fantina, Florida International University; Lynne Graft, Saginaw Valley State University; Peggy Jolly, University of Alabama at Birmingham; Beth Madison, West Virginia University; Patricia Medeiros, Scottsdale Community College; Christine Miller, California State University, Sacramento; Sarah R. Morrison, Morehead State University; Angela Rhoe, University of Cincinnati; James Sodon, St. Louis Community College; Mary Torio, University of Toledo; Julie Wakeman-Linn, Montgomery College; Sandra Zapp, Paradise Valley Community College; and Tom Zimmerman, Washtenaw Community College; Jennifer Almjeld, Bowling Green State University; Richard Fantina, Florida International University; John C. Gooch, University of Texas at Dallas; Matthew Hartman, Ball State University; William Lawton, James Madison University; Cynthia Marshall, Wright State University; Sarah Quirk, Waubonsee Community College; Ana Schnellmann, Lindenwood University; Molly Sides, Rock Valley College; Effie Siegel, Montgomery College; Linda VanVickle, St. Louis Community College; Desiree Ward, University of Texas at Dallas; Joan Wedes, University of Houston–Downtown; and Sandra Zapp, Paradise Valley Community College.

April Wells-Hayes of Fairplay Publishing Service, our production editor, and Barbara Armentrout, our copyeditor, went far beyond the call of duty in helping us refine and complete the revised manuscript. Finally, Christopher Bennem and Joshua Feldman, our editors, showed their usual brilliance and lent their unflagging energy throughout the process that led to this new edition of *Aims*.

A special thanks to Marcella Stark, research librarian at SMU, for all her help with updating the research chapter.

Timothy Crusius
Carolyn Channell
Dallas, Texas

Our goal in this book is not just to show you how to construct an argument but also to make you more aware of why people argue and what purposes argument serves. Consequently, Part Two of this book introduces four specific aims that people have in mind when they argue: to inquire, to convince, to persuade, and to mediate. Part One precedes the aims of argument and focuses on understanding argumentation in general, reading and analyzing arguments, doing research, and working with such forms of visual persuasion as advertising.

The selections in Parts One and Two offer something to emulate. All writers learn from studying the strategies of other writers. The object is not to imitate what a more experienced writer does but to understand the range of strategies you can use in your own way for your own purposes.

Included are arguments made with words and images. We have examples of editorial cartoons, advertisements, and photographs.

The additional readings in Parts Three and Four serve another function. To learn argument, we have to argue; to argue, we must have something to argue about. So we have grouped essays and images around central issues of current public discussion. Part Three's two casebooks offer expanded treatment of two subjects we think you'll find especially interesting: the consumer society, and sex and relationships. We selected the essays of Part Four rather than others for two main reasons. One is that the included essays have worked better than those we tried and rejected. The other is that most of the topics of these essays deal centrally with difference, which causes people to disagree with one another in the first place.

People argue with one another because they do not see the world the same way, and they do not see the world the same way because of different backgrounds. Therefore, in dealing with how people differ, a book about argument must deal with what makes people different, with the sources of disagreement itself—including gender, race/ethnicity, class, sexual orientation, and religion. Rather than ignoring or glossing over difference, the readings in Parts Three and Four will help you better understand it.

This book concludes with two appendixes. The first is on editing, the art of polishing and refining prose, and finding common errors. The second deals with fallacies and critical thinking. Consult these references often as you work through the text's assignments.

Arguing well is difficult for anyone. We have tried to write a text no more complicated than it has to be. We welcome your comments to improve future editions. Write us at

The Rhetoric Program
Dallas Hall
Southern Methodist University
Dallas, Texas 75275

or e-mail your comments to

cchannel@mail.smu.edu

Timothy W. Crusius is professor of English at Southern Methodist University, where he teaches beginning and advanced composition. He's the author of books on discourse theory, philosophical hermeneutics, and Kenneth Burke. He resides in Dallas with his wife, Elizabeth, and their children, Micah and Rachel.

Carolyn E. Channell taught high school and community college students before coming to Southern Methodist University, where she is now a senior lecturer and specialist in first-year writing courses. She resides in Richardson, Texas, with her husband, David, and "child," a boxer named Gretel.

BRIEF CONTENTS

CONTENTS

PART ONE
RESOURCES FOR READING AND WRITING ARGUMENTS 1

CHAPTER 1
Understanding Argument 3

CHAPTER 4

Reading and Writing about Visual Arguments   61

CHAPTER 5

Writing Research-Based Arguments   93

CHAPTER 8

Making Your Case: Arguing to Convince   209

CHAPTER 9

Motivating Action: Arguing to Persuade   247

CHAPTER 17

Genetics and Enhancement: Better Than Human?   653

APPENDIXES

BOXES BY TYPE

Concept Close-Up Boxes

Best Practices Boxes

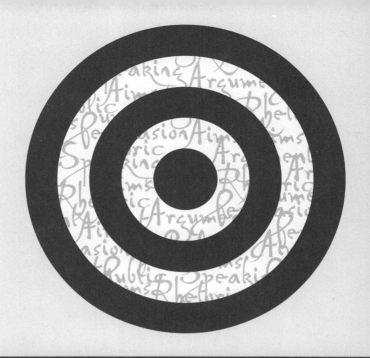

Resources for
Reading and Writing
Arguments

RESOURCES FOR READING AND WRITING ARGUMENTS

CHAPTER 1

Understanding Argument

The Aims of Argument is based on two key concepts: argument and rhetoric. These days, unfortunately, the terms *argument* and *rhetoric* have acquired bad reputations. The popular meaning of *argument* is *disagreement;* we think of raised voices, hurt feelings, winners and losers. Most people think of *rhetoric,* too, in a negative sense—as language that sounds good but evades or hides the truth. In this sense, rhetoric is the language we hear from the politician who says anything to win votes, the public relations person who puts "positive spin" on dishonest business practices, the buck-passing bureaucrat who blames the foul-up on someone else, the clever lawyer who counterfeits passion to plead for the acquittal of a guilty client.

The words *argument* and *rhetoric,* then, are commonly applied to the darker side of human acts and motives. This darker side is real—arguments are often pointless and silly, ugly and destructive; all too often, rhetoric is empty words contrived to mislead or to disguise the desire to exert power. But this book is not about that kind of argument or that kind of rhetoric. Here we develop the meanings of *argument* and *rhetoric* in an older, fuller, and far more positive sense—as the language and art of mature reasoning.

WHAT IS ARGUMENT?

In this book, **argument** means *mature reasoning*. By *mature,* we mean an attitude and approach to argument, not an age group. Some older adults are incapable of mature reasoning, whereas some young people reason very well. And all of us, regardless of age, sometimes fall short of mature reasoning. What is "mature" about the kind of argument we have in mind? One meaning of *mature* is "worked out fully by the mind" or "considered" (*American Heritage Dictionary*). Mature decisions, for example, are thoughtful ones, reached slowly after full consideration of all the consequences. And this is true also of mature reasoning.

The second term in this definition of argument also needs comment: *reasoning.* If we study logic in depth, we find many definitions of reasoning, but for practical purposes, *reasoning* here means *an opinion plus a reason (or reasons) for holding that opinion.* As we will see in detail later in this chapter, good arguments require more than this; to be convincing, reasons must be developed with evidence like specific facts and examples. However, understanding the basic form of "opinion-plus-a-reason" is the place to begin when considering your own and other people's arguments.

One way to understand argument as mature reasoning is to contrast it with *debate.* In debate, opponents take a predetermined, usually assigned, side and attempt to defend it, in much the same way that an army or a football team must hold its ground. The point is to win, to best one's opponent. In contrast, rather than starting with a position to defend, mature reasoners work toward a position. If they have an opinion to start with, mature reasoners think it through and evaluate it rather than rush to its defense. To win is not to defeat an opponent but rather to gain insight into the topic at hand. The struggle is with the problem, question, or issue we confront. Rather than seeking the favorable decision of the judges, as in debate, we are after a sound opinion in which we can believe—an opinion consistent with the facts and that other people will respect and take seriously.

Of course, having arrived at an opinion that seems sound to us, we still must *make our case*—argue in the sense of providing good reasons and adequate evidence in support of them. But whereas debaters must hold their positions at all costs, mature reasoners may not. The very process of making a case will often show us that what we thought was sound really isn't. We try to defend our opinion and find that we can't—or at least, not very well. And so we rethink our position until we arrive at one for which we *can* make a good case. From beginning to end, therefore, mature reasoning is a process of discovery.

WHAT IS RHETORIC?

Over time, the meanings of most words in most languages change—sometimes only a little, sometimes a lot. The word *rhetoric* is a good example of a big change. As indicated already, the popular meaning of *rhetoric* is empty verbiage—the art of sounding impressive while saying

Defining Mature Reasoning

Argument as mature reasoning means

- Defending *not the first position* you might take on an issue *but the best position,* determined through open-minded inquiry
- Providing reasons for holding that position that can earn the respect of an opposing audience

little—or the art of verbal deception. This meaning of *rhetoric* confers a judgment, and not a positive one.

In contrast, in ancient Greece, where rhetoric was invented about 2,500 years ago, *rhetoric* referred to the art of public speaking. The Greeks recognized that rhetoric could be abused, but, for their culture in general, it was not a negative term. They had a goddess of persuasion (see Figure 1.1), and they respected the power of the spoken word to move

Figure 1.1

Peitho, the goddess of persuasion, was often involved in seductions and love affairs. On this piece (a detail from a terra-cotta kylix, c. 410 BCE), Peitho, the figure on the left, gives advice to a dejected-looking woman, identified as Demonassa. To the right, Eros, the god of love, stands with his hand on Demonassa's shoulder, suggesting the nature of this advice.

ONCEPT

Defining Rhetoric

Rhetoric is the art of argument as mature reasoning. The study of rhetoric develops self-conscious awareness of the principles and practices of mature reasoning and effective arguing.

Bust of the great ancient Greek orator, Demosthenes (384–322 BCE). Louvre, Paris

people. It dominated their law courts, their governments, and their public ceremonies and events. As an art, the spoken word was an object of study. People enrolled in schools of rhetoric to become effective public speakers. Further, the ancient rhetoricians put a high value on good character. Not just sounding ethical but being ethical contributed to a speaker's persuasive power.

This old, highly valued meaning of rhetoric as oratory survived well into the nineteenth century. In Abraham Lincoln's day, Americans assembled by the thousands to hear speeches that went on for hours. For them, a good speech held the same level of interest as a big sporting event does for people today.

In this book, we are interested primarily in various ways of using *written* argument, but the rhetorical tradition informs our understanding of mature reasoning. Mature reasoning has nothing to do with the current definition of rhetoric as speech that merely sounds good or deceives people. The ancient meaning of *rhetoric* is more relevant, but we update it here to connect it directly with mature reasoning.

If argument is mature reasoning, then rhetoric is its *art*—that is, how we go about arguing with some degree of success. Just as there is an art of painting or sculpture, so is there an art of mature reasoning. Since the time of Aristotle, teachers of rhetoric have taught their students *self-conscious* ways of reasoning well and arguing successfully. The study of rhetoric, therefore, includes both what we have already defined as reasoning *and* ways of appealing to an audience. These include efforts to project oneself as a good and intelligent person as well as efforts to connect with the audience through humor, passion, and image.

AN EXAMPLE OF ARGUMENT

So far, we've been talking about argument in the abstract—definitions and explanations. To really understand argument, especially as we define it here, we need a concrete example. One thing mature reasoning does is to challenge unexamined belief, the stances people take out of habit without much thought. The following argument by a syndicated columnist would have us consider more carefully our notion of "free speech."

You Also Have the Right
to Tell a Bigot What You Think

LEONARD PITTS

For the record, I have no idea who let the dogs out. I didn't even know the gate was open.

We Americans get hooked on saying some pretty silly things, you know? "Where's the beef?" "Make my day."

Generally, it is pretty harmless stuff. Granted, after the fifteenth time someone avows that he feels your pain, you probably are ready to inflict some of your own. But overall, yeah—pretty harmless.

There is, however, one expression that never fails to make me nuts. Truth be told, it is less a catchphrase than a cop-out, a meaningless thing people say—usually when accusations of racism, sexism, anti-Semitism or homophobia have been leveled and they are being asked to defend the indefensible.

"Entitled to my opinion," they say. Or "entitled to his opinion," as the case 5 may be. The sense of it is the same even when the words vary: People clamber atop the First Amendment and remind us that it allows them or someone they decline to criticize to say or believe whatever they wish.

It happened again just the other day, on the eve of the Grammys. One of the entertainment news programs did an informal poll of musicians, asking them to comment on the rapper Eminem's violently homophobic and misogynistic music. You would have sworn they all were reading from the same script: "He is entitled to say what he feels," they said.

In that, they echoed the folks who thought John Rocker was unfairly maligned for his bigotry: "He is entitled to his opinion," the ballplayer's defenders told us. And that, in turn, was an echo of what happened in 1993 when a reporter asked a student at City University of New York about Dr. Leonard Jeffries' claim of a Jewish conspiracy against black people. "He had a right to say whatever he chooses to say," the student replied.

As I said, it makes me crazy—not because the observation isn't correct, but because it is beside the point.

Anybody who is a more ardent supporter of the First Amendment than I probably ought to be on medication. I believe the liberties it grants are meaningless unless extended as far as possible into the ideological hinterlands. Only in this way can you preserve and defend those liberties for the rest of us. So, as far as I am concerned, every sexist, homophobe, communist, flag burner, Jew baiter, Arab hater and racist must be protected in the peaceful expression of his or her beliefs.

But after acknowledging the right of the hateful to be hateful and the vile to 10 be vile, it seems to me that the least I can do is use my own right of free speech to call those people what they are. It seems to me, in fact, that I have a moral obligation to do so. But many people embrace moral cowardice instead and blame it on the First Amendment.

It is a specious claim. The First Amendment is violated when the government seeks to censor expression. That didn't happen to Eminem. That didn't happen to

John Rocker, either. What did happen was that the media and private citizens criticized them and demanded that some price—public condemnation or professional demotion—be extracted as a penalty for the stupid things they said.

Friends and neighbors, that isn't a violation of free speech. That *is* free speech. And if some folks confuse the issue, well, that is because too many of us believe freedom of speech means freedom from censure, the unfettered right to say whatever you please without anyone being allowed to complain. Worse, many of us accept that stricture for fear of seeming "judgmental." These days, of course, "judgmental" is a four-letter word.

I make no argument for being closed-minded. People ought to open themselves to the widest possible variety of ideas and expressions. But that doesn't mean losing your ability to discern or abdicating your responsibility to question, criticize . . . *think.* All ideas aren't created equal. To pretend otherwise is to create a rush from judgment—to free a bigot from taking responsibility for his beliefs and allow him a facade of moral validity to hide behind.

So I could happily live the rest of my life without being reminded that this fool or that has the right to say what he thinks. Sure, he does. But you know what? We all do.

Leonard Pitts, "You Also Have the Right to Tell a Bigot What You Think," *Miami Herald,* March 1, 2001, p. 1E. Copyright 2001 by McClatchy Interactive West. Reproduced with permission of McClatchy Interactive West in the format Textbook via Copyright Clearance Center.

Discussion of "You Also Have the Right . . ."

Leonard Pitts's argument is an example of a certain type or *genre* of written argument, the opinion column we find in the editorial section of newspapers. Arguments of this genre are usually brief and about some issue of general public concern, often an issue prominent in recent news stories. Most arguments written for college assignments are longer and deal with academic topics, but if we want to grasp the basics of mature reasoning, it's good to begin with the concise and readable arguments of professional columnists. Let's consider both the argument Pitts makes and his rhetoric—the art he uses to make his argument appealing to readers.

Pitts's Reasoning

In defining argument as mature reasoning, we stressed the process of arriving at an opinion as much as defending it. Arriving at an opinion is part of the aim of argument we call **inquiry,** and it's clearly very important for college writers who must deal with complex subjects and digest much information. Unfortunately, we can't see how authors arrived at their opinions by reading their finished work. As readers, we "come in" at the point where the writer states and argues for a position; we can't "go behind" it to appreciate how he or she got there. Consequently, all we can do with a published essay is discover how it works.

Let's ask the first question we must ask of any argument we're analyzing: What is Pitts's opinion, or claim? If a piece of writing is indeed an argument, we should be able to see that the author has a clear position or opinion. We can call this the **claim** of the argument. It is what the author wants the audience to believe or to do.

All statements of opinion are answers to questions, usually **implied questions** because the question itself is too obvious to need spelling out. But when we study an argument, we must be willing to be obvious and spell it out anyway to see precisely what's going on. The question behind Pitts's argument is: What should we do when we hear someone making clearly bigoted remarks? His answer: We have the right and even the moral obligation to "call those people what they are." That is his claim.

What reasons does Pitts give his readers to convince them of his claim? He tells them that the common definition of freedom of speech is mistaken. Freedom of speech does not give everyone the right to say whatever he or she wants without fear of consequences, without even the expectation of being criticized. He thinks people use this definition as an excuse not to speak up when they hear or read bigotry.

In developing his reason, Pitts explains that this common definition is beside the point because no one is suggesting that people aren't entitled to their opinions. Of course they are, even if they are uninformed and full of hatred for some person or group of people. But freedom of speech is not the right to say anything without suffering consequences; rather, as Pitts says, it's a protection against government censorship, what's known in law as *prior restraint.* In other words, if a government authority prevents you from saying or printing something, that is censorship and a violation of the First Amendment in most cases. We should not feel that someone's rights have been taken away if a high price—for instance, "public condemnation or professional demotion" (paragraph 11)—must be paid for saying stupid things. The First Amendment does not protect us from the social or economic consequences of what we say or write. "All ideas aren't created equal," as Pitts maintains. Some deserve the condemnation they receive.

Now that we understand what Pitts is arguing, we can ask another question: What makes Pitts's argument mature, an example of the kind of reasoning worth learning how to do? First, it's mature in contrast to the opinion about free speech he criticizes, which clearly does not result from a close examination of what free speech means. Second, it's mature because it assumes civic responsibility. It's not a cop-out. It argues for doing the difficult thing because it is right and good for our society. It shows mature reasoning when it says: "People ought to open themselves to the widest possible variety of ideas and expressions. But that doesn't mean losing your responsibility to question, criticize . . . *think.*" Finally, it's mature in contrast to another common response to bigotry that Pitts doesn't discuss—the view that "someone ought to shut that guy up" followed by violence or the threat of violence directed at the offending person. Such an attitude is neither different from nor better than the attitude of a playground bully, and the mature mind does not accept it.

In recognizing the maturity of Pitts's argument, we should not be overly respectful of it. Ultimately, the point of laying out an argument is to respond to it maturely ourselves, and that means asking our own questions. For instance, we might ask:

When we say, "He's entitled to his opinion," are we *always* copping out, or is such a response justified in some circumstances?

Does it do any good to call a bigot a bigot? Is it wiser sometimes to just ignore hate speech?

How big a price is too big for stating a foolish opinion? Does it matter if a bigot later retracts his opinion, admits he was wrong, and apologizes?

One of the good things about mature arguments is that we can pursue them at length and learn a lot from discussing them.

◎◎ FOLLOWING THROUGH

Select an opinion column on a topic of interest to your class from your local city or campus newspaper. Choose an argument that you think exemplifies mature reasoning. Discuss its reasoning as we have here with Pitts's essay. Can you identify the claim or statement of the author's opinion? The claim or opinion is what the author wants his or her readers to believe or to do. If you can find no exact sentence to quote, can you nevertheless agree on what it is he or she wants the readers to believe or to do? Can you find in the argument one or more reasons for doing so?   •

Other Appeals in Pitts's Argument

Finally, we ask, what makes Pitts's argument effective? That is, what makes it succeed with his readers? We have said that reasoning isn't enough when it comes to making a good argument. A writer, like a public speaker, must employ more than reason and make a conscious effort to project personality, to connect with his or her readers. Most readers seem to like Leonard Pitts because of his T-shirt-and-shorts informality and his conversational style, which includes remarks like "it makes me crazy" and sentence fragments like "But overall, yeah—pretty harmless."

We can't help forming impressions of people from reading what they write, and often these impressions correspond closely to how authors want us to perceive them anyway. Projecting good character goes all the way back to the advice of the ancient rhetoric teachers. Showing intelligence, fairness, and other signs of maturity will help you make an argument effectively.

Pitts also makes a conscious effort to appeal to his readers (that is, to gain their support) by appealing to their feelings and acknowledging their attitudes. Appreciating Pitts's efforts here requires first that we think for a moment about who these people probably are. Pitts writes for the *Miami Herald,* but his column appears in many local papers across the United States. It's safe to say that the general public are his readers. Because he is writing an argument, we assume he envisions them as not already seeing the situation as he sees it. They might be "guilty" of saying, "Everyone's entitled to an opinion." But he is not angry with them. He just wants to correct their misperception. Note that he addresses them as "friends and neighbors" in paragraph 12.

He does speak as a friend and neighbor, opening with some small talk, alluding to a popular song that made "Who let the dogs out" into a catchphrase. Humor done well is subtle, as here, and it tells the readers he knows they are as tired of this phrase as he is. Pitts is getting ready to announce his serious objection to one particular catchphrase, and he wants to project himself as a man with a life, an ordinary guy with common sense, not some neurotic member of the language police about to get worked up over nothing. Even though he shifts to a serious tone in the fourth paragraph, he doesn't completely abandon this casual and humorous personality—for example, in paragraph 9, where he jokes about his "ardent" support of the First Amendment.

But Pitts also projects a dead serious tone in making his point and in presenting his perspective as morally superior. One choice that conveys this attitude is his comment about people in the "ideological hinterlands": "every sexist, homophobe, communist, flag burner, Jew baiter, Arab hater and racist must be protected in the peaceful expression of his or her beliefs."

◎◎ FOLLOWING THROUGH

For class discussion: What else in Pitts's argument strikes you as particularly good, conscious choices? What choices convey his seriousness of purpose? Pay special attention to paragraphs 9 and 13. Why are they there? How do they show audience awareness? Which of Pitts's strategies or choices seem particularly appropriate for op-ed writing? Which might not be appropriate in an academic essay? One reason for noticing the choices professional writers make in their arguments is to learn some of their strategies, which you can use when writing your own arguments.　　　　　•

FOUR CRITERIA OF MATURE REASONING

Students often ask, "What does my professor want?" Although you will be writing many different kinds of papers in response to the assignments in this textbook, your professor will most likely look for evidence of mature reasoning. When we evaluate student work, we look for four criteria that we consider marks of mature reasoning.

Mature Reasoners Are Well Informed

Your opinions must develop from knowledge and be supported by reliable and current evidence. If the reader feels that the writer "doesn't know his or her stuff," the argument loses all weight and force.

You may have noticed that people have opinions about all sorts of things, including subjects they know little or nothing about. The general human tendency is to have the strongest opinions on matters about which we know the least. Ignorance and inflexibility go together because it's easy to form an opinion when few or none of the facts get in the way and we can just assert our prejudices. Conversely, the more we know about most topics, the harder it is to be dogmatic. We find ourselves changing or at least refining our opinions more or less continuously as we gain more knowledge.

Mature Reasoners Are Self-Critical and Open to Constructive Criticism from Others

We have opinions about all sorts of things that don't matter much to us, casual opinions we've picked up somehow and may not even bother to defend if challenged. But we also have opinions in which we are heavily invested, sometimes to the point that our whole sense of reality, right and wrong, good and bad—our very sense of ourselves—is tied up in them. These opinions we defend passionately.

On this count, popular argumentation and mature reasoning are alike. Mature reasoners are often passionate about their convictions, as committed

"I don't listen to the evidence. I like to make up my own mind."

This classic cartoon from the New Yorker *(1954) captures well the still-common attitude "don't confuse me with the facts." It also reflects gender stereotypes unquestioned in 1954 and sometimes still evident today.*

to them as the fanatic on the street corner is to his or her cause. A crucial difference, however, separates the fanatic from the mature reasoner. The fanatic is all passion; the mature reasoner is able and willing to step back and examine even deeply held convictions. "I may have believed this for as long as I can remember," the mature reasoner says, "but is this conviction really justified? Do the facts support it? When I think it through, does it really make sense? Can I make a coherent and consistent argument for it?" These are questions that don't concern the fanatic and are seldom posed in the popular argumentation we hear on talk radio.

In practical terms, being self-critical and open to well-intended criticism boils down to this: Mature reasoners can and do change their minds when they have good reasons to do so. In popular argumentation, changing one's mind can be taken as a weakness, as "wishy-washy," and so people tend to go on advocating what they believe, regardless of what anyone else says. But there's nothing wishy-washy about, for example, confronting the facts, about realizing that what we thought is not supported by the available evidence. In such a case, changing one's mind is a sign of intelligence and the very maturity mature reason values. Nor is it a weakness to recognize a good point made against one's own argument. If we don't listen and take seriously what others say, they won't listen to us.

Mature Reasoners Argue with Their Audiences or Readers in Mind

Nothing drains energy from argument more than the feeling that it will accomplish nothing. As one student put it, "Why bother? People just go on thinking what they want to." This attitude is understandable. Popular, undisciplined argument often does seem futile: minds aren't changed; no progress is made; it's doubtful that anyone learned anything. Sometimes the opposing positions only harden, and the people involved are more at odds than before.

Why does this happen so often? One reason we've already mentioned—nobody's really listening to anyone else. We tend to hear only our own voices and see only from our own points of view. But there's another reason: The people making the arguments have made no effort to reach their audience. This is the other side of the coin of not listening—when we don't take other points of view seriously, we can't make our points of view appealing to those who don't already share them.

To have a chance of working, arguments must be *other-directed*, attuned to the people they want to reach. This may seem obvious, but it's also commonly ignored and not easy to do. We have to imagine the other guy. We have to care about other points of view, not just see them as obstacles to our own. We have to present and develop our arguments in ways that won't turn off the very people for whom we're writing. In many ways, *adapting to the audience* is the biggest challenge of argument.

Four Criteria of Mature Reasoning

MATURE REASONERS ARE WELL INFORMED

Their opinions develop out of knowledge and are supported by reliable and current evidence.

MATURE REASONERS ARE SELF-CRITICAL AND OPEN TO CONSTRUCTIVE CRITICISM

They balance their passionate attachment to their opinions with willingness to evaluate and test them against differing opinions, acknowledge when good points are made against their opinions, and even, when presented with good reasons for doing so, change their minds.

MATURE REASONERS ARGUE WITH THEIR AUDIENCES OR READERS IN MIND

They make a sincere effort to understand and connect with other people and other points of view because they do not see differences of opinion as obstacles to their own points of view.

MATURE REASONERS KNOW THEIR ARGUMENTS' CONTEXTS

They recognize that what we argue about now was argued about in the past and will be argued about in the future, that our contributions to these ongoing conversations are influenced by who we are, what made us who we are, where we are, what's going on around us.

Mature Reasoners Know Their Arguments' Contexts

All arguments are part of an ongoing conversation. We think of arguments as something individuals make. We think of our opinions as *ours*, almost like private property. But arguments and opinions have pasts: Other people argued about more or less the same issues and problems before—often long before—we came on the scene. They have a present: Who's arguing what now, the current state of the argument. And they have a future: What people will be arguing about tomorrow, in different circumstances, with knowledge we don't have now.

So most arguments are not the isolated events they seem to be. Part of being well informed is knowing something about the history of an argument. By understanding an argument's past, we learn about patterns that will help us develop our own position. To some extent, we must know what's going on now and what other people are saying to make our own reasoning relevant. And although we can't know the future, we can imagine the drift of the argument, where it might be heading. In other words, there's a larger context we need to join—a big conversation of many voices to which our few belong.

WHAT ARE THE AIMS OF ARGUMENT?

The heart of this book is Part Two, the section entitled "The Aims of Argument." In conceiving this book, we worked from one basic premise: Mature reasoners do not argue just to argue; rather, they use argument to accomplish something: *to inquire* into a question, problem, or issue (commonly part of the research process); *to convince* their readers to assent to an opinion, or claim; *to persuade* readers to take action, such as buying a product or voting for a candidate; and *to mediate* conflict, as in labor disputes, divorce proceedings, and so on.

Let's look at each of these aims in more detail.

Arguing to Inquire

Arguing to **inquire** is using reasoning to determine the best position on an issue. We open the "Aims" section with inquiry because mature reasoning is not a matter of defending what we already believe but of questioning it. Arguing to inquire helps us form opinions, question opinions we already have, and reason our way through conflicts or contradictions in other people's arguments on a topic. Inquiry is open minded, and it requires that we make an effort to find out what people who disagree think and why.

The ancient Greeks called argument as inquiry **dialectic;** today we might think of it as dialogue or serious conversation. There is nothing confrontational about such conversations. We have them with friends, family, and colleagues, even with ourselves. We have these conversations in writing, too, as we make notations in the margins of the arguments we read. Listserv groups engage in inquiry about subjects of mutual interest.

Inquiry centers on questions and involves some intellectual legwork to answer them—finding the facts, doing research. This is true whether you are inquiring into what car to buy, what major to choose in college, what candidate to vote for, or what policy our government should pursue on any given issue.

Arguing to Convince

We've seen that the goal of inquiry is to reach some kind of conclusion on an issue. Let's call this conclusion a **conviction** and define it as "an earned opinion, achieved through careful thought, research, and discussion." Once we arrive at a conviction, we usually want others to share it. The aim of further argument is to secure the assent of people who do not share our conviction (or who do not share it fully).

Argument to **convince** centers on making a case, which means offering reasons and evidence in support of our opinion. Arguments to convince are all around us. In college, we find them in scholarly and professional writing. In everyday life, we find arguments to convince in editorials, courtrooms, and political speeches. Whenever we encounter an opinion supported by reasons and asking us to agree, we are dealing with argument to convince.

Arguing to Persuade

Like convincing, persuasion attempts to earn agreement, but it wants more. **Persuasion** attempts to influence not just thinking but also behavior. An advertisement for Mercedes-Benz aims to convince us not only that the company makes a high-quality car but also that we should go out and buy one. A Sunday sermon asks for more than agreement with some interpretation of a biblical passage; the minister wants the congregation to live according to its message. Persuasion asks us to do something—spend money, give money, join a demonstration, recycle, vote, enlist, acquit. Because we don't always act on our convictions, persuasion cannot rely on reasoning alone. It must appeal in broader, deeper ways.

Persuasion appeals to readers' emotions. It tells stories about individual cases of hardship that move us to pity. It often uses photographs, as when charities confront us with pictures of poverty or suffering. Persuasion uses many of the devices of poetry, such as patterns of sound, repetitions, metaphors, and similes to arouse a desired emotion in the audience.

Persuasion also relies on the personality of the writer to an even greater degree than does convincing. The persuasive writer attempts to represent something "higher" or "larger" than him- or herself—some ideal with which the reader would like to be associated. For example, a war veteran and hero like John McCain naturally brings patriotism to the table when he makes a speech.

Arguing to Mediate

By the time we find ourselves in a situation where our aim is to **mediate**, we will have already attempted to convince an opponent to settle a conflict or dispute our way. Our opponent will have done the same. Yet neither side has secured the assent of the other, and "agreeing to disagree" is not a practical solution because the participants must decide what to do.

In most instances of mediation, the parties involved try to work out the conflict themselves because they have some relationship they wish to preserve—as employer and employee, business partners, family members, neighbors, even coauthors of an argument textbook. Common differences requiring mediation include the amount of a raise or the terms of a contract. In private life, mediation helps roommates live together and families decide on everything from budgets to vacation destinations.

Just like other aims of argument, arguing to mediate requires sound logic and the clear presentation of positions and reasons. However, mediation challenges our interpersonal skills more than do the other aims. Each side

Comparing the Aims of Argument

The aims of argument have much in common. For example, besides sharing argument, they all tend to draw on sources of knowledge (research) and to deal with controversial issues. But the aims also differ from one another, mainly in terms of purpose, audience, situation, and method, as summarized here and on the inside front cover.

	Purpose	Audience	Situation	Method
Inquiry	Seeks truth	Oneself, friends, and colleagues	Informal; a dialogue	Questions
Convincing	Seeks assent to a thesis	Less intimate; wants careful reasoning	More formal; a monologue	Case-making
Persuading	Seeks action	More broadly public, less academic	Pressing need for a decision	Appeals to reason and emotions
Mediating	Seeks consensus	Polarized by differences	Need to cooperate, preserve relations	"Give-and-take"

We offer this chart as a general guide to the aims of argument. Think of it as the "big picture" you can always return to as you work your way through Part Two, which deals with each of the aims in detail.

must listen closely to understand not just the other's case but also the emotional commitments and underlying values. When mediation works, the opposing sides begin to converge. Exchanging viewpoints and information and building empathy enable all parties to make concessions, to loosen their hold on their original positions, and finally to reach consensus—or at least a resolution that all participants find satisfactory.

A GOOD TOOL FOR UNDERSTANDING AND WRITING ARGUMENTS: THE WRITER'S NOTEBOOK

Argumentation places unique demands on readers and writers. One of the most helpful tools that you can use to meet these demands is a writer's notebook.

The main function of a writer's notebook is to help you sort out what you read, learn, accomplish, and think as you go through the stages of creating a finished piece of writing. A writer's notebook contains the writing you do before you write; it's a place to sketch out ideas, assess research, order what you have to say, and determine strategies and goals for writing.

Ways to Use a Writer's Notebook

Any entry that you may want to use for future reference is appropriate to add to your writer's notebook. It's for private exploration, so don't worry about organization, spelling, or grammar. Following are some specific possibilities.

TO EXPLORE ISSUES YOU ENCOUNTER IN AND OUT OF CLASS

Bring your notebook to class each day. Use it to respond to ideas presented in class and in every reading assignment. When you're assigned a topic, write down your first impressions and opinions about it. When you're to choose your own topic, use the notebook to respond to controversial issues in the news or on campus. Your notebook then becomes a source of ideas for your essays.

TO RECORD AND ANALYZE ASSIGNMENTS

Staple your instructor's handouts to a notebook page, or write the assignment down word for word. Take notes as your instructor explains the assignment. Later, look it over more carefully, circling and checking key words, underlining due dates and other requirements. Record your questions, ask your instructor as soon as possible, and jot down the answers.

TO WORK OUT TIMETABLES FOR COMPLETING ASSIGNMENTS

To avoid procrastination, schedule. Divide the task into blocks—preparing and researching, writing a first draft, revising, editing, final typing and proofreading—and work out how many days you can devote to each. Your schedule may change, but making one and attempting to stick to it helps avoid last-minute scrambling.

TO MAKE NOTES AS YOU RESEARCH

Record ideas, questions, and preliminary conclusions that occur to you as you read, discuss your ideas with others, conduct experiments, compile surveys and questionnaires, and consult with experts. Keep your notebook handy at all times; write down ideas as soon as possible and assess their value later.

TO RESPOND TO ARGUMENTS YOU HEAR OR READ

To augment the notes you make in the margins of books, jot down extended responses in your notebook. Evaluate the strengths and weaknesses of texts,

Why Keep a Notebook?

Some projects require extensive research and consultation, which involve compiling and assessing large amounts of data and working through complex chains of reasoning. Under such conditions, even the best memory will fail without the aid of a notebook. Given life's distractions, we often forget too much and imprecisely recall what we do manage to remember. With a writ-

compare an argument with other arguments; make notes on how to use what you read to build your own arguments. Note page numbers to make it easier to use this information later.

TO WRITE A RHETORICAL PROSPECTUS

A *prospectus* details a plan for proposed work. In your notebook, explore

Your thesis: What are you claiming?

Your aim: What do you want to accomplish?

Your audience: Who should read this? Why? What are these people like?

Your persona: What is your relationship to the audience? How do you want them to perceive you?

Your subject matter: What does your thesis obligate you to discuss? What do you need to learn more about? How do you plan to get the information?

Your organizational plan: What should you talk about first? Where might that lead? What might you end with?

TO RECORD USEFUL FEEDBACK

Points in the writing process when it is useful to seek feedback from other students and the instructor include

When your *initial ideas* have taken shape, to discover how well you can explain your ideas to others and how they respond

After you and other students have *completed research* on similar topics, to share information and compare evaluations of sources

Upon completion of a *first draft,* to uncover what you need to do in a second draft to accommodate readers' needs, objections, and questions

At the end of the *revising process,* to correct surface problems such as awkward sentences, usage errors, misspellings, and typos

Prepare specific questions to ask others, and use your notebook to jot them down; leave room to sum up the comments you receive.

TO ASSESS A GRADED PAPER

Look over your instructor's comments carefully, and write down anything useful for future reference. For example, what did you do well? What might you carry over to the next assignment? Is there a pattern in the shortcomings your instructor has pointed out?

er's notebook, we can preserve the ideas that come to us as we walk across campus or stare into space over our morning coffee. Often, a writer's notebook even provides sections of writing that can be incorporated into your papers and so can help you save time.

In the chapters that follow, we refer frequently to your writer's notebook. We hope you'll use this excellent tool.

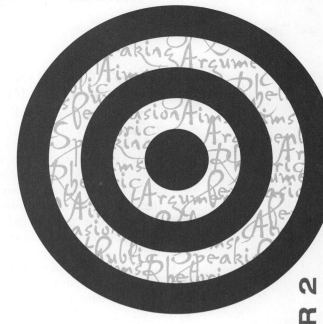

Reading an Argument

In a course in argumentation, you will read many arguments. Our book contains a wide range of argumentative essays, some by students, some by established professionals. In addition, you may find arguments on your own in books, newspapers, and magazines, or on the Internet. You'll read them to develop your understanding of argument. That means you will analyze and evaluate these texts—known as **critical reading.** Critical reading involves special skills and habits that are not essential when you read a book for information or entertainment. This chapter discusses those skills and habits.

By the time most students get to high school, reading is no longer taught. While there's plenty to read, any advice on *how to read* is usually about increasing vocabulary or reading speed, not reading critically. This is too bad, because in college you are called on to read more critically than ever.

Have patience with yourself and with the texts you work with in this book. Reading will involve going through a text more than once, no matter how careful that single reading may be. You will go back to a text several times, asking new questions with each reading. That takes time, but it's time well spent. Just as when you see a film a second time, you notice new details, so each reading increases your knowledge of a text.

Before we start, a bit of advice: Attempt critical reading only when your mind is fresh. Find a place conducive to concentration—such as a table in the library. Critical reading requires an alert, active response.

THE FIRST ENCOUNTER: SEEING THE TEXT IN CONTEXT

Critical reading begins not with a line-by-line reading but with a fast over-view of the whole text, followed by some thinking about how the text fits into a bigger picture, or *context*, which we describe shortly.

We first **sample** a text rather than read it through. Look at the headings and subdivisions. They will give a sense of how the text is organized. Note what parts look interesting and/or hard to understand. Note any information about the author provided before or after the text itself, as well as any pub-lication information (where and when the piece was originally published). Look at the opening and closing paragraphs to discern the author's main point or view.

Reading comprehension depends less on a large vocabulary than on the ability to see how the text fits into contexts. Sampling will help you consider the text in two contexts that are particularly important:

1. *The general climate of opinion* surrounding the topic of the text. This includes debate on the topic both before and since the text's publication.
2. *The rhetorical context* of the text. This includes facts about the author, the intended audience, and the setting in which the argument took place.

Considering the Climate of Opinion

Familiarity with the climate of opinion will help you view any argument critically, recognize a writer's biases and assumptions, and spot gaps or errors in the information. Your own perspective, too, will affect your interpretation of the text. So think about what you know, how you know it, what your opinion is, and what might have led to its formation. You can then interact with a text, rather than just read it passively.

◎◎ FOLLOWING THROUGH

An argument on the topic of body decoration (tattoos and piercing) appears later in this chapter. "On Teenagers and Tattoos" is about motives for decorat-ing the body. As practice in identifying the climate of opinion surrounding a topic, think about what people say about tattooing. Have you heard people argue that it is "low-class"? a rebellion against middle-class conformity? immoral? an artistic expression? a fad? an affront to school or parental author-ity? an expression of individuality? If you would not want a tattoo, why not? If you have a tattoo, why did you get it? In your writer's notebook, jot down some positions you have heard debated, and state your own viewpoint. •

Considering the Rhetorical Context

Critical readers also are aware of the **rhetorical context** of an argument. They do not see the text merely as words on a page but as a contribution to some debate among interested people. Rhetorical context includes the author, the intended audience, and the date and place of publication. The reader who knows something about the author's politics or affiliations will have an advantage over the reader who does not. Also, knowing if a periodical is liberal, like *The Nation,* or conservative, like *National Review,* helps.

An understanding of rhetorical context comes from both external and internal clues—information outside the text and information you gather as you read and reread it. You can glean information about rhetorical context from external evidence such as publishers' notes about the author or about a magazine's editorial board or sponsoring foundation. You can find this information in any issue of a periodical or by following an information link on the home page of an online publication.

You may also have prior knowledge of rhetorical context—for example, you may have heard of the author. Or you can look in a database such as *InfoTrac* (see pages 108, 109–113) to see what else the author has written. Later, when you read the argument more thoroughly, you will enlarge your understanding of rhetorical context as you discover what the text itself reveals about the author's bias, character, and purpose for writing.

In sum, the first encounter with a text is preliminary to a careful, close reading. It prepares you to get the most out of the second encounter. If you are researching a topic and looking for good sources of information and viewpoints about it, the first encounter with any text will help you decide whether you want to read it at all. A first encounter can be a time-saving last encounter if the text does not seem appropriate or credible.

◎◎ FOLLOWING THROUGH

Note the following information about "On Teenagers and Tattoos."

When published: In 1997, reprinted fall 2000.

Where published: In the *Journal of Child and Adolescent Psychiatry,* published by the American Academy of Child and Adolescent Psychiatry, then reprinted in *Reclaiming Children and Youth.*

Written by *whom:* Andres Martin, MD. Martin is an associate professor of child psychiatry at the Yale Child Study Center in New Haven, CT.

Then do a fast sampling of the text itself. In your writer's notebook, make some notes about what you expect to find in this argument. What do you think the author's perspective will be, and why? How might it differ from that of a teen, a parent, a teacher? Do the subheadings give you any idea of the main point? Do you notice at the opening or closing any repeated ideas that might give a clue to the author's claim? To whom do you imagine the author was writing, and what might be the purpose of an essay in a journal such as the one that published his argument?   •

Guidelines for Determining Rhetorical Context

To determine an argument's rhetorical context, answer the following questions:

Who wrote this argument, and what are his or her occupation, personal background, and political leanings?

To whom do you think the author is writing? Arguments are rarely aimed at "the general public" but rather at a definite target audience, such as "entertainment industry moguls," "drivers in Dallas," or "parents of teenagers."

Where does the article appear? If it is reprinted, where did it appear originally? What do you know about the publication?

When was the argument written? If not recently, what do you know about the time during which it appeared?

Why was the article written? What prompted its creation, and what purpose does the author have for writing?

AN ARGUMENT FOR CRITICAL READING

On Teenagers and Tattoos

ANDRES MARTIN

The skeleton dimensions I shall now proceed to set down are copied verbatim from my right arm, where I had them tattooed: as in my wild wanderings at that period, there was no other secure way of preserving such valuable statistics.

—Herman Melville, *Moby Dick*

Tattoos and piercing have become a part of our everyday landscape. They are ubiquitous, having entered the circles of glamour and the mainstream of fashion, and they have even become an increasingly common feature of our urban youth. Legislation in most states restricts professional tattooing to adults older than 18 years of age, so "high end" tattooing is rare in children and adolescents, but such tattoos are occasionally seen in older teenagers. Piercings, by comparison, as well as self-made or "jailhouse" type tattoos, are not at all rare among adolescents or even among school-age children. Like hairdo, makeup, or baggy jeans, tattoos and piercings can be subject to fad influence or peer pressure in an effort toward group affiliation. As with any other fashion statement, they can be construed as bodily aids in the inner struggle toward identity consolidation, serving as adjuncts to the defining and sculpting of the self by means of external manipulations. But unlike most other body decorations, tattoos and piercings are set apart by their irreversible and permanent nature, a quality at the core of their magnetic appeal to adolescents.

Adolescents and their parents are often at odds over the acquisition of bodily decorations. For the adolescent, piercing or tattoos may be seen as personal and

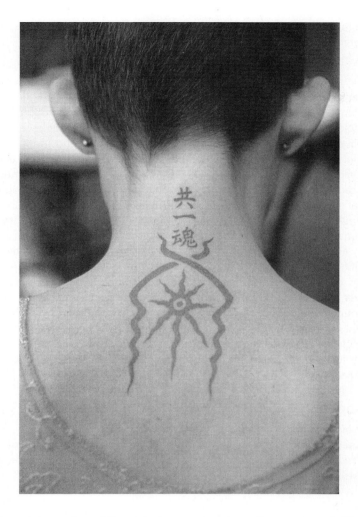

beautifying statements, while parents may construe them as oppositional and enraging affronts to their authority. Distinguishing bodily adornment from self-mutilation may indeed prove challenging, particularly when a family is in disagreement over a teenager's motivations and a clinician is summoned as the final arbiter. At such times it may be most important to realize jointly that the skin can all too readily become but another battleground for the tensions of the age, arguments having less to do with tattoos and piercings than with core issues such as separation from the family matrix. Exploring the motivations and significance [underlying] tattoos (Grumet, 1983) and piercings can go a long way toward resolving such differences and can become a novel and additional way of getting to know teenagers. An interested and nonjudgmental appreciation of teenagers' surface presentations may become a way of making contact not only in their terms but on their turfs: quite literally on the territory of their skins.

The following three sections exemplify some of the complex psychological underpinnings of youth tattooing.

IDENTITY AND THE ADOLESCENT'S BODY

Tattoos and piercing can offer a concrete and readily available solution for many of the identity crises and conflicts normative to adolescent development. In using such decorations, and by marking out their bodily territories, adolescents can support their efforts at autonomy, privacy, and insulation. Seeking individuation, tattooed adolescents can become unambiguously demarcated from others and singled out as unique. The intense and often disturbing reactions that are mobilized in viewers can help to effectively keep them at bay, becoming tantamount to the proverbial "Keep Out" sign hanging from a teenager's door.

Alternatively, feeling prey to a rapidly evolving body over which they have no 5 say, self-made and openly visible decorations may restore adolescents' sense of normalcy and control, a way of turning a passive experience into an active identity. By indelibly marking their bodies, adolescents can strive to reclaim their bearings within an environment experienced as alien, estranged, or suffocating or to lay claim over their evolving and increasingly unrecognizable bodies. In either case, the net outcome can be a resolution to unwelcome impositions: external, familial, or societal in one case; internal and hormonal in the other. In the words of a 16-year-old girl with several facial piercings, and who could have been referring to her body just as well as to the position within her family: "If I don't fit in, it is because I say so."

INCORPORATION AND OWNERSHIP

Imagery of a religious, deathly, or skeletal nature, the likenesses of fierce animals or imagined creatures, and the simple inscription of names are some of the time-tested favorite contents for tattoos. In all instances, marks become not only memorials or recipients for dearly held persons or concepts: they strive for incorporation, with images and abstract symbols gaining substance on becoming a permanent part of the individual's skin. Thickly embedded in personally meaningful representations and object relations, tattoos can become not only the ongoing memento of a relationship, but at times even the only evidence that there ever was such a bond. They can quite literally become the relationship itself. The turbulence and impulsivity of early attachments and infatuations may become grounded, effectively bridging oblivion through the visible reality to tattoos.

Case Vignette: "A," a 13-year-old boy, proudly showed me his tattooed deltoid. The coarsely depicted roll of the dice marked the day and month of his birth. Rather disappointed, he then uncovered an immaculate back, going on to draw for me the great "piece" he envisioned for it. A menacing figure held a hand of cards: two aces, two eights, and a card with two sets of dates. "A's" father had belonged to Dead Man's Hand, a motorcycle gang named after the set of cards (aces and eights) that the legendary Wild Bill Hickock had held in the 1890s when shot dead over a poker table in Deadwood, South Dakota. "A" had only the vaguest memory of and sketchiest information about his father, but he knew he had died in a motorcycle accident: The fifth card marked the dates of his birth and death.

The case vignette also serves to illustrate how tattoos are often the culmination of a long process of imagination, fantasy, and planning that can start at an early age. Limited markings, or relatively reversible ones such as piercings, can at a later time scaffold toward the more radical commitment of a permanent tattoo.

THE QUEST OF PERMANENCE

The popularity of the anchor as a tattoo motif may historically have had to do less with guild identification among sailors than with an intense longing for rootedness and stability. In a similar vein, the recent increase in the popularity and acceptance of tattoos may be understood as an antidote or counterpoint to our urban and nomadic lifestyles. Within an increasingly mobile society, in which relationships are so often transient—as attested by the frequencies of divorce, abandonment, foster placement, and repeated moves, for example—tattoos can be a readily available source of grounding. Tattoos, unlike many relationships, can promise permanence and stability. A sense of constancy can be derived from unchanging marks that can be carried along no matter what the physical, temporal, or geographical vicissitudes at hand. Tattoos stay, while all else may change.

Case Vignette: A proud father at 17, "B" had had the smiling face of his 10 4-month-old baby girl tattooed on his chest. As we talked at a tattoo convention, he proudly introduced her to me, explaining how he would "always know how beautiful she is today" when years from then he saw her semblance etched on himself.

The quest for permanence may at other times prove misleading and offer premature closure to unresolved conflicts. At a time of normative uncertainties, adolescents may maladaptively and all too readily commit to a tattoo and its indefinite presence. A wish to hold on to a current certainty may lead the adolescent to lay down in ink what is valued and cherished one day but may not necessarily be in the future. The frequency of self-made tattoos among hospitalized, incarcerated, or gang-affiliated youths suggests such motivations: A sense of stability may be a particularly dire need under temporary, turbulent, or volatile conditions. In addition, through their designs teenagers may assert a sense of bonding and allegiance to a group larger than themselves. Tattoos may attest to powerful experiences, such as adolescence itself, lived and even survived together. As with Moby Dick's protagonist, Ishmael, they may bear witness to the "valuable statistics" of one's "wild wandering(s)": those of adolescent exhilaration and excitement on the one hand; of growing pains, shared misfortune, or even incarceration on the other.

Adolescents' bodily decorations, at times radical and dramatic in their presentation, can be seen in terms of figuration rather than disfiguration, of the natural body being through them transformed into a personalized body (Brain, 1979). They can often be understood as self-constructive and adorning efforts, rather than prematurely subsumed as mutilatory and destructive acts. If we bear all of this in mind, we may not only arrive at a position to pass more reasoned clinical judgment, but become sensitized through our patients' skins to another level of their internal reality.

REFERENCES

Brain, R. (1979). *The decorated body.* New York: Harper & Row.
Grumet, G. W. (1983). Psychodynamic implications of tattoos. *American Journal of Orthopsychiatry, 53,* 482–92.

Andres Martin, "On Teenagers and Tattoos," *Journal of the American Academy of Child & Adolescent Psychiatry,* vol. 36, no. 6 (June 1997), pp. 860–861. Reprinted by permission of Lippincott Williams & Wilkins.

THE SECOND ENCOUNTER: READING AND ANALYZING THE TEXT

We turn now to suggestions for reading and analyzing. These are our own "best practices," what we do when we prepare to discuss or write about a written text. Remember, when you read critically, your purpose goes beyond merely finding out what an argument says. The critical reader is different from the target audience. As a critical reader, you are more like the food critic who dines not merely to eat but to evaluate the chef's efforts.

To see the difference, consider the different perspectives that an ant and a bird would have when looking at the same suburban lawn. The ant is down among the blades of grass, climbing one and then the next. It's a close look, but the view is limited. The bird in the sky above looks down, noticing the size and shape of the yard, the brown patches, the difference between the grass in this yard and the grass in the surrounding yards. The bird has the big picture, the ant the close-up. Critical readers move back and forth between the perspective of the ant and the perspective of the bird, each perspective enriching the other. The big picture helps one notice the patterns, even as the details offer clues to the big picture.

Because critical reading means interacting with the text, be ready with pencil or pen to mark up the text. Highlighting or underlining is not enough. Write comments in the margin.

Wrestling with Difficult Passages

Because one goal of the second encounter is to understand the argument fully, you will need to determine the meanings of unfamiliar words and difficult passages. In college reading, you may encounter new words. You may find allusions or references to other books or authors that you have not read. You may encounter metaphors and irony. The author may speak ironically or for another person. The author may assume that readers have lived through all that he or she has or share the same political viewpoint. All of this can make reading harder. Following are common features that often make reading difficult.

Unfamiliar Contexts

If the author and his or her intended audience are removed from your own experience, you will find the text difficult. Texts from a distant culture or time will include concepts familiar to the writer and original readers but not to you. This is true also of contemporary writing intended for specialists. College increases your store of specialized knowledge and introduces you to new (and old) perspectives. Accepting the challenge of difficult texts is part of college. Look up concepts you don't know. Your instructors can also help you to bridge the gap between your world and the text's.

Contrasting Voices and Views

Authors may state viewpoints that contradict their own. They may concede that part of an opposing argument is true, or they may put in an opposing view to refute it. These voices and viewpoints may come as direct quotations or paraphrases. To avoid misreading these views as the author's, be alert to words that signal contrast. The most common are *but* and *however*.

Allusions

Allusions are brief references to things outside the text—to people, works of art, songs, events in the news—anything in the culture that the author assumes he or she shares knowledge of with readers. Allusions are one way for an author to form a bond with readers—provided the readers' and authors' opinions are the same about what is alluded to. Allusions influence readers. They are persuasive devices that can provide positive associations with the author's viewpoint.

In "On Teenagers and Tattoos," the epigraph (the quotation that appears under the title of the essay) is an allusion to the classic novel *Moby Dick*. Martin alludes to the novel again in paragraph 11. He assumes that his readers know the work—not just its title but also its characters, in particular, the narrator, Ishmael. And he assumes his readers would know that the "skeleton dimensions" of a great whale were important and that readers would therefore understand the value of preserving these statistics. The allusion predisposes readers to see that there are valid reasons for permanently marking the body.

Specialized Vocabulary

If an argument is aimed at an audience of specialists, it will undoubtedly contain vocabulary peculiar to that group or profession. Martin's essay contains social science terminology: "family matrix" and "surface presentations" (paragraph 2), "individuation" (paragraph 4), "grounded" (paragraph 6), "sense of constancy" (paragraph 9), and "normative uncertainties" (paragraph 11).

The text surrounding these terms provides enough help for most lay readers to get a fair understanding. For example, the text surrounding *individuation* suggests that the person would stand out as a separate physical presence; this is not quite the same as *individuality,* which refers more to one's character. Likewise, the text around *family matrix* points to something the single word *family* does not: it emphasizes the family as the surroundings in which one develops.

If you need to look up a term and a dictionary does not seem to offer an appropriate definition, go to one of the specialized dictionaries available on the library reference shelves. (See pages 100–106 for more on these.)

If you encounter an argument with more jargon than you can handle, you may have to accept that you are not an appropriate reader for it. Some readings are aimed at people with highly specialized graduate degrees or training. Without advanced courses, no one could read these articles with full comprehension, much less critique their arguments.

◎◎ FOLLOWING THROUGH

Find other words in Martin's essay that sound specific to the field of psychology. Use the surrounding text to come up with laymen's terms for these concepts.   •

Missing Persons

A common difficulty with scientific writing is that it can sound disembodied and abstract. You won't find a lot of people doing things in it. Sentences are easiest to read when they take a "who-does-what" form. However, these can be rare in scientific writing. Many of Martin's sentences have abstract subjects and nonaction verbs like *be* and *become:*

> *An interested and nonjudgmental appreciation of teenagers' surface presentations* may become a way of making contact not only in their terms but on their turfs. . . .

In at least one other sentence, Martin goes so far in leaving people out that his sentence is grammatically incorrect. Note the dangling modifier:

> Alternatively, *feeling prey to a rapidly evolving body over which they have no say,* self-made and openly visible decorations may restore adolescents' sense of normalcy and control, a way of turning passive experience into active identity.

The italicized phrase describes adolescents, not decorations. If you have trouble reading passages like this, take comfort in the fact that the difficulty is not your fault. Recasting the idea into who-does-what can clear things up:

> Teens may feel like helpless victims of the changes taking place in their bodies. They may mark themselves with highly visible tattoos and piercings to regain a sense of control over their lives.

Passive Voice

Passive voice is another common form of the missing-person problem. In an active-voice sentence, we see our predictable who-does-what pattern:

Active voice: The rat ate the cheese.

In passive-voice sentences, the subject of the verb is not an agent; it does not act.

Passive voice: The cheese was eaten by the rat.

At least in this sentence, we know who the agent is. But scientists often leave out any mention of agents. Thus, in Martin's essay we have sentences like this one:

> Adolescents' bodily decorations . . . *can be seen* in terms of figuration rather than disfigurement. . . .

Who can see them? Martin means that *psychiatrists should see tattoos* as figuration rather than disfigurement. But that would sound too committed, not scientific. Passive-voice sentences are common in the sciences, part of an effort to sound objective.

If you learn to recognize passive voice, you can often mentally convert the troublesome passage into active voice, making it clearer. Passive voice takes this pattern:

> A helping verb in some form of the verb *to be: Is, was, were, has been, will be, will have been, could have been,* and so forth.

> Followed by a main verb, a past participle: Past participles end in *ed, en, g, k,* or *t.*

Some examples:

> The car *was being driven* by my roommate when we had the wreck.

> Infections *are spread* by bacteria.

> The refrain *is sung* three times.

◎◎ FOLLOWING THROUGH

Convert the following sentences into active voice. We have put the passive-voice verbs in bold type, but you may need to look at the surrounding text to figure out who the agents are.

> A sense of constancy **can be derived** from unchanging marks that **can be carried** along no matter what the physical, temporal, or

geographical vicissitudes at hand. (paragraph 9) To edit this one, ask *who* can derive what and *who* can carry what.

The intense and often disturbing reactions that ***are mobilized*** in viewers can help to effectively keep them at bay, becoming tantamount to the proverbial "Keep Out" sign hanging from a teenager's door. (paragraph 4) To edit, ask *what* mobilizes the reactions in other people.

Using Paraphrase to Aid Comprehension

As we all know, explaining something to someone else is the best way to make it clear to ourselves. Putting an author's ideas into your own words, **paraphrasing** them, is like explaining the author to yourself. For more on paraphrasing, see Chapter 5, pages 125–127.

Paraphrase is often longer than the original because it loosens up what is dense. In paraphrasing, try to make both the language and the syntax (word order) simpler. Paraphrase may require two sentences where there was one. It looks for plainer, more everyday language, converts passive voice to active voice, and makes the subjects concrete.

Analyzing the Reasoning of an Argument

As part of your second encounter with the text, pick out its reasoning. The reasoning is the author's case, which consists of the *claim* (what the author wants the readers to believe or do) and the *reasons* and *evidence* offered in support of it. State the case in your own words and describe what else is going on in the argument, such as the inclusion of opposing views or background information.

If a text is an argument, we can state what the author wants the readers to believe or do, and just as importantly, *why*. We should look for evidence presented to make the reasons seem believable. Note claims, reasons, and evidence in the margins as you read.

Reading Martin's Essay

Complex arguments require critical reading. Two critical-reading skills will help you: **subdividing the text** and **considering contexts.**

Finding Parts

Critical readers break texts down into parts. By *parts,* we mean groups of paragraphs that work together to perform some role in the essay. Examples of such roles are to introduce, to provide background, to give an opposing view, to conclude, and so on.

Discovering the parts of a text can be simple. Authors often make them obvious with subheadings and blank space. Even without these, transitional

Guidelines for Paraphrasing

- Use your own words, but don't strain to find a different word for every single one in the original. Some of the author's plain words are fine.

- If you take a phrase from the original, enclose it in quotation marks.

- Use a simpler sentence pattern than the original, even if it means making several short sentences. Aim for clarity.

- Check the surrounding sentences to make sure you understand the passage in context. You may want to add an idea from the context.

- Try for who-does-what sentences.

expressions and clear statements of intention make subdividing a text almost as easy as breaking a Hershey bar into its already well-defined segments. However, some arguments are more loosely constructed, their subdivisions less readily discernible. Even so, close inspection will usually reveal subdivisions and you should be able to see the roles played by the various chunks.

We have placed numbers next to every fifth paragraph in the essays reprinted in our text. Numbering makes it easier to refer to specific passages and to discuss parts.

Martin helps us see the parts of his essay by announcing early on, in paragraph 3, that it will have three sections, each "[exemplifying] some of the complex psychological underpinnings of youth tattooing." Martin's essay can thus be subdivided as follows:

1. Epigraph

2. Paragraphs 1, 2, and 3: the introduction

3. Paragraphs 4 and 5: an example

4. Paragaphs 6, 7, and 8: another example

5. Paragraphs 9, 10, and 11: a third example

6. Paragraph 12: the conclusion

Using Context

Taking the larger view again, we can use context to help pick out the reasoning. While a quick reading might suggest that Martin is arguing that teens have good reasons for decorating their bodies, we need to recall that the essay appeared in a journal for psychiatrists—doctors, not parents or teachers. Martin is writing to other psychiatrists and psychologists, clinicians who work with families. Reading carefully, we learn that his audience is an even smaller portion of this group: clinicians who have been "summoned as the final arbiter" in family disputes involving tattoos and other body decoration (paragraph 2). Because journals such as the *Journal of Child and Adolescent Psychiatry* are aimed at improving the practice of medicine, we want to note sentences that tell these readers what they ought to do and how it will make them better doctors.

Identifying the Claim and Reasons

The claim: Martin is very clear about his claim, repeating it three times, using just slightly different wording:

> His readers should "[explore] **the motivations and significance [underlying] tattoos and piercings. . . ."** (paragraph 2)

> His readers should have "[a]n **interested and nonjudgmental appreciation of teenagers' surface presentations. . . ."** (paragraph 2)

> His readers should see "[a]dolescents' **bodily decorations . . . in terms of figuration rather than disfigurement. . . ."** (paragraph 12)

Asked to identify Martin's claim, you could choose any one of these statements.

The reason: The reason is the "because" part of the argument. Why should the readers believe or do as Martin suggests? We can find the answer in paragraph 2, in the same sentences with his claim:

> Because doing so "**can go a long way toward resolving . . . differences and can become a novel and additional way of getting to know teenagers."**

> Because doing so "**may become a way of making contact not only in their terms but on their turfs. . . ."**

And the final sentence of Martin's essay offers a third version of the same reason:

> Because "**we may not only arrive at a position to pass more reasoned clinical judgment, but become sensitized through our patients' skins to another level of their internal reality."**

Again, we could choose any one of these sentences as the stated reason or paraphrase his reason. Using paraphrase, we can begin to outline the case structure of Martin's argument:

> **Claim:** Rather than dismissing tattoos as disfigurement, mental health professionals should take a serious interest in the meaning of and motivation behind the tattoos.

> **Reason:** Exploring their patients' body decorations can help them gain insight and make contact with teenagers on teenagers' own terms.

Where is Martin's evidence? Martin tells us that the three subsections will "exemplify some of the complex psychological underpinnings of youth tattooing." In each, he offers a case, or vignette, as evidence.

> **Example and evidence** (paragraphs 4 and 5): Tattoos are a way of working out identity problems when teens need either to mark

themselves off from others or to regain a sense of control of a changing body or an imposing environment. The sixteen-year-old-girl who chose not to fit in.

Example and evidence (paragraphs 6, 7, and 8): Tattoos can be an attempt to make the intangible a tangible part of one's body. The thirteen-year-old boy remembering his father.

Example and evidence (paragraphs 9, 10, and 11): Tattoos are an "antidote" to a society that is on the run. The seventeen-year-old father.

THE THIRD ENCOUNTER: RESPONDING CRITICALLY TO AN ARGUMENT

Once you feel confident that you have the argument figured out, you are ready to respond to it, which means evaluating and comparing it with other perspectives, including your own. Only by *writing words* can you respond critically. As the reading expert Mortimer Adler says in *How to Read a Book,*

> Reading, if it is active, is thinking, and thinking tends to express itself in words, spoken or written. The person who says he knows what he thinks but cannot express it in words usually does not know what he thinks. (49)

Annotation Is Key

We suggest that you annotate heavily. **Annotation** simply means making a note. Use the margins, and/or writer's notebook, for these notes of critical response. Many writers keep reading journals to practice active interaction with what they read and to preserve the experience of reading a text they want to remember.

What should you write about? Think of questions you would ask the author if he or she were in the room with you. Think of your own experience with the subject. Note similarities and contrasts with other arguments you have read or experiences of your own that confirm or contradict what the author is saying. Write about anything you notice that seems interesting, unusual, brilliant, or wrong. *Comment, question*—the more you actually write on the page, the more the text becomes your own. And you will write more confidently about a text you own than one you are just borrowing.

The list in the Best Practices box on page 37 will give you more ideas for annotations.

A concluding comment about responses: Even if you agree with an argument, think about who might oppose it and what their objections might be. Challenge the views you find most sympathetic.

Following is an example of annotation for part of Martin's argument.

Sample Annotations

How is he defining "solution"? Do tattoos solve a problem or just indicate one?

It seems like there are more mature ways to do this.

Or would it cause parents to pay attention to them rather than leave them alone?

Is he implying that the indelible mark is one they will not outgrow? What if they do?

Tattoos and piercing can offer a concrete and readily available solution for many of the identity crises and conflicts normative to adolescent development. In using such decorations, and by marking out their bodily territories, adolescents can support their efforts at autonomy, privacy, and insulation. Seeking individuation, tattooed adolescents can become unambiguously demarcated from others and singled out as unique. The intense and often disturbing reactions that are mobilized in viewers can help to effectively keep them at bay, becoming tantamount to the proverbial "Keep Out" sign hanging from a teenager's door.

Alternatively, feeling prey to a rapidly evolving body   5
over which they have no say, self-made and openly visible decorations may restore adolescents' sense of normalcy and control, a way of turning a passive experience into an active identity. By indelibly marking their bodies, adolescents can strive to reclaim their bearings within an environment experienced as alien, estranged, or suffocating or to lay claim over their evolving and increasingly unrecognizable bodies. In either case, the net outcome can be a resolution to unwelcome impositions: external, familial, or societal in one case, internal and hormonal in the other. In the words of a 16-year-old girl with several facial piercings, and who could have been referring to her body just as well as to the position within her family: "If I don't fit in, it is because I say so."

What is normal?

Would he say the same about anorexia?

Does he assume this family needs counseling—or will not need it? He says the problem is "resolved."

WRITING ASSIGNMENT: A CRITICAL RESPONSE TO A SINGLE ARGUMENT

This assignment asks you to write an essay about your critical reading of an argument. Writing about your encounters with a text will make you more conscious about your critical thinking, exposing your habits and practices. Here, write for your classmates. The goal of your paper is to

Ways to Annotate

- Paraphrase the claim and reasons next to where you find them stated.

- Consider: Does the author support his or her reasons with evidence? Is the evidence sufficient in terms of both quantity and quality?

- Circle the key terms. Note how the author defines or fails to define them.

- Ask: What does the author assume? Behind every argument, there are assumptions. For example, a baseball fan wrote to our local paper arguing that the policy of fouls after the second strike needs to be changed. His reason was that the fans would not be subjected to such a long game. The author assumed that a fast game of hits and outs is more interesting than a slow game of strategy between batters and hitters. Not every baseball fan shares that assumption.

- Note any contradictions you see, either within the text itself or with anything else you've read or learned.

- Consider the implications of the argument. If we believe or do what the author argues, what is likely to happen?

- Think of someone who would disagree with this argument, and say what that person might object to.

- If you see any opposing views in the argument, question the author's fairness in presenting them. Consider whether the author has represented opposing views fairly or has set them up to be easily knocked down.

- Ask: What is the author overlooking or leaving out?

- Consider: Where does the argument connect with anything else you have read?

- Consider: Does the argument exemplify mature reasoning as explained in Chapter 1, "Understanding Argument"?

- Ask: What aim does the argument seem to pursue? One of the four in the box on page 17, or some combination of them?

- Ask: What kind of person does the author sound like? Mark places where you hear the author's voice. Describe the tone. How does the author establish credibility—or fail to?

- Note the author's values and biases, places where the author sounds liberal or conservative, religious or materialistic, and so on.

- Note places where you see clues about the intended audience of the argument, such as appeals to their interests, values, tastes, and so on.

help your classmates better comprehend and criticize an essay you have all read.

In Part One

The project has two parts. In Part One, explain the rhetorical context, including who the author is and his or her point of view, as well as the intended audience as you infer it from clues outside and inside the text. Describe what you see as the claim and reason. Comment on the organization, referring to groups of paragraphs and the role they play in the argument. Tell about your experience of reading the essay—whether you found it easy, difficult, or confusing, and why. Be specific, and refer to actual passages.

In Part Two

In Part Two, evaluate the argument. How effective might it have been for its target audience? Focus on the text of the argument, but talk about its strengths and weaknesses. Your point is not simply to agree or disagree with the author; instead, show your understanding of the qualities of mature argumentation. In developing Part Two, use the suggestions for annotation on pages 35–37 as well as the criteria for mature reasoning on pages 11–14. Although your responses may be critical in the sense of negative, we use the term here to mean "a careful and exact evaluation and judgment" (*American Heritage Dictionary*).

Other Advice for Both Parts

- Refer to paragraphs in the text by number.
- Quote exactly and use quotation marks. Indicate in parentheses the paragraph they come from.
- Use paraphrase when talking about key ideas in the essay, and cite the paragraph in which the idea appeared.
- Use first person.
- Refer to the author by full name on first mention and by last name only after.

STUDENT SAMPLE ESSAY: CRITICAL RESPONSE TO A SINGLE ARGUMENT

Here we have reproduced another argument on the topic of tattoos and body decorations. Following it is one student's critical response to this essay, which follows the structure laid out above.

Once outlawed, the tradition of tribal tattooing has undergone a recent renewal among the Maori people of New Zealand and other Polynesian cultures. Full facial markings, or moko, *such as this Maori chief has, are the most common in New Zealand.*

Called the Tribe, these men (gathered under the Golden Gate Bridge in San Francisco) are leaders of the local Modern Primitivism movement. The Tribe has a tattoo parlor that does only tribal marking. Several of the tattoo artists have traveled to Borneo and learned the craft from tribal masters.

The Decorated Body

FRANCE BOREL

Nothing goes as deep as dress nor as far as the skin; ornaments have the dimensions of the world.

—Michel Serres, *The Five Senses*

Human nakedness, according to social custom, is unacceptable, unbearable, and dangerous. From the moment of birth, society takes charge, managing, dressing, forming, and deforming the child—sometimes even with a certain degree of violence. Aside from the most elementary caretaking concerns—the very diversity of which shows how subjective the motivation is—an unfathomably deep and universal tendency pushes families, clans, and tribes to rapidly modify a person's physical appearance.

One's genuine physical makeup, one's given anatomy, is always felt to be unacceptable. Flesh, in its raw state, seems both intolerable and threatening. In its naked state, body and skin have no possible existence. The organism is acceptable only when it is transformed, covered with signs. The body only speaks if it is dressed in artifice.

For millennia, in the four quarters of the globe, mothers have molded the shape of their newborn babies' skulls to give them silhouettes conforming to prevalent criteria of beauty. In the nineteenth century, western children were tightly swaddled to keep their limbs straight. In the so-called primitive world, children were scarred or tattooed at a very early age in rituals which were repeated at all the most important steps of their lives. At a very young age, children were fitted with belts, necklaces, or bracelets; their lips, ears, or noses were pierced or stretched.

Some cultures have designed sophisticated appliances to alter physical structure and appearance. American Indian cradleboards crushed the skull to flatten it; the Mangbetus of Africa wrapped knotted rope made of bark around the child's head to elongate it into a sugar-loaf shape, which was considered to be aesthetically pleasing. The feet of very young Chinese girls were bound and spliced, intentionally and irreversibly deforming them, because this was seen to guarantee the girls' eventual amorous and matrimonial success.[1]

Claude Lévi-Strauss said about the Caduveo of Brazil: "In order to be a man, 5 one had to be painted; whoever remained in a natural state was no different from the beasts."[2] In Polynesia, unless a girl was tattooed, she would not find a husband. An unornamented hand could not cook, nor dip into the communal food bowl. Pink lips were despicable and ugly. Anyone who refused the test of the tattoo was seen to be marginal and suspect.

Among the Tivs of Nigeria, women called attention to their legs by means of elaborate scarification and the use of pearl leg bands; the best decorated calves were known for miles around. Tribal incisions behind the ears of Chad men rendered the skin "as smooth and stretched as that of a drum." The women would laugh at any man lacking these incisions, and they would never accept him as a husband. Men would subject themselves willingly to this custom, hoping for scars deep enough to leave marks on their skulls after death.

At the beginning of the eighteenth century, Father Laurent de Lucques noted that any young girl of the Congo who was not able to bear the pain of scarification and who cried so loudly that the operation had to be stopped was considered "good for nothing."[3] That is why, before marriage, men would check to see if the pattern traced on the belly of their intended bride was beautiful and well-detailed.

The fact that such motivations and pretexts depend on aesthetic, erotic, hygienic, or even medical considerations has no influence on the result, which is always in the direction of transforming the appearance of the body. Such a transformation is wished for, whether or not it is effective.

The body is a supple, malleable, and transformable prime material, a kind of modeling clay, easily molded by social will and wish. Human skin is an ideal subject for inscription, a surface for all sorts of marks which make it possible to differentiate the human from the animal. The physical body offers itself willingly for tattooing or scarring so that, visibly and recognizably, it becomes a social entity.

The absolutely naked body is considered as brutish, reduced to the level of 10 nature where no distinction is made between man and beast. The decorated body, on the other hand, dressed (if even only in a belt), tattooed, or mutilated, publicly exhibits humanity and membership in an established group. As Theophile Gautier said, "The ideal disturbs even the roughest nature, and the taste for ornamentation distinguishes the intelligent being from the beast more exactly than anything else. Indeed, dogs have never dreamed of putting on earrings."

So, it is by their categorical refusal of nakedness that human beings are distinguished from nature. The "mark makes unremarkable"—it creates an interval between what is biologically and brutally given in the animal realm and what is won in the cultural realm. The body is tamed continuously; social custom demands, at any price—including pain, constraint, or discomfort—that wildness be abandoned.

Each civilization chooses—through a network of elective relationships which are difficult to determine—which areas of the body deserve transformation. These areas are as difficult to define and as shifting as those of eroticism or modesty. An individual alone eludes bodily modifications; they are the expression of a homogeneous collectivity which, at a chosen moment, comes to a tacit agreement to attack one or another part of the anatomy.

Whatever the choices, options, or differences may be, that which remains constant is the transformation of appearance. In spite of our contemporary western belief that the body is perfect as it is, we are constantly changing it: clothing it in musculature, suntan, or makeup; dying its head hair or pulling out its bodily hair. The seemingly most innocent gestures for taking care of the body very often hide a persistent and disguised tendency to make it adhere to the strictest of norms, reclothing it in a veil of civilization. The total nudity offered at birth does not exist in any region of the world. Man puts his stamp on man. The body is not a product of nature, but of culture.

NOTES

1. Of course, there are also many different sexual mutilations, including excisions and circumcisions, which we will not go into at this time as they constitute a whole study in themselves.
2. C. Lévi-Strauss, *Tristes Tropiques* (Paris: Plon, 1955), p. 214.
3. J. Cuvelier, *Relations sur le Congo du Père Laurent de Lucques* (Brussels: Institut royal colonial belge, 1953), p. 144.

The Decorated Body from *Le Vêtement incarné—Les Métamorphoses du corps* by France Borel, translated by Ellen Dooling Draper. © Editions Calmann-Lévy, 1992.

A SAMPLE STUDENT RESPONSE

Analysis of "The Decorated Body"
Katie Lahey

Part One

"The Decorated Body" by France Borel addresses the idea of external body manipulation not only as an issue prevalent to our own culture and time but also as a timeless concept that exists beyond cultural boundaries. It was published in *Parabola*, a magazine supported by the Society for the Study of Myth and Tradition. Borel discusses the ways in which various cultures both ancient and modern modify the natural body. Borel, who has written books on clothing and on art, writes with a style that is less a critique than an observation of his populations. This style suggests an anthropological approach rather than a psychological one, focusing on the motivations of people as a whole and less on the specific individuals within the societies. It seems, therefore, that she may be targeting an academic audience of professional anthropologists or other readers who are interested in the similarities of both "primitive" and "modern" cultures and the whole idea of what it means to be human.

Borel makes the claim that "social custom" dictates that all humans manipulate their bodies to brand themselves as humans. She says in the first paragraph that "an unfathomably deep and universal tendency pushes families, clans, and tribes to rapidly modify a person's physical appearance." She restates the idea in paragraph 2: The body "is acceptable only when it is transformed, covered with signs." She believes that in all cultures this type of branding or decorating is essential to distinguish oneself as legitimate within a civilization. Man has evolved from his original body; he has defied nature. We are no longer subject to what we are born with; rather, we create our bodies and identities as we see fit.

Borel reasons that this claim is true simply because all cultures conform to this idea and do so in such diverse ways. As she says, "the very diversity . . . shows how subjective the motivation is . . ." (paragraph 1). She provides ample evidence to support this reasoning in paragraphs 3 through 7, citing various cultures and examples of how they choose to decorate the body.

Part Two

However, Borel does not provide a solid explanation as to why the human race finds these bodily changes necessary to distinguish itself as human. It serves her argument to state that the various specific motivations behind these changes are irrelevant. All she is interested in proving is that humans must change their bodies, and she repeats this concept continually throughout the essay, first saying that a man remaining "in a natural state was no different from the beasts" in paragraph 5 and again in paragraphs 9 and 10. Maybe some readers would think this reiteration makes her point stronger, but I was unsatisfied.

I found myself trying to provide my own reasons why humans   5 have this need to change their bodies. What makes this essay so unsatisfying to me is that, once I thought about it, it does in fact matter why cultures participate in body decoration. For example, why did the Chinese find it necessary to bind the feet of their young girls, a tradition so painful and unhealthy and yet so enduring? In such traditions, it becomes obvious that ulterior motives lie beneath the surface. The binding of the feet is not simply a tradition that follows the idea of making oneself human. In fact, it methodically attempts to put women below men. By binding the feet, a culture disables the young women not only physically but emotionally as well. It teaches them that they do not deserve the same everyday comforts as men and belittles them far beyond simply having smaller feet. Borel, however, fails to discuss any of these deeper motives. She avoids supplying her own opinion because she does not want to get into the politics of the practices she describes. She wants to speak in generalizations about body modification as a mark of being human, even though people in modern Western culture might see some of these activities as violations of human rights.

Borel barely touches on modern Western civilization. She really only addresses our culture in the final paragraph, where she alleges that everyday things we do to change ourselves, whether it be shaving, tanning, toning, dying, or even applying makeup, are evidence that we have the same need to mark ourselves as human. She challenges our belief that "the body is perfect as it is" by showing that "we are constantly changing it" (paragraph 13). But many people today, especially women, *do* doubt that their individual bodies are perfect and would concede that they are constantly trying to "improve" them. What does Borel mean by "perfect as it is"? Is she talking about an ideal we would like to achieve?

Her placement of this paragraph is interesting. I wondered why she leaves this discussion of our own culture until the very end of the essay so that her ideas of European and American culture appear as an afterthought. She spends the majority of the essay discussing other, more "primitive cultures" that yield many more examples of customs, such as the American Indian cradleboards, that clearly mark one as a member of a tribe. Perhaps Borel tends to discuss primitive cultures as opposed to our modern Western culture because primitive cultures generally back up her thesis, whereas American culture, in particular, veers from her claim that people decorate themselves in order to demonstrate what they have in common.

Borel ignores any controversy over tattoos and piercing, which people in Western culture might do to mark themselves as different from other people in their culture. In America, we value individualism, where everyone tries to be unique, even if in some small way. Other authors like Andres Martin, who wrote "On Teenagers and Tattoos," look at American culture and claim that we use body decoration as a means to show and celebrate our individuality. Martin says one good reason for teens to tattoo themselves is for "individuation"—to mark themselves as distinct from their peers and their families. This goes completely opposite from Borel's claim that "[a]n individual alone eludes bodily modifications; they are the expression of a homogeneous collectivity . . ." (paragraph 12).

Borel makes a sound argument for her claim that human existence is something more complex or more unnatural than simply being alive. But we know this already through humans' use of speech, social organization, and technology. Before I read her argument and even after the first time I read it, I wasn't swayed by Borel. I was looking for something more specific than what she is saying. In fact, all she is showing is that we decorate to symbolize our humanity. She does support this claim with good evidence. In this sense, the argument holds. But I cannot help but prefer to think about the other, more specific things we symbolize through our body decorations.

CHAPTER 3

Analyzing Arguments:
A Simplified Toulmin Method

In Chapter 2, we discussed the importance of reading arguments critically: breaking them down into their parts to see how they are put together, noting in the margins key terms that are not defined, and raising questions about the writer's claims or evidence. Although these general techniques are sufficient for analyzing many arguments, sometimes—especially with intricate arguments and with arguments we sense are faulty but whose weaknesses we are unable to specify—we need a more systematic technique.

In this chapter, we explain and illustrate such a technique based on the work of Stephen Toulmin, a contemporary philosopher who has contributed a great deal to our understanding of argumentation. This method will allow you to analyze the logic of any argument; you will also find it useful in examining the logic of your own arguments as you draft and revise them. Keep in mind, however, that because it is limited to the analysis of logic, the Toulmin method is not sufficient by itself. It is also important to question an argument through dialogue (see Chapter 7) and to look at the appeals of character, emotion, and style (see Chapter 9).

A PRELIMINARY CRITICAL READING

Before we consider Toulmin, let's first explore the following argument carefully. Use the general process for critical reading we described in Chapter 2.

Rising to the Occasion of Our Death

WILLIAM F. MAY

> William F. May (b. 1927) is a distinguished professor of ethics at Southern Methodist University. The following essay appeared originally in *The Christian Century* (1990).

For many parents, a Volkswagen van is associated with putting children to sleep on a camping trip. Jack Kevorkian, a Detroit pathologist, has now linked the van with the veterinarian's meaning of "putting to sleep." Kevorkian conducted a dinner interview with Janet Elaine Adkins, a 54-year-old Alzheimer's patient, and her husband and then agreed to help her commit suicide in his VW van. Kevorkian pressed beyond the more generally accepted practice of passive euthanasia (allowing a patient to die by withholding or withdrawing treatment) to active euthanasia (killing for mercy).

Kevorkian, moreover, did not comply with the strict regulations that govern active euthanasia in, for example, the Netherlands. Holland requires that death be imminent (Adkins had beaten her son in tennis just a few days earlier); it demands a more professional review of the medical evidence and the patient's resolution than a dinner interview with a physician (who is a stranger and who does not treat patients) permits; and it calls for the final, endorsing signatures of two doctors.

So Kevorkian-bashing is easy. But the question remains: Should we develop a judicious, regulated social policy permitting voluntary euthanasia for the terminally ill? Some moralists argue that the distinction between allowing to die and killing for mercy is petty quibbling over technique. Since the patient in any event dies—whether by acts of omission or commission—the route to death doesn't really matter. The way modern procedures have made dying at the hands of the experts and their machines such a prolonged and painful business has further fueled the euthanasia movement, which asserts not simply the right to die but the right to be killed.

But other moralists believe that there is an important moral distinction between allowing to die and mercy killing. The euthanasia movement, these critics contend, wants to engineer death rather than face dying. Euthanasia would bypass dying to make one dead as quickly as possible. It aims to relieve suffering by knocking out the interval between life and death. It solves the problem of suffering by eliminating the sufferer.

The impulse behind the euthanasia movement is understandable in an age 5 when dying has become such an inhumanly endless business. But the movement may fail to appreciate our human capacity to rise to the occasion of our death. The best death is not always the sudden death. Those forewarned of death and given time to prepare for it have time to engage in acts of reconciliation. Also, advanced grieving by those about to be bereaved may ease some of their pain.

Psychiatrists have observed that those who lose a loved one accidentally have a more difficult time recovering from the loss than those who have suffered through an extended period of illness before the death. Those who have lost a close relative by accident are more likely to experience what Geoffrey Gorer has called limitless grief. The community, moreover, may need its aged and dependent, its sick and its dying, and the virtues which they sometimes evince—the virtues of humility, courage, and patience—just as much as the community needs the virtues of justice and love manifest in the agents of care.

On the whole, our social policy should allow terminal patients to die, but it should not regularize killing for mercy. Such a policy would recognize and respect that moment in illness when it no longer makes sense to bend every effort to cure or to prolong life and when one must allow patients to do their own dying. This policy seems most consonant with the obligations of the community to care and of the patient to finish his or her course.

Advocates of active euthanasia appeal to the principle of patient autonomy—as the use of the phrase "voluntary euthanasia" indicates. But emphasis on the patient's right to determine his or her destiny often harbors an extremely naïve view of the uncoerced nature of the decision. Patients who plead to be put to death hardly make unforced decisions if the terms and conditions under which they receive care already nudge them in the direction of the exit. If the elderly have stumbled around in their apartments, alone and frightened for years, or if they have spent years warehoused in geriatrics barracks, then the decision to be killed for mercy hardly reflects an uncoerced decision. The alternative may be so wretched as to push patients toward this escape. It is a huge irony and, in some cases, hypocrisy to talk suddenly about a compassionate killing when the aging and dying may have been starved for compassion for many years. To put it bluntly, a country has not earned the moral right to kill for mercy unless it has already sustained and supported life mercifully. Otherwise we kill for compassion only to reduce the demands on our compassion. This statement does not charge a given doctor or family member with impure motives. I am concerned here not with the individual case but with the cumulative impact of a social policy.

I can, to be sure, imagine rare circumstances in which I hope I would have the courage to kill for mercy—when the patient is utterly beyond human care, terminal, and in excruciating pain. A neurosurgeon once showed a group of physicians and an ethicist the picture of a Vietnam casualty who had lost all four limbs in a landmine explosion. The catastrophe had reduced the soldier to a trunk with his face transfixed in horror. On the battlefield I would hope that I would have the courage to kill the sufferer with mercy.

But hard cases do not always make good laws or wise social policies. Regularized mercy killings would too quickly relieve the community of its obligation to provide good care. Further, we should not always expect the law to provide us with full protection and coverage for what, in rare circumstances, we may morally need to do. Sometimes the moral life calls us out into a no-man's-land where we cannot expect total security and protection under the law. But no one said that the moral life is easy.

Dr. Jack Kevorkian served a prison sentence for assisting with voluntary euthanasia.

A STEP-BY-STEP DEMONSTRATION OF THE TOULMIN METHOD

The Toulmin method requires an analysis of the claim, the reasons offered to support the claim, and the evidence offered to support the reasons, along with an analysis of any refutations offered.

Analyzing the Claim

Logical analysis begins with identifying the *claim*, the thesis or central contention, along with any specific qualifications or exceptions.

Identify the Claim

First, ask yourself, *What statement is the author defending?* In "Rising to the Occasion of Our Death," for example, William F. May spells out his claim in paragraph 6:

> [O]ur social policy should allow terminal patients to die, but it should not regularize killing for mercy.

In his claim, May supports passive euthanasia (letting someone die by withholding or discontinuing treatment) but opposes "regularizing" (making legal or customary) active euthanasia (administering, say, an overdose of morphine to cause a patient's death).

Much popular argumentation is sometimes careless about what exactly is being claimed: Untrained arguers too often content themselves with merely taking sides ("Euthanasia is wrong"). Note that May, a student of ethics trained in philosophical argumentation, makes a claim that is both specific and detailed. Whenever an argument does not include an explicit statement of its claim, you should begin your analysis by stating the writer's claim yourself. Try to state it in sentence form, as May's claim is stated.

Look for Qualifiers

Next, ask, *How is the claim qualified?* Is it absolute, or does it include words or phrases to indicate that it may not hold true in every situation or set of circumstances?

May qualifies his claim in paragraph 6 with the phrase "On the whole," indicating that he recognizes possible exceptions. Other qualifiers include "typically," "usually," and "most of the time." Careful arguers are wary of making absolute claims. Qualifying words or phrases are used to restrict a claim and improve its defensibility.

Find the Exceptions

Finally, ask, *In what cases or circumstances would the writer not press his or her claim?* Look for any explicit exceptions the writer offers.

May, for example, is quite clear in paragraph 8 about when he would not press his claim:

> I hope I would have the courage to kill for mercy—when the patient is utterly beyond human care, terminal, and in excruciating pain.

Once he has specified these abstract conditions, he offers a chilling example of a case in which mercy killing would be appropriate. Nevertheless, he insists that such exceptions are rare and thus do not justify making active euthanasia legal or allowing it to become common policy.

Critical readers respond to unqualified claims skeptically—by hunting for exceptions. With qualified claims, they look to see what specific exceptions the writer will admit and what considerations make restrictions necessary or desirable.

Summarize the Claim

At this point it is a good idea to write out in your writer's notebook the claim, its qualifiers, and its exceptions so that you can see all of them clearly. For May, they look like this:

(qualifier)   "On the whole"

(claim)   "our social policy should allow terminal patients to die, but it should not regularize killing for mercy"

(exception)   "when the patient is utterly beyond human care, terminal, and in excruciating pain"

Analyzing the Reasons

Once you have analyzed the claim, you should next identify and evaluate the reasons offered for the claim.

List the Reasons

Begin by asking yourself, *Why is the writer advancing this claim?* Look for any statement or statements that are used to justify the thesis. May groups all of his reasons in paragraph 5:

The dying should have time to prepare for death and to reconcile with relatives and friends.

Those close to the dying should have time to come to terms with the impending loss of a loved one.

The community needs examples of dependent but patient and courageous people who sometimes do die with dignity.

The community needs the virtues ("justice and love") of those who care for the sick and dying.

When you list reasons, you need not preserve the exact words of the arguer; often, doing so is impossible because reasons are not always explicit but may have to be inferred. Be very careful, however, to adhere as closely as possible to the writer's language. Otherwise, your analysis can easily go astray, imposing a reason of your own that the writer did not have in mind.

Note that reasons, like claims, can be qualified. May does not say, for instance, that "the aged and dependent" *always* show "the virtues of humility, courage, and patience." He implicitly admits that they can be ornery and cowardly as well. But for May's purposes it is enough that they sometimes manifest the virtues he admires.

Use your writer's notebook to list the reasons following your summary of the claim, qualifiers, and exceptions. One possibility is to list them beneath the summary of the claim in the form of a tree diagram (see the model diagram in the Concept Close-Up box on page 53).

Examine the Reasons

There are two questions to ask as you examine the reasons. First, ask, *Are they really good reasons?* A reason is only as good as the values it invokes or implies. A value is something we think is good—that is, worth pursuing for its own sake or because it leads to attaining other goods. For each reason, specify the values involved and then determine whether you accept those values as generally binding.

Second, ask, *Is the reason relevant to the thesis?* In other words, does the relationship between the claim and the reason hold up to examination? For example, the claim "You should buy a new car from Fred Freed" cannot be supported by the reason "Fred is a family man with three cute kids."

Be careful as you examine whether reasons are good and whether they are relevant. No other step is as important in assessing the logic of an argument, and no other can be quite as tricky.

To illustrate, consider May's first reason: Those who know they are about to die should have time to prepare for death and to seek reconciliation with people from whom they have become estranged. Is this a good reason? Yes, because we value the chance to prepare for death and to reconcile with estranged friends or family members.

But is the reason relevant? May seems to rule out the possibility that a dying person seeking active euthanasia would be able to prepare for death and reconcile with others. But this is obviously not the case. Terminally ill people who decide to arrange for their own deaths may make any number of preparations beforehand, so the connection between this reason and May's claim is really quite weak. To accept a connection, we would have to assume that active euthanasia necessarily amounts to a sudden death without adequate preparation. We are entitled to question the relevance of the reason, no matter how good it might be in itself.

◎◎ FOLLOWING THROUGH

Now examine May's second, third, and fourth reasons on your own, as we have just examined the first one. Make notes about each reason, evaluating how good each is in itself and how relevant it is to the thesis. In your writer's notebook, create your own diagram based on the model on page 53.   •

Analyzing the Evidence

Once you have finished your analysis of the reasons, the next step is to consider the evidence offered to support any of those reasons.

List the Evidence

Ask, *What kinds of evidence (data, anecdotes, case studies, citations from authority, and so forth) are offered as support for each reason?* Some arguments advance little in the way of evidence. May's argument is a good example of a moral argument about principles; such an argument does not require much evidence. Lack of evidence, then, is not always a fault. For one of his reasons, however, May does offer some evidence: After stating his second reason in paragraph 5—the chance to grieve before a loved one dies—he invokes authorities who agree with him about the value of advanced grieving.

Examine the Evidence

Two questions apply. First, ask, *Is the evidence good?* That is, is it sufficient, accurate, and credible? Second, ask, *Is it relevant to the reason it supports?* The evidence May offers in paragraph 5 is sufficient. We assume his citations are accurate and credible as well. We would also accept them as relevant because, apart from our own experience with grieving, we have to rely on expert opinion. (See Chapter 5 for a fuller discussion of estimating the adequacy and relevance of evidence.)

Noting Refutations

A final step is to assess an arguer's refutations. In a refutation, a writer anticipates potential objections to his or her position and tries to show why they do not undermine the basic argument. A skilled arguer uses them to deal with any obvious objections a reader is likely to have.

First, ask, *What refutations does the writer offer?* Summarize them. Then, ask, *How does the writer approach each objection?* May's refutation occupies paragraph 7. He recognizes that the value of free choice lends weight to the proeuthanasia position, and so he relates this value to the question of "voluntary euthanasia." Because in our culture individual freedom is so strong a value, May doesn't question the value itself; rather, he leads us to question whether voluntary euthanasia is actually a matter of free choice. He suggests that unwanted people may be coerced into "choosing" death or may be so isolated and neglected that death becomes preferable. Thus, he responds to the objection that dying people should have freedom of choice where death is concerned.

Summarizing Your Analysis

Once you have completed your analysis, it is a good idea to summarize the results in a paragraph or two. Be sure to set aside your own position on the issue, confining your summary to the argument the writer makes.

Although May's logic is strong, it doesn't seem fully compelling. He qualifies his argument and uses exceptions effectively, and his single use of refutation is skillful. However, he fails to acknowledge that active euthanasia need not be a sudden decision leading to sudden death. Consequently, his reasons for supporting passive euthanasia can be used to support at least some cases of active euthanasia as well. It is here—in

Model Toulmin Diagram for Analyzing Arguments

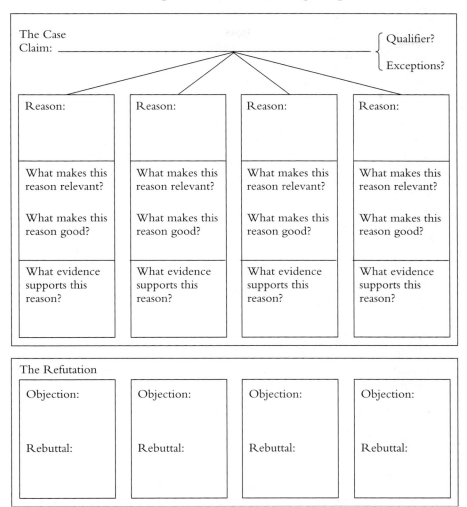

The Case
Claim: _____   ⎧ Qualifier?
                                                            ⎨
                                                            ⎩ Exceptions?

Reason:	Reason:	Reason:	Reason:
What makes this reason relevant?	What makes this reason relevant?	What makes this reason relevant?	What makes this reason relevant?
What makes this reason good?	What makes this reason good?	What makes this reason good?	What makes this reason good?
What evidence supports this reason?	What evidence supports this reason?	What evidence supports this reason?	What evidence supports this reason?

The Refutation

Objection:	Objection:	Objection:	Objection:
Rebuttal:	Rebuttal:	Rebuttal:	Rebuttal:

the linkage between reasons and claim—that May's argument falls short. Furthermore, we may question whether the circumstances under which May would permit active euthanasia are in fact as rare as he suggests. Many people are beyond human care, terminal, and in pain, and many others suffer acute anguish for which they might legitimately seek the relief of death.

Toulmin Analysis

A. ANALYZE THE CLAIM

1. **Find the claim.** In many arguments, the claim is never explicitly stated. When it isn't, try to make the implied claim explicit by stating it in your own words. (Note: If, after careful analysis, you aren't sure *exactly* what the writer is claiming, you've found a serious fault in the argument.)

2. **Look for qualifiers.** Is the claim absolute? Or is it qualified by some word or phrase like *usually* or *all things being equal*? If the claim is absolute, can you think of circumstances in which it might not apply? If the claim is qualified, why is it not absolute? That is, is there any real thought or content in the qualifier—good reasons for qualifying the claim?

3. **Look for explicit exceptions to the claim.** If the writer has pointed out conditions in which he or she would not assert the claim, note them carefully.

Summarize steps 1–3. See the diagram on page 53.

B. ANALYZE THE REASONS

1. **Find the reason or reasons advanced to justify the claim.** All statements of reason will answer the question "Why are you claiming what you've claimed?" They can be linked to the claim with *because*. As with claims, reasons may be implied. Dig them out and state them in your own words. (Note: If, after careful analysis, you discover that the reasons aren't clear or relevant to the claim, you should conclude that the argument is either defective and in need of revision or invalid and therefore unacceptable.)

2. **Ponder each reason advanced.** Is the reason good in itself? Is the reason relevant to the thesis? Note any problems.

List the reasons underneath the claim. See the diagram on page 53.

C. ANALYZE THE EVIDENCE

1. **For each reason, locate all evidence offered to back it up.** Evidence is not limited to hard data. Anecdotes, case studies, and citations from authorities also count as evidence. (Note: Not all reasons require extensive evidence. But we should be suspicious of reasons without evidence, especially when it seems that evidence ought to be available. Unsupported reasons are often a sign of bad reasoning.)

2. **Ponder each piece of evidence.** Is it good? That is, is it accurate and believable? Is it relevant to the reason it supports? Note any problems.

List the evidence underneath the claim. See the diagram on page 53.

D. EXAMINE THE REFUTATIONS

If there are refutations—efforts to refute objections to the case—examine them. If not, consider what objections you think the writer should have addressed.

◎◎ FOLLOWING THROUGH

Following is a student-written argument on capital punishment. Read it through once, and then use the Toulmin method as described in this chapter to analyze its logic systematically.

STUDENT SAMPLE An Argument for Analysis

Capital Punishment: Society's Self-Defense
Amber Young

Just after 1:00 a.m. on a warm night in early June, Georgeann, a pretty college student, left through the back door of a fraternity house to walk the ninety feet down a well-lighted alley to the back door of her sorority house. Lively and vivacious, Georgeann had been an honor student, a cheerleader, and Daffodil Princess in high school, and now she was in the middle of finals week, trying to maintain her straight A record. That evening, several people saw Georgeann walk to within about forty feet of the door of her sorority house. She never arrived. Somewhere in that last forty feet, she met a tall, handsome young man on crutches, his leg in a cast, struggling with a briefcase. The young man asked Georgeann if she could help him get to his car, which was parked nearby. She consented. Then, a housemother sleeping by an open window in a nearby fraternity house was awakened by a high-pitched, terrified scream that suddenly stopped. That was the last anyone ever heard or saw of Georgeann Hawkins. Her bashed skull and broken body were dumped on a hillside many miles away, along with the bodies of several other young female victims who had also been lured to their deaths by the good-looking, clean-cut, courteous, intelligent, and charming Ted Bundy.

By the time Ted Bundy was caught in Utah with his bashing bar and other homemade tools of torture, he had bludgeoned and strangled to death at least thirty-two young women, raping and savaging many of them in the process. His "hunting" trips had extended into at least five Western states, including Washington, Oregon, Idaho, Utah, and Colorado.

Bundy was ultimately convicted of the attempted kidnapping of Carol DeRonche and imprisoned. For this charge he probably would have been paroled within eighteen months. However, before parole could be approved, Bundy was transferred to a jail in Colorado to stand trial for the murder of Caryn Campbell. With Bundy in jail, no

www.mhhe.com/**crusius**

For additional information an writing analysis essays, go to

Writing >
Writing Tutors >
Interpretive Analysis and
Writing about Litature

one else died. Young women could go about their lives normally, "safe" and separated from Ted Bundy by prison walls. Yet any number of things could have occurred to set him free—an acquittal, some sympathetic judge or parole board, a psychiatrist pronouncing him rehabilitated and safe, a state legislature passing shorter sentencing or earlier parole laws, inadequate prison space, a federal court ruling abolishing life in prison without any possibility for parole, or an escape.

In Bundy's case, it was escape—twice—from Colorado jails. The first time, he was immediately caught and brought back. The second time, Bundy made it to Florida, where fifteen days after his escape he bludgeoned and strangled Margaret Bowman, Lisa Levy, Karen Chandler, and Kathy Kleiner in their Tallahassee sorority house, tearing chunks out of Lisa Levy's breast and buttock with his teeth. Ann Rule, a noted crime writer who became Bundy's confidant while writing her book The Stranger Beside Me, described Bundy's attack on Lisa Levy as like that of a rabid animal. On the same night at a different location, Bundy sneaked through an open window and so savagely attacked Cheryl Thomas in her bed that a woman in the apartment next door described the clubbing as seeming to reverberate through the whole house. Then, three weeks later, less than forty days after his escape from the Colorado jail, Bundy went hunting again. He missed his chance at one quarry, junior high school student Leslie Ann Parmenter, when her brother showed up and thwarted her abduction. But Bundy succeeded the next day in Lake City, where he abducted and killed twelve-year-old Kimberly Diane Leach and dumped her strangled, broken body in an abandoned pig barn.

The criminal justice system did not keep Margaret Bowman,   5
Lisa Levy, Karen Chandler, Kathy Kleiner, Cheryl Thomas, Leslie Ann Parmenter, or little Kimberly Leach safe from Ted Bundy. The state of Florida, however, with its death penalty, has made every other young woman safe from Ted Bundy forever. Capital punishment is society's means of self-defense. Just as a person is justified in using deadly force in defending herself against a killer, so society also has a right to execute those who kill whenever the opportunity and the urge arise.

However, while everyone wants a safe society, some people would say that capital punishment is too strong a means of ensuring it. Contemporary social critic Hendrick Hertzberg attacks the death penalty, using arguments that are familiar, but not compelling, to those who do not share his absolute value-of-life position. For example, in one article he paints a graphic picture of how horrible and painful even lethal injection is to the prisoner ("Premeditated"). Elsewhere he dismisses the deterrence argument as "specious," since "[n]o one has ever been able to show that capital punishment lowers the murder rate" ("Burning" 4). But the Florida death penalty has, in fact, made certain that Ted Bundy will never kill again. A needle prick in the arm is hardly cruel and unusual. Thousands of good people with cancer and other diseases or injuries endure much greater pain every day.

Of course, the possibility of executing an innocent person is a serious concern. However, our entire criminal justice system is tilted heavily toward the accused, who is protected from the start to the end of the criminal justice procedure by strong individual-rights guarantees in the Fourth, Fifth, Sixth, and Seventh Amendments of the U.S. Constitution. The burden of proof in a criminal case is on the government, and guilt must be proved beyond a reasonable doubt. The chances of a guilty person going free in our system are many times greater than those of an innocent person being convicted.

If, however, a mistake occurs despite all the safeguards, such an innocent death would be tragic, just as each of the nearly 50,000 deaths of innocent people each year on our highways is tragic. As much as we value human life, we inevitably weigh that value against social costs and benefits, whether we like to admit it or not. If the possibility that an innocent person might be executed is bad enough to require abolition of capital punishment, then why don't we also demand the abolition of automobiles as well? We don't because we accept the thousands of automobile deaths per year to keep our cars. It is interesting to note that opponents of capital punishment like Hertzberg do not demand abolition of the automobile. So preservation of life must not be the highest value in all cases.

Just as society has decided that the need for automobiles outweighs their threat to innocent life, so capital punishment is necessary for the safety and well-being of the general populace. The strongest reason for capital punishment is not retribution or deterrence, but simply self-defense. We have a right to demand that government remove forever first-degree murderers, like Bundy, who hunt and kill their victims with premeditation and malice.

There are only two alternatives—life in prison or death. We base our approval or disapproval of capital punishment on fundamental values relating to life itself, rather than on statistics or factual evidence. Few in our society go so far as to believe that we must preserve life above all else. Our founding fathers wrote in the Declaration of Independence that all men are endowed by their Creator with unalienable rights, including "life, liberty, and the pursuit of happiness." However, there is no indication that life was more sacred to them than liberty. In fact, Patrick Henry, who would later be instrumental in the adoption of the Bill of Rights to the U.S. Constitution, is most famous for his defiant American Revolutionary declaration, "I know not what course others may take, but as for me, give me liberty or give me death!"   10

The sentiment that some things are worse than death remains. Millions of soldiers have put themselves in harm's way and lost their lives to preserve and defend freedom. Many people will admit to their willingness to use deadly force to protect themselves or their families from a murderer. The preservation of life, any life, regardless of everything else, is not an absolute value for most people.

In fact, many prisoners would prefer to die than to languish in prison. Bundy himself, in his letters from prison to Ann Rule, declared, "My world is a cage," as he tried to describe "the cruel metamorphosis that occurs in captivity" (qtd. in Rule 148). After his sentencing in Utah, Bundy described his attempts to prepare mentally for the "living hell of prison" (qtd. in Rule 191). Thus, some condemned prisoners, including Gary Gilmore, the first person to be executed after the U.S. Supreme Court found that Utah's death penalty law met Constitutional requirements, refused to participate in the appeals attempting to convert his death sentence to life in prison because he preferred death. In our society, founded on the principle that liberty is more important than life, the argument that it is somehow less cruel and more civilized to deprive someone of liberty for the rest of his or her life than to end the life sounds hollow. The Fifth Amendment of the U.S. Constitution prohibits the taking of either life or liberty without due process of law, but it does not place one at a higher value than the other.

The overriding concerns of the Constitution, however, are safety and self-defense. The chance of a future court ruling, a release on parole, a pardon, a commutation of sentence, or an escape—any of which could turn the murderer loose to prey again on society—creates a risk that society should not have to bear. Lisa Levy, Margaret Bowman, Karen Chandler, Kathy Kleiner, Cheryl Thomas, and Kimberly Leach were not protected from Bundy by the courts and jails in Utah and Colorado, but other young women who were potential victims are now safe from Bundy thanks to the Florida death penalty.

Capital punishment carries with it the risk that an innocent person will be executed; however, it is more important to protect innocent, would-be victims of convicted murderers. On balance, society was not demeaned by the execution of Bundy in Florida, as Hertzberg claimed ("Burning" 49). On the contrary, society is better off with Ted Bundy and others like him gone.

Works Cited

Hertzberg, Hendrick. "Burning Question." The New Republic 20 Feb. 1989: 4+.

---. "Premeditated Execution." Time 18 May 1992: 49.

Rule, Ann. The Stranger Beside Me. New York: Penguin, 1989.

A FINAL NOTE ABOUT LOGICAL ANALYSIS

No method for analyzing arguments is perfect, and no method can guarantee that everyone using it will assess an argument the same way. Uniform results are not especially desirable anyway. What would be left to talk about? The point of argumentative analysis is to step back and examine an argument carefully, to detect how it is structured, to assess the cogency and power of its logic. The Toulmin method helps us move beyond a hit-or-miss approach to logical analysis, but it cannot yield a conclusion as compelling as mathematical proof.

Convincing and persuading always involve more than logic, and, therefore, logical analysis alone is never enough to assess the strength of an argument. For example, William May's argument attempts to discredit those like Dr. Jack Kevorkian who assist patients wishing to take their own lives. May depicts Kevorkian as offering assistance without sufficient consultation with the patient. Is his depiction accurate? Clearly, we can answer this question only by finding out more about how Kevorkian and others like him work. Because such questions are not a part of logical analysis, they have not been of concern to us in this chapter. But any adequate and thorough analysis of an argument must also address questions of fact and the interpretation of data.

CHAPTER 4

Reading and Writing about Visual Arguments

We live in a world awash in pictures. We turn on the TV and see not just performers, advertisers, and talking heads but also dramatic footage of events from around the world, commercials as visually creative as works of art, and video images to accompany popular music. We boot up our computers and surf the Net; many of the waves we ride are visual swells, enticing images created or enhanced by the very machines that take us out to sea. We drive our cars through a gallery of street art—on billboards and buildings and on the sides of buses and trucks. We go to malls and window-shop, entertained by the images of fantasy fulfillment each retailer offers. Print media are full of images; in our newspapers, for instance, photos, drawings, and computer graphics vie with print for space. Even college textbooks, once mostly blocks of uninterrupted prose with an occasional black-and-white drawing or photo, now often have colorful graphics and elaborate transparency overlays.

Like language, visual images are rhetorical. They persuade us in obvious and not-so-obvious ways. And so we need some perspective on visual rhetoric; we need to understand its power and how to use it effectively and responsibly.

UNDERSTANDING VISUAL ARGUMENTS

Visual rhetoric is *the use of images, sometimes coupled with sound or appeals to the other senses, to make an argument or persuade us to act as the image-maker would have us act.* Probably the clearest examples are advertisements and political cartoons, a few of which we will examine shortly. But visual rhetoric is everywhere. We do not ordinarily think, say, of a car's body style as "rhetoric," but clearly it is, because people are persuaded to pay tens of thousands of dollars for the sleekest new body style when they could spend a few thousand for an older car that would get them from home to work or school just as well.

Consider also the billions of dollars we spend on clothes, hairstyles, cosmetics, diets, and exercise programs—all part of the rhetoric of making the right "visual statement" in a world that too often judges us solely by how we look. We spend so much because our self-images depend in part on others' responses to our cars, bodies, offices, homes—to whatever represents "us." No doubt we all want to be appreciated for our true selves, but distinguishing this "inside" from the "outside" we show the world has never been easy. Because we tend to become the image we cultivate, the claim that "image is everything" may not be as superficial as it sounds.

"READING" IMAGES

Rhetorical analysis of visual rhetoric involves examining images to see how they attempt to convince or persuade an audience. Pictures are symbols that must be read, just as language is read. To read an argument made through images, a critic must be able to recognize allusions to popular culture. For example, Americans knew that the white mustaches on the celebrities in the milk commercials referred to the way children drink milk; more recently, the milk mustache symbolizes the ad campaign itself, now part of our culture.

As with inquiry into any argument, we ought to begin with questions about rhetorical context: When was the visual argument created and by whom? To what audience was it originally aimed and with what purpose? Then we can ask what claim a visual argument makes and what reasons it offers in support of that claim. Then, as with verbal texts that make a case, we can examine visual arguments for evidence, assumptions, and bias, and we can ask what values they favor and what the implications of accepting their argument are.

However, many visuals do not even attempt reasoning; they rely instead on emotional appeals. Such appeals are most obvious in advertising, where the aim is to move a target audience to buy a service or product. In many advertisements, especially for products like beer, cigarettes, and perfume, where the differences are subjective, emotional appeal is all there is. Most emotional appeals work by promising to reward our desires for love, status, peace of mind, or escape from everyday responsibilities.

Advertisements also use ethical appeals, associating their claim with values the audience approves of and wants to identify with—such as images that show nature being preserved, races living in harmony, families staying in touch, and people attaining the American dream of upward mobility.

In evaluating the ethics of visual rhetoric, we need to consider whether the argument is at least reasonable: Does the image demonstrate reasoning, or does it oversimplify and mislead? We will want to look at the emotional and ethical appeals to decide if they pander to audience weaknesses and prejudices or manipulate fantasies and fears.

ANALYSIS: FIVE COMMON TYPES OF VISUAL ARGUMENT

In this section, we analyze some visual arguments in various genres: advertisements, editorial cartoons, public sculpture, news photographs, and graphics. We show how "reading" visual texts requires interpretive skills and how interpretive skills, in turn, depend on cultural knowledge.

Advertisements

We begin with a classic ad for Charlie perfume from 1988 that created quite a stir when it first appeared (see Figure C-1 in the color section). As James B. Twitchell noted in his *Twenty Ads That Shook the World,* the shot of a woman giving a man an encouraging fanny pat "subverted sexism, turned it on its head, [and] used it against itself." At first the editors at the *New York Times* "refused to run the ad, saying it was in 'poor taste.'" But the ad proved irresistibly appealing when it appeared in women's magazines. Why did it work so well?

Twitchell argues that "Charlie is not just in charge, she is clearly enjoying dominance."

> She is taller than her partner. . . . Not only does he have part of his
> anatomy removed from the picture so that the Charlie bottle can be fore-
> grounded, and not only does she have the jaunty scarf and the cascading
> hair of a free spirit, but she is delivering that most masculine of signifiers,
> the booty pat. . . . In football especially, the pat signifies comradeship . . .
> and is applied dominant to submissive. . . . The coach delivers it to a
> hulking [player] returning to the field of battle. . . . When Charlie bestows
> it on her gentleman friend . . . , she is harvesting a rich crop of meaning.
> The tide has turned, and now men are getting their butts slapped, by of
> all people, women. (170)

It's possible, of course, to read the pat in other ways—for example, as the kind of thing a dominant man might do to a subordinate woman at the office, inappropriate behavior now widely understood as sexual harassment. But no matter how you read it, there's no doubt that the ad tapped into the woman's movement at a time when women routinely endured sexism at work. No wonder that the ad was hugely popular.

The other ads in our color section work in different ways. Try your hand at analyzing their persuasive power.

◎◎ FOLLOWING THROUGH

1. Figure C-2 may look like a poster but it is actually a "semi-postal" stamp, so called because a percentage of its cost goes to the cause it advocates. This stamp has raised over $22 million for breast cancer research since it was issued in 1998. What are the sources of its appeal?

2. Figure C-3, from the Southampton Anti-Bias Task Force, depends for full impact on remembering a crayon labeled *flesh* that was the color of the center crayon in the photo. People in their forties and fifties or older remember that crayon. What, then, is the ad's appeal for them? What does it say about skin color to younger people who don't remember the crayon?

3. Figure C-4 is a striking example of the power of photography and probably digital and other ways of enhancing photographs. How might women respond to it? How might men?

4. If Figure C-4 features the art of photography in selling glamour, C-5 is deliberately unglamorous, playing with the stereotype of the computer nerd. How does it work to promote the services of the Geek Squad?

5. Figure C-6, the Adidas ad, ingeniously exploits how the eye can be fooled by what it *expects* to see rather than what is actually there. Did you see the shadow at first simply as the runner's shadow? What made you reevaluate what you were seeing? What's the impact of playing with perception in this case?

6. As a class project, find ads for the same product in magazines that appeal to different market segments, as defined by age, income, sex, ethnicity, and so on. Compare and contrast the ads to see how they are designed to appeal to their target audiences.   •

Editorial Cartoons

Editorial cartoons comment on events and issues in the news. They are funny but offer concise arguments too. Most political cartoons rely on captions and dialogue to make their argument, combining the visual and verbal. Consider the one by Mike Keefe (Figure 4.1, page 65) that comments on the impact of computers.

The cartoon illustrates well how "reading" a visual argument depends on shared cultural knowledge. The image of a thirsty man crawling on hands and knees through a desert stands for anything important that humans lack. The cartoon depicts our common metaphor for the Internet, the "information superhighway," literally. The man has too much information and not enough

Figure C-1

Figure C-2

SOUTHAMPTON ANTI-BIAS TASK FORCE · 516-287-5734

Figure C-3

LOUIS VUITTON

Figure C-4

Figure C-5

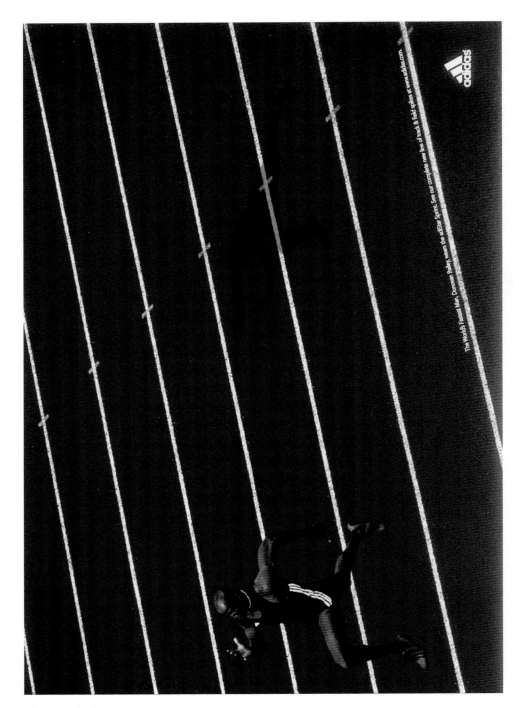

Figure C-6

Figure C-7

Figure C-8

Figure 4.1

Mike Keefe, dePIXion Studios. Reprinted with permission.

wisdom. To read the argument of the cartoon and appreciate its humor, the viewer has to know about the overwhelming glut of information on the Internet, suggested by the size of the letters on the road. The cartoon "argues" that relying on the Internet will deprive a civilization of the wisdom to sustain a good life.

◎◎ FOLLOWING THROUGH

1. Cartoons probably are most persuasive when they satirize a familiar problem, as in the information superhighway example in Figure 4.1. A similar cartoon is Stuart Carlson's in Figure 4.3 (page 67). However, although most Americans struggle with the Net's information glut, fewer, but still a large percentage, drive gas-guzzling vehicles. If you don't, how do you react to Carlson's cartoon? Why do you react the way you do? If you drive a gas guzzler or would like to, is the cartoon still amusing? Why or why not?

2. Some cartoons are "factional," created by one side in a controversy to ridicule the position of the other side. Contrasting examples appear in Figure 4.2 (page 66). Clearly, neither cartoon will persuade anyone whose position is held up to ridicule. Yet, factional cartoons are common. They must serve some purpose. How do you think they work?

3. Find a recent editorial cartoon on an issue prominent in the news. Bring it to class and be prepared to explain its persuasive tactics. Consider also the fairness of the cartoon. Does the cartoon minimize the complexity of the issue it addresses? •

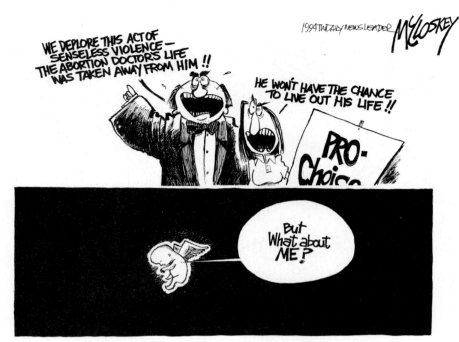

Jim McCloskey, *The News Leader*, Staunton, Virginia. Reprinted by permission.

By permission of Mike Luckovich and Creators Syndicate, Inc.

Figure 4.2

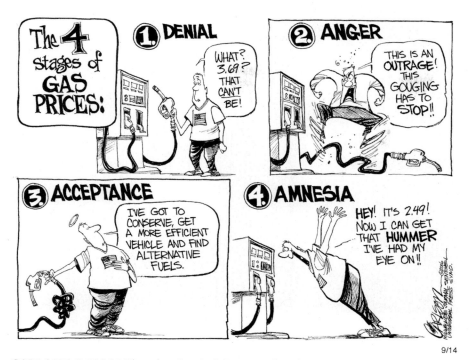

CARLSON © 2006 Milwaukee Sentinel. Reprinted with permission of Universal Press Syndicate. All rights reserved.

Figure 4.3

Public Sculpture

Public sculptures, such as war memorials, aim to teach an audience about a nation's past and to honor its values. An example that can be read as an argument is the Marine Corps Memorial, erected in 1954 on the Mall in Washington, D.C. (see Figure 4.4, page 68). It honors all Marines who have given their lives by depicting one specific act of bravery, the planting of the American flag on Iwo Jima, a Pacific island captured from the Japanese in 1945. The claim the sculpture makes is clear: Honor your country. The image of the soldiers straining every muscle gives the reason: These men made extreme sacrifices to preserve the values symbolized by this flag. The sculpture also communicates through details like the wind-whipped flag.

The Iwo Jima sculpture is traditional, glorifying victory on enemy soil. Compare it with the Vietnam War Memorial, dedicated in Washington, D.C., in November 1982. Maya Lin designed what we now call "the Wall" while an undergraduate student at Yale. Her design was controversial because it was so unconventional (see Figures 4.5 and 4.6, page 69). and anti-war. Its black granite slates are etched with the names of war dead; it honors individuals who died in a war that tore the nation apart.

Figure 4.4

⊙⊙ FOLLOWING THROUGH

1. Because it does not portray a realistic scene as the Iwo Jima Memorial does, the Wall invites interpretation and analysis. If you have visited it, try to recall your reaction. What details led to your interpretation? Could you characterize the Wall as having logical, ethical, and emotional appeals?

2. Find public sculpture or monuments to visit and analyze. Alone or with some classmates, take notes and photographs. Then develop your interpretation of the sculpture's argument, specifying how visual details contribute to the case, and present your analysis to the class. Compare your interpretation with those of your classmates.

News Photographs

While some news photographs may seem merely to record an event, the camera is not objective. The photographer makes many decisions—whether to snap a picture, when to snap it, what to include and exclude from the image—and decisions about light, depth of field, and so on. Figure 4.7 (page 70), a photograph that appeared in the *New York Times*, shows a scene photographer Bruce Young encountered covering a snowstorm that hit Washington, D.C., in January 1994. The storm was severe enough to shut down the city and most government offices. Without the caption supplied by the

Figure 4.5

Figure 4.6

Figure 4.7

New York Times, readers might not recognize the objects in the foreground as human beings, homeless people huddled on benches, covered by undisturbed snow.

The picture depicts homelessness in America as a national disgrace. The White House in the background is our nation's "home," a grand and lavishly decorated residence symbolic of national wealth. In the foreground, the homeless people look like bags of garbage, marring the picture of the snow-covered landscape. No blame attaches to the homeless for their condition; they are too pathetic under their blankets of snow. The picture shows the homeless as a fact of life in our cities, challenging the idealized image of our nation.

FOLLOWING THROUGH

1. Figure C-7 in the color section depicts the family of Sgt. Jose M. Velez watching over his casket. Sgt. Velez was killed in Iraq. Any thoughtful response to such a photo has to be complex. How would you describe your response? To what extent is your view of the war in Iraq relevant?

2. Figure C-8 is a shot of the Tour de France, the annual bicycling race that Lance Armstrong made almost as big an event in the United States as it is in Europe. What impression does the photo convey? What details in the photo convey the impression?

3. The two news photos in Figure 4.8 (page 72) were both included in a collection of shots *Time* magazine published on the Net as "The Best Photos of the Year 2006." The top one had the title "Sweet Home, New Orleans" and depicts people in a lounge during Mardi Gras, a sign that normal life was returning to the city after Hurricane Katrina's devastation. The bottom one captures refugees in Chad, fleeing from Arab militias, one of several murderous conflicts going on in Africa and not getting much attention in the United States. What details make the photos so effective? Why are such photos almost indispensable to news stories? Put together, as they are in Figure 4.8, what thoughts and feelings do these photographs stimulate in you?

4. In a recent newspaper or news magazine, look for photos you think are effective when combined with a story about a controversial issue. What perspective or point of view do the pictures represent? How do you read their composition, including camera angle, light conditions, foreground and background, and so on?

 www.mhhe.com/**crusius**　To find more photographs to analyze, check out:
Writing > Visual Rhetoric Tutorial > Catalyst Image Bank

Graphics

Visual supplements to a longer text such as an essay, article, or manual are known as **graphics.** Most graphics fall into one of the following categories:

If you want information on using PowerPoint to create graphics, go to

Writing > PowerPoint Tutorial

> Tables and charts (typically an arrangement of data in columns and rows that summarizes the results of research)
>
> Graphs (including bar, line, and pie graphs)
>
> Photographs
>
> Drawings (including maps and cartoons)

Although charts and tables are not images, they present data in visual form. Tables display information economically in one place so that readers can assess it as they read and find it easily afterward if they want to refer to it again. Consider Figure 4.9 (page 73), which combines a table with bar graphs. It comes from a study of poverty in the United States. Note how much information is packed into this single visual and how easy it is to read, moving top to bottom and left to right through the categories. Consider how many long and boring paragraphs it would take to say the same thing in prose.

Graphs are usually no more than tables transformed into visuals we can interpret more easily. Bar graphs are best at showing comparisons at some single point in time. In contrast, line graphs reveal trends—for example, the performance of the stock market. Pie graphs highlight relative proportions well. When newspapers want to show us how the federal budget is spent,

Figure 4.8

for example, they typically use pie graphs with the pieces labeled in some way to represent categories such as national defense, welfare, and entitlement programs. What gets the biggest pieces of the pie becomes *instantly clear* and *easy to remember*—the two major purposes of all graphs. Graphs don't make arguments, but they deliver evidence powerfully.

Figure 4.9

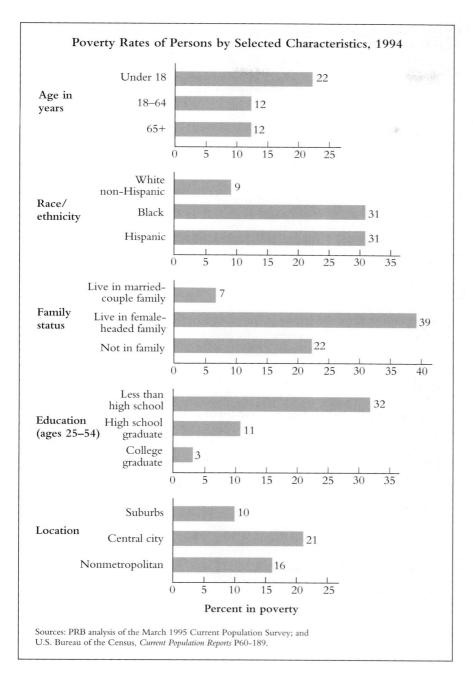

Poverty Rates of Persons by Selected Characteristics, 1994

Age in years
- Under 18: 22
- 18–64: 12
- 65+: 12

Race/ethnicity
- White non-Hispanic: 9
- Black: 31
- Hispanic: 31

Family status
- Live in married-couple family: 7
- Live in female-headed family: 39
- Not in family: 22

Education (ages 25–54)
- Less than high school: 32
- High school graduate: 11
- College graduate: 3

Location
- Suburbs: 10
- Central city: 21
- Nonmetropolitan: 16

Percent in poverty

Sources: PRB analysis of the March 1995 Current Population Survey; and U.S. Bureau of the Census, *Current Population Reports* P60-189.

www.mhhe.com/crusius For more help with visual design, go to:

Writing > Visual Rhetoric Tutorial > Visualizing Data

and

Writing > Visual Rhetoric Tutorial > Designing Documents

As graphics, photographs represent people, objects, and scenes realistically. For instance, owner's manuals for cars often have a shot of the engine compartment that shows where fluid reservoirs are located. Clearly, such photos serve highly practical purposes, such as helping us locate the dipstick. But they're also used, for example, in biographies; we get a better sense of, say, Abraham Lincoln's life and times when pictures of him, his family, his home, and so on are included. But photographs can do much more than inform. They can be highly dramatic and powerfully emotional in ways that only the best writers can manage with prose. Photos are often potent persuaders.

Photographs, however, are not analytical—by their nature, they give us the surface, only what the camera can "see." A different type of graphic, the drawing, is preferable when we want to depict how something is put together or structured. For instance, instructions for assembling and installing a ceiling fan or a light fixture usually have many diagrams—a large one showing how all the parts fit together and smaller ones that depict steps in the process in more detail. Corporate publications often include diagrams of the company's organizational hierarchy. Scientific articles and textbooks are full of drawings or illustrations created with computer graphics; science writers want us to understand structures, particularly internal structures, impossible to capture on film. For example, our sense of DNA's double-helical structure comes entirely from diagrams.

The following article illustrates how a variety of graphics can contribute to the effectiveness of a written text.

The Rise of Renewable Energy

DANIEL M. KAMMEN

This article appeared in the September 2006 issue of *Scientific American*. Daniel Kammen is Distinguished Professor of Energy at the University of California, Berkeley, where he founded and directs the Renewable and Appropriate Energy Laboratory.

Renewable energy refers to any source of power that does not depend on the limited supply of fossil fuels, such as oil or coal, and produces relatively little or none of the greenhouse gases that contribute significantly to global warming. There are many renewable energy sources. Kammen discusses the potential of solar power, wind power, and biofuels such as ethanol.

No plan to substantially reduce greenhouse gas emissions can succeed through increases in energy efficiency alone. Because economic growth continues to boost the demand for energy—more coal for powering new factories, more oil for fueling new cars, more natural gas for heating new cars, more natural gas for heating new homes—carbon emissions will keep climbing despite the introduction of more energy-efficient vehicles, buildings and appliances. To counter the alarming trend of global warming, the U.S. and other countries must make a major commitment to developing renewable energy sources that generate little or no carbon.

Renewable energy technologies were suddenly and briefly fashionable three decades ago in response to the oil embargoes of the 1970s, but the interest and support were not sustained. In recent years, however, dramatic improvements in the performance and affordability of solar cells, wind turbines and biofuels—ethanol and other fuels derived from plants—have paved the way for mass commercialization. In addition to their environmental benefits, renewable sources promise to enhance America's energy security by reducing the country's reliance on fossil fuels from other nations. What is more, high and wildly fluctuating prices for oil and natural gas have made renewable alternatives more appealing.

We are now in an era where the opportunities for renewable energy are unprecedented, making this the ideal time to advance clean power for decades to come. But the endeavor will require a long-term investment of scientific, economic and political resources. Policymakers and ordinary citizens must demand action and challenge one another to hasten the transition.

LET THE SUN SHINE

Solar cells, also known as photovoltaics, use semiconductor materials to convert sunlight into electric current. They now provide just a tiny slice of the world's electricity: their global generating capacity of 5,000 megawatts (MW) is only 0.15 percent of the total generating capacity from all sources. Yet sunlight could potentially supply 5,000 times as much energy as the world currently consumes. And thanks to technology improvements, cost declines and favorable policies in many states and nations, the annual production of photovoltaics has increased by more than 25 percent a year for the past decade and by a remarkable 45 percent in 2005. The cells manufactured last year added 1,727 MW to worldwide generating capacity, with 833 MW made in Japan, 353 MW in Germany and 153 MW in the U.S.

Solar cells can now be made from a range of materials, from the traditional 5 multicrystalline silicon wafers that still dominate the market to thin-film silicon cells and devices composed of plastic or organic semiconductors. Thin-film photovoltaics are cheaper to produce than crystalline silicon cells but are also less efficient at turning light into power. In laboratory tests, crystalline cells have achieved efficiencies of 30 percent or more; current commercial cells of this type range from 15 to 20 percent. Both laboratory and commercial efficiencies for all kinds of solar cells have risen steadily in recent years, indicating that an expansion of research efforts would further enhance the performance of solar cells on the market.

Solar photovoltaics are particularly easy to use because they can be installed in so many places—on the roofs or walls of homes and office buildings, in vast

A world of clean energy could rely on wind turbines and solar cells to generate its electricity and biofuels derived from switchgrass and other plants to power its vehicles.

KENN BROWN

arrays in the desert, even sewn into clothing to power portable electronic devices. The state of California has joined Japan and Germany in leading a global push for solar installations; the "Million Solar Roof" commitment is intended to create 3,000 MW of new generating capacity in the state by 2018. Studies done by my research group, the Renewable and Appropriate Energy Laboratory at the University of California, Berkeley, show that annual production of solar photovoltaics in the U.S. alone could grow to 10,000 MW in just 20 years if current trends continue.

The biggest challenge will be lowering the price of the photovoltaics, which are now relatively expensive to manufacture. Electricity produced by crystalline cells has a total cost of 20 to 25 cents per kilowatt-hour, compared with four to six cents for coal-fired electricity, five to seven cents for power produced by burning natural gas, and six to nine cents for biomass power plants. (The cost of nuclear power is harder to pin down because experts disagree on which expenses to include in the analysis; the estimated range is two to 12 cents per kilowatt-hour.) Fortunately, the prices of solar cells have fallen consistently over the past decade, largely because of improve-

ments in manufacturing processes. In Japan, where 290 MW of solar generating capacity were added in 2005 and an even larger amount was exported, the cost of photovoltaics has declined 8 percent a year; in California, where 50 MW of solar power were installed in 2005, costs have dropped 5 percent annually.

Surprisingly, Kenya is the global leader in the number of solar power systems installed per capita (but not the number of watts added). More than 30,000 very small solar panels, each producing only 12 to 30 watts, are sold in that country annually. For an investment of as little as $100 for the panel and wiring, the system can be used to charge a car battery, which can then provide enough power to run a fluorescent lamp or a small black-and-white television for a few hours a day. More Kenyans adopt solar power every year than make connections to the country's electric grid. The panels typically use solar cells made of amorphous silicon; although these photovoltaics are only half as efficient as crystalline cells, their cost is so much lower (by a factor of at least four) that they are more affordable and useful for the two billion people worldwide who currently have no access to electricity. Sales of

GROWING FAST, BUT STILL A SLIVER

Solar cells, wind power and biofuels are rapidly gaining traction in the energy markets, but they remain marginal providers compared with fossil-fuel sources such as coal, natural gas and oil.

THE RENEWABLE BOOM

Since 2000 the commercialization of renewable energy sources has accelerated dramatically. The annual global production of solar cells, also known as photo-voltaics, jumped 45 percent in 2005. The construction of new wind farms, particularly in Europe, has boosted the worldwide generating capacity of wind power 10-fold over the past decade. And the production of ethanol, the most common biofuel, soared to 36.5 billion liters last year, with the lion's share distilled from American-grown corn.

Photovoltaic Production

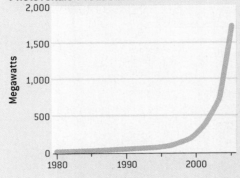

Wind Energy Generating Capacity

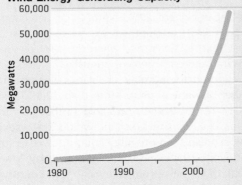

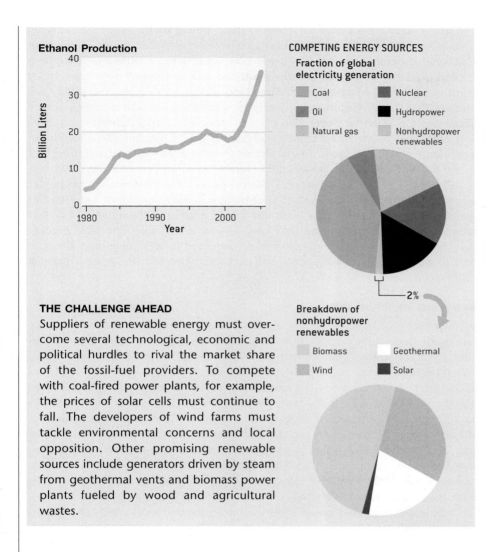

Ethanol Production

Billion Liters

COMPETING ENERGY SOURCES

Fraction of global
electricity generation

- Coal
- Oil
- Natural gas
- Nuclear
- Hydropower
- Nonhydropower renewables

—2%

Breakdown of
nonhydropower
renewables

- Biomass
- Wind
- Geothermal
- Solar

THE CHALLENGE AHEAD

Suppliers of renewable energy must overcome several technological, economic and
political hurdles to rival the market share
of the fossil-fuel providers. To compete
with coal-fired power plants, for example,
the prices of solar cells must continue to
fall. The developers of wind farms must
tackle environmental concerns and local
opposition. Other promising renewable
sources include generators driven by steam
from geothermal vents and biomass power
plants fueled by wood and agricultural
wastes.

small solar power systems are booming in other African nations as well, and
advances in low-cost photovoltaic manufacturing could accelerate this trend.

Furthermore, photovoltaics are not the only fast-growing form of solar power.
Solar-thermal systems, which collect sunlight to generate heat, are also undergoing
a resurgence. These systems have long been used to provide hot water for homes
or factories, but they can also produce electricity without the need for expensive
solar cells. In one design, for example, mirrors focus light on a Stirling engine, a
high-efficiency device containing a working fluid that circulates between hot and
cold chambers. The fluid expands as the sunlight heats it, pushing a piston that,
in turn, drives a turbine.

In the fall of 2005 a Phoenix company called Stirling Energy Systems announced   10
that it was planning to build two large solar-thermal power plants in southern
California. The company signed a 20-year power purchase agreement with Southern
California Edison, which will buy the electricity from a 500-MW solar plant to be
constructed in the Mojave Desert. Stretching across 4,500 acres, the facility will
include 20,000 curved dish mirrors, each concentrating light on a Stirling engine
about the size of an oil barrel. The plant is expected to begin operating in 2009
and could later be expanded to 850 MW. Stirling Energy Systems also signed a 20-
year contract with San Diego Gas & Electric to build a 300-MW, 12,000-dish plant
in the Imperial Valley. This facility could eventually be upgraded to 900 MW.

The financial details of the two California projects have not been made public,
but electricity produced by present solar-thermal technologies costs between five
and 13 cents per kilowatt-hour, with dish-mirror systems at the upper end of that
range. Because the projects involve highly reliable technologies and mass production, however, the generation expenses are expected to ultimately drop closer to
four to six cents per kilowatt-hour—that is, competitive with the current price of
coal-fired power.

BLOWING IN THE WIND

Wind power has been growing at a pace rivaling that of the solar industry. The
worldwide generating capacity of wind turbines has increased more than 25 percent a year, on average, for the past decade, reaching nearly 60,000 MW in 2005.
The growth has been nothing short of explosive in Europe—between 1994 and
2005, the installed wind power capacity in European Union nations jumped from
1,700 to 40,000 MW. Germany alone has more than 18,000 MW of capacity thanks
to an aggressive construction program. The northern German state of Schleswig-
Holstein currently meets one quarter of its annual electricity demand with more
than 2,400 wind turbines, and in certain months wind power provides more than
half the state's electricity. In addition, Spain has 10,000 MW of wind capacity,
Denmark has 3,000 MW, and Great Britain, the Netherlands, Italy and Portugal
each have more than 1,000 MW.

In the U.S. the wind power industry has accelerated dramatically in the past
five years, with total generating capacity leaping 36 percent to 9,100 MW in 2005.
Although wind turbines now produce only 0.5 percent of the nation's electricity,
the potential for expansion is enormous, especially in the windy Great Plains states.
(North Dakota, for example, has greater wind energy resources than Germany, but
only 98 MW of generating capacity is installed there.) If the U.S. constructed
enough wind farms to fully tap these resources, the turbines could generate as
much as 11 trillion kilowatt-hours of electricity, or nearly three times the total
amount produced from all energy sources in the nation last year. The wind industry has developed increasingly large and efficient turbines, each capable of yielding
4 to 6 MW. And in many locations, wind power is the cheapest form of new electricity, with costs ranging from four to seven cents per kilowatt-hour.

The growth of new wind farms in the U.S. has been spurred by a production
tax credit that provides a modest subsidy equivalent to 1.9 cents per kilowatt-hour,

enabling wind turbines to compete with coal-fired plants. Unfortunately, Congress has repeatedly threatened to eliminate the tax credit. Instead of instituting a long-term subsidy for wind power, the lawmakers have extended the tax credit on a year-to-year basis, and the continual uncertainty has slowed investment in wind farms. Congress is also threatening to derail a proposed 130-turbine farm off the coast of Massachusetts that would provide 468 MW of generating capacity, enough to power most of Cape Cod, Martha's Vineyard and Nantucket.

The reservations about wind power come partly from utility companies that 15 are reluctant to embrace the new technology and partly from so-called NIMBY-ism. ("NIMBY" is an acronym for Not in My Backyard.) Although local concerns over how wind turbines will affect landscape views may have some merit, they must be balanced against the social costs of the alternatives. Because society's energy needs are growing relentlessly, rejecting wind farms often means requiring the construction or expansion of fossil fuel–burning power plants that will have far more devastating environmental effects.

GREEN FUELS

Researchers are also pressing ahead with the development of biofuels that could replace at least a portion of the oil currently consumed by motor vehicles. The most common biofuel by far in the U.S. is ethanol, which is typically made from corn and blended with gasoline. The manufacturers of ethanol benefit from a substantial tax credit: with the help of the $2-billion annual subsidy, they sold more than 16 billion liters of ethanol in 2005 (almost 3 percent of all automobile fuel by volume), and production is expected to rise 50 percent by 2007. Some policymakers have questioned the wisdom of the subsidy, pointing to studies showing that it takes more energy to harvest the corn and refine the ethanol than the fuel can deliver to combustion engines. In a recent analysis, though, my colleagues and I discovered that some of these studies did not properly account for the energy content of the by-products manufactured along with the ethanol. When all the inputs and outputs were correctly factored in, we found that ethanol has a positive net energy of almost five megajoules per liter.

We also found, however, that ethanol's impact on greenhouse gas emissions is more ambiguous. Our best estimates indicate that substituting corn-based ethanol for gasoline reduces greenhouse gas emissions by 18 percent, but the analysis is hampered by large uncertainties regarding certain agricultural practices, particularly the environmental costs of fertilizers. If we use different assumptions about these practices, the results of switching to ethanol range from a 36 percent drop in emissions to a 29 percent increase. Although corn-based ethanol may help the U.S. reduce its reliance on foreign oil, it will probably not do much to slow global warming unless the production of the biofuel becomes cleaner.

But the calculations change substantially when the ethanol is made from cellulosic sources: woody plants such as switch-grass or poplar. Whereas most makers of corn-based ethanol burn fossil fuels to provide the heat for fermentation, the producers of cellulosic ethanol burn lignin—an unfermentable part of the organic material—to heat the plant sugars. Burning lignin does not add any greenhouse

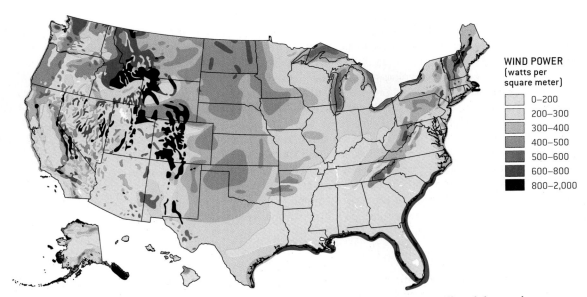

America has enormous wind energy resources, enough to generate as much as 11 trillion kilowatt-hours of electricity each year. Some of the best locations for wind turbines are the Great Plains states, the Great Lakes and the mountain ridges of the Rockies and the Appalachians.

gases to the atmosphere, because the emissions are offset by the carbon dioxide absorbed during the growth of the plants used to make the ethanol. As a result, substituting cellulosic ethanol for gasoline can slash greenhouse gas emissions by 90 percent or more.

Another promising biofuel is so-called green diesel. Researchers have produced this fuel by first gasifying biomass—heating organic materials enough that they release hydrogen and carbon monoxide—and then converting these compounds into long-chain hydrocarbons using the Fischer-Tropsch process. (During World War II, German engineers employed these chemical reactions to make synthetic motor fuels out of coal.) The result would be an economically competitive liquid fuel for motor vehicles that would add virtually no greenhouse gases to the atmosphere. Oil giant Royal Dutch/Shell is currently investigating the technology.

THE NEED FOR R&D

Each of these renewable sources is now at or near a tipping point, the crucial stage 20 when investment and innovation, as well as market access, could enable these attractive but generally marginal providers to become major contributors to regional and global energy supplies. At the same time, aggressive policies designed to open markets for renewables are taking hold at city, state and federal levels around the world. Governments have adopted these policies for a wide variety of reasons: to promote market diversity or energy security, to bolster industries and jobs, and to protect the environment on both the local and global scales. In the U.S. more than

20 states have adopted standards setting a minimum for the fraction of electricity that must be supplied with renewable sources. Germany plans to generate 20 percent of its electricity from renewables by 2020, and Sweden intends to give up fossil fuels entirely.

Even President George W. Bush said, in his now famous State of the Union address this past January, that the U.S. is "addicted to oil." And although Bush did not make the link to global warming, nearly all scientists agree that humanity's addiction to fossil fuels is disrupting the earth's climate. The time for action is now, and at last the tools exist to alter energy production and consumption in ways that simultaneously benefit the economy and the environment. Over the past 25 years, however, the public and private funding of research and development in the energy sector has withered. Between 1980 and 2005 the fraction of all U.S. R&D spending devoted to energy declined from 10 to 2 percent. Annual public R&D funding for energy sank from $8 billion to $3 billion (in 2002 dollars); private R&D plummeted from $4 billion to $1 billion (see box, "R&D Is key").

To put these declines in perspective, consider that in the early 1980s energy companies were investing more in R&D than were drug companies, whereas today investment by energy firms is an order of magnitude lower. Total private R&D funding for the entire energy sector is less than that of a single large biotech company. (Amgen, for example, had R&D expenses of $2.3 billion in 2005.) And as R&D spending dwindles, so does innovation. For instance, as R&D funding for photovoltaics and wind power has slipped over the past quarter of a century, the number of successful patent applications in these fields has fallen accordingly. The lack of attention to long-term research and planning has significantly weakened our nation's ability to respond to the challenges of climate change and disruptions in energy supplies.

Calls for major new commitments to energy R&D have become common. A 1997 study by the President's Committee of Advisors on Science and Technology and a 2004 report by the bipartisan National Commission on Energy Policy both recommended that the federal government double its R&D spending on energy. But would such an expansion be enough? Probably not. Based on assessments of the cost to stabilize the amount of carbon dioxide in the atmosphere and other studies that estimate the success of energy R&D programs and the resulting savings from the technologies that would emerge, my research group has calculated that public funding of $15 billion to $30 billion a year would be required—a fivefold to 10-fold increase over current levels.

Greg F. Nemet, a doctoral student in my laboratory, and I found that an increase of this magnitude would be roughly comparable to those that occurred during previous federal R&D initiatives such as the Manhattan Project and the Apollo program, each of which produced demonstrable economic benefits in addition to meeting its objectives. American energy companies could also boost their R&D spending by a factor of 10, and it would still be below the average for U.S. industry overall. Although government funding is essential to supporting early-stage technologies, private-sector R&D is the key to winnowing the best ideas and reducing the barriers to commercialization.

R&D IS KEY

Spending on research and development in the U.S. energy sector has fallen steadily since its peak in 1980. Studies of patent activity suggest that the drop in funding has slowed the development of renewable energy technologies. For example, the number of successful patent applications in photovoltaics and wind power has plummeted as R&D spending in these fields has declined.

U.S. R&D SPENDING IN THE ENERGY SECTOR

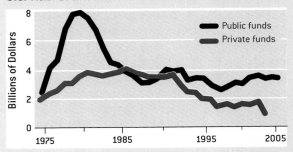

LAGGING INNOVATION IN PHOTOVOLTAICS . . .

. . . AND IN WIND POWER

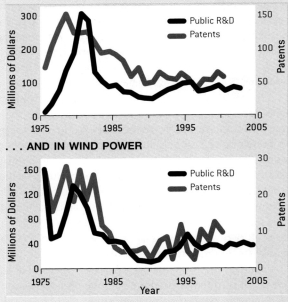

Spending amounts are expressed in 2002 dollars to adjust for inflation.

Raising R&D spending, though, is not the only way to make clean energy a 25
national priority. Educators at all grade levels, from kindergarten to college, can
stimulate public interest and activism by teaching how energy use and production
affect the social and natural environment. Nonprofit organizations can establish a
series of contests that would reward the first company or private group to achieve
a challenging and worthwhile energy goal, such as constructing a building or appli-
ance that can generate its own power or developing a commercial vehicle that can
go 200 miles on a single gallon of fuel. The contests could be modeled after the
Ashoka awards for pioneers in public policy and the Ansari X Prize for the developers of space vehicles. Scientists and entrepreneurs should also focus on finding
clean, affordable ways to meet the energy needs of people in the developing world.
My colleagues and I, for instance, recently detailed the environmental benefits of
improving cooking stoves in Africa.

But perhaps the most important step toward creating a sustainable energy
economy is to institute market-based schemes to make the prices of carbon fuels
reflect their social cost. The use of coal, oil and natural gas imposes a huge collective toll on society, in the form of health care expenditures for ailments caused by
air pollution, military spending to secure oil supplies, environmental damage from
mining operations, and the potentially devastating economic impacts of global
warming. A fee on carbon emissions would provide a simple, logical and transpar-
ent method to reward renewable, clean energy sources over those that harm the
economy and the environment. The tax revenues could pay for some of the social
costs of carbon emissions, and a portion could be designated to compensate low-
income families who spend a larger share of their income on energy. Furthermore,
the carbon fee could be combined with a cap-and-trade program that would set
limits on carbon emissions but also allow the cleanest energy suppliers to sell permits to their dirtier competitors. The federal government has used such programs
with great success to curb other pollutants, and several northeastern states are
already experimenting with greenhouse gas emissions trading.

Best of all, these steps would give energy companies an enormous financial
incentive to advance the development and commercialization of renewable energy
sources. In essence, the U.S. has the opportunity to foster an entirely new industry.
The threat of climate change can be a rallying cry for a clean-technology revolution
that would strengthen the country's manufacturing base, create thousands of jobs
and alleviate our international trade deficits—instead of importing foreign oil, we
can export high-efficiency vehicles, appliances, wind turbines and photovoltaics. This
transformation can turn the nation's energy sector into something that was once
deemed impossible: a vibrant, environmentally sustainable engine of growth.

Understanding Kammen's Graphics

The article certainly informs, and the graphics present information economically, clearly, and memorably. However, Kammen's central purpose is to convince us that renewable energy has enormous potential and needs significantly

more public attention, research investment, and commercial development than it is currently getting. "Let's commit ourselves to renewable energy" is its central message, and so this apparently informative article is actually an argument. The graphics, therefore, function mainly as evidence to back up Kammen's main contentions. Let's examine the first two and reserve the others for your own analysis.

The opening drawing, an example of what's called an "artist's conception," depicts a green world, powered entirely by renewables, where agriculture and city exist side by side. The combine in the field runs on electricity generated by huge solar panels, perhaps using biofuels on days without sun, while wind (note the turbines in the background) and sun (note the solar panels on the roof of the houses in the right foreground) work together to provide all the power needed by the city. In the original color drawing, the sky is deep blue merging into purple, suggesting lack of pollution, and the fields are various shades of green and gold, with obvious implications.

"Why an artist's conception?" you might ask. The obvious answer, of course, is no such communities exist today to photograph. The article needs a way to stimulate our imagination, to help us envision a world that could be, where energy is cheap, abundant, inexhaustible, and, most of all, clean. Caught as we are in a world that burns oil, natural gas, and coal to supply nearly all energy, we have trouble conceiving a world powered by renewables. Anything we can't conceive, we can't aspire to—hence the importance of establishing this vision of the future.

The drawing, then, is persuasive: "Just imagine the possibilities" is the message. The box titled "Growing Fast . . ." (pages 78–79), in contrast, gives us the facts. Solar, wind, and ethanol production are all sharply up worldwide, as the three line graphs show, but the top pie graph puts the upswing in perspective—only a tiny sliver, 2%, of the world's power comes currently from renewables. The pie graph on the bottom depicts the relative proportions of green energy in use, showing us, among other things, that the enormous potential of wind and solar power has yet to be aggressively exploited. Finally, the prose combined with the visuals summarizes knowledge that the graphs and photos couldn't supply, making the box a fine example of combining visuals with words.

The "Growing Fast . . ." box packs a lot of information into an attractive space; it would take many pages to describe it in prose, boring pages of data that would not have half the impact of the graphics. That's part of why it's persuasive—we can see the big picture without trudging through many pages of text. But to appreciate its full persuasive power, the implications of the box and the opening drawing must be combined. The drawing seems almost futuristic, as if we will wait a long time to see anything like it, while the box shows us that it's all tantalizingly within reach. We just have to do more with what we've got. And so, in sum, the message is simple and upbeat: "We can do it."

◎◎ FOLLOWING THROUGH

1. Graphics, we must always remember, *supplement* texts. Reread the section "Blowing in the Wind," an allusion to a famous song by Bob Dylan, and then examine the map of the United States (page 82), which depicts the 11 trillion kilowatt-hours of wind energy that could be generated in the United States each year. What does text and graphic working together "say"?

2. We see what could happen in the map—wind power harnessed to full potential. And so we ask, Why not? The box "R&D Is Key" (page 84) tells us what the main problem is—not nearly enough R&D. The problem is not putting enough money in research and scientific innovation. We're not going to get there if we don't. Work backwards from this box: How do all the graphics link to one another to answer closely related questions? How much of Kammen's case for renewables is made in the graphics? If we had only the text without the graphics, how much persuasive power would be lost?

3. To see the potential for adding graphics in your own writing, bring a recent paper you wrote to class. If you didn't use graphics, consider whether the paper can be improved with graphic support. If so, given your audience and purposes, what graphic types would you use and why? If you did use graphics, be prepared to discuss them—what you did and why, and how you went about securing or creating the visuals. If you now see ways to improve them, discuss what you would do as well.   •

WRITING ASSIGNMENTS

Assignment 1: Analyzing an Advertisement or Editorial Cartoon

Choose an ad or cartoon from a current magazine or newspaper. First, inquire into its rhetorical context: What situation prompted its creation? What purpose does it aim to achieve? Where did it originally appear? Who is its intended audience? What would they know or believe about the product or issue? Then inquire into the argument being made. To do this, you should consult the questions for inquiry on pages 181–182 to the extent that they apply to visual rhetoric. You should also consider the following points: What visual metaphors or allusions appear? What prior cultural knowledge and experiences would the audience need to "read" the image? Consider how the visual argument might limit the scope of the issue or how it might play to the audience's biases, stereotypes, or fears. After thorough inquiry, reach some conclusion about the effectiveness and ethics of your ad or cartoon. Write your conclusion as a thesis or claim. Use your analysis to convince, supporting it with evidence gathered during inquiry.

The following student essay is an example of Assignment 1. Before you begin your own essay, read it and discuss the conclusions reached about an advertisement for Eagle Brand condensed milk. We were unable to obtain permission to reprint the advertisement under discussion, but the descriptions of it should make the analysis easy to follow.

A Mother's Treat
Kelly Williams

Advertisements are effective only if they connect with their audiences. Advertisers study the group of people they hope to reach and know what the group values and what images they have of themselves. Often these images come from social expectations that tell businessmen, mothers, fathers, teens that they should look or act a certain way. Most people adhere to the norms because they give social status. Advertisers tend to look to these norms as a way to sell their products. For example, an ad depicts a man in an expensive suit driving a luxury car, and readers assume he is a lawyer, physician, or business executive. Such people will buy this car because they associate it with the status they want to project. Likewise, some advertisements manipulate women with children by associating a product with the ideal maternal image.

An advertisement for Eagle Brand condensed milk typifies this effort. The advertisement appeared in magazines aimed at homemakers and in *People* magazine's "Best and Worst Dressed" issue of September 1998. The readers are predominantly young women; those with children may be second-income producers or single mothers. They are struggling to raise a family and have many demands on their time. They feel enormous pressure to fulfill ideal work and domestic roles.

The advertisement creates a strong connection with a maternal audience. The black-and-white photograph depicts a young girl about kindergarten age. The little girl's facial expression connotes hesitation and sadness. In the background is a school yard. Other children are walking toward the school, their heads facing down, creating a feeling of gloom. All readers will recognize the situation. The little girl is about to attend her first day of school. One could easily guess that she is looking back at her mother with a sense of abandonment, pleading for support.

The wording of the text adds some comic relief. The ad is not intended to make the readers sad. The words seem to come from the mind of the child's mother. "For not insisting on bunny slippers for shoes, for leaving Blankie behind, for actually getting out of the car. . . ." These words show that the mother is a good mother, very empathetic. Even the print type is part of the marketing strategy. It mimics a "proper" mother's handwriting. There are no sharp edges, implying softness and gentleness.

The intent is to persuade mothers that if they buy Eagle   5 Brand milk and make the chocolate bar treat, they will be good mothers like the speaker in the ad. It tells women that cooking such treats helps alleviate stressful situations in everyday family life. The little girl reminds mothers of their duty to comfort their kids. She evokes the "feminine" qualities of compassion, empathy, and protectiveness.

The ad also suggests that good mothers reward good behavior. As the ad says, "It's time for a treat." But good mothers would also know that "Welcome Home Chocolate Bars" are rich, so this mother has to say, "I'll risk spoiling your dinner." The invisible mother in the ad is ideal because she does care about her child's nutrition, but more about the emotional state of her child.

In many ways this ad is unethical. While the ad looks harmless and cute, it actually reinforces social pressures on women to be "perfect" mothers. If you don't bake a treat to welcome your child back home after school, you are failing as a mother. The recipe includes preparation time, showing that the treat can be made with minimal effort. It gives mothers no excuse for not making it. Moreover, the advertisement obviously exploits children to sell their product.

Desserts do not have much nutritional value. It would be hard to make a logical case for Welcome Home Bars, so Eagle Brand appeals to emotion. There's nothing wrong with a treat once in a while, but it is wrong to use guilt and social pressure to persuade mothers to buy a product.

Assignment 2: Analyzing and Creating Posters or Flyers

As a class project, collect copies of posters or flyers you find around your campus. It's true that information in our culture is plentiful and cheap but attention is at a premium. Creators of posters and flyers must compete not only with each other but with all other visual sources of information to catch and keep our attention. How well do the posters and flyers your class found work? Why do some catch and hold attention better than others?

Create a poster or flyer to publicize an event, an organization, a student government election, or anything else relevant to your campus life. Use the best posters and flyers you found as a model, but don't be reluctant to use color, type sizes, images, and so on in your own way.

Assignment 3: Using Visual Rhetoric to Promote Your School

Colleges and universities compete fiercely for students and are therefore as concerned about their image as any corporation or politician. As a class project, collect images your school uses to promote itself, including brochures for prospective students, catalogs, class lists, and Web home pages. Choose three or four of the best ones, and in class discussions analyze them. Then, working in groups of three or four students or individually, do one or all of the following:

1. Find an aspect of your college or university overlooked in the publications that you believe is a strong selling point. Employing photographs, drawings, paintings, or some other visual medium, create an image appropriate for one of the school publications. Compose an appealing text to go with it. Then, in a page or two, explain why you think your promotional image would work well.

2. If someone in the class has the computer knowledge, create an alternative to your school's home page, or make changes that would make it more appealing to prospective students and their parents.

3. Imagine that for purposes of parody or protest you wanted to call attention to aspects of your school that the official images deliberately omit. Proceed as in item 1. In a short statement, explain why you chose the image you did and what purpose(s) you want it to serve.

4. Select a school organization (a fraternity or sorority, a club, etc.) whose image you think could be improved. Create a promotional image for it either for the Web or for some other existing publication.

5. As in item 3, create a visual parody of the official image of a school organization, perhaps as an inside joke intended for other members of the organization.

Assignment 4: Analyzing Your Own Visual Rhetoric

Study all the images your class created as argument and/or persuasion in the previous assignment. Select an image to analyze in depth. Write an essay that addresses these questions:

> What audience does the image intend to reach?
> What goal did the creator of the image seek to accomplish?

If something is being argued, ask:

> What thesis is advanced by the image or accompanying text?
> Do aspects of the image or text function as reasons for holding the thesis?

If an image persuades more than it argues, attempt to discover and understand its major source of appeal. Persuasion appeals to the whole person in an effort to create **identification,** a strong linking of the reader's interests and values with the image that represents something desired. Hence, we can ask

How do the images your class created appeal to the audience's interests and values?

Do the images embody emotional appeals? If so, how?

Assignment 5: Writing to Convince

Newspapers have been criticized for printing pictures that used to be considered too gruesome for publication. Highly respected newspapers like the *New York Times* have offered defenses of graphic photos. Look into what publishers, readers, and critics have to say on this topic. What issues and questions come up in these debates? Draw a conclusion of your own, and write an essay supporting it.

Assignment 6: Using Graphics to Supplement Your Own Writing or Other Texts

Select an essay that could be improved either by adding graphics or by revising the graphics used. Working alone or collaboratively with a writing group, revise it. For help with using graphics effectively in your writing, see the Best Practices box "Guidelines for Using Visuals." You have many revision options: Besides adding visuals, you can cut unneeded ones, redesign existing ones, change media (for example, from a photo to a drawing), change image types (for example, from a table to a graph), and so on. Revising graphics always means reworking the text as well. Expect changes in one to require changes in the other.

Assignment 7: Presenting Information Using PowerPoint

Revise and present the written text in Assignment 6 as an oral presentation using PowerPoint. If you don't know how to use PowerPoint, have another student who does show you how, or use the tutorial that comes with the program.

PowerPoint is a powerful tool for presenting visuals in a talk. *But it is more often used poorly, as a crutch for nervous speakers, than it is used well, to supplement a talk.* Inexperienced speakers want the audience's eyes on anything else but them, so they pack everything they have to say into the PowerPoint slides and have the audience looking at the projections all through the speech. Don't do this. Use PowerPoint to present your graphics to the audience and to summarize major points. Otherwise, keep the audience looking at and listening to you, not staring at a projection screen. Show them a graphic, for instance, and then discuss it, but don't leave it on screen to

www.mhhe.com/**crusius**

For further help on using Power-Point, visit the online tutorial at:

Writing > PowerPoint Tutorial

Guidelines for Using Visuals

Graphics come in a variety of useful forms: as tables to display numerical data economically, as graphs to depict data in a way that permits easy comparison of proportions or trends, as photographs to convey realism and drama, and as drawings to depict structures. Whatever graphics you use, be sure to do the following:

- Make sure every graphic has a definite function. Graphics are not decorative and should never be "thrown" into an essay.

- Choose the kind or form of visual best suited to convey the point you are trying to make.

- Design graphics so that they are easy to interpret. That is, keep them simple, make them large enough to be read without strain, and use clear labeling.

- Place graphics as close as possible to the text they explain or illustrate. Remember, graphics should be easier to understand than the text they supplement.

- Refer to all your graphics in the text. Readers usually need both the graphic and a text discussion for full understanding.

- Acknowledge the creator or source of each graphic next to the graphic itself. As long as you acknowledge the source or creator, you can borrow freely, just as you can with quotations from texts. Of course, if you wish to publish an essay that includes borrowed graphics, you must obtain written permission.

distract attention from you. Don't read from your text or memorize it, but talk from a few notes to remind yourself of what you need to say. Remember: PowerPoint complements a speech in much the same way graphics complement a written text. Don't let it take over or allow anxiety to cause you to lean on it too hard.

Writing Research-Based Arguments

Most arguments are researched writing. You need to read sources to inform yourself about your topic, and then you need to cite sources in order to convince your readers that you have a good case. An argument with no research behind it is generally weak. Many published arguments may not appear to have research behind them. In journalism, sources may not be documented, but the authors have had to dig to learn the facts, and when they use someone else's views, they introduce that person as an authority because naming authorities' credentials strengthens a case.

Nevertheless, a researched argument must be your own case, with your own angle on the topic, not a case borrowed from your sources. The trick to writing well with sources is to keep them from taking over. You must be in charge, using your sources as supporting characters in what must remain your own show. This chapter will cover finding sources, evaluating them, using them in your own writing, and citing them correctly. To help you stay in charge through this whole process, we will emphasize the role of writing "behind the scenes" *before* you begin drafting your paper. The more you use writing to interact with your sources, to know them well, and to see what supporting parts they might play, the more you will be ready to write

www.mhhe.com/**crusius**

For a wealth of research resources, go to:

Research

as the author—the authority—of an argument of your own: an argument with your own claim, your own voice, your own design.

Using your sources with this kind of confidence helps reduce the possibility of misusing a source. Misuse of a source includes

- Taking material out of context and misrepresenting the viewpoint of the author. Most texts include "multiple voices"—that is, writers may describe opposing views, or they may speak ironically, so a casual reader may misunderstand their viewpoint. Applying the critical reading skills described in Chapter 2 will keep you from misusing a source.

www.mhhe.com/crusius

For more information on plagiarism, go to:

Research > Plagiarism

- Using material without giving credit to the source. If you use someone else's words, you must put quotation marks around them. If you use someone else's ideas, even in your own words, you must give that other person credit. Failure to do so is plagiarism. Because plagiarism is a growing problem, partly owing to the ease with which material can be cut and pasted from online sources, we have devoted the next chapter, Chapter 6, to ethical writing and plagiarism. Because some plagiarism is not intentional—students may not understand what constitutes fair use of a source or may not realize how to paraphrase adequately and accurately—we recommend that you read this brief chapter before you start working with the sources you find.

Research takes time and patience; it takes initiative; it takes genuine curiosity. You have to recognize what you do not know and be willing to accept good evidence even if it contradicts what you previously believed. The first step in research is finding an issue that is appropriate.

FINDING AN ISSUE

Let's say you have been assigned to write an argument on an issue of current public concern. If you have no idea what to write about, what should you do?

Understand the Difference between a Topic and an Issue

People argue about issues, not about topics. For example, global warming is a topic. It is the warming of the earth's atmosphere, a scientific observation. However, people argue about many issues related to the topic of global warming, such as whether human activity has contributed to the temperature increase. This was the argument made by the film *An Inconvenient Truth*. The conversation on that issue is subsiding because even the oil companies have come to accept the evidence about the effects of manmade greenhouse gases. But other issues remain, such as what sources of energy are the best alternatives to the fuels that produce greenhouse gases and how individuals might change their lifestyles to make less of an impact on global climate. The point here: To write a good argument, you must explore genuine questions at issue, not just topics. Furthermore, you should explore a question that really interests you. You will need to care about your issue because research takes time, patience, and—most of all—initiative.

Find Issues in the News

Pay attention to the news and to the opinions of newsmakers, leaders, and commentators. College students are busy, but there are some easy ways to keep abreast of issues in the news. Here are hints for various news sources.

The Internet

- Set one of the major news organizations or newspapers as your home page so that when you turn on your computer, the news will be the first thing you see. Some options are

Cable News Network	<http://www.cnn.com>
Microsoft NBC News	<http://www.msnbc.com>
National Public Radio News	<http://www.npr.org/>
The *New York Times*	<http://www.nytimes.com>
The *Wall Street Journal*	<http://www.wsj.com>

  If you moved away to go to college, choose the online version of your hometown paper as a way of keeping in touch with events back home as well as around the world.

- Visit the index of mainstream and alternative online news sources listed on the Web site of FAIR (Fairness and Accuracy in Reporting) at <http://www.fair.org/index.php?page=134>. This Web site also provides links to media criticism and other resources for doing research into the news media.

- Visit CQ Researcher Online. This division of *Congressional Quarterly* allows you to search for issues and browse for in-depth reports and pro and con statements from public figures. This resource is located at <http://library.cqpress.com/cqresearcher/>.

Magazines and Newspapers

Browse your campus bookstore or library for magazines devoted to news and current affairs. In the library, ask for directions to the "recent periodicals" area. In addition to the obvious choices such as *Time* and *Newsweek*, look for the more opinionated magazines such as *Utne Reader, New Republic*, and *National Review*. For more coverage of issues, look for *Atlantic Monthly, Harper's, Science,* and *National Geographic.*

Lectures, Panel Discussions, Class Discussions, Conversations

Hearing in person what others have to say on an issue will help expose the important points and raise questions for research. Seek out discussion of issues you are considering for research.

Personal Observations

The best way to find an engaging issue is to look around you. Your instructor may not give you total freedom to choose an issue, but many current events and social concerns touch our daily lives. For example, the student whose paper we use as an example of researched writing found her issue when she realized the connection between something close to home that had been bothering her and the general topic area her instructor had specified for the class: global warming.

Finding an Issue on the Topic of Global Warming: A Student Example

Student Julie Ross was in a class that had been assigned the topic of global warming. To find an issue, Julie attended an on-campus screening of *An Inconvenient Truth,* followed by a panel discussion featuring representatives of government agencies, environmentalists, and professors of earth science. Julie asked the panelists what individual citizens could do to reduce their contributions to greenhouse gases. One panelist suggested that consuming "less stuff" would make a difference, since the production of consumer goods contributes to carbon dioxide and other greenhouse gases. Because Julie was already fuming about old houses on her street being torn down and replaced with supersized McMansions, she decided to research the question of how destructive this kind of development is, not just to the immediate neighborhood, but also to the planet. She began wondering about its contribution to global warming and how much more energy it demands, because the new houses use much more energy than the ones they replace. She decided to write her paper to an audience of home buyers. If she could discourage them from buying these huge new houses, the developers would have to stop building them. To make a convincing case, Julie needed to find good arguments for preserving the older homes and evidence about how much more energy the large new homes use than the older, smaller ones. Julie's paper appears at the end of this chapter.

 www.mhhe.com/**crusius** | You'll find more tools to help you find an issue at:
Learning > Links Across the Curriculum > Refdesk.com

FINDING SOURCES

The prospect of doing research can be overwhelming, given the many possible avenues to explore: the Internet, newspapers, magazines and journals, and all kinds of books. You need a strategy to guide you most efficiently to the best sources on your topic. The quality of your paper depends on its ingredients; you want to find not just *any* sources but the most credible, appropriate, and—if you are writing about current events—the most recent.

As you begin your research, two tips will make the journey much more efficient and orderly—and less stressful.

1. Keep a research log. Students often complain that they found a reference to an article but didn't save it or print it out, and then they could not find their way back to it. They waste precious time because they didn't take the time to write down the title and author, the journal it appeared in, and the index which led them to it. So our first advice on research strategy is to use your notebook to mark your trail

to anything that looks interesting. Better yet, if you think you might use a source, print it out right then or photocopy it.

2.   Make complete photocopies and printouts. When you make printouts and photocopies, get *all* the information you will need later to cite these sources even if you are not sure you will use them. It's easier to take the time when you have the source at hand than to retrace your steps later. If you use a book that you cannot check out of the library, take the time to photocopy the title page and the copyright page with the date of publication. Also, photocopy the page (usually near the front or back if there is one) that gives information about the author. Be sure to place the book carefully on the copy machine to make sure you get the entire page copied, with no text cut off, including the page number.

Field Research

Consider beginning your research with what you can observe. That means going out into the "field," as researchers call it, and recording what you see, either in written notes or with photographs or drawings. Field research can also include recording what you hear, in audiotapes and in notes of interviews and conversations. An interview can also take place online, through e-mails or a chat, if you can preserve it. Following are some suggestions for field research.

Observations

Do not discount the value of your own personal experiences as evidence in making a case. You will notice that many writers of arguments offer as evidence what they themselves have seen, heard, and done.

Alternatively, you may seek out a specific personal experience as you inquire into your topic. For example, one student writing about homelessness in Dallas decided to visit a shelter. She called ahead to get permission and schedule the visit. Her paper was memorable because she was able to include the stories and physical descriptions of several homeless women, with details of their conversations.

Julie Ross began her research by walking the streets of her neighborhood, photographing the stark contrasts of size and style between the older homes and the new ones built on the sites of torn-down houses. Her photographs provided evidence for her case against super-sized homes in historic communities.

Questionnaires and Surveys

You may be able to get information on some topics, especially if they are campus related, by doing surveys or questionnaires. This can be done very efficiently in electronic versions (Web-based or e-mail). Be forewarned, however, that it is very difficult to conduct a reliable survey.

First, there is the problem of designing a clear and unbiased survey instrument. If you have ever filled out an evaluation form for an instructor or a course, you will know what we mean about the problem of clarity. For example, one evaluation might ask whether an instructor returns papers "in a reasonable length of time"; what is "reasonable" to some students may be too long for others. As for bias, consider the question "Have you ever had trouble getting assistance from the library's reference desk?" To get a fair response, this questionnaire had better also ask how many requests for help were handled promptly and well. If you do decide to draft a questionnaire, we suggest you do it as a class project so that students on all sides of the issue can contribute and troubleshoot for ambiguity.

Second, there is the problem of getting a representative response. For the same reasons we doubt the results of certain magazine-sponsored surveys of people's sex lives, we should be skeptical about the statistical accuracy of surveys targeting a group that may not be representative of the whole. For example, it would be impossible to generalize about all first-year college students in the United States based on a survey of only your English class—or even the entire first-year class at your college.

Surveys can be useful, but design, administer, and interpret them carefully.

Interviews

You can get a great deal of current information by talking to experts. As with any kind of research, the first step in conducting an interview is to decide exactly what you want to find out. Write down your questions.

The next step is to find the right person to interview. As you read about an issue, note the names (and possible biases) of any organizations mentioned; these may have local offices, the telephone numbers of which you could easily find. In addition, institutions such as hospitals, universities, and large corporations have public relations offices whose staffs provide information. Also, do not overlook the expertise available from faculty members at your own school.

Once you have determined possible sources for interviews, you must begin a patient and courteous round of telephone calls, continuing until you connect with the right person; this can take many calls. If you have a subject's e-mail address, you might write to introduce yourself and request an appointment for a telephone interview.

Whether your interview is face to face or over the telephone, begin by acknowledging that the interviewee's time is valuable. Tell the person something about the project you are working on, but withhold your own position on any controversial matters. Sound neutral and be specific about what you want to know. Take notes, and include the title and background of the person being interviewed and the date of the interview, which you will need to cite this source. If you want to tape the interview, ask permission first. Finally, if you have the individual's mailing address, send a thank-you note after the interview.

If everyone in your class is researching the same topic and more than one person wants to contact the same expert, avoid flooding that person with requests. One or two students could do the interview and report to the class, or the expert could visit the class.

Library and Internet Research

Since 80% of what is now published in print is also available online, the distinction between library and Internet research has blurred. You will be able to find many magazines, scholarly journals, and newspapers through the Internet, and many Internet sites through your library's online directories. Because so many documents are now electronic—even if they appeared first in print—librarians have coined the term "born digital" to distinguish purely cyberspace documents from documents that were born in print but have been made available online.

With the daily additions to information, articles, images, and even books available online, the resources for searching it are constantly being upgraded. The advice in this chapter should get you started, but it's always a good idea to consult your library's reference librarians for help with finding sources on your topic. They know what is in your school's library, what is online, and what the latest tools are for finding any kind of source. You will find these librarians at the reference desk; every library has one.

 **www.mhhe.com/crusius** To find online guidance for using the library, check out:
Research > Using the Library

Kinds of Sources

The various kinds of sources available in print and online include books and periodicals as well as electronic media.

Books Nonfiction books generally fall into three categories:

Monographs: Monographs are sustained arguments on a single topic. To use them responsibly, you should know the complete argument; that means reading the entire book, which time may not allow. Possibly, reading the introduction to a book will acquaint you with the author's argument well enough that you can selectively read sections of the book. Decide if you have time to use a book responsibly. Sometimes you can find a magazine or journal article by the author that covers some of the same ground as the book but in a condensed way.

Anthologies: These are collections of essays and articles, usually by many different writers, selected by an editor, who writes an introductory essay. Anthologies are good sources for short papers because they offer multiple voices, and each argument can be read in one sitting. Pay attention to whether a book is an anthology because you will cite these anthology selections differently from a regular book. Look near the back of the book for information about the author of any selection you choose to use.

Reference books: These are good for gathering background information and specific facts on your topic. You can find these online and in the library shelves; they cannot be checked out. Reference books include specialized encyclopedias on almost any subject, such as *The Encyclopedia of Serial Killers,* a 391-page book. We will tell you below how to search for encyclopedias and other reference books. Many reference books are now available electronically.

A *note of caution about* Wikipedia: *Wikipedia* is not a scholarly publication. In fact, it encourages a democratic notion of knowledge in which anyone can contribute, add to, alter, or delete material that has been posted on a topic. Although the editors scan it regularly for misinformation, errors, and deliberate lies, there is no guarantee that what you find there is credible. We suggest you use it for background information and for links to other, more authoritative sources whose authors' credentials you can confirm. Check any facts you plan to use in your papers against other, more scholarly sources.

A *note of caution about general encyclopedias:* Multi-volume online and print encyclopedias such as *Britannica* and *Microsoft Encarta* are good for background knowledge as you begin research on a topic or for fact-checking while you are writing. However, college students should not use general encyclopedias as primary sources. The entries do not cover topics in depth and are not usually products of original research. It is better to use specialized encyclopedias and reference works or books and articles by specialists in your topic.

Periodicals Periodicals are published periodically—daily, weekly, monthly, quarterly. They include the following types:

Articles in scholarly journals: These journals are usually published by university presses and aimed at readers in a particular scholarly discipline: Both the authors and intended readers are professors and graduate students. Scholarly articles are contributions to ongoing debates within a discipline. Therefore, they are credible sources, but scan them for accessibility. If you are not familiar with the debate they are joining, you may not find them accessible enough to use responsibly. Seek your instructor's help if you find a source hard to comprehend. Scholarly journals are usually born in print and put online, but some are born digital.

Articles in magazines: Magazines—print, online, and the born digital "e-zines"—are all good sources for short papers. Magazine articles vary greatly, depending on their intended readership. Some magazines, such as *Atlantic Monthly, Harper's, National Review, New Republic,* the *New Yorker,* and even *Rolling Stone,* offer articles by scholars and serious journalists. They give arguments on current public issues by the same people who write for scholarly journals, but the articles are aimed at an educated public readership, not other scholars. These are perfect for familiarizing yourself with viewpoints on an issue. You can find even more accessible articles and arguments in weekly newsmagazines, including columns by nationally syndicated writers. Trade magazines are good for business-related topics; Julie Ross found several online magazines published for the building industry. Many advocacy groups also publish magazines in print and online. Julie found ecological advocacy groups' magazines, such as *E: The Environmental Magazine,* helpful in her research.

Newspapers: Newspapers are ideal sources for arguments and information on current as well as historical issues. Feature articles, which are long and in-depth, usually present the reporter's angle on the topic; opinion columns are arguments and therefore good for getting perspectives on your topic. Major national newspapers such as the *Washington Post, Wall Street Journal,* and *New York Times* should be available online through your library's catalogue, as will the local newspaper for your college's city or town. Below, we tell more about how to search for newspaper articles, including those from student-run college papers and small-town and regional papers.

Audiovisual Materials Visuals so often supplement verbal arguments that you should be aware of the many resources for finding visuals to use in your papers and also to view as sources of information. Your library's book catalogue includes films available on campus; search engines like Google help you find visuals on the Internet.

Web Sites Web sites include nearly every kind of source described above and more. You have to evaluate everything you find in the wild and open world of cyberspace, but nearly all research institutes and centers associated with universities, advocacy groups, government bureaus, and political organizations are excellent sources for your arguments. Also, nearly all writers these days have their own page on the Web, where you can go to find more about their lives, views, and other writing, so the Web is a great resource for learning more about your sources. The only problem is searching the Web efficiently, and we offer advice later in this chapter on how to zero in on the best sites for your topic.

Blogs, Listservs, Usenet Groups, Message Boards The Web has become an exciting place for dialogue, where scholars within an area of interest can argue with each other and ask each other for help with their research. Although a first-year student may not feel ready to enter these discussions, "lurking"—reading a discussion without contributing to it—is a great way to learn about the debates firsthand. And an intelligent question will find people ready to share their knowledge and opinions. We'll tell you later in this chapter about directories that will take you to the most relevant resources for your topic.

Choose the Best Search Terms

The success of your search depends on what terms you use. Before beginning, write down, in your notebook or research log, possible terms that you might use in searching for sources on your topic. Do this by examining your research question to find its key terms. As you begin doing your research, you will discover which of these terms are most productive and which you can cross out. Adapt your search terms as you discover which ones are most productive.

We'll use Julie's search to illustrate how to find the best search terms. Julie's research question was, What are the negative effects of tearing down older homes and replacing them with bigger new ones? Julie wanted to know more about the environmental effects of large homes, both on climate change globally and on the local neighborhoods.

Use Phrase Searching Whether you are in a Google search, a directory or index search, or an online catalogue, put *quotation marks* around phrases to tell your search engine to search for the combined words, not the individual words. Put the words in the order you want them to appear and put quotation marks around the phrase; for example,

"neighborhood preservation"

Start with General Words What are the most obvious words for your topic? Julie's topic about the big new houses replacing old ones fits into the larger category of *residential construction* or *home building*.

Think of Synonyms When Julie could not find any books in her library's catalogue on home building, she thought, What is a synonym for *home*? Answer: *house*. She looked again for books under the subject *house building*.

Use Unique or Specific Words and Phrases What words most specifically describe your topic? You may be able to think of these words, or they may show up as you search. Julie quickly discovered that the sources she found used the term *teardowns*. When she began using this as a search term, she found many relevant sources. As she began reading about the effects of residential construction on the environment, Julie also encountered the term *green building* to describe the more sustainable kinds of home construction materials and designs.

Use Boolean Searching Boolean searching (named after nineteenth-century English logician George Boole) allows you to narrow or broaden your search by joining words with AND OR NOT

AND: "home size" AND "energy consumption"

Using AND narrowed Julie's search. However, she found nothing by combining "home size" AND "global warming." She needed to think more specifically about the connection between home size and global warming: Energy consumption is the link. (Note: Google and most other search engines automatically put AND in when you type words in succession.)

OR: "green houses" OR "sustainable homes"

Using OR broadened the search, yielding more hits. Using OR is helpful if you know your subject has many synonyms, such as *youth, teenagers, students*.

NOT: "green house" NOT agriculture

Using NOT limited the search by eliminating references to hothouses in agriculture.

Searching Your Library

Because much of the research material on the Internet is available for free through your school's library, it makes sense to start with your library's resources. Why pay for something that you already have free access to through your college or university? Also, unlike much of what you find on the Internet, the materials available through your library have been selected by scholars, editors, and librarians, so you can be more confident about the credibility of what you find.

Don't assume that searching the library means using bound books and periodicals only, or even going there in person. Libraries are going electronic, giving you online access to more high quality, full-text sources than you will find on the Web. Libraries subscribe to online indexes and journals that cannot be found through search engines, such as Google and Yahoo. These resources are on what is called the "Deep Web" or the "Invisible Web." Your enrollment at school gives you access to these resources, which are described later in this chapter. Your library's online home page is the gateway to all the library's resources. Figure 5.1 is an example of a library home page.

Your Library's Online Catalogue

Your library's online catalogue is the gateway to a wealth of sources: books, both printed and online in the form of e-books that you can "check out" and download; full-text online newspapers, including the complete archives of these papers; indexes to individual articles in magazines, newspapers, and scholarly journals, including links to the full text of most of them online; audiovisual materials; maps; and reference books of all kinds. Visit the home page of your library's online catalogue and explore the places it will take you. In the library catalogue, you can search for books by title, author, subject, and key word, as well as their Library of Congress call numbers. Here are some tips:

> *In a title search:* If you know a title you are looking for, do a title search with as much of the title needed to distinguish it from other titles. Omit initial articles (*a, the, an*).

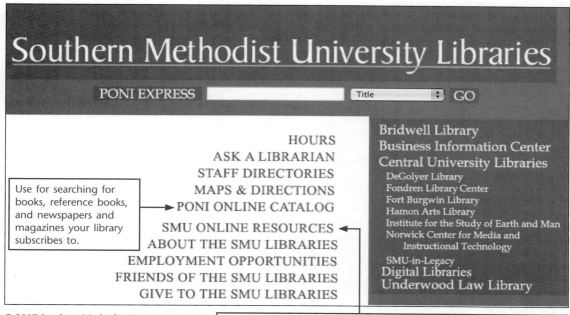

In a subject search: You will need to know what "subject heading" the Library of Congress has given your topic. Julie, for example, found no books in her library catalogue when she typed in "home construction" but found twenty-five books when she typed in "house construction." If you cannot find books with your term, you can try other synonyms or go to <http://authorities.loc.gov/> and put your search term in the "Search Authorities" box. It will tell you the right term to use according to the Library of Congress cataloging system. Or just try a key word search, described below.

In a key word search: This kind of search is more forgiving than a subject search and can be helpful if you don't know the exact right word. Put quotation marks around phrases: "global warming." You can use AND or OR to combine terms: "teardowns" AND "neighborhood preservation."

Figure 5.1

An example library home page

The library's online catalogue will also tell you if your library subscribes to a particular newspaper or magazine. The catalogue will not tell you about individual articles or stories in these periodicals, but you can find them by searching the publication's own online index or the online databases in your library, described below. Most university libraries now subscribe to major U.S. newspapers and have full-text archives online. Do a title search to find if your library has a particular newspaper.

To locate reference books, combine your key word search with words like *encyclopedia, dictionary,* or *almanac,* and you will find both online and on-the-shelf reference books. For an example of such a search and an example of a result, see Figures 5.2 and 5.3.

Your Library's Online Resources (The Deep Web)

Your school library's purchased online resources are available only to students, faculty, and staff. Your library has to subscribe to them in order for you to see them. They are known as the "Deep Web" or the "Invisible Web" because outsiders do not have access to them. Students can access them on campus or off campus by using computers connected to the campus server or by using a password. The main Web page of most university libraries offers a link to a page listing the online resources available to you. These usually include reference resources: dictionaries such as the Oxford English Dictionary; electronic encyclopedias, journals, and magazines; and most important, licensed databases to help you search for a wide variety of sources on any topic, both on and off the Web.

These databases are indexes to articles in periodicals: magazines, scholarly journals, and newspapers. You search them by typing in a subject, key word, author, or title. In most cases the search will produce a list of articles, an abstract of the article, and often, a link to full text of the article, which you can then save or print out.

If the full text is not available online, the database will tell you if the periodical is in your library's holdings. You may be able to access it electronically through the online catalogue. This is why it is good to know which magazines, journals, and newspapers are catalogued along with the books in your library's online catalogue.

Never use the abstract of an article as a source. Abstracts may not be written by the source's author; they may not be accurate. Most important, you cannot get the in-depth understanding of a source that would allow you to use it accurately.

The following are some common licensed databases you can link to from your library's online resources page:

- EBSCO Host Research Databases: If your library subscribes to EBSCO Host, you may have access to as many as fifty databases at a click of your mouse. Choose EBSCO Host and then the tab that says "Choose Databases." The list should include Academic Search Premier. This is the most useful, all-around database for multidiscipline searches, providing access to full-text documents in over 4,500 journals. While in Academic Search Premier, use the "Other Databases" tab to find a pull-down menu to other EBSCO databases. Some EBSCO databases are

Business Source Complete
Communication and Mass Media Complete
Film and Television Literature Index

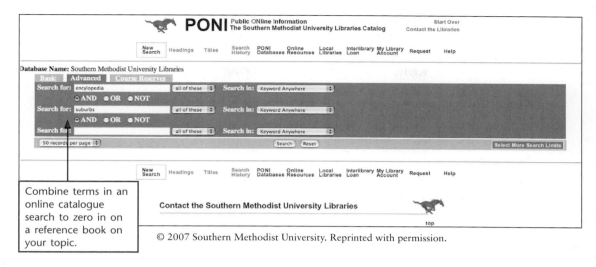

Combine terms in an online catalogue search to zero in on a reference book on your topic.

© 2007 Southern Methodist University. Reprinted with permission.

Figure 5.2

A search in online catalogue for specialized encyclopedias about suburbs

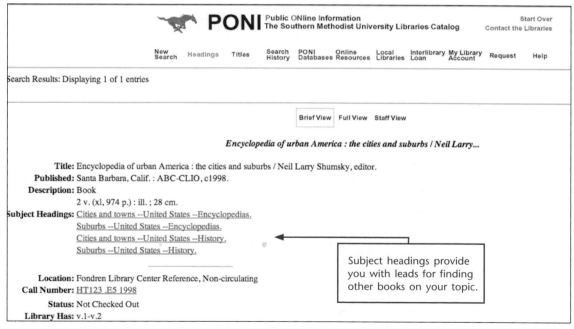

Subject headings provide you with leads for finding other books on your topic.

© 2007 Southern Methodist University. Reprinted with permission.

Figure 5.3

The result of an online search for encyclopedias about suburbs

Religion and Philosophy Collection

TOPICsearch (good for social, political, and other topics popular in classroom discussions)

- *InfoTrac* (for articles in magazines, journals, and major newspapers)
- *InfoTrac* Newspaper (good for finding articles in local newspapers; browse the titles to find if yours is here)
- UMI ProQuest Direct (similar to Infotrac)
- Lexis-Nexis (good for newspaper articles, including articles and editorials in many college campus papers; find the "university wire" index under the tab for "university news")

In addition to these common databases, most schools' online resources page will also give you access to more specialized databases. You can find them grouped according to subject, such as anthropology, economics, or psychology. For example, a search within the subject "communications" brought up this list of over twenty indexes:

Academic OneFile
All movie guide
American Film Institute catalog
American memory
Arts & humanities citation index
Arts and humanities search
Communication & mass media complete
Film & television literature index
Film literature Index
FITA
International Children's Digital Library
Journalist's toolbox
JSTOR
Mintel reports
MLA international bibliography
MRI+
NewPages.com
PollingReport.com
Population Reference Bureau
Poynter online
Project Muse
Redbooks
Social sciences citation index
SocioSite
Trademark Electronic Search System (TESS)

Of these, the JSTOR index (which stands for *Journal Storage*) is itself an index to over seven hundred scholarly journals in approximately forty disciplines. Clearly, the library's licensed databases are an expansive chain of resources for research.

 **www.mhhe.com/crusius** You can find more tools organized by discipline at:
Research > Discipline-Specific Resources

An advanced search in databases like *InfoTrac* and EBSCO Academic Premier (illustrated in Figure 5.4) allows you to combine terms to narrow your search. Julie Ross eliminated all hits not related to housing by including "houses" as a second term in her search. Note that EBSCO and *InfoTrac* allow you to select from academic journals, popular magazines, newspapers, or all three. The search in Figure 5.4 targeted newspapers only.

Internet Research

Because the Internet is so large—estimated to contain over 50 billion documents—we want to caution you about the potential for wasting time if you start browsing with one of the common search engines such as Yahoo or Google. However, there are some ways to use search engine features to narrow your search. One of those ways is to limit your search to certain domains.

 **www.mhhe.com/crusius**
For further advice on using the Internet to conduct research, go to:
Research > Using the Internet

Domains

Every Internet address or URL (Uniform Resource Locator) has certain components; it helps to know a little about them. What is known as the "top level domain name" tells you something about who put the site on the Web.

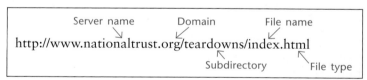

For Web sites from the United States, the following are the four most common top level domain names. Web sites from other nations typically have instead an abbreviation of the country's name.

Commercial (.com) "Dot com" sites include businesses and their publications—such as the real estate newsletter at <http://www.teardowns.com>—other commercial publications, such as magazines; and personal Web pages and blogs, such as those created on Blogger.com. The example, teardowns. com, is a site assisting builders who want to construct on the sites of torn-down houses. Although you will find magazine and newspaper articles through search engines like Yahoo and Google, a better way to ensure that you get them in full text for free is to find them through your library's licensed databases, as described on page 106. Because so much of the Web is commercial

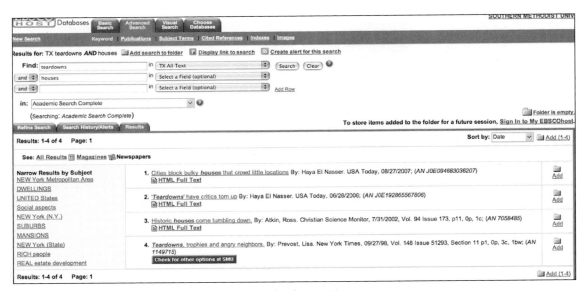

© 2007 EBSCO Industries, Inc. All rights reserved. Reprinted with permission.

Figure 5.4

Results of a search for articles in a database

sites, you will probably want to use the advanced search options explained in the next section to filter "dot com" sites from your search.

Nonprofit Organizations (.org) "Dot org" sites include organizations and advocacy groups, such as the National Trust for Historic Preservation at <http://www.nationaltrust.org/teardowns/>. Their purpose is to raise awareness of, participation in, and donations to their causes.

Educational Institutions (.edu) "Dot edu" sites contain research and course materials of public and private schools, colleges, and universities. The URL <http://sciencepolicy.colorado.edu/> is a site for a center at University of Colorado at Boulder doing research on science, technology, and public policy. Although mostly what you find at these sites is the work of professors, some of the material may be by graduate and undergraduate students, so as always, check out the author's credentials.

Government Agencies (.gov) "Dot gov" sites are useful for getting the latest information about any aspect of American government or about government agencies and policies. The URL <http://www.census.gov/Press-Release/www/releases/archives/housing/007127.html> leads to an article published by the U.S. Census Bureau on the size of houses in 2006.

Advanced Features for Searching the Web

Search engines provide a variety of ways to focus your search, and Google has some that are especially useful for students.

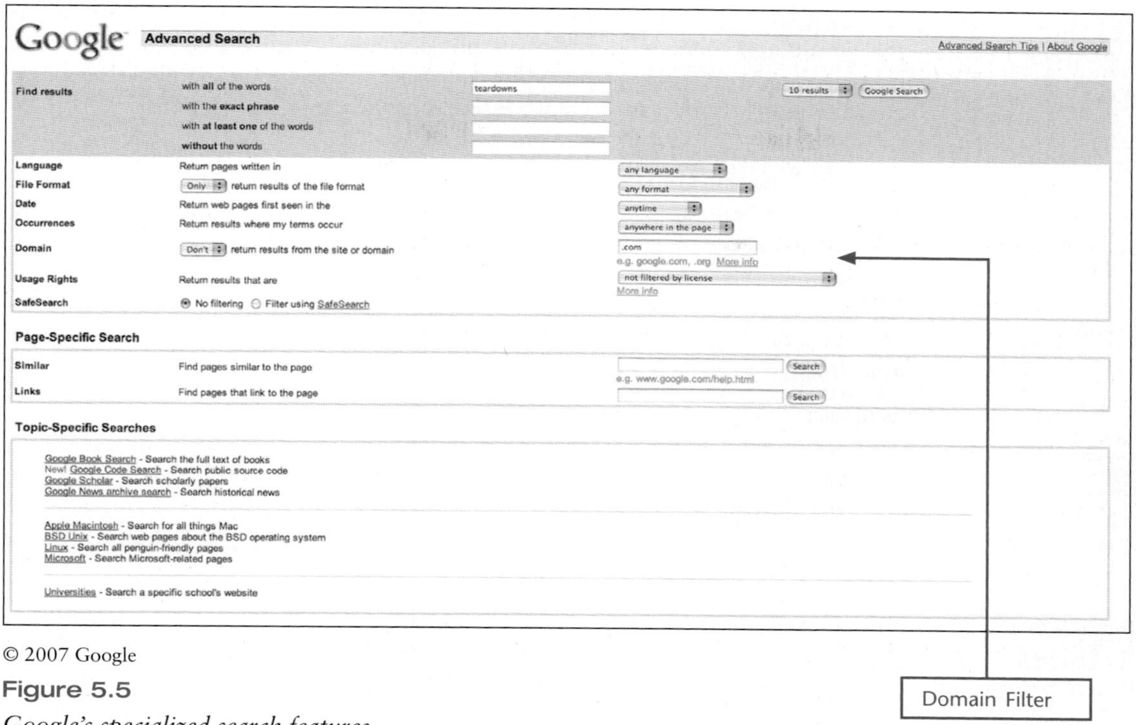

© 2007 Google

Figure 5.5

Google's specialized search features

Advanced Searches Search engines will let you customize your search, allowing you to limit your search to just one or two of the domains listed above, or to exclude one. Filtering out the "dot com" sites is like turning on a spam blocker, so you will get fewer hits by writers with no academic or professional credentials. (See Figure 5.5.)

Google Specialized Searches Google offers an ever-increasing number of specific kinds of searches, such as News Archives, Books, Images, and Earth. Many link you to materials that you will have to pay for. However, you can probably find many of these for free through your school library, which subscribes to the archives of many magazines and newspapers. See the earlier section, "Your Library's Online Catalogue."

Google Book Google Book Search can find your key word as it appears on a specific page in a book, even if the title may not indicate that the book contains information on that topic. So, for example, when Julie typed in "teardowns" in Google Book, she was taken to a list of books where that term appeared. By choosing one, she could see the actual page where the term was used. This feature is both helpful and dangerous, however. Google Book shows you one page only, not the whole book, although it gives you information about the whole book. You should not use Google Book as a source. Using material taken so far out of context, knowing very little about the whole argument of the book is not a solid way of doing research, even if you cite the book correctly. On the other hand, knowing that the book contains something you are interested in, you can then look for a copy of the book in your library or a bookstore.

Google Scholar Google Scholar is where your library and the Internet intersect. Google Scholar is an index to scholarly articles and book reviews, many of them available at your university library. If you open Google Scholar from a computer on campus or if your home computer connects to your school's network (or if you have a password that will grant you off-campus access to your school's network), you will be able to access full texts of materials available from your school's library.

Subject Directories to the Web

You can narrow your search for Web sites by going first to a subject directory that organizes Web sites by topic. Some examples are

Google Directory

Yahoo Directory

Figure 5.6
An example Web directory page

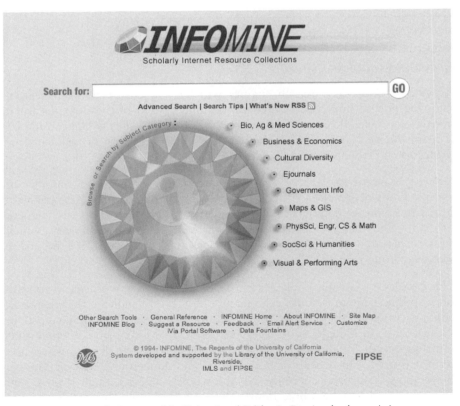

Infomine (assembled by librarians, not machines)

About.com

Other Web Resources: Blogs, Listservs, Message Boards, and Chat Groups

Don't overlook the potential of interactive sites on the Internet. Many authors of your sources have blogs and personal Web pages where they try out new ideas and get feedback from others interested in their topics. As a student, you may not feel ready to join these conversations, but you can learn a lot by lurking—that is, just reading them. You can find them by using "blogs," "listservs," "message board," or "chat room" as a search term in your browser. By searching for "academic blogs," we found this good portal to professors' blogs: <http://www.academicblogs.net/wiki/index.php/Main_Page>.

 www.mhhe.com/**crusius** For more online research resources, go to:

Research > Additional Links on Research

EVALUATING SOURCES

Before beginning to read and evaluate your sources, you may need to reevaluate your issue. If you have been unable to find many sources that address the question you are raising, consider changing the focus of your argument.

For example, one student, Michelle, had the choice of any issue under the broad category of the relationship between humans and other animals. Michelle decided to focus on the mistreatment of circus animals, based on claims made in leaflets handed out at the circus by animal-rights protestors. Even with a librarian's help, however, Michelle could find no subject headings that led to even one source in her university's library. She then called and visited animal-rights activists in her city, who provided her with more materials written and published by the animal-rights movement. She realized, however, that researching the truth of their claims was more than she could undertake, so she had to acknowledge that her entire argument was based on heavily biased sources.

Once you have reevaluated your topic, use the following method to record and evaluate sources.

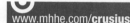 www.mhhe.com/**crusius**

For a tutorial on evaluating sources, go to:

Research > Source Evaluation Tutor: CARS

Eliminate Inappropriate Sources

You may find that some books and articles are intended for audiences with more specialized knowledge than you have. If you have trouble using a source, put it aside, at least temporarily.

Also, carefully review any electronic sources you are using. While search engines make it easy to find material on the Web, online documents often have met no professional standards for scholarship. Material can be "published" electronically without review by experts, scholars, and editors that must occur in traditional publishing. Nevertheless, you will find legitimate scholarship on the Internet—news reports, encyclopedias, government documents, and even scholarly journals appear online. While the freedom of electronic publishing creates an exciting and democratic arena, it also puts a much heavier burden on students and researchers to ensure that the sources they use are worthy of readers' respect.

Carefully Record Complete Bibliographic Information

For every source you consider using, be sure to record full bibliographic information. Take this information from the source itself, not from an index, which may be incomplete or inaccurate. If you make a record of this information immediately, you will not have to go back later to fill in omissions. We recommend that you use a separate index card for each source, but whatever you use, record the following:

1. For a book:

   Author's full name (or names)
   Title of book
   City where published
   Name of publisher
   Year published

   For an article or essay in a book, record all of the information for the book, including the name(s) of the book's author or editor and the title and the author(s) of the article; also record the inclusive page numbers of the article or chapter (for example, "pp. 100–150").

2. For a periodical:

   Author's full name (or names)
   Title of the article
   Title of the periodical
   Date of the issue
   Volume number, if given
   Inclusive page numbers

3. For a document found on the World Wide Web:

   Author's full name (or names)
   Title of the work
   Original print publication data, if applicable
   Title of the database or Web site
   Full URL
   Date you accessed the document

4. For material found through listservs and Usenet newsgroups:

   Author's full name (or names)
   Author's e-mail address
   Subject line from the posting
   Date of the posting
   Address of the listserv or newsgroup
   Date you accessed the document

Read the Source Critically

As discussed in Chapter 2, critical reading depends on having some prior knowledge of the subject and the ability to see a text in context. As you research a topic, your knowledge naturally becomes deeper with each article you read. But your sources are not simply windows, giving you a clear view; whether argumentative or informative, they have bias. Before looking through them, you must look *at* your sources. Therefore, devote conscious attention to the rhetorical context of each source. Keep these questions in mind.

Who Is the Writer, and What Is His or Her Bias?

Is there a note that tells about the writer's professional title or institutional affiliation? If not, search the Internet for the writer's personal home page or university Web site. Or look in the *Dictionary of American Biographies,* or the *Biography and Genealogy Master Index,* which will send you to numerous specialized biographical sketches.

How Reliable Is the Source?

Again, checking for credibility is particularly important when you are working with electronic sources. For example, one student found two sites on the Web, both through a key word search on "euthanasia." One, entitled "Stop the Epidemic of Assisted Suicide," was posted by a person identified only by name, the letters MD, and the affiliation "Association for Control of Assisted Suicide." There was no biographical information, and the "snail mail" address was a post office box. The other Web site, "Ethics Update: Euthanasia," was posted by a professor of philosophy at the University of San Diego whose home page included a complete professional biography detailing his education, titles, and the publishers of his many books and articles. The author gave his address at USD in the Department of Philosophy. The student decided that, although the first source had some interesting information—including examples of individual patients who were living with pain rather than choosing suicide—it was not a source that skeptical readers would find credible. Search engines often land you deep within a Web site, and you have to visit the site's home page to get any background information about the source and its author. Be suspicious

Additional Guidelines for Evaluating Internet Sources

1. Look at the last segment of the domain name, which will tell you who developed the site. The most reliable ones are developed by colleges and universities (.edu) or by the government (.gov). Of course, commercial sites (.com, .biz) are profit-minded.

2. Check whether the name of the creator of the Web page or its Webmaster appears, complete with an e-mail address and the date of the last update, near either the top or the bottom of the page.

3. Check whether the source includes a bibliography, a sign of scholarly work.

4. Ask yourself if the links are credible.

5. A tilde (~) indicates a personal page; these pages must be evaluated with special care.

of sites that do not contain adequate source information; they probably aren't reliable.

When Was This Source Written?

If you are researching a current issue, decide what sources are too old. Arguments on current issues often benefit from earlier perspectives.

Where Did This Source Appear?

If you are using an article from a periodical, be aware of the periodical's readership and editorial bias. For example, *National Review* is conservative, *The Nation* liberal. An article in the *Journal of the American Medical Association* will usually defend the medical profession. Looking at the table of contents and scanning editorial statements will give you a feel for the periodical's politics. Also look at the page that lists the publisher and editorial board. You will find, for example, that *New American* is published by the ultra-right-wing John Birch Society. If you need help determining bias, ask a librarian. A reference book that lists periodicals by subject matter and explains their bias is *Magazines for Libraries*.

Why Was the Book or Article Written?

Although some articles are occasioned by news events, most books and arguments are written as part of an ongoing conversation among scholars or journalists. Being aware of the issues and the participants in this conversation is essential, as you will be joining it with your own researched argument. You can check *Book Review Index* to find where a book has been reviewed, and then consult some reviews to see how the book was received.

"I just feel fortunate to live in a world with so much disinformation at my fingertips."

What Is the Author's Aim?

First, determine whether the source informs or argues. Both are useful and both will have some bias. When your source is an argument, note whether it aims primarily to inquire, to convince, to persuade, or to mediate.

How Is the Source Organized?

If the writer doesn't use subheadings or chapter titles, break the text into parts yourself and note what function each part plays in the whole.

Special Help with Evaluating Web Sites

The Internet is a dangerous place for researchers in a hurry. If you are not careful to look closely at what you find on the Web, you could embarrass yourself badly. For example, why would a college student want to cite a paper written for a high school class? Many high school teachers put their best student papers on class sites—good papers, but nevertheless, not exactly the kind of authority a college student should be citing. So before choosing to use something from the Web, go through the following checklist:

1. **Know the site's domain.** See pages 109–110 for how to read a Web address and what the various domain suffixes tell you about the site.

Note if the site is commercial, educational, governmental, or some kind of advocacy group, usually indicated by *.org* in the domain name. Commercial sites may be advertising something—they are not disinterested sources.

2. **Find the home page.** A search engine or online directory may take you to a page deep within the site; always look for links back to the home page because that is where you can find out more about the bias of the site and the credentials of the people behind it.

3. **Read about the bias and mission of the site.** At the home page, you should see a link to more information about the site—often the link is called "About Us" or "Mission Statement." Follow it and learn about the ideology of the site and how it compares with your own bias and that of other sources you are using.

4. **Read about the credentials of the site's creators.** The creators' degrees and professional affiliations should be easy to find. Regard any site as bogus if the only link to finding more about the authors is an e-mail address. Also, note whether the credentials of its board of directors or trustees are in the fields of specialization for your topic. For example, many writers for some Web sites on global warming dispute scientific findings, but are not scientists. They may be economists or historians.

5. **Note if the site reports on its funding and donors.** The rule of "follow the money" becomes important when you are using sources outside of the academic world. Think tanks and advocacy groups receive money from large corporations. Consider how the funding might influence their research and reported findings. There should be a link to material about funding, corporate sponsors, and the group's annual tax reports.

6. **Note how current the site is.** Near the beginning or the end of any Web site or part of a Web site, you should be able to find a note about when the site was last updated. You will need this information in order to cite the site—a site that has not been updated in years is not a good choice.

The Web site for the National Trust for Historic Preservation, where Julie found a speech about the effects of teardowns on neighborhoods, checks out as a credible site. From the home page, Julie was able to link to a page titled "About the National Trust," where she learned that it is a private, nonprofit organization founded in 1949 and dedicated to saving historical places. It advocates for legislation to protect communities and places of cultural heritage. The home page also provides a link titled "Funding," with information about donations, corporate sponsors, and tax returns. A link to the organization's "Management" gave the credentials of its trustees and its executive staff, including Richard Moe, the author of the speech. Julie learned that

Figure 5.7

The home page of the Web site of the National Trust for Historic Preservation

Moe graduated from Williams College in 1959 and from the University of Minnesota Law School in 1966. He has been president of the National Trust since 1993. He is an honorary member of The American Institute of Architects and co-author of a book titled *Changing Places: Rebuilding Community in the Age of Sprawl,* published in 1997. Clearly, this source from a Web site passed the test.

USING SOURCES

The first way to use your sources is to familiarize yourself with viewpoints on your topic. Your thesis will grow out of your research; you do not do research to find information to support a position you have not investigated. In high school, you may have grabbed quotations or facts from a source; in college you must know the source itself, including something about the author and the author's argument, unless your source is an encyclopedia or almanac or other reference work. For more on getting to know sources, read Chapter 2, "Reading an Argument," and the preceding section in this chapter, "Evaluating Sources," pages. 113–119.

When you have gathered and evaluated some sources, you should next spend some time with each one, reading it, marking it up, and writing about it in your notebook or on a notepad. This essential step will help you use your sources confidently and accurately in a paper with your own angle and voice. One teacher calls this step "writing in the middle" since it bridges the gap between the sources you have found and the paper you will turn in. If you skip this step, you risk misrepresenting your source, taking material out of context, plagiarizing (see Chapter 6, "Ethical Writing and Plagiarism"), or, more commonly, letting your sources take over with too much of their voice and wording, resulting in a paper that sounds patched together.

Because you should not use a source that you have not read in its entirety, we reproduce below one of Julie Ross's sources for her argument on neighborhood preservation. We will demonstrate various kinds of "writing in the middle" about this source.

Note that we have annotated this reading, an important "writing in the middle" step you should perform for every source you plan to use.

Battling Teardowns, Saving Neighborhoods

Note author's credentials

RICHARD MOE, president of the National Trust for Historic Preservation

Speech given to the Commonwealth Club, San Francisco, CA; June 28, 2006

A growing disaster is tearing apart many of America's older neighborhoods. They're being devoured, one house at a time, here in the Bay Area, across California, and in scores of communities from coast to coast.

Quotable passage here

I'm talking about teardowns—the practice of purchasing and demolishing an existing house to make way for a new, much bigger house on the same site. Teardowns wreck neighborhoods. They spread through a community like a cancer, destroying the character and livability that are a neighborhood's lifeblood. I believe teardowns represent the biggest threat to America's older neighborhoods since the heyday of urban renewal and interstate highway construction during the 1950s and 60s.

Claim

Here's how it works: Developers and home-buyers look through desirable neighborhoods for a building lot that can lawfully accommodate a much bigger house than that which currently stands on it. The property is acquired, the existing house is torn down and a bigger house is constructed in its place. There are variations: Sometimes a large estate is leveled and subdivided to accommodate several new houses; in others, several smaller houses are cleared to make way for a single, massive new one.

Extent of the problem

It's a simple process, but it can totally transform the streetscape of a neighborhood and destroy its character. It's especially destructive in older and historic communities.

Teardowns are occurring all over America—from fashionable resorts such as Palm Beach and Palm Springs to the inner-ring suburbs around Washington and Chicago and the Richmond District here in San Francisco. The trend has become so alarming that the National Trust included "Teardowns in Historic Neighborhoods" on our list of America's 11 Most Endangered Historic Places in 2002. Back then, we identified 100 communities in 20 states that were having major problems with teardowns. That statistic was troubling in 2002—but four years later, the news is much worse: Today we can document the impact of teardowns in more than 300 communities in 33 states. The National Association of Home Builders says that 75,000 houses are razed and replaced with larger homes each year. . . .

Background information [margin note, line 5]

This disaster goes by many names. In New Jersey, the practice is often called "bash-and-build." In Colorado, teardowns are known as "scrape-offs." In Oregon, the new houses are sometimes called "snout houses" because of the big, protruding garages that dominate their facades. In other places they're known simply—and aptly—as "bigfoots" or "monster homes."

Extent of the problem [margin note]

Whatever you call it, one teardown usually sparks others. A New Jersey builder says, "It's a trend that keeps on rolling. Builders used to be afraid to be the first person in a neighborhood to tear a house down. Now they're looking around and saying they don't mind taking the risk."

Why is this happening?

Three factors are at work in the spread of teardowns.

The first is the rise in real-estate prices. In some areas, home values have doubled or tripled over the past decade, and this leads developers to look for "undervalued" properties—many of which exist in older neighborhoods.

More background [margin note, line 10]

The second factor is the trend toward bigger houses. In 1950, the average American home incorporated less than 1,000 sq. ft. By 2005, the average new home had more than doubled in size, to 2,412 sq. ft. According to the National Association of Home Builders, almost 40% of new homes have four or more bedrooms; that's more than twice as many as in the early 1970s—despite the fact that the average family size decreased during that same period. Subdivisions of luxury homes of 5,000 sq. ft. and more are becoming commonplace. Clearly, burgers and french fries aren't the only things in America being "super-sized."

Reasons for teardowns [margin note]

The final factor is that many people are looking for an alternative to long commutes or are simply fed up with the soulless character of sprawling new subdivisions. For these people, older in-town neighborhoods and inner-ring suburbs are enormously appealing because of their attractive architecture, mature landscaping, pedestrian orientation, easy access to public transportation and amenities such as local shopping districts, libraries and schools.

Other reasons for teardowns [margin note]

The problem is that too many people try to impose their preference for suburban-style mini-mansions on smaller-scale neighborhoods where they just don't fit. And since most of these older areas offer few vacant lots for new construction, the pressure to demolish existing houses can be intense. A modest cottage gets torn down and hauled off to the landfill, and what goes up in its place is "Tara" on a quarter-acre lot.

Neighborhood livability is diminished as trees are removed, backyards are eliminated, and sunlight is blocked by bulky new structures built right up to the property lines. Economic and social diversity are reduced as costly new "faux chateaux" replace more affordable houses—including the modest "starter homes" that our parents knew and that first-time homebuyers still search for today. . . .

While the destruction of historic houses is wasteful, environmentally unsound 15 and unnecessary, it's often just the beginning of the problems caused by teardowns.

It's not uncommon for a demolished older home to be replaced with a new one that is three times as big as any other house on the block. These structures loom over their neighbors and break the established building patterns of the area. Front yards are often given over to driveways, and three- or four-car garages are the dominant elements in the façade. Floor plans are often oriented to private interior spaces, making the new houses look like fortresses that stand totally aloof from their surroundings. . . .

Apart from their visual impact, teardowns can profoundly alter a neighborhood's economic and social environment. A rash of teardowns can cause property taxes to rise—and while this may be a good thing for communities in search of revenue, it can drive out moderate-income or fixed-income residents. Those who remain start to feel they've lost control of their neighborhood to developers and speculators. A house that once might have been praised as "charming and historic" now gets marketed as "older home on expansive lot"—which is realtor language for "teardown." Once that happens—once the value of an older house is perceived to be less than that of the land it's built on—the house's days are probably numbered. And sadly, the neighborhood's days as a viable historic enclave may be numbered too.

It doesn't have to be this way. There are alternatives to teardowns.

First of all, prospective builders should realize that most older, established neighborhoods simply can't accommodate the kind of sprawling new mini-mansion that is appropriate on a suburban cul-de-sac. People who want to move into the city can often find development opportunities in underused historic buildings and vacant land in older areas. Even in areas where vacant land is scarce, existing older houses can be enlarged in sensitive ways: A new zoning ordinance in Coronado, California, for example, gives homebuilders "bonus" square footage if they incorporate design elements that maintain the historic character of the community.

No one is saying that homebuyers shouldn't be able to alter or expand their 20 home to meet their needs, just as no one is saying that older neighborhoods should be frozen in time like museum exhibits. A neighborhood is a living thing, and change is both inevitable and desirable. The challenge is to manage change so that it respects the character and distinctiveness that made these neighborhoods so appealing in the first place.

Let me mention a few things that people and communities can do.

First and most important, communities must realize that they aren't helpless in the face of teardowns. They have choices: They can simply take the kind of community they get, or they can go to work to get the kind of community they want. They have to decide what they like about the community and don't want to lose. They must develop a vision for the future of their community, including where and how to accommodate growth and change. Then they must put in place mechanisms to ensure that their vision is not compromised.

Ideally, this consensus-building should take place as part of a comprehensive planning process—but that can take time, and sometimes the pressure of teardowns calls for immediate action. In those situations, some communities have provided a "cooling-off" period by imposing a temporary moratorium on demolition. This moratorium prevents the loss of significant structures while allowing time for residents and city officials to develop effective means of preserving neighborhood character.

One of those means is local historic district designation. Notice that I said "local historic district." Many people believe that listing a property in the National Register of Historic Places is enough to protect it, but that isn't true. The only real protection comes through the enactment of a local ordinance that regulates demolition, new construction and alteration in a designated historic area. More than 2,500 communities across the country have enacted these ordinances. Most of them require that an owner get permission before demolishing or altering a historic building; many also offer design guidelines to ensure that new buildings will harmonize with their older neighbors.

More solutions

If historic district designation isn't feasible or appropriate, other forms of regu- 25 lation may work. Conservation districts or design-review districts can address issues such as demolition and new construction with less administrative burden than historic districts. Floor-area ratios or lot-coverage formulas can remove the economic incentive for teardowns by limiting the size of new buildings. In the same way, setback requirements, height limits and open-space standards can help maintain traditional neighborhood building patterns. At least two communities in San Mateo County have recently adopted regulations of this sort to limit the height and floor area of newly built homes.

Not all approaches require government involvement. Local preservation organizations or neighborhood groups can offer programs to educate realtors and new residents about the history of older neighborhoods and provide guidance in rehabbing or expanding older houses. They can acquire easements to ensure that the architectural character of historic buildings is permanently protected. They can provide low-interest loans to help encourage sensitive rehabilitation. Incentives such as these are particularly effective when combined with technical assistance and some form of tax abatement from state or local government.

Some people go so far as to claim that teardowns actually support smart growth by directing new-home construction to already-developed areas, thereby increasing density and offering an alternative to suburban sprawl. Again, I disagree.

Opposing view and rebuttal

Tearing down a smaller house to build a bigger one simply adds square footage, not population density. In addition, teardowns affect neighborhood livability, reduce affordability, consume energy, and send thousands of tons of demolition debris to landfills. That doesn't sound like smart growth to me.

Equally important, teardowns exact too high a price in the wasteful destruction of our nation's heritage. Of course we need to encourage investment in existing communities as an alternative to sprawl—but not at the expense of the historic character that makes older neighborhoods unique, attractive and livable. Some say that change is simply the price of progress—but this kind of change isn't progress at all; it's chaos.

The National Trust is committed to helping local residents put the brakes on 30 teardowns. It will be a huge job—but it's eminently worthy of our best efforts.

America's older neighborhoods are important chapters in the story of who we are as a nation and a people. Working together, we can keep that story alive. Working together, we can keep America's older and historic communities intact so that generations to come can live in them, learn from them, be sheltered and inspired by them—just as we are today.

Ways of "Writing-in-the-Middle" to Gain Mastery over Your Sources

We borrow the term "writing-in-the-middle" from Bruce Ballenger, whose excellent book *The Curious Researcher* contains many suggestions for bridging the chasm between the writing that you read and the writing that you produce as a result of reading. The more you engage your sources with "talk-back" such as annotations, notebook responses to the ideas in the sources, notebook entries that make connections between and among ideas in sources, and paraphrases and summaries that make you really think about the key points and passages, the easier it will be for you to assume the voice of authority when it is time to start drafting your paper. Here are some suggestions for writing in the middle zone between researching and drafting.

1. Annotate the Source

Use the advice in Chapter 2, "Reading an Argument," which suggests things to look for in sources that are arguments. If a source is not an argument, note the author's angle, bias, and main points.

2. Respond to the Source in Your Notebook

After annotating, write more in your notebook about how you might use the source. If you have roughed out a case, note which reason or reasons of your own case this source could help you develop. If you find a new reason for your case, note it and think how you could develop it with your own observations and other sources you have found.

If you think the source will be mainly useful for facts, make a note about what kind of facts it has and the page numbers, so that when you start drafting, you can find them quickly.

If the author is an expert or authority, note the credentials or at least where you can go to find these as you start drafting—perhaps the author's Web page or a biographical note at the end of the book or article.

If this will be a major source for your paper, you should be sure you grasp the most important concepts in it. Look for the passages that pose a challenge; to use the source with authority, you need to own, not borrow, these ideas. That means instead of just dropping them in as quotations, you will have to work them in, explaining them in your own words. Try out *paraphrases* (see more on paraphrases in item 3 in this list) to make these points completely clear to you and then respond to the major ideas with what you think about them: If it's a good idea, why do you think so? What in your own experiences (field research) confirms it? What can you add of your own as you discuss this idea in your paper?

Look for memorable passages that are worth *direct quotations* (see more on direct quotations in this chapter's section on incorporating source material). The best quotes are strongly worded opinions and writing that cannot be paraphrased without losing its punch.

Think about how additional research might help you develop an idea given to you by this source.

Here are some notes Julie put in her notebook after deciding to use the National Trust source.

Notes on Moe, Richard. "Battling Teardowns."

- *Perfect source for my paper. I need to mention the National Trust for Historic Preservation. This source supports my "preserve the neighborhood character" reason. Good description of the garages—"snout houses." Also mention the way these new houses block the sunlight. Good on the economic impact on the older people in my neighborhood. Many can't afford to stay. This source helps explain why.*

- *I also hadn't thought about how these homebuyers are destroying the very thing that makes them want to live here. Old charm won't last if everybody does what they are doing. This could appeal to their interest—restore, not tear down.*

- *I like the part about allowing for change. I'll use this quote: "A neighborhood is a living thing. Change is both inevitable and desirable." What kinds of changes would I consider OK? Could a new house of different architectural style actually add character to the neighborhood? Maybe look for a source that describes some kind of acceptable change.*

- *He mentions the other part of my case, the environment, but not enough to use this source for that part.*

---

3. Paraphrase Important Ideas from the Source

Although you will use paraphrases as you incorporate material from your sources into your essay, consider paraphrase as a study skill that helps you understand key ideas by putting them into your own words. It helps you to "own" the key ideas rather than simply borrowing the author's words to insert into your paper. Here are some suggestions for paraphrasing:

- Read the entire source or section in which the passage appears. You cannot write a good paraphrase of a passage you have taken out of context.

Surrounding sentences will provide information essential for understanding the material you are paraphrasing, and to make the idea clear to yourself, you may need to add some of that information to your paraphrase. Later, if you use the paraphrase in your paper, you will need to provide enough context so that your readers will understand the idea as well.

- Read the passage several times through, including surrounding text, until you think you understand it. Annotate it. Look up any words that are even slightly unfamiliar to you.

- Put the text away so that you will not be tempted to look at it. Then think of the main ideas and try to put each one into your own words and your own wording. A paraphrase must not be an echo of the original's sentence patterns with synonyms plugged in. That is really a form of plagiarism, since it involves "stealing" the author's sentence pattern. You may want to break up complex sentences into shorter, more simple ones that make the idea easier to comprehend.

- Do not feel that you must find a substitute word for every ordinary word in the passage. For example, if a passage has the word *children,* don't feel you have to say *kids.*

- Go back and check your paraphrase against the original to see if you have accurately represented the full content of the original passage. Make adjustments as needed.

Examples of Adequate and Inadequate Paraphrasing
Original Passage:

> Some people go so far as to claim that teardowns actually support smart growth by directing new-home construction to already-developed areas, thereby increasing density and offering an alternative to suburban sprawl. Again, I disagree. Tearing down a smaller house to build a bigger one simply adds square footage, not population density.

Inadequate Paraphrase: This example borrows too much of the wording and sentence patterns (underlined) from the original text by Moe.

> Some people even claim that tearing down old houses supports smart growth by increasing new-home construction and density in already developed areas. Therefore, teardowns are an alternative to suburban sprawl. Moe disagrees because tearing down small houses and building bigger ones only adds more square footage, not more people.

Inadequate Paraphrase: The paraphrase below doesn't do justice to the idea: It does not include the concept of smart growth; it does not mention the problem of new development in suburban areas versus rebuilding in existing neighborhoods; and it does not give Moe credit for the opinion.

> It's not smart to tear down old houses and replace them with bigger ones because you don't get more population density.

Good Paraphrase: This explains "smart growth," gives Moe credit, and represents all the points in original sentence patterns. It even offers an interpretation at the end.

> Smart growth is an attempt to develop cities while minimizing suburban
> sprawl. According to Moe, tearing down older, small homes in close-in
> neighborhoods and replacing them with bigger ones is not really "smart
> growth" because bigger houses do not necessarily increase population
> density; they just offer more square footage for the same size household.
> So they are really a kind of urban sprawl.

4. Write Summaries of Portions of a Source

As a way to help get your own handle on important sections of a source, write a summary of it in your notebook. That means putting just the most important parts of the text into your own words (paraphrase) and joining them into a smooth paragraph. To write a summary, follow these steps.

1. Read and reread the portion of a text you want to summarize, looking up unfamiliar words.
2. Choose the main points.
3. Paraphrase them, using the advice on paraphrasing above.
4. Combine sentences to make the new version as concise as possible.

Here is an example of a portion of Richard Moe's speech that Julie used in her paper by shortening it and presenting it in her own words. The underlined sections are the ones she deemed important enough to go into the summary.

Original Passage:

> Three factors are at work in the spread of teardowns.
>
> The first is the rise in real-estate prices. In some areas, home values have doubled or tripled over the past decade, and this leads developers to look for "undervalued" properties—many of which exist in older neighborhoods. The second factor is the trend toward bigger houses. In 1950, the average American home incorporated less than 1,000 sq. ft. By 2005, the average new home had more than doubled in size, to 2,412 sq. ft. According to the National Association of Home Builders, almost 40% of new homes have four or more bedrooms; that's more than twice as many as in the early 1970s—despite the fact that the average family size decreased during that same period. Subdivisions of luxury homes of 5,000 sq. ft. and more are becoming commonplace. Clearly, burgers and french fries aren't the only things in America being "super-sized."
>
> The final factor is that many people are looking for an alternative to long commutes or are simply fed up with the soulless character of sprawling new subdivisions. For these people, older in-town neighborhoods and inner-ring suburbs are enormously appealing because of their attractive architecture, mature landscaping, pedestrian orientation, easy access to public transportation and amenities such as local shopping districts, libraries and schools.

Guidelines for Summarizing

1. Read and reread the original text until you have identified the claim and the main supporting points. You ought to be able to write an outline of the case, using your own words. Depending on your purpose for summarizing and the amount of space you can devote to the summary, decide how much, if any, of the evidence to include.

2. Make it clear at the start whose ideas you are summarizing.

3. If you are summarizing a long passage, break it down into subsections and work on summarizing one at a time.

4. As with paraphrasing, work from memory. Go back to the text to check your version for accuracy.

5. Maintain the original order of points, with this exception: If the author delayed presenting the thesis, refer to it earlier in your summary.

6. Use your own words.

7. Avoid quoting entire sentences. If you want to quote key words and phrases, incorporate them into sentences of your own, using quotation marks around the borrowed words.

Julie's Summary:

Moe sees three reasons for the increase in teardowns:

- In the past decade, the value of houses has doubled or tripled, except in some older neighborhoods. Developers look for these "'undervalued' properties" to build on.

- Homebuyers want more space, with the average home size going from 1,000 square feet in 1950 to 2,412 square feet in 2005.

- Some homebuyers desire to move from the "soulless . . . sprawling subdivisions" to close-in neighborhoods that have more character and more amenities, such as public transportation and local shopping.

5. Write Capsule Summaries of Entire Sources

Writers frequently have to summarize the content of an entire source in just a brief paragraph. Such summaries appear in the introduction to a volume of collected essays, in an opening section of scholarly articles in which the author reviews previously published literature on the topic, and at the end of books or articles in annotated bibliographies or works cited lists. The purpose of these is to let other scholars know about sources they might also want to consult.

If your class is working on a common topic, your instructor may ask the class to assemble a working bibliography of sources all of you have found, including a brief summary of each one to let other students know what the source contains. This is called an "annotated bibliography." Following is some advice on creating capsule summaries and annotated bibliographies.

Sample Entry in an Annotated Bibliography

Here is an annotated bibliography entry for Julie's National Trust source.

Moe, Richard. "Battling Teardowns, Saving Neighborhoods." The National Trust for Historic Preservation. June 28, 2006. <http://www.national-trust.org/news/2006/20060628_speech_sf.html> Jan. 21, 2007.

In this transcript of a speech given to a San Francisco civic organization, Moe, who is president of the National Trust for Historic Preservation, argues that builders should respect the integrity of older neighborhoods and that local residents should join the Trust's efforts to block the teardown trend, which is fueled by rising real estate values, homebuyers' desire for bigger houses, and fatigue with life in the distant suburbs. Teardowns "wreck neighborhoods" by removing trees and backyards, blocking the sun, ruining historic character, raising taxes so that poorer residents are forced out, and generating environmental waste. Communities can organize to fight teardowns by applying for historical designation or other kinds of government regulations on building as well as offering incentives for realtors and new buyers to respect neighborhood quality.

1. As explained in Chapter 2, "Reading an Argument," read and annotate the entire source, noting claims, reasons, the subdivisions into which the text breaks down, and definitions of words you looked up.
2. Working with one subdivision at a time, write paraphrases of the main ideas in each. Decide how much specific evidence would be appropriate to include, depending on the purpose of your summary. As with any paraphrase, work from memory and recheck the original later for accuracy.
3. You may include brief direct quotations, but avoid quoting whole sentences. That is not efficient.
4. Join your paraphrases into a coherent and smooth paragraph.
5. Edit your summary to reduce repetitions and to combine points into single sentences where possible.

Note that a good capsule summary restates the main points; it doesn't just describe them.

Not: Moe gives three reasons for the rise of the teardown trend.

But: Moe argues that the teardown trend is fueled by rising real estate values, homebuyers' desire for bigger houses, and fatigue with life in the distant suburbs.

Guidelines for Writing with Sources

Avoid plagiarism by *distinguishing sharply* between quoting and paraphrasing. Anytime you take exact words from a source, even if it is only a phrase or a significant word, you are quoting. You must use quotation marks and documentation. If you make any change at all in the wording of a quotation, you must indicate the change with square brackets. If you remove any words from a direct quotation, use ellipses (three spaced dots) to indicate the deletion. If you use your own words to summarize or paraphrase portions of a source, name that source in your text and document it. Be careful to use your own words when paraphrasing and summarizing.

1. Use an attributive tag such as "According to . . ." to introduce quotations both direct and indirect. Don't just drop them in.

2. Name the person whose words or idea you are using. Provide the full name on first mention.

3. Identify the author(s) of your source by profession or affiliation so that readers will understand the significance of what he or she has to say. Omit this if the speaker is someone readers are familiar with.

4. Use transitions into quotations to link the ideas they express to whatever point you are making.

5. If your lead-in to a quotation is a phrase, follow it with a comma. But if your lead-in can stand alone as a sentence, follow it with a colon.

6. Place the period at the end of a quotation or paraphrase, after the parenthetical citation, except with block quotations. (See page 134 for treatment of block quotations.)

6. Dialogue about Sources

Inside or outside of class, any conversations you can have about your research with others researching the same topic will help you get an angle and an understanding of your sources. This is the reason many scholars keep blogs—a blog is a place to converse about ideas. Your instructor may set up an electronic bulletin board for students to chat about their research, or you might make your own blog with friends and start chatting.

INCORPORATING AND DOCUMENTING SOURCE MATERIAL

We turn now to the more technical matter of how to incorporate source material in your own writing and how to document it. You incorporate material through direct quotation or through summary or paraphrase; you document material by naming the writer and providing full publication details of the source—a two-step process. In academic writing, documenting sources is essential, with one exception: You do not need to document sources of factual information that can easily be found in common references, such as an encyclopedia or atlas, or of common knowledge. See page 155 in Chapter 6, "Ethical Writing and Plagiarism," for more explanation of common knowledge.

Different Styles of Documentation

Different disciplines have specific conventions for documentation. In the humanities, the most common style is the Modern Language Association (MLA). In the physical, natural, and social sciences, the American Psychological Association (APA) style is most often used. We will illustrate both in the examples that follow. Both MLA and APA use parenthetical citations in the text and simple, alphabetical bibliographies at the end, making revision and typing much easier. (For a detailed explanation of these two styles, visit the Web sites for the MLA at <http://www.mla.org> and the APA at <http://apa.org>.)

In both MLA and APA formats, you provide some information in the body of your paper and the rest of the information under the heading "Works Cited" (MLA) or "References" (APA) at the end of your paper. The following summarizes the essentials of both systems.

www.mhhe.com/**crusius**

For Web sites with information on documentation styles, go to:

Research > Annotated Links to Documentation Sites

www.mhhe.com/**crusius**

You can find more documentation information at:

Research > Links to Documentation Sites

Instructions for Using MLA and APA Styles

MLA Style

In parentheses at the end of both direct and indirect quotations, supply the last name of the author of the source and the exact page number(s) where the quoted or paraphrased words appear. If the name of the author appears in your sentence that leads into the quotation, omit it in the parentheses.

www.mhhe.com/**crusius**

For a student sample of a paper in MLA format, go to:

Research > Sample Paper in MLA Style

Direct quotation with source identified in the lead-in:

> According to Jessie Sackett, a member of the U.S. Green Building Council, home ownership is "the cornerstone of the American dream. Recently, however, we've realized that keeping that dream alive for future generations means making some changes to how we live today" (36).

Indirect quotation with source cited in parenthetical citation:

> A spokesperson for the U.S. Green Building Council reminds us that home ownership is fundamental to the American dream; however, in order to preserve that dream for the generations to come, we need to develop more energy efficient houses and lifestyles today (Sackett 36).

APA Style

In parentheses at the end of direct or indirect quotations, place the author's last name, the date published, and the page number(s) where the cited material appears. If the author's name appears in the sentence, the date of publication should follow it in parentheses; the page number still comes at the end of the sentence. Unlike MLA, the APA style uses commas between the parts of the citation and "p." or "pp." before the page numbers.

www.mhhe.com/**crusius**

For a student sample of a paper in APA format, go to:

Research > Sample Paper in APA Style

Direct quotation with source cited in the lead-in:

> Jessie Sackett (2006), a member of the U.S. Green Building Council, writes, "Owning a home is the cornerstone of the American dream. Recently, however, we've realized that keeping that dream alive for future generations means making some changes to how we live today" (p. 36).

Indirect quotation with source cited in parenthetical citation:

> A spokesperson for the U.S. Green Building Council reminds us that home ownership is fundamental to the American dream; however, in order to preserve that dream for the generations to come, we need to develop more energy efficient houses and lifestyles today (Sackett, 2006, p. 36).

Direct Quotations

Direct quotations are exact words taken from a source. The simplest direct quotations are whole sentences worked into your text, as illustrated in the following excerpt.

MLA Style

> Richard Moe of the National Trust for Historic Preservation explains, "The problem is that too many people try to impose their preference for suburban-style mini-mansions on smaller scale neighborhoods where they just don't fit."

This source will be listed in the MLA Works Cited list as follows:

> Moe, Richard. "Battling Teardowns, Saving Neighborhoods." The National Trust for Historic Preservation. 28 June 2006. 15 Jan. 2007 <http://www.nationaltrust.org/news/2006/20060628_speech_sf.html>.

APA Style

> Richard Moe (2006) of the National Trust for Historic Preservation explains, "The problem is that too many people try to impose their preference for suburban-style mini-mansions on smaller scale neighborhoods where they just don't fit."

This source will be listed in the APA reference list as follows:

> Moe, R. (2006, June 28). Battling teardowns, saving neighborhoods. Retrieved Jan. 15, 2007, from *The National Trust for Historic Preservation* web site: http://www.nationaltrust.org/news/2006/20060628_speech_sf.html

Note that for both MLA and APA format, a page number is usually required with any citation. Because the source does not use page numbers, in this instance they are not included.

Altering Direct Quotations with Ellipses and Square Brackets

Although there is nothing wrong with quoting whole sentences, it is often more economical to quote some words or parts of sentences from the original in your own sentences. When you do this, use *ellipses* (three evenly spaced periods) to signify the omission of words from the original; use square *brackets* to substitute words, to add words for purposes of clarification, and to change the wording of a quotation so that it fits gracefully into your own sentence. (If ellipses already appear in the material you are quoting and you are omitting additional material, place your ellipses in square brackets to distinguish them.)

The following passage illustrates quoted words integrated into the sentence, using ellipses and square brackets. The citation is in MLA style.

Square Brackets   Use square brackets to indicate any substitutions or alterations to a direct quotation.

Original passage:

> Teardowns wreck neighborhoods. They spread through a community like a cancer, destroying the character and livability that are a neighborhood's lifeblood.

Passage worked into the paper: Part of the quotation has been turned into paraphrase.

> Moe compares the teardown trend to a cancer on the community: "Teardowns wreck neighborhoods. They [destroy] the character and livability that are a neighborhood's lifeblood."

Ellipses   Use three spaced periods to indicate where words have been removed from a direct quotation.

Original passage:

> Almost every one of these new, large homes is made out of wood— roughly three-quarters of an acre of forest. Much of the destructive logging around the world is fueled by our demand for housing. But home-building doesn't have to translate into forest destruction. By using smart design and forest-friendly products, builders can create new homes that save trees and money.
>
>   Many houses today are still built using outdated, inefficient construction methods. About one-sixth of the wood delivered to a construction site is never used, but simply hauled away as waste.

Passage worked into the paper: Two entire sentences have been removed, replaced with ellipses, because they were not relevant to the point Julie was making. There are no quotation marks because this will be a blocked quotation in the paper.

> Almost every one of these new, large homes is made out of wood—roughly three-quarters of an acre of forest. Much of the destructive logging around the world is fueled by our demand for housing. . . . Many houses today are still built using outdated, inefficient construction methods. About one-sixth of the wood delivered to a construction site is never used, but simply hauled away as waste.

Using Block Quotations

If a quoted passage runs to four or more lines of text in your essay, indent it one inch (ten spaces of type) from the left margin, double-space it as with the rest of your text, and omit quotation marks. In block quotations, a period is placed at the end of the final sentence, followed by one space and the parenthetical citation.

> In a consumer society, when people see their neighbors driving a new car, they think they need to buy a new one too. This is called "keeping up with the Joneses." Gregg Easterbrook has coined a new phrase, "call and raise the Joneses." He explains his new term this way:
>
> > In call-and-raise-the-Joneses, Americans feel compelled not just to match the material possessions of others, but to stay ahead. Bloated houses, for one, arise from a desire to call-and-raise-the-Joneses— surely not from a belief that a seven-thousand-square-foot house that comes right up against the property setback line would be an ideal place in which to dwell. (140)

Indirect Quotations

Indirect quotations are paraphrases or summaries of a source. Here is how this quotation might be incorporated in a paper as an indirect quotation.

MLA Style

> A spokesperson for the U.S. Green Building Council reminds us that home ownership is fundamental to the American dream; however, in order to preserve that dream for the generations to come, we need to develop more energy efficient houses and lifestyles today (Sackett 36).

The entry in the Works Cited list would appear as follows:

> Sackett, Jessie. "The Green American Dream: LEED for Homes Is Currently Being Piloted." <u>The LEED Guide: Environmental Design & Construction.</u> 9.6 (2006): 36+. InfoTrac Thomson Gale. Southern Methodist U, Fondren Lib., Dallas, TX. 18 Oct. 2006 <http://find.galegroup.com>.

APA Style

> A spokesperson for the U.S. Green Building Council reminds us that home ownership is fundamental to the American dream; however, in order to

Leading into Direct Quotations

Direct quotations need to be set up, not dropped into your paper. Setting up a quotation means leading into it with words of your own. A lead-in may be a short introductory tag such as "According to Smith," if you have already introduced Smith, but lead-ins usually need more thought. You need to connect the quotation to the ideas surrounding it in the original source.

Provide enough of the original context to fit the quotation coherently into your paragraph. You may need to paraphrase some of the surrounding sentences from the original source from which the quotation was taken. If you have not done so already, you may need to introduce the speaker of the words, along with his or her credentials if the speaker is an important writer or authority.

Here is an example of a quotation that does not fit coherently into the student's paper.

Quotation dropped in:

> Affluent Americans are buying new super-sized homes in older, urban residential areas. These lots were once occupied by historic and humble homes. "Teardowns wreck neighborhoods. They [destroy] the character and livability that are a neighborhood's lifeblood" (Moe).

Here is how Julie Ross led into the same quotation so that her readers would know more about the speaker and his point.

Quotation worked in:

> Affluent Americans are buying new super-sized homes in older, urban residential areas. These lots were once occupied by historic and humble houses. The older houses are now known as "teardowns." In their place, towering "McMansions" dominate the street. Richard Moe, President of the National Trust for Historic Preservation, reports that teardowns affect over 300 U.S. cities, with a total of 75,000 older houses razed each year. Moe compares the teardown trend to a cancer on the community: "Teardowns wreck neighborhoods. They [destroy] the character and livability that are a neighborhood's lifeblood" (QQO).

Introduces the speaker.

Provides context for the quotation.

Parenthetical citation of author's name not needed because author is cited in text.

> preserve that dream for the generations to come, we need to develop more energy efficient houses and lifestyles today (Sackett, 2006, p. 36).

The entry in the References list would appear as follows:

> Sackett, J. (2006). The green American dream: LEED for homes is currently being piloted. *The LEED Guide: Environmental Design & Construction*. 9.6 (2006): 36+. Retrieved 18 Oct. 2006, from InfoTrac Thomson Gale.

In-Text References to Electronic Sources

The conventions just described apply to print sources. Adapt the examples to Internet and other electronic sources. Because you must include the electronic sources in your works-cited or reference list, your in-text citations should connect the material quoted or paraphrased in your text to the matching work or posting on the list. Therefore, your in-text citation should begin with the author's name or, lacking that, the title of the work or posting. The APA format requires that you also include the posting date.

CREATING WORKS-CITED AND REFERENCE LISTS

www.mhhe.com/crusius

For an electronic tool that helps create properly formatted works-cited pages, go to:

Research > Bibliomaker

At the end of your paper, include a bibliography of all sources that you quoted, paraphrased, or summarized. If you are using MLA style, your heading for this list will be *Works Cited;* if you are using APA style, it will be *References.* In either case, the list is in alphabetical order based on either the author's (or editor's) last name or—in the case of unidentified authors—the first word of the title, not counting the articles *a, an, the.* The entire list is double-spaced both within and between entries. See the works-cited page of the sample student paper at the end of this chapter for the correct indentation and spacing. Note that MLA format requires that the first line of each entry be typed flush with the left margin; subsequent lines of each entry are indented half an inch (five spaces on a typewriter). The APA recommends the same indentation.

The following examples illustrate the correct MLA and APA style for the types of sources you will most commonly use.

Books

Book by One Author

MLA: Crusius, Timothy W. <u>Discourse: A Critique & Synthesis of Major Theories</u>. New York: MLA, 1989.

APA: Crusius, T. W. (1989). *Discourse: A critique & synthesis of major theories*. New York: Modern Language Association.

(Note that APA uses initials rather than the author's first name and capitalizes only the first word and proper nouns in titles and subtitles.)

Two or More Works by the Same Author

MLA: Crusius, Timothy W. <u>Discourse: A Critique & Synthesis of Major Theories</u>. New York: MLA, 1989.

--- <u>A Teacher's Introduction to Philosophical Hermeneutics</u>. Urbana: NCTE, 1991.

(Note that MLA arranges works alphabetically by title and uses three hyphens to show that the name is the same as the one directly above.)

APA: Crusius, T. W. (1989). *Discourse: A critique & synthesis of major theories*. New York: Modern Language Association.

Crusius, T. W. (1991). *A teacher's introduction to philosophical hermeneutics*. Urbana, IL: National Council of Teachers of English.

(Note that APA repeats the author's name and arranges works in chronological order.)

Book by Two or Three Authors

MLA: Deleuze, Gilles, and Felix Guattari. <u>Anti-Oedipus: Capitalism and Schizophrenia.</u> New York: Viking, 1977.

APA: Deleuze, G., & Guattari, F. (1977). *Anti-Oedipus: Capitalism and schizophrenia.* New York: Viking.

(Note that MLA style inverts only the first author's name. APA style, however, inverts both authors' names and uses an ampersand [&] between authors instead of the word "and.")

Book by Four or More Authors

MLA: Bellah, Robert N., et al. <u>Habits of the Heart: Individualism and Commitment in American Life</u>. New York: Harper, 1985.

(Note that the Latin abbreviation *et al.*, meaning "and others," stands in for all subsequent authors' names. MLA style also accepts spelling out all authors' names instead of using *et al.*)

APA: Bellah, R., Madsen, R., Sullivan, W., Swidler, A., & Tipton, S. (1985). *Habits of the heart: Individualism and commitment in American life.* New York: Harper & Row.

(Note that APA uses *et al.* only for more than six authors.)

Book Prepared by an Editor or Editors

MLA: Connors, Robert J., ed. <u>Selected Essays of Edward P. J. Corbett</u>. Dallas: Southern Methodist UP, 1989.

APA: Connors, R. J. (Ed.). (1989). *Selected essays of Edward P. J. Corbett.* Dallas: Southern Methodist University Press.

Work in an Edited Collection

MLA: Jackson, Jesse. "Common Ground: Speech to the Democratic National Convention." <u>The American Reader</u>. Ed. Diane Ravitch. New York: Harper, 1991. 367–71.

APA: Jackson, J. (1991). Common ground: Speech to the Democratic National Convention. In D. Ravitch (Ed.), *The American reader* (pp. 367–371). New York: HarperCollins.

Translated Book

MLA: Vattimo, Gianni. <u>The End of Modernity: Nihilism and Hermeneutics in Postmodern Culture</u>. Trans. Jon R. Snyder. Baltimore: Johns Hopkins UP, 1988.

APA: Vattimo, G. (1988). The end of modernity: *Nihilism and hermeneutics in postmodern culture.* (J. R. Snyder, Trans.). Baltimore: Johns Hopkins University Press.

Periodicals

Article in a Journal with Continuous Pagination

MLA: Herron, Jerry. "Writing for My Father." <u>College English</u> 54 (1992): 928–37.

APA: Herron, J. (1992). Writing for my father. *College English, 54,* 928–937.

(Note that in APA style the article title is not fully capitalized, but the journal title is. Note also that the volume number is italicized in APA style.)

Article in a Journal Paginated by Issue

MLA: McConnell, Margaret Liu. "Living with <u>Roe v. Wade</u>." <u>Commentary</u> 90.5 (1990): 34–38.

APA: McConnell, M. L. (1990). Living with *Roe v. Wade. Commentary,* 90(5), 34–38.

(In both examples, "90" is the volume number and "5" is the number of the issue.)

Article in a Magazine

MLA: D'Souza, Dinesh. "Illiberal Education." <u>Atlantic</u> Mar. 1990: 51+.

(Note that the plus sign indicates that the article runs on nonconsecutive pages.)

APA: D'Souza, D. (1990, March). Illiberal education. *Atlantic,* pp. 51–58, 62–65, 67, 70–74, 76, 78–79.

(Note that APA requires all page numbers to be listed.)

Anonymous Article in a Newspaper

MLA: "Clinton Warns of Sacrifice." <u>Dallas Morning News</u> 7 Feb. 1993: A4.

APA: Clinton warns of sacrifice. (1993, February 7). *The Dallas Morning News,* p. A4.

(In both examples, the "A" refers to the newspaper section in which the article appeared.)

Editorial in a Newspaper

MLA: Lewis, Flora. "Civil Society, the Police and Abortion." Editorial. <u>New York Times</u> 12 Sept. 1992, late ed.: A14.

APA: Lewis, F. (1992, September 12). Civil society, the police and abortion [Editorial]. *The New York Times,* p. A14.

(Note that in MLA style the edition of the newspaper must be specified.)

Nonprint Sources

Interview

MLA: May, William. Personal interview. 24 Apr. 1990.

(Note that APA style documents personal interviews only parenthetically within the text: "According to W. May [personal interview, April 24, 1990], . . ." Personal interviews are not included on the reference list.)

Sound Recording

MLA: Glass, Philip. Glassworks. CBS Sony, MK 37265, 1982.

APA: Glass, P. (1982). *Glassworks* [CD Recording No. MK 37265]. Tokyo: CBS Sony.

Film

MLA: Scott, Ridley, dir. Thelma and Louise. Perf. Susan Sarandon, Geena Davis, and Harvey Keitel. 1991. Videocassette. MGM/UA Home Video, 1996.

APA: Scott, R. (Director). (1991). *Thelma and Louise* [Motion picture]. Culver City, CA: MGM/UA Home Video.

(Note that with nonprint media, you identify the medium—CD, DVD, videocassette, film, and so forth. MLA includes the principal actors, but APA does not. APA specifies the place of production, but MLA does not.)

Electronic Sources

Although the documentation requirements for MLA and APA citations of electronic sources contain much of the same information, there are also differences. Use the following lists as general guides when you cite Internet sources.

MLA Style: Citing Internet Sources

1. Author's or editor's name, followed by a period
2. Title of the article or short work (such as a short story or poem) followed by a period and enclosed by quotation marks
3. Name of the book, journal, or other longer work underlined
4. Publication information, followed by a period:
   City, publisher, and date for books
   Volume and year for journals
   Date for magazines
   Date for and description of government documents
5. Date on which you accessed the information (no period)
6. URL, placed inside angle brackets, followed by a period

APA Style: Citing Internet Sources

1. Author's or editor's last name, followed by a comma and the initials
2. Year of publication, followed by a comma, with the month and day for magazine and newspaper articles, within parentheses and followed by a period
3. Title of the article, book, or journal (follow APA conventions for titles of works)
4. Volume number
5. Page numbers
6. The words "Retrieved from," followed by the date of access, followed by the source (such as the World Wide Web) and a colon
7. URL, without a period

Online Book

MLA: Strunk, William. <u>The Elements of Style</u>. 1st ed. Geneva: Humphrey, 1918. May 1995. Columbia U Academic Information Systems, Bartleby Lib. 12 Apr. 1999 <http://www.Columbia.edu/acis/bartleby/strunk/strunk100.html>.

APA: Strunk, W. (1918). *The elements of style* (1st ed.). [Online]. Retrieved April 12, 1999, from http://www.Columbia.edu/acis/bartleby/strunk/strunk100.html

(Note that MLA requires that the original publication data be included if it is available for works that originally appeared in print. The APA, however, requires only an online availability statement.)

World Wide Web Site

MLA: <u>Victorian Women Writers Project</u>. Ed. Perry Willett. Apr. 1999. Indiana U. 12 Apr. 1999 <http://www.indiana.edu/~letrs/vwwp>.

APA: Willett, P. (1999, April). *Victorian women writers project* [Web page]. Retrieved April 12, 1999, from http://www.indiana.edu/~letrs/vwwp

Document on a Web Site

MLA: Moe, Richard. "Battling Teardowns, Saving Neighborhoods." <u>The National Trust for Historic Preservation</u>. 28 June 2006. 15 Jan. 2007 <http://www.nationaltrust.org/news/2006/20060628_speech_sf.html>.

APA: Moe, R. (2006, June 28). Battling teardowns, saving neighborhoods. Retrieved Jan. 15, 2007, from *The National Trust for Historic Preservation* Web site: http://www.nationaltrust.org/news/2006/20060628_speech_sf.html

Article in an Electronic Journal

MLA: Harnack, Andrew, and Gene Kleppinger. "Beyond the *MLA Handbook:* Documenting Sources on the Internet." <u>Kairos</u> 1.2 (Summer 1996). 7 Jan. 1997 <http://english.ttu.edu/Kairos/1.2/index.html>.

APA: Harnack, A., & Kleppinger, G. (1996). Beyond the *MLA Handbook:* Documenting sources on the Internet. *Kairos* [Online], *1*(2). Retrieved January 7, 1997, from http://english.ttu.edu/Kairos/1.2/index. html

Encyclopedia Article on CD-ROM

MLA: Duckworth, George. "Rhetoric." <u>Microsoft Encarta</u> '95. CD-ROM. Redmond: Microsoft, 1995.

APA: Duckworth. G. (1995). Rhetoric. In *Microsoft encarta '95* [CD-ROM]. Redmond, WA: Microsoft.

Encyclopedia Article Online

MLA: "Toni Morrison." <u>Encyclopaedia Britannica Online</u>. 1994–1999. Encyclopaedia Britannica. 4 Mar. 1999 <http://members.eb.com/bol/topic?eu=55183&sctn=#s_top>.

APA: (1994–1999). Toni Morrison. In *Encyclopaedia Britannica Online* [Online]. Retrieved March 4, 1999, from http://members.eb.com/bol/topic?eu=55183&sctn=#s_top

E-Mail, Listserv, and Newsgroup Citations

For MLA, give in this order the author's name, the title of the document (in quotation marks), followed by the description *Online posting,* the date when the material was posted, the name of the forum (if known), the date of access, and in angle brackets the online address of the list's Internet site or, if unknown, the e-mail address of the list's moderator.

MLA: Stockwell, Stephen. "Rhetoric and Democracy." Online posting. 13 Jan. 1997. 22 Jan. 1997 <H-Rhetor@msu.edu>.

For APA, the custom is not to include e-mail, listservs, and newsgroups in a reference list but rather to give a detailed in-text citation as follows: (S. Stockwell, posting to H-Rhetor@msu.edu, January 13, 1997).

However, if the content of the message is scholarly, many researchers do include messages in the references:

APA: Stockwell, S. (1997, January 13). Rhetoric and democracy. Retrieved January 22, 1997, from e-mail: H-Rhetor@msu.edu

STUDENT SAMPLE: A RESEARCH PAPER (MLA STYLE)

Ross 1

Standard heading

Julie Ross
ENGL 1301, Section 009
April 20, 2007
Professor Channell

Title centered

Why Residential Construction Needs to Get a Conscience

www.mhhe.com/cru

For another model essay in format, go to:

Research > Sample Paper MLA Style

Entire essay is double-spaced

Introduction announces topic

Poses issue the argument will address

No word breaks at end of lines

Author's last name and page number in MLA style

Full name and credentials of authors who have expertise

Home ownership is a significant part of the American dream. Americans take great pride in putting down roots and raising a family in a good neighborhood. And, if a recent boom in residential construction is any indication, more Americans are realizing that dream. In addition to the number of new homes being built, the average home size has also grown significantly, almost twice as large as in the 1960s ("How to Build"). The question is: what is the impact of super-sized houses on our neighborhoods and our environment?

In big cities like Dallas, huge new houses are springing up in the outer-ring suburbs like Frisco and Flower Mound. The National Association of Homebuilders reports that the average size of a single-family home has grown from 983 square feet in 1950 to 2,434 square feet in 2005, "even as the average household shrunk from 3.4 to 2.6 people" (Brown 23). This desire for more living space keeps cities sprawling outward as developers look for open land. However, urban residential areas are also now impacted by new building. Affluent Americans are buying new super-sized homes in older, urban residential areas. These lots were once occupied by historic and humble houses. The older houses are now known as "teardowns." In their place, towering "McMansions" dominate the street. Richard Moe, President of the National Trust for Historic Preservation, reports that

Ross 2

teardowns affect over 300 U.S. cities, with a total of 75,000 older houses razed each year.

Moe compares the teardown trend to a cancer on the community: "Teardowns wreck neighborhoods. They [destroy] the character and livability that are a neighborhood's life-blood." He sees three reasons for the rise in teardowns:

- In the past decade, the value of houses has doubled or tripled, except in some older neighborhoods. Developers look for these "'undervalued' properties" to build on.

- Homebuyers demand more space.

- Some homebuyers want to move from the "soulless . . . sprawling subdivisions" to close-in neighborhoods that have more character and more amenities, such as public transportation and local shopping.

Moe explains, "The problem is that too many people try to impose their preference for suburban-style mini-mansions on smaller scale neighborhoods where they just don't fit."

My neighborhood in Dallas, known as Lakewood Heights, has been plagued by more than its share of tearing down and building up. Once famous for its 1920s Craftsman and Tudor architecture, my quiet residential street is now marred by rows of McMansions, bustling traffic, and noisy, new construction. These colossal residences vary little in outward appearance from one to the next. "Starter mansions" as they are often called, have no particular architectural style and only remotely resemble Tudor or Craftsman styles. No matter where you look, these giants tower over their single-story neighbors, blocking the sunlight and peering into once-private backyards from their tall, garish peaks.

Paraphrases for information from source, quotations for opinions

Colon after full-sentence as introductory tag

Reasons against teardowns begin

Personal observation as support for this reason

Another reason against tearing down

Ross 3

A super-sized new home towers over its older next-door neighbor.

The builders and buyers of these giant homes are callous to community and environmental concerns. Preserving an old Dallas neighborhood's rich architectural history and green landscape is of little importance to them. For example, most McMansions occupy an extremely large footprint, leaving little or no yard space. Original homes in my neighborhood occupied about a third of their rectangular lot. This design permitted a sizable back yard with room for a small one-car garage as well as an inviting front lawn where children could play. By contrast, mega homebuilders show no appreciation for conventional site planning. They employ bulldozers to flatten the lot and uproot native trees. Their goal is to make room for as much house as possible, raking in more profit with each square foot. Furthermore, each tall fortress has a wide cold, concrete driveway leading to the grandiose two-Tahoe garage, equivalent to nearly half the size of my one-story house.

Ross 4

What was once a grassy lawn is now paved with concrete.

Only ten years ago pecan trees, the official state tree of Texas, and flowering magnolias graced every lawn on my block. These beautiful native trees, some over a century old, shaded our homes from the harsh Texas sun and our sidewalks from the triple-digit, summer heat. There is no way the new home owners' landscaping can replace what is lost. The charm of the neighborhood is being destroyed.

Aside from changing the face of my neighborhood, these monster houses, many selling for half a million or more, have skyrocketed property taxes and pushed out many older, lower-income, long-time residents. As a result, several senior citizens and other long-time residents of Lakewood have been forced to sell their homes and move to apartments. Many custom homeowners argue that more expensive, larger homes positively contribute to a neighborhood by increasing the resale value of smaller, older homes. This may be true to a certain extent. However, from a wider perspective, short-term

Transition into another reason

Ross 5

gains in resale prices are no compensation for the irreversible harm done to our neighborhoods.

But the destruction of a neighborhood is only half the story. These over-sized homes, and others like them everywhere, are irresponsible from a larger environmental perspective. According to Peter Davey, editor of the <u>Architectural Review,</u> "Buildings [residential and commercial combined] take up rather more than half of all our energy use: they add more to the pollution of the atmosphere than transport and manufacture combined." Not only is pollution a consequence of this surge in residential structure size, but also the building of larger homes drains our natural resources, such as lumber. The National Resource Defense Council notes that forested areas, necessary for absorbing greenhouse gas emissions, are being depleted by the super-sizing trend in residential building:

> Almost every one of these new, large homes is made out of wood—roughly three-quarters of an acre of forest. Much of the destructive logging around the world is fueled by our demand for housing. . . . Many houses today are still built using outdated, inefficient construction methods. About one-sixth of the wood delivered to a construction site is never used, but simply hauled away as waste. And much of the wood that goes into the frame of a house is simply unnecessary. ("How to Build")

Obviously, residential construction must "go green" in an effort to save valuable resources and conserve energy. But what does it mean to "go green"? As Earth Advantage, a green building certification organization, explains: "Green building entails energy efficiency, indoor air quality, durability and minimal site impact" (Kaleda). However, whether a home can be designated as "green" depends on more than just

Double-space blocked quotations; use no quotation marks

Period ends sentence. Ellipses of three dots indicates material omitted

With block form, period goes before parenthetical citation

Ross 6

energy-efficient construction methods and materials. According to Martin John Brown, an ecologist and independent consultant, green homebuilding is being used to describe a wide range of residential construction, and not all homes should qualify. Essentially, while some homebuilders are selling "environmentally-friendly" design, the epic scale of these new homes outweighs any ecological benefits provided through materials and construction methods. So, size does matter. A recent article in the <u>Journal of Industrial Energy</u>, published by M.I.T. Press, reports that a 1,500 square foot house with "mediocre energy-performance standards" will consume far less energy than a 3,000 square foot house with all the latest energy-saving materials and details (Wilson 284). In Boston, a house rated "poor" in terms of energy standards used 66% less energy than one rated "good" but twice the size (Wilson 282).

> For articles by reporters or staff writers, rather than experts and authorities, their names can be cited parenthetically only

Brown argues that practically minded, ecologically conscious homebuilding should be part of our overall effort to decrease our consumption of limited resources and energy. Evidence from the Department of Energy supports his claim: "From 1985 to 2002, total residential energy consumption per capita climbed eight percent, and residential consumption for the nation—the figure most relevant to global effects like carbon dioxide (CO_2) emissions—climbed 32 percent" (Brown 23).

Unfortunately, many Americans who can afford it won't stop buying environmentally irresponsible, un-humble abodes. Their motives may stem from the competitive nature of consumer society. When people see their neighbors driving a new car, they think they need to buy a new one too. This is called "keeping up with the Joneses." Discussing the supersized house, best-selling author Gregg Easterbrook has coined a new phrase, "call and raise the Joneses." As he explains it,

Ross 7

> In call-and-raise-the-Joneses, Americans feel compelled
> not just to match the material possessions of others,
> but to stay ahead. Bloated houses . . . arise from a
> desire to call-and-raise-the-Joneses—surely not from a
> belief that a seven-thousand-square-foot house that
> comes right up against the property setback line
> would be an ideal place in which to dwell. (140)

Daniel Chiras, the author of <u>The Natural House: A Complete
Guide to Healthy, Energy-Efficient, Environmental Homes,</u> warns:
"People tell themselves that if they can afford a 10,000-
square-foot house, then that's what they should have . . .
but I wonder if the earth can afford it" (qtd. in Iovine).

Cite author of
article, not speaker.
Use "qtd." to
indicate quotation
appeared in the
source

Fortunately, other Americans are starting to recognize
the folly of buying more space than they need. A survey by
Lowe's and Harris Interactive found that "46% of homeowners
admit to wasting up to half of their home" ("Are McMansions
Giving Way"). Felicia Oliver of <u>Professional Builder</u> magazine
suggests that the marriage of conservation and construction
is the next natural step in the evolution of residential building.
One example of a builder taking this step is the Cottage
Company in Seattle, which specializes in "finely detailed and
certified-green" houses of between 1,000 and 2,000 square
feet. Company co-owner Linda Pruitt says Cottage Company
houses "'live as big' as McMansions because they're better
designed, with features like vaulted ceilings and abundant
built-ins. 'It's kind of like the design of a yacht,' she says.
The theme is quality of space, not quantity" (qtd. in Brown
24).

If no author, use
shortened form
of title
Shows possible
solution to problem

Even Richard Moe of the National Trust for Historic
Preservation admits that responsible new construction has a
place in older neighborhoods:

Ross 8

Trees tower over this stretch of original modest-scale homes in Lakewood Heights, reminding us of what is being lost.

No one is saying that homebuyers shouldn't be able to alter or expand their home to meet their needs, just as no one is saying that older neighborhoods should be frozen in time like museum exhibits. A neighborhood is a living thing, and change is both inevitable and desirable. The challenge is to manage change so that it respects the character and distinctiveness that made these neighborhoods so appealing in the first place. This is the challenge that must be met in my own neighborhood. If new construction and additions are as architecturally interesting as the older homes and comparable with them in size and footprint, preserving lawns and trees, the neighborhood can retain its unique character.

> Conclusion returns to idea used in introduction

Jessie Sackett, a member of the U.S. Green Building Council, writes: "Owning a home is the cornerstone of the American dream. Recently, however, we've realized that keeping that

Ross 9

dream alive for future generations means making some changes to how we live today" (36). We must ensure that the American Dream doesn't translate into a horrific nightmare for our planet or future generations. Therefore, I ask would-be homebuyers to consider only the more conscientious construction in both urban and suburban areas. When we demand more modest and responsible homebuilding, we send a clear message: younger generations will know that we value our planet and our future more than we value excessive personal living space.

Works Cited

"Are 'McMansions' Giving Way to Smaller, Cozy Homes?" <u>Coatings World</u>. Aug. 2004: 12. <u>InfoTrac</u> Thomson Gale. Southern Methodist U, Fondren Library, Dallas, TX. 12 Jan. 2007. <http://find.galegroup.com>.

Brown, Martin John. "Hummers on the Homefront: At 4,600 square feet, Is It an Eco-House?" <u>E, The Environmental Magazine</u>. Sept–Oct 2006: 23–24. <u>InfoTrac</u> Thomson Gale. Southern Methodist U, Fondren Lib., Dallas, TX. 6 Oct. 2006. <http://find.galegroup.com>.

Davey, Peter. "Decency and Forethought: It Is Foolish to Behave As If We as a Race Can Go on Treating the Planet As We Have Been Doing Since the Industrial Revolution." <u>The Architectural Review</u> 213.1281 (2003): 36–37. <u>InfoTrac</u> Thomson Gale. Southern Methodist U, Fondren Lib., Dallas, TX. 18 Oct. 2006 <http://find. galegroup.com>.

Easterbrook, Gregg. <u>The Progress Paradox: How Life Gets Better While People Feel Worse</u>. New York: Random House, 2003.

"How to Build a Better Home: A New Approach to Homebuilding Saves Trees and Energy—and Makes for Economical,

Use alphabetical order according to author's last name or if no author, according to first word in title, ignoring articles (a, an, the)

Double-space in and between entries

Ross 10

Comfortable Homes." <u>National Resources Defense Council</u>. 22 July 2004. 22 Oct. 2006. <http://www.nrdc.org/cities/ building/fwoodus.asp>.

Iovine, Julie V. "Muscle Houses Trying to Live Lean; Solar Panels on the Roof, Five Cars in the Garage." <u>The New York Times</u>. 30 Aug. 2001. B9. <u>InfoTrac</u> Thomson Gale. Southern Methodist U, Fondren Lib., Dallas, TX. 18 Oct. 2006 <http://find.galegroup.com>.

Kaleda, Colleen. "Keeping It 'Green' With Panels and More." <u>The New York Times</u>. 15 Oct. 2006: 11. <u>InfoTrac</u> Thomson Gale. Southern Methodist U, Fondren Lib., Dallas, TX. 22 Oct. 2006 <http://find.galegroup.com>.

Moe, Richard. "Battling Teardowns, Saving Neighborhoods." <u>The National Trust for Historic Preservation</u>. 28 June 2006. 23 Jan. 2007 <http://www.nationaltrust.org/ news/2006/20060628_speech_sf.html>.

Oliver, Felicia. "The Case for Going Green." <u>Professional Builder (1993)</u>. 2.5. (2006): 38. <u>InfoTrac</u> Thomson Gale. Southern Methodist U, Fondren Lib., Dallas, TX. 6 Oct. 2006 <http://find.galegroup.com>.

Sackett, Jessie. "The Green American Dream: LEED for Homes Is Currently Being Piloted." <u>The LEED Guide: Environmental Design & Construction</u>. 9.6 (2006): 36+. <u>InfoTrac</u> Thomson Gale. Southern Methodist U, Fondren Lib., Dallas, TX. 18 Oct. 2006 <http://find.galegroup.com>.

Wilson, Alex and Jessica Boehland. "Small Is Beautiful: U.S. House Size, Resource Use, and the Environment." <u>Journal of Industrial Energy</u>. 9.1 (Winter/Spring 2005) 277–287. EBSCO Academic Host. Southern Methodist U, Fondren Lib., Dallas, TX. 17 Feb. 2007 <http://ebscohost.com>.

Ethical Writing and Plagiarism

CHAPTER 6

WHY ETHICS MATTER

To write well, you need to be informed about your topic, which means doing research into what others have already said about it. You will want to put some of these ideas into your papers, but it is unethical to do so in a way that does not give credit to the source.

By citing your sources, you earn your reader's respect as well. Readers are more likely to accept your views if you project good character, what the ancient rhetoricians called *ethos*. Honesty is part of good character. Part of writing honestly is distinguishing your ideas from the ideas of others.

The news has been filled in recent years with stories about unethical writers, people who have been caught using other writers' words and ideas without citing the source. This is *plagiarism*, which we will define shortly. Although painters and poets often borrow freely from each other's ideas, in the academic world, such borrowing is a serious breach of ethics, with serious consequences. One university president who borrowed too freely in a convocation speech without mentioning his source was forced to resign. Recently, some history professors' books were found to contain long passages taken verbatim from sources, the result—they claimed—of careless

www.mhhe.com/**crusius**

For more information on plagiarism, go to:

Research > Plagiarism

note-taking. Whether deliberate or accidental, such mistakes can destroy a person's career.

Plagiarism by students has also become an increasing problem, partly as a result of the Internet. Students may plagiarize by accident, not realizing that material that is so easy to copy and paste from the Web must be treated as a quotation and cited as a source. The Internet has also become part of the solution to this problem: Professors using programs like Turnitin.com can check submitted work for originality. At schools using this software, plagiarized work dropped by 82%.*

For students, the consequences of plagiarizing are severe, ranging from failure on the writing project to failure in the course and even to suspension or expulsion from the university. Many universities will indicate on a student's transcript if there has been an honor violation, something that potential employers will see.

The purpose of this chapter is to help you avoid plagiarizing, even by accident. Also, we will show that failure to cite sources is not the only kind of unethical writing. Students can get too much help through misuse of tutoring, study groups, and other sources in the process of writing a paper.

---

*"Largest Study of Cheating in the World Reveals 82% Drop in Plagiarism After Using Turnitin.com for Five or More Years." *PR Newswire*. Oct. 4, 2006.

Plagiarism: The Presentation or Submission of Another's Work as Your Own

This includes summarizing, paraphrasing, copying, or translating words, ideas, artworks, audio, video, computer programs, statistical data, or any other creative work, without proper attribution.

Plagiarism can be deliberate or accidental. It can be partial or complete. No matter which, the penalties are often similar. Understanding what constitutes plagiarism is your first step to avoiding it.

SOME ACTS OF PLAGIARISM:

- Copying and pasting from the Internet without attribution
- Buying, stealing, or ghostwriting a paper
- Using ideas or quotations from a source without citation
- Paraphrasing an author too lightly

—"What Constitutes Plagiarism?" by Ramona Islam, Senior Reference Librarian and Instruction Coordinator at Fairfield University. Reprinted with permission.

WHAT PLAGIARISM IS

We like the definition of plagiarism on Fairfield University's online honor tutorial because it includes the various kinds of media that count as sources and must be acknowledged when you draw from them in academic writing. See Concept Close-Up, above, to read this definition.

As we explain in Chapter 5, "Writing Research-Based Arguments," you must document the sources of all direct quotations, all paraphrased ideas taken from sources, and even information paraphrased from sources, unless it is "common knowledge."

A good definition of *common knowledge* comes from Bruce Ballenger's excellent book *The Curious Researcher:* "Basically, common knowledge means facts that are widely known and about which there is no controversy."* If you already knew something that shows up in your research, that's a good indication that it is common knowledge, but you also have to consider whether your *readers* would already know it. If your readers know less about your topic than you do, it is good to cite the source, especially if the information might surprise them. Consider, too, that "common knowledge" shifts with time. When Ballenger wrote his book in the early 1990s, he gave as an example of common knowledge the fact that

---

*Bruce Ballenger, *The Curious Researcher: A Guide to Writing Research Papers*, 3rd ed. Boston: Allyn and Bacon, 2001, p. 236.

Understanding the Ethics of Plagiarism

A student who plagiarizes faces severe penalties: a failing grade on a paper, perhaps failure in a course, even expulsion from the university and an ethics violation recorded on his or her permanent record. Outside of academe, in the professional world, someone who plagiarizes may face public humiliation, loss of a degree, rank, or job, perhaps even a lawsuit. Why is plagiarism such a serious offense?

Plagiarism is theft. If someone takes our money or our car, we rightly think that person should be punished. Stealing ideas or the words used to express them is no less an act of theft. That's why we have laws that protect *intellectual property* such as books and essays.

Plagiarism is a breach of ethics. In our writing, we are *morally obligated* to distinguish between our ideas, information, and language and somebody else's ideas, information, and language. If we don't, it's like taking someone else's identity, pretending to be what we're not. Human society cannot function without trust and integrity—hence the strong condemnation of plagiarism.

Plagiarism amounts to taking an unearned and unfair advantage. You worked hard to get that "B" on the big paper in your political science class. How would you feel if you knew that another student had simply purchased an "A" paper, thereby avoiding the same effort? At the very least, you'd resent it. We hope you'd report the plagiarism. Plagiarism is not just a moral failure with potentially devastating consequences for an individual. *Plagiarism, like any form of dishonesty intended to gain an unfair advantage, damages human society and hurts everyone.*

Ronald Reagan made a movie with a chimpanzee. You may have known that, but do you think most college students today know it? The decision about when to cite information depends on to whom it is "common knowledge." Remember, if you use direct quotation to present any information, you must cite the source.

THE ETHICS OF USING SOURCES

There are five major kinds of violations of ethics in using sources.

Purchasing a Paper

A simple Internet browser search for most topics will turn up services that offer pre-written essays for sale. These services claim that the essays are merely "examples" of what could be written on the topic, but we all know better. In almost every arena of life, people are ruthlessly trying to make a buck off the gullible or the desperate. These services are counting on college students to take the bait. It's a bad idea for all these reasons:

- You learn nothing about writing, so you are cheating yourself.
- You can be charged with an honor violation.
- College professors can find the same essays by searching the Internet and by using more sophisticated search engines designed by textbook publishers to help them find plagiarism.
- The paper will be a poor fit with the prompt your teacher has given you, and the style of the writing will not match previous examples of your own voice and style—red flags professors are able to see from miles away.
- Some of these papers are poorly written and produced at sweatshop pace, so they are often filled with generalizations, bad thinking, and errors of grammar and punctuation. The example below is taken from the opening of one essay available for purchase online. We've under-lined some of the grammar, punctuation, and spelling errors.

> All the choices we make reveal something about our personality, <u>sur-rounding and our upbringing influences</u> these choices. The <u>way we speak, dress, the food we eat, the music</u> we listen to tells <u>allot</u> about us and how we came to be. Everywhere we look in <u>America we</u> can see different cultural signs. It's really amazing how we can tell the difference between an American <u>person, and</u> a <u>non American</u> just by looking at <u>them; and between people</u> from different parts of our own country.

Using a Paper Found Online

Many college professors and high school teachers have class Web sites where they post the best work of their students. These papers will often turn up in online searches. Don't be tempted to use these papers or parts of them without citing them, and that includes giving the qualifications of the author. Many of the other reasons for not buying a paper apply here:

- The paper may be inferior in writing quality and use of sources, so you may be borrowing someone else's mistakes or even someone else's plagiarism.
- You learn nothing about how to write.
- You can be charged with an honor violation.
- Professors can find these papers online even more easily than you can.

Using Passages from Online Sources without Citing the Source

It is easy to cut and paste material from the Internet, and much of it is not protected by copyright. Nevertheless, to take passages, sentences, or even phrases or single significant words from another text is plagiarism. Significant words express strong judgment or original style, such as metaphors.

Compare the source text below with the uses of it. It comes from an interview with Al Gore about his film *An Inconvenient Truth.* The interview appeared in *Sierra Magazine,* found on the Sierra Club Web site.*

Sierra: In your movie, you cite U.S. determination in World War II as an example of the kind of resolve we need to confront global warming. But it took the attack on Pearl Harbor to galvanize the country. Are we going to have a similar moment in this crisis?

Gore: Obviously, we all hope it doesn't come to that, but for hundreds of thousands of people in New Orleans, that moment has already been reached. And for millions of people in Africa's Sahel, that moment has already been reached with the disappearance of Lake Chad. For an untold number of species, it has been reached. The challenge for the rest of us is to connect the dots and see the picture clearly. H. G. Wells wrote that "history is a race between education and catastrophe." And this is potentially the worst catastrophe in the history of civilization. The challenge now is to seize our potential for solving this crisis without going through a cataclysmic tragedy that would be the climate equivalent of wartime attack. And it's particularly important because, by the nature of this crisis, when the worst consequences begin to manifest themselves, it will already be too late.

Unethical use of source:

> It will take an environmental crisis to galvanize the country into confronting the problem of global warming, and for hundreds of thousands of people in New Orleans, that moment has already been reached. The challenge for the rest of us is to connect the dots and see the picture clearly. H. G. Wells wrote that "history is a race between education and catastrophe." And this is potentially the worst catastrophe in the history of civilization, so we must step up our efforts to learn about global warming and the means to keep it in check.

In this example, the writer has made no reference to the source of the words or ideas. This is wholesale theft of another's words and ideas. This kind of borrowing from sources is every bit as unethical as buying a paper online and turning it in as your own writing.

Ethical use of source:

> There are two routes to discovering the need to confront the problem of global warming, as Al Gore explained to *Sierra* magazine. We can wait for catastrophes like Hurricane Katrina, or we can learn from other environmental crises that are occurring around the globe and take action now. Quoting H. G. Wells, who said that "history is a race between education and catastrophe," Gore argues that we need to get educated because global

---

warming is "potentially the worst catastrophe in the history of civilization. . . ." (Joseph).

The ethical way to use a source is

- to integrate paraphrase and direct quotation into a paragraph of your own, and
- to cite the source.

Notice that good paraphrasing does not borrow either the language or the sentence pattern of the original text. The source is cited and the style of the sentences is the student's own.

Inadequate Paraphrasing

Paraphrasing is tricky because paraphrases must be *entirely* your own words, not a mixture of your words and the words of the source. Even if you cite the source, it is plagiarism to borrow words and phrases from another author. Therefore, you must put quotation marks around sentences, parts of sentences, and even significant words taken directly from another text.

Here is a source text, and opposite is the picture, to which the examples of paraphrase that follow refer:

> Subversive masculine modes in the second half of this century began with the tee-shirts and blue jeans of rural laborers, later adopted by rebellious urban youth.
>
> —Anne Hollander, *Sex and Suits* (New York: A. A. Knopf, 1994)

Unethical use of source:

> Marlon Brando symbolizes the subversive masculine mode of the second half of the twentieth century with the tee-shirts and blue jeans of rural laborers (Hollander 186).

Even though the student cited his source, this is plagiarism because his sentence contains words from the source without quotation marks. This example illustrates the most common kind of unintentional plagiarism. This passage also fails to identify Hollander as the interpreter of the image.

To avoid this accidental plagiarism:

- When taking notes, highlight in color any wording that you copy directly from a source.
- When paraphrasing, study the original passage but then put it aside when you write your paraphrase, so that you will not be tempted to use the wording of the source. Then go back and check your paraphrase for accuracy and for originality of expression. As the ethical version below shows, any quoted parts must be treated as quotations.

Ethical use of source:

> According to art historian Anne Hollander, Marlon Brando's tee-shirt and blue jeans illustrate a rebellious kind of late-twentieth-century masculinity, a look originally associated with "rural laborers" (186).

Marlon Brando in A Streetcar Named Desire, *1951.*

This version has reworded the sentence into an adequate paraphrase and used quotation marks around a phrase taken word for word from Hollander. It also identifies Hollander as an art historian, which establishes her credibility. When you tell your readers something about your source, you increase the credibility of your own writing.

Paraphrasing Ideas or Information without Naming the Source

Although it is not necessary to cite sources of commonly available information, such as the percentage of high school graduates who go to college, you must give credit when a source presents someone's idea, interpretation, or opinion, or when the information would be difficult for your readers to verify on their own. If in doubt, it is always better to cite. The source text below comes from a book about the college experience:

> Many [college] seniors single out interdisciplinary classes as the courses that meant the most to them. As a corollary, they cite faculty members who, while expert in their own fields, are able to put the fields in proper perspective. Students find this important. They believe that the real world, and the way people think about the world, does not divide neatly into categories called history, chemistry, literature, psychology, and politics.
>
> —Richard J. Light, *Making the Most of College: Students Speak Their Minds* (Cambridge: Harvard UP, 2001)

Unethical use of source:

> Studies have shown that college students find interdisciplinary courses the most meaningful. They also prefer professors who can think outside the box of their own areas of academic specialization.

Richard Light's research led him to this information; he deserves credit for his work.

Ethical use of source:

> In interviews with seniors at Harvard, where he teaches, Richard Light found that college students say that interdisciplinary courses are the most meaningful. They also prefer professors who can think outside the box of their own areas of academic specialization (126).

By citing Light as the source of this information, the writer has also added credibility to his or her own essay.

When Opinions Coincide

Students often ask what to do when they have an idea, opinion, or interpretation and then encounter that same idea, opinion, or interpretation as they are doing research. For example, after looking into the problem of global warming, a student could easily come to the conclusion that rising temperatures and ocean levels could become a threat to civilization. Reading the *Sierra* interview with Al Gore, that student sees that she and Gore share the opinion that global warming "is potentially the worst catastrophe in the history of civilization." If the student doesn't use Gore's exact words, is it plagiarism to use the opinion without citing him? A classic book on the subject of research, *The Craft of Research,* advises the cautious approach: "In the world of research, priority counts not for everything, but for a lot. If you do not cite that prior source, you risk having people think that you plagiarized it, even though you did not."* You don't have to check to see that all of your own ideas are not already out there; however, if you encounter one of your own in a source, you should acknowledge that source.

THE ETHICS OF GIVING AND RECEIVING HELP WITH WRITING

Writing is not a solitary act. Most professional writers seek feedback from colleagues, editors, family, and friends, and they thank those who have contributed in the acknowledgments section of the book. Students benefit from help with their projects—in conferences with their instructors, peer exchanges with other students in class, and visits to their campus's tutorial services. Whether you are giving help or receiving it, you need to realize that inappropriate help is also plagiarism because it involves using someone else's ideas and language. If someone tells you what to write, rewrites your work for you, or even proofreads or "edits" your work, that is plagiarism, because you are using someone else's work as if it were your own. Likewise, it is unethical for you to provide such help to anyone else, a practice known as "facilitating plagiarism" and equally punishable at most schools.

The following list describes three unethical ways of giving and receiving help.

1. **Having someone "ghostwrite" your paper.** College campuses attract unscrupulous people who offer to "help" students with their writing. It is dangerous to use an off-campus tutor because his or her primary interest is income, not education. If someone offers to write a paper for you or to write parts of it, do not agree to work with that person. Likewise, parents may not understand the line between constructive advice and doing the writing for you. Instructors can detect writing that does not sound like the voice of an undergraduate or that is not consistent with your in-class work and other papers.

2. **Having someone edit your paper for style.** It is plagiarism to have someone else change your wording and word choices for you. Your instructor will teach you about elements of style and illustrate principles of editing. This textbook covers such material in Appendix A.

   After you have used this advice to edit your own paper, it is okay to ask someone else to point out passages that need more attention and even to explain why those passages are wordy or unclear. But it is up to you to improve the expression. Reworking awkward passages is problem solving. The one who does it gets the benefit of the experience and deserves the credit. That should be you.

3. **Having someone proofread your paper for grammar and punctuation.** As with editing for style, proofreading is your responsibility. You plagiarize if you hand your paper to someone else to "clean it up," whether

---

*Wayne C. Booth, Gregory Colomb, and Joseph M. Williams, *The Craft of Research.* Chicago: U of Chicago P, 2003, p. 203.

B. Smaller

"My parents didn't write it—they just tweaked it."

as a favor or for money. Many students need help with proofreading, and your instructor or on-campus tutorial service can offer instruction that will help you catch errors in the future. Instead of making "corrections" line by line, a good tutor will look over your draft for patterns of error. Then he or she can explain the "rule" or convention, show you how to detect and correct the problem, give you some examples for practice, and finally, watch as you go through your draft to find the places that need correction.

ETHICAL WRITING AND GOOD STUDY HABITS

Good study habits are central to ethical writing.

- **Do not procrastinate.** Students who procrastinate are more likely to make the kind of careless errors that lead to accidental plagiarism. They are also more likely to use intentional plagiarism as the only way to meet a deadline.

- **Take careful notes.** Use your notebook or notecards to write about your sources, being sure to distinguish your own ideas from the material you copy directly or paraphrase. Use quotation marks around any words you take directly from a source. You may even want to highlight these to mark them as material that you will have to cite if it goes into your paper.

- **Ask your instructor about proper sources of help with your writing.** Avoid using untrained family members and friends as tutors. Avoid off-campus tutors who work for profit. If your school has a writing center, take advantage of the tutors there.

- **Work on improving your reading skills.** Good reading skills will empower you to use sources more confidently. Read Chapter 2, "Reading an Argument," for advice on how to improve your comprehension and analysis of texts.

The Aims
of Argument

THE AIMS OF ARGUMENT

CHAPTER 7

Looking for Some Truth: Arguing to Inquire

To inquire is to look into something. Inquiry can be a police investigation or a doctor's effort to diagnose a patient's illness, a scientist's experiment or an artist's attempt to see the world differently. According to singer and songwriter Lucinda Williams, one of the joys of life in this "sweet old world" is "looking for some truth."

It is satisfying to be able to say, "This is true." If we are religious, we find truth in the doctrines of our faith. But in our daily lives, we often must discern for ourselves what is true. We look for truth in messages from family and friends and lovers, in nature, and in art, music, and literature. Often we have to work to decide what to believe, for newspapers and textbooks offer differing versions of fact. The search for truth, then, is closely allied to the question "What is knowledge?" The pursuit of both is inquiry.

INQUIRY AND INTERPRETATION IN ACADEMIC WRITING

Inquiry is an important part of college learning because college is where we learn that one "true" body of knowledge or facts about the world does not exist. Take, for example, something usually considered fact:

Columbus discovered America in 1492.

If this statement were on a true/false test, would your answer be "true," "false," or "that depends"? With hardly any inquiry at all, we see that this "fact" depends on

- the calendar you use to mark time on this Earth
- your definition of the word "discover"
- your definition of "America"
- whether your ancestors were here before Columbus
- whether you know anything about Vikings and other early explorers

So what we accept as fact, as truth, is *an interpretation*. Most significant claims to truth are *efforts to understand and explain;* as such, they are interpretations that need defending. Later in this chapter, you will read several arguments, each claiming to know the truth about whether violence on television causes children to act out violently. All offer data to prove their claims, but data are meaningless without interpretation. And interpretations are open to inquiry.

The current state of knowledge on any given topic depends on who is doing the interpreting and whether the data are of interest to people in a particular culture. Some facts remain unknown for centuries because no one thought they mattered. What one considers knowledge or truth, then, depends on the perspective of the interpreters, which in turn depends on the interpreters' social class, politics, religion, and a host of other factors that make up who they are and how they see the world.

Like the high school research paper, college writing requires research. Unlike the high school paper, which typically requires only that you obtain information, organize it, and restate it in your own words, most college assignments will require *inquiry* into sources.

It's important to gather information and viewpoints. But research itself is not the goal of inquiry. The most important part of inquiry is the thinking you do before and after gathering sources. The quality of your paper will depend on your initial thinking as well as on your sources and your understanding of them. Nothing is more vital to writing well than learning how to inquire well.

As we begin to inquire, it is important not to try to "prove" anything. Argument as inquiry is not confrontational; rather, it is conversational. It is conversation with friends, family, and colleagues. We can have these kinds of conversations with ourselves, too, asking and answering questions about the arguments we read.

To inquire well, we must question our initial viewpoints instead of holding on to them. We need to ask hard questions, even if the answers threaten our preconceptions and beliefs. Before Copernicus, "common sense" held that the Earth was stationary and religious beliefs reinforced this "truth." To question our truths makes us uncomfortable. But inquiry requires holding a question open. The scientist whose theory wins respect from other scientists must test its truth rather than protect it from further inquiry. Likewise, a college student needs to test received wisdom from his or her past to grow intellectually. After inquiry, you may still hold the same belief, but because you have tested it, your belief will be a claim to truth that you have earned, not just been told.

This chapter offers guidelines for inquiring and shows how writing plays a part in it. The writing project is the exploratory essay, through which the following pages will guide you.

THE WRITING PROJECT: PART 1

The exploratory essay is an account of inquiry. Your goal is to share the experience of questioning your opinions and the arguments of others on your chosen topic. The paper will be a journey with a starting point, a tour of viewpoints on the issue, and a destination, a claim you can defend. The essay has three parts, one written before inquiry, the other two written after. In this informal paper, you will refer to yourself and your own thoughts and experiences. Write in first person.

Here is an overview of the paper:

In Part 1, you will tell what question or issue interests you most about a given topic and express your initial opinion.

Part 2 will be the exploration itself. The point is to open the question and keep it open, testing your opinions and exploring the issue through conversations and research that connect you to a range of expert opinions. You are not trying to support your initial opinion but to test it. You'll write about readings that confirm and contradict your thinking and evaluate these arguments fairly.

Part 3, the conclusion, will be a statement of your thinking after inquiry, an explanation of the truth as you now see it. Think of exploration as the process of *arriving* at a claim.

Your instructor may follow this paper with Chapter 8, "Making Your Case: Arguing to Convince," and an assignment to convince others to assent to your claim. But in this paper you'll explore, not make a case.

We illustrate inquiry and the steps of writing the exploratory essay by exploring violence in the media and its relation to violence in society. We show some students' initial thinking about this issue and take you through their exploration of it.

Step 1: Choosing a Topic for Inquiry

If your instructor has not assigned a topic, begin by looking at newspapers. Current events offer good topics that need interpretation. If you are familiar with a news topic, you probably already have an opinion, and that is a good place to begin inquiry. We came upon our violence in the media topic by noticing an op-ed column in the *New York Times,* but yours could come from a front-page story or an item on television news.

www.mhhe.com/**crusius**

For more sources of a potential topic, go to:

Research > Discipline-Specific Resources in the Library and on the Internet

Once you have selected a topic, consider what you already know about it and consider narrowing the focus. Violence in the media is a huge subject. There's staged or *pretend violence*—the quarrels, muggings, rapes, and so on of television and movie dramas. There's *virtual violence* in computer games. And there's *actual violence,* the staple of broadcast news. "If it bleeds, it leads": Local TV news programs often start with an account of a brutal murder or a big traffic accident.

The more you narrow your topic, the easier it will be to find issues to argue about and sources that converse with each other. For example, narrowing media violence to video games or music lyrics is a good strategy.

Step 2: Finding an Issue

An issue is a controversial question. With the example topic, such questions include: Why do people find violence so engrossing, so entertaining? Why do we like to see it in sports like football, hockey, and auto racing? Why do we go to movies that feature violence? Is it our nature or our culture? How is it related to gender?

All are worthwhile questions, but we need to identify a central or primary issue. In this instance, that issue is whether pretend violence can be connected to aggressive acts. It's central because most articles about the topic address it and because our answer determines what the other issues are.

Inquiry looks for order or hierarchy among issues; that is, our answer to one question leads to the next. *If* there is a link between fantasy violence and actual violence, *then* the next question is, How significant is the connection? We can't ask the second question until we answer the first. *If* we decide that pretend violence is a major contributor to actual aggression, *then* we must decide what action should be taken—and this leads to issues of censorship. For media violence, then, we can list this hierarchy of issues:

- Is there a link between fantasy violence and real-world violence? If so, what is it exactly?
- How strong is the link? Does media violence make people more aggressive and less sensitive to the suffering of others? Does it contribute to murders and assaults?
- If the contribution is significant, should we consider censorship, or does the Constitution prohibit taking this kind of action?
- If we can't censor, what other action(s) can we suggest to reduce the negative effect?

Locating the issues is usually not difficult. Often we can supply them from general knowledge and experience. We need only ask, What have we heard people arguing about when this topic came up? What have we ourselves argued about it? If we can't identify the issues before research, sources will reveal them. Once you begin reading what others have said about your topic, you may discover an issue more interesting than ones you thought of beforehand.

◎◎ FOLLOWING THROUGH

In preparation for writing your exploratory paper, select a topic of current interest. What do you see as the main issue that people debate? With answers to that question, draw up a chain of questions that follow one another. Which interests you most? •

◎◎ FOLLOWING THROUGH

Read an argument on the topic you intend to explore. What issue does this argument primarily address? What is the author's answer to this question—in other words, what is the author's claim? Restate it in your own words. What other issues are raised in the argument? What *other* issues do you know about? •

Step 3: Stating Your Initial Opinions

In this step, you will write Part 1 of your exploratory essay, where you state your initial ideas before inquiry. Write this part of your paper before doing any serious research. Begin by introducing your topic and the issue or issues you intend to consider. State your opinions on those issues now and explain your reasoning. Include some explanation of what, in your own experiences or observations, has contributed to your opinions.

Below is an example on the media violence topic.

STUDENT SAMPLE Exploratory Essay, Part 1—Lauren's Initial Opinions

---

I have to admit that I am somewhat biased when it comes to the topic of the relation between entertainment and violence in children. I have been involved in several life-altering experiences before this assignment that made me feel very strongly that virtual violence and aggressive behavior in children are causally related. When I was in high school, a group of kids I grew up with got mixed up in the whole "gangster" scene. They listened to rap music about murder and drugs. Ultimately, these boys took the life of a fellow student at the McDonald's down the street from my school. They used a shotgun to murder him in a drug deal gone bad. Because I knew these kids when they were younger, I can say that when they were in the seventh grade they were incapable of committing such a crime. Did the rap music influence them? They had to get the idea from somewhere, and I cannot think of another reasonable explanation.

Even though music may not plant evil in a child's mind, it can lead to problems. Throughout my senior year, I did volunteer work at the Salvation Army recreation center. It's located in the so-called ghetto of Lincoln, Nebraska, and intended for children to walk to after school when their parents are still working. Working here opened my eyes to how the future of America is growing up.

My first encounter was with a six-year-old boy who called me profane names. Not only was I verbally abused, but also pushed, shoved, and kicked. Later, after discussing the situation with the boy in time-out, I found out that he had heard these names in an Eminem song that bashes women.

Because of these experiences, my negative opinion about media violence is strong.

◎◎ FOLLOWING THROUGH

Draft Part 1 of your paper. In the opening paragraph or two, state what your opinions were before you researched the topic. Describe and explain experiences that influenced your outlook. Refer to specific films or music or news broadcasts. If you've read or heard about the topic before or discussed it in school or elsewhere, recall both context and content and share them with your readers. Edit for clarity and correctness.   •

Step 4: Exploring an Issue

Once you have written Part 1, concentrate on exploring—reading and talking about your topic. Because you will eventually write about these experiences in Part 2, use your writer's notebook and make good annotations in the margins of what you read, to record your thoughts. These notes are the raw material from which you will eventually write the account of your exploration.

CONVERSATION AND DIALOGUE IN INQUIRY

A good way to begin inquiry is to talk through your position in serious conversation with a friend, family member, classmate, or teacher. Inquiry often takes the form of discussion or conversation. And conversation is a big part of higher education. Many college classes are devoted to discussion rather than lecture; even lecturers encourage classes to discuss controversial questions. Out of class, students can talk with professors and each other.

As you know from watching talk shows, conversation is not always a search for truth. There's an art to productive conversation. In Chapter 2, we noted that critical reading depends on developing certain practices and habits. Conversation aimed at finding some truth also depends on good practices and habits. Participants need to move beyond ordinary conversation, often just an exchange of opinions, to *dialogue*, a *questioning* of opinions.

Let's begin by looking at a conversation about violence in entertainment.

An Example Conversation

The conversation that follows took place shortly after the Columbine High School killings. It was recorded and transcribed, and an excerpt of it appeared in the May 17, 1999, issue of *Newsweek*. The conversation is neither especially good nor especially bad but rather typical, the sort of thing we encounter routinely in media-arranged talk. Read it carefully. Comments follow explaining what we can learn from it.

Moving beyond the Blame Game

JONATHAN ALTER, MODERATOR

A month after the Littleton tragedy, the conversation continues—in schools, in homes and at this week's White House conference on youth violence. The theories of why Eric Harris and Dylan Klebold went on their rampage have given way to a broader discussion of the deeper sources of the problem and where to go from here. Obviously, there are no quick fixes; everything from more values [in] education to better supervision of antidepressant medication has been introduced into the debate. But Americans have singled out a few issues for special attention. According to the new *Newsweek* Poll, about half of all Americans want to see the movie industry, the TV industry, computer-game makers, Internet services and gun manufacturers and the NRA make major policy changes to help reduce teen violence. Slightly fewer want the music industry to change fundamentally. Younger Americans are less concerned about media violence than their elders are. On guns, there's a racial gap, with 72 percent of nonwhites and 41 percent of whites seeking major changes.

To further the conversation, *Newsweek* assembled a panel last week to explore the complexities. One after another, the people who actually make heavily violent movies, records and games declined to participate, just as they did when the White House called. This could be a sign that they are feeling the heat—or perhaps just avoiding it. Those who did take part in the *Newsweek* forum include Wayne LaPierre, executive director of the NRA; Jack Valenti, president of the Motion Picture Association of America; Hillary Rosen, president of the Recording Industry Association of America; Doug Lowenstein, president of the Interactive Digital Software Association; Marshall Herskovitz, TV and movie producer and director; and Jonah Green, a 15-year-old New York high-school student. *Newsweek's* Jonathan Alter moderated the discussion.

Excerpts:

Alter: Youth shall be served, so I want to start with Jonah. You seem to think that there's [a] lot of scapegoating going on.

Green: Well, I have to say that America is very confused and scared. There's no one simple answer to teen violence. It's understandable because we're seeking answers, but right now people are focusing too much on putting the blame somewhere. We should be focusing on solutions.

Alter: OK, Wayne, wouldn't making guns less easily accessible be at least a   5
partial solution?

LaPierre: You can't talk about easy access to guns by people we all don't want to have guns without talking about the shameful secret that really hasn't been reported. Which is the complete collapse of enforcement of the existing firearm laws on the books by the Department of Justice [in] the last six years. The proof is in the statistics. Six thousand kids illegally brought guns to school the last two years. We've only had 13 [federal] prosecutions. And only 11 prosecutions for illegally transferring guns to juveniles.

Alter: Do you think that if an 11-year-old brings his father's gun to school, the child should be prosecuted?

LaPierre: Yes, I do. They did not prosecute Kip Kinkel out in Oregon after he was blowing up cats, threatening people. He walks into school with a gun. They do nothing to him except send him home. And he comes back to the school two days later with a gun and shoots those kids. I mean, the fact is we're either serious about this situation or we're not.

Alter: How about Clinton's gun-limit proposal? Why does anyone need to buy more than one gun a month?

LaPierre: That's just a sound bite.   10

Alter: Doug, some of your industry's games are a long way from Pac-Man, right?

Lowenstein: Oh, absolutely. There are some very violent videogames, although they represent only a small fraction of the market. There's a critical parental role here: It costs over $1,000 to own a computer. A hundred dollars plus to own a videogame machine. There's a very conscious choice involved in bringing this kind of entertainment into your home. And the parent needs the tools to make an informed choice.

Alter: You don't think it desensitizes kids to violence to play games over and over?

Green: Personally, I think some kids use videogames, especially the violent ones, just as some violent movies, as a vent. You know, they like to live vicariously and vent their anger through that. And Doug was right that we can't really map out everything a kid has and how they use it and what makes them able to kill somebody.

Alter: Hillary, MTV is doing a stop-the-violence campaign, but then they   15
air—and you supported—something like Eminem's song about stuffing a
woman into the trunk of a car. Don't you see a contradiction here?

Rosen: Young people are so much smarter than anybody—the media or politicians or most adults, in fact—may give them credit for being. They understand the difference between fantasy and reality, and that's why giving them
concrete steps to take when they face personal conflict or when they face a
gang conflict or school bullying, or those sorts of things, are much more
productive means for giving them tools to be nonviolent in their lives than
taking away their culture.

Alter: Do you think that a music-rating system just makes it forbidden fruit
and makes kids want to play or see it more?

Rosen: We've done surveys that show it doesn't encourage young people
to buy artists. People buy music that they connect with, that they like, that
has a good beat, that sounds good. The label is there for parents and for
retailers.

Green: I actually think artists like Eminem are very sarcastic. It is more playful than hard core. I find rap being a little more human than it used to be.
Gangsta rap isn't as big anymore, and now sampling is.

Rosen: It's true.   20

Green: Edgar Allan Poe talked about death—he was dark, but he was a celebrated poet. It's about having an edge, a hook. That can be violence.

Alter: You don't have any problem with Marilyn Manson naming himself
after a serial killer?

Green: I think it's in bad taste. It was just stupid and controversial.

Alter: Hillary, how about you?

Rosen: Well, I agree with Jonah that it's bad taste, but that's the point.   25
Marilyn Manson is an act. It's an act that's sort of designed to create a persona of empowering the geek. Unfortunately, Charles Manson was a real
person. People don't have to make up horrible tragedies in this world.

Green: Entertainment and the media were never really for getting across
good, moral messages like "I love my school and my mother." People rarely
feel they need to express bland feelings like that.

Rosen: But it is on some level, because Britney Spears sells more records
than Marilyn Manson. You know there's been a resurgence of young pop
music. B*Witched and the Dixie Chicks and Britney Spears and 'N Sync.
I mean, these artists are selling a hell of a lot more records than Marilyn
Manson.

Alter: Do you think that kids have kind of gotten that message and are less
interested in gratuitously violent lyrics than they used to be? Because they've
seen so much death, either in their own neighborhoods or on TV?

Rosen: Well, there's no question that what used to be known as gangsta rap is definitely played out. Rap is much more light-hearted. It's about getting money and getting women. The music has evolved.

Alter: Why is that?   30

Rosen: Well, this might be controversial, but I'm actually one of those people who believes that young people are a lot more positive about the world today than most of the media is giving them credit for in the last couple of weeks. Surveys have shown that young people are more optimistic about their future, they're more positive, they're more connected to their parents than they have been in generations. And these all speak to really good, positive things.

Alter: Marshall, what do you think are some of Hollywood's responsibilities in this area?

Herskovitz: I think we now have virtual reality available to people that is nihilistic, anarchic and violent. And it is possible for a person to so completely live in that virtual reality that they come to confuse it for the real world around them.

Alter: But you know from firsthand experience that violence sells.

Herskovitz: "Legends of the Fall" was a very violent movie. I think violence   35
has a potentially strong part in any artistic venture. It's not something I would ever want to talk about legislatively. I would like to talk about it in terms of individual responsibility, yes.

Alter: So where should the thoughtful consumer of all of this draw the line between gratuitous violence and necessary violence for dramatic purposes?

Herskovitz: Oh, I think that's the point. The thoughtful consumers feel it in their gut. I think the problem in this culture is that thoughtful consumers are not particularly influencing their children.

Alter: But isn't it a little too easy to just say it's all the parent's responsibility?

Valenti: Well, I don't think the movie industry can stand in *loco parentis*. Over 30 years ago I put in place a movie-rating system, voluntary, which gives advanced cautionary warnings to parents so that parents can make their own judgments about what movies they want their children to see.

Alter: I think what a lot of parents wonder is, why is it that NC-17 is not   40
applied to gratuitously violent movies?

Valenti: Well, it's because the definition of "gratuitous" is shrouded in subjectivity. There is no way to write down rules. I think Marshall can tell you that creative people can shoot a violent scene a hundred different ways. Sex and language are different, because there are few ways that you can couple on the screen that—there's only a few. And language is language. It's there or it isn't. But violence is far more difficult to pin down. It's like picking up mercury with a fork.

Alter: A movie director told me recently that he went to see "The Matrix," and there was a 5-year-old at the film with his mother. Isn't that a form of child abuse?

Valenti: If a parent says he wants his 5-year-old to be with him, who is to tell this parent he can't do it? Who is to tell him?

Alter: But if it was NC-17, that 5-year-old wouldn't be allowed to go, right?

Valenti: Well, that's right. 45

Alter: So why allow them in when it's R?

Valenti: Because the way our system is defined, we think there's a dividing line.

Alter: When parents aren't doing their job properly, where does the responsibility of everybody else begin?

LaPierre: I was talking with John Douglas, the FBI's criminal profiler. And he said, "Wayne, never underestimate the fact that there are some people that are just evil." And that includes young people. We go searching for solutions, and yet some people are just plain bad apples. You look around the country—the cities that are making progress across the board are really combining prevention and working with young people when you get the first warning signs. And making sure they find mentors. Making sure they're put into programs. And they're combining that with very, very tough enforcement of things like the gun laws.

Herskovitz: I have a fear that modern society, and in particular television, 50 may be beyond the ability of parents to really control. I think movies are different, because the kid has to go out of the house and go there. TV is a particular problem because it's in the house.

Alter: But Marshall, maybe that's because the values that are being propagated by the media, broadly speaking, are so much more powerful that parents can't compete as easily as they used to.

Herskovitz: I don't believe that. I accept a lot of responsibility for the picture the media create of the world. But I don't think there's a conflict between that and the responsibility of parents to simply sit down and talk with their children. Most violent crime is committed by males. Young men are not being educated in the values of masculinity by their fathers.

Alter: So why then let all of these boys see scenes of gratuitous violence that don't convey human values to them?

Valenti: There are only three places where a child learns what Marshall was talking about, values. You learn them in the church. You learn them in school. And you learn them at home. And if you don't have these moral shields built in you by the time you're 10 or 12 years old, forget it.

Alter: I'm not sure that people in Hollywood are thinking, "Is what we do 55 part of the solution on this values question, or does it just contribute to the problem?"

Herskovitz: The answer is the people who aren't contributing to the problem are thinking about it a lot, and the people who are contributing to the problem are not thinking about it.

Valenti: Well, how does *Newsweek* then condone its putting on the cover of your magazine Monica Lewinsky? What kind of a value system does that convey?

Alter: Well, that's a separate discussion.

Valenti: Oh, I don't think it is.

Alter: Well, let me say this. We very explicitly did not put Dylan Klebold   60
and Eric Harris on our cover the first week. We're wrong in these judgments sometimes, but we do at least try to think about the consequences of what we put out there, instead of just saying it's up to the parents. That seems to me a cop-out.

Lowenstein: What you're looking for is an elimination of any problematic content.

Alter: No, I'm not. I'm looking for a sense of shame and a sense of responsibility. I'm wondering where it is in all of the industries that we have represented here today.

Herskovitz: Most people, especially in electronic journalism, don't think at all about this, and their role is incredibly destructive, just like most people in the movie and television business don't think at all about this. And their role is destructive. I think there's a great need for shame. Most people I know and speak to are very ashamed, but unfortunately they're not the people who make violent movies.

Analysis of "Moving beyond the Blame Game"

It's obvious that the *Newsweek* excerpts are not part of a natural, spontaneous conversation, the sort of thing we might have with friends around a campfire or at a bar after work. It's been *arranged*. The participants didn't just happen to come together some place and start talking; they were invited. Furthermore, they knew why they were invited—each represents a group or industry implicated in teen violence. Even Jonah Green, the fifteen-year-old, is cast (that's the right word) as "youth," as if one young person could stand for all young people. Each participant knew his or her role in advance, then, and what was at stake. Except perhaps for Jonah Green, each had an agenda and an interest in protecting their reputations and the public image of their businesses and organizations. Therefore, unlike the conversations in which we ask you to engage, theirs from the start was something less than an open-minded search for truth. In a genuine dialogue, people do not attack each other or become defensive.

In addition to its adversarial tone, this discussion falls short of good inquiry because it lacks depth. It is an extreme example of what tends to go wrong with *all* discussions, including class discussions. In the classroom, the teacher plays Alter's role, trying to get students to talk. When a question is greeted by silence from the class, sometimes teachers do what Alter does: solicit opinions by addressing questions to individuals, who then have no choice but to answer. Often the instructor is happy to get any opinion just to get things going. Once the ice is broken, students usually join in. It can be stimulating just to hear what everybody else is thinking. Before long, we're caught up in the discussion and don't perceive what it is: a superficial exchange of opinions, like the *Newsweek* example. Much is said, but almost nothing is *examined, pursued, genuinely explored.*

Exactly what do we mean? Look at the first few exchanges in the *Newsweek* example. Alter addresses Jonah Green, the fifteen-year-old high school student, who had apparently talked enough previously to reveal an opinion. Alter summarizes that opinion: "There's a lot of scapegoating going on." Green himself immediately offers two more intelligent observations, better than anything we get from the adult participants: "There's no one simple answer to teen violence" and "we should be focusing on solutions" rather than on blame.

These statements merit attention. But what happens? Alter must get the others into the discussion, so he turns to LaPierre and asks if better gun control might be part of the solution. *The secret of a good discussion is not to allow intelligent comments to go unquestioned.* Imagine, for example, what the following line of questioning might lead to. ("Q" stands for "questioner," who could be anyone involved in the discussion.)

> Green: There's a lot of scapegoating going on.
>
> Q: What do you mean by "scapegoating"?
>
> Green: A scapegoat is someone who gets blamed or punished for doing something everyone is guilty of or responsible for.
>
> Q: So you're saying that youth violence is a collective problem that everyone contributes to in one way or another. Is that right?
>
> Green: Yes.

Now that we know what Green's assertion actually means, we can really discuss it, look for whatever truth it may convey. Are we *all* really implicated in youth violence? How exactly? If we are, what can each of us do?

We handle Green's comment about looking for solutions the same way. All we need to ask is, What might be part of the solution? It would be interesting to hear Jonathan's ideas. Maybe he has an idea how high schools could build more community or how parents could get involved. But no—the conversation moves in a new direction.

Our intent is not to put down conversation. Exchanging opinions is one of the great pleasures of social life. For inquiry, however, we need genuine dialogue.

To help your conversations become dialogue, we offer "Questions for Inquiry" on pages 181–182. These same questions will help you inquire into written texts, such as the sources encountered in research. Most of the questions on this list can be traced to the origins of dialogue in ancient Greece

Understanding the Art of Dialogue

To be useful for inquiry, conversations must become dialogues. They become dialogues when someone questions, in a nonhostile way, what someone else has said. Only then are we really discussing something, not just stating our opinion and talking for talking's sake.

and have demonstrated their value for about 2,500 years. Commit the list to memory, and practice asking these questions until they become second nature.

FOLLOWING THROUGH

Mark up the *Newsweek* dialogue. Use the "Questions for Inquiry" to probe the participants' comments. For example, one question suggests that you inquire about analogies and comparisons. You might ask Jonah if Edgar Allen Poe's "darkness" is truly comparable to the creations of Marilyn Manson. Aren't there some significant differences in the context in which these art forms present violence? Be ready to point out places where the discussants failed to answer questions directly or where you would have posed a good question if you had been there. Note places where the discussion moved toward dialogue and where it moved toward mere venting of opinion. Does Alter do a good job as moderator, or is he mainly concerned with going broader rather than deeper? Be ready to discuss your annotations in class.   •

Step 5: Engaging in a Dialogue about Your Initial Opinions

Earlier, you wrote Part 1 of your exploratory essay, a statement of your initial opinions. A good way to begin exploration is with what you said in Part 1. Exchanging these initial statements with a classmate and then asking each other questions will get you thinking more deeply about what you already believe.

Read the examples on page 182, which show one student's first thoughts and the dialogue that he and another student had. These students used a software program that allowed them to record their conversation, and what follows is a transcript of a real-time chat. They had printouts of each other's initial opinions in front of them as they took turns being each other's friendly questioner. First, read Matt's initial thoughts and then the dialogue he had with Lauren, whose own first thoughts we reproduced earlier. Note where the dialogue seems to be a conversation and where Lauren attempts to make it an inquiry. Where does it succeed as inquiry, and where does it not?

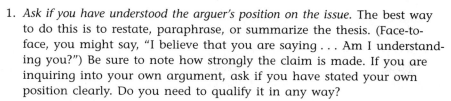

Questions for Inquiry

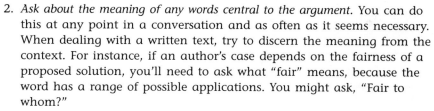

1. *Ask if you have understood the arguer's position on the issue.* The best way to do this is to restate, paraphrase, or summarize the thesis. (Face-to-face, you might say, "I believe that you are saying . . . Am I understanding you?") Be sure to note how strongly the claim is made. If you are inquiring into your own argument, ask if you have stated your own position clearly. Do you need to qualify it in any way?

2. *Ask about the meaning of any words central to the argument.* You can do this at any point in a conversation and as often as it seems necessary. When dealing with a written text, try to discern the meaning from the context. For instance, if an author's case depends on the fairness of a proposed solution, you'll need to ask what "fair" means, because the word has a range of possible applications. You might ask, "Fair to whom?"

3. *Ask what reasons support the thesis.* Paraphrasing reasons is a good way to open up a conversation to further questions about assumptions, values, and definitions.

4. *Ask about the assumptions on which the thesis and reasons are based.* Most arguments are based on one or more unstated assumptions. For example, if a college recruiter argues that the school he or she represents is superior to most others (thesis) because its ratio of students to teachers is low (reason), the unstated assumptions are (1) that students there will get more attention and (2) that more attention results in a better education. As you inquire into an argument, note the assumptions, and ask if they are reasonable.

5. *Ask about the values expressed or implied by the argument.* For example, if you argue that closing a forest to logging operations is essential even at the cost of dozens of jobs, you are valuing environmental preservation over the livelihoods of the workers who must search for other jobs.

6. *Ask how well the reasons are supported.* Are they offered as opinions only, or are they supported with evidence? Is the evidence recent? sufficient? What kind of testimony is offered? Who are the authorities cited? What are their credentials and biases?

7. *Consider analogies and comparisons.* If the author makes an argument by analogy, does the comparison hold up? For example, advocates of animal rights draw an analogy with civil rights when they claim that just as we have come to recognize the immorality of exploiting human beings, so we should recognize the immorality of exploiting other species. But is this analogy sound?

8. *Ask about the arguer's biases and background.* What past experiences might have led the arguer to take this position? What does the holder of this position stand to gain? What might someone gain by challenging it?

(continued)

9. *Ask about implications.* Where would the argument ultimately lead if we accept what the speaker advocates? For example, if someone contends that abortion is murder, asking about implications would lead to the question "Are you willing to put women who get abortions on trial for murder and, if they are convicted, to punish them as murderers are usually punished?"

10. *Ask whether the argument takes opposing views into account.* If it does, are they presented fairly and clearly or with mockery and distortion? Does the author take them seriously or dismiss them? Are they effectively refuted?

STUDENT SAMPLE Example Dialogue for Analysis—Matt's Initial Opinions

I think the issue of violence in the media is overdone. I believe that violence is a conscious act by people who are evil, not people motivated by what they have seen or heard in the media. Some people are violent, and they cannot be stopped from committing their crimes simply by censoring media violence. Violence is natural, an instinct all humans have, yet most restrain themselves from acting on their impulse. Though I have seen and heard my share of violence in the media, I am not a violent person. Sure, sometimes after watching a violent movie, I think about what it would be like to do some of that stuff, but I am not stupid enough to act out my curiosity.

STUDENT SAMPLE Example Dialogue between Matt and Lauren

Lauren: You don't think there is any relation between violence and the entertainment industry?

Matt: Not really. I don't see how music could influence someone to the point of violence.

Lauren: I kind of agree with you, but I don't know. I think that sometimes it gives a person the mentality to do that kind of stuff when their friends are—when people are impressionable like that, they will do a lot of stupid things. When I was in high school, a group of kids I grew up with started getting into the whole "gangster" scene. They listened to rap talking about murder, drugs, and destruction. They murdered a fellow student at the McDonalds down the street from the school. Did the music make them do this? We'll never know, but they had to get the idea from somewhere.

Matt: What happened to the guys that killed that person?

Lauren: They are all in jail now. Only one has gone to trial. 5

Matt: That's crazy. I listened to all kinds of music, and I am not violent.

Lauren: You can't assume everyone is like you. How do you explain kids doing the kind of stuff they are doing?

Matt: There are just some violent, evil people. They just aren't right, if you know what I mean.

Lauren: Do you mean they are crazy?

Matt: Yes, they're crazy. 10

Lauren: I think you said violence is an act of nature. Does that mean we are born violent? Is it normal to be violent?

Matt: I think everyone has a violent side, but they act on it in different ways. I go play sports or work out to get rid of the aggression.

Lauren: But is violence the same thing as evil? Or aggression? Those kids at my school were evil, not natural. I think you need to think more about what you mean by violent when you say it's natural. Maybe it's natural for animals to have aggression and to attack and kill to stay alive, but is that evil? When you say people are "just not right," do you mean that they are natural or not natural?

Matt: Okay, I think we are born violent, but some of us are also born evil.

Lauren: So, are you saying that nothing good could change these 15
people for the better, like having a good family or going to church? Are they just how they were born?

Matt: I'd have to think about that. They could maybe be taught.

Lauren: Well, I'm just saying, if they can be influenced for the better, why not for the worse—that the media could influence them to be worse?

Matt: I don't know.

Lauren: What about real life? When the media pays too much attention to one issue, like the school shooting in Columbine, do you think it makes other people want to do the same thing?

Matt: I don't know. A good friend of mine got kicked out of school 20
for calling in a bomb threat. He probably wouldn't have done that if all that hadn't been on the news.

◎◎ FOLLOWING THROUGH

Look at Matt's initial opinion statement on page 182. Use the "Questions for Inquiry" (pages 181–182) to suggest questions you would have asked him if you had been his partner.   •

◎◎ FOLLOWING THROUGH

Writing should be a rhythm between "drawing in"—the solo act of composing— and "reaching out" through dialogues during every phase of the composing process.

Exchange initial opinion statements with a classmate. Take turns asking each other questions based on the "Questions for Inquiry" on pages 181–182. Explore one person's thinking at a time. After twenty minutes, trade roles. If you do not have a software program that allows you to make a transcript of the discussion, tape it, or simply take notes after each questioning session. Be ready to report on how the dialogue clarified or modified your thinking. What did the dialogue make you realize you need to think and read about more?

We should never think of dialogue as something unrelated to writing. Dialogue can help us write better. The notes and written records of dialogues will provide material for your paper, so save them as we turn to the next step, reading about the topic.   •

Step 6: Engaging in Dialogue with a Reading

Inquiry into a text begins with a critical reading of it, including attention to its rhetorical context, as discussed in Chapter 2 (pages 22–23). Sample the text quickly to see if it is worth your attention. If it is, read it thoroughly and mark it up, noting its subdivisions and case structure—that is, mark claims and note evidence.

What we have just discussed about turning conversation into dialogue also applies to reading, but obviously conversations and written arguments can't be approached the same way.

In conversations, we mostly encounter simple statements of opinion. People say what they think without much explanation or support unless someone asks for it. In contrast, writers *argue* their opinions. That is, a written piece typically contains a *thesis* or *claim*. That claim is *explained* and justified or defended with reasons backed up by evidence. A text must stand on its own—a writer cannot respond to a reader's questions. Instead, *the writer must anticipate the questions an alert, critical reader will have and answer them in advance.*

Consequently, whereas in conversation we can question simple statements of opinion as they occur, with written arguments we question *entire cases*. We need to use "Questions for Inquiry" (pages 181–182), which lead us to question all parts of a case. We should also note whether opposing views appear in the argument and how the author handles them.

Example Dialogue with a Reading

As an example of how to engage in dialogue with a written text, let's work with "Hollow Claims about Fantasy Violence," by Richard Rhodes, which appeared September 17, 2000, in the *New York Times*. Rhodes has won awards for his books on the making of the atomic and hydrogen bombs. This essay appeared after the publication of *Why They Kill*, based on interviews with convicted murderers.

Hollow Claims about Fantasy Violence

RICHARD RHODES

The moral entrepreneurs are at it again, pounding the entertainment industry for advertising its Grand Guignolesque confections to children. If exposure to this mock violence contributes to the development of violent behavior, then our political leadership is justified in its indignation at what the Federal Trade Commission has reported about the marketing of violent fare to children. Senators John McCain and Joseph Lieberman have been especially quick to fasten on the F.T.C. report as they make an issue of violent offerings to children.

But is there really a link between entertainment and violent behavior?

The American Medical Association, the American Psychological Association, the American Academy of Pediatrics and the National Institute of Mental Health all say yes. They base their claims on social science research that has been sharply criticized and disputed within the social science profession, especially outside the United States. In fact, no direct, causal link between exposure to mock violence in the media and subsequent violent behavior has ever been demonstrated, and the few claims of modest correlation have been contradicted by other findings, sometimes in the same studies.

History alone should call such a link into question. Private violence has been declining in the West since the media-barren late Middle Ages, when homicide rates are estimated to have been 10 times what they are in Western nations today. Historians attribute the decline to improving social controls over violence—police forces and common access to courts of law—and to a shift away from brutal physical punishment in child-rearing (a practice that still appears as a common factor in the background of violent criminals today).

The American Medical Association has based its endorsement of the media 5 violence theory in major part on the studies of Brandon Centerwall, a psychiatrist in Seattle. Dr. Centerwall compared the murder rates for whites in three countries from 1945 to 1974 with numbers for television set ownership. Until 1975, television broadcasting was banned in South Africa, and "white homicide rates remained stable" there, Dr. Centerwall found, while corresponding rates in Canada and the United States doubled after television was introduced.

A spectacular finding, but it is meaningless. As Franklin E. Zimring and Gordon Hawkins of the University of California at Berkeley subsequently pointed out, homicide rates in France, Germany, Italy and Japan either failed to change with increasing television ownership in the same period or actually declined, and American homicide rates have more recently been sharply declining despite a proliferation of popular media outlets—not only movies and television, but also video games and the Internet.

Other social science that supposedly undergirds the theory, too, is marginal and problematic. Laboratory studies that expose children to selected incidents of televised mock violence and then assess changes in the children's behavior have sometimes found more "aggressive" behavior after the exposure—usually verbal, occasionally physical.

But sometimes the control group, shown incidents judged not to be violent, behaves more aggressively afterward than the test group; sometimes comedy produces the more aggressive behavior; and sometimes there's no change. The only obvious conclusion is that sitting and watching television stimulates subsequent physical activity. Any kid could tell you that.

As for those who claim that entertainment promotes violent behavior by desensitizing people to violence, the British scholar Martin Barker offers this critique: "Their claim is that the materials they judge to be harmful can only influence us by trying to make us be the same as them. So horrible things will make us horrible—not horrified. Terrifying things will make us terrifying—not terrified. To see something aggressive makes us feel aggressive—not aggressed against. This idea is so odd, it is hard to know where to begin in challenging it."

Even more influential on national policy has been a 22-year study by two 10 University of Michigan psychologists, Leonard D. Eron and L. Rowell Huesmann, of boys exposed to so-called violent media. The Telecommunications Act of 1996, which mandated the television V-chip, allowing parents to screen out unwanted programming, invoked these findings, asserting, "Studies have shown that children exposed to violent video programming at a young age have a higher tendency for violent and aggressive behavior later in life than children not so exposed."

Well, not exactly. Following 875 children in upstate New York from third grade through high school, the psychologists found a correlation between a preference for violent television at age 8 and aggressiveness at age 18. The correlation—0.31— would mean television accounted for about 10 percent of the influences that led to this behavior. But the correlation only turned up in one of three measures of aggression: the assessment of students by their peers. It didn't show up in students' reports about themselves or in psychological testing. And for girls, there was no correlation at all.

Despite the lack of evidence, politicians can't resist blaming the media for violence. They can stake out the moral high ground confident that the First Amendment will protect them from having to actually write legislation that would be likely to alienate the entertainment industry. Some use the issue as a smokescreen to avoid having to confront gun control.

But violence isn't learned from mock violence. There is good evidence—causal evidence, not correlational—that it's learned in personal violent encounters, beginning with the brutalization of children by their parents or their peers.

The money spent on all the social science research I've described was diverted from the National Institute of Mental Health budget by reducing support for the construction of community mental health centers. To this day there is no standardized reporting system for emergency-room findings of physical child abuse. Violence is on the decline in America, but if we want to reduce it even further, protecting children from real violence in their real lives—not the pale shadow of mock violence—is the place to begin.

Inquiring into sources presents a special challenge: to overcome the authority the source projects. When ideas are in print, we tend to accept them uncritically, especially when they support our own opinion. If the argument appears in a leading newspaper like the *New York Times,* the piece can seem to have such authority that people just quote it and don't bother to assess it critically, especially when the author is as respected as Rhodes. We think, Who am I to question what he says? After all, I've gone to him to find out about fantasy violence. Shouldn't I just accept what he says, at least until I read other sources that oppose his view?

Our earlier chapters on reading and analyzing an argument show how we can overcome this natural tendency to be passive when we encounter an authoritative text. It's true that we are only inquirers, not experts, and so we cannot question Rhodes as another expert might. But we are hardly powerless. We can put into practice the critical-reading habits and skills discussed in Chapter 2. And we can use the "Questions for Inquiry" on pages 181–182 to open an argument to scrutiny.

A Dialogue with Rhodes

Looking at the "Questions for Inquiry," note that some seem perfect entry points into Rhodes's argument. We have no problems understanding his claim, but we might ask about the second item on our list, "the meaning of any words central to the argument." How does Rhodes define "violence"? In the fourth, fifth, and sixth paragraphs, he refers to declining homicide rates despite proliferating media violence. But when we think of violence today, we think not only of homicide but also of date rape, domestic violence, bullying, and even road rage.

⊚⊚ FOLLOWING THROUGH

After sampling Rhodes's essay and reading it through, mark it up. What are the introduction and the conclusion? Are there any other subsections besides the presentation of the reasoning? Do you see the claim, reasons, and evidence? (See Chapter 3, "Analyzing Arguments," pages 45–59.) Mark and annotate them. How does Rhodes handle opposing views? Finally, use the "Questions for Inquiry" on pages 181–182. Make marginal annotations in response to Rhodes, and compare them with our discussion of the argument's strengths and weaknesses, pages 187–189. •

⊚⊚ FOLLOWING THROUGH

If you are working on a different topic, find an argument that addresses one of the topic's central issues. Do it as we have done it with Rhodes. •

We could also question the thinking of one of Rhodes's sources, Martin Barker, who says it is "odd" to assume that watching "horrible things will make us horrible—not horrified." There are many depictions of violent acts shown in the media, and some glorify violence or make it seem funny. Barker's language oversimplifies the problem.

We might also ask the sixth question for inquiry, about evidence. In the third paragraph, Rhodes acknowledges that the American Medical Association, the American Psychological Association, the American Academy of Pediatrics, and the National Institute of Mental Health all affirm "a link between entertainment and violent behavior." Much of the rest of the article is an effort to undermine the science that claims to establish such a link. Is it likely that the AMA, APA, and the other institutions mentioned are *all* wrong? Is it likely that the AMA based its opinion "in major part" on only *one* study of fantasy violence, as Rhodes claims in paragraph 5? Neither seems very likely. We should be suspicious enough to visit one of the Web sites for these organizations to find out more about the basis of their opinion.

And we might question an assumption Rhodes makes, using question 4 as our inspiration. When he says that the rates of television ownership rose in France, Germany, Italy, and Japan while homicide rates did not change, is he assuming that the same shows were broadcast in these countries as in the United States and Canada, where homicide rates doubled? He seems to assume that the technology rather than the programs is an appropriate basis for comparison.

Finally, we might question Rhodes's assumption that if one thing is not necessary for another thing to happen, it therefore cannot be a factor at all. For example, cell phone use is not necessary for a car wreck to occur. However, cell phone use does *contribute* to automobile accidents. Rhodes claims that "violence isn't learned from mock violence. There is good evidence—causal evidence, not correlational—that it's learned in personal violent encounters, beginning with the brutalization of children by their parents or their peers." Does anyone doubt that real violence in children's lives contributes more than fantasy violence to aggressive behavior? Of course not. But that doesn't mean that fantasy violence contributes *nothing*. We can't dismiss something altogether just because something else contributes more.

◎◎ FOLLOWING THROUGH

If you are inquiring into a topic of your own, use the "Questions for Inquiry" to open it up, as we have with Rhodes's essay. Do not try to pose all possible questions; find those that point to areas of weakness in the argument.   •

Another Example of Dialogue with a Reading

Let's also examine a book on violent entertainment, Sissela Bok's *Mayhem* (1998). Following is a chapter in which Bok assesses various ways to resist the effects of media violence. The chapter is especially interesting because it focuses on what children can do "to think for themselves and to become discriminating viewers."

Formerly professor of philosophy at Brandeis University, Sissela Bok is now a senior visiting fellow at the Harvard Center for Population and Development Studies.

Media Literacy

SISSELA BOK

How can children learn to take a more active and self-protective part in evaluating what they see? For an example of such learning, consider a class of second-graders in Oregon that Peter Jennings introduced on ABC's evening news in March 1995. With the help of their teacher, these children had arranged to study the role that television violence played in their lives: now they were presenting their "Declaration of Independence from Violence" to the rest of the student body. Their assignment had been to watch half an hour of television at home for several days running and to count the incidents of violence in each one—kicking, shooting, bombarding, killing. To their amazement, they had found nearly one such incident a minute in the programs they watched. The media mayhem they had taken for granted as part of their daily lives was suddenly put in question. One girl acknowledged that "before, I didn't even know what violence was."

The children then discussed the role of media violence in their own lives and concluded that what they saw on TV did affect them. Together, they considered different types of responses, often also discussing these choices in their homes. In their "Declaration of Independence from Violence," they addressed not only their school but the county board of education and community service organizations. Some pledged to limit their intake of violent programming and to refuse to watch certain shows; others wrote letters to television stations; a few organized a boycott of the products advertised on the programs they considered most violent.

These children were learning the rudiments of critical judgment and experiencing the pleasure of thinking for themselves about the messages beamed at them by advertisers and programmers. They were beginning to draw distinctions with respect to types of violence and their effects and to consider what might lie in their power to do in response. Throughout, they were learning to make active use of the media, including having their own initiative beamed to millions via the Jennings broadcast.

In so doing, the second-graders were participating in what has come to be called "media literacy education."[1] The media literacy movement, begun in Australia in the 1980s, views all media as offering scope for participants to learn not to submit passively to whatever comes along, but instead to examine offerings critically while recognizing the financial stakes of programmers and sponsors, to make informed personal and group choices, and to balance their own TV intake with participation in other activities. The hope is that children who become able to take such an approach will be more self-reliant, more informed, and correspondingly less fearful and passive, when it comes to their use of modern media. And since few adults have acquired critical viewing skills, such education is important at all ages.

Maturing, learning how to understand and deal with violence, coping better 5 with its presence on the screen as in the world, knowing its effects, and countering them to the extent possible involves exploring distinctions such as the following:

- between physical violence and psychological and other forms of violence
- between actual and threatened violence
- between direct and indirect violence
- between active violence and violence made possible by neglect or inaction
- between unwanted violence and, say, surgery, performed with consent
- between violence done to oneself and that done to others
- between seeing real violence and witnessing it on the screen
- between portrayals of "real" and fictional violence
- between violence conveyed as information and as entertainment
- between levels of violence in the media and in real life
- between oneself as viewer and as advertising or programming target
- between gratuitous portrayals of violence and others
- between violence glamorized or not

Learning to deal with violence involves sorting out such distinctions and categories and seeking to perceive when they overlap and interact and shade into one another. It is as inaccurate to view all these distinctions as utterly blurred as to imagine each category in a watertight compartment. Exploring these distinctions and their interactions is facilitated by talking them over with others and by seeing them illuminated, first in the simplest stories and pictures, later in literature and works of art.

Because the approach must be gradual and attuned to children's developmental stage, a film such as Steven Spielberg's *Schindler's List,* which offers searing insight into most of the distinctions listed above, is inappropriate for small children, who have not learned to make the necessary distinctions.[2] If they are exposed to such a film before they have learned to draw even rudimentary distinctions with respect to violence, they can respond with terror, numbing, sometimes even misplaced glee. As far as they are concerned, it is beside the point whether the horrors the film conveys are gratuitous or not, real or fictional, or meant as entertainment or not. They cannot tell the difference and should not be exposed to such material before they can do so. The film can be misunderstood, too, by those who would ordinarily be old enough to perceive such distinctions but whose capacity to respond to them has been thwarted or numbed, through personal experience, perhaps from violence in the home, or through overexposure to entertainment violence. The half-embarrassed, half-riotous laughter with which some high school audiences greeted the film troubled many: it was as if these students had lost their ability to make even the most basic distinctions.

A number of these distinctions are hard even for the most experienced media critics to pin down. Take the concept of "gratuitous" violence, violence not needed for purposes of the story being told but added for its shock or entertainment value. Some regard it as a characterization primarily in the eye of the beholder, while others insist that it can be clearly identified in particular films and television programs. Whatever the answer, there are borderline cases of violence where it is hard for anyone to be sure whether it is gratuitous or not. Works such as Spielberg's *Schindler's List* show instances of extreme cruelty that are necessary to convey the horror and inhumanity of the work's subject, and are thus not gratuitous in their own right; yet that film also explores how gratuitous violence is inflicted, even enjoyed, by its perpetrators. The film is about gratuitous violence, then, without in any sense exploiting it or representing an instance of it; and it is emphatically not meant as entertainment violence. Perhaps this is part of what Spielberg meant in saying that he made the film "thinking that if it did entertain, then I would have failed. It was important to me not to set out to please. Because I always had."[3]

Long before callous or uncomprehending ways of responding become ingrained, children can learn, much as the second-graders in the Jennings program were learning, to play a greater part in sorting out the distinctions regarding violence and media violence and to consider how they wish to respond. They can learn to think for themselves and to become discriminating viewers and active participants, rather than passive consumers of the entertainment violence beamed at them daily. Such learning helps, in turn, with the larger goal of achieving resilience—the ability to bounce back, to resist and overcome adversity.

Just as "buyer beware" is an indispensable motto in today's media environment 10 but far from sufficient, so is a fuller understanding of the role of violence in public entertainment. Individuals, families, and schools can do a great deal; but unless they can join in broader endeavors devoted to enhancing collective resilience, the many admirable personal efforts now under way will not begin to suffice. When neither families nor schools, churches, and neighborhoods can cope alone, what is the larger social responsibility?

NOTES

1. See Neil Anderson, *Media Works* (Oxford: Oxford University Press, 1989); and Madeline Levine, *Viewing Violence* (New York: Doubleday, 1996).
2. When *Schindler's List* was about to be broadcast on television, Spielberg was quoted as saying that the film was not, in his opinion, one that should be shown to the very young. His own children, of elementary school age, had not seen it in 1997; but he would want them to once they were of high school age. See Caryn James, "Bringing Home the Horror of the Holocaust," *New York Times,* February 23, 1997, p. 36 H.
3. Steven Spielberg, quoted by Stephen Schiff in "Seriously Spielberg," *New Yorker,* March 21, 1994, p. 101.

Possibilities for Dialogue with "Media Literacy"

There's no one right way to have a dialogue, just as there's no magic question that will always unlock the text in front of us. But it's a good idea to begin with the question *What exactly is the arguer's position?* It's clear that Bok favors "media literacy education." She advocates it, but as only part of the solution to children's exposure to media violence. Her last paragraph implies that we will need other measures as well. And so we might ask, "Why is media education not the only solution?" or "Why isn't media education enough?" Can we tell what she thinks the limitations are?

Having begun with the position question, where we go from there *depends on the nature of the text.* In this case, we need to ask question 2, *What do certain key terms mean?* Paragraph 5 is about the kind of distinctions necessary to a mature understanding of violence. But are we sure about the distinctions? What is "psychological violence"? Bok doesn't say. How would we answer? If there are both physical and psychological forms of violence, what other forms are there? Again, Bok provides no explanation or examples. Can we? It's far from clear what she means. We must figure this out ourselves or work through these distinctions in class discussion.

We should also ask about assumptions and implications. Bok admits that "[a] number of these distinctions are hard even for the most experienced media critics to pin down" (paragraph 8). As adults and college students, we're certainly having our troubles with them; how can we assume that the second-graders referred to in the first paragraph can make them? Do they really understand whatever distinctions their teacher is helping them to make?

Once we question what the argument assumes—that young children (about seven or eight years old) can make meaningful distinctions and understand them—we begin to wonder about implications as well. For instance, the students present what they call a "Declaration of Independence from Violence" to "the rest of the student body." Does the declaration imply that violence is *not* part of the human condition? Are we ignoring reality or learning how to cope with it? More broadly, Bok's discussion implies that media education must continue as students grow up. Is this practical? realistic? Is it something our schools can or should undertake?

◎◎ FOLLOWING THROUGH

In class discussion, continue the dialogue with "Media Literacy." What other questions are relevant from our list of "Questions for Inquiry"? What questions can we ask that do not appear on the list? Be sure to consider the rather unusual case of *Schindler's List.* Why might high school students laugh at it? Is the *only* explanation the one that Bok offers, that the students didn't understand the horror of Nazi violence? Does a movie like *Schindler's List,* when audiences understand and react appropriately to it, help us in "achieving resilience—the ability to bounce back, to resist and overcome adversity"?   ●

◎◎ FOLLOWING THROUGH

As prewriting for Part 2 of your exploratory essay, read one substantial argument on the topic. Write a brief summary of the argument, noting its claim and reasons. Then write a few paragraphs of response to it, as we have done with Rhodes's essay and Bok's chapter, showing how the "Questions for Inquiry" opened up that argument to closer inspection. How did the argument compare with your own initial opinions? Was your thinking changed in any way? Why or why not?   ●

INQUIRY AGAIN: DIGGING DEEPER

Inquiry can always lead to more inquiry. For example, if, after reading Bok, we doubt that media literacy can work, we can find out more about it, including what went on in Australia in the 1980s. If we question what second-graders can understand about media violence, we can research the cognitive development of young children. If we aren't sure about the impact of *Schindler's List,* we can watch it ourselves or read about Spielberg's making of the film and the popular and critical reception of it. There's nothing important in "Media Literacy" that can't be researched and explored further. Digging deeper means getting more information. But mere quantity is not the goal. Moving deeper also means moving closer to genuine expertise. For example, Richard Rhodes is a journalist, not a social scientist. He consulted social scientists to write his argument. To evaluate Rhodes's claims we need to do the same. Digging deeper should take us closer to people who ought to know the most.

Digging deeper also means sharpening the focus of inquiry. As we said earlier, the narrow but deep inquiry will produce a better argument than a broad survey. Look for arguments and informative sources that address the same aspect of a topic. You may find two or more arguments that debate each other.

To find good sources, read the sections on finding and evaluating sources, pages 97–119. There are always resources for digging deeper into a question. Reference librarians can help. They are experts at finding the experts.

When should you stop digging deeper? You can tell when you're near the end of inquiry. You'll be reading but not finding much you haven't seen already. That's the time to stop—or find another avenue for further research.

Most important, *seek out some sources with points of view that differ from your own.* The whole point of inquiry is to seek the new and challenging. *Remember: We are not defending what we think but putting it to the test.*

◎◎ FOLLOWING THROUGH

Read pages 97–119 on finding and evaluating sources. Using the library and electronic indexes available, find at least five good articles and arguments about your chosen issue. Be sure to find sources that contain a variety of opinions but that address the same issues. Read each carefully, and write notes and annotations based on the "Questions for Inquiry."   •

When the Experts Disagree

A professor once advised his classes, "If you want to think you know something about a subject, read one book, because reading a second will just confuse you." Some confusion is unavoidable in inquiry. Digging deeply will reveal sources that conflict. Instead of avoiding conflicting sources (the professor was mocking those who do), seek out conflict and analyze it. Decide which sources to accept, which to reject. We illustrate some strategies for dealing with conflict in the following exploration of two articles that assess the research linking fantasy violence to actual violence.

An Example of Experts Disagreeing

When we left Richard Rhodes, we still wondered, Does violent entertainment contribute to violence in our society? He made a good case against such a link, but we can't ignore all the experts he mentions who do take it seriously. Nor can we put aside the results of our own inquiry into the article, which gave us good reason to doubt his position. So we went to the social scientists themselves to see how they interpret the research. We located the following exchange from the *Harvard Mental Health Letter* (1996). Jonathan L. Freedman, a professor of psychology at the University of Toronto, argues much as Rhodes did—that there's no proof linking fantasy violence to actual violence. L. Rowell Huesmann, a professor of psychology at the University of Michigan, and his graduate assistant, Jessica Moise, defend the link, based in part on their own research.

Now we have conflicting arguments. Read the following articles and assess them on your own. Ask yourself, Who makes the better case?

Children watching violence on TV.

Violence in the Mass Media and Violence in Society: The Link Is Unproven[1]

JONATHAN L. FREEDMAN

Imagine that the Food and Drug Administration (FDA) is presented with a series of studies testing the effectiveness of a new drug. There are some laboratory tests that produce fairly consistent positive effects, but the drug does not always work as expected and no attempt has been made to discover why. Most of the clinical tests are negative; there are also a few weak positive results and a few results suggesting that the drug is less effective than a placebo. Obviously the FDA would reject this application, yet the widely accepted evidence that watching television violence causes aggression is no more adequate.

In laboratory tests of this thesis, some children are shown violent programs, others are shown nonviolent programs, and their aggressiveness is measured immediately afterward. The results, although far from consistent, generally show some increase in aggression after a child watches a violent program. Like most laboratory studies of real-world conditions, however, these findings have limited value. In the first place, most of the studies have used dubious measures of aggression. In one experiment, for example, children were asked, "If I had a balloon, would you want me to prick it?" Other measures have been more plausible, but none is unimpeachable. Second, there is the problem of distinguishing effects of violence from effects of interest and excitement. In general, the violent films in these experiments are more arousing than the neutral films. Anyone who is aroused will display more of

[1]Jonathan L. Freedman, "Violence in the Mass Media and Violence in Society: The Link Is Unproven." Excerpted from the *Harvard Mental Health Letter,* May 1996. © 1996, President and Fellows of Harvard College. For more information, visit www.health.harvard.edu/mental. Harvard Health Publications does not endorse any products or medical procedures.

almost any behavior; there is nothing special about aggression in this respect. Finally and most important, these experiments are seriously contaminated by what psychologists call demand characteristics of the situation: the familiar fact that people try to do what the experimenter wants. Since the children know the experimenter has chosen the violent film, they may assume that they are being given permission to be aggressive.

PUTTING IT TO THE TEST

The simplest way to conduct a real-world study is to find out whether children who watch more violent television are also more aggressive. They are, but the correlations are small, accounting for only 1% to 10% of individual differences in children's aggressiveness. In any case, correlations do not prove causality. Boys watch more TV football than girls, and they play more football than girls, but no one, so far as I know, believes that television is what makes boys more interested in football. Probably personality characteristics that make children more aggressive also make them prefer violent television programs.

To control for the child's initial aggressiveness, some studies have measured children's TV viewing and their aggression at intervals of several years, using statistical techniques to judge the effect of early television viewing on later aggression. One such study found evidence of an effect, but most have found none.

For practical reasons, there have been only a few truly controlled experiments 5 in which some children in a real-world environment are assigned to watch violent programs for a certain period of time and others are assigned to watch nonviolent programs. Two or three of these experiments indicated slight, short-lived effects of TV violence on aggression; one found a strong effect in the opposite of the expected direction, and most found no effect. All the positive results were obtained by a single research group, which conducted studies with very small numbers of children and used inappropriate statistics.

SCRUTINIZING THE EVIDENCE

An account of two studies will give some idea of how weak the research results are and how seriously they have been misinterpreted.

A study published by Lynette Friedrichs and Aletha Stein is often described (for example, in reports by the National Institute of Mental Health and the American Psychological Association) as having found that children who watched violent programs became more aggressive. What the study actually showed was quite different. In a first analysis the authors found that TV violence had no effect on physical aggression, verbal aggression, aggressive fantasy, or object aggression (competition for a toy or other object). Next they computed indexes statistically combining various kinds of aggression, a technique that greatly increases the likelihood of connections appearing purely by chance. Still they found nothing.

They then divided the children into two groups—those who were already aggressive and those who were not. They found that children originally lower in aggression seemed to become more aggressive and children originally higher in aggression seemed to become less aggressive no matter which type of program they watched. This is a well-known statistical artifact called regression toward the mean, and it has no substantive significance. Furthermore, the less aggressive children actually became more aggressive after watching the neutral program than after watching the violent program. The only comfort for the experimenters was that the level of aggression in highly aggressive children fell more when they watched a neutral program than when they watched a violent program. Somehow that was sufficient for the study to be widely cited as strong evidence that TV violence causes aggression.

An ambitious cross-national study was conducted by a team led by Rowell Huesmann and Leonard Eron and reported in 1986. In this widely cited research the effect of watching violent television on aggressiveness at a later age was observed in seven groups of boys and seven groups of girls in six countries. After controlling for initial aggressiveness, the researchers found no statistically significant effect for either sex in Australia, Finland, the Netherlands, Poland, or kibbutz children in Israel. The effect sought by the investigators was found only in the United States and among urban Israeli children, and the latter effect was so large, so far beyond the normal range for this kind of research and so incongruous with the results in other countries, that it must be regarded with suspicion. Nevertheless, the senior authors concluded that the pattern of results supported their position. The Netherlands researchers disagreed; they acknowledged that they had not been able to link TV violence to aggression, and they criticized the methods used by some of the other groups. The senior authors refused to include their chapter in the book that came out of the study, and they had to publish a separate report.

A SECOND LOOK

If the evidence is so inadequate, why have so many committees evaluating it con- 10 cluded that the link exists? In the first place, these committees have been composed largely of people chosen with the expectation of reaching that conclusion. Furthermore, committee members who were not already familiar with the research could not possibly have read it all themselves, and must have relied on what they were told by experts who were often biased. The reports of these committees are often seriously inadequate. The National Institute of Mental Health, for example, conducted a huge study but solicited only one review of the literature, from a strong advocate of the view that television violence causes aggression. The review was sketchy—it left out many important studies—and deeply flawed.

The belief that TV violence causes aggression has seemed plausible because it is intuitively obvious that this powerful medium has effects on children. After all, children imitate and learn from what they see. The question, however, is what they see on television and what they learn. We know that children tend to imitate actions that are rewarded and avoid actions that are punished. In most violent television programs villains start the fight and are punished. The programs also show heroes using violence to fight violence, but the heroes almost always have special legal or moral authority; they are police, other government agents, or protectors of society like Batman and the Power Rangers. If children are learning anything from these programs, it is that the forces of good will overcome evil assailants who are the first to use violence. That may be overoptimistic, but it hardly encourages the children themselves to initiate aggression.

TELLING THE DIFFERENCE

Furthermore, these programs are fiction, and children know it as early as the age of five. Children watching Power Rangers do not think they can beam up to the command center, and children watching "Aladdin" do not believe in flying carpets. Similarly, children watching the retaliatory violence of the heroes in these programs do not come to believe they themselves could successfully act in the same way. (Researchers concerned about mass media violence should be more interested in the fights that occur during hockey and football games, which are real and therefore may be imitated by children who play those sports.)

Recently I testified before a Senate committee, and one Senator told me he knew TV made children aggressive because his own son had met him at the door with a karate kick after watching the Power Rangers. The Senator was confusing aggression with rough play, and imitation of specific actions with learning to be aggressive. Children do imitate what they see on television; this has strong effects on the way they play, and it may also influence the forms their real-life aggression takes. Children who watch the Ninja Turtles or Power Rangers may practice martial arts, just as years ago they might have been wielding toy guns, and long before that, wrestling or dueling with wooden swords. If there had been no television, the Senator's son might have butted him in the stomach or poked him in the ribs with a gun. The question is not whether the boy learned his karate kick from TV, but whether TV has made him more aggressive than he would have been otherwise.

Television is an easy target for the concern about violence in our society but a misleading one. We should no longer waste time worrying about this subject. Instead let us turn our attention to the obvious major causes of violence, which include poverty, racial conflict, drug abuse, and poor parenting.

Media Violence: A Demonstrated Public Health Threat to Children[2]

L. ROWELL HUESMANN AND JESSICA MOISE

Imagine that the Surgeon General is presented with a series of studies on a widely distributed product. For 30 years well-controlled experiments have been showing that use of the product causes symptoms of a particular affliction. Many field surveys have shown that this affliction is always more common among people who use the product regularly. A smaller number of studies have examined the long-term effects of the product in different environments, and most have shown at least some evidence of harm, although it is difficult to disentangle effects of the product itself from the effects of factors that lead people to use it. Over all, the studies suggest that if a person with a 50% risk for the affliction uses the product, the risk rises to 60% or 70%. Furthermore, we have a fairly good understanding of how use of the product contributes to the affliction, which is persistent, difficult to cure, and sometimes lethal.

[2]L. Rowell Huesmann and Jessica Moise, "Media Violence: A Demonstrated Public Health Threat to Children." Excerpted from *Harvard Mental Health Letter,* June 1996. © 1996, President and Fellows of Harvard College. For more information, visit www.health.harvard.edu/mental. Harvard Health Publications does not endorse any products or medical procedures.

The product is economically important, and its manufacturers spend large sums trying to disparage the scientific research. A few scientists who have never done any empirical work in the field regularly point out supposed flaws in the research and belittle its conclusions. The incidence of the affliction has increased dramatically since the product was first introduced. What should the Surgeon General do?

This description applies to the relationship between lung cancer and cigarettes. It also applies to the relationship between aggression and children's viewing of mass media violence. The Surgeon General has rightly come to the same conclusion in both cases and has issued similar warnings.

CAUSE AND EFFECT

Dr. Freedman's highly selective reading of the research minimizes overwhelming evidence. First, there are the carefully controlled laboratory studies in which children are exposed to violent film clips and short-term changes in their behavior are observed. More than 100 such studies over the last 40 years have shown that at least some children exposed to visual depictions of dramatic violence behave more aggressively afterward both toward inanimate objects and toward other children. These results have been found in many countries among boys and girls of all social classes, races, ages, and levels of intelligence.

Freedman claims that these studies use "dubious measures of aggression." He cites only one example: asking children whether they would want the researcher to prick a balloon. But this measure is not at all representative. Most studies have used such evidence as physical attacks on other children and dolls. In one typical study Kaj Bjorkqvist exposed five- and six-year-old Finnish children to either violent or non-violent films. Observers who did not know which kind of film each child had seen then watched them play together. Children who had just seen a violent film were more likely to hit other children, scream at them, threaten them, and intentionally destroy their toys.

Freedman claims that these experiments confuse the effects of arousal with the   5 effects of violence. He argues that "anyone who is aroused will display more of almost any behavior." But most studies have shown that prosocial behavior decreases after children view an aggressive film. Finally, Freedman says the experiments are contaminated by demand characteristics. In other words, the children are only doing what they think the researchers want them to do. That conclusion is extremely implausible, considering the wide variety of experiments conducted in different countries by researchers with different points of view.

LARGE BODY OF EVIDENCE

More than 50 field studies over the last 20 years have also shown that children who habitually watch more media violence behave more aggressively and accept aggression more readily as a way to solve problems. The relationship usually persists when researchers control for age, sex, social class, and previous level of aggression. Disbelievers often suggest that the correlation is statistically small. According to Freedman, it accounts for "only 1% to 10% of individual differences in children's aggressiveness." But an increase of that size (a more accurate figure would be 2%

to 16%) has real social significance. No single factor has been found to explain more than 16% of individual differences in aggression.

Of course, correlations do not prove causality. That is the purpose of laboratory experiments. The two approaches are complementary. Experiments establish causal relationship, and field studies show that the relationship holds in a wide variety of real-world situations. The causal relationship is further confirmed by the finding that children who view TV violence at an early age are more likely to commit aggressive acts at a later age. In 1982 Eron and Huesmann found that boys who spent the most time viewing violent television shows at age eight were most likely to have criminal convictions at age 30. Most other long-term studies have come to similar conclusions, even after controlling for children's initial aggressiveness, social class, and education. A few studies have found no effect on some measures of violence, but almost all have found a significant effect on some measures.

Freedman singles out for criticism a study by Huesmann and his colleagues that was concluded in the late 1970s. He says we found "no statistically significant effect for either sex in Australia, Finland, the Netherlands, Poland, or kibbutz children in Israel." That is not true. We found that the television viewing habits of children [as] young as six or seven predicted subsequent increases in childhood aggression among boys in Finland and among both sexes in the United States, in Poland, and in Israeli cities. In Australia and on Israeli kibbutzim, television viewing habits were correlated with simultaneous aggression. Freedman also suggests that another study conducted in the Netherlands came to conclusions so different from ours that we banned it from a book we were writing. In fact, the results of that study were remarkably similar to our own, and we did not refuse to publish it. The Dutch researchers themselves chose to publish separately in a different format.

CULTURAL DIFFERENCES

Freedman argues that the strongest results reported in the study, such as those for Israeli city children, are so incongruous that they arouse suspicion. He is wrong. Given the influence of culture and social learning on aggressive behavior, different results in different cultures are to be expected. In fact, the similarity of the findings in different countries is remarkable here. One reason we found no connection between television violence viewing and aggression among children on [kib]butzim is the strong cultural prohibition against intra-group aggression in those communities. Another reason is that kibbutz children usually watched television in a group and discussed the shows with an adult caretaker afterward.

Two recently published meta-analyses summarize the findings of many studies 10 conducted over the past 30 years. In an analysis of 217 experiments and field studies, Paik and Comstock concluded that the association between exposure to television violence and aggressive behavior is extremely strong, especially in the data accumulated over the last 15 years. In the other meta-analysis, Wood, Wong, and Chachere came to the same conclusion after combined analysis of 23 studies of unstructured social interaction.

We now have well-validated theoretical explanations of these results. Exposure to media violence leads to aggression in at least five ways. The first is imitation, or observational learning. Children imitate the actions of their parents, other children, and

media heroes, especially when the action is rewarded and the child admires and identifies with the model. When generalized, this process creates what are sometimes called
cognitive scripts for complex social problem-solving: internalized programs that guide
everyday social behavior in an automatic way and are highly resistant to change.

TURNING OFF

Second, media violence stimulates aggression by desensitizing children to the
effects of violence. The more televised violence a child watches, the more acceptable aggressive behavior becomes for that child. Furthermore, children who watch
violent television become suspicious and expect others to act violently—an attribu-
tional bias that promotes aggressive behavior.

Justification is a third process by which media violence stimulates aggression. A
child who has behaved aggressively watches violent television shows to relieve guilt
and justify the aggression. The child then feels less inhibited about aggressing again.

A fourth process is cognitive priming or cueing—the activation of existing aggressive thoughts, feelings, and behavior. This explains why children observe one kind of
aggression on television and commit another kind of aggressive act afterward. Even
an innocuous object that has been associated with aggression may later stimulate
violence. Josephson demonstrated this . . . in a study of schoolboy hockey players.
She subjected the boys to frustration and then showed them either a violent or a
non-violent television program. The aggressor in the violent program carried a walkie-
talkie. Later, when the referee in a hockey game carried a similar walkie-talkie, the boys
who had seen the violent film were more likely to start fights during the game.

A NUMBING EFFECT

The fifth process by which media violence induces aggression is physiological 15
arousal and desensitization. Boys who are heavy television watchers show lower
than average physiological arousal in response to new scenes of violence. Similar
short-term effects are found in laboratory studies. The arousal stimulated by viewing violence is unpleasant at first, but children who constantly watch violent television become habituated, and their emotional and physiological responses decline.
Meanwhile the propensity to aggression is heightened by any pleasurable arousal,
such as sexual feeling, that is associated with media violence.

Freedman argues that in violent TV shows, villains start the fight and are punished
and the heroes "almost always have special legal or moral authority." Therefore, he
concludes, children are learning from these programs that "the forces of good will
overcome evil assailants." On the contrary, it is precisely because media heroes are
admired and have special authority that children are likely to imitate their behavior
and learn that aggression is an acceptable solution to conflict. Freedman also claims
that media violence has little effect because children can distinguish real life from fiction. But children under 11 do not make this distinction very well. Studies have shown
that many of them think cartoons and other fantasy shows depict life as it really is.

The studies are conclusive. The evidence leaves no room for doubt that exposure to media violence stimulates aggression. It is time to move on and consider
how best to inoculate our children against this insidious threat.

Commentary on the Experts' Disagreement

When experts disagree, the rest of us can respond in only a few ways. We can throw up our hands and say, "Who knows?" But this response doesn't work because expert disagreement is so common. We'd have to give up on most issues. Another response is to take seriously only those experts who endorse the opinion we favor and ignore the rest, a common tactic in debate, legal pleadings, business, and politics whenever truth gives way to self-interest. We can also "go with our gut," opting for the opinion that "feels right." But gut feelings amount to little more than our prejudices talking. And so we are left with the only response appropriate to inquiry: *rational assessment of the competing arguments.* We should take as true the better or best case.

How can we decide which of two or several arguments is better or best?

In this instance, let's recognize that Huesmann and Moise have an advantage simply because they wrote second, after Freedman, who has no opportunity to respond to what they've said. Huesmann and Moise can *both* refute Freedman *and* make their own case without the possibility of rebuttal. Granting this it's still hard to find Freedman's case more convincing. Why?

We'll offer only a few reasons for assenting to the Huesmann–Moise argument. You and your class can take the analysis further—it's a good opportunity to practice critical reading and thinking.

Both articles begin with an analogy. Freedman compares the research on violent TV programs with the research required to approve a drug. Huesmann and Moise compare the research linking cigarettes to lung cancer with the research linking violent TV to aggressive behavior in children. The second comparison is better because the two instances of research compared are more nearly alike. Furthermore, the fact that the Surgeon General has issued warnings both for cigarettes and for violent entertainment's effect on children shows how seriously research on the latter is taken by qualified authorities. In fact, one of the more convincing aspects of the Huesmann–Moise case is the amount of support they claim for their position. They are specific about the numbers: "50 field studies over the last 20 years" (paragraph 6); "an analysis of 217 experiments and field studies" (paragraph 10)—all confirm their conclusion. If Freedman has evidence to rival this, he does not cite it. We must assume he doesn't because he doesn't have it.

Another strength of the Huesmann–Moise article is that they go beyond linking TV violence to aggression by offering five *explanations* for the negative impact of fantasy violence (paragraphs 11–15). We come away not only convinced that the link exists but also understanding why it exists. Freedman has no well-developed explanation to support his position. What he offers, such as the assertion that children know the difference between pretend and real violence, is refuted by Huesmann and Moise.

If you are thinking that the better or best case isn't always so easy to discern, you're right. Comparative assessment will not always yield a clearly superior case. We will sometimes argue with ourselves and others over whose case merits our support. Nonetheless, when we encounter opposing positions, we should set aside our prejudices and study the arguments made. We should resolve the conflict by taking the better or best case as the closest thing we have to the truth.

In most cases, the better or best argument will emerge as you think your way through the arguments, comparing their strengths and weaknesses. What's hard is to let go of a position we're attracted to when another one has the better case. *The real challenge of inquiry is to change or revise our own opinions as we encounter arguments stronger than our own.*

◎◎ FOLLOWING THROUGH

Even if they do not speak directly to each other, as our examples here do, find two sources that present conflicting data or information or conflicting interpretations of the same information. Write an evaluation of these arguments, telling which one has the better case. Explain why you think so. Did you find that comparing these arguments influenced your own thinking? If so, how? •

THE WRITING PROJECT: PART 2

By now you have many notes that you can use as raw material for writing Part 2 of your essay. You have had a serious dialogue with at least one other person about your ideas. You should have notes about this dialogue and maybe a recording or transcript of it. Look over this material, and make more notes about how this conversation modified your ideas—by clarifying them, by presenting you with a new idea, or by solidifying a belief you already held.

You have also read several printed arguments. You have written evaluations of these arguments and marked them up. Now note places where they touch upon the same points. Use highlighters to color-code passages that connect across the readings. Draft paragraphs about what different experts have to say on the same question, including an estimate of how sound their points are and how they increased your own knowledge. Which viewpoints seemed most persuasive, and why?

You are ready to draft the body of your paper. It should contain at least four well-developed paragraphs that describe your inquiry. Discuss the conversations you had and the materials you read, and show how these lines of inquiry influenced your thinking. Assess the arguments you read, consider their rhetorical context, include the names of the authors and the biases they might have. Talk about why an author's argument was sound or not sound, why it influenced your initial opinion or why it did not.

Part 2 could be organized around a discussion of initial opinions strengthened by your research versus those reconsidered because of it. Did a source offer new information that caused you to reconsider what you thought? Tell what the information was, and explain why it's changed your outlook. Did you encounter a well-developed argument defending a position different from your own? How did you react? What aspects of the argument do you take seriously enough to modify or change your own opinion? Explain why. If you found sources who disagreed, which side did you find more convincing, and why?

Some paragraphs could be devoted to a single source. Others could compare an idea across two or more sources; you could point out ways in which they agree or disagree, showing how each contributed to changing your opinion.

No matter how you organize your paper, *be specific about what you have read.* You will need to quote and paraphrase; when you refer to sources, do so very specifically. See our advice about using sources on pages 119–130.

Don't merely summarize your sources or use them to support and illustrate your own argument. *You are evaluating the thinking expressed in the sources,* not making your own case.

Rhetorical context is vital and it should be part of your consideration of each source. *Be selective.* Your readers don't want to get bogged down in needless detail; they want the information that altered your understanding of the topic and the arguments that opened up new considerations. *The point is to show how your research-inquiry refined, modified, or changed your initial opinions and to explain why.* Anything that doesn't do this should be cut from the final draft of your paper.

THE WRITING PROJECT: PART 3

In preparation for writing the conclusion of your essay, reread Part 1, the overview of your exploration. Have you arrived at a claim you could defend in an essay to convince or persuade an audience? If so, what is it? Perhaps you're still unsure—what then? One option is to conclude your paper by explaining what you are unsure of and why, and what you'd like to learn from further research. An inconclusive but honest ending is better than a forced one making a claim you don't really believe.

Draft a conclusion in which you honestly discuss the results of your exploration, whatever they were. This section is about *where you stand now,* but it needn't be final or conclusive. If you have doubts, state them and indicate how you might resolve them through further research and inquiry.

AFTER DRAFTING YOUR ESSAY

Revise your draft to make sure each paragraph is unified around one point and to remove any unnecessary summarizing. Check your work against the guidelines for incorporating source material in your own writing (pages 130–135).

Edit your paper for wordiness, repetition, and excessive passive voice. See the suggestions for editing in Appendix A.

Proofread your paper. Read it aloud to catch omissions and errors of grammar and punctuation.

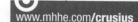

STUDENT SAMPLE An Exploratory Essay

Exploratory Essay
Sydney Owens

Part 1

I think that the relationship between violence and the media is hard to define. There is definitely some relation between them, but to what extent it is hard to say. Media itself is only one word, but it includes television, radio, CDs, video games, papers, books, the Internet, and more. It's hard to say what each contributes. Also, you have to look at what kind of violence you are talking about. Do media influence extreme aggressive behavior, such as killing? Lastly, a child's environment, personality, and parents also have to be considered. It is difficult to say why people do anything, including acts of violence.

Each human is unique so that it's hard to say that media violence makes people more violent. One person could watch gruesome violence every day and remain caring and loving, whereas another individual might see minimal violent media and go out and kill. How do you explain the difference? You have to define a norm. But that norm only defines "normal" people's reactions to media violence. A person outside of the norm may still commit acts of violence.

When I see or hear violence in the media, I know that I am not inclined to do anything more violent than if I had not. Granted, a high-action movie thriller has given me that feeling of kick-ass satisfaction and exposure to rap has caused me to use strong language. But feelings and slang are not acts of violence. These examples do show that there is a connection between the media and people's behavior.

Part 2

When I read "Violence in the Mass Media and Violence in Society: The Link Is Unproven," I began to think that there really is not much evidence indicating that media violence leads to violent behavior. The author, Jonathan Freedman, argued that you could not prove the link because the "studies . . . used dubious measures of aggression," they could not "distinguish effects of violence from effects of interest and excitement," and the studies were "seriously contaminated by . . . demand characteristics of the situation." All of this made sense to me. I especially agreed with the contamination of the demand characteristics because I had just learned about this in my psychology class. I was taught that experimenters have to take into

account that subjects alter their own behavior to meet what they
think the experimenter wants.

Freedman also gave an example that stuck in my mind as proof 5
that there is not a strong enough link to prove anything. He said to
imagine that the FDA was testing the effectiveness of a new drug.
The results came out negative, even less effective than a placebo. He
said that obviously the FDA would reject this drug and that, similarly,
media should be rejected as having a significant effect on violence.
This made perfect sense until I compared it to "Media Violence: A
Demonstrated Public Health Threat to Children," an article by L. Rowell Huesmann and Jessica Moise that counters Freedman's position.
The FDA analogy that had sounded so good now looked faulty compared with Huesmann's Surgeon General analogy. In Huesmann's
analogy, he points out that if something has shown even the slightest
negative effect, it can't be dismissed. Freedman was right to say that
we cannot prove for certain that media violence leads to violent
behavior, but what he failed to acknowledge is that we should still
warn about negative effects. After contrasting these two articles, I had
changed my mind and decided that media violence does play a role in
violent behavior.

With this new state of mind, I read several other articles that
reinforced the claim that media violence promotes violent behavior.
In the article "We Are Training Our Kids to Kill," Dave Grossman
claims that "the desensitizing techniques used for training soldiers
are being replicated in contemporary mass media movies, television,
and video games, giving rise to the alarming rate of homicide and
violence in our schools and communities." Not only was this article
interesting, but it also made sense. Grossman, who travels the
world training medical, law enforcement, and U.S. military personnel about the realities of warfare, supported his claim by showing
how classical and operant conditioning used in the military parallel
the effects of violent media on young children. Grossman's article
was simple and straightforward. I followed his argument and
agreed that the desensitizing effects of media train our kids to kill.

To be sure that his argument was true, I tried looking for
some evidence that would prove that desensitizing did not have an
effect. The only text I could find was the article by Richard
Rhodes, "Hollow Claims about Fantasy Violence." In this article,
there is one short and very confusing paragraph (paragraph 9) in
which Rhodes offers "a British scholar's" critique of the desensitization argument:

> [T]heir claim is that the materials they judge to be harmful can only
> influence us by trying to make us be the same as them. So horrible
> things will make us horrible—not horrified. . . . This idea is so odd,
> it is hard to know where to begin in challenging it.

After reading this, I felt like saying the same thing to Rhodes. His paragraph was so confusing I had a hard time knowing where to begin in challenging it. In reality, it is not really an argument at all because Rhodes offers only a quote without explanation. The quote lumps all forms of violence together and ignores the different ways violence is depicted. I stuck with my new view that desensitization does promote violent behavior.

Part 3

After reading all of these articles and deciding that I do think that media contributes to violent behavior, I began thinking about my own personal experiences again. I thought about that "kick-ass feeling" I get when I watch certain action movies, and I began feeling somewhat ashamed. As film producers Edward Zwick and Marshall Herskovitz pointed out in their New York Times column "When the Bodies Are Real," written after 9/11, "perhaps what this event has revealed, with its real bodies blown to bits and real explosions bringing down buildings, is the true darkness behind so much of the product coming out of Hollywood today."

Annotated Bibliography

Freedman, Jonathan L. "Violence in the Mass Media and Violence in Society: The Link Is Unproven." Harvard Mental Health Letter May 1996: 4–6.

This article claims that there is not solid proof that mass media leads to violence. The author, Jonathan Freedman, proves his claim by showing that the studies have used dubious measures of aggression, by showing that it is hard to distinguish effects of violence from effects of excitement, and to separate either from the effects of demand characteristics. This would be a good article to use to prove that media does not influence aggressive behavior; however, I used the article's weak points to prove that media does lead to aggressive behavior.

Grossman, Dave. "We Are Training Our Kids to Kill." Saturday Evening Post July/Aug. 1999: 64–70.

This article explains the killings committed by America's youth as a result of media violence. First the author discusses how killing is unnatural. He then goes on to show how several military techniques for training soldiers resemble the ways the media interact with children. This article gives logical support to the claim that media influences violent behavior.

Herskovitz, Marshall, and Edward Zwick. "When the Bodies Are Real." Editorial. New York Times 23 Sept. 2001.

This is a short article written in response to the horrible tragedy of 9/11. It is written for the general public but focuses

specifically on how the media community will respond to this
tragedy. The authors, Marshall Herskovitz and Edward Zwick,
are producers, directors, and writers. They point out how 9/11
has caused Hollywood, and all of us, to reexamine violence.

Huesmann, L. Rowell, and Jessica Moise. "Media Violence: A Demonstrated Public Health Threat to Children." <u>Harvard Mental Health
Letter</u> June 1996: 5–7.

This article responds to Jonathan Freedman's article, "Violence
in the Mass Media and Violence in Society: The Link Is
Unproven." The authors refute most of Freedman's article with
research. The article offers good support for the link between
media and real violence.

Rhodes, Richard. "Hollow Claims about Fantasy Violence." Editorial.
<u>New York Times</u> 17 Sept. 2000.

This essay attempts to prove that there is not enough evidence
to claim that media violence leads to real violence. The author
says that people (in particular, politicians) use media as a
scapegoat for not looking at the real problems behind violence.

Note: For a discussion of how to create an annotated bibliography, see Chapter 5, pages 128–129.

INQUIRY: SUMMING UP THE AIM

In this chapter, we've introduced you to college-level inquiry. Here are the
key points:

- In college, we don't just ransack sources for information and quotes.
  We interact with them. "Interact" means be critical of sources and
  allow them to influence, even change, our point of view.

- Informal conversation is a valuable medium of inquiry. But it becomes
  more valuable when we turn conversation into dialogue. *Assert opinions less, and question opinions more.* When a good question elicits a
  good response, pursue it with more questions.

- The best and most stimulating sources need dialogue. *Think of texts as
  something to "talk with."* Such dialogues will uncover more research
  possibilities. Pursue these, and you'll approach the depth of inquiry
  valued in college work and beyond, in graduate school and the work-
  place.

Inquiry is learning. Inquiry is finding what we really think and have to
say. It's the most creative part of the writing process. Invest in it. It will repay
your best efforts.

CHAPTER 8

Making Your Case: Arguing to Convince

The last chapter ended where inquiry ends—with the attempt to formulate a position, an opinion that we can assert with some confidence. Once our aim shifts from inquiring to convincing, everything changes.

The most significant change is in audience. In inquiry, our audience consists of our fellow inquirers—friends, classmates, and teachers we can talk with face to face. We seek assurance that our position is at least plausible and defensible, a claim to truth that can be respected whether or not the audience agrees with it. In convincing, however, our audience consists of readers whose positions differ from our own or who have no position at all. The audience changes from a small, inside group that helps us develop our argument to a larger, public audience who will either accept or reject it.

As the audience changes, so does the situation or need for argument. Inquiry is a cooperative use of argument; it cannot take place unless people are willing to work together. Conversely, convincing is competitive. We pit our case against the case(s) of others to win the assent of readers who will compare the various arguments and ask, Who makes the best case? With whom should I agree? Our arguments now compete for "best or better" status, just as do the disagreeing arguments of experts.

From Inquiry to Convincing

Inquiry ⟶	Convincing
Intimate audience	Public readership
Cooperative	Competitive
Earns a conviction	Argues a thesis
Seeks a case convincing *to us*	Makes a case convincing *to them,* the readers

We take the position we discovered through inquiry and turn it into a thesis supported by a case designed to gain the assent of a specific group of readers.

Because of the change in audience and situation, our thinking also changes, becomes more strategic and calculated to influence readers. In inquiry, we make a case we can believe in; in convincing, we make a case readers can believe in. What we find compelling in inquiry will sometimes also convince our readers, but *in convincing we must adapt our reasoning to appeal to their beliefs, values, and self-interest.* We will also likely offer reasons that did not occur to us at all in inquiry but come as we attempt to imagine the people we hope to convince. Convincing, however, does not mean abandoning the work of inquiry. Our version of the truth, our convictions, gained through inquiry, are what we argue for.

In this chapter, we look first at the structure and strategy of complete essays that aim to convince. Then we provide a step-by-step analysis of the kind of thinking necessary to produce such an essay.

THE NATURE OF CONVINCING: STRUCTURE AND STRATEGY

An argument is an assertion supported by a reason. To convince an audience, writers need to expand on this structure. They usually must offer more than one reason and support all reasons with evidence. We use **case structure** to describe a flexible plan for making *any argument to any audience* who expects sound reasoning. We use **case strategy** to describe the reader-centered moves writers make *to shape a particular argument*—selecting reasons, ordering them, developing evidence, and linking the sections of the argument together for maximum impact.

Case Structure

All cases have at least three levels of assertion. The first level is the thesis, or central claim, which everything else in the case supports. The second level is the reason or reasons the arguer advances for holding the thesis. The third

Key Questions for Case-Making

1. Who is your **target audience**?
2. What **preconceptions** and **biases** might they hold about your topic?
3. What **claim** do you want your readers to accept?
4. What **reasons** are likely to appeal to this audience?
5. How should you **arrange** these reasons for **maximum impact** on your target audience?
6. How might you **introduce** your case?
7. How might you **conclude** it?
8. How can you gain the **trust** and **respect** of your audience?

Convincing is audience centered. Every choice we make must be made with the target audience in mind.

---

level is the evidence offered to support each reason, typically drawn from some authoritative source.

In the abstract, then, cases look like this:

Figure 8.1

Our diagram shows three reasons, but good cases can be built with only one reason or with more than three.

Case Strategy

In Chapter 2, we explain that you can read an argument with greater comprehension if you have a sense of the rhetorical context in which the writer worked. Likewise, in preparing to write an argument, consider your own context by using the Concept Close-Up "Key Questions for Case-Making."

By working out answers to these questions in your writer's notebook, you'll create a **rhetorical prospectus** that will help you envision a context within which to write and a tentative plan to follow.

To demonstrate case strategy, we'll look at "Arrested Development: The Conservative Case against Racial Profiling" (pp. 214–217). The author, James

Forman, Jr., is an educator and fellow at the New American Foundation in Washington, D.C. His article was published in *The New Republic,* September 10, 2001.

Thinking about Audience

To make an effective case for his position, Forman envisions an audience who favors racial profiling, and his strategy is to use reasons and evidence to convince readers who will resist his thesis. Therefore, he had to consider their likely responses. He posed questions like these:

- Who will my readers be?
- How will they be predisposed to view racial profiling?
- What will they have on their minds as soon as they see that my argument is against it?

Based on these questions, Forman assumes something like the following about the intended audience:

> My conservative audience supports the police and approves of or at least tolerates racial profiling as a tactic for apprehending criminals. I want to show them not only that profiling doesn't work but also, more importantly, that it violates fundamental conservative principles.

Strategy, then, must begin with thoughts about the audience, its values and preconceptions. Next, we examine how Forman shapes the elements of case structure—thesis, reasons, and evidence—to appeal to his readers.

Formulating the Thesis

Your thesis may not be explicitly stated but it must be *strongly implied,* clear to you and your reader. It must be clear to you because you must build a case around it. It must be clear to your readers so that they know what you're claiming and what to expect from your case. Forman's thesis is implied and can be stated as follows: *Political conservatives, most of whom now support racial profiling, ought to oppose it.*

Choosing Reasons

Forman constructs his case around four reasons, all designed to appeal to his audience and undercut their support of racial profiling.

Thesis: Political conservatives, most of whom now support racial profiling, ought to oppose it.

> *Reason 1:* Racial profiling is ineffective—it doesn't reliably identify criminals. (Strategy: Forman wants to take away the major justification for profiling, that it helps the police catch lawbreakers.)

> *Reason 2:* Racial profiling harasses law-abiding blacks just because they are black. (Strategy: Forman wants his readers, most of whom

have not been stopped and frisked by the police, to appreciate how discriminatory profiling is and the damage it does to people's respect for authority.)

Reason 3: Racial profiling violates the conservative principle that equates equal rights with equal responsibilities. (Strategy: Forman wants his readers to see that racial profiling contradicts his audience's values—in this instance, the relationship of individual achievement to full, equal participation in the community.)

Reason 4: Racial profiling violates the conservative ideal of a color-blind society. (Strategy: Forman wants his audience to see that their reasons for opposing affirmative action apply with equal force to racial profiling.)

As you read Forman's argument, note how he arranges his reasons; the order of presentation matters. Note also his strategies for developing reasons, especially his use of evidence.

Figure 8.2

Hulbert Waldroup, the artist who painted the controversial mural of Amadou Diallo in the Bronx near where Diallo was shot, signs his initials to his latest work, a painting on racial profiling, after unveiling it in New York's Times Square, Tuesday, July 24, 2001. Waldroup says his work portrays racial profiling "through the eyes of a cop—what he sees, what he thinks, the stereotypes we are all responsible for."

Arrested Development: The Conservative Case against Racial Profiling

JAMES FORMAN, JR.

The Maya Angelou Public Charter School in Washington, D.C., is the kind of institution conservatives love—a place that offers opportunity but demands responsibility. Students are in school ten and a half hours per day, all year long, mostly studying core subjects like reading, writing, math, and history. When not in class, they work in student-run businesses, where they earn money and learn job skills. Those who achieve academically are held in high esteem not only by their teachers but by their peers. Those who disrupt class or otherwise violate the rules are subject to punishment, including expulsion, as determined by a panel of students and teachers.

The results have been impressive. Most Maya Angelou students had academic difficulty at their previous schools. In fact, more than one-half had stopped even attending school on a regular basis before they came to Maya Angelou, while more than one-third had been in the juvenile court system. Yet more than 90 percent of its graduates go on to college, compared with a citywide rate of just 50 percent. This success stems in part from the school's small classes, innovative curriculum, and dedicated staff. But it is also due to its fundamentally conservative ethos: If you work hard and don't make excuses, society will give you a chance, no matter what your background is.

I can speak to this with some authority because I helped establish the school four years ago and still teach an elective there today. But, for all the school's accomplishments, we keep running up against one particularly debilitating problem. It's awfully hard to convince poor, African American kids that discrimination isn't an obstacle, that authority must be respected, and that individual identity matters more than racial identity when experiences beyond school walls repeatedly contradict it. And that's precisely what's happening today, thanks to a policy many conservatives condone: Racial profiling by the police.

The prevalence of racial profiling is no secret. Numerous statistical studies have shown that being black substantially raises the odds of a person being stopped and searched by the police—even though blacks who are stopped are no more likely than whites to be carrying drugs. As David Cole and John Lamberth recently pointed out in *The New York Times,* in Maryland "73 percent of those stopped and searched on a section of Interstate 95 were black, yet state police reported that equal percentages of the whites and blacks who were searched, statewide, had drugs or other contraband." Blacks were actually far less likely than whites to be found carrying drugs in New Jersey, a state whose police force has acknowledged the use of racial profiling. According to Cole and Lamberth, consensual searches "yielded contraband, mostly drugs, on 25 percent of whites, 13 percent of blacks and only 5 percent of Latinos."

Behind these statistics are hundreds if not thousands of well-chronicled anec- 5 dotes, some from America's most prominent black citizens. Erroll McDonald, vice president and executive editor of Pantheon publishing, was driving a rented Jaguar in New Orleans when he was stopped—simply "to show cause why I shouldn't be deemed a problematic Negro in a possibly stolen car.". . .

Even off-duty black police frequently tell of being harassed by their unsuspecting white colleagues. Consider the case of Robert Byrd, an eleven-year veteran of the D.C. police, who was off duty and out of uniform when he tried to stop a carjacking and robbery in Southeast Washington last March. After witnessing the crime, Byrd used his police radio to alert a police dispatcher, then followed the stolen van in his own. Byrd got out of his van as marked police vehicles arrived. According to Byrd, white officers then began beating him in the belief that he was the African American suspect. The real perpetrators were caught later that night.

None of these stories would surprise the students at Maya Angelou. Almost weekly this past spring, officers arrived at the corner of 9th and T Streets NW (in front of our school), threw our students against the wall, and searched them. As you might imagine, these are not polite encounters. They are an aggressive show of force in which children are required to "assume the position": legs spread, face against the wall or squad car, hands behind the head. Police officers then search them, feeling every area of their bodies. Last spring, a police officer chased one male student into the school, wrestled him to the ground, then drew his gun. Another time, when a student refused a police request to leave the corner in front of our school (where the student was taking a short break between classes, in complete compliance with school rules and D.C. law), the officer grabbed him, cuffed him, and started putting him into a police van, before a school official intervened. These students committed no crime other than standing outside a school in a high-drug-use neighborhood. Indeed, despite the numerous searches, no drugs have ever been discovered, and no student has ever been found in violation of the law.

Liberals generally decry such incidents; conservatives generally deny that they take place. "[T]he racial profiling we're all supposed to be outraged about doesn't actually happen very much," explained Jonah Goldberg in his *National Review Online* column last spring. And even those conservatives who admit the practice's frequency often still insist it does more good than harm. "The evidence suggests," William Tucker wrote in a recent issue of *The Weekly Standard*, "that racial profiling is an effective law enforcement tool, though it undeniably visits indignity on the innocent."

In other words, liberals—who are generally more concerned about individual rights and institutionalized racism—believe racial profiling contradicts their principles. Conservatives, on the other hand—who tolerate greater invasions of privacy in the name of law and order—consider racial profiling to be generally consistent with theirs. But conservatives are wrong—racial profiling profoundly violates core conservative principles.

It is conservatives, after all, who remind us that government policy doesn't 10 affect only resources; it affects values, which in turn affect people's behavior. This argument was at the heart of the conservative critique of welfare policy. For years, conservatives (along with some liberals) argued that welfare policies—like subsidizing unmarried, unemployed women with children—fostered a culture of dependency. Only by demanding that citizens take responsibility for their own fates, the argument went, could government effectively combat poverty.

But if sending out welfare checks with no strings attached sends the wrong message, so does racial profiling. For the conservative ethos about work and responsibility to resonate, black citizens must believe they are treated the same way as white citizens—that with equal responsibilities go equal rights. In *The Dream and the Nightmare,* which President Bush cites as one of the most influential books he has ever read, the conservative theorist Myron Magnet writes: "[W]hat underclass kids need most . . . is an authoritative link to traditional values of work, study, and self-improvement, and the assurance that these values can permit them to claim full membership in the larger community." Magnet quotes Eugene Lange, a businessman who promised scholarships to inner-city kids who graduated from high school: "It's important that [inner-city kids] grow up to recognize that they are not perpetuating a life of the pariah, but that the resources of the community are legitimately theirs to take advantage of and contribute to and be a part of."

Magnet is right. But random and degrading police searches radically undermine this message. They tell black kids that they are indeed pariahs—that, no matter how hard they study, they remain suspects. As one Maya Angelou first-year student explained to me: "We can be perfect, perfect, doing everything right, and they still treat us like dogs. No, worse than dogs, because criminals are treated worse than dogs." Or, as a junior asked me, noting the discrepancy between the message delivered by the school and the message delivered by the police: "How can you tell us we can be anything if they treat us like we're nothing?"

Indeed, people like myself—teachers, counselors, parents—try desperately to convince these often jaded kids that hard work really will pay off. In so doing, we are quite consciously pursuing an educational approach that conservatives have long advocated. We are addressing what conservative criminologist James Q. Wilson calls "intangible problems—problems of 'values,'" the problems that sometimes make "blacks less likely to take advantage of opportunities." But we are constantly fighting other people in the neighborhood who tell kids that bourgeois norms of work, family, and sexuality are irrelevant and impossible. Since the state will forever treat you as an outlaw, they say, you might as well act like one. Every time police single out a young black man for harassment, those other people sound more credible—and we sound like dupes.

Then there's that other vaunted conservative ideal: color-blindness. In recent years, conservatives have argued relentlessly for placing less emphasis on race. Since discrimination is on the wane, they suggest, government itself must stop making race an issue—i.e., no more affirmative action in admissions, no more set-asides in contracting, no more tailoring of government programs to favor particular racial or ethnic groups. In the words of affirmative action critics Abigail and Stephen Thernstrom, it's essential to fight the "politics of racial grievance" and counter the "suspicion that nothing fundamental [has] changed." Society, says Magnet, "needs to tell [blacks] that they can do it—not that, because of past victimization, they cannot."

But it's hard to tell young black men that they are not victims because of their 15 race when police routinely make them victims because of their race. Students at Maya Angelou are acutely aware that the police do not treat young people the same way at Sidwell Friends and St. Albans, schools for Washington's overwhelmingly white elite. As another Maya Angelou first-year told me, "You think they would try that stuff with white kids? Never." Such knowledge makes them highly suspicious of the conservative assertion that blacks should forego certain benefits—such as racial preferences in admissions—because of the moral value of color-blindness. Why, they wonder, aren't white people concerned about that principle when it hurts blacks as well as when it benefits them? And racial profiling makes them cynical about the conservative demand that blacks not see the world in racialized, group-identity terms. Why, they wonder, don't white people demand the same of the police?

Most conservatives who support racial profiling are not racist; they simply consider the practice an essential ingredient of effective law enforcement. But it isn't. Indeed, the great irony of conservative support for racial profiling is that conservative principles themselves explain why racial profiling actually makes law enforcement less effective.

. . . [D]iscriminatory police practices create unnecessary and unproductive hostility between police and the communities they serve. Imagine that you are 17, standing outside your school during a break from class, talking to friends, laughing, playing, and just relaxing. Imagine that squad cars pull up; officers jump out, shouting, guns drawn; and you are thrown against the wall, elbowed in the back, legs kicked apart, and violently searched. Your books are strewn on the ground. You ask what's going on, and you are told to "shut the fuck up" or you will be taken downtown. When it finally ends, the officers leave, giving no apology, no explanation, and you are left to fix your clothes, pick up your books, and gather your pride. Imagine that this is not the first time this has happened to you, that it has happened repeatedly, in one form or another, throughout your adolescence. Now imagine that, the day after the search, there is a crime in your neighborhood about which you hear a rumor. You know the police are looking for information, and you see one of the officers who searched you yesterday (or indeed any officer) asking questions about the crime. How likely are you to help? . . .

Arranging Reasons

Conservative support for racial profiling depends on belief in its effectiveness, especially in combating illegal drugs. Forman therefore challenges this belief first. If he can show that profiling doesn't produce the results claimed for it, his readers should then be more receptive to his other reasons, all of which establish its negative impact.

His second reason has force because no law-abiding citizen wants to be treated as if she or he were suspected of criminal activity. No matter who you are, however, and no matter what you are doing, you can be so treated if you fit the profile. Such harassment would not be tolerated by the conservative, mostly white audience Forman is trying to reach and so should not be condoned by that audience when directed toward other racial and ethnic groups. It's a matter of fairness.

Forman's first two reasons engage relatively concrete and easily grasped issues: Does racial profiling work? Are innocent people harassed when it's used? His third and fourth reasons are more abstract and depend on the reader's recognition of contradiction. If we oppose welfare because it encourages dependency and lack of personal responsibility, shouldn't we oppose racial profiling because it "tell[s] black kids that they are indeed pariahs—that, no matter how hard they study, they remain suspects"? Similarly, if we oppose affirmative action because it favors people because of race, shouldn't we also oppose profiling because it also singles out race? Rational people want to be consistent; Forman shows his readers that they haven't been—a powerful strategy after showing that profiling doesn't work and harasses innocent people.

Using Evidence

How well does Forman use the third level of case structure, the supporting evidence for each reason?

Note that he uses different *kinds* of evidence appropriately. To support his contention that racial profiling doesn't work, he cites *data*—in this case, statistics—showing that blacks are less likely than whites or Latinos to be caught with contraband (paragraph 4). Profiling blacks, therefore, makes no sense. Next, he uses *individual examples* to confirm that innocent people, including police officers, are treated as suspects simply because they're black. These individual examples may have more impact than statistics because they personalize the problem. Used together, individual examples and statistics complement each other.

Then, in paragraph 7, Forman draws on *personal experience* as evidence, what he himself has observed. He's seen police shake down students at the school where he teaches. He wants his readers to *feel* the sense of violation involved and so offers a graphic description. Clearly, personal experience can be a powerful source of evidence.

Finally, to back up his last two reasons, Forman cites *well-known authorities,* prominent conservatives such as Myron Magnet and Abigail and Stephen Thernstrom (paragraphs 11 and 14). He cites these sources, obviously, because his audience considers them representative of their own viewpoint and respects them. Forman combines these authorities with the voices of his own students, who gain additional credibility simply by being cited along with the experts.

Forman's essay merits close study for its use of evidence alone. He employs different kinds of evidence, combines different types well, and never forgets that evidence must appeal to his audience.

Introducing and Concluding the Argument

We have analyzed Forman's strategies for using the three levels of case structure—thesis, reasons, and evidence—to build a convincing argument. Arguing to convince also requires a writer to think about effective ways to open and close the case.

The Introduction When you read Forman's essay the first time, you may have thought that somehow we had attached the wrong title to an essay about school reform. Not until the end of the third paragraph does the author announce his actual subject, racial profiling. Why this long introduction about the Maya Angelou Public Charter School?

The introduction accomplishes at least the following key purposes. Conservatives are strong supporters of alternatives to public schools. One of these is the charter school, and the author uses his story about a highly successful one to confirm conservative policy. Note how he emphasizes the seriousness of the curriculum and other school activities. He also points to the strict rules and discipline and how the Maya Angelou school has turned around standard public school failures, including kids headed for serious trouble with the law. All of this is likely to sound especially good to conservatives.

The story also establishes the author's authority as someone who makes conservative ideas work. Later on, when he cites his students' words to confirm his points, we do not doubt their authenticity. We can see, then, how crucial the introduction is to setting up the case.

Finally, the introduction anticipates the contradictions he'll address later, especially in reasons 3 and 4. The Maya Angelou school has succeeded in educating the kind of student that other schools often don't reach. Kids who could be a public danger now and adult criminals later are apparently becoming good citizens instead. But everything the school has accomplished can be undone by racial profiling. Thus, conservative educational reform clashes with conservative law enforcement policy. They don't fit together, and clearly the former is more important than the latter because the school is creating students who will stay on the right side of the law. Forman is already implying that racial profiling must go, which is the whole point of his essay.

The point for us is that introductions shouldn't be dashed off carelessly, thrown together just because we know we need one. Our introductions must prepare the way for our case.

The Conclusion Paragraphs 16 and 17 conclude his argument. What do they achieve?

Paragraph 16 states that most conservatives are not racists, that they just have been misled into thinking profiling works. In effect, these assertions release conservatives from the common accusation that they don't care about blacks and support policies that discriminate against them. Forman also reminds his readers that he has used *conservative principles* to explain why racial profiling diminishes police effectiveness.

Paragraph 17 explains in a concrete and memorable way how police tactics like profiling can interfere with law enforcement. Forman wants his

Case Strategy

1. Your thesis can be stated or implied, but **you and your readers must have no doubt about what you're contending.**

2. **Begin with your most important reason.** (For example, if your audience supports racial profiling because they think it works, begin your case against profiling by showing them that it doesn't.)

3. In general, **provide the kind of evidence each reason requires.** (For example, if you contend that helmet laws will reduce head injuries in motorcycle accidents, such a reason requires *data* for support. In contrast, if you contend that helmet laws do not seriously intrude upon personal freedom, data won't help—you must show that helmet laws are no more restrictive than other laws we accept as justified, such as seat belt or maximum speed laws.)

4. Use the **full range** of evidence available (data, individual examples, personal experience, expert opinion, etc.). When possible and appropriate, **mix different kinds of evidence to support a single reason.**

5. **Devote serious effort to introductions and conclusions.** They should accomplish definite tasks, such as generating interest at the beginning and leaving your reader with something memorable at the end. Avoid "throwaway," high school introductions that begin with "In this essay, I will discuss . . ." or "In conclusion . . ." conclusions.

---

readers to remember the harshness of the procedures and that the experience makes minorities suspicious of and uncooperative with police. We see the damage profiling does from the inside, and we cannot help but appreciate its negative consequences. The implied message is: If you value law and order, be against racial profiling. In this way, Forman advances his major point from another conservative value—support for the police.

Like introductions, conclusions are not throwaways, not merely hasty summaries. Like introductions, they should do something, not just repeat what we've said already. *The conclusion must clinch our case by ending it forcefully and memorably.*

◉◉ FOLLOWING THROUGH

A successful essay has smooth transitions between its opening and its first reason and between its last reason and its conclusion, as well as between each reason in the body of the essay. In your writer's notebook, describe how Forman (1) announces that he is moving from his introduction to the first reason, from the first reason to the second, and so on and (2) at the same time links each section to what has come before.

WRITING A CONVINCING ARGUMENT

Few people draft an essay sequentially, beginning with the first sentence of the first paragraph and ending with the last sentence of the last paragraph. But the final version of any essay must read as if it had been written sequentially, with the writer fully in control.

A well-written essay is like a series of moves in a chess game, in which each move is part of an overall plan. In the case of convincing, the purpose is to gain the agreement of the reader.

Although readers may not be fully aware of the "moves" that make up a convincing argument, the writer probably made most of them consciously. As we have seen in this chapter, we can learn much about how to convince by studying finished essays. However, it is one thing to understand how something works and quite another to make it work ourselves. Part of the difficulty is that we cannot see in the final product everything that went into making it work so well. Just as a movie audience typically cannot imagine all the rehearsals, the many takes, and the editing that make a scene powerful, so it is hard for us to imagine all the research and thinking, the many drafts, and the process of editing and proofreading that Forman must have gone through to make "Arrested Development" effective. Yet it's precisely this process you must understand and immerse yourself in to produce convincing arguments of your own.

The following discussion of the composing process assumes that the work of research (Chapter 5) and inquiry (Chapter 7) has already been done. It also assumes that you have worked out a rhetorical prospectus (see Chapter 1, pages 18–19) to guide you in combining structure with strategy.

www.mhhe.com/**crusius**

For some electronic guidance on writing arguments, go to:

Writing > Writing Tutors > Argument

Preparing a Brief

Before you begin to draft, it is a good idea to prepare a **brief,** which shows the thesis and reasons you plan to use and gives some indication of how you will support each reason with evidence. The brief ought to arrange the reasons in order, but the order may change as you draft and revise.

Working toward a Position

First, we need to distinguish a position from a thesis. A **position** (or a stance or opinion) amounts to an overall, summarizing attitude or judgment about some issue. "Universities often exploit student athletes" is an example of a position. A **thesis** is not only more specific and precise but also more strategic, designed to appeal to readers and be consistent with available evidence. For example, "Student athletes in revenue-generating sports ought to be paid for their services" is one possible thesis representing the preceding position, perhaps for an audience of college students. We cannot construct a case without a thesis. But without a position, we cannot experiment with various thesis formulations. Positions precede theses.

Finding a position can be a significant challenge in itself. What often happens is that we begin with a strong opinion, find it failing under scrutiny, discover other positions that do not fully satisfy us, and so emerge from inquiry uncertain about what we do think. Another common path is to start with no opinion at all, find ourselves attracted to parts of several conflicting positions, and so wind up unsure, confused, even vexed because we can't decide what to think.

In such situations, resolve to be patient with yourself. The best, most mature positions typically come only after a struggle. Second, take out your writer's notebook and start making lists. Look over your research materials, especially the notecards on which you have recorded positions and evidence from your sources. Make lists in response to these questions:

What positions have you encountered in research and class discussion?

What seems strongest and weakest in each position? What modifications might be made to eliminate or minimize the weak points? Are there other possible positions? What are their strong and weak points?

What evidence impressed you? What does each piece of evidence imply or suggest? What connections can you draw among the pieces of evidence given in various sources? If there is conflict in the implications of the evidence, what is that conflict?

While all this list-making may seem only doodling, you'll begin to sort things out.

Bear in mind that, although emotional commitment to ideas and values is important, it can impede clear thought. Sometimes we find our stance by relinquishing a strongly held opinion—perhaps for lack of compelling reasons or evidence. The more emotional the issue—abortion or pornography, for instance—the more likely we are to cling to a position that is difficult to defend. When we sense deep conflict, when we want to argue a position even in the face of strong contradictory evidence, it's time to consider changing our minds.

Finally, if you find yourself holding out for the "perfect" position, all strength and no weakness, give up. Controversial issues are controversial precisely because no single stance convinces everyone, because there is always room for counter-argument and for other positions that have their own power to convince.

STUDENT SAMPLE   Working toward a Position

Justin Spidel's class began by reading many arguments about homosexuality and discussing issues related to gay rights. Justin decided to investigate whether same-sex marriage should be legal. His initial position was that same-sex marriage ought to be legal because gays and lesbians should be treated like everyone else. Research revealed that a majority of Americans oppose same-sex marriage because they believe its legalization would change the definition of marriage and alter its sacred bond. Justin read articles opposing gay marriage by such well-known public figures as William Bennett, an advocate of conservative causes, but he also read many in favor. He found especially convincing the arguments by gays and lesbians who were in stable, loving, monogamous relationships but barred from marrying. Justin's initial round of research led him to the position "Gays and lesbians should be able to marry."

During the inquiry stage, Justin discussed his position with his classmates and instructor. Knowing that gays and lesbians do sometimes get married in churches, Justin's classmates asked him to clarify "able to marry." Justin explained that he meant *legal recognition* of same-sex marriages by all state governments. When asked if other countries recognize same-sex marriage, Justin said that some do. He thought that the United States should be among the leaders in valuing equality and individual rights. He was asked about the implications of his position: Would granting legal status to same-sex marriage devalue the institution? He said that the people fighting for legalization have the deepest respect for marriage and that marriage is about love and commitment, not sexual orientation.

◎◎ FOLLOWING THROUGH

Formulate a tentative position on a topic that you have researched and into which you have inquired. Write it up with a brief explanation of why you support this stand. Be prepared to defend your position in class or with a peer in a one-on-one exchange of position statements. •

Analyzing the Audience

Before you decide on a thesis, give some thought to the rhetorical context of your argument. Who needs to hear it? What are their values? What common ground might you share with them? How might you have to qualify your position to influence their opinions?

To provoke thought, people occasionally make cases for theses that they know have little chance of winning assent. One example is the argument for legalizing all drug use; although a reasonably good case can be made, most Americans find it too radical. If you want to convince rather than provoke, formulate a thesis that *both* represents your position *and* creates as little resistance in your readers as possible. Instead of arguing for legalizing all drug use, for example, you might argue that much of the staggering amount spent on the war on drugs should be diverted to rehabilitation and dealing with social problems connected with drug abuse. Because positions allow for many possible theses, you should analyze your audience before settling on one.

STUDENT SAMPLE   Analyzing the Audience

Justin knew that many people would view same-sex marriage as radical. Some audiences, such as conservative Christians, would never assent to it. So Justin targeted an audience he had some chance of convincing—people who opposed same-sex marriage but were tolerant of homosexuals. Justin wrote the following audience profile:

> My audience would be heterosexual adults who accept that some people are homosexual or lesbian; they know people who are. They would be among the nearly 47 percent of Americans who do not object to same-sex relationships between consenting adults. They may be fairly well educated and could belong to any age group. They are not likely to have strong religious objections, so my argument will not focus on whether homosexuality is a sin. However, these readers oppose legalizing marriage between gays and lesbians because they think it would threaten the traditional role of marriage as the basis of family life. They think that marriage is troubled enough by divorce, and they want to preserve its meaning. Their practical position is that, if same-sex couples want to live together and act like they're married, there's nothing to stop them—so leave things as they are. They believe in the value of heterosexual marriage; I can appeal to that. They also hold basic American principles of equal rights and the right to the "pursuit of happiness." But mainly I want to show my readers that gays and lesbians are missing out on basic civil rights and that permitting marriage would benefit everyone.

◎◎ FOLLOWING THROUGH

Write a profile of the audience you hope to reach through an argument you want to make. Be as specific as possible; include any information—age, gender, economic status, and so forth—that may contribute to your audience's outlook and attitudes. What interests, beliefs, and values might they hold? How might you have to phrase your thesis to give your argument a chance of succeeding? What reasons might they be willing to consider? What would you have to rule out?   •

Developing a Thesis

A good thesis grows out of many factors: your position, your research, your exploration of reasons to support your position, and your understanding of the audience. During drafting, you may refine the thesis by phrasing it more precisely, but for now concentrate on stating a thesis that represents your position clearly and directly.

Your thesis should present only the claim. Save the reasons for the body of the paper.

STUDENT SAMPLE Developing a Thesis

Justin's original statement, "Gays and lesbians should be able to marry," expresses a position, but it could be more precise and better directed toward the readers Justin defined in his audience profile. He refined his position to the following:

> A couple's right to marry should not be restricted because of sexual orientation.

This version emphasized that marriage is a right everyone should enjoy, but it did not clarify why readers should recognize it as a right. Justin tried again:

> Every couple who wishes to commit to each other in marriage should have the right to do so, regardless of sexual preference.

Justin was fairly satisfied with this version because it appealed to a basic value—commitment.

He then started thinking about how committed relationships benefit society, an argument that would appeal to his readers. He wanted to portray the thesis not just as an issue of rights for homosexuals but also as a benefit for everyone, broadening its appeal. He tried one more time and settled on the following thesis:

> Everyone, gay and straight, will benefit from extending the basic human right of marriage to all couples, regardless of sexual preference.

◉◉ FOLLOWING THROUGH

1. Refine your thesis as Justin did for the essay on which you are currently working. Why did you settle on one way of stating it?

2. As we saw in analyzing William May's case against assisted suicide (Chapter 3), sometimes a thesis needs to be qualified and exceptions to the thesis stated and clarified. Now is a good time to think about qualifications and exceptions.

You can handle qualifications and exceptions in two ways. First, you can add a phrase to your thesis that limits it, as William May did in his argument on assisted suicide: "*On the whole,* our social policy . . . should not regularize killing for mercy." May admits that a few extreme cases of suffering justify helping someone die. The other method is to word the thesis in such a way that exceptions or qualifications are implied rather than spelled out. For example, "Life sentences with no parole are justifiable for all sane people found guilty of first-degree murder." Here the exceptions would be "those who are found insane" and "those tried on lesser charges."

Using your best thesis statement, decide whether qualifications and exceptions are needed. If so, decide how best to handle them.   •

Analyzing the Thesis

Once you have a thesis, *unpack* it to determine what you must argue. To do this, put yourself in the place of your readers. To be won over, what must they find in your argument? Answering that question requires looking very closely at both what the thesis says and what it implies. It also requires thinking about the position and attitudes of your readers as you described them earlier in your audience profile.

Many thesis sentences appear simple, but analysis shows they are complex. Let's consider a thesis on the topic of whether Mark Twain's *Huckleberry Finn* should be taught in public schools. Some people have argued that Twain's classic novel should be removed from reading lists because some readers, especially African-Americans, find its subject matter and language offensive. In some schools the novel is not assigned, whereas in others it's optional. In our example thesis, the writer supports teaching the novel: "Mark Twain's *Huckleberry Finn* should be required reading for all high school students in the United States."

Unpacking this thesis, we see that the writer must first argue for *Huckleberry Finn* as *required* reading—not merely a good book but an indispensable one. The writer must also argue that the book should be required at the high school level rather than in middle school or college. Finally, the author must defend the novel from charges of racism, even though the thesis does not explicitly state, "*Huckleberry Finn* is not a racist book." Otherwise, these charges stand by default; to ignore them is to ignore the context of the issue.

STUDENT SAMPLE Analyzing the Thesis

By analyzing his thesis—"Everyone, gay and straight, will benefit from extending the basic human right of marriage to all couples, regardless of sexual preference"—Justin realized that his main task was to explain specific benefits that would follow from allowing gays to marry. He knew that his readers would agree that marriage is a "basic human right" for heterosexual adults, but could not assume that they would see it that way for homosexual couples. Therefore, he had to lead them to see that same-sex couples have the same needs as other couples. He also wanted his readers to understand that he was arguing only that *the law* should recognize such marriages. Churches would not have to sanctify them.

⊙⊙ FOLLOWING THROUGH

Unpack a thesis of your own or one that your instructor gives you to see what key words and phrases an argument based on that thesis must address. Also consider what an audience would expect you to argue given the current context of the dispute.

Finding Reasons

For the most part, no special effort goes into finding reasons to support a thesis. They come to us as we attempt to justify our opinions, as we listen to the arguments of our classmates, as we encounter written arguments in research, and as we think about how to reach the readers we hope to convince. Given good writing preparation, we seldom formulate a thesis without already having some idea of the reasons we will use to defend it. Our problem, rather, is usually selection—picking out the best reasons and shaping and stating them in a way that appeals to our readers. When we do find ourselves searching for reasons, however, it helps to be aware of their common sources.

The Audience's Belief System Ask yourself, What notions of the real, the good, and the possible will my readers entertain? Readers will find any reason unconvincing if it is not consistent with their understanding of reality. For example, based on their particular culture's notions about disease, people will accept or reject arguments about how to treat illness. Likewise, people have differing notions of what is good. Some people think it is good to exploit natural resources so that we can live with more conveniences; others see more good in preserving the environment. Finally, people disagree about what is possible. Those who believe that some aspects of human nature can't be changed will not accept arguments that certain types of criminals can be rehabilitated.

Special Rules or Principles Good reasons can also be found in a community's accepted rules and principles. For example, we believe that a person is innocent until proven guilty. We apply this principle in even nonlegal situations when someone is accused of misconduct.

The law is only one source of special rules or principles. We also find them in politics ("one person, one vote"), in business (the principle of seniority, which gives preference to employees who have been on the job longest), and even in the home, where each family formulates its own house rules. In other words, all human settings and activities have norms and we can draw on them.

Expert Opinion and Hard Evidence We rely on expert opinion when we lack direct experience with a particular subject. Most readers respect the opinion of trained professionals with advanced degrees and prestige in their fields. Especially when you can show that most experts agree, you have a good basis for a reason.

Hard evidence can also yield good reasons. Research shows, for example, that wearing a bicycle helmet significantly reduces the incidence of head injuries in accidents. Therefore, we can support the thesis "Laws should require bicycle riders to wear helmets" with the reason "because statistics show that fewer serious head injuries occurred in bicycle accidents when the riders were wearing helmets."

Tradition   We can sometimes strengthen a position by citing or alluding to well-known sources that are part of our audience's cultural tradition—for example, the Bible and the sayings or writings of people our readers recognize and respect. Although reasons drawn from tradition may lose force if audience members identify with different cultures or resist tradition itself, they will be effective when readers revere the source.

Comparison   A reason based on similarity argues that what is true in one instance should be true in another. For example, we could make a case for legalizing marijuana by showing that it is similar in effect to alcohol, which is legal—and also a drug. The argument might look like this:

> *Thesis:* Marijuana use should be decriminalized.
>
> *Reason:* Marijuana is no more harmful than alcohol.

Many comparison arguments attempt to show that present situations are similar to past ones. For example, many who argue for the civil rights of gays and lesbians say that discrimination based on sexual preference should not be tolerated today just as discrimination based on race, common thirty-five years ago, is no longer tolerated.

A special kind of argument based on similarity is *analogy,* which attempts to explain one thing, usually abstract, in terms of something else, usually more concrete. For example, in an argument opposing sharing the world's limited resources, philosopher Garrett Hardin reasons that requiring the wealthy nations of the world to feed the starving ones is like requiring the occupants of a lifeboat filled to capacity to take on those still in the water until the lifeboat sinks and everyone perishes.

Arguments of comparison can also assert difference, showing how two things are not the same. For example, some Americans supported participation in the 1991 Persian Gulf War by arguing that, unlike the disastrous conflict in Vietnam, this war was winnable. The argument went as follows:

> *Thesis:* America can defeat Iraq's military.
>
> *Reason:* Warfare in the deserts of Kuwait and Iraq is very different from warfare in the jungles of Vietnam.

The Probable or Likely   All reasoning about controversial issues relies on making a viewpoint seem probable or likely, but specific reasons drawn from the probable or likely come into play when we want to defend one account of events over another or when we want to attack or support a proposed policy. For example, in 1991 defenders of Supreme Court nominee Clarence Thomas attempted to discredit Anita Hill's accusations of sexual harassment in a number of ways, all related to probability: Is it likely, they asked, that she would remember so clearly and in such detail events that happened as long as ten years ago? Is it probable that a woman who had been harassed would follow Thomas from one job to another, as Hill did?

Cause and Effect People think that most circumstances result from causes and that most changes in circumstances result in new effects. Belief in cause-and-effect relationships can provide reasons for certain arguments. For example, environmentalists have successfully argued for reductions in the world's output of hydrofluorocarbons by showing that the chemicals damage the Earth's ozone layer.

Cause-and-effect arguments are difficult to prove; witness the fact that cigarette manufacturers argued for years that the connection between smoking and lung disease cannot be demonstrated. Responsible arguments from cause and effect depend on credible and adequate hard evidence and expert opinion. And they must always acknowledge the possible existence of hidden factors; smoking and lung disease, for example, may be influenced by genetic predisposition.

Definition Arguments often require definitions for clarification. However, a definition can also provide a reason in support of a thesis. If we define a term by placing it in a category, we are saying that whatever is true for the category is true for the term we are defining. For example, Elizabeth Cady Stanton's landmark 1892 argument for women's rights ("The Solitude of Self") was based on the definition "women are individuals":

> *Thesis:* Women must have suffrage, access to higher education, and sovereignty over their own minds and bodies.
>
> *Reason:* Women are individuals.

Stanton's audience, the American Congress, believed that all individuals are endowed with certain inalienable rights. Stanton's definition reminded them that women belong in the category "individual" as much as men and deserve the same rights.

Most good reasons come from one or a combination of these eight sources. However, simply knowing the sources will not automatically provide you with good reasons. Nothing can substitute for research and thoughtful inquiry.

Also, do not feel that quantity is crucial in finding good reasons. Be selective: focus on those reasons that appeal most to your audience and that you can develop thoroughly. A good argument is often based on one or two good reasons.

STUDENT SAMPLE Finding Reasons

Justin used five of the eight sources listed in this section to help find some of his reasons. Here are the possible reasons he found; note that each reason is stated as a complete sentence.

From the audience's belief system:

> Marriage is primarily about love and commitment, not sex.
> Marriage is a stabilizing influence in society.

From rules or principles the audience would hold:

> Everyone has an equal right to life, liberty, and the pursuit of happiness.

From expert opinion (in this case, a lawyer and some noted authors on gay rights):

> Denying gays and lesbians the right to marry is discrimination.
> Allowing gays and lesbians to marry will promote family values such as monogamy and the two-parent family.

From comparison or analogy:

> Just as many people once thought marriage between blacks and whites should be illegal, now a majority think same-sex marriage should be illegal. Gay and lesbian couples can love each other just as devotedly as heterosexual couples.

From cause and effect:

> Marriage is a way for people to take care of each other rather than being a burden on society should they become ill or unemployed.

Justin now had far more reasons for his case than he needed. He now had to evaluate his list.

◎◎ FOLLOWING THROUGH

Here is one way to brainstorm for reasons. First, list the eight sources for finding reasons discussed on pages 227–229 in your writer's notebook, perhaps on the inside front cover or on the first or last page—someplace where you can easily find them. Practice using these sources by writing your current thesis at the top of another page and going through the list, writing down reasons as they occur to you.

Selecting and Ordering Reasons

Selecting reasons depends on two considerations: your thesis and your readers. Any thesis demands a certain line of reasoning. For example, the writer contending that *Huckleberry Finn* should be required reading in high school must offer a compelling reason for accepting no substitute—not even another novel by Mark Twain. Such a reason might be "Because many critics and novelists see *Huckleberry Finn* as the inspiration for much subsequent American fiction, we cannot understand the American novel if we are not familiar with *Huckleberry Finn*." A reason of this kind should appeal to teachers or school administrators.

It is often difficult to see how to order reasons prior to drafting. Because we can easily reorder reasons as we rewrite, in developing our case we need only attempt an order that seems right. The writer advocating *Huckleberry Finn*, for example, might first defend the novel from the racism charge. Readers unaware of the controversy will want to know why the book needs defending, and well-informed readers will expect an immediate response to the book's critics who want to remove it from the classroom. Once racism has been disposed of, readers will be prepared to hear the reasons for keeping the book on required-reading lists.

Besides thinking about what your readers need and expect and how one reason may gain force by following another one, keep in mind a simple fact about memory: We recall best what we read last; next best, what we read first. A good rule of thumb, therefore, is to begin and end your defense of a thesis with your strongest reasons. A strong beginning also helps keep the reader reading; a strong conclusion avoids a sense of anticlimax.

STUDENT SAMPLE   Selecting and Ordering Reasons

Justin generated eight possible reasons to support his position on gay and lesbian marriage. To help decide which ones to use, he looked again at his audience profile. What had he said about the concerns of people who oppose same-sex marriage? Which of his potential reasons would best address these concerns?

Because his audience did not believe that the ban on same-sex marriage was a great loss to gays and lesbians, Justin decided to use the lawyer's point that the ban is discriminatory. The audience's other main concern was with the potential effect of gay marriage on the rest of society, particularly traditional marriage and family. Therefore, Justin decided to use the reasons about the benefits of same-sex marriage to society: that family values would be reinforced and that marriage keeps people from burdening society if they become unable to support themselves.

Justin noticed that some of his reasons overlapped. For example, the point that marriage is stabilizing was better expressed in combination with his more specific reasons about economic benefits and family values. And discrimination overlapped with his point about "life, liberty, and the pursuit of happiness." Overlap is common and requires some consolidation of reasons.

What is the best strategy for arranging the reasons? Initially, Justin wanted to begin with the point about discrimination, but then he decided to appeal to his audience's interests by listing the advantages of same-sex marriage first. Saving discrimination until the second half of his essay would let him end more strongly with an appeal to the readers' sense of fairness.

Then Justin rechecked his thesis to confirm that the reasons really supported it. He decided that his readers might not accept that marriage is a "basic human right" for those of the same sex, so he decided to add one more reason to support the similarities between heterosexuals and homosexuals.

Justin outlined his argument:

> Thesis: Everyone, gay and straight, will benefit from extending the basic human right of marriage to all couples, regardless of sexual preference.
>
> Reason: It would reinforce family values such as monogamy and the two-parent family.
>
> Reason: It would help keep people from burdening society.
>
> Reason: Denying people the right to marry is discrimination.
>
> Reason: The love homosexuals have for each other is no different from love between heterosexuals.

◎◎ FOLLOWING THROUGH

We call case structure flexible because as long as you maintain the three-level structure of thesis, reasons, and evidence, you can change everything else: throw out one thesis for another or alter its wording, add or take away reasons or evidence, or reorder both to achieve the desired impact. Order your reasons based on these questions:

What will my audience need or expect to read first?

Will one reason help set up another?

Which of my reasons are stronger? Can I begin and conclude my argument with the better reasons I have?

To a thesis you have already refined, now add the second level of your brief, the reason or reasons. Be ready to explain your decisions about selection and arrangement. Final decisions about ordering may come late in drafting—in a second or third writing. Spending a little time now thinking about order-ings can save time later and make composing less difficult. •

Using Evidence

The skillful use of evidence involves many judgments. Let's begin with some basic questions.

What Counts as Evidence? Because science and technology rely on the hard data of quantified evidence—especially statistics—some people assume that hard data are the only really good form of evidence. Such a view, how-ever, is far too narrow. Besides hard data, evidence includes

- Quotation from authorities: expert opinion and traditional authorities such as respected political leaders, philosophers, and well-known authors. Besides printed sources, you can gather quotations from interviews and electronic sources.

- Constitutions, statutes, court rulings, organizational bylaws, company policy statements, and the like

- Examples and case histories (that is, extended narratives about an individual's or an organization's experience)

- The results of questionnaires that you devise and administer

- Personal experience

In short, evidence includes anything that confirms a good reason or that might increase your readers' acceptance of a reason.

What Kind of Evidence Is Best? It depends on the particular reason. To argue for bicycle helmet legislation, we need facts and figures—hard data—to back up our claim that wearing helmets reduces the number of serious head injuries. To defend *Huckleberry Finn* by saying that it indicts racism will require quoted passages from the novel itself, statements from respected interpreters, and so forth.

When you have many pieces of evidence to choose from, select based on the quality of the evidence itself and its likely impact on readers. In general the best evidence is the most recent. The more trusted and prestigious the source, the more authority it will have. Arguments about AIDS in the United States, for example, often use data from the Centers for Disease Control in Atlanta, a research facility that specializes in the study of epidemics.

Finally, always look for evidence that will give you an edge in winning reader assent. For example, given the charge that *Huckleberry Finn* is offensive to blacks, its defense by an African-American literary scholar would carry more weight than its defense by a white scholar.

How Much Evidence Is Needed? The amount of evidence required depends on two judgments: (1) how crucial a reason is to your case and (2) how much resistance readers are likely to have. Most cases have a pivotal reason, one point on which the whole case is built and therefore either stands or falls. Forman's case against racial profiling turns on accepting its unreliability. Such a reason needs much evidence; about one-fourth of Forman's essay supports this reason alone.

Of course, the pivotal reason may also be one which readers will resist. For instance, many arguments supporting women's right to abortion depend on a fetus not being considered fully human until it reaches a certain stage of development. This reason is obviously both pivotal and likely to be resisted, so devoting much space to evidence would be justified.

STUDENT SAMPLE STUDENT SAMPLE Using Evidence

Justin took the brief showing his case so far and on a table laid out all of his notecards and the material he had photocopied and marked up during research. He needed to select the expert opinions, quotations, statistics, dates, and other evidence to support his reasons. Doing this before drafting reveals where evidence is lacking or thin and what further research is necessary. To handle many sources, use different-colored markers to indicate which passages will work with which reasons. Justin then added evidence to his case structure, including noting the sources and page numbers.

Thesis: Everyone, gay and straight, will benefit from extending the basic human right of marriage to all couples, regardless of sexual preference.

Reason: It would reinforce family values such as monogamy and the two-parent family.

Evidence: Marriage stabilizes relationships. (Sources: Rauch 23; Dean 114)

Evidence: Children of gays and lesbians should not be denied having two parents. (Sources: Dean 114; Sullivan; Salholz)

Evidence: If gays can have and adopt children, they should be able to marry. (Source: Salholz)

Reason: It would provide a means of keeping people from burdening society.

Evidence: Spouses take care of each other. (Source: Rauch)

Reason: Denying gays and lesbians the right to marry is discriminatory.

Evidence: Marriage includes rights to legal benefits. (Source: Dean 112)

Evidence: Domestic partnerships fail to provide these rights. (Sources: Dean 112; Salholz)

Evidence: Barring these marriages violates many democratic principles. (Sources: "Declaration"; Dean 113; Salholz)

Reason: The love homosexuals have for each other is no different from love between heterosexuals.

Evidence: Many gays and lesbians are in monogamous relationships. (Source: Ayers 5)

Evidence: They have the same need to make a public, legal commitment. (Source: Sullivan)

◎◎◎ FOLLOWING THROUGH

Prepare a complete brief for an argument. Include both reasons and evidence and note sources. Remember that a brief is flexible, not engraved in stone. It can change as you draft and revise.

The Brief

1. A position or general outlook on a topic is not a thesis. A thesis is a carefully worded **claim** that your entire essay backs up with reasons and evidence. **Experiment with various ways of stating your thesis** until it says *exactly* what you want it to say and creates the least resistance in your readers.

2. Be willing to give up or modify significantly a thesis you find you cannot support with good reasons and strong evidence that appeal *to your readers*. We **must argue a thesis that fits the available** evidence, which may differ a little or a lot from what we really believe.

3. Take the time to create a specific **audience profile**. What are the age, gender, and economic status of your target audience? What interests, beliefs, and values might they bring to your topic and thesis? Remember: There is no such thing as a "general audience." **We are always trying to convince some definite group of possible readers.**

4. **Unpack your thesis** to discover what you must argue. If you say, for instance, that *Huckleberry Finn* should be *required* reading in high school, you must show why *this particular novel* should be an experience shared by all American high school students. It won't be enough to argue that it's a good book.

5. Select your reasons based on what you must argue to defend your thesis combined with what you should say **given your audience's prior knowledge, preconceptions, prejudices, and interests.**

6. Be prepared to **try out different ways of ordering your reasons.** The order that seemed best in your brief might not work best as you draft and redraft your essay.

From Brief to Draft

Turning a brief into a paper is never easy. You will have to create parts of the essay that are not represented in the brief, such as an effective introduction and conclusion. You may also need paragraphs that provide background on your topic, clarify or define an important term, or present and rebut an opposing argument. Following are suggestions and examples that should help.

The Introduction

Introductions are among the hardest things to write well. *Remember that an introduction need not be one paragraph;* it is often two or even three short ones. A good introduction (1) meets the needs of the audience by setting up the topic with just enough background information and (2) goes right to the heart of the issue as it relates to the audience's concerns.

Should the introduction end with the thesis statement? Such placement can work well in offering a transition to the reasons. However, the thesis need not be the last sentence in the introduction; it need not appear until much later—or at all, provided that readers can tell what it is from the title or from reading the essay.

STUDENT SAMPLE The Introduction

Justin had to consider whether he should refer to the history of marriage and why people feel strongly about its value. Because his readers oppose same-sex marriage, presumably they were familiar with the traditions underpinning the institution. What would these readers need in the introduction? That the gay and lesbian rights movement calls for extending to same-sex couples the legal right to marry and that Justin's argument supports its position.

If Justin had opened with "The current intolerant attitudes toward homosexuality are excluding a whole class of citizens from exercising the right to marry," he would have been assuming that no valid reasons exist for denying same-sex marriage. Such a statement would offend his target audience members, who are not homophobic and would resent the implication that their view is based on prejudice. Justin's introduction attempts to establish some common ground with his readers:

> When two people fall deeply in love, they want to share every part of their lives with each other. For some, that could mean making a commitment, living together, and having children. But most people want more than that; they want to make their commitment public and legal through marriage, a tradition thousands of years old that has been part of almost every culture.
>
> But not everyone has the right to make that commitment. In this country and in most others, gays and lesbians are denied the right to marry. According to many Americans, allowing them to marry would destroy the institution and threaten traditional family values. Nevertheless, "advances in gay and lesbian civil rights [are] bringing awareness and newfound determination to many," and hundreds of same-sex couples are celebrating their commitment in religious ceremonies (Ayers 6). These couples would like to make their unions legal, and we should not prohibit them. Everyone, gay and straight, will benefit from extending the basic human right of marriage to all couples, regardless of sexual orientation.

Justin's first paragraph builds common ground by offering an overview of marriage that his readers are likely to share. In the second paragraph, he goes on to introduce the conflict, showing his awareness of the main objections to same-sex marriage. Note the tone: he's presenting himself as fair and responsible. Finally, Justin builds common ground by showing gays and lesbians positively, as people who love and commit to each other just as heterosexuals do.

A good introduction gains reader interest. To do this, writers use a number of techniques. They may open with the story of a person whose experience illustrates some aspect of the topic. Or they may begin with a surprising fact or opinion, as Jonathan Rauch, one of Justin's sources, did when he began his essay with this: "Whatever else marriage may or may not be, it is certainly falling apart." Usually, dictionary definitions are dull openers, but a *Newsweek* writer used one effectively to start her article on gay marriage: "Marry. 1 a) to join as husband and wife; unite in wedlock, b) to join (a man) to a woman as her husband, or (a woman) to a man as his wife." All of these are fairly dramatic techniques, but the best advice about openings is that *specifics work better than generalizations.* The *Newsweek* article just mentioned had this statement: "Say marriage and the mind turns to three-tiered cakes, bridal gowns, baby carriages."

How you open depends on your audience. Popular periodicals like *Newsweek* are more appropriate for dramatics than academic journals and college papers, but readers appreciate a memorable opening.

The Body: Presenting Reasons and Evidence

We now turn to drafting the body paragraphs. Although it's possible for one paragraph to develop a reason, *avoid thinking in terms of only one paragraph per reason.* Multiple paragraphs are the norm.

Paragraphs perform some function in presenting the case. You ought to be able to say what the function of a given paragraph is—and your readers ought to be able to sense it. Does it introduce a reason? Does it define a term? Does it support a reason by setting up an analogy? Does another paragraph support the same reason by offering examples or data or an illustrative case?

Not all paragraphs need topic sentences. Try instead to open each paragraph with hints that allow readers to see its function. For example, a transitional word or phrase announces that you are turning from one reason to a new one. When you introduce a new reason, be sure that readers can see how it relates to the thesis.

STUDENT SAMPLE Presenting Reasons and Evidence

Let's look at how Justin developed his first reason. Recall that he decided to put the two reasons about benefits to society ahead of his reasons against discrimination. Of the two benefits he planned to cite, strengthening family values seemed the stronger one, so he led with it. Note how Justin's transitional phrase connects his first reason to the introduction, which had mentioned opposing views. Observe how he *develops his reason over a number of paragraphs,* drawing upon multiple sources, using both paraphrase and direct quotation.

> In contrast to the critics, allowing gays and lesbians to marry promotes family values because it encourages monogamy and two-parent homes. As Jonathan Rauch, a gay writer, explains, marriage stabilizes relationships:
>
>> One of the main benefits of publicly recognized marriage is that it binds couples together not only in their own eyes but also in the eyes of society at large. Around the partners is woven a web of expectations that they will spend nights together, go to parties together, take

out mortgages together, buy furniture . . . together, and so on—all of which helps tie them together and keep them off the streets and at home. (23)

Some people would say that gays and lesbians can have these things without marriage by living together, but if marriage is not necessary for gays, it's not necessary for heterosexuals either. If it's immoral to live together outside marriage, then gays and lesbians should marry too. Craig Dean, a Washington, D.C., lawyer and gay-marriage activist, says that it is "paradoxical that mainstream America stereotypes Gays and Lesbians as unable to maintain long-term relationships, while at the same time denying them the very institutions to stabilize such relationships" (114).

Furthermore, many homosexual couples have children from previous marriages or by adoption. According to a study by the American Bar Association, gay and lesbian families with children make up six percent of all families in the United States (Dean 114). A secure environment is important for raising children, and allowing same-sex couples to marry would help. It would also send children the positive message that marriage is the foundation for family life. As Andrew Sullivan, a senior editor of *The New Republic,* says, why should gays be denied the very same family values that many politicians are arguing everyone else should have? Why should their children be denied these values? *Newsweek* writer Eloise Salholz describes the problem: If "more and more homosexual pairs are becoming parents . . . but cannot marry, what kind of bastardized definition of family is society imposing on their offspring?"

At this point, Justin is ready to take up his next reason: Marriage provides a system by which people take care of each other, lessening the burden on society. Justin's entire essay appears on pages 243–246. Look it over carefully before you draft your essay. Note which paragraphs bring in the remaining reasons and which paragraphs present and rebut opposing views.

The Conclusion

Once you have presented your case, what else is there to say? Short papers don't need summaries. And the conclusion is not a place for new points.

Strategically, in your conclusion you want to imply, "Case made!" Here are some suggestions for doing so:

1. Look back at your introduction. Perhaps a question you posed there has an answer, a problem a solution.

2. Think about larger contexts for your argument. For example, the *Huckleberry Finn* case could end by pointing out that education becomes diluted and artificial when the curriculum avoids controversy.

3. If you end with a memorable quotation, comment on it as you would whenever you quote.

4. Be aware that many conclusions should be shorter. If you are dissatis-
    fied with yours, lop off the last sentence or so. You may uncover the
    real ending.

5. Pay attention to style, especially in the last sentence. An awkwardly
    worded sentence will not have a sound of finality, but one with some
    rhythmic punch or consciously repeated sounds can wrap up an essay
    neatly.

STUDENT SAMPLE   The Conclusion

Following is Justin's conclusion.

> It's only natural for people in love to want to commit to each other; this
> desire is the same for homosexuals and lesbians as it is for heterosexuals.
> One recent survey showed that "over half of all lesbians and almost 40% of
> gay men" live in committed relationships and share a home together (Ayers
> 5). As Sullivan, who is gay, explains, "At some point in our lives, some of us
> are lucky enough to meet the person we truly love. And we want to commit
> to that person in front of family and country for the rest of our lives. It's the
> most simple, the most natural, the most human instinct in the world. How
> could anyone seek to oppose that?" And what does anyone gain when that
> right is denied? That's a question that everyone needs to ask themselves.

◎◎ FOLLOWING THROUGH

Using your brief as a guide, write a draft version of your argument to convince.
In addition to the advice in this chapter, refer to Chapter 5, which covers
paraphrasing, summarizing, quoting, incorporating, and documenting source
material.   •

www.mhhe.com/**crusius**   For further writing coverage, including information on writing in the
traditional modes, visit:

Writing > Writing Tutors

Revising the Draft

Too often, revising is confused with editing. Revising makes large changes in
content and organization, not sentence-level corrections or stylistic changes,
which are part of editing.

To get a sense of what is involved in revising, you should know that
the brief of Justin Spidel's essay on page 234 is actually a revised version.
Justin had originally written a draft with his reasons presented in a different
order and without three of the sources that now appear in his paper. When

Justin exchanged drafts with another classmate who was writing on the same topic, he discovered that some of her sources would also help him. The following paragraph was the original third paragraph of Justin's draft, immediately following the thesis. Compare it to the revised essay, printed on pages 243–246. Justin improved this part of his argument by developing the point more thoroughly in two paragraphs and by placing them toward the end of the paper.

> Not to allow same-sex marriage is clearly discriminatory. The
> Human Rights Act of 1977 in the District of Columbia "prohibits
> discrimination based on sexual orientation. According to the Act,
> 'every individual shall have an equal opportunity to participate in
> the economic, cultural, and intellectual life of the District and
> have an *equal opportunity to participate in all aspects of life*' "
> (Dean 112). If politicians are going to make such laws, they
> need to recognize all their implications and follow them. Not
> allowing homosexuals to marry is denying the right to "participate"
> in an aspect of life that is important to every couple that has found
> love in each other. Also, the Constitution guarantees equality to every
> man and woman; that means nondiscrimination, something that
> is not happening for gays and lesbians in the present.

Reading Your Own Writing Critically

Chapter 2 discussed critical or analytical reading. Apply what you learned to reading your own writing.

Read for Structure   Remember, different parts of an argument perform different jobs. Read to see if you can divide your draft easily into its strategic parts and can identify the role each group of paragraphs plays in the paper. If you have trouble identifying the parts and how they fit together, you need to see where you repeat yourself or separate connected points. This may be the time for scissors and tape, or electronic cutting and pasting.

Read for Rhetorical Context   You may need to revise to make the rhetorical context clearer: Why are you writing and to whom? You establish this reader awareness in the introduction, and you need to think about your readers' values and beliefs that underlie their position on the issue. You may need to revise your introduction to engage your readers better. The more specific you can make your opening, the more likely you are to succeed.

Inquire into Your Own Writing   Have a dialogue with yourself about it. Some of the questions listed on pages 181–182 are relevant:

1. Ask what you mean by the words that are central to the argument. Have you provided definitions as needed?

Reader's Checklist for Revision

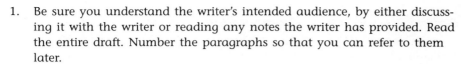

1. Be sure you understand the writer's intended audience, by either discussing it with the writer or reading any notes the writer has provided. Read the entire draft. Number the paragraphs so that you can refer to them later.

2. If you can find an explicit statement of the author's thesis, underline or highlight it. If you cannot find one, ask yourself whether it is necessary. If the thesis is easily inferred, restate it in your own words at the top of the first page.

3. Think about how the thesis could be improved. Is it offensive, vague, too general? Does it have a single focus? Is it clearly stated?

4. Circle the words most central to the thesis. Could there be disagreement about the meaning of any of them? If so, has the author clarified what he or she means?

5. Look for the argument's structure and strategy. Underline the sentences that present the reasons. If you can't identify the reasons, let the author know. Also think about the order of the reasons. Suggest improvements if you can.

6. Identify the author's best reason. How would it appeal to the audience? Has the author placed it in a good position for emphasizing it?

7. What reasons need more or better support? Indicate what factual information seems lacking, what sources don't seem solid or credible, what statements sound too general, or what reasoning—such as analogies—seems shaky.

8. Ask whether the author shows awareness of opposing arguments. If not, should this be added? What are the best challenges you can make to anything the author has said?

9. Evaluate the introduction and conclusion.

2. Find the reasons, and ask about their relation to the thesis. State the connection with the word "because."

3. Explore the assumptions behind your thesis and your reasons. Ask yourself, What's not said that someone has to believe? Be sure your audience will share the assumption. If not, state the assumption and argue for it.

4. Look at your comparisons and analogies. Are they plausible?

5. Look at your evidence. Have you offered facts, expert opinion, illustrations, and so on? Have you presented these in a way that would not raise doubts but eliminate them?

6. Consider your own bias. What do you stand to gain from advocating the position you take? Is your argument self-serving or truth-serving?

Getting Feedback from Other Readers

Because it's hard to be objective about our own work, getting feedback from a friend, classmate, or teacher is a good way to see where revision would help. Ask your readers to use a revision checklist, such as the one on page 241.

◎◎ FOLLOWING THROUGH

1. After you have written a draft of your own argument, revise it using the suggestions in the preceding section. Then exchange your revised draft for a classmate's, and use the "Reader's Checklist for Revision" on page 241 to guide you in making suggestions for each other's drafts.

2. Read the final version of Justin Spidel's argument, following. Then apply the questions for inquiry listed on pages 181–182 to assess his argument.

3. If you were assigned to suggest ways to improve Justin's argument, what would you advise? Reread his audience profile (page 224), and use the "Reader's Checklist for Revision" (page 241) to help you decide.   •

www.mhhe.com/**crusius**

For help editing your essay, go to:

Editing

Editing and Proofreading

The final steps of writing any argument are editing and proofreading, which we discuss in the Appendix A.

STUDENT SAMPLE An Essay Arguing to Convince

Who Should Have the Right to Marry?
Justin Spidel

When two people fall deeply in love, they want to share their
lives. For some, that could mean making a commitment, living together,
and maybe having children. But most people in love want more: they
want to make their commitment public and legal through marriage, a
tradition thousands of years old and part of almost every culture.

But not everyone has the opportunity to make that commitment.
In this country and most others, gays and lesbians are denied the
right to marry. According to many citizens and politicians, allowing
them that right would destroy the institution and threaten traditional
family values. Nevertheless, "advances in gay and lesbian civil rights
[are] bringing awareness and newfound determination to many," and
hundreds of same-sex couples are celebrating their commitment to
each other in religious ceremonies (Ayers 6). These couples would
like to make their unions legal, and we should not prohibit them.
Everyone, gay and straight, will benefit from extending marriage to
all couples, regardless of sexual orientation.

In contrast to the critics, allowing gays and lesbians to marry
promotes family values because it encourages monogamy and two-
parent homes. As Jonathan Rauch, a gay writer, explains, marriage
stabilizes relationships:

> One of the main benefits of publicly recognized marriage is that
> it binds couples together not only in their own eyes but also in
> the eyes of society at large. Around the partners is woven a
> web of expectations that they will spend nights together, go to
> parties together, take out mortgages together, buy furniture . . .
> together, and so on—all of which helps tie them together and
> keep them off the streets and at home. (23)

Some people would say that gays and lesbians can have these things
without marriage by living together, but if marriage is not necessary
for gays, it's not necessary for heterosexuals either. If it's immoral
to live together outside of marriage, then gays and lesbians should
marry too. Craig Dean, a Washington, D.C., lawyer and gay-marriage
activist, says that it is "paradoxical that mainstream America stereotypes Gays and Lesbians as unable to maintain long-term relationships, while at the same time denying them the very institutions to
stabilize such relationships" (114).

Furthermore, many homosexual couples have children from previous marriages or by adoption. According to a study by the American Bar Association, gay and lesbian families with children make up six percent of all families in the United States (Dean 114). A secure environment is important for raising children, and allowing same-sex couples to marry would help. It would also send children the positive message that marriage is the foundation for family life. As Andrew Sullivan, a senior editor of <u>The New Republic</u>, asks, why should gays be denied the very same family values that many politicians are arguing everyone else should have? Why should their children be denied these values? <u>Newsweek</u> writer Eloise Salholz describes the problem: If "more and more homosexual pairs are becoming parents . . . but cannot marry, what kind of bastardized definition of family is society imposing on their offspring?"

Binding people together in marriage also benefits society because 5 marriage encourages people to take care of each other. Marriage means that individuals are not a complete burden on society when they become sick, injured, old, or unemployed. Jonathan Rauch argues, "If marriage has any meaning at all, it is that when you collapse from a stroke, there will be at least one other person whose 'job' it is to drop everything and come to your aid" (22). This benefit of marriage may be even more important for homosexuals because their relationships with parents and other relatives may be strained. Same-sex couples already show such devotion to each other; recognition of legal marriage would strengthen that devotion.

In spite of the benefits, some say that same-sex marriage would upset our society's conventional idea of marriage. According to William Bennett, letting people of the same sex marry "would obscure marriage's enormously consequential function—procreation and childrearing." Procreation may be a consequence of marriage, but it is not the main reason people get married. Today "even for heterosexuals, marriage is becoming an emotional union and commitment rather than an arrangement to produce . . . children" ("Marriage" 770). And what about sterile heterosexual couples? No one would say they should not be allowed to marry. If the right to marry is based on the potential to have children, "then a post-menopausal woman who applies for a marriage license should be turned away at the courthouse door" (Rauch 22). No one expects couples who get married to prove that they can have children and intend to do so.

In the same way, to outlaw same-sex marriage is clearly discriminatory. According to Craig Dean, "Marriage is an important civil right because it gives societal recognition and legal protection to a relationship and confers numerous benefits to spouses" (112). Denying same-sex marriage means that gays and lesbians cannot enjoy such benefits as health insurance through a spouse's employer, life insurance benefits, tax preferences, leaves for bereavement, and

A marriage in San Francisco, February 13, 2004. At 79 and
83, these women had lived together fifty years before they
were allowed to marry.

inheritance. In some states, laws about domestic partnership give
same-sex couples some of these rights, but they are not as secure
as they would be if the couple were legally next of kin. Thomas
Stoddard, a lawyer, says that domestic partnership is the equivalent
of "second-class citizenship" (qtd. in Salholz).

Aside from these concrete forms of discrimination, denying
same-sex marriage keeps gay and lesbian citizens from enjoying
the basic human right to "life, liberty, and the pursuit of happiness." The Human Rights Act of 1977 in the District of Columbia
makes one of the strongest stands against discrimination based on
sexual orientation. According to the Act, "every individual shall
have an equal opportunity to participate in the economic, cultural,
and intellectual life of the District and have an equal opportunity
to participate in all aspects of life" (qtd. in Dean 113). Not allowing homosexuals to marry does deny them the right to participate
in an aspect of life important to almost every loving couple.

Of course, some churches will never agree to perform same-sex
marriages because they believe that homosexuality is a sin. The
separation of church and state allows all churches to follow their
own doctrines; many things that are legal in this country are
opposed by some churches. The government should not deny the
legal right to marry because some churches oppose it.

It's only natural for people in love to want to commit to each 10
other; this desire is the same for homosexuals and lesbians as it is
for heterosexuals. One recent survey showed that "over half of all
lesbians and almost 40% of gay men" live in committed relationships and share a house together (Ayers 5). As Sullivan explains,

"At some point in our lives, some of us are lucky enough to meet the person we truly love. And we want to commit to that person in front of family and country for the rest of our lives. It's the most simple, the most natural, the most human instinct in the world. How could anyone seek to oppose that?" And what does anyone gain when the right is denied? That's a question that everyone needs to ask themselves.

Works Cited

Ayers, Tess, and Paul Brown. The Essential Guide to Lesbian and Gay Weddings. San Francisco: Harper, 1994.

Bennett, William, "Leave Marriage Alone." Newsweek 3 June 1996: 27.

Dean, Craig R. "Gay Marriage: A Civil Right." The Journal of Homosexuality 27.3–4 (1994): 111–15.

"Marriage." The Encyclopedia of Homosexuality. Ed. Wayne R. Dynes. New York: Garland, 1990.

Rauch, Jonathan. "For Better or Worse?" The New Republic 6 May 1996: 18–23.

Salholz, Eloise. "For Better or For Worse." Newsweek 24 May 1993: 69.

Sullivan, Andrew. "Let Gays Marry." Newsweek 3 June 1996: 26.

CHAPTER 9

Motivating Action: Arguing to Persuade

In Chapter 1, we defined persuasion as "convincing *plus*" because, in addition to reason, three other forms of appeal come into play: (1) appeal to the writer's character, (2) appeal to the emotions of the audience, and (3) appeal to style, the artful use of language itself. Building on what you learned about making cases in Chapter 8, this chapter's goal is to help you understand and control persuasion's wider range of appeals. (See Concept Close-Up, page 248.)

WHEN TO CONVINCE AND WHEN TO PERSUADE: A MATTER OF EMPHASIS

When should you aim to persuade rather than convince? Always notice what an assignment calls for because the full range of persuasive appeal is not always appropriate in college. In general, the more academic the audience or the more purely intellectual the issue, the less appropriate the full resources of persuasion are. Philosophy or science papers require you to convince, but seldom to persuade. Good reasons and evidence are all that matters.

When you are working with public issues, matters of policy or questions of right and wrong, persuasion's fuller range of appeal is usually appropriate. Arguments in these areas affect not just how we think but also how we act.

The Four Forms of Appeal

Form	Function	Presence in Text
Reason	Logical cogency	Your case; any supported contention
Character	Personal appeal	Indications of author's status and values
Emotion	Appeals to feelings	Concrete descriptions, moving images
Style	Appeals through language	Word choice, sentence structure, metaphor

Essentially, persuasion differs from convincing in seeking action, not just agreement; it integrates rational appeal with other ways to influence people.

Convincing requires control over case-making. In persuasion we must also (1) gain our readers' confidence and respect, (2) touch our readers' emotions, and (3) focus on language itself. We want an essay that integrates all appeals so that they work together.

ANALYZING YOUR READERS

Successful persuasion brings readers and writer together, creating a sense of connection between people previously separated by viewpoint. What can we do to overcome difference and create identity? First, we need to understand our readers' frame of mind.

Who Is the Audience, and How Do They View the Topic?

Good persuaders are able to empathize and sympathize with other people, building solidarity. To aid audience analysis, ask these questions:

- Who are my readers? How do I define them in terms of age, economic and social class, gender, education, and so forth?
- What typical attitudes or stances toward my topic do they have?
- What in their background or daily experiences helps explain their point of view?
- What are they likely to know about my topic?
- How might they be uninformed or misinformed about it?
- How would they like to see the problem, question, or issue resolved, answered, or handled? Why? That is, what *personal stake* do they have in the topic?
- In what larger framework—religious, ethical, political, economic—do they see my topic? That is, what general beliefs and values are involved?

What Are Our Differences?

Audience analysis isn't complete until you specify exactly what divides you from your readers. These questions can help:

- Is the difference a matter of assumptions? If so, how can I shake my readers' confidence in their assumptions and offer others favorable to my position?

- Is the difference a matter of principle, the application of general rules to specific cases? If so, should I dispute the principle itself and offer a competing one the audience also values? Or should I show why the principle does not apply to my subject?

- Is the difference a matter of a hierarchy of values—that is, do we value the same things but in a different order of priority? If so, how might I restructure my readers' values?

- Is the difference a matter of ends or of means? If ends, how can I show that my vision of what ought to be is better or that realizing my ends will also secure the ends of my readers? If a difference of means, how can I show that my methods are justified and effective, preferable to others?

- Is the difference a matter of interpretation? If so, how can I show that my interpretation is better, accounting more adequately for the facts?

- Is the difference a matter of implications or consequences? If so, how can I convince my readers that what they fear may happen will not happen, or that the outcome will not be as bad as they think, or that any negatives will be outweighed by positives?

What Do We Have in Common?

In seeking common ground with your readers, remember that, no matter how sharply you and your readers disagree, resources for identification always exist. Ask

- Do we have a shared local identity—as members of the same organization or as students at the same university?

- Do we share a more abstract, collective identity—citizens of the same region or nation, worshippers in the same religion, and so forth?

- Do we share a common cause—such as preventing child abuse or overcoming racial prejudice?

- Is there a shared experience or human activity—raising children, caring for aging parents, helping a friend in distress, struggling to make ends meet?

- Can we connect through a well-known event or cultural happening—a popular movie, a best-selling book, something in the news of interest to both you and your readers?

- Is there a historical event, person, or document we both respect?

READING A PERSUASIVE ESSAY

To illustrate the importance of audience analysis, we turn to a classic persuasive essay of the twentieth century, Martin Luther King's "Letter from Birmingham Jail." As we will see, King masterfully analyzed his audience and used the full range of appeals for his readership.

Background

To appreciate King's persuasive powers, we must first understand the events that led to the "Letter" and the actions King wanted his readers to take. In 1963, as president of the Southern Christian Leadership Conference, King had been organizing and participating in civil rights demonstrations in Birmingham, Alabama. He was arrested, and while he was in jail, eight white Alabama clergymen of various denominations issued a public statement critical of his activities. Published in a local newspaper, the statement deplored the demonstrations as "unwise and untimely":

> We the undersigned clergymen are among those who, in January, issued "An Appeal for Law and Order and Common Sense," in dealing with racial problems in Alabama. We expressed understanding that honest convictions in racial matters could properly be pursued in the courts, but urged that decisions of those courts should in the meantime be peacefully obeyed.
>
> Since that time there had been some evidence of increased forbearance and a willingness to face facts. Responsible citizens have undertaken to work on various problems which cause racial friction and unrest. In Birmingham, recent public events have given indication that we all have opportunity for a new constructive and realistic approach to racial problems.
>
> However, we are now confronted by a series of demonstrations by some of our Negro citizens, directed and led in part by outsiders. We recognize the natural impatience of people who feel that their hopes are slow in being realized. But we are convinced that these demonstrations are unwise and untimely.
>
> We agree rather with certain local Negro leadership which has called for honest and open negotiation of racial issues in our area. And we believe this kind of facing of issues can best be accomplished by citizens of our own metropolitan area, white and Negro, meeting with their knowledge and experience of the local situation. All of us need to face that responsibility and find proper channels for its accomplishment.
>
> Just as we formerly pointed out that "hatred and violence have no sanction in our religious and political traditions," we also point out that such actions as incite to hatred and violence, however technically peaceful those actions may be, have not contributed to the resolution of our local problems. We do not believe that these days of new hope are days when extreme measures are justified in Birmingham.
>
> We commend the community as a whole, and the local news media and law enforcement officials in particular, on the calm manner in which these

Audience Analysis

To understand any audience we hope to persuade, we must know *both* what separates us from them *and* what common ground we share.

We may **differ** from our audience in:

Kind of Difference	Example
Assumptions	Western writers assume that separation of church and state is normal; some Muslim audiences do not make the distinction.
Principles	Most conservative writers believe in the principle of the open market; labor audiences often believe in protecting American jobs from foreign competition.
Value rankings	Some writers value personal freedom over duty and obligation; some audiences place duty and obligation above personal freedom.
Ends and means	Writer and audience may agree about purpose (for example, making America safe from terrorism) but disagree about what policies will best accomplish this end.
Interpretation	Some writers understood the September 11, 2001, attacks as acts of war; some audiences saw them as criminal acts that demanded legal rather than military measures.
Consequences	Some writers think making divorce harder would keep more couples together; some audiences think it would only promote individual unhappiness.

We may **share** with our audience:

Kind of Identification	Example
Local identity	Students and teachers at the same university
Collective identity	Citizens of the same state or the same nation
Common cause	Improving the environment
Common experience	Pride in the success of American Olympic athletes
Common history	Respect for soldiers who have died defending the United States

Essentially, we must understand differences to discover how we need to argue; we must use the resources of identification to overcome differences separating us from our readers.

---

demonstrations have been handled. We urge the public to continue to show restraint should the demonstrations continue, and the law enforcement officials to remain calm and continue to protect our city from violence.

We further strongly urge our own Negro community to withdraw support from these demonstrations, and to unite locally in working peacefully for a better Birmingham. When rights are consistently denied, a cause should be pressed in the courts and in negotiations among local leaders,

Figure 9.1

Rosa Parks, whose refusal to move to the back of a bus touched off the Montgomery bus boycott and the beginning of the civil rights movement, is fingerprinted by Deputy Sheriff D. H. Lackey in Montgomery, Alabama, February 22, 1956. She was among some 100 people charged with violating segregation laws.

and not in the streets. We appeal to both our white and Negro citizenry to observe the principles of law and order and common sense.

Signed by:

C. C. J. Carpenter, D.D., LL.D., Bishop of Alabama

Joseph A. Durick, D.D., Auxiliary Bishop, Diocese of Mobile, Birmingham

Rabbi Milton L. Grafman, Temple Emanu-El, Birmingham, Alabama

Bishop Paul Hardin, Bishop of the Alabama-West Florida Conference of the Methodist Church

Bishop Nolan B. Harmon, Bishop of the North Alabama Conference of the Methodist Church

George M. Murray, D.D., LL.D., Bishop Coadjutor, Episcopal Diocese of Alabama

Edward V. Ramage, Moderator, Synod of the Alabama Presbyterian Church in the United States

Earl Stallings, Pastor, First Baptist Church, Birmingham, Alabama

Martin Luther King, Jr., with his son, about 1963.

In his cell, King began his letter on the margins of that newspaper page, addressing it specifically to the eight clergymen, hoping to move them from disapproval to support, to recognizing the need for demonstrations. King knew that his letter would reach a larger audience, including the demonstrators themselves, who were energized by its message when 50,000 copies were later distributed. King's letter has since reached a global audience with its argument for nonviolent protest in the service of moral law.

Letter from Birmingham Jail

MARTIN LUTHER KING, JR.

My Dear Fellow Clergymen: *April 16, 1963*

While confined here in the Birmingham city jail, I came across your recent statement calling my present activities "unwise and untimely." Seldom do I pause to answer criticism of my work and ideas. If I sought to answer all the criticisms that cross my desk, my secretaries would have little time for anything other than such correspondence in the course of the day, and I would have no time for constructive work. But since I feel that you are men of genuine good will and that your criticisms are sincerely set forth, I want to try to answer your statement in what I hope will be patient and reasonable terms.

I think I should indicate why I am here in Birmingham, since you have been influenced by the view which argues against "outsiders coming in." I have the honor of serving as president of the Southern Christian Leadership Conference, an organization operating in every southern state, with headquarters in Atlanta, Georgia. We have some eighty-five affiliated organizations across the South, and one of them is the Alabama Christian Movement for Human Rights. Frequently we share staff, educational, and financial resources with our affiliates. Several months ago the affiliate here in Birmingham asked us to be on call to engage in a nonviolent direct-action program if such were deemed necessary. We readily consented, and when the hour came we lived up to our promise. So I, along with several members of my staff, am here because I was invited here. I am here because I have organizational ties here.

But more basically, I am in Birmingham because injustice is here. Just as the prophets of the eighth century BC left their villages and carried their "thus saith the Lord" far beyond the boundaries of their home towns, and just as the Apostle Paul left his village of Tarsus and carried the gospel of Jesus Christ to the far corners of the Greco-Roman world, so am I compelled to carry the gospel of freedom beyond my own home town. Like Paul, I must constantly respond to the Macedonian call for aid.

Moreover, I am cognizant of the interrelatedness of all communities and states. I cannot sit idly by in Atlanta and not be concerned about what happens in Birmingham. Injustice anywhere is a threat to justice everywhere. We are caught in an inescapable network of mutuality, tied in a single garment of destiny. Whatever affects one directly, affects all indirectly. Never again can we afford to live with the narrow, provincial "outside agitator" idea. Anyone who lives inside the United States can never be considered an outsider anywhere within its bounds.

You deplore the demonstrations taking place in Birmingham. But your statement, I am sorry to say, fails to express a similar concern for the conditions that brought about the demonstrations. I am sure that none of you would want to rest content with the superficial kind of social analysis that deals merely with effects and does not grapple with underlying causes. It is unfortunate that demonstrations are taking place in Birmingham, but it is even more unfortunate that the city's white power structure left the Negro community with no alternative. 5

In any nonviolent campaign there are four basic steps: collection of the facts to determine whether injustices exist; negotiation; self-purification; and direct action. We have gone through all these steps in Birmingham. There can be no gainsaying the fact that racial injustice engulfs this community. Birmingham is probably the most thoroughly segregated city in the United States. Its ugly record of brutality is widely known. Negroes have experienced grossly unjust treatment in the courts. There have been more unsolved bombings of Negro homes and churches in Birmingham than in any other city in the nation. These are the hard, brutal facts of the case. On the basis of these conditions, Negro leaders sought to negotiate with the city fathers. But the latter consistently refused to engage in good-faith negotiation.

Then, last September, came the opportunity to talk with leaders of Birmingham's economic community. In the course of the negotiations, certain promises were made by the merchants—for example, to remove the stores' humiliating racial signs. On the basis of these promises, the Reverend Fred Shuttlesworth and the leaders of the Alabama Christian Movement for Human Rights agreed to a moratorium on all demonstrations. As the weeks and months went by, we realized that we were the victims of a broken promise. A few signs, briefly removed, returned; the others remained.

As in so many past experiences, our hopes had been blasted, and the shadow of deep disappointment settled upon us. We had no alternative except to prepare for direct action, whereby we would present our very bodies as a means of laying our case before the conscience of the local and the national community. Mindful of the difficulties involved, we decided to undertake a process of self-purification. We began a series of workshops on nonviolence, and we repeatedly asked ourselves: "Are you able to accept blows without retaliating?" "Are you able to endure the ordeal of jail?" We decided to schedule our direct-action program for the Easter season, realizing that except for Christmas, this is the main shopping period of the year. Knowing that a strong economic-withdrawal program would be the by-product of direct action, we felt that this would be the best time to bring pressure to bear on the merchants for the needed change.

Then it occurred to us that Birmingham's mayoral election was coming up in March, and we speedily decided to postpone action until after election day. When we discovered that the Commissioner of Public Safety, Eugene "Bull" Connor, had piled up enough votes to be in the run-off, we decided again to postpone action until the day after the run-off so that the demonstrations could not be used to cloud the issues. Like many others, we waited to see Mr. Connor defeated, and to this end we endured postponement after postponement. Having aided in this community need, we felt that our direct-action program could be delayed no longer.

You may well ask: "Why direct action? Why sit-ins, marches and so forth? Isn't 10 negotiation a better path?" You are quite right in calling for negotiation. Indeed, this is the very purpose of direct action. Nonviolent direct action seeks to create such a crisis and foster such a tension that a community which has constantly refused to negotiate is forced to confront the issue. It seeks so to dramatize the issue that it can no longer be ignored. My citing the creation of tension as part of the work of the nonviolent-resister may sound rather shocking. But I must confess that I am not afraid of the word "tension." I have earnestly opposed violent tension, but there is a type of constructive, nonviolent tension which is necessary for growth. Just as Socrates felt that it was necessary to create a tension in the mind so that individuals could rise from the bondage of myths and half-truths to the unfettered realm of creative analysis and objective appraisal, so must we see the need for nonviolent gadflies to create the kind of tension in society that will help men rise from the dark depths of prejudice and racism to the majestic heights of understanding and brotherhood.

The purpose of our direct-action program is to create a situation so crisis-packed that it will inevitably open the door to negotiation. I therefore concur with you in your call for negotiation. Too long has our beloved Southland been bogged down in a tragic effort to live in monologue rather than dialogue.

One of the basic points in your statement is that the action that I and my associates have taken in Birmingham is untimely. Some have asked: "Why didn't you give the new city administration time to act?" The only answer that I can give to this query is that the new Birmingham administration must be prodded about as much as the outgoing one, before it will act. We are sadly mistaken if we feel that the election of Albert Boutwell as mayor will bring the millennium to Birmingham. While Mr. Boutwell is a much more gentle person than Mr. Connor, they are both segregationists, dedicated to maintenance of the status quo. I have hope that Mr. Boutwell will be reasonable enough to see the futility of massive resistance to desegregation. But he will not see this without pressure from devotees of civil rights. My friends, I must say to you that we have not made a single gain in civil rights without determined legal and nonviolent pressure. Lamentably, it is an historical fact that privileged groups seldom give up their privileges voluntarily. Individuals may see the moral light and voluntarily give up their unjust posture; but, as Reinhold Niebuhr has reminded us, groups tend to be more immoral than individuals.

We know through painful experience that freedom is never voluntarily given by the oppressor; it must be demanded by the oppressed. Frankly, I have yet to engage in a direct-action campaign that was "well timed" in the view of those who have not suffered unduly from the disease of segregation. For years now I have heard the word "Wait!" It rings in the ear of every Negro with piercing familiarity. This "Wait" has almost always meant "Never." We must come to see, with one of our distinguished jurists, that "justice too long delayed is justice denied."

We have waited for more than 340 years for our constitutional God-given rights. The nations of Asia and Africa are moving with jetlike speed toward gaining political independence, but we still creep at horse-and-buggy pace toward gaining a cup of coffee at a lunch counter. Perhaps it is easy for those who have never felt the stinging darts of segregation to say, "Wait." But when you have seen vicious mobs lynch your mothers and fathers at will and drown your sisters and brothers at whim; when you have seen hate-filled policemen curse, kick, and even kill your black brothers and sisters; when you see the vast majority of your twenty million Negro brothers smothering in an airtight cage of poverty in the midst of an affluent society; when you suddenly find your tongue twisted and your speech stammering as you seek to explain to your six-year-old daughter why she can't go to the public amusement park that has just been advertised on television, and see tears welling up in her eyes when she is told that Funtown is closed to colored children, and see ominous clouds of inferiority beginning to form in her little mental sky, and see her beginning to distort her personality by developing an unconscious bitterness toward white people; when you have to concoct an answer for a five-year-old son who is asking: "Daddy, why do white people treat colored people so mean?"; when you take a cross-country drive and find it necessary to sleep night after night in the uncomfortable corners of your automobile because no motel will accept you; when you are humiliated day in and day out by nagging signs reading "white" and "colored"; when your first name becomes "nigger," your middle name becomes "boy" (however old you are), and your last name becomes "John," and your wife and mother are never given the respected title "Mrs."; when you are harried by day and haunted by night by the fact that you are a Negro, living constantly at tiptoe stance, never quite knowing what to expect next, and are plagued with inner fears and outer resentments; when you are forever fighting a degenerating sense of "nobodiness"—then you will understand why we find it difficult to wait. There comes a time when the cup of endurance runs over, and men are no longer willing to be plunged into the abyss of despair. I hope, sirs, you can understand our legitimate and unavoidable impatience.

You express a great deal of anxiety over our willingness to break laws. This is 15 certainly a legitimate concern. Since we so diligently urge people to obey the Supreme Court's decision of 1954 outlawing segregation in the public schools, at first glance it may seem rather paradoxical for us consciously to break laws. One may well ask: "How can you advocate breaking some laws and obeying others?" The answer lies in the fact that there are two types of laws: just and unjust. I would be the first to advocate obeying just laws. One has not only a legal but a moral responsibility to obey just laws. Conversely, one has a moral responsibility to disobey unjust laws. I would agree with St. Augustine that "an unjust law is no law at all."

Now, what is the difference between the two? How does one determine whether a law is just or unjust? A just law is a man-made code that squares with the moral law or the law of God. An unjust law is a code that is out of harmony with the moral law. To put it in the terms of St. Thomas Aquinas: An unjust law is a human law that is not rooted in eternal law and natural law. Any law that uplifts human personality is just. Any law that degrades human personality is unjust. All segregation statutes are unjust because segregation distorts the soul and damages the personality. It gives the segregator a false sense of superiority and the segregated a false sense of inferiority. Segregation, to use the terminology of the Jewish philosopher Martin Buber, substitutes an "I–it" relationship for an "I–thou" relationship and ends up relegating persons to the status of things. Hence, segregation is not only politically, economically, and sociologically unsound, it is morally wrong and sinful. Paul Tillich has said that sin is separation. Is not segregation an existential expression of man's tragic separation, his awful estrangement, his terrible sinfulness? Thus it is that I can urge men to obey the 1954 decision of the Supreme Court, for it is morally right; and I can urge them to disobey segregation ordinances, for they are morally wrong.

Let us consider a more concrete example of just and unjust laws. An unjust law is a code that a numerical or power majority group compels a minority group to obey but does not make binding on itself. This is *difference* made legal. By the same token, a just law is a code that a majority compels a minority to follow and that it is willing to follow itself. This is *sameness* made legal.

Let me give another explanation. A law is unjust if it is inflicted on a minority that, as a result of being denied the right to vote, had no part in enacting or devising the law. Who can say that the legislature of Alabama which set up that state's segregation laws was democratically elected? Throughout Alabama all sorts of devious methods are used to prevent Negroes from becoming registered voters, and there are some counties in which, even though Negroes constitute a majority of the population, not a single Negro is registered. Can any law enacted under such circumstances be considered democratically structured?

Sometimes a law is just on its face and unjust in its application. For instance, I have been arrested on a charge of parading without a permit. Now, there is nothing wrong in having an ordinance which requires a permit for a parade. But such an ordinance becomes unjust when it is used to maintain segregation and to deny citizens the First-Amendment privilege of peaceful assembly and protest.

I hope you are able to see the distinction I am trying to point out. In no sense 20 do I advocate evading or defying the law, as would the rabid segregationist. That would lead to anarchy. One who breaks an unjust law must do so openly, lovingly, and with a willingness to accept the penalty. I submit that an individual who breaks a law that conscience tells him is unjust, and who willingly accepts the penalty of imprisonment in order to arouse the conscience of the community over its injustice, is in reality expressing the highest respect for law.

Of course, there is nothing new about this kind of civil disobedience. It was evidenced sublimely in the refusal of Shadrach, Meshach, and Abednego to obey the laws of Nebuchadnezzar, on the ground that a higher moral law was at stake. It was practiced superbly by the early Christians, who were willing to face hungry lions and the excruciating pain of chopping blocks rather than submit to certain unjust laws of the Roman Empire. To a degree, academic freedom is a reality today because Socrates practiced civil disobedience. In our own nation, the Boston Tea Party represented a massive act of civil disobedience.

We should never forget that everything Adolf Hitler did in Germany was "legal" and everything the Hungarian freedom fighters did in Hungary was "illegal." It was "illegal" to aid and comfort a Jew in Hitler's Germany. Even so, I am sure that, had I lived in Germany at the time, I would have aided and comforted my Jewish brothers. If today I lived in a Communist country where certain principles dear to the Christian faith are suppressed, I would openly advocate disobeying that country's antireligious laws.

I must make two honest confessions to you, my Christian and Jewish brothers. First, I must confess that over the past few years I have been gravely disappointed with the white moderate. I have almost reached the regrettable conclusion that the Negro's great stumbling block in his stride toward freedom is not the White Citizen's Counciler or the Ku Klux Klanner, but the white moderate, who is more devoted to "order" than to justice; who prefers a negative peace which is the presence of tension to a positive peace which is the presence of justice; who constantly says: "I agree with you in the goal you seek, but I cannot agree with your methods of direct action"; who paternalistically believes he can set the timetable for another man's freedom; who lives by a mythical concept of time and who constantly advises the Negro to wait for a "more convenient season." Shallow understanding from people of good will is more frustrating than absolute misunderstanding from people of ill will. Lukewarm acceptance is much more bewildering than outright rejection.

I had hoped that the white moderate would understand that law and order exist for the purpose of establishing justice and that when they fail in this purpose they become the dangerously structured dams that block the flow of social progress. I had hoped that the white moderate would understand that the present tension in the South is a necessary phase of the transition from an obnoxious negative peace, in which the Negro passively accepted his unjust plight, to a sub-stantive and positive peace, in which all men will respect the dignity and worth of human personality. Actually, we who engage in nonviolent direct action are not the creators of tension. We merely bring to the surface the hidden tension that is already alive. We bring it out in the open, where it can be seen and dealt with. Like a boil that can never be cured so long as it is covered up but must be opened with all its ugliness to the natural medicines of air and light, injustice must be exposed, with all the tension its exposure creates, to the light of human conscience and the air of national opinion before it can be cured.

In your statement you assert that our actions, even though peaceful, must be 25 condemned because they precipitate violence. But is this a logical assertion? Isn't this like condemning a robbed man because his possession of money precipitated the evil act of robbery? Isn't this like condemning Socrates because his unswerving commitment to truth and his philosophical inquiries precipitated the act by the misguided populace in which they made him drink hemlock? Isn't this like con-demning Jesus because his unique God-consciousness and never-ceasing devotion to God's will precipitated the evil act of crucifixion? We must come to see that, as the federal courts have consistently affirmed, it is wrong to urge an individual to cease his efforts to gain his basic constitutional rights because the quest may pre-cipitate violence. Society must protect the robbed and punish the robber.

I had also hoped that the white moderate would reject the myth concerning time in relation to the struggle for freedom. I have just received a letter from a white brother in Texas. He writes: "All Christians know that the colored people will receive equal rights eventually, but it is possible that you are in too great a religious hurry. It has taken Christianity almost two thousand years to accomplish what it has. The teachings of Christ take time to come to earth." Such an attitude stems from a tragic misconception of time, from the strangely irrational notion that there is something in the very flow of time that will inevitably cure all ills. Actually, time itself is neutral; it can be used either destructively or constructively. More and more I feel that the people of ill will have used time much more effec-tively than have the people of good will. We will have to repent in this generation not merely for the hateful words and actions of the bad people but for the appall-ing silence of the good people. Human progress never rolls in on wheels of inev-itability; it comes through the tireless efforts of men willing to be coworkers with God, and without this hard work, time itself becomes an ally of the forces of social stagnation. We must use time creatively, in the knowledge that the time is always ripe to do right. Now is the time to make real the promise of democracy and transform our pending national elegy into a creative psalm of brotherhood. Now is the time to lift our national policy from the quicksand of racial injustice to the solid rock of human dignity.

You speak of our activity in Birmingham as extreme. At first I was rather disap-pointed that fellow clergymen would see my nonviolent efforts as those of an extremist. I began thinking about the fact that I stand in the middle of two oppos-ing forces in the Negro community. One is a force of complacency, made up in part of Negroes who, as a result of long years of oppression, are so drained of self-respect and a sense of "somebodiness" that they have adjusted to segregation; and in part of a few middle-class Negroes who, because of a degree of academic and economic security and because in some ways they profit by segregation, have become insensitive to the problems of the masses. The other force is one of bitterness and hatred, and it comes perilously close to advocating violence. It is expressed in the various black nationalist groups that are springing up across the nation, the largest and best-known being Elijah Muhammad's Muslim movement. Nourished by the Negro's frustration over the continued existence of racial discrimination, this movement is made up of people who have lost faith in America, who have absolutely repudiated Christianity, and who have concluded that the white man is an incorrigible "devil."

I have tried to stand between these two forces, saying that we need emulate neither the "do-nothingism" of the complacent nor the hatred and despair of the black nationalist. For there is the more excellent way of love and nonviolent protest. I am grateful to God that, through the influence of the Negro church, the way of nonviolence became an integral part of our struggle.

If this philosophy had not emerged, by now many streets of the South would, I am convinced, be flowing with blood. And I am further convinced that if our white brothers dismiss as "rabble-rousers" and "outside agitators" those of us who employ nonviolent direct action, and if they refuse to support our nonviolent efforts, millions of the Negroes will, out of frustration and despair, seek solace and security in black-nationalist ideologies—a development that would inevitably lead to a frightening racial nightmare.

Oppressed people cannot remain oppressed forever. The yearning for freedom 30 eventually manifests itself, and that is what has happened to the American Negro. Something within has reminded him of his birthright of freedom, and something without has reminded him that it can be gained. Consciously or unconsciously, he has been caught up by the *Zeitgeist,* and with his black brothers of Africa and his brown and yellow brothers of Asia, South America, and the Caribbean, the United States Negro is moving with a sense of great urgency toward the promised land of racial justice. If one recognizes this vital urge that has engulfed the Negro community, one should readily understand why public demonstrations are taking place. The Negro has many pent-up resentments and latent frustrations, and he must release them. So let him march; let him make prayer pilgrimages to the city hall; let him go on freedom rides—and try to understand why he must do so. If his repressed emotions are not released in nonviolent ways, they will seek expression through violence; this is not a threat but a fact of history. So I have not said to my people: "Get rid of your discontent." Rather, I have tried to say that this normal and healthy discontent can be channeled into the creative outlet of nonviolent direct action. And now this approach is being termed extremist.

But though I was initially disappointed at being categorized as an extremist, as I continued to think about the matter I gradually gained a measure of satisfaction from the label. Was not Jesus an extremist for love: "Love your enemies, bless them that curse you, do good to them that hate you, and pray for them which despitefully use you, and persecute you." Was not Amos an extremist for justice:

"Let justice roll down like waters and righteousness like an ever-flowing stream."
Was not Paul an extremist for the Christian gospel: "I bear in my body the marks
of the Lord Jesus." Was not Martin Luther an extremist: "Here I stand; I cannot do
otherwise, so help me God." And John Bunyan: "I will stay in jail to the end of my
days before I make a butchery of my conscience." And Abraham Lincoln: "This
nation cannot survive half slave and half free." And Thomas Jefferson: "We hold
these truths to be self-evident, that all men are created equal. . . ." So the question
is not whether we will be extremists, but what kind of extremists we will be. Will
we be extremists for hate or for love? Will we be extremists for the preservation of
injustice or for the extension of justice? In that dramatic scene on Calvary's hill
three men were crucified. We must never forget that all three were crucified for
the same crime—the crime of extremism. Two were extremists for immorality, and
thus fell below their environment. The other, Jesus Christ, was an extremist for love,
truth and goodness, and thereby rose above his environment. Perhaps the South,
the nation and the world are in dire need of creative extremists.

I had hoped that the white moderate would see this need. Perhaps I was too
optimistic; perhaps I expected too much. I suppose I should have realized that few
members of the oppressor race can understand the deep groans and passionate
yearnings of the oppressed race, and still fewer have the vision to see that injustice
must be rooted out by strong, persistent, and determined action. I am thankful,
however, that some of our white brothers in the South have grasped the meaning
of this social revolution and committed themselves to it. They are still all too few
in quantity, but they are big in quality. Some—such as Ralph McGill, Lillian Smith,
Harry Golden, James McBride Dabbs, Anne Braden, and Sarah Patton Boyle—have
written about our struggle in eloquent and prophetic terms. Others have marched
with us down nameless streets of the South. They have languished in filthy, roach-
infested jails, suffering the abuse and brutality of policemen who view them as
"dirty nigger-lovers." Unlike so many of their moderate brothers and sisters, they
have recognized the urgency of the moment and sensed the need for powerful
"action" antidotes to combat the disease of segregation.

Let me take note of my other major disappointment. I have been so greatly
disappointed with the white church and its leadership. Of course, there are some
notable exceptions. I am not unmindful of the fact that each of you has taken some
significant stands on this issue. I commend you, Reverend Stallings, for your Christian stand on this past Sunday, in welcoming Negroes to your worship service on
a nonsegregated basis. I commend the Catholic leaders of this state for integrating
Spring Hill College several years ago.

But despite these notable exceptions, I must honestly reiterate that I have been
disappointed with the church. I do not say this as one of those negative critics who
can always find something wrong with the church. I say this as a minister of the
gospel, who loves the church; who was nurtured in its bosom; who has been sustained by its spiritual blessings and who will remain true to it as long as the cord
of life shall lengthen.

When I was suddenly catapulted into the leadership of the bus protest in 35
Montgomery, Alabama, a few years ago, I felt we would be supported by the white

church. I felt that the white ministers, priests, and rabbis of the South would be among our strongest allies. Instead, some have been outright opponents, refusing to understand the freedom movement and misrepresenting its leaders; all too many others have been more cautious than courageous and have remained silent behind the anesthetizing security of stained-glass windows.

In spite of my shattered dreams, I came to Birmingham with the hope that the white religious leadership of this community would see the justice of our cause and, with deep moral concern, would serve as the channel through which our just grievances could reach the power structure. I had hoped that each of you would understand. But again I have been disappointed.

I have heard numerous southern religious leaders admonish their worshipers to comply with a desegregation decision because it is the law, but I have longed to hear white ministers declare: "Follow this decree because integration is morally right and because the Negro is your brother." In the midst of blatant injustices inflicted upon the Negro, I have watched white churchmen stand on the sideline and mouth pious irrelevancies and sanctimonious trivialities. In the midst of a mighty struggle to rid our nation of racial and economic injustice, I have heard many ministers say: "Those are social issues, with which the gospel has no real concern." And I have watched many churches commit themselves to a completely otherworldly religion which makes a strange, un-Biblical distinction between body and soul, between the sacred and the secular.

I have traveled the length and breadth of Alabama, Mississippi, and all the other southern states. On sweltering summer days and crisp autumn mornings I have looked at the South's beautiful churches with their lofty spires pointing heavenward. I have beheld the impressive outlines of her massive religious-education buildings. Over and over I have found myself asking: "What kind of people worship here? Who is their God? Where were their voices when the lips of Governor Barnett dripped with words of interposition and nullification? Where were they when Governor Wallace gave a clarion call for defiance and hatred? Where were their voices of support when bruised and weary Negro men and women decided to rise from the dark dungeons of complacency to the bright hills of creative protest?"

Yes, these questions are still in my mind. In deep disappointment I have wept over the laxity of the church. But be assured that my tears have been tears of love. There can be no deep disappointment where there is not deep love. Yes, I love the church. How could I do otherwise? I am in the rather unique position of being the son, the grandson, and the great-grandson of preachers. Yes, I see the church as the body of Christ. But, oh! How we have blemished and scarred that body through social neglect and through fear of being nonconformists.

There was a time when the church was very powerful—in the time when the early Christians rejoiced at being deemed worthy to suffer for what they believed. In those days the church was not merely a thermometer that recorded the ideas and principles of popular opinion; it was a thermostat that transformed the mores of society. Whenever the early Christians entered a town, the people in power became disturbed and immediately sought to convict the Christians for being "disturbers of the peace" and "outside agitators." But the Christians pressed on, in the conviction that they were "a colony of heaven," called to obey God rather than man. Small in number, they were big in commitment. They were too God-intoxicated to be "astronomically intimidated." By their effort and example they brought an end to such ancient evils as infanticide and gladiatorial contests.

Things are different now. So often the contemporary church is a weak, ineffectual voice with an uncertain sound. So often it is an archdefender of the status quo. Far from being disturbed by the presence of the church, the power structure of the average community is consoled by the church's silent—and often even vocal—sanction of things as they are.

But the judgment of God is upon the church as never before. If today's church does not recapture the sacrificial spirit of the early church, it will lose its authenticity, forfeit the loyalty of millions, and be dismissed as an irrelevant social club with no meaning for the twentieth century. Every day I meet young people whose disappointment with the church has turned into outright disgust.

Perhaps I have once again been too optimistic. Is organized religion too inextricably bound to the status quo to save our nation and the world? Perhaps I must turn my faith to the inner spiritual church, the church within the church, as the true *ekklesia* and the hope of the world. But again I am thankful to God that some noble souls from the ranks of organized religion have broken loose from the paralyzing chains of conformity and joined us as active partners in the struggle for freedom. They have left their secure congregations and walked the streets of Albany, Georgia, with us. They have gone down the highways of the South on tortuous rides for freedom. Yes, they have gone to jail with us. Some have been dismissed from their churches, have lost the support of their bishops and fellow ministers. But they have acted in the faith that right defeated is stronger than evil triumphant. Their witness has been the spiritual salt that has preserved the true meaning of the gospel in these troubled times. They have carved a tunnel of hope through the dark mountain of disappointment.

I hope the church as a whole will meet the challenge of this decisive hour. But even if the church does not come to the aid of justice, I have no despair about the future. I have no fear about the outcome of our struggle in Birmingham, even if our motives are at present misunderstood. We will reach the goal of freedom in Birmingham and all over the nation, because the goal of America is freedom. Abused and scorned though we may be, our destiny is tied up with America's destiny. Before the pilgrims landed at Plymouth, we were here. Before the pen of Jefferson etched the majestic words of the Declaration of Independence across the pages of history, we were here. For more than two centuries our forebears labored in this country without wages; they made cotton king; they built the homes of their masters while suffering gross injustice and shameful humiliation—and yet out of a bottomless vitality they continued to thrive and develop. If the inexpressible cruelties of slavery could not stop us, the opposition we now face will surely fail. We will win our freedom because the sacred heritage of our nation and the eternal will of God are embodied in our echoing demands.

Before closing I feel impelled to mention one other point in your statement 45 that has troubled me profoundly. You warmly commended the Birmingham police force for keeping "order" and "preventing violence." I doubt that you would have so warmly commended the police force if you had seen its dogs sinking their teeth into unarmed, nonviolent Negroes. I doubt that you would so quickly commend the policemen if you were to observe their ugly and inhumane treatment of Negroes here in the city jail; if you were to watch them push and curse old Negro women and young Negro girls; if you were to see them slap and kick old Negro men and young boys; if you were to observe them, as they did on two occasions, refuse to give us food because we wanted to sing our grace together. I cannot join you in your praise of the Birmingham police department.

It is true that police have exercised a degree of discipline in handling the demonstrators. In this sense they have conducted themselves rather "nonviolently" in public. But for what purpose? To preserve the evil system of segregation. Over the past few years I have consistently preached that nonviolence demands that the means we use must be as pure as the ends we seek. I have tried to make clear that it is wrong to use immoral means to attain moral ends. But now I must affirm that it is just as wrong, or perhaps even more so, to use moral means to preserve immoral ends. Perhaps Mr. Connor and his policemen have been rather nonviolent in public, as was Chief Pritchett in Albany, Georgia, but they have used the moral means of nonviolence to maintain the immoral end of racial injustice. As T. S. Eliot has said: "The last temptation is the greatest treason: To do the right deed for the wrong reason."

I wish you had commended the Negro sit-inners and demonstrators of Birmingham for their sublime courage, their willingness to suffer and their amazing discipline in the midst of great provocation. One day the South will recognize its real heroes. They will be the James Merediths, with the noble sense of purpose that enables them to face jeering and hostile mobs, and with the agonizing loneliness that characterizes the life of the pioneer. They will be old, oppressed, battered Negro women, symbolized in a seventy-two-year-old woman in Montgomery, Alabama, who rose up with a sense of dignity and with her people decided not to ride segregated buses, and who responded with ungrammatical profundity to one who inquired about her weariness: "My feets is tired, but my soul is at rest." They will be the young high school and college students, the young ministers of the gospel and a host of their elders, courageously and nonviolently sitting in at lunch counters and willingly going to jail for conscience's sake. One day the South will know that when these disinherited children of God sat down at lunch counters, they were in reality standing up for what is best in the American dream and for the most sacred values in our Judaeo-Christian heritage, thereby bringing our nation back to those great wells of democracy which were dug deep by the founding fathers in their formulation of the Constitution and the Declaration of Independence.

Never before have I written so long a letter. I'm afraid it is much too long to take your precious time. I can assure you that it would have been much shorter if I had been writing from a comfortable desk, but what else can one do when he is alone in a narrow jail cell, other than write long letters, think long thoughts, and pray long prayers?

If I have said anything in this letter that overstates the truth and indicates an unreasonable impatience, I beg you to forgive me. If I have said anything that understates the truth and indicates my having a patience that allows me to settle for anything less than brotherhood, I beg God to forgive me.

I hope this letter finds you strong in faith. I also hope that circumstances will 50 soon make it possible for me to meet each of you, not as an integrationist or a civil-rights leader but as a fellow clergyman and a Christian brother. Let us all hope that the dark clouds of racial prejudice will soon pass away and the deep fog of misunderstanding will be lifted from our fear-drenched communities, and in some not too distant tomorrow the radiant stars of love and brotherhood will shine over our great nation with all their scintillating beauty.

Yours for the cause of Peace and Brotherhood

Martin Luther King, Jr.

King's Analysis of His Audience: Identification and Overcoming Difference

King's letter is worth studying for the resources of identification alone. For example, he appeals in his salutation to "My Dear Fellow Clergymen," which emphasizes at the outset that he and his readers share a role. Elsewhere he calls them "my friends" (paragraph 12) and "my Christian and Jewish brothers" (paragraph 23). In many other places, King alludes to the Bible and to other religious figures; these references put him on common ground with his readers. King's letter also deals with that which separates him from his readers. We can use the list in the Concept Close-Up on page 251 to analyze how he addressed those differences:

Assumptions: King's readers assumed that if black people waited long enough, their situation would inevitably grow better. King, in paragraph 26, questions "the strangely irrational notion that . . . the very flow of time . . . will inevitably cure all ills." Against this common assumption that "time heals," King offers the view that "time . . . can be used either destructively or constructively."

Principles: King's readers believed in always obeying the law, a principle blind to intent and application. King substitutes another principle: Obey just laws, but disobey, openly and lovingly, unjust laws (paragraphs 15–22).

Hierarchy of Values: King's readers elevated reducing racial tension over securing racial justice. In paragraph 10, King's strategy is to talk about "constructive, nonviolent tension," an effort to get his readers to see tension as not necessarily a bad thing.

Ends and Means: King's audience seems to disagree with him not about the ends for which he was working but about the means. King focuses not on justifying civil rights but on justifying civil disobedience.

Interpretation: King's audience interpreted extremism as always negative. King counters by showing, first, that he is actually a moderate, neither a "do-nothing" nor a militant (paragraph 28). But then he redefines extremism, arguing that extremism for good causes is justified and citing historical examples to support his point (paragraph 31).

Consequences: King's readers doubtless feared the consequences of supporting civil rights too strongly—losing the support of conservative members of their congregations. But as King warns, "If today's church does not recapture the sacrificial spirit of the early church, it will . . . be dismissed as an irrelevant social club" (paragraph 42). King's strategy is to emphasize long-term consequences—the church's loss of vitality and relevance.

◎◎ FOLLOWING THROUGH

As a class, look closely at one of the essays from an earlier chapter, and do an audience analysis. What audience did the writer attempt to reach? How did the writer connect or fail to connect with the audience's experience, knowledge, and concerns? What exactly divides the author from his or her audience, and how did the writer attempt to overcome the division? How effective were the writer's strategies for achieving identification? What can you suggest that might have worked better?

USING THE FORMS OF APPEAL

We turn now to the forms of appeal in persuasion, noting how King used them. For a summary of the forms, see the Concept Close-Up on page 248.

The Appeal to Reason

Persuasion uses the same appeal to reason as convincing. King chose to respond to the clergymen's statement with a personal letter, organized around their criticisms. Most of King's letter amounts to self-defense and belongs to the genre called *apologia*. An **apologia** is an effort to explain and justify what one has done, or chosen not to do, in the face of disapproval or misunderstanding.

Rather than making a single case, King uses a series of short arguments, occupying from one to as many as eight paragraphs, to respond to the criticisms. These include

Refutation of the "outside agitator" concept (paragraphs 2–4)

Defense of nonviolent civil disobedience (paragraphs 5–11)

Definitions of "just" versus "unjust" laws (paragraphs 15–22)

Refutation and defense of the label "extremist" (paragraphs 27–31)

Rejection of the ministers' praise for the conduct of the police during the Birmingham demonstration (paragraphs 45–47)

In addition to defending himself and his cause, King advances his own criticisms, most notably of the "white moderate" (paragraphs 23–26) and the "white church and its leadership" (paragraphs 33–44). This concentration on rational appeal confirms King's character as a man of reason.

King also cites evidence that his readers must respect. In paragraph 16, for example, he cites St. Thomas Aquinas, Martin Buber, and Paul Tillich—representing, respectively, the Catholic, Jewish, and Protestant traditions—to defend his position on just and unjust laws. He has chosen these authorities so that each of his eight accusers has someone from his own tradition with whom to identify.

◎◎ FOLLOWING THROUGH

1. Look at paragraphs 2–4 of King's letter. What reasons does he give to justify being in Birmingham? How does he support each reason? Do his reasons and evidence indicate a strategy aimed at his clergy audience?

2. King's argument for civil disobedience (paragraphs 15–22) is based on one main reason. What is it, and how does he support it?

3. What are the two reasons King gives to refute his audience's charge of extremism (paragraphs 27–31)?

4. Think about a time in your life when you did (or did not do) something for which you were unfairly criticized. Choose one or two of the criticisms, and defend yourself in a short case of your own. Remember to persuade *your accusers,* not yourself. Ask, as King did, How can I appeal to them? What will they find reasonable?   •

The Appeal to Character

In Chapter 8, our concern was how to make a good case. We did not discuss self-presentation there, but when you make a good case you are also creating a positive impression. A good argument will always reveal the writer's values, intelligence, and knowledge. We respect and trust a person who reasons well, even when we do not agree.

The appeal to character in persuasion differs from convincing only in degree. In convincing, the appeal is implicit and diffused throughout the argument; in persuading, the appeal is often explicit and concentrated in a specific section of the essay. The effect on readers is consequently different: In convincing, we are seldom aware of the writer's character; in persuading, the writer's character assumes a major role.

Perception of character was a special problem for King when he wrote his letter. He was not a national hero in 1963 but rather a controversial civil rights leader whom many viewed as a troublemaker. Furthermore, he wrote this now celebrated document while in jail—hardly a condition that inspires respect and trust. Self-presentation, then, was something he concentrated on, especially at the beginning and end.

In his opening paragraph, King acknowledges that he is currently in jail. But he goes on to establish himself as a professional person like his readers, with secretaries, correspondence, and important work to do.

Just prior to his conclusion, King offers a strongly worded critique of the white moderate and the mainstream white church, taking the offensive in a way that his readers are certain to perceive as an attack. In paragraph 48, however, he suddenly becomes self-deprecating: "Never before have I written so long a letter." As unexpected as it is, this sudden shift of tone disarms the reader. Then, with gentle irony (the letter, he says, would have been shorter "if I had been writing from a comfortable desk"), King explains the length of his letter as the result of his having no other outlet for action. What can one do in jail but "write long letters, think long thoughts, and pray long prayers?" King turns the negative of jail into a positive, an opportunity rather than a limitation.

His next move is equally surprising, especially after the assertive tone of his critique of the church. He begs forgiveness—from his readers if he has overstated his case, from God if he has understated it. This daring, dramatic move is just the right touch, the perfect gesture of reconciliation. Because he asks so humbly, his readers *must* forgive him. What else can they do? The subordination of his own will to God's is the stance of the sufferer and martyr in both Jewish and Christian traditions.

Finally, King sets aside that which divides him from his readers—integration and civil rights—in favor of that which unifies them: All are men of God, brothers in faith. Like an Old Testament prophet, he envisions a time when the current conflicts will be over, when "the radiant stars of love and brotherhood will shine over our great nation." In other words, King holds out the possibility for transcendence, for rising above racial prejudice to a new age. In the end, his readers are encouraged to soar with him into hope for the future.

The key to identification is to reach beyond the individual self, associating one's character with something larger—the Christian community, the history of the struggle for freedom, national values, "spaceship Earth," or any appropriate cause or movement in which readers can also participate.

◎◎ FOLLOWING THROUGH

Look at the list of questions for creating audience identification on page 249. Other than in the conclusion, find some examples in King's letter in which he employs some of these resources of identification. What methods does King use that any persuader might use? •

The Appeal to Emotion

Educated people aware of the techniques of persuasion are often deeply suspicious of emotional appeal. Among college professors this prejudice can be especially strong because all fields of academic study claim to value reason, dispassionate inquiry, and critical analysis. Many think of emotional appeal as the opposite of sound thinking.

We can all cite examples of the destructive power of emotional appeal. But to condemn it wholesale, without qualification, exhibits lack of self-awareness. Most scientists will concede, for instance, that they are passionately committed to their methods, and mathematicians say that they are moved by the elegance of certain equations. All human activity has some emotional dimension, a strongly felt adherence to a common set of values.

Moreover, we ought to have strong feelings about certain things: revulsion at the horrors of the Holocaust, pity and anger over the abuse of children, happiness when a war is concluded or when those kidnapped by terrorists are released, and so on. We cease to be human if we are not responsive to emotional appeal.

Clearly, then, we must distinguish between legitimate and illegitimate emotional appeals. Distinguishing the two is not always easy, but answering certain questions can help:

Do the emotional appeals substitute for knowledge and reason?

Do they employ stereotypes and pit one group against another?

Do they offer a simple, unthinking reaction to a complex situation?

Whenever the answer is yes, our suspicions should be aroused.

Perhaps an even better test is to ask yourself, If I act on the basis of how I feel, who will benefit and who will suffer? You may be saddened, for example, to see animals used in medical experiments, but an appeal showing only the animals and ignoring the benefits for humans panders to emotions.

In contrast, legitimate emotional appeal *supplements* argument, drawing on knowledge and often firsthand experience. At its best, it can bring alienated groups together and create empathy or sympathy. Many examples could be cited from King's letter, but the most effective passage is surely paragraph 14:

> We have waited for more than 340 years for our constitutional God-given rights. The nations of Asia and Africa are moving with jetlike speed toward gaining political independence, but we still creep at horse-and-buggy pace toward gaining a cup of coffee at a lunch counter. Perhaps it is easy for those who have never felt the stinging darts of segregation to say, "Wait." But when you have seen vicious mobs lynch your mothers and fathers at will and drown your sisters and brothers at whim; when you have seen hate-filled policemen curse, kick, and even kill your black brothers and sisters; when you see the vast majority of your twenty million Negro brothers smothering in an airtight cage of poverty in the midst of an affluent society; when you suddenly find your tongue twisted and your speech stammering as you seek to explain to your six-year-old daughter why she can't go to the public amusement park that has just been advertised on television, and see tears welling up in her eyes when she is told that Funtown is closed to colored children, and see ominous

clouds of inferiority beginning to form in her little mental sky, and see her beginning to distort her personality by developing an unconscious bitterness toward white people; when you have to concoct an answer for a five-year-old son who is asking: "Daddy, why do white people treat colored people so mean?"; when you take a cross-country drive and find it necessary to sleep night after night in the uncomfortable corners of your automobile because no motel will accept you; when you are humiliated day in and day out by nagging signs reading "white" and "colored"; when your first name becomes "nigger," your middle name becomes "boy" (however old you are), and your last name becomes "John," and your wife and mother are never given the respected title "Mrs."; when you are harried by day and haunted by night by the fact that you are a Negro, living constantly at tiptoe stance, never quite knowing what to expect next, and are plagued with inner fears and outer resentments; when you are forever fighting a degenerating sense of "nobodiness"—then you will understand why we find it difficult to wait. There comes a time when the cup of endurance runs over, and men are no longer willing to be plunged into the abyss of despair. I hope, sirs, you can understand our legitimate and unavoidable impatience.

Just prior to this paragraph, King has concluded an argument justifying the use of direct action to dramatize social inequities and to demand rights and justice denied to oppressed people. Direct-action programs are necessary, he says, because "freedom is never voluntarily given by the oppressor; it must be demanded by the oppressed." It is easy for those not oppressed to urge an underclass to wait. But "[t]his 'Wait' has almost always meant 'Never'."

At this point, King creates a sense of outrage in his readers. Having ended paragraph 13 by equating "wait" with "never," King next refers to a tragic historical fact: For 340 years, since the beginning of slavery in the American colonies, black people have been waiting for their freedom. He sharply contrasts the "jetlike speed" with which Africa is overcoming colonialism with the "horse-and-buggy pace" of integration in the United States. In African homelands, black people are gaining their political independence; but here, in the land of the free, they are denied even "a cup of coffee at a lunch counter." Clearly, this is legitimate emotional appeal, based on fact and reinforcing reason.

In the long and rhythmical sentence that takes up most of the rest of the paragraph, King unleashes the full force of emotional appeal in a series of concrete images designed to make his privileged white readers feel the anger, frustration, and humiliation of the oppressed. In rapid succession, King alludes to mob violence, police brutality, and economic discrimination—the more public evils of racial discrimination—and then moves to the personal, everyday experience of segregation, concentrating especially on what it does to innocent children. For any reader with even the least capacity for sympathy, these images strike home, creating identification with the suffering of the oppressed and impatience with the evil system that perpetuates it. In sum, through the use of telling detail drawn from his own experience, King succeeds in getting his audience to feel what he feels.

What have we learned from King about the available means of emotional appeal? Instead of telling his audience what they should feel, he has evoked that emotion using five specific rhetorical techniques:

Concrete examples

Personal experiences

Metaphors and similes

Sharp contrasts and comparisons

Sentence rhythm, particularly the use of intentional repetition

We next consider how style contributes to persuasion.

◎◎ FOLLOWING THROUGH

1. Emotional appeals need to be both legitimate and appropriate—honest and suitable for the subject matter and the audience. Find examples of arguments from books, newspapers, magazines, and professional journals and discuss the use or avoidance of emotional appeal in each. On the basis of this study, generalize about what subjects and audiences allow direct emotional appeal.

2. Write an essay analyzing the tactics of emotional appeal in editorials in your campus or local newspaper. Compare the strategies with those used by King. Evaluate the appeals. How effective are they? How well do they reinforce the reasoning offered? Be sure to discuss their legitimacy and appropriateness.
   •

The Appeal through Style

Style refers to the choices a writer makes at the level of words, phrases, and sentences. Style is not merely a "dressing up" of an argument. Ideas and arguments do not get expressed apart from style, and all the appeals involve stylistic choices. Style works hand-in-hand with reason, character, and emotion.

Furthermore, style makes what we say memorable. Because persuasive impact depends largely on what readers remember, style matters as much as any of the other appeals.

Style means choice from options. One choice involves the degree of formality. King strikes a formal and professional tone through most of his letter, choosing words like *cognizant* (paragraph 4) rather than the more common *aware*. Writers also choose words based on **connotation** (what a word implies or what we associate with it) as much as on **denotation** (a word's literal meaning). For example, King opens his letter with "While confined here in the Birmingham city jail." The word *confined* denotes the same condition as *incarcerated* but has more favorable connotations, because people can be *confined* in ways that evoke sympathy.

Memorable writing often appeals to sight and sound. Concrete words paint a picture; in paragraph 45, for example, King tells about "dogs sinking their teeth" into nonviolent demonstrators. Writers may also evoke images through metaphor and simile. King's "the stinging darts of segregation" (paragraph 14) is an example of metaphor. In this same paragraph, King refers to the "airtight cage of poverty," the "clouds of inferiority" forming in his young daughter's "mental sky," and the "cup of endurance" that has run over for his people—each a powerful metaphor.

Even when read silently, language has sound. Style also includes variety in sentence length and rhythms. For example, writers may emphasize a short, simple sentence by placing it at the end of a series of long ones, as King does in paragraph 14. Or they may repeat certain phrases to emphasize a point. In the fourth sentence of paragraph 14, King repeats "when you" a number of times, piling up examples of racial discrimination and creating a powerful rhythm that carries readers through this unusually long sentence. Another common rhythmic pattern is parallelism. Note the following phrases, again from the fourth sentence of paragraph 14:

"lynch your mothers and fathers at will"

"drown your sisters and brothers at whim"

Here King uses similar words in the same places, even the same number of syllables in each phrase. The parallelism is further emphasized by *alliteration*, repetition of consonant sounds. In yet another passage from paragraph 14, King suggests violence when he describes police who "curse, kick, and even kill" black citizens. Repetition of the hard *k* sound, especially in one-syllable words, makes the violence sound as brutal as it was.

FOLLOWING THROUGH

1. Analyze King's style in paragraphs 6, 8, 23, 24, 31, and 47. Compare what King does in these paragraphs with paragraph 14. How are they similar? How are they different? Why?

2. To some extent, style is a gift or talent. But it is also learned by imitating authors we admire. Use your writer's notebook to increase your stylistic options; whenever you hear or read something stated well, copy it down and analyze why it's effective. Make up a sentence of your own using the same techniques with different subject matter. In this way, you can begin to use analogy, metaphor, repetition, alliteration, parallelism, and other stylistic devices. Begin by imitating six or so sentences or phrases that you especially liked in King's letter.

3. Write an essay analyzing your own style in a previous essay. What would you do differently now? Why?

DRAFTING A PERSUASIVE ESSAY

Persuasion addresses real needs and moves people to act. Begin, therefore, by conceiving the need you want to address and the audience you want to reach.

Establishing Need

Sometimes the need for action is so widely and well understood that saying much about it isn't necessary. We need a cure for cancer, for instance. Everybody knows this, so a paper about it would at most remind readers of how many people die annually from various types of cancer.

Most of the time, however, need has to be established—or if you are arguing against taking action proposed by someone else, arguing that no need exists that requires action. *Establishing need depends on the extent of common knowledge about your subject and the common attitudes toward it.* By now, for instance, everyone has heard about global warming. You can assume general awareness. However, knowledge of the science is not widespread. You'll need to explain what global warming is and how it's related to human activities. Because attitudes toward it range from casual dismissal to taking it as the biggest problem we face, you must be clear about your own attitude and communicate it forcefully. You can't assume that your audience either understands global warming or is willing to take action that requires self-sacrifice or even inconvenience. Consequently, a substantial portion of your paper will be devoted to establishing need.

In contrast, sometimes there's general acceptance of the need to act when you think no compelling need exists. This situation is common. Politicians and news media, for instance, often pump up minor nuisances into major problems. Soon many people are saying, "We've got to do something." Sometimes the action they want or can be persuaded to accept will do more damage than doing nothing at all. When you write about such a topic, obviously your paper will be devoted to showing that no need exists.

No matter what situation your topic requires you to face, thinking about need—the motivation for action—comes first. The temptation is to think that everyone sees the need as you do, which is rarely the case. Take the time to think through need. It will always be time well spent.

Choosing a Readership

Because we have to consider common knowledge and attitudes about our topic in thinking about need, readers are already in the picture. Such thinking, however, isn't specific enough to envision a readership.

Begin by eliminating the vague, nearly useless concept of "general public." Even when people say they are writing for the general public, they are actually writing for a more limited readership. Also ignore readers who agree with you already. There's nothing to gain by persuading the already persuaded. Finally, you can eliminate readerships so strongly opposed to your position that nothing you could say has a chance of reaching them.

Writing Persuasively: Key Points

The following list summarizes pages 273–281, "Drafting a Persuasive Essay."

1. Choose a **specific** audience whose characteristics you **know well** and who have some capacity for **taking action** or **influencing events.**

2. Identify your audience early in the process.

3. In your case, show **need** and emphasize **urgency.**

4. Your readers must feel that you are **well-informed, confident, fair, honest,** and have their **interests** and **values** in mind. Avoid ridicule of other positions. Recognize and respond to the main objections your readers are likely to have to your proposal.

5. Arouse emotions you genuinely feel. Concentrate on those feelings your audience may lack or not feel strongly enough.

6. Favor a **middle style** for persuasion, conversational without being too familiar or informal.

There's nothing to gain by wasting effort trying to persuade those who won't listen.

What's left? Readerships that are

- *uncommitted*—On most topics, there are people who have not yet formed an opinion.

- *weakly supportive*—There will also be people inclined toward your position but who lack sufficient knowledge and arguments to agree strongly enough to take action.

- *opposed but still open to reason*—For most topics and most efforts to persuade, this is the prime target group. King, for instance, did not try to appeal to white racists but to church leaders who opposed his methods but not his goals.

These categories are useful for thinking about readerships but still not specific enough. Consider two other criteria. First, who is best able to take action or influence outcomes? If you want some change in a local public school policy, for example, parents, especially those active in parent-teacher organizations, may be the best target. But if you want change in public school policy at the state level, probably legislators should be your target readership. Second, among the groups that can take action or influence those that can, which group do you know the best? Obviously, you can appeal most effectively to people you know well.

Selecting a readership demands at least as much careful thought as pondering the need for action. *People who want to persuade go wrong most often by not identifying the most appropriate readership or by not keeping an appropriate readership firmly in mind as they compose.* Therefore, try to identify your readership early in the process. Of course, you can change your mind later, but doing so will require rewriting. Devoting time to discovering your intended audience early in the process can save time and effort later.

◎◎ FOLLOWING THROUGH

For a persuasive argument you are about to write, determine your audience; that is, decide who can make a difference with respect to this issue and what they can do to make a difference. In your writer's notebook, respond to the questions "Who is my audience?" and "What are our differences?" (refer to the lists of questions on pages 248–249 to help formulate answers). Use your responses to write an audience profile. •

STUDENT SAMPLE Need and Audience

Elizabeth Baxley's persuasive essay, "Be a Parent, Not a Friend," appears on pages 281–284 of this chapter. At the time the paper was assigned, local newspapers were covering the resolution of a dispute that had taken place at her high school while she was in her senior year. Her notebook entry shows her exploring the need for action prompted by the incident behind the dispute.

Elizabeth's notebook entry:

My high school has been in the news because of an incident that took place while I was a senior on the cheerleading squad. Several members of the squad were acting wild and even posed for pictures at a condom store while wearing their cheerleading outfits. Then our coach was fired because she tried to discipline them. It's been in the news lately because the fired coach sued the principal. I feel ashamed about the bad publicity for my school. I would like to write to keep this kind of thing from happening again—at any school. You could say it is the girls' fault for acting out, but I know these girls and I think the problem is a lack of parenting. Too many parents are allowing kids to get away with too much. Guidance isn't happening because parents want to be friends rather than parents.

Elizabeth's audience profile:

The audience for this paper will be parents of high school children. Readers could be both mothers and fathers, but I'll aim the paper more toward the mothers because I've observed them firsthand. The readers for my paper are typical mothers in my upper-middle-class suburb. They are into looking young, buying fashionable clothes, and shopping with their daughters. They want a close relationship with their daughters; they want their daughters to confide in them as if they were peers. They think that their children will love them if they are permissive and will hate them if they discipline them. Many of these mothers don't work; they are in an upper-level bracket because of their husbands' income. Having money they don't earn might make them think that they don't have to worry about preparing their children for the hard realities of life. These mothers know that they should be good parents, but they need more motivation to actually do what needs to be done.

Discovering the Resources of Appeal

Before and during drafting, you will be making choices about

How to formulate a case and support it with research

How to present yourself

How to arouse your readers' emotions

How to make the style of your writing contribute to the argument's effectiveness

All these decisions will be influenced by the audience you want to persuade.

Appealing through Reason

One difference between convincing and persuading is that persuasion argues for a course of action. Therefore, (1) show that there is a need for action; (2) show urgency—we must act and act now; and show that what you're proposing satisfies the need.

Sometimes your goal will be to persuade your audience *not* to act because what they want to do is wrong or inappropriate. Need is still the issue. The difference, obviously, is to show that no need exists or that awaiting further developments will enable a proposed action to work better.

◎◎ FOLLOWING THROUGH

Prepare a brief of your argument (see Chapter 8). Be ready to present an overview of your audience and to defend your brief, either before the class or in small groups. Pay special attention to how well the argument establishes a need to act (or shows that there is no need).   •

Appealing through Character

Readers should feel that you are

Well-informed

Confident, honest, and sincere

Fair and balanced in dealing with other positions

Sensitive to their concerns and objections

Sympathetic to what they value

What can you do to communicate these impressions? You must earn them. There are no shortcuts.

To seem well-informed, you must be well-informed. This requires digging into the topic, thinking about it carefully, researching it thoroughly, and taking good notes. This work will enable you to

Make passing references to events and people connected with the issue now or recently

Create a context or provide background information, which may include comments on the history of the question or issue

Produce sufficient high-quality evidence to back up contentions

Draw upon personal experience when it has played a role in determining your position, and don't be reluctant to reveal your own stake in the issue. Make your case boldly, qualifying it as little as possible.

Represent other positions accurately and fairly; then present evidence that refutes those positions or show that the reasoning is inadequate or inconsistent. Indicate agreement with parts of other opinions when they are consistent with your own. Partial agreement can play a major role in overcoming reader resistance.

STUDENT SAMPLE Elizabeth Baxley's Brief

Claim: Parents must take an active role in disciplining their children.

Reason: Children actually want parents to make and enforce rules.

Evidence: "Everyday Rules" from PBS Web site

Evidence: My own family

Reason: When parents don't assume authority, kids will have unrealistic ideas about their own power at home and at school.

Evidence: Twenge on kids with too much power in decisions.

Evidence: The incident at my high school.

Reason: Children suffer the consequence when parents don't act like parents.

Evidence: Girls from my high school

Evidence: Levine on how kids will not be able to meet demands of adult life.

Note that Elizabeth's brief "blocks out" (separates into clear, distinct points) what she intends to say. No matter how closely related they are, *don't allow your points to run together.* If they do, your reader won't be able to detect or follow a sequence of reasons that justify the claim you're defending. Note also that Elizabeth uses both statements from experts and personal experience as evidence, mixing the two well. The experts confirm her outlook, whereas the personal experience makes her stance more concrete and shows her firsthand knowledge of the consequences of bad parenting.

◎◎ FOLLOWING THROUGH

The "Following Through" assignment on page 275 asked you to prepare an audience profile and explore your key areas of difference. Now use the results to think through how you can appeal to these readers. Use the questions on page 249 to help establish commonality. ●

Appealing to Emotion

As in King's essay, argument is the star performer, and emotional appeal plays a supporting role, taking center stage only occasionally. Consequently, you need to decide

What emotions to arouse and by what means

How frequent and intense the appeals should be

Where to include them

The first of these decisions is usually the easiest. Arouse emotions that you genuinely feel; what moved you should move your readers. If your emotions come from direct experience, use it for concrete descriptive detail, as King did.

Deciding how often, at what length, and how intensely to make emotional appeals presents a greater challenge. Much depends on the topic, the audience, and your own range and intensity of feeling.

As always in persuasion, your audience matters most. What attitudes and feelings do they have already? Which of these help your case? Which hinder it? Emphasize those feelings consistent with your position.

Ask also, What does my audience not feel or not feel strongly enough? King decided that his readers' greatest emotional deficit was their inability to feel what victims of racial discrimination feel—hence paragraph 14, the most intense emotional appeal in the letter.

How often and where to include emotional appeals are important considerations. Take your shots sparingly, getting as much as you can each time. Use them to lead into or clinch a point.

◎◎ FOLLOWING THROUGH

After you have a first draft of your essay, reread it with an eye to emotional appeal. Highlight the places where you have sought to arouse the audience's emotions.

Decide if you need more attention to emotional appeal. Consider how you could make each appeal more effective and whether each appeal is located well.   •

Strategies of Appeal in the Student Sample Essay "Be a Parent, Not a Friend"

We wager that you found Elizabeth Baxley's essay persuasive. Most people do because common sense tells them that parents must be parents. But did she reach her target audience, those parents who want to be their children's friends? If so, how did she do it?

As we've seen, Elizabeth had no problem identifying need or audience. The difficulty, rather, was how she viewed the audience she hoped to persuade.

In notebook entries and a first draft, the challenge became clear: How could she reach a readership she saw as almost unreachable—an audience whose behavior seemed to her so completely irrational and misguided that nothing she could say would make any difference?

She began with satire, using a movie that exposes the Mrs. Georges of the world to ridicule. She hoped to accomplish several purposes this way. First, she wanted parents not living up to their role to recognize themselves. Second, she wanted them to admit that how they behave is indefensible. And third, because the purpose of satire is to move deviant behavior toward a desired norm, she saw her opening as strongly implying the action she wanted from her audience.

Undeniably, as she realized, the opening is risky. It's not usually good strategy to ridicule the audience you're trying to persuade. However, she could discover no better way to appeal initially. Furthermore, she followed it with a case that relies on evidence drawn from expert opinion and her own experience, a case that shows erring parents the serious damage they are doing to the children they profess to love. So the ridicule stops after the opening, and rational appeal dominates the rest of the essay.

Insofar as Elizabeth's audience can be reached at all, we think her approach has a chance. Do you agree? If not, how would you try to appeal to her audience?

Appealing through Style

Stylistic choices are part of drafting, but refining them belongs to revision. In the first draft, set an appropriate level of formality. Most persuasive prose is like dignified conversation—the way people talk when they respect one another but do not know each other well. We can see some of the hallmarks of persuasive prose in King's letter:

- It uses *I, you,* and *we.*
- It avoids technical jargon and slang.
- It inclines toward strong action verbs.
- It chooses examples and images familiar to the reader.

These and other features characterize the **middle style.**

As we discovered, King varies his style from section to section, depending on his purpose. He sounds formal in his introduction (paragraphs 1–5), where he wants to establish authority, but more informal when he narrates the difficulties he and other black leaders had in their efforts to negotiate with city leaders (paragraphs 6–9).

Just as King matches style with function, so you need to vary your style based on what each part of your essay is doing. This variation creates *pacing,* the sense of overall rhythm. As you write your first draft, concern yourself with matching style to purpose from section to section, depending

Reader's Checklist for Revising a Persuasive Essay

The following list will direct you to specific features of good persuasion. Exchange drafts with another student and help each other. After you have revised your draft, use the suggestions in the appendix to edit for style and check for errors at the sentence level.

- Read the audience profile. Then read the draft, taking the role of the target audience. Mark the essay's divisions. You may also want to number paragraphs so that you can refer to them easily.

- Inspect the case first. Underline the thesis and mark the reasons. Note any reasons that need more evidence or other support, such as examples.

- Evaluate the plan. Are the reasons well ordered? Does the argument build to a strong conclusion? Can you envision a better arrangement? Make suggestions, referring to paragraphs by number.

- Persuasion requires the writer to present him- or herself as worthy of the reader's trust and respect. Reread the draft, marking specific places where the writer has sought identification from the target audience. Has the writer made an effort to find common ground with readers by using any of the ideas listed on page 249? Suggest improvements.

- Persuasion also requires emotional appeal through concrete examples and imagery, analogies and metaphors, first-person reporting, quotations, and so on. Locate the emotional appeals. Are they successful? What improvements can you suggest?

- Examine the draft for any instances of

  Poor transitions between sentences or paragraphs

  Wordy passages, especially those containing the passive voice (see "Editing for Clarity and Conciseness" in the appendix)

  Awkward sentences

  Poor diction—that is, incorrect or inappropriate words

- After studying the argument, ask whether you are sure what action the writer wants or expects from the audience. Has he or she succeeded in persuading the audience? Why or why not?

on whether you are providing background information, telling a story, developing a reason in your case, mounting an emotional appeal, and so on. Save detailed attention to style for editing a second or third draft.

◎◎ FOLLOWING THROUGH

When you have completed your draft, select one paragraph which you think is stylistically effective. Share the paragraph with your class, describing your choices as we have done with passages from King's letter.

 **FOLLOWING THROUGH**

Read the student essay that begins below, and be ready to discuss its effectiveness as persuasion. Build your evaluation around the suggestions listed in the "Reader's Checklist for Revising a Persuasive Essay," opposite. •

---

www.mhhe.com/crusius For further writing coverage, including information on writing in the traditional modes, visit:

Writing > Writing Tutors

STUDENT SAMPLE: An Essay to Persuade

Be a Parent, Not a Friend
Elizabeth Baxley

Many moms are dropping the parenting role for a much more glamorous one—a role full of Juicy Couture track suits accessorized with a mini-Chihuahua. They lack the ability to act their age, which means being a parent. Instead, they live through their children's social life. The recent movie <u>Mean Girls</u> makes fun of these irritating mothers with the character Mrs. George, who thinks that she is one of the gang.

"Hey, hey, hey. How are my best girlfriends?" asks Mrs. George shortly after serving mocktails to her daughter's friends. "Hey, you guys! Happy hour is from four to six!"

Cady, one of her daughter's friends, asks, "Um, is there alcohol in this?"

Mrs. George replies, "Oh, God, honey, no! What kind of mother do you think I am? Why, do you want a little bit? Because if you're going to drink, I'd rather you do it in the house."

The scene worsens when Mrs. George assures her daughter's 5
friends: "There are <u>no</u> rules in the house. I'm not like a regular mom—I'm a cool mom. . . . I'm a cool mom! Right, Regina?"

However, Mrs. George's desperate attempt to be one of the gang only irritates Regina, who has no respect for her mother. Why should she? Mrs. George doesn't deserve it. Regina should be the kid, not Mrs. George.

Although this scene is amusing, the growing problem is not a laughing matter. As a recent high school graduate from an affluent neighborhood, I have witnessed too many of these instances. Many

www.mhhe.com/crusius

For many additional examples of student writing, go to:

Writing

parents nowadays don't know how to handle their role. Rather than instill values, they just want to be their child's friend. Robert Billingham, an associate professor of human development and family studies at Indiana University, says the problem occurs when "parents are no longer eager to be 'parents.' They want to love and guide their children as a trusted friend" (Twenge 30).

Many parents don't understand that their child wants a parent—one that enforces rules. The Web site of Mr. Rogers' Neighborhood, a show known for its dedication to teaching young children important lessons, discusses this desire for structure: "Even though children may test the limits, they really do feel safer when they know what the rules are—when they've been told by people they love what to do" (Hooper). They want to be part of a family that has traditional roles, one with structure, because structure brings security.

I was thankful (and often envied) for my parents, who were able to provide the guidance I needed. Rules are a part of that process. Ever since I was a little girl, I have loved my parents (despite my resentment at times) because they always knew what I needed even when I didn't. I was taught what is right and wrong. My house had curfews, discipline, and non-negotiable rules. Boundaries allowed me to grow up safely. The kids my age who were also brought up well come from homes with this sort of structure. I am thankful because my parents have prepared me and kept me safe. They always had my best interests at heart.

My view isn't shared by everyone. A group of teens and their   10
families were surveyed for a recent newspaper article. The survey found that "forty percent of teens see their opinions as 'very important' in making family decisions." There was one teenage girl who had actually helped her father select his new job (Twenge 30-31). How can someone in their teens make such a decision? Her father was allowing her to have authority he should assert.

I am dismayed by the frequent encounters I have had with out-of-control teenagers because their parents simply exerted no authority. I was a member of the varsity cheerleading squad throughout high school. Each new year brought a different coach. The school joked that the position was cursed, but the truth was that no one could deal with the insubordination from the girls. Although many of my fellow teammates showed no disrespect to our coach, the second the coach attempted to discipline us, all hell broke loose among some who were not used to being disciplined. Many of the girls had never had to follow any rules in their homes, so they did not know how to follow rules at school. The word "no" was incomprehensible—even listening wasn't necessary.

This year's coach, Mrs. Ward, resigned after being told by the principal, who happened to have a daughter on the team, that she was not allowed to discipline the squad. Mrs. Ward was the first coach to enforce a demerit system. It included punishment for misconduct ranging from skipping classes to representing the school poorly. Mrs. Ward suspended one group of girls for taking sexually suggestive pictures in their cheerleading uniforms in front of the Condom Sense store and then posting them on the Net. However, these attempts at punishment were overturned by the principal, whose daughter was one of the offenders.

It got to the point where there were no rules for our squad. The UIL contracts stating that we would not drink or do drugs were violated without penalty. In the case of the Condom Sense photographs, the guilty party's suspension was reduced from 30 days to only 15. The girls only had to sit out one game. One girl's mother even hired a lawyer to sue Mrs. Ward. Although she agreed that what her daughter did was wrong, she didn't think that it was the coach's job to discipline her daughter. What kind of message was she sending her daughter? These parents were not teaching their children that actions have consequences. They shielded them from the punishment they deserved.

The time will come when parents can't shield their children any longer. Eventually, the girls will pay for their parents' poor job. Of the girls on my squad, some didn't even want to go to college because they had never had the discipline to excel in school. One girl hoped to attend SMU but didn't even apply because of poor grades. She also worked at the country club tennis shop with me, but she was fired because she couldn't follow a few simple rules. For instance, she would leave work while still on the clock. Other cheerleaders were into alcohol, drugs, and sex. None of them understood why any of this was unacceptable because their parents never taught them.

Children need to learn how to live in the real world. Mel Levine, 15 M.D., a child and adolescent development expert, says, "The adult world is full of nonnegotiable expectations. Grown-ups, for example, must fulfill the demands of their jobs and pay their bills on time" (Asnes 97). There will be penalties for careless, irresponsible behavior. So, do your kids a favor and teach them how to be successful. "Teens gain the tools they need to meet [real world] demands by living up to their parents' expectations at home, where people who love them can help them when they fail," says Dr. Levine (Asnes 97). If not for that reason, then do it for your child's protection. You only get one chance with a precious life. It is in your hands. Teens are going to try to push the limits to get away with as much as possible. It is your job to make sure that they are making healthy decisions. Don't just ignore a problem because it is easier than dealing with it.

It is up to parents to instill respect in their children. You must take an active role in your children's lives. Most importantly, you must be their parent, not their friend. Be a role model, someone your kids can look up to. Be someone they can learn from. Do it for your child's safety. Do it for your child's future.

Works Cited

Asnes, Marion. "When Your Teen Wants You to Say No." Good Housekeeping. Apr. 2005: 94–97.

"Everyday Rules and Limits." PBS Kids.com. 13 November 2006 <http://pbskids.org/rogers/parentsteachers/theme/1541_t_art.html>.

"Memorable Quotes from Mean Girls (2004)." Internet Movie Database. 15 November 2006 <http://www.imdb.com/title/tt0377092/quotes>.

Twenge, Jean M. Generation Me: Why Today's Young Americans Are More Confident, Assertive, Entitled—And More Miserable Than Ever Before. New York: Free Press, 2006.

www.mhhe.com/**crusius**

For an electronic tool that helps create properly formatted works-cited pages, go to:

Research > Bibliomaker

CHAPTER 10

Resolving Conflict:
Arguing to Mediate

Private citizens can avoid the big conflicts that concern politicians and activist groups: debates over gay marriage, abortion, taxes, foreign policy, and so on. However, we cannot hide from all conflict. Family members have different preferences about budgeting, major purchases, where to go on vacation, and much else. Furthermore, if you care about what goes on beyond your front door, you will find conflict close to home. The school down the street, for example, wants to expand its athletic stadium. Some parents support the decision because their children play sports at the school. Others oppose it because they think the expansion will bring more traffic, noise, and bright lights to the neighborhood.

One way to resolve conflict is through reasoned arguments. The chapters on convincing and persuading show how appeals to logic and emotion can change minds. But what if we cannot change someone's mind and can't impose our will in other ways?

Some conflicts don't have to be resolved. The Republican husband can live happily with the Democratic wife. Other conflicts are resolved by compromise. We can go to the mountains this year, the seashore the next. Compromise is better than shouting matches, but it does not result in a common understanding.

Characteristics of Mediation

1. Aims to **resolve conflict** between opposing and usually **hardened** positions, often because action of some kind must be taken.

2. Aims to reduce hostility and promote understanding between or among conflicting parties; **preserving human relationships and promoting communication** are paramount.

3. Like inquiry, mediation **involves dialogue** and requires that one understand all positions and strive for an **open mind.**

4. Like convincing, mediation involves making a case that **appeals to all parties in the controversy.**

5. Like persuasion, mediation depends on the **good character** of the negotiator and on sharing **values and feelings.**

6. Mediation depends on conflicting parties' desire to **find solutions to overcome counterproductive stalemates.**

Essentially, mediation comes into play when convincing and persuading have resulted in sharply differing viewpoints. The task is first to understand the positions of all parties involved and second to uncover a mediating position capable of producing consensus and a reduction in hostility.

This chapter presents mediation as argument whose aim is to resolve conflict by thinking more critically about it. People too often see disputes uncritically by simplifying them to their extreme positions, pro and con. The news media does little to help us see conflicts as complex and many-sided, with related issues and shades of gray. *Mediation aims to move disputants beyond the polarized thinking that makes conflicts impossible to resolve.*

MEDIATION AND THE OTHER AIMS OF ARGUMENT

Mediation uses the other three aims of argument: inquiry, convincing, and persuading. Like inquiry, it open-mindedly examines the range of positions on an issue. Mediation requires knowledge of case structure. The mediator must scrutinize the arguments offered by all sides. A mediatory essay must also present a well-reasoned case of its own. Finally, like persuasion, mediation considers the values, beliefs, and assumptions of the people who hold the conflicting positions. Mediators must appeal to all sides and project a character all sides will trust and find attractive.

President Ronald Reagan and Premier Mikhail Gorbachev at the Reykjavik summit, 1986. They met to negotiate about arms control and human rights.

In short, mediation requires the mediator to rise above a dispute, including his or her own preferences, to see what is reasonable and right in conflicting positions. The mediator's best asset is wisdom.

THE PROCESS OF MEDIATION

Mediation takes place more often in conversation, through dialogue with the opposing sides, than in writing. But essays can mediate by attempting to argue for middle ground in a conflict. Whether it eventually takes the form of an essay or a dialogue, mediation begins where all arguments should—with inquiry.

MEDIATION AND ROGERIAN ARGUMENT

Arguing to mediate resembles an approach to communication developed by a psychologist, Carl Rogers (1902–1987). In "Communication: Its Blocking and Its Facilitation," he urged people in conflict to listen carefully and with empathy to each other as a first step toward resolving differences. The second step is to go beyond listening in an effort to understand one another's background, the context in which viewpoints take root and grow into hardened positions. Finally, a third step is for each person involved in a dispute to state the position of his or her opponents in a way the opponents can agree is accurate and fair. The total approach reduces misunderstanding and helps to clarify what the genuine points of difference are, thus opening up the potential to resolve conflict.

In their textbook *Rhetoric: Discovery and Change* (1970), Richard Young, Alton Becker, and Kenneth Pike outlined four stages for Rogerian argument:

1. An introduction to the problem and a demonstration that the opponent's position is understood

2. A statement of the contexts in which the opponent's position may be valid

3. A statement of the writer's position, including the contexts in which it is valid

4. A statement of how the opponent's position would benefit if he were to adopt elements of the writer's position. If the writer can show that the positions complement each other, that each supplies what the other lacks, so much the better.[1]

Our approach to mediation draws on Rogerian argument. As a mediator, rather than a participant in a dispute, you'll need to consider the validity of opposing positions, including the personal backgrounds of the people involved. In light of these backgrounds, you look for what is good and right in each position.

Rather than face-to-face verbal arguments, in this chapter you will be reading written arguments on a controversial issue and exploring these arguments to uncover exactly how and why their authors disagree. Instead of sitting around a table with parties in conflict as mediators do, you'll write a mediatory essay proposing a point of view designed to appeal to both sides.

A Conflict to Mediate

The United States is a nation of immigrants, but recently the immigrant population includes a wider array of races, ethnicities, religions, and cultures than in the past. The result is a population less white and less Protestant. Should we become a multicultural nation or maintain a single culture based on the original northern European settlers?

Some people argue that the influx of diverse people should have no impact on the traditional Eurocentric identity of America. According to this position, America has a distinctive and superior culture, traceable to the Puritan settlers and based more broadly on Western civilization. This culture is the source of our nation's strength. To keep it strong, newcomers need to assimilate, adopting its values and beliefs. In other words, people holding this position advocate the melting-pot metaphor. Because they believe cultural differences should dissolve as new immigrants become "true Americans," they oppose multiculturalism. We have chosen a recent essay by Roger Kimball,

---

[1]This summary of the four stages comes from Douglas Brent, "Rogerian Rhetoric: An Alternative to Traditional Rhetoric," *Argument Revisited, Argument Redefined: Negotiating Meaning in the Composition Classroom,* ed. Barbara Emmel, Paula Resch, and Deborah Tenney (Thousand Oaks, CA: Sage, 1996) <http://www.acs.ucalgary.ca/~dabrent/art/rogchap.html>.

an art critic and editor at the conservative journal *The New Criterion,* to represent the assimilationist position.

Opponents argue that newcomers should preserve their distinctive cultures, taking pride in being Mexican, Chinese, African, and so on. Their metaphor is the mosaic, with each culture remaining distinct but contributing to the whole, like the tiles in a mosaic. We have chosen an essay by Elizabeth Martínez to represent the multiculturalist perspective. Martínez is a Chicana writer and an activist on issues of social justice, including racism and women's rights.

Understanding the Positions

Any attempt to mediate positions requires an understanding of opposing cases. Printed below are the two arguments, followed by our analyses.

Institutionalizing Our Demise: America vs. Multiculturalism

ROGER KIMBALL

The following abridged article appeared in *The New Criterion* (June 2004). Roger Kimball's books include *The Long March: How the Cultural Revolution of the 1960s Changed America* (Encounter, 2000) and *Tenured Radicals: How Politics Has Corrupted Our Higher Education* (HarperCollins, 1990).

There is no room in this country for hyphenated Americanism. When I refer to hyphenated Americans, I do not refer to naturalized Americans. Some of the very best Americans I have ever known were naturalized Americans, Americans born abroad. But a hyphenated American is not an American at all. This is just as true of the man who puts "native" before the hyphen as of the man who puts German or Irish or English or French before the hyphen.

—Theodore Roosevelt, 1915

It is often said that the terrorist attacks of September 11 precipitated a new resolve throughout the nation. There is some truth to that. Certainly, the extraordinary bravery of the firefighters and other rescue personnel in New York and Washington, D.C., provided an invigorating spectacle—as did Todd "Let's roll" Beamer and his fellow passengers on United Airlines Flight 93. Having learned from their cell phones what had happened at the World Trade Center and the Pentagon, Beamer and his fellows rushed and overpowered the terrorists who had hijacked their plane. As a result, the plane crashed on a remote Pennsylvania farm instead of on Pennsylvania Avenue. Who knows how many lives their sacrifice saved?

The widespread sense of condign outrage—of horror leavened by anger and elevated by resolve—testified to a renewed sense of national purpose and identity after 9/11. Attacked, many Americans suddenly (if temporarily) rediscovered the virtue of patriotism. At the beginning of his remarkable book *Who Are We? The Challenges to America's National Identity* (2004), the Harvard political scientist

Samuel Huntington recalls a certain block on Charles Street in Boston. At one time, American flags flew in front of a U.S. Post Office and a liquor store. Then the Post Office stopped displaying the flag, so on September 11, 2001, the flag was flying only in front of the liquor store. Within two weeks, seventeen American flags decorated that block of Charles Street, in addition to a huge flag suspended over the street close by. "With their country under attack," Huntington notes, "Charles Street denizens rediscovered their nation and identified themselves with it."

Was that rediscovery anything more than a momentary passion? Huntington reports that within a few months, the flags on Charles Street began to disappear. By the time the first anniversary rolled around in September 2002, only four were left flying. True, that is four times more than were there on September 10, 2001, but it is less than a quarter of the number that populated Charles Street at the end of September 2001.

There are similar anecdotes from around the country—an access of flag-waving followed by a relapse into indifference. Does it mean that the sudden upsurge of patriotism in the weeks following 9/11 was only, as it were, skin deep? Or perhaps it merely testifies to the fact that a sense of permanent emergency is difficult to maintain, especially in the absence of fresh attacks. Is our sense of ourselves as Americans patent only when challenged? "Does it," Huntington asks, "take an Osama bin Laden . . . to make us realize that we are Americans? If we do not experience recurring destructive attacks, will we return to the fragmentation and eroded Americanism before September 11?"

One hopes that the answer is No. . . . But I fear that for every schoolchild 5 standing at attention for the National Anthem, there is a teacher or lawyer or judge or politician or ACLU employee militating against the hegemony of the dominant culture, the insupportable intrusion of white, Christian, "Eurocentric" values into the curriculum, the school pageant, the town green, etc., etc. . . .

The threat shows itself in many ways, from culpable complacency to the corrosive imperatives of "multiculturalism" and political correctness. . . . In essence, as Huntington notes, multiculturalism is "anti-European civilization. . . . It is basically an anti-Western ideology.". . . [W]herever the imperatives of multiculturalism have touched the curriculum, they have left broad swaths of anti-Western attitudinizing competing for attention with quite astonishing historical blindness. Courses on minorities, women's issues, the Third World proliferate; the teaching of mainstream history slides into oblivion. "The mood," Arthur Schlesinger wrote in *The Disuniting of America* (1992), his excellent book on the depredations of multiculturalism, "is one of divesting Americans of the sinful European inheritance and seeking redemptive infusions from non-Western cultures."

A profound ignorance of the milestones of American culture is one predictable result of this mood. The statistics have become proverbial. Huntington quotes one poll from the 1990s showing that while 90 percent of Ivy League students could identify Rosa Parks, only 25 percent could identify the author of the words "government of the people, by the people, for the people." (Yes, it's the Gettysburg Address.) In a 1999 survey, 40 percent of seniors at fifty-five top colleges could not say within half a century when the Civil War was fought. Another study found that more high school students knew who Harriet Tubman was than knew that Washington commanded the American army in the revolution or that Abraham Lincoln wrote the Emancipation Proclamation. Doubtless you have your own favorite horror story.

But multiculturalism is not only an academic phenomenon. The attitudes it fosters have profound social as well as intellectual consequences. One consequence has been a sharp rise in the phenomenon of immigration without—or with only partial—assimilation: a dangerous demographic trend that threatens American identity in the most basic way. These various agents of dissolution are also elements in a wider culture war: the contest to define how we live and what counts as the good in the good life. Anti-Americanism occupies such a prominent place on the agenda of the culture wars precisely because the traditional values of American identity—articulated by the Founders and grounded in a commitment to individual liberty and public virtue—are deeply at odds with the radical, de-civilizing tenets of the "multiculturalist" enterprise.

To get a sense of what has happened to the institution of American identity, compare Robert Frost's performance at John F. Kennedy's inauguration in 1961 with Maya Angelou's performance thirty-two years later. As Huntington reminds us, Frost spoke of the "heroic deeds" of America's founding, an event, he said, that with "God's approval" ushered in "a new order of the ages." By contrast, Maya Angelou never mentioned the words "America" or "American." Instead, she identified twenty-seven ethnic or religious groups that had suffered repression because of America's "armed struggles for profit," "cynicism," and "brutishness.". . .

A favorite weapon in the armory of multiculturalism is the lowly hyphen. When 10 we speak of an African-American or Mexican-American or Asian-American these days, the aim is not descriptive but deconstructive. There is a polemical edge to it, a provocation. The hyphen does not mean "American, but hailing at some point in the past from someplace else." It means "only provisionally American: my allegiance is divided at best.". . . The multicultural passion for hyphenation is not simply a fondness for syntactical novelty. It also bespeaks a commitment to the centrifugal force of anti-American tribalism. The division marked by the hyphen in African-American (say) denotes a political stand. It goes hand-in-hand with other items on the index of liberal desiderata—the redistributive impulse behind efforts at "affirmative action," for example. . . .

Multiculturalism and "affirmative action" are allies in the assault on the institution of American identity. As such, they oppose the traditional understanding of what it means to be an American—an understanding hinted at in 1782 by the French-born American farmer J. Hector St. John de Crèvecoeur in his famous image of America as a country in which "individuals of all nations are melted into a new race of men." This crucible of American identity, this "melting pot," has two aspects. The negative aspect involves disassociating oneself from the cultural imperatives of one's country of origin. One sheds a previous identity before assuming a new one. One might preserve certain local habits and tastes, but they are essentially window-dressing. In essence one has left the past behind in order to become an American citizen.

The positive aspect of advancing the melting pot involves embracing the substance of American culture. The 1795 code for citizenship lays out some of the formal requirements.

> I do solemnly swear (1) to support the Constitution of the United States; (2) to renounce and abjure absolutely and entirely all allegiance and fidelity to any foreign prince, potentate, state, or sovereignty of whom or which the applicant was before a subject or citizen; (3) to support and defend the Constitution and the laws of the United States against all enemies, foreign and domestic; (4) to bear true faith and allegiance to the same; and (5) (A) to bear arms on behalf of the United States when required by law, or (B) to perform noncombatant service in the Armed Forces of the United States when required by law. . . .

For over two hundred years, this oath had been required of those wishing to become citizens. In 2003, Huntington tells us, federal bureaucrats launched a campaign to rewrite and weaken it.

I shall say more about what constitutes the substance of American identity in a moment. For now, I want to underscore the fact that this project of Americanization has been an abiding concern since the time of the Founders. "We must see our people more Americanized," John Jay declared in the 1780s. Jefferson concurred. Teddy Roosevelt repeatedly championed the idea that American culture, the "crucible in which all the new types are melted into one," was "shaped from 1776 to 1789, and our nationality was definitely fixed in all its essentials by the men of Washington's day."

It is often said that America is a nation of immigrants. In fact, as Huntington points out, America is a country that was initially a country of *settlers*. Settlers precede immigrants and make their immigration possible. The culture of those mostly English-speaking, predominantly Anglo-Protestant settlers defined American culture. Their efforts came to fruition with the generation of Franklin, Washington, Jefferson, Hamilton, and Madison. The Founders are so denominated because they founded, they inaugurated a state. Immigrants were those who came later, who came from elsewhere, and who became American by embracing the Anglophone culture of the original settlers. The English language, the rule of law, respect for individual rights, the industriousness and piety that flowed from the Protestant work ethic—these were central elements in the culture disseminated by the Founders. And these were among the qualities embraced by immigrants when they became Americans. "Throughout American history," Huntington notes, "people who were not white Anglo-Saxon Protestants have become Americans by adopting America's Anglo-Protestant culture and political values. This benefited them and the country."

Justice Louis Brandeis outlined the pattern in 1919. Americanization, he said, means that the immigrant "adopts the clothes, the manners, and the customs generally prevailing here . . . substitutes for his mother tongue the English language" and comes "into complete harmony with our ideals and aspirations and cooperate[s] with us for their attainment." Until the 1960s, the Brandeis model mostly prevailed. Protestant, Catholic, and Jewish groups, understanding that assimilation was the best ticket to stability and social and economic success, eagerly aided in the task of integrating their charges into American society.

The story is very different today. In America, there is a dangerous new tide of immigration from Asia, a variety of Muslim countries, and Latin America, especially from Mexico. The tide is new not only chronologically but also in substance. First, there is the sheer matter of numbers. More than 2,200,000 legal immigrants came to the U.S. from Mexico in the 1990s alone. The number of illegal Mexican immigrants is staggering. So is their birth rate. Altogether there are more than 8 million Mexicans in the U.S. Some parts of the Southwest are well on their way to becoming what Victor Davis Hanson calls "Mexifornia," "the strange society that is emerging as the result of a demographic and cultural revolution like no other in our times." A professor of Chicano Studies at the University of New Mexico gleefully predicts that by 2080 parts of the Southwest United States and Northern Mexico will join to form a new country, "La Republica del Norte."

The problem is not only one of numbers, though. Earlier immigrants made—and were helped and goaded by the ambient culture to make—concerted efforts to assimilate. Important pockets of these new immigrants are not assimilating, not learning English, not becoming or thinking of themselves primarily as Americans. The effect of these developments on American identity is disastrous and potentially irreversible.

Such developments are abetted by the left-wing political and educational elites of this country, whose dominant theme is the perfidy of traditional American values. Hence the passion for multiculturalism and the ideal of ethnic hyphenation that goes with it. This has done immense damage in schools and colleges as well as in the population at large. By removing the obligation to master English, multiculturalism condemns whole subpopulations to the status of permanent second-class citizens. . . .

As if in revenge for this injustice, however, multiculturalism also weakens the social bonds of the community at large. The price of imperfect assimilation is imperfect loyalty. Take the movement for bilingualism. Whatever it intended in theory, in practice it means *not* mastering English. It has notoriously left its supposed beneficiaries essentially monolingual, often semi-lingual. The only *bi* involved is a passion for bifurcation, which is fed by the accumulated resentments instilled by the anti-American multicultural orthodoxy. Every time you call directory assistance or some large corporation and are told "Press One for English" and "Para español oprime el numero dos" it is another small setback for American identity. . . .

We stand at a crossroads. The future of America hangs in the balance. Huntington outlines several possible courses that the country might take, from the loss of our core culture to an attempt to revive the "discarded and discredited racial and ethnic concepts" that, in part, defined pre-mid-twentieth century America. Huntington argues for another alternative. If we are to preserve our identity as a nation we need to preserve the core values that defined that identity. This is a point that the political philosopher Patrick, Lord Devlin made in his book *The Enforcement of Morals* (1965): 20

> [S]ociety means a community of ideas; without shared ideas on politics, morals, and ethics no society can exist. Each one of us has ideas about what is good and what is evil; they cannot be kept private from the society in which we live. If men and

women try to create a society in which there is no fundamental agreement about good and evil they will fail; if having based it upon a common set of core values, they surrender those values, it will disintegrate. For society is not something that can be kept together physically; it is held by the invisible but fragile bonds of common beliefs and values. . . . A common morality is part of the bondage of a good society, and that bondage is part of the price of society which mankind must pay.

What are those beliefs and values? They embrace several things, including religion. You wouldn't know it from watching CNN or reading *The New York Times,* but there is a huge religious revival taking place now, affecting just about every part of the globe except Western Europe, which slouches towards godlessness almost as fast as it slouches towards bankruptcy and demographic collapse. (Neither Spain nor Italy are producing enough children to replace their existing populations, while the Muslim birthrate in France continues to soar).

Things look different in America. For if America is a vigorously secular country—which it certainly is—it is also a deeply religious one. It always has been. Tocqueville was simply minuting the reality he saw around him when he noted that "[o]n my arrival in the United States the religious aspect of the country was the first thing that struck my attention." As G. K. Chesterton put it a century after Tocqueville, America is "a nation with the soul of a church." Even today, America is a country where an astonishing 92 percent of the population says it believes in God and 80 to 85 percent of the population identifies itself as Christian. Hence Huntington's call for a return to America's core values is also a call to embrace the religious principles upon which the country was founded, "a recommitment to America as a deeply religious and primarily Christian country, encompassing several religious minorities adhering to Anglo-Protestant values, speaking English, maintaining its cultural heritage, and committed to the principles" of political liberty as articulated by the Founders. . . . Huntington is careful to stress that what he offers is an "argument for the importance of Anglo-Protestant culture, not for the importance of Anglo-Protestant people." That is, he argues not on behalf of a particular ethnic group but on behalf of a culture and set of values that "for three and a half centuries have been embraced by Americans of all races, ethnicities, and religions and that have been the source of their liberty, unity, power, prosperity, and moral leadership."

American identity was originally founded on four things: ethnicity, race, ideology, and culture. By the mid-twentieth century, ethnicity and race had sharply receded in importance. Indeed, one of America's greatest achievements is having eliminated the racial and ethnic components that historically were central to its identity. Ideology—the package of Enlightened liberal values championed by the Founders—[is] crucial but too thin for the task of forging or preserving national identity by themselves. ("A nation defined only by political ideology," Huntington notes, "is a fragile nation.") Which is why Huntington, like virtually all of the Founders, explicitly grounded American identity in religion. . . .

Opponents of religion in the public square never tire of reminding us that there is no mention of God in the Constitution. This is true. Neither is the word "virtue" mentioned. But both are presupposed. For the American Founders, as the historian

Gertrude Himmelfarb points out, virtue, grounded in religion, was presumed "to be rooted in the very nature of man and as such . . . reflected in the *moeurs* of the people and in the traditions and informal institutions of society." It is also worth mentioning that if the Constitution is silent on religion, the Declaration of Independence is voluble, speaking of "nature's God," the "Creator," "the supreme judge of the world," and "divine Providence.". . . Benjamin Rush, one of the signers of the Declaration of Independence, summed up the common attitude of the Founders toward religion when he insisted that "[t]he only foundation for a useful education in a republic is to be laid in religion. Without it there can be no virtue, and without virtue there can be no liberty, and liberty is the object of all republican governments." George Washington concurred: "Reason and experience both forbid us to expect that national morality can prevail in exclusion of religious principles."

No nation lasts forever. An external enemy may eventually overrun and subdue it; internal forces of dissolution and decadence may someday undermine it, leaving it prey to more vigorous competitors. Sooner or later it succumbs. The United States is the most powerful nation the world has ever seen. Its astonishing military might, economic productivity, and political vigor are unprecedented. But someday, as Huntington reminds us, it too will fade or perish as Athens, Rome, and other great civilizations have faded or perished. Is the end, or the beginning of the end, at hand?

So far, the West—or at least the United States—has disappointed its self-appointed undertakers. How do we stand now, at the dawn of the twenty-first century? It is worth remembering that besieged nations do not always succumb to the forces, external or internal, that threaten them. Sometimes, they muster the resolve to fight back successfully, to renew themselves. Today, America faces a new external enemy in the form of militant Islam and global terrorism. That minatory force, though murderous, will fail in proportion to our resolve to defeat it. Do we still possess that resolve? Inseparable from resolve is self-confidence, faith in the essential nobility of one's regime and one's way of life. To what extent do we still possess, still practice that faith?

Reinventing "America": Call for a New National Identity

ELIZABETH MARTÍNEZ

Elizabeth Martínez has written six books, including one on Chicano history. This essay comes from her 1998 book, *De Colores Means All of Us: Latina Views for a Multi-Colored Century.*

For some 15 years, starting in 1940, 85 percent of all U.S. elementary schools used the Dick and Jane series to teach children how to read. The series starred Dick, Jane, their white middle-class parents, their dog Spot and their life together in a home with a white picket fence.

"Look, Jane, look! See Spot run!" chirped the two kids. It was a house full of glorious family values, where Mom cooked while Daddy went to work in a suit and mowed the lawn on weekends. The Dick and Jane books also taught that you should do your job and help others. All this affirmed an equation of middle-class with whiteness with virtue.

In the mid-1990s, museums, libraries and 80 Public Broadcasting Service (PBS) stations across the country had exhibits and programs commemorating the series. At one museum, an attendant commented, "When you hear someone crying, you know they are looking at the Dick and Jane books." It seems nostalgia runs rampant among many Euro-Americans: a nostalgia for the days of unchallenged White Supremacy—both moral and material—when life was "simple."

We've seen that nostalgia before in the nation's history. But today it signifies a problem reaching a new intensity. It suggests a national identity crisis that promises to bring in its wake an unprecedented nervous breakdown for the dominant society's psyche.

Nowhere is this more apparent than in California, which has long been on the 5 cutting edge of the nation's present and future reality. Warning sirens have sounded repeatedly in the 1990s, such as the fierce battle over new history textbooks for public schools, Proposition 187's ugly denial of human rights to immigrants, the 1996 assault on affirmative action that culminated in Proposition 209, and the 1997 move to abolish bilingual education. Attempts to copycat these reactionary measures have been seen in other states.

The attack on affirmative action isn't really about affirmative action. Essentially it is another tactic in today's war on the gains of the 1960s, a tactic rooted in Anglo resentment and fear. A major source of that fear: the fact that California will almost surely have a majority of people of color in 20 to 30 years at most, with the nation as a whole not far behind.

Check out the February 3, 1992, issue of *Sports Illustrated* with its double-spread ad for *Time* magazine. The ad showed hundreds of newborn babies in their hospital cribs, all of them Black or brown except for a rare white face here and there. The headline says, "Hey, whitey! It's your turn at the back of the bus!" The ad then tells you, read *Time* magazine to keep up with today's hot issues. That manipulative image could have been published today; its implication of shifting power appears to be the recurrent nightmare of too many potential Anglo allies.

Euro-American anxiety often focuses on the sense of a vanishing national identity. Behind the attacks on immigrants, affirmative action and multiculturalism, behind the demand for "English Only" laws and the rejection of bilingual education, lies the question: with all these new people, languages and cultures, what will it mean to be an American? If that question once seemed, to many people, to have an obvious, universally applicable answer, today new definitions must be found. But too often Americans, with supposed scholars in the lead, refuse to face that need and instead nurse a nostalgia for some bygone clarity. They remain trapped in denial.

An array of such ostriches, heads in the sand, began flapping their feathers noisily with the publication of Allan Bloom's 1987 best-selling book, *The Closing of the American Mind.* Bloom bemoaned the decline of our "common values" as a society, meaning the decline of Euro-American cultural centricity (shall we just call it cultural imperialism?). Since then we have seen constant sniping at "diversity" goals across the land. The assault has often focused on how U.S. history is taught. And with reason, for this country's identity rests on a particular narrative about the historical origins of the United States as a nation.

THE GREAT WHITE ORIGIN MYTH

Every society has an origin narrative that explains that society to itself and the world 10 with a set of stories and symbols. The origin myth, as scholar-activist Roxanne Dunbar Ortiz has termed it, defines how a society understands its place in the world and its history. The myth provides the basis for a nation's self-defined identity. Most origin narratives can be called myths because they usually present only the most flattering view of a nation's history; they are not distinguished by honesty.

Ours begins with Columbus "discovering" a hemisphere where some 80 million people already lived but didn't really count (in what became the United States, they were just buffalo-chasing "savages" with no grasp of real estate values and therefore doomed to perish). It continues with the brave Pilgrims, a revolution by independence-loving colonists against a decadent English aristocracy and the birth of an energetic young republic that promised democracy and equality (that is, to white male landowners). In the 1840s, the new nation expanded its size by almost one-third, thanks to a victory over that backward land of little brown people called Mexico. Such has been the basic account of how the nation called the United States of America came into being as presently configured.

The myth's omissions are grotesque. It ignores three major pillars of our nationhood: genocide, enslavement and imperialist expansion (such nasty words, who wants to hear them?—but that's the problem). The massive extermination of indigenous peoples provided our land base; the enslavement of African labor made our economic growth possible; and the seizure of half of Mexico by war (or threat of renewed war) extended this nation's boundaries north to the Pacific and south to the Rio Grande. Such are the foundation stones of the United States, within an economic system that made this country the first in world history to be born capitalist.

Those three pillars were, of course, supplemented by great numbers of dirt-cheap workers from Mexico, China, the Philippines, Puerto Rico and other countries, all of them kept in their place by White Supremacy. In history they stand alongside millions of less-than-supreme white workers and sharecroppers.

Any attempt to modify the present origin myth provokes angry efforts to repel such sacrilege. In the case of Native Americans, scholars will insist that they died from disease or wars among themselves, or that "not so many really did die." At worst it was a "tragedy," but never deliberate genocide, never a pillar of our nationhood. As for slavery, it was an embarrassment, of course, but do remember that Africa also had slavery and anyway enlightened white folk finally did end the practice here.

In the case of Mexico, reputable U.S. scholars still insist on blaming that coun- 15 try for the 1846–48 war. Yet even former U.S. President Ulysses Grant wrote in his memoirs that "[w]e were sent to provoke a fight [by moving troops into a disputed border area] but it was essential that Mexico should commence it [by fighting back]" (*Mr. Lincoln's General: Ulysses S. Grant, an illustrated autobiography*). President James Polk's 1846 diary records that he told his cabinet his purpose in declaring war as "acquiring California, New Mexico, and perhaps other Mexican lands" (*Diary of James K. Polk 1845–49*). To justify what could be called a territorial drive-by, the Mexican people were declared inferior; the U.S. had a "Manifest Destiny" to bring them progress and democracy.

Even when revisionist voices expose particular evils of Indian policy, slavery or the war on Mexico, they remain little more than unpleasant footnotes; the core of the dominant myth stands intact. PBS's eight-part documentary series of 1996 titled "The West" is a case in point. It devoted more than the usual attention to the devastation of Native Americans, but still centered on Anglos and gave little attention to why their domination evolved as it did. The West thus remained the physically gorgeous backdrop for an ugly, unaltered origin myth.

In fact, "The West" series strengthens that myth. White Supremacy needs the brave but inevitably doomed Indians to silhouette its own inevitable conquest. It needs the Indian-as-devil to sustain its own holy mission. Remember Timothy Wight, who served as pastor to Congress in the late 1700s and wrote that, under the Indians, "Satan ruled unchallenged in America" until "our chosen race eternal justice sent." With that self-declared moral authority, the "winning of the West" metamorphosed from a brutal, bloody invasion into a crusade of brave Christians marching across a lonely, dangerous landscape.

RACISM AS LINCHPIN OF THE U.S. NATIONAL IDENTITY

A crucial embellishment of the origin myth and key element of the national identity has been the myth of the frontier, analyzed in Richard Slotkin's *Gunfighter Nation,* the last volume of a fascinating trilogy. He describes Theodore Roosevelt's belief that the West was won thanks to American arms, "the means by which progress and nationality will be achieved." That success, Roosevelt continued, "depends on the heroism of men who impose on the course of events the latent virtues of their 'race.'" Roosevelt saw conflict on the frontier producing a species of virile "fighters and breeders" who would eventually generate a new leadership class. Militarism thus went hand in hand with the racialization of history's protagonists.

No slouch as an imperialist, Roosevelt soon took the frontier myth abroad, seeing Asians as Apaches and the Philippines as Sam Houston's Texas in the process of being seized from Mexico. For Roosevelt, Slotkin writes, "racial violence [was] the principle around which both individual character and social organization develop." Such ideas have not remained totally unchallenged by U.S. historians, nor was the frontier myth always applied in totally simplistic ways by Hollywood and other media. (The outlaw, for example, is a complicated figure, both good and bad.) Still, the frontier myth traditionally spins together virtue and violence, morality and war, in a convoluted, Calvinist web. That tortured embrace defines an essence of the so-called American character—the national identity—to this day.

The frontier myth embodied the nineteenth-century concept of Manifest Destiny, a doctrine that served to justify expansionist violence by means of intrinsic racial superiority. Manifest Destiny saw Yankee conquest as the inevitable result of 20 a confrontation between enterprise and progress (white) versus passivity and backwardness (Indian, Mexican). "Manifest" meant "God-given," and the whole doctrine is profoundly rooted in religious conviction going back to the earliest colonial times. In his short, powerful book *Manifest Destiny: American Expansion and the Empire of Right,* Professor Anders Stephanson tells how the Puritans reinvented the Jewish notion of chosenness and applied it to this hemisphere so that territorial expansion became God's will. . . .

MANIFEST DESTINY DIES HARD

The concept of Manifest Destiny, with its assertion of racial superiority sustained by military power, has defined U.S. identity for 150 years. Only the Vietnam War brought a serious challenge to that concept of almightiness. Bitter debate, moral anguish, images of My Lai and the prospect of military defeat for the first time in U.S. history all suggested that the long-standing marriage of virtue and violence might soon be on the rocks. In the final years of the war the words leaped to mind one day: this country is having a national nervous breakdown.

Perhaps this is why the Vietnam War continues to arouse passions today. Some who are willing to call the war "a mistake" still shy away from recognizing its immorality or even accepting it as a defeat. A few Americans have the courage to conclude from the Vietnam War that we should abandon the idea that our identity rests on being the world's richest, most powerful and indeed *best* nation. Is it possible that the so-called Vietnam syndrome might signal liberation from a crippling self-definition? Is it possible the long-standing belief that "American exceptionalism" had made freedom possible might be rejected someday?

The Vietnam syndrome is partly rooted in the fact that, although other societies have also been based on colonialism and slavery, ours seems to have an insatiable need to be the "good guys" on the world stage. That need must lie at least partially in a Protestant dualism that defines existence in terms of opposites, so that if you are not "good" you are bad, if not "white" then Black, and so on. Whatever the cause, the need to be seen as virtuous, compared to someone else's evil, haunts U.S. domestic and foreign policy. Where on earth would we be without Saddam Hussein, Qaddafi, and that all-time favorite of gringo demonizers, Fidel Castro? Gee whiz, how would we know what an American really is?

Today's origin myth and the resulting concept of national identity make for an intellectual prison where it is dangerous to ask big questions about this society's superiority. When otherwise decent people are trapped in such a powerful desire not to feel guilty, self-deception becomes unavoidable. To cease our present falsification of collective memory should, and could, open the doors of that prison. When together we cease equating whiteness with Americanness, a new day can dawn. As David Roediger, the social historian, has said, "[Whiteness] is the empty and therefore terrifying attempt to build an identity on what one isn't, and on whom one can hold back."

Redefining the U.S. origin narrative, and with it this country's national identity, 25 could prove liberating for our collective psyche. It does not mean Euro-Americans should wallow individually in guilt. It does mean accepting collective responsibility to deal with the implications of our real origin. A few apologies, for example, might be a step in the right direction. In 1997, the idea was floated in Congress to apologize for slavery; it encountered opposition from all sides. But to reject the notion because corrective action, not an apology, is needed misses the point. Having defined itself as the all-time best country in the world, the United States fiercely denies the need to make a serious, official apology for anything. . . . To press for any serious, official apology does imply a new origin narrative, a new self-image, an ideological sea change.

Accepting the implications of a different narrative could also shed light on today's struggles. In the affirmative-action struggle, for example, opponents have said that that policy is no longer needed because racism ended with the Civil Rights Movement. But if we look at slavery as a fundamental pillar of this nation, going back centuries, it becomes obvious that racism could not have been ended by 30 years of mild reforms. If we see how the myth of the frontier idealized the white male adventurer as the central hero of national history, with the woman as sunbonneted helpmate, then we might better understand the dehumanized ways in which women have continued to be treated. A more truthful origin narrative could also help break down divisions among peoples of color by revealing common experiences and histories of cooperation.

A new origin narrative and national identity could help pave the way to a more livable society for us all. A society based on cooperation rather than competition, on the idea that all living creatures are interdependent and that humanity's goal should be balance. Such were the values of many original Americans, deemed "savages." Similar gifts are waiting from other despised peoples and traditions. We might well start by recognizing that "America" is the name of an entire hemisphere, rich in a stunning variety of histories, cultures and peoples—not just one country.

The choice seems clear, if not easy. We can go on living in a state of massive denial, affirming this nation's superiority and virtue simply because we need to believe in it. We can choose to believe the destiny of the United States is still manifest: global domination. Or we can seek a transformative vision that carries us forward, not backward. We can seek an origin narrative that lays the groundwork for a multicultural, multinational identity centered on the goals of social equity and democracy. We do have choices.

There is little time for nostalgia. Dick and Jane never were "America," they were only one part of one community in one part of one country in one part of one continent. Yet we have let their image define our entire society and its values. Will the future be marked by ongoing denial or by steps toward a new vision in which White Supremacy no longer determines reality? When on earth will we transcend the assumptions that imprison our minds?

At times you can hear the clock ticking.   30

Analysis of the Writers' Positions

The first step in resolving conflict is to understand what the parties are claiming and why. Below is our paraphrase of Kimball's and Martínez's arguments.

Kimball's Position He opposes multiculturalism and wants to preserve an American identity based in Anglo-Protestant culture.

> *Thesis:* Multiculturalism weakens America by keeping people of different cultures from assimilating to the core values of America's Anglo-Protestant identity.
>
> > *Reason:* Educational multiculturalism degrades traditional American values and ignores mainstream history and culture.
> >
> > > *Evidence:* Opinions of Samuel Huntington and Arthur Schlesinger, Jr. Examples of college students' ignorance about history. Maya Angelou's speech at Clinton's inauguration.
> >
> > *Reason:* Multiculturalism "weakens the social bond" by denying that immigrants need to assimilate to the language and values of the dominant culture.
> >
> > > *Evidence:* Rise of hyphenization. Rise of non-English-speaking communities. Calls for affirmative action, which violates the idea of success based on merit.
> >
> > *Reason:* America should be defined by one culture and nationality, not many.
> >
> > > *Evidence:* Quotations from de Crèvecoeur on the "new race of men." Quotations from Theodore Roosevelt, John Jay, Thomas Jefferson, Benjamin Franklin. The 1795 oath of allegiance for citizenship.
> >
> > *Reason:* The single, unifying identity of America should be based in Anglo-Saxon Protestant Christianity.
> >
> > > *Evidence:* Religious beliefs of original settlers. Historian Himmelfarb on American virtue as deeply rooted in religion. Quotes from Founding Fathers on relation of virtue to religion. Huntington on the need for national identity based in religion.

Martínez's Position She wants to replace traditional Anglo-American identity with a multicultural one.

> *Thesis:* The United States needs to discard its "white supremacist" identity.
>
> > *Reason:* It's based on racism, genocide, and imperialist expansion.
> >
> > > *Evidence:* The "origin myth" in common accounts of U.S. history. The historical record of slavery, takeover of Native American land, wars of expansion. Primary sources such as Presidents Grant and Polk. Theodore Roosevelt's statements about racial superiority. Historian Richard Slotkin's analysis of frontier myth.

Reason: It's based on a false sense of moral superiority and favor in the eyes of God.

Evidence: Professor Anders Stephanson on the concept of Manifest Destiny. Protestant moral dualism—seeing the world in terms of good and evil. Social historian David Roediger on the Anglo sense of superiority.

Reason: America will be a more fair and democratic country if we revise our identity to acknowledge Anglo faults and adopt the values of non-Anglo cultures.

Evidence: Racism and sexism not eliminated. The valuable gifts of other cultures, such as cooperation over competition.

◎◎ FOLLOWING THROUGH

If you and some of your classmates have written arguments taking opposing views on the same issue, prepare briefs of your respective positions to share with one another. (You might also create briefs of your opponents' positions to see how well you have understood one another's written arguments.)

Alternatively, write briefs summarizing the opposing positions offered in several published arguments as a first step toward mediating these viewpoints. •

Locating the Areas of Agreement and Disagreement

Differences over Facts

Most conflicts result from interpreting facts differently rather than disagreement about the facts themselves. For example, in the arguments of Kimball and Martínez, we see agreement on many factual points:

- Whites are becoming the minority in some parts of the United States.
- Assimilation has meant conformity to a culture defined by Anglo-Protestant values.
- Christianity has played a large role in America's sense of identity.

If a mediator finds disagreement over facts, he or she needs to look into it and provide evidence from credible sources that would resolve these details. Or the problem might be that one or both sides are arguing without enough information. The mediator can help here by doing the needed research or advising the parties to find out more about what they are arguing over. If they know each other personally, doing the research jointly is a good idea.

◎◎ FOLLOWING THROUGH

For the arguments you are mediating, make a list of facts that the authors both accept. Note facts offered by one side but denied or not considered by the other. Where your authors don't agree on the facts, do research to decide how valid the facts cited on both sides are. Explain the discrepancies. If your class is mediating the same conflict, compare your findings. •

Differences over Interests, Values, and Interpretations

Facts alone cannot resolve entrenched disputes such as the debate over multiculturalism. For example, a history lesson about white settlers' treatment of Native Americans would not change Kimball's mind. Nor would a lesson in Enlightenment philosophy alter what Martínez thinks. When we attempt to mediate, *we have to look into why people hold the positions they do.* Like persuasion, mediation looks at the contexts of a dispute.

To identify these differences, we can ask questions similar to those that are useful in persuasion for identifying what divides us from our audience (see "Questions for Understanding Difference," page 304). We apply below the questions about difference to Kimball's and Martínez's positions.

Is the Difference a Matter of Assumptions? Every argument has assumptions—unstated assertions that the audience must share to find the reasoning valid and persuasive. Kimball assumes that Anglo-Protestant culture is moral; therefore, he does not show how Christianity has made America a moral nation. Martínez disputes the very assumption that America is moral. But she also makes assumptions. She assumes that the "origin narrative" of the white man's conquest and exploitation is the sole basis for the nation's past and present identity. This assumption allows her to argue that the culture of the United States is simply white supremacist.

These two assumptions show polarized thinking—one assumes that Anglo-Protestant values are all good, the other that Anglo-Protestant values are all evil. Such polarized assumptions are common in disputes because, as philosopher of ethics Anthony Weston explains, we polarize not just to simplify but to justify: "We polarize . . . to be able to picture ourselves as totally justified, totally right, and the 'other side' as totally unjustified and wrong."[2] It's precisely this tactic that mediation must resist and overcome.

Is the Difference a Matter of Principle? By principles, we mean informal rules that guide our actions, like the "rule" in sales: "The customer is always right." Kimball's principle is patriotism: Americans should be undivided in loyalty and allegiance to the United States. Martínez's principle is fairness and justice for all, which means rewriting the origin narrative, admitting past mistakes, and recognizing the richness and morality of all the cultures that make up America. A mediator might ask: Can we be patriotic *and* self-critical? Must we repudiate the past entirely to fashion a new national identity?

Is the Difference a Matter of Values or Priorities? The principles just discussed reflect differing priorities. In the post–9/11 world, Kimball is concerned with America's strength on the world stage, whereas Martínez concentrates more on America's compassion in its domestic policies. This is a significant difference because Martínez supports programs like affirmative action and

---

[2]Anthony Weston, *A Practical Companion to Ethics* (New York: Oxford, 2005) 50.

Questions for Understanding Difference

1. Is the difference a matter of *assumptions?* As we discussed in Chapter 3 on the Toulmin method of analysis and in Chapter 7 on inquiry, all arguments are based on some assumptions.

2. Is the difference a matter of *principle?* Are some parties to the dispute following different principles, or general rules, from others?

3. Is the difference a matter of *values* or a matter of having the same values but giving them different *priorities?*

4. Is the difference a matter of *ends* or *means?* That is, do people want to achieve different goals, or do they have the same goals in mind but disagree on the means to achieve them?

5. Is the difference a matter of *interpretation?*

6. Is the difference a matter of *implications* or *consequences?*

7. Is the difference a result of *personal background, basic human needs,* or *emotions?*

To our list of questions about difference in persuasive writing, we add this last question because mediators must look not just at the arguments but also at the disputants as people with histories and feelings. It is not realistic to think that human problems can be solved without taking human factors into consideration. Mediators must take into account such basic human needs as personal security, economic well-being, and a sense of belonging, recognition, and people's control over their own lives. If you are mediating among printed texts, you must use the texts themselves as evidence of these human factors.

multicultural education, the very policies Kimball claims weaken our social bonds (paragraph 10). Once we see this difference, we can see the dispute in the context of liberal and conservative opinion in general. Kimball is arguing for a national identity acceptable to conservatives, Martínez for one acceptable to liberals. But what we need, obviously, is something that can cross this divide and appeal to all or most Americans.

Is the Difference a Matter of Ends or Means?   Martínez and Kimball have different ends in mind, so they also have different means to achieve the ends. For Martínez, a multicultural identity is the means to a more fair and livable society for all. For Kimball, a common identity in Anglo-Protestant culture is the means to remaining "the most powerful nation the world has ever seen." A mediator could reasonably ask: Couldn't we have both? Couldn't the United States be a powerful nation that is also fair and livable for all its citizens?

Is the Difference a Matter of Implications or Consequences?   The mediator has to consider what each side fears will happen if the other side prevails. Kimball fears that multiculturalism will lead Americans to self-doubt, loss of confidence. He also forecasts a large population of "permanent second-class citizens" if subgroups of the population do not assimilate. Martínez fears continuing oppression of minorities if our national self-conception doesn't change to fit our country's actual diversity. The mediator must acknowledge the fears of both sides while not permitting either to go unquestioned. Fear is a powerful motivator that must be confronted squarely.

Is the Difference a Matter of Interpretation? A major disagreement here is over how to interpret the values of Anglo-Protestant culture. To Kimball, these values are "individual liberty and public virtue" (paragraph 8), "the rule of law" (paragraph 14), "respect for individual rights" (paragraph 14), devotion to God and a strong work ethic (paragraph 14). In contrast, Martínez interprets Anglo-Protestant values as a belief in whites' moral superiority and favor in the eyes of God (paragraph 20) that enabled them to see their own acts of "genocide, enslavement, and imperialist expansion" (paragraph 12) as morally acceptable and even heroic (paragraph 19). These interpretations stem from the different backgrounds of the writers, which we consider next.

Is the Difference a Matter of Personal Background, Basic Human Needs, or Emotions? When mediating between positions in written arguments such as these, it's a good idea to go to the library or an online source for biographical information about the authors. It will pay off with insight into why they disagree.

Kimball and Martínez obviously come from very different backgrounds that are representative of others who hold the same positions they do. For example, as a white male with the financial means to have attended Yale, Kimball represents the group that has benefited most from the traditional national identity. His conservative views have pitted him against liberal academics and social activists.

Martínez identifies herself as a Chicana, an American woman of Mexican descent (her father was an immigrant). She is an activist for social justice and heads the Institute for MultiRacial Justice in San Francisco and has taught women's studies and ethnic studies in the California State University system. She knows the burden of discrimination from personal experience and from her work and research. As a proponent of bilingual and multicultural education, she sees people like Kimball as the opposition.

◎◎ FOLLOWING THROUGH

If you are mediating among printed arguments, write an analysis based on applying the questions in the Best Practices box on page 304 to two or more arguments. You could write out your analysis in list form, as we did in analyzing the differences between Kimball and Martínez, or you could treat it as an exploratory essay.

As a creative variation for your analysis, write a dialogue with yourself as mediator, posing questions to each of the opposing parties. Have each side respond to your questions just as we demonstrated in our sample dialogue on pages 182–183.

Finding Creative Solutions: Exploring Common Ground

Using critical thinking to mediate means looking closely at what people want and why they want it. It also means seeing the dispute in larger contexts. For example, the dispute over national identity is part of a larger debate between liberals and conservatives over politics, social policy, and education.

Mediation won't and shouldn't try to reach everyone. Some people hold extreme views that reason cannot touch. An example would be the professor Kimball cites who predicts that the southwestern United States and northern Mexico will eventually become a new and separate country. Mediation between this person and Kimball is about as likely as President Bush and Osama bin Laden having dinner together. But mediators can bring reasonable people closer together by trying to arrive at creative solutions that appeal to some of the interests and values of all parties.

Taking a simple example of conflicting interests, consider the family divided about their vacation destination, mountains or seashore. If the seashore lovers go for swimming and sunbathing and the mountain enthusiasts hiking and mountain biking, why not look for places that have both—mountains *and* seashore?

In complex conflicts, such as the one over multiculturalism and national identity, creative solutions are possible if people can move beyond polarized to cooperative thinking. The ethicist Anthony Weston suggests trying to see conflict in terms of what each side is right about. He says, "If both sides (or all sides) are to some extent right, then we need to try to honor what is right in each of them."[3]

Weston points to the debate over saving owls in old-growth forests versus logging interests that employ people. Preserving the environment and endangered species is good, but so is saving jobs. If jobs could be created that use wood in craft-based ways, people could make a living without destroying massive amounts of timber. This solution is possible if the parties cooperate—but not if greedy corporations are deadlocked with radical environmentalists, neither willing to concede anything or give an inch.

Mediators should aim for "win-win" solutions, which resolve conflict by dissolving it. The challenge for the mediator is keeping the high ground and looking for the good and reasonable in what each side wants. Perfect neutrality isn't necessary and mediators do have to expose bad thinking or factual errors, but they must not fall into advocating one side over the other.

---

[3]Weston, *Practical Companion* 56.

Exploring Common Ground in the Debate over National Identity

To find integrative solutions for the national identity–multiculturalism dispute, we analyzed our list of questions for understanding difference to find interests and values Kimball and Martínez might share or be persuaded to share. Here's what we found.

Both want Americans to know their history. Kimball is right. It's a disgrace that college students can't recognize a famous phrase from the Gettysburg Address. But they need to know that *and* the relevance of Harriet Tubman to those words. Martínez is right also that history should not be propaganda for one view of events. The history of all nations is a mix of good and bad.

Neither Kimball nor Martínez wants a large population of second-class citizens, living in isolated poverty, not speaking English, not seeing themselves as Americans, and not having a say in the democratic process. Martínez's multiculturalism would "break down divisions among peoples of color by revealing common experiences and histories of cooperation" with the goal of "social equity and democracy." She would be more likely, however, to achieve her goal if she considered white men and women *as participants* in this multicultural discussion. To exclude whites keeps people of color where they too often are—on the margins, left out. Kimball needs to be reminded that failure to assimilate is not typically a choice. First-generation immigrants usually learn little English partly because they work several jobs to survive. Living in segregated neighborhoods with others like them provides security and support and can make success easier for their children. Studies show that children who assimilate to the culture of America's poor neighborhoods do less well in school than those whose parents raise them in traditional ways. As in the past, assimilation works only when educational and economic opportunities exist. Kimball needs to look into solutions to the problem of poverty among immigrants.

There is agreement too on the need for a national identity. Martínez calls for "a new identity," implying that we need something deep to define us as Americans. But asking what culture should provide it is the wrong question. Concentrating on the values themselves will help everyone see that most values are shared across races and cultures. For example, Martínez takes Anglo-Protestant culture as competitive, not cooperative. While competition drives capitalism, we need to recall that early Protestant settlers also valued community. The Puritans tried to establish utopian communities devoted to charity; John Winthrop almost went bankrupt making himself an example of generosity to his neighbors. Kimball's "Protestant" work ethic can be found in every ethnic group—for example, in the predominantly Catholic Mexican laborers who do backbreaking work in agriculture and construction. Instead of getting hung up on which religion or ethnic group provided the values, those arguing for a strong American identity can agree on the values themselves: justice, equality, democracy, productivity, charity toward one another, respect for human rights, and love of country.

Finally, what agreement could be reached about assimilation? What does it mean to become "Americanized"? Kimball suggests that immigrants follow Justice Louis Brandeis's advice—adopting "the clothes, the manners, and the customs generally prevailing here." But would such advice mean that what "prevails" here is based in Protestantism and Anglo-Saxon culture? A more realistic idea of "Americanization" comes from our third writer, Bharati Mukherjee, who suggests in her mediatory essay that "assimilation" is a two-way transformation, with immigrants and mainstream culture interacting, influencing each other. Such a conception *requires* both the preservation of tradition Kimball wants and the respect for diversity Martínez wants.

Mediating any controversy involves opening up the thinking of all parties by questioning assumptions, checking facts, and searching for what pulls together rather than tears apart.

◎◎ FOLLOWING THROUGH

Either in list form or as an informal exploratory essay, explore possible areas of agreement between the various positions you have been analyzing. End your list or essay with a summary of a position that all sides might be willing to acknowledge has some validity.   •

THE MEDIATORY ESSAY

The natural human tendency in argument is to polarize—to see conflict as simply "us" versus "them," like children choosing up sides in a game. Modern media, often striving only for ratings by playing up the dramatic and the sensational, can make matters worse by featuring representatives of extreme positions locked in verbal combat. The result is rarely arguments intended to persuade but rather arguments aimed at solidifying the support of those already in agreement with one or the other sides.

That's why mediation is necessary and matters so much as a way of moving beyond polarized thinking. An example of mediation in the multiculturalism debate appears below. The essay's author is the novelist Bharati Mukherjee. She was born into a wealthy family in Calcutta but became an American citizen. She is now Distinguished Professor of English at the University of California at Berkeley.

She has been faulted by some Indians and other South Asians for depicting India and its culture too harshly in her fiction; her characters are immigrants who embrace, rather than resist, American culture. These critics, whom Mukherjee denounces near the end of her essay, are part of the academic multiculturalists Kimball describes as anti-American. Obviously, Mukherjee is not writing to them nor to "rabid Eurocentrists" on the other side, people she mentions who want to close our borders and stop even legal immigration. She's writing to people who accept either Kimball's position—

preserve the Euro-Protestant "core" of American identity—or Martínez's—create a new national identity based on the multicultural mosaic.

There's no single model for a mediatory essay. In this case, Mukherjee's essay mediates by making a case against both radical extremes, one way of seeking to bring people together on the remaining middle ground.

Beyond Multiculturalism:
A Two-Way Transformation

BHARATI MUKHERJEE

The United States exists as a sovereign nation with its officially stated Constitution, its economic and foreign policies, its demarcated, patrolled boundaries. "America," however, exists as image or idea, as dream or nightmare, as romance or plague, constructed by discrete individual fantasies, and shaded by collective paranoias and mythologies.

I am a naturalized U.S. citizen with a certificate of citizenship; more importantly, I am an American for whom "America" is the stage for the drama of self-transformation. I see American culture as a culture of dreamers, who believe material shape (which is not the same as materialism) can be given to dreams. They believe that one's station in life—poverty, education, family background—does not determine one's fate. They believe in the reversal of omens; early failures do not spell inevitable disaster. Outsiders can triumph on merit. All of this happens against the backdrop of the familiar vicissitudes of American life.

I first came to the United States—to the state of Iowa, to be precise—on a late summer evening nearly thirty-three years ago. I flew into a placid, verdant airport in Iowa City on a commercial airliner, ready to fulfill the goals written out in a large, lined notebook for me by my guiltlessly patriarchal father. Those goals were unambiguous: I was to spend two years studying Creative Writing at Paul Engle's unique Writers Workshop; then I was to marry the perfect Bengali bridegroom selected by my father and live out the rest of a contented, predictable life in the city of my birth, Calcutta. In 1961, I was a shy, pliant, well-mannered, dutiful young daughter from a very privileged, traditional, mainstream Hindu family that believed women should be protected and provided for by their fathers, husbands, sons, and it did not once occur to me that I might have goals of my own, quite distinct from those specified for me by my father. I certainly did not anticipate then that, over the next three decades, Iowans—who seemed to me so racially and culturally homogeneous—would be forced to shudder through the violent paroxysms of a collective identity in crisis.

When I was growing up in Calcutta in the fifties, I heard no talk of "identity crisis"—communal or individual. The concept itself—of a person not knowing who she or he was—was unimaginable in a hierarchical, classification-obsessed society. One's identity was absolutely fixed, derived from religion, caste, patrimony, and mother tongue. A Hindu Indian's last name was designed to announce his or her forefathers' caste and place of origin. A Mukherjee could *only* be a Brahmin from Bengal. Indian tradition forbade inter-caste, inter-language, inter-ethnic marriages.

Bengali tradition discouraged even emigration; to remove oneself from Bengal was to "pollute" true culture.

Until the age of eight, I lived in a house crowded with forty or fifty relatives. We 5 lived together because we were "family," bonded by kinship, though kinship was interpreted in flexible enough terms to include, when necessary, men, women, children who came from the same *desh*—which is the Bengali word for "homeland"—as had my father and grandfather. I was who I was because I was Dr. Sudhir Lal Mukherjee's daughter, because I was a Hindu Brahmin, because I was Bengali-speaking, and because my *desh* was an East Bengal village called Faridpur. I was encouraged to think of myself as indistinguishable from my dozen girl cousins. Identity was viscerally connected with ancestral soil and family origins. I was first a Mukherjee, then a Bengali Brahmin, and only then an Indian.

Deep down I knew, of course, that I was not quite like my girl cousins. Deeper down, I was sure that pride in the purity of one's culture has a sinister underside. As a child I had witnessed bloody religious riots between Muslims and Hindus, and violent language riots between Bengalis and Biharis. People kill for culture, and die of hunger. Language, race, religion, blood, myth, history, national codes, and manners have all been used, in India, in the United States, are being used in Bosnia and Rwanda even today, to enforce terror, to "otherize," to murder.

I do not know what compelled my strong-willed and overprotective father to risk sending us, his three daughters, to school in the United States, a country he had not visited. In Calcutta, he had insisted on sheltering us from danger and temptation by sending us to girls-only schools, and by providing us with chaperones, chauffeurs, and bodyguards.

The Writers Workshop in a quonset hut in Iowa City was my first experience of coeducation. And after not too long, I fell in love with a fellow student named Clark Blaise, an American of Canadian origin, and impulsively married him during a lunch break in a lawyer's office above a coffeeshop.

That impulsive act cut me off forever from the rules and ways of upper-middle-class life in Bengal, and hurled me precipitously into a New World life of scary improvisations and heady explorations. Until my lunchtime wedding, I had seen myself as an Indian foreign student, a transient in the United States. The five-minute ceremony in the lawyer's office had changed me into a permanent transient.

Over the last three decades the important lesson that I have learned is that in this 10 era of massive diasporic movements, honorable survival requires resilience, curiosity, and compassion, a letting go of rigid ideals about the purity of inherited culture.

The first ten years into marriage, years spent mostly in my husband's *desh* of Canada, I thought myself an expatriate Bengali permanently stranded in North America because of a power surge of destiny or of desire. My first novel, *The Tiger's Daughter*, embodies the loneliness I felt but could not acknowledge, even to myself, as I negotiated the no-man's-land between the country of my past and the continent of my present. Shaped by memory, textured with nostalgia for a class and culture I had abandoned, this novel quite naturally became my expression of the *expatriate consciousness*.

It took me a decade of painful introspection to put the smothering tyranny of nostalgia into perspective, and to make the transition from expatriate to immigrant. I have found my way back to the United States after a fourteen-year stay in Canada. The transition from foreign student to U.S. citizen, from detached onlooker to committed immigrant, has not been easy.

The years in Canada were particularly harsh. Canada is a country that officially—and proudly—resists the policy and process of cultural fusion. For all its smug rhetoric about "cultural mosaic," Canada refuses to renovate its national self-image to include its changing complexion. It is a New World country with Old World concepts of a fixed, exclusivist national identity. And all through the seventies when I lived there, it was a country without a Bill of Rights or its own Constitution. Canadian official rhetoric designated me, as a citizen of non-European origin, one of the "visible minority" who, even though I spoke the Canadian national languages of English and French, was straining "the absorptive capacity" of Canada. Canadians of color were routinely treated as "not real" Canadians. In fact, when a terrorist bomb, planted in an Air India jet on Canadian soil, blew up after leaving Montreal, killing 329 passengers, 90 percent of whom were Canadians of Indian origin, the prime minister of Canada at the time, Brian Mulroney, cabled the Indian prime minister to offer Canada's condolences for India's loss, exposing the Eurocentricity of the "mosaic" policy of immigration.

In private conversations, some Canadian ambassadors and External Affairs officials have admitted to me that the creation of the Ministry of Multiculturism in the seventies was less an instrument for cultural tolerance, and more a vote-getting strategy to pacify ethnic European constituents who were alienated by the rise of Quebec separatism and the simultaneous increase of non-white immigrants.

The years of race-related harassments in a Canada without a Constitution have 15 politicized me, and deepened my love of the ideals embedded in the American Bill of Rights.

I take my American citizenship very seriously. I am a voluntary immigrant. I am not an economic refugee, and not a seeker of political asylum. I am an American by choice, and not by the simple accident of birth. I have made emotional, social, and political commitments to this country. I have earned the right to think of myself as an American.

But in this blood-splattered decade, questions such as who is an American and what is American culture are being posed with belligerence and being answered with violence. We are witnessing an increase in physical, too often fatal, assaults on Asian Americans. An increase in systematic "dot-busting" of Indo-Americans in New Jersey, xenophobic immigrant-baiting in California, minority-on-minority violence during the south-central Los Angeles revolution.

America's complexion is browning daily. Journalists' surveys have established that whites are losing their clear majority status in some states, and have already lost it in New York and California. A recent *Time* magazine poll indicated that 60 percent of Americans favor limiting *legal* immigration. Eighty percent of Americans polled favor curbing the entry of undocumented aliens. U.S. borders are too extensive and too porous to be adequately policed. Immigration, by documented and undocumented aliens, is less affected by the U.S. Immigration and Naturalization Service, and more by wars, ethnic genocides, famines in the emigrant's own country.

Every sovereign nation has a right to formulate its immigration policy. In this decade of continual, large-scale diasporic movements, it is imperative that we come to some agreement about who "we" are now that the community includes old-timers, newcomers, many races, languages, and religions; about what our expectations of happiness and strategies for its pursuit are; and what our goals are for the nation.

Scapegoating of immigrants has been the politicians' easy instant remedy. Hate 20 speeches fill auditoria, and bring in megabucks for those demagogues willing to profit from stirring up racial animosity.

The hysteria against newcomers is only minimally generated by the downturn in our economy. The panic, I suspect, is unleashed by a fear of the "other," the fear of what Daniel Stein, executive director of the Federation for American Immigration Reform, and a champion of closed borders, is quoted as having termed "cultural transmogrification."

The debate about American culture has to date been monopolized by rabid Eurocentrists and ethnocentrists; the rhetoric has been flamboyantly divisive, pitting a phantom "us" against a demonized "them." I am here to launch a new discourse, to reconstitute the hostile, biology-derived "us" versus "them" communities into a new *consensual* community of "we."

All countries view themselves by their ideals. Indians idealize, as well they should, the cultural continuum, the inherent value system of India, and are properly incensed when foreigners see nothing but poverty, intolerance, ignorance, strife, and injustice. Americans see themselves as the embodiments of liberty, openness, and individualism, even when the world judges them for drugs, crime, violence, bigotry, militarism, and homelessness. I was in Singapore when the media was very vocal about the case of an American teenager sentenced to caning for having allegedly vandalized cars. The overwhelming local sentiment was that caning Michael Fay would deter local youths from being tempted into "Americanization," meaning into gleefully breaking the law.

Conversely, in Tavares, Florida, an ardently patriotic school board has legislated that middle school teachers be required to instruct their students that American culture—meaning European-American culture—is inherently "superior to other foreign or historic cultures." The sinister, or at least misguided, implication is that American culture has not been affected by the American Indian, African American, Latin American, and Asian American segments of its population.

The idea of "America" as a nation has been set up in opposition to the tenet 25 that a nation is a collection of like-looking, like-speaking, like-worshiping people. Our nation is unique in human history. We have seen very recently, in a Germany plagued by anti-foreigner frenzy, how violently destabilizing the traditional concept of nation can be. In Europe, each country is, in a sense, a tribal homeland. Therefore, the primary criterion for nationhood in Europe is homogeneity of culture, and race, and religion. And that has contributed to blood-soaked balkanization in the former Yugoslavia and the former Soviet Union.

All European Americans, or their pioneering ancestors, gave up an easy homogeneity in their original countries for a new idea of Utopia. What we have going for us in the 1990s is the exciting chance to share in the making of a new American culture, rather than the coerced acceptance of either the failed nineteenth-century model of "melting pot" or the Canadian model of the "multicultural mosaic."

The "mosaic" implies a contiguity of self-sufficient, utterly distinct culture. "Multiculturism" has come to imply the existence of a central culture, ringed by peripheral cultures. The sinister fallout of official multiculturalism and of professional multiculturists is the establishment of one culture as the norm and the rest as aberrations. Multiculturism emphasizes the differences between racial heritages. This emphasis on the differences has too often led to the dehumanization of the different. Dehumanization leads to discrimination. And discrimination can ultimately lead to genocide.

We need to alert ourselves to the limitations and the dangers of those discourses that reinforce an "us" versus "them" mentality. We need to protest any official rhetoric or demagoguery that marginalizes on a race-related and/or religion-related basis any segment of our society. I want to discourage the retention of cultural memory if the aim of that retention is cultural balkanization. I want to sensitize you to think of culture and nationhood *not* as an uneasy aggregate of antagonistic "them" and "us," but as a constantly re-forming, transmogrifying "we."

In this diasporic age, one's biological identity may not be the only one. Erosions and accretions come with the act of emigration. The experiences of violent unhousing from a biological "homeland" and rehousing in an adopted "homeland" that is not always welcoming to its dark-complected citizens have tested me as a person, and made me the writer I am today.

I choose to describe myself on my own terms, that is, as an American without 30 hyphens. It is to sabotage the politics of hate and the campaigns of revenge spawned by Eurocentric patriots on the one hand and the professional multiculturists on the other, that I describe myself as an "American" rather than as an "Asian-American." Why is it that hyphenization is imposed only on non-white Americans? And why is it that only non-white citizens are "problematized" if they choose to describe themselves on their own terms? My outspoken rejection of hyphenization is my lonely campaign to obliterate categorizing the cultural landscape into a "center" and its "peripheries." To reject hyphenization is to demand that the nation deliver the promises of the American Dream and the American Constitution to *all* its citizens. I want nothing less than to invent a new vocabulary that demands, and obtains, an equitable power-sharing for all members of the American community.

But my self-empowering refusal to be "otherized" and "objectified" has come at tremendous cost. My rejection of hyphenization has been deliberately misrepresented as "race treachery" by some India-born, urban, upper-middle-class Marxist "green card holders" with lucrative chairs on U.S. campuses. These academics strategically position themselves as self-appointed spokespersons for their ethnic communities, and as guardians of the "purity" of ethnic cultures. At the same time, though they reside permanently in the United States and participate in the capitalist economy of this nation, they publicly denounce American ideals and institutions.

They direct their rage at me because, as a U.S. citizen, I have invested in the present and the future rather than in the expatriate's imagined homeland. They condemn me because I acknowledge erosion of memory as a natural result of emigration; because I count that erosion as net gain rather than as loss; and because I celebrate racial and cultural "mongrelization." I have no respect for these expatriate fence-straddlers who, even while competing fiercely for tenure and promotion within the U.S. academic system, glibly equate all evil in the world with the United States, capitalism, colonialism, and corporate and military expansionism. I regard the artificial retentions of "pure race" and "pure culture" as dangerous, reactionary illusions fostered by the Eurocentric and the ethnocentric empire builders within the academy. I fear still more the politics of revenge preached from pulpits by some minority demagogues. . . .

As a writer, my literary agenda begins by acknowledging that America has transformed *me.* It does not end until I show that I (and the hundreds of thousands of recent immigrants like me) am minute by minute transforming America. The transformation is a two-way process; it affects both the individual and the national cultural identity. The end result of immigration, then, is this two-way transformation: that's my heartfelt message.

Others often talk of diaspora, of arrival as the end of the process. They talk of arrival in the context of loss, the loss of communal memory and the erosion of an intact ethnic culture. They use words like "erosion" and "loss" in alarmist ways. I want to talk of arrival as gain. . . .

What excites me is that we have the chance to retain those values we treasure 35 from our original cultures, but we also acknowledge that the outer forms of those values are likely to change. In the Indian American community, I see a great deal of guilt about the inability to hang on to "pure culture." Parents express rage or despair at their U.S.-born children's forgetting of, or indifference to, some aspects of Indian culture. Of those parents, I would ask: What is it we have lost if our children are acculturating into the culture in which we are living? Is it so terrible that our children are discovering or inventing homelands for themselves? Some first-generation Indo-Americans, embittered by overt anti-Asian racism and by unofficial "glass ceilings," construct a phantom more-Indian-than-Indians-in-India identity as defense against marginalization. Of them I would ask: Why not get actively involved in fighting discrimination through protests and lawsuits?

I prefer that we forge a national identity that is born of our acknowledgment of the steady de-Europeanization of the U.S. population; that constantly synthesizes—fuses—the disparate cultures of our country's residents; and that provides a new, sustaining, and unifying national creed.

Analyzing Mukherjee's Essay

Let's see what we can learn about how to appeal to audiences in mediatory essays. We'll look at *ethos* (how Mukherjee projects good character), *pathos* (how she arouses emotions favorable to her case), and *logos* (how she wins assent through good reasoning).

Ethos: Earning the Respect of Both Sides

Mediatory essays are not typically as personal as this one. But the author is in an unusual position, which makes the personal relevant. By speaking in the first person and telling her story, Mukherjee seeks the goodwill of people on both sides. She presents herself as patriotic, a foreigner who has assimilated to American ways, clearly appealing to those on Kimball's side. But she is also a "person of color," who's been "tested" by racial prejudices in the United States, clearly appealing to Martínez's side. She creates negative ethos for the radical extremists in the identity debate, depicting them as lacking morality and/or honesty. That's why she cites the violence committed by both whites and minorities, the scapegoating by politicians pandering to voter fears, the hypocrisy of professors who live well in America while denouncing its values. She associates her own position with words like *commitment, compassion, consensus, equality,* and *unity.*

By including her own experiences in India and Canada and her references to Bosnia, Rwanda, Germany, and the former Soviet Union, Mukherjee is able to place this American debate in a larger context—parts of the world in which national identity incites war and human rights violations.

Pathos: Using Emotion to Appeal to Both Sides

Appealing to the right emotions can help to move parties in conflict to the higher ground of consensus. Mukherjee displays a range of emotions, including pride, anger, and compassion. In condemning the extremes on both sides, her tone becomes heated. She uses highly charged words like *rabid, demagogues, scapegoaters, fence-straddlers,* and *reactionaries* to describe them. Her goal is to distance the members of her audience who are reasonable from those who aren't, so her word choice is appropriate and effective.

Patriotism is obviously emotional. Mukherjee's repeated declaration of devotion to her adopted country stirs audience pride. So does the contrast with India and Canada and the celebrating of individual freedom in the United States.

Her own story of arrival, nostalgia, and transformation arouses compassion and respect because it shows that assimilation is not easy. She understands the reluctance of Indian parents to let their children change. This shows her ability to empathize.

Finally, she appeals through hope and optimism. Twice she describes the consensus she proposes as *exciting*—and also fresh, new, vital, alive—in contrast to the rigid and inflexible ethnic purists.

Logos: Integrating Values of Both Sides

Mukherjee's thesis is that the opposing sides in the national identity debate are two sides of the wrong coin: the mistaken regard for ethnic purity. Making an issue of one's ethnicity, whether it be Anglo, Chicano, Indian-American, or whatever, is not a means to harmony and equality. Instead, America needs a unifying national identity that blends the ever-changing mix of races and cultures that make up our population.

Mukherjee offers reasons to oppose ethnic "purity":

Violence and wars result when people divide according to ethnic and religious differences. It creates an "us" versus "them" mentality.

The multicultural Canadian program created second-class, marginal populations.

Hyphenization in America makes a problem out of non-whites in the population.

We said that mediation looks for the good in each side and tries to show what they have in common. Mukherjee shows that her solution offers gains for both sides, a "win-win" situation. She concedes that her solution would mean some loss of "cultural memory" for immigrants, but these losses are offset by the following gains:

The United States would be closer to the strong and unified nation that Kimball wants because *everyone's* contributions would be appreciated.

The cultural barriers between minorities would break down, as Martínez wants. This would entail speaking to each other in English, but being free to maintain diverse cultures at home.

The barriers between "Americans" and hyphenated Americans would break down, as both Kimball and Martínez want. In other words, there would be assimilation, as Kimball wants, but not assimilation to one culture, which Martínez strongly resists.

By removing the need to prove one's own culture superior, we could all recognize the faults in our past as well as the good things. We would have no schools teaching either the superiority or the inferiority of any culture.

Emphasizing citizenship instead of ethnicity is a way of standing up for and demanding equal rights and equal opportunity, helping to bring about the social justice and equality Martínez seeks.

The new identity would be "sustaining," avoiding future conflicts because it would adapt to change.

Mukherjee's essay mediates by showing that a definition of America based on either one ethnic culture or many ethnic cultures is not satisfactory. By dropping ethnicity as a prime concern, both sides can be better off and freer in pursuit of happiness and success.

FOLLOWING THROUGH

Look over the essays by Elizabeth Martínez and Roger Kimball. Do you think either of them would find Bharati Mukherjee's essay persuasive? What does Mukherjee say that might cause either of them to relax their positions about American identity? Do you think any further information might help to bring either side to Mukherjee's consensus position? For example, Kimball mentions the "Letter from an American Farmer" by de Crèvecoeur, who describes Americans as a new "race" of blended nationalities, leaving behind their ties and allegiances to former lands. How is Crèvecouer's idea of the "new race" similar to Mukherjee's?   •

Writing a Mediatory Essay

Prewriting

If you have been mediating the positions of two or more groups of classmates or two or more authors of published arguments, you may be assigned to write a mediatory essay in which you argue for a compromise position, appealing to an audience of people on all sides. In preparing to write such an essay, you should work through the steps of mediation as described on pages 302–305. In your writer's notebook, prepare briefs of the various conflicting positions, and note areas of disagreement; think hard about the differing interests of the conflicting parties, and respond to the questions about difference on page 304.

If possible, give some thought to each party's background—age, race, gender, and so forth—and how it might contribute to his or her viewpoint on the issue. For example, in a debate about whether *Huckleberry Finn* should be taught and read aloud in U.S. high schools, an African-American parent whose child is the only minority student in her English class might well have a different perspective from that of a white teacher. Can the white teacher be made to understand the embarrassment that a sole black child might feel when the white characters speak with derision about "niggers"?

In your writer's notebook, describe the conflict in its full complexity, not just its polar opposites. For example, considering the controversy over *Huckleberry Finn,* you might find some arguments in favor of teaching it anytime, others opposed to teaching it at all, others suggesting that it be an optional text for reading outside of class, and still others proposing that it be taught only in twelfth grade, when students are mature enough to understand Twain's satire. Try to find the good values in each position: a desire to teach the classics of American literature for what they tell us about the human condition and our country's history and values; a desire to promote respect for African-American students; a desire to ensure a comfortable learning climate for all students; and so on. You may be able to see that people's real interests are not as far apart as they might seem. You may be able to find common ground. For example, those who advocate teaching *Huckleberry Finn* and those who are opposed may both have in mind the goal of eliminating racial prejudice.

At this point in the prewriting process, think of some solutions that would satisfy at least some of the interests on all sides. It might be necessary for you to do some additional research. What do you think any of the opposing parties might want to know more about in order to accept your solution?

Finally, write up a clear statement of your solution. Can you explain how your solution appeals to the interests of all sides? In the *Huckleberry Finn* debate, we might propose that the novel be taught at any grade level provided that it is presented as part of a curriculum to educate students about the African-American experience with the involvement of African-American faculty or visiting lecturers.

Drafting

There is no set form for the mediatory essay. In fact, it is an unusual, even somewhat experimental, form of writing. As with any argument, the important thing is to have a plan for arranging your points and to provide clear signals to your readers. One logical way to organize a mediatory essay is in three parts:

Overview of the conflict. Describe the conflict and the opposing positions in the introductory paragraphs.

Discussion of differences underlying the conflict. Here your goal is to make all sides more sympathetic to one another and to sort out the important real interests that must be addressed by the solution.

Proposed solution. Here you make a case for your compromise position, giving reasons why it should be acceptable to all—that is, showing that it does serve at least some of their interests.

Revising

When revising a mediatory essay, you should look for the usual problems of organization and development that you would be looking for in any essay to convince or persuade. Be sure that you have inquired carefully and fairly into the conflict and that you have clearly presented the cases for all sides, including your proposed solution. At this point, you also need to consider how well you have used the persuasive appeals:

The appeal to character. Think about what kind of character you have projected as a mediator. Have you maintained neutrality? Do you model open-mindedness and genuine concern for the sensitivities of all sides?

The appeal to emotions. To arouse sympathy and empathy, which are needed in negotiation, you should take into account the emotional appeals discussed on pages 268–271. Your mediatory essay should be a moving argument for understanding and overcoming difference.

The appeal through style. As in persuasion, you should put the power of language to work. Pay attention to concrete word choice, striking metaphors, and phrases that stand out because of repeated sounds and rhythms.

For suggestions about editing and proofreading, see Appendix A.

www.mhhe.com/**crusius**

For help editing your essay,
go to:

Editing

STUDENT SAMPLE An Essay Arguing to Mediate

The following mediatory essay was written by Angi Grellhesl, a first-year student at Southern Methodist University. Her essay examines opposing written views on the institution of speech codes at various U.S. colleges and its effect on freedom of speech.

Mediating the Speech Code Controversy
Angi Grellhesl

The right to free speech has raised many controversies over the years. Explicit lyrics in rap music and marches by the Ku Klux Klan are just some examples that test the power of the First Amendment. Now, students and administrators are questioning if, in fact, free speech ought to be limited on university campuses. Many schools have instituted speech codes to protect specified groups from harassing speech.

Both sides in the debate, the speech code advocates and the free speech advocates, have presented their cases in recent books and articles. Columnist Nat Hentoff argues strongly against the speech codes, his main reason being that the codes violate students' First Amendment rights. Hentoff links the right to free speech with the values of higher education. In support, he quotes Yale president Benno Schmidt, who says, "Freedom of thought must be Yale's central commitment. . . . [U]niversities cannot censor or suppress speech, no matter how obnoxious in content, without violating their justification for existence . . . " (qtd. in Hentoff 223). Another reason Hentoff offers against speech codes is that universities must teach students to defend themselves in preparation for the real world, where such codes cannot shield them. Finally, he suggests that most codes are too vaguely worded; students may not even know they are violating the codes (216).

Two writers in favor of speech codes are Richard Perry and Patricia Williams. They see speech codes as a necessary and fair limitation on free speech. Perry and Williams argue that speech codes promote multicultural awareness, making students more sensitive to the differences that are out there in the real world. These authors do not think that the codes violate First Amendment rights, and they are suspicious of the motives of those who say they do. As Perry and Williams put it, those who feel free speech rights are being threatened "are apparently unable to distinguish between a liberty interest on the one hand and, on the other, a quite specific interest in being able to spout racist, sexist, and homophobic epithets completely

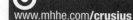

www.mhhe.com/**crusius**

For many additional examples of students writing, go to:

Writing

unchallenged—without, in other words, the terrible inconvenience of feeling bad about it" (228).

Perhaps if both sides trusted each other a little more, they could see that their goals are not contradictory. Everyone agrees that students' rights should be protected. Hentoff wishes to ensure that students have the right to speak their minds. He and others on his side are concerned about freedom. Defenders of the codes argue that students have the right not to be harassed, especially while they are getting an education. They are concerned about opportunity. Would either side really deny that the other's goal had value?

Also, both sides want to create the best possible educational   5
environment. Here the difference rests on the interpretation of what benefits the students. Is the best environment one most like the real world, where prejudice and harassment occur? Or does the university have an obligation to provide an atmosphere where potential victims can thrive and participate freely without intimidation?

I think it is possible to reach a solution that everyone can agree on. Most citizens want to protect constitutional rights; but they also agree that those rights have limitations, the ultimate limit being when one person infringes on the rights of others to live in peace. All sides should agree that a person ought to be able to speak out about his or her convictions, values, and beliefs. And most people can see a difference between that protected speech and the kind that is intended to harass and intimidate. For example, there is a clear difference between expressing one's view that Jews are mistaken in not accepting Christ as the son of God, on the one hand, and yelling anti-Jewish threats at a particular person in the middle of the night, on the other. Could a code not be worded in such a way as to distinguish between these two kinds of speech?

Also, I don't believe either side would want the university to be an artificial world. Codes should not attempt to ensure that no one is criticized or even offended. Students should not be afraid to say controversial things. But universities do help to shape the future of the real world, so shouldn't they at least take a stand against harassment? Can a code be worded that would protect free speech and prevent harassment?

The current speech code at Southern Methodist University is a compromise that ought to satisfy free speech advocates and speech code advocates. It prohibits hate speech at the same time that it protects an individual's First Amendment rights.

First, it upholds the First Amendment by including a section that reads, "[D]ue to the University's commitment to freedom of speech and expression, harassment is more than mere insensitivity or offensive conduct which creates an uncomfortable situation for certain members of the community" (Peruna 92). The code therefore should satisfy those, like Hentoff, who place a high value on the basic rights our nation was built upon. Secondly, whether or not there is a need for protection, the current code protects potential victims from hate speech or "any words or acts deliberately designed to disregard the safety or rights of another, and which intimidate, degrade, demean, threaten, haze, or otherwise interfere with another person's rightful action" (Peruna 92). This part of the code should satisfy those who recognize that some hurts cannot be overcome. Finally, the current code outlines specific acts that constitute harassment: "Physical, psychological, verbal and/or written acts directed toward an individual or group of individuals which rise to the level of 'fighting words' are prohibited" (Peruna 92).

The SMU code protects our citizens from hurt and from unconstitutional censorship. Those merely taking a position can express it, even if it hurts. On the other hand, those who are spreading hatred will be limited as to what harm they may inflict. Therefore, all sides should respect the code as a safeguard for those who use free speech but a limitation for those who abuse it.

10

Works Cited

Hentoff, Nat. "Speech Codes on the Campus and Problems of Free Speech." Debating P.C. Ed. Paul Berman. New York: Bantam, 1992. 215–24.

Perry, Richard, and Patricia Williams. "Freedom of Speech." Debating P.C. Ed. Paul Berman. New York: Bantam, 1992. 225–30.

Peruna Express 1993–1994. Dallas: Southern Methodist U, 1993.

www.mhhe.com/**crusius**

For an electronic tool that helps create properly formatted works-cited pages, go to:

Research > Bibliomaker

Two Casebooks for Argument

TWO CASEBOOKS FOR ARGUMENT

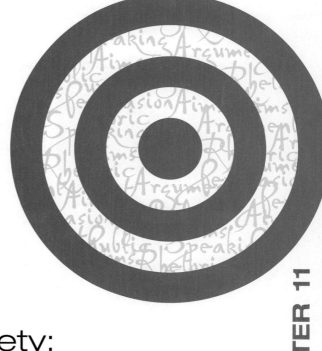

CHAPTER 11

Consumer Society: The Urge to Splurge

PHOTO MONTAGE: BLACK FRIDAY EVE

Dedicated consumers waited in line for the 5:00 a.m. opening of Best Buy on the day after Thanksgiving.

GENERAL INTRODUCTION: WHAT IS A CONSUMER SOCIETY?

When we say we live in a consumer society, we commonly mean that we live with more products and services than our parents and grandparents did; more choices within a product category, including premium labels at the high-priced end; and more information about it all in the form of advertising, media images, and product placement in music, movies, and TV. We would have to live in a remote corner of the world to escape the consumer society, and even then, we would have to keep the TV off in order to preserve the purity of our ignorance. Even people who would never in their lives buy a pair of Manolo Blahnik shoes have heard of them because of the show *Sex and the City*. So, yes, life in a consumer society means having more stuff and, for many people, more debt. This casebook, however, will take a closer and more critical look at how active membership in a consumer society affects people's sense of identity and quality of life.

Scholars who observe consumer societies describe not just the amount of goods available but the importance people place on goods. Says Paul Elkins: "A consumer society is one in which the possession and use of an increasing number and variety of goods and services is the principal cultural aspiration and the surest perceived route to personal happiness, social status, and national success."[1] In contrast to an earlier America where people's identity depended on their occupation, in consumer societies people's identity is tied to what they consume. James Twitchell, one of the writers in this chapter, puts it bluntly: "In the way we live now, you are not what you make. You are what you consume." People buy goods to create "lifestyles." Another contributor to this chapter, Jean Kilbourne, explains, "The consumer culture encourages us not only to buy more but to seek our identity and fulfillment through what we buy."

The readings in this chapter focus on the United States, but the consumer society is really a global village, including the middle- and upper-class populations of developing nations whose workers supply most of the products we buy. In China, for example, parts of Shanghai and other booming cities epitomize the consumer society. A serious problem for China, however, is the disparity of income between rich and poor. A measure of income inequality, called the Gini coefficient, stands currently at 0.46 in China, a rate that is considered alarmingly high. When vast numbers of a population are excluded from the "good life," social instability results.

Since the year 2000, the United States has also been experiencing an increase in disparity between rich and poor. Although nowhere near Brazil's, the income gap in the United States is larger than that of any other advanced industrialized country, as illustrated in Figure 11.1.

Some other statistics to bear in mind: According to the U.S. Census Bureau, the median household income in the United States in 2005 rose to

---

[1]Paul Elkins, qtd. in Neva R. Goodwin, "Overview Essay," *The Consumer Society*, ed. Neva R. Goodwin, Frank Ackerman, and David Kiron (Washington, D.C.: Island Press, 1997), 2.

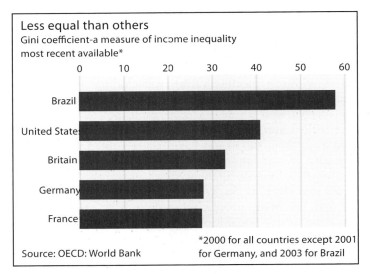

Figure 11.1[2]

$46,326, while the poverty rate in that year remained unchanged, at 12.6% of the population, about 37 million people. However, the rich are getting much, much richer:

> According to Emmanuel Saez of the University of California, Berkeley, and Thomas Piketty of the École Normale Supérieure in Paris, the share of aggregate income going to the highest-earning 1% of Americans has doubled from 8% in 1980 to over 16% in 2004. That going to the top tenth of 1% has tripled from 2% in 1980 to 7% today. And that going to the top one-hundredth of 1%—the 14,000 taxpayers at the very top of the income ladder—has quadrupled from 0.65% in 1980 to 2.87% in 2004.[3]

These statistics are worth remembering as you read the arguments in this chapter. Some of the authors address the problem of those excluded from the consumer society; others do not. And, as Juliet Schor argues, even those who can afford to participate at some level feel inadequate because they constantly compare themselves to the biggest spenders at the top. Thanks to the media, the "lifestyles of the rich and famous" are highly visible while the lives of the poor can easily be ignored by those who choose not to look.

Many issues are connected with this topic, too many to include in our casebook. The readings do not go into depth about the income disparities in rich countries or the exploitation of workers in poor ones. There is only brief

---

[2, 3]From "Inequality in America: The Rich, the Poor, and the Growing Gap between Them," *The Economist*, June 15, 2006. Copyright 2006 by Economist Newspaper Group. Reproduced with permission of Economist Newspaper Group in the format Textbook via Copyright Clearance Center.

mention of mass consumption's consequences for the environment, but the richest countries devour the most of Earth's resources and contribute the most to pollution and global warming. We are also not including articles about alternatives to the consumer society, although there is such a backlash against it that advice about how to live a more simple and sustainable lifestyle is now readily available.

Instead, we have chosen essays that examine the quality of life for those who are indeed part of the consumer society, looking at such questions as, Why do people buy what they do not need? How does the consumer society affect our values and our quality of life? How much power does advertising have? Does advertising reflect who we are or define who we are? Finally, we ask, How does living in a consumer society affect our psychological well-being? How can we build meaningful lives in a materialistic world?

SECTION 1: THE MEANING OF SPENDING
Overview

This section opens with three arguments about why people buy what we might call "unnecessary" things: goods and services that are upscale, stylish, and in some cases, over-the-top luxurious. The authors—Virginia Postrel, James Twitchell, and Juliet Schor—are leading scholars, and they present a range of opinion about consumer society, from highly enthusiastic to harshly critical. All note that America has changed since the 1950s. Americans used to have modest goals for houses, cars, and lifestyles, but today, it's not enough to just be comfortable. People want more. The question is, Is this change for the better?

The arguments are complex, but in essence, Postrel offers a strong endorsement of the rise of style in everyday products and environments, such as Starbucks. The consumer society has enhanced daily life for many Americans. Of course, it is nicest of all for those who can afford a five-dollar cup of coffee. According to Postrel, we buy for pleasure: Today's consumer society allows us to satisfy our innate appreciation for aesthetic objects and to express our individuality through a wide selection of styles.

Twitchell also takes a positive view. He agrees with Postrel that we have an innate love for material things, but he sees today's consumption as more meaningful socially: We buy to fit in with others who like the same products and brands. Luxury spending, available to everyone to some degree (even if only as a cup of coffee or a designer wastebasket at Target) is a democratizing trend: There are benefits to a society where what you buy has become more important than older status markers, such as race, family name, and religious affiliation.

Schor, an economist, sees consumer societies as destructive of people's quality of life. People buy not for pleasure but to keep up with the Joneses. She sees status anxiety behind Americans' spending, and she notes the consequences of spending beyond one's income, including a constant feeling of dissatisfaction because the richest Americans' lifestyles are constantly on display in the media.

The second half of this section provides three readings that illustrate more concretely the motives of consumers. We visit a suburban Home Depot where Dad buys a barbeque grill, a strip of transient stores in a ghetto where teenagers buy brand-name shoes, and a cyberspace community of young people making friends by exchanging information about their personal possessions.

The Aesthetic Imperative

VIRGINIA POSTREL

Virginia Postrel, whose degree from Princeton is in English literature, has made a career writing on the subjects of economics, progress, and design. She writes regular columns for *The Atlantic* and *Forbes* magazines and has published two books, *The Future and Its Enemies* (Free Press 1998) and *The Substance of Style: How the Rise of Aesthetic Value Is Remaking Commerce, Culture, and Consciousness* (HarperCollins 2003), from which this selection is excerpted.

The twenty-first century isn't what the old movies imagined. We citizens of the future don't wear conformist jumpsuits, live in utilitarian high-rises, or get our food in pills. To the contrary, we are demanding and creating an enticing, stimulating, diverse, and beautiful world. We want our vacuum cleaners and mobile phones to sparkle, our bathroom faucets and desk accessories to express our personalities. We expect every strip mall and city block to offer designer coffee, several different cuisines, a copy shop with do-it-yourself graphics workstations, and a nail salon for manicures on demand. We demand trees in our parking lots, peaked roofs and decorative façades on our supermarkets, auto dealerships as swoopy and stylish as the cars they sell.

Aesthetics has become too important to be left to the aesthetes. To succeed, hard-nosed engineers, real estate developers, and MBAs must take aesthetic communication, and aesthetic pleasure, seriously. We, their customers, demand it.

"We are by nature—by deep, biological nature—visual, tactile creatures," says David Brown, the former president of the Art Center College of Design in Pasadena, California, and a longtime observer of the design world. That is a quintessential turn-of-our-century statement, a simultaneous affirmation of biological humanity and aesthetic power. Our sensory side is as valid a part of our nature as the capacity to speak or reason, and it is essential to both. Artifacts do not need some other justification for pleasing our visual, tactile, emotional natures. Design, says Brown, is moving from the abstract and ideological—"this is good design"—to the personal and emotional—"I *like* that." In this new age of aesthetics, we are acknowledging, accepting, and even celebrating what a design-museum curator calls our "quirky underside."

This trend doesn't mean that a particular style has triumphed or that we're necessarily living in a period of unprecedented creativity. It doesn't mean everyone or everything is now beautiful, or that people agree on some absolute standard of taste. The issue is not *what* style is used but rather *that* style is used, consciously and conscientiously, even in areas where function used to stand alone. Aesthetics is more pervasive than it used to be—not restricted to a social, economic, or artistic elite, limited to only a few settings or industries, or designed to communicate only power, influence, or wealth. Sensory appeals are everywhere, they are increasingly personalized, and they are intensifying.

Of course, saying that aesthetics is pervasive does not imply that look and feel 5 trump everything else. Other values have not gone away. We may want mobile phones to sparkle, but first we expect them to work. We expect shops to look good, but we also want service and selection. We still care about cost, comfort, and convenience. But on the margin, aesthetics matters more and more. When we decide how next to spend our time, money, or creative effort, aesthetics is increasingly likely to top our priorities.

In this context, "aesthetics" obviously does not refer to the philosophy of art. Aesthetics is the way we communicate through the senses. It is the art of creating reactions without words, through the look and feel of people, places, and things. Hence, aesthetics differs from entertainment that requires cognitive engagement with narrative, word play, or complex, intellectual allusion. While the sound of poetry is arguably aesthetic, the meaning is not. Spectacular special effects and beautiful movie stars enhance box-office success in foreign markets because they offer universal aesthetic pleasure; clever dialogue, which is cognitive and culture-bound, doesn't travel as well. Aesthetics may complement storytelling, but it is not itself narrative.

Aesthetics shows rather than tells, delights rather than instructs. The effects are immediate, perceptual, and emotional. They are not cognitive, although we may analyze them after the fact. As a mid-century industrial designer said of his field, aesthetics is "fundamentally the art of using line, form, tone, color, and texture to arouse an emotional reaction in the beholder."

Whatever information aesthetics conveys is prearticulate—the connotation of the color and shapes of letters, not the meanings of the words they form. Aesthetics conjures meaning in a subliminal, associational way, as our direct sensory experience reminds us of something that is absent, a memory or an idea. Those associations may be universal, the way Disney's big-eyed animals play on the innate human attraction to babies. Or they may change from person to person, place to place, moment to moment.

Although we often equate aesthetics with beauty, that definition is too limited. Depending on what reaction the creator wants, effective presentation may be strikingly ugly, disturbing, even horrifying. The title sequence to *Seven*—whose rough, backlit type, seemingly stuttering film, and unsettling sepia images established a new style for horror films—comes to mind. Or aesthetics may employ novelty, allusion, or humor, rather than beauty, to arouse a positive response. Philippe Starck's fly swatter with a face on it doesn't represent timeless beauty. It's just whimsical fun.

Aesthetic effects begin with universal reactions, but these effects always oper- 10 ate in a personal and cultural context. We may like weather-beaten paint because it seems rustic, black leather because it makes us feel sexy, or fluffy pop music because it reminds us of our youth. Something novel may be interesting, or something familiar comforting, without regard to ideal beauty. The explosion of tropical colors that hit women's fashion in 2000 was a relief from the black, gray, and beige of the late 1990s, while those neutrals looked calm and sophisticated after the riot of jewel tones that preceded them. Psychologists tell us that human beings perceive changes in sensory inputs—movement, new visual elements, louder or softer sounds, novel smells—more than sustained levels.

Because aesthetics operates at a prerational level, it can be disquieting. We have a love-hate relationship with the whole idea. As consumers, we enjoy sensory appeals but fear manipulation. As producers, we'd rather not work so hard to keep up with the aesthetic competition. As heirs to Plato and the Puritans, we suspect sensory impressions as deceptive, inherently false. Aesthetics is "the power of provocative surfaces," says a critic. It "speaks to the eye's mind, overshadowing matters of quality or substance."

But the eye's mind is identifying something genuinely valuable. Aesthetic pleasure itself has quality and substance. The look and feel of things tap deep human instincts. We are, as Brown says, "visual, tactile creatures." We enjoy enhancing our sensory surroundings. That enjoyment is real. The trick is to appreciate aesthetic pleasure without confusing it with other values.

Theorist Ellen Dissanayake defines art as "making special," a behavior designed to be "sensorily and emotionally gratifying and more than strictly necessary." She argues that the instinct for "making special" is universal and innate, a part of human beings' evolved biological nature. Hers may or may not be an adequate definition of art, but it does offer a useful insight into our aesthetic age. Having spent a century or more focused primarily on other goals—solving manufacturing problems, lowering costs, making goods and services widely available, increasing convenience, saving energy—we are increasingly engaged in making our world special. More people in more aspects of life are drawing pleasure and meaning from the way their persons, places, and things look and feel. Whenever we have the chance, we're adding sensory, emotional appeal to ordinary function.

"Aesthetics, whether people admit it or not, is why you buy something," says a shopper purchasing a high-style iMac, its flat screen pivoting like a desk lamp on a half-spherical base. He likes the computer's features, but he particularly likes its looks. A computer doesn't have to be a nondescript box. It can express its owner's taste and personality.

"Deciding to buy an IBM instead of a Compaq simply because you prefer black 15 to gray is absolutely fine as long as both machines meet your other significant criteria," a writer advises computer shoppers on the female-oriented iVillage Web site. "Not that color can't or shouldn't be a significant criterion; in truth, the market is filled with enough solid, affordable machines that you finally have the kind of freedom of choice previously reserved only for the likes of footwear." Computers all used to look pretty much the same. Now they, too, can be special.

A Salt Lake City grocery shopper praises her supermarket's makeover. Gone are the gray stucco exterior, harsh fluorescent lighting, and tall, narrow aisles. In their place are warm red brick, spot and track lighting, and low-rise departments of related items. The "crowning glory" is the Starbucks in the front, which provides both a welcoming aroma and a distinctive look and feel. "The experience is a lot more calm, a lot more pleasant," she says, "an extraordinary change, and a welcome one." Grocery shopping is still a chore, but at least now the environment offers something special.

A political writer in Washington, D.C., a city noted for its studied ignorance of style, says he pays much more attention to his clothes than he did ten or fifteen years ago, and enjoys it a lot more. "One thing I try to do is not to wear the same combination of suit, shirt, and tie in a season," he says. "It's another way of saying every day is special." Once seen as an unnecessary luxury, even a suspect indulgence, "making special" has become a personal, social, and business imperative.

NOTES

333 "*We are by nature*" David Brown, interview with the author, November 9, 2000.
333 "*quirky underside*" Martin Eidelberg, quoted in Linda Hales, "When Designs Delight," *The Washington Post,* November 12, 1998, p. T12.

334 *As a midcentury industrial designer* Harold Van Doren, *Industrial Design: A Practical Guide to Product Design and Development,* 2nd ed. (New York: McGraw-Hill, 1954), p. 166.

334 *"The power of provocative surfaces"* Stuart Ewen, *All Consuming Images: The Politics of Style in Contemporary Culture* (New York: Basic Books, 1988), p. 2.

335 *"making special"* Ellen Dissanayake, *Homo Aestheticus: Where Art Comes From and Why* (Seattle: University of Washington Press, 1992, 1995), p. 56.

335 *"Aesthetics, whether people admit it . . . "* Dave Caldwell, quoted in Vikas Bajaj, "Electronic Manufacturers Emphasize Form with Function," *The Dallas Morning News,* April 4, 2002, p. 5D.

335 *"Deciding to buy an IBM"* Heidi Pollock. "How to Buy a Computer, Part I," iVillage, http://www.iVillage.com/click/experts/goodbuygirl/articles/0,5639,38862,00.html.

335 *"A Salt Lake City grocery shopper"* Deborah Moeller, e-mail to the author, December 27, 2001, and interview with the author, April 8, 2002.

335 *A political writer* Michael Barone, interview with the author, April 8, 2002.

Needing the Unnecessary

JAMES B. TWITCHELL

James B. Twitchell is an English professor at University of Florida who also teaches advertising. His interests range from Romanticism to popular commercial culture, especially shopping. Among his most recent books are *Branded Nation: The Marketing of Megachurch, College, Inc., and Museumworld* (Simon & Schuster, 2005) and *Living It Up: Our Love Affair with Luxury* (Columbia, 2002), from which the following selection was originally excerpted and published in *Reason* magazine.

THE DEMOCRATIZATION OF LUXURY

If you want to understand material culture at the beginning of the 21st century, you must understand the overwhelming importance of unnecessary material. If you are looking for the one unambiguous result of modern capitalism, of the industrial revolution, and of marketing, here it is. In the way we live now, you are not what you make. You are what you consume. And most of what you consume is totally unnecessary yet remarkably well made.

The most interesting of those superfluous objects belong in a socially constructed and ever-shifting class called luxury. Consuming those objects, objects as rich in meaning as they are low in utility, causes lots of happiness and distress. As well they should. For one can make the argument that until all necessities are had by all members of a community, no one should have luxury. More complex still is that, since the 1980s, the bulk consumers of luxury have not been the wealthy but the middle class, your next-door neighbors and their kids. And this is happening not just in the West but in many parts of the world.

When I was growing up in the middle class of the 1950s, luxury objects were lightly tainted with shame. You had to be a little cautious if you drove a Cadillac, wore a Rolex, or lived in a house with more than two columns out front. The rich could drip with diamonds, but you should stay dry. Movie stars could drive convertibles; you should keep your top up. If you've got it, don't flaunt it. Remember, the people surrounding you had lived through the Depression, a time that forever lit the bright lines between have-to-have, don't-need-to-have, and have-in-order-to-show-off.

The best definition of this old-style off-limits luxury came to me from my dad. I was just a kid, and it was my first trip to a cafeteria: Morrison's Cafeteria in Pompano Beach, Florida, February 1955. When I got to the desserts, I removed the main course from my tray and loaded up on cake and Jell-o. My dad told me to put all the desserts back but one. I said that wasn't fair. To me the whole idea of cafeteria was to have as much as you want of what you want. My dad said no, that was not the idea of cafeteria. The idea of cafeteria is that you can have just one of many choices.

LUXURIFICATION

Look around American culture, and you will see how wrong he was. Almost every 5 set of consumables has a dessert at the top. And you can have as much of it as you can get on your tray or as much of it as your credit card will allow. This is true not just for expensive products like town cars and McMansions but for everyday objects.

In bottled water, for instance, there is Evian, advertised as if it were a liquor. In coffee, there's Starbucks; in ice cream, Häagen-Dazs; in sneakers, Nike; in whiskey, Johnnie Walker Blue; in credit cards, American Express Centurian; in wine, Chateau Margaux; in cigars, Arturo Fuente Hemingway; and, well, you know the rest.

Name the category, no matter how mundane, and you'll find a premium or, better yet, a super-premium brand at the top. And having more than you can conceivably use of such objects is not met with opprobrium but with genial acceptance. This pattern persists regardless of class: The average number of branded sneakers for adolescent males? It's 4.8 pairs. And regardless of culture: A favorite consumer product in China? Chanel lipstick dispensers sans lipstick.

Basil Englis and Michael Solomon, professors of marketing in the School of Business at Rutgers University, have studied the effects of brand consumption, particularly how college students cluster around top-brand knowledge. They drew guinea pigs from undergraduate business majors at their institution and presented them with 40 cards, each containing a description of a different cluster of consumers.

The professors sifted the clusters to make four groups—lifestyles, if you will—representative of undergraduate society. They were Young Suburbia, Money & Brains, Smalltown Downtown, and Middle America. Then Englis and Solomon gathered images of objects from four product categories (automobiles, magazines/newspapers, toiletries, and alcoholic beverages) that fit into each group. The students were asked to put the various images together into coherent groups; they were also to state their current proximity to, or desire to be part of, each group in the future.

As might be expected, the Money & Brains cluster was the most popular aspirational niche. What Englis and Solomon did not expect was how specific and knowledgeable the students were about the possessions that they did not have but knew that members of that cluster needed.

When asked what brand of automobile they would drive, here's what they said: 10 BMWs (53.6 percent), Mercedes (50.7), Cadillacs (30.4), Volvos (23.2), Porsches (21.7), Acuras (17.4), and Jaguars (15.9). They knew what they wanted to read: travel magazines (21.7 percent), *Vogue* (21.7), *BusinessWeek* (20.3), *Fortune* (17.9), and *GQ* (15.9). Again, this is not what they did read but what they took to be the reading material of the desired group. What they were actually reading (or so they said) were *Forbes, Barron's, The New Yorker,* and *Gourmet*. No mention of *Rolling Stone, Playboy, Spin,* or *Maxim* for this group. They certainly knew what to drink: Heineken beer (33.3 percent), expensive wines (26.1), scotch (18.8), champagne (17.4), and Beck's beer (15). They also knew what to sprinkle on their bodies: Polo (27.5 percent), Obsession (15.9), and Drakkar (15.9).

What the professors found was not just that birds of a feather had started to flock together, but that these young birds already knew what flock to shy away from. They were not ashamed of smoking, for instance, but of smoking the wrong brand. Their prime avoidance group corresponded to the Smalltown Downtown cluster.

The Money & Brainers knew a lot about the Smalltowners. They knew about favored pickup trucks, Chevys (23.2 percent) and Fords (18.8). They knew that this group reads *People* (30.4), *Sports Illustrated* (26.1), *TV Guide* (24.6), *Wrestling* (21.7), fishing magazines (20.3), and *The National Enquirer* (18.8). They assumed that Smalltowners preferred Budweiser (59.4), followed by Miller (24.6) and Coors

(18.8). Essentially, the Money & Brainers had learned not just what to buy but what to avoid (or at least what to say to avoid).

Such shared knowledge is the basis of culture. This insight was, after all, the rationale behind a liberal arts education. John Henry Newman and Matthew Arnold argued for state-supported education in the 19th century precisely because cultural literacy meant social cohesion. No one argued that it was important to know algebraic functions or Latin etymologies or what constitutes a sonnet because such knowledge allows us to solve important social problems. We learn such matters because it is the basis of how to speak to each other, how we develop a bond of shared history and commonality. This is the secular religion of the liberal arts and sciences, what French sociologist Pierre Bourdieu calls cultural capital.

In our postmodern world we have, it seems, exchanged knowledge of history and science (a knowledge of production) for knowledge of products and how such products interlock to form coherent social patterns (a knowledge of consumption). Buy this and don't buy that has replaced make/learn this, don't make/learn that. After all, in the way we live now, everyone is a consumer, but not everyone is a worker. As Marcel Duchamp, sly observer of the changing scene, said, "Living is more a question of what one spends than what one makes." Thus a new denomination of cultural capital.

A shift in currency has clear ramifications. A producer culture focuses on the 15 independent self of the worker: self-help, self-discipline, self-respect, self-control, self-reliance, self-interest. Responsibility is situated in the individual: Can she get work? A consumer culture, however, focuses on community: Fit in, don't stand out. Be cool. The standard of judgment becomes the ability to interact effectively with others, to win their affection and admiration—to merge with others of the same lifestyle. Can he consume the right brands? . . .

From time to time in Western history there is vociferous antipathy toward high-end consumption. From Plato to the early Christians to the Renaissance, luxury was thought to effeminize and weaken. But this was hardly a pressing problem, because just getting to the necessities of life was a full-time job for most.

With increasing affluence this view shifted. Luxury became dangerous not because of debasement but because it was a sign of overreaching, of getting out of place. An interesting transformation shows how fluid this category can be. In the Renaissance, luxury objects became those things thought worthy of being painted. Such objects were called objets d'art. Now, of course, the luxury object is the painting itself. But you can see that even before the industrial revolution there was a growing desire to show stuff off, to use the material world as marker of social dominance, to strut, to flaunt.

By the 18th century, social critics like Bernard Mandeville and economists like Adam Smith were beginning to suggest that, for improving the weal of humanity, the promise of consuming luxury might be a better carrot than the stick of shame. Yet there was still deep resentment for consuming out of your class, beyond your means.

This suspicion about consuming beyond your class continued well into the 19th century. In fact, ancient sumptuary laws, explaining exactly what objects were forbidden by church and state, were read from the Anglican pulpit until the 1860s. Reading these laws took two hours of church time to complete, and the laws kept people in their places, if only to have to listen to them.

Clerics, clearly supported by the aristocracy, were not alone in stiff-arming luxury. 20 With the onset of industrial surpluses, secular pundits like Henry David Thoreau railed against what they took to be the excesses of mass production. "Most of the luxuries, and many of the so-called comforts, of life are not only not indispensable, but positive hindrances to the elevation of mankind," he pointed out in *Walden*.

By the fin de siècle this view of high-end consumption had so exploded that Thorstein Veblen unloosed the first modern sustained attack on luxury in his thoroughly entertaining *Theory of the Leisure Class* (1899). Coining all manner of nifty concepts like conspicuous consumption, invidious comparison, bandwagon effect, symbolic pantomime, vicarious leisure, and parodic display, Veblen had at the excesses of robber-baron shopping. . . .

THE LEISURE CLASSIC

Here is Veblen's argument: As wealth spreads, what drives consumers' behavior is increasingly neither subsistence nor comfort but the attainment of "the esteem and envy of fellow men." Because male wage earners are too circumspect to indulge themselves, they deposit consumption on surrogates, on loved ones. Vicarious ostentation—the way that plainly dressed Victorian men encouraged their wives and daughters to wear complicated trappings of wealth—is how this unfolds. Ditto their servants, horses, and even house pets.

In retrospect, Veblen was too successful, too neat, too sharp. Veblen thought that the purpose of acquisition was public consumption of esteem, status anxiety resolved by material display. Not much more. Wealth, he argued, confers honor; it suggests prowess and achievement. But wealth would have no social meaning were it simply consumed or possessed. "In order to gain and to hold the esteem of men," he wrote, "it is not sufficient merely to possess wealth or power. The wealth or power must be put in evidence, for esteem is awarded only on evidence." . . . With insights like this, Veblen proved himself to be too strong a critic to dismiss. You don't need to have read a word he wrote to know him. He set the tone of modern criticism. . . .

Veblen's descendants are still at it. Following in the footsteps of Galbraith have been two moralists passing as economists: Juliet Schor, a professor now at Boston College, who has published *The Overspent American: Why We Want What We Don't Need*, and Robert Frank, a professor at Cornell, who contributed *Luxury Fever: Why Money Fails to Satisfy in an Era of Excess*. Just read the subtitles.

The modern attack usually centers around a specific object as an exemplum. 25 While Galbraith disliked Cadillac tail fins, Schor disdains granite countertops in the kitchen, and Frank holds up expensive watches as symptomatic of bad habits. On the surface they have such good points: How do those fins help the car move, are those stone countertops better than Formica, does a Lucian Picard keep better time than a Timex?

But here's the problem. The 1958 Cadillac has been featured in the Museum of Modern Art's retrospective show celebrating industrial design as art, and if you now want to buy one in mint condition, you'll pay about 20 times the purchase price. The granite countertop really makes more sense as a cutting surface than as a slab to lay down over the dead body of Uncle Louie, and—who knows?—it might even be passed from generation to generation, while the sensible Formica is carted out to the dump. And had Frank invested in Lucian Picard watches at the beginning of the bull market, he would have made more on his watch investment than on the S&P 500. Drats! That this stuff could have increased in value tells us how slippery these slopes can be.

No matter. Critics of consumption love to point out that people with these things are no happier than people without them. Ergo, why buy extra stuff? But people who can't buy unnecessary opuluxe are definitely unhappier for not being let into the cycle; buying this notational stuff and having such stuff are different experiences; consumers move in definite stages, from adolescence, where consumption is central, to middle age, where it ceases to be so important, to old age, where having things is positively a hindrance. Religious fanatics invariably rank highest on happiness scales, irrespective of culture or religion. Let's give happiness a rest. Consumption of the new luxury is about far more interesting sensations.

Whereas Veblen contended that male aggression caused the crazed consumption of deluxe items at the end of his century, these modern critics are more au courant in putting forth their etiology. They medicalize consumption, in large part because the bulk consumers of luxe are now young women. The diagnosis, although they would never use this precise term, is addiction. We are addicted to luxury. That's what causes the fever. That's why we yearn for what we don't want. Diagnosis from the National Public Radio crowd: not just Sudden Wealth Syndrome but the dreaded "affluenza."

OVER THE TOP

I must say that I found most of the luxury objects that I've looked at, from Patek Philippe watches to Porsche Turbos to the men's room of the Bellagio Hotel, to be a little over the top. But I am not so oblivious to the world around me that I can't appreciate how important the new luxury has become. And I can't overlook how high-end consumption promises to do exactly what critics of the stuff have always yearned for, namely, to bring us together, often traumatically. Yes, indeed, the transgenerational poor are excluded, as the bottom fifth of our population has not budged an inch in the luxe explosion. Yet more people than ever are entering the much-vaunted global village because of consumption, not despite it.

In fact, one could argue, as Dinesh D'Souza, Virginia Postrel, and W. Michael 30 Cox and Richard Alm have recently done, that the aspiration of the poor to get at these unnecessary goods has done more than any social program to motivate some of the disenchanted to become enfranchised. While one may be distressed at seeing a dish antenna atop a ramshackle house or a Caddie out front, the yearning to have superfluous badges of affluence may promise a more lasting peace around the world than any religion or political system has ever delivered. I don't mean to overlook the complexities here.

This is not a universal phenomenon, as the al Qaeda have wickedly demonstrated. Some of the world's poor are most certainly not becoming better off in absolute or relative terms. I only want to say that, given a choice between being mugged for your sneakers or having your ethnic or religious heritage cleansed, the lust for sneakers may prove a more lasting way to improve the general lot of humanity.

Let's face it. In the world that I grew up in, your religion, your family name, the color of your skin, your language skills, your gender, where you went to school, your accent, and your marriage partner were doing the work that luxury consumption does now. My dad went to Exeter, Williams, and Harvard Med, and he never drove anything fancier than a Plymouth. He never had to. Today I wouldn't go to a doctor who drove a Plymouth. I would figure that if she doesn't drive a Lexus, she is having trouble with her practice.

So I admit the ugly truth. After spending the last few years trying to understand the pull of the material world, I am far more sympathetic to its blandishments and far more forgiving of its excesses. The democratization of luxury has been the single most important marketing phenomenon of modern times. And it has profound political implications. It may not be as bad as some lifestyle scolds make it out to be. In its own way it is a fair, albeit often wasteful, system, not just of objects but of meaning. Don't get me wrong: It's not that I came to mock and stayed to pray, but I do feel that getting and spending has some actual worth. Nobody checks the number of vowels in your name, or the color of your skin, or whether you know the difference between *like* and *as* when you are buying your Prada parka—that's got to mean something.

Although luxury has become a mallet with which one pounds the taste of others, this misses some essential points. One is that humans are consumers by nature. We are tool users because we like to use what tool using can produce. In other words, tools are not the ends but the means. So too materialism does not crowd out spiritualism; spiritualism is more likely a substitute when objects are scarce. When we have few things, we make the next world luxurious. When we have plenty, we enchant the objects around us.

Second, consumers are rational. They are often fully aware that they are more 35 interested in consuming aura than objects, sizzle than steak, meaning than material. In fact, if you ask them—as academic critics are usually loath to do—they are quite candid in explaining that the Nike swoosh, the Polo pony, the Guess? label, the DKNY logo are what they are after. They are not duped by advertising, packaging, branding, fashion, and merchandising. They actively seek and enjoy the status that surrounds the object, especially when they are young.

Third, we need to question the standard argument that consumption of opuluxe almost always leads to disappointment. Admittedly, the circular route from desire to purchase to disappointment to renewed desire is never-ending, but we may follow it because the other route—from melancholy to angst—is worse. In other words, in a world emptied of inherited values, consuming what looks to be overpriced fripperies may be preferable to consuming nothing.

Finally, we need to rethink the separation between production and consumption, for they are more alike than separate and occur not at different times and places but simultaneously. Instead of wanting less luxury, we might find that just the opposite—the paradoxical luxury for all—is a suitable goal of communal aspiration. After all, luxury before all else is a social construction, and understanding its social ramifications may pave the way for a new appreciation of what has become a characteristic contradiction of our time, the necessary consumption of the unnecessary.

When Spending Becomes You

JULIET SCHOR

Juliet Schor, professor of sociology at Boston College, is a noted public speaker and best-selling writer on economic and social issues, particularly the relationship of work, consumer spending, and family life in America. Her books include *The Overworked American: The Unexpected Decline of Leisure* (Basic Books, 1992), *The Overspent American: Why We Want What We Don't Need* (HarperPerennial, 1998), and *Born to Buy: The Commercialized Child and the New Consumer Culture* (Scribner, 2004). The selection below is excerpted from *The Overspent American*.

The most striking feature of household spending in modern America is its sheer volume. The typical middle- to upper-middle-class household occupies more than two thousand square feet of floor space, owns at least two cars, a couple of couches, numerous chairs, beds, and tables, a washer and dryer, more than two televisions, a VCR, and has cable. The kitchen contains a conventional oven, a microwave, a frost-free refrigerator, a blender, a coffee maker, a tea kettle, a food processor, and so many pots, pans, dishes, cups and glasses, storage containers, kitchen utensils, and pieces of flatware that they aren't even counted. Elsewhere in the house are a personal computer and printer, telephones, an answering machine, a calculator, a stereo or CD player, musical instruments, and many pieces of art—in addition to paintings and reproductions, there are decorative items such as vases, plates, and statuettes, photographs in frames, and knickknacks. In the bathroom are a hair dryer, a scale, perhaps an electric toothbrush or shaver, and cabinets overflowing with towels, shampoos, conditioners, face creams, and other cosmetics. The closets are stuffed with clothes and shoes of all types: dresses, suits, pants, shirts, sweaters, coats, hats, boots, sneakers, flats, pumps, walking shoes, patent leathers, and loafers. And don't forget the jewelry. In addition to watches, the diamond ring, and other high-value items, there's usually a large collection of costume jewelry: bead necklaces, bracelets, and earrings, earrings, earrings. The family room is filled with books, videos, tapes, CDs, magazines, and more photos and knickknacks. The floors are covered with rugs or carpet, and throughout the house are scattered other pieces of furniture, accented perhaps with dried or silk flowers. Stored in the garage or basement is all the sports equipment, such as bicycles and skis, as well as luggage and totes, lawn and garden tools, and broken appliances. (Some developers now routinely build three-car garages—two spaces for the cars, one for the junk.) In addition to all these durable products (of which this is a very incomplete inventory), households spend heavily on services such as child care, movies, restaurants and bars, hotel stays, airplane trips, haircuts, massages, visits to Disney World, lawyer bills, insurance premiums, interest payments, and, sometimes, rental on the storage space where even more stuff resides.

If you are a typical American consumer, you did not always have so much. There was probably a time in your adult life when you could fit everything you owned into your car and drive off into the sunset. Now you need professionals to transport your possessions. You spend hundreds, perhaps thousands of dollars a year to insure or protect them. As you survey your material landscape, you may wonder how this state of affairs came to be. You certainly didn't intend to imitate those medieval armies that became sitting ducks—unable to move on account of the creature comforts they started lugging around. Each purchase made sense at the time. Many were truly necessary. Some were captivating, giving you that "I just have to have this" feeling. But added together, they raise the possibility that yours is a lifestyle of excess.

How does it happen? And so quickly? To understand how your possessions came to fill a full-size moving van, or why you never seem to have enough closet space, we need to begin with the acquisition process. The sequence of events starts with a social act—being exposed to consumer goods. It proceeds through the mental stages of fantasizing, wishing, and rationalizing. Borrowing may be the next step before the process culminates with a purchase. See, want, borrow, buy. . . .

Inner desires are prompted first and foremost by exposure. The seeds are "planted" by seeing what people at work wear or drive; by visiting others' homes and observing their private spaces; by hearing about a coworker's new purchase; by window and in-store shopping; by looking at mail-order catalogs; and by viewing (or to a lesser extent, hearing about) consumer items in advertisements and films or on television. As the North American president of Montblanc Pen put it, referring to the Euro Classique, the company's entry-level ($90) pen, "They will see their friend with one and go out and get the same." While most critics of consumer society focus on ads and the media, it's important to remember that the more powerful stimulator of desire is what friends and family have.

For Lauren Vandermeer, work was the place where her desires were stimulated. 5 After graduating from a Seven Sisters college, Lauren wanted only three things: a camera, a stereo, and a bike. In her sales job at a large corporation, she quickly acquired them. "Then I became aware of people going on vacation, and then I wanted to go on vacation. I went to Mexico for a week. I really liked it." The townhouse came next. "Very quickly after [the vacation], several of my colleagues started buying houses and townhouses. And all these people were moving to York and Yardley and Newtown, Pennsylvania. It's a great little yuppie area, and it's all very beautiful. It was like one started and then everybody else followed suit. Everybody was looking, everybody was putting down payments down. And so I jumped on board too. But I will admit, the only reason I did it is because everybody else was doing it. And I felt not so much keeping up with the Joneses as their logic. I bought into the logic of not wanting to pay rent, and that it was worth it to have a mortgage and the deductions for your taxes and all of that.". . .

Between seeing and buying lies the inner world of desire. Recent literature has focused on fantasy, imagination, and vicarious experience as key aspects of modern consumer behavior. Spending fantasies are prevalent, indeed commonplace. People anticipate, they daydream, and they plan their participation in the "enchanted domain" of consumer culture. In their study of inner desire, Susan Fournier and Michael Guiry found that 61 percent of respondents "*always* have something in mind that [they] look forward to buying." Twenty-seven percent of the sample said that they "dream about things they do not own" very often.

In fact, these desires were rather structured; many respondents had well-articulated "wish lists." Defined as "things that you would like to own or do someday," these lists contained an average of 6.3 items and were heavily dominated by material possessions.

(Consumption wishes outnumbered idealistic ones by three to one.) The most popular item (on 67 percent of all lists) was an exotic vacation. Then came the everyday-life items. Forty-seven percent of people wanted a "better, bigger, or more beautifully situated home." Another 28 percent wanted a vacation house. Forty-two percent wanted new cars, mainly luxury models. (As the title to Fournier and Guiry's article suggests, what Americans dream about is "An Emerald Green Jaguar, a House on Nantucket, and an African Safari.") Of course, respondents wanted other things beyond the house, car, and travel trio. About one-quarter cited household electronics—big-screen TVs, home computers, VCRs. Fifteen percent wanted a boat, 10 percent yearned for nice clothes, and 16 percent just asked for the money—enough to buy anything they could possibly want. These wish lists did not vary by sex, income, education, or standard of living. Apparently consumerism is an equal opportunity ideology. . . .

Our fantasies also reveal the centrality of gaining others' esteem. The ideal house fantasy is not complete without "showing the house to admiring others." In the words of one dreamer, "The awe and respect and wonder of my guest are basic to every daydream about my house." This is also true of the luxury goods featured in the standard "material wealth" fantasy. Displaying goods and gaining respect for them are crucial to our preoccupation with things. . . .

Not everyone earns before buying. Most of what we purchase we finance through borrowing. The earning comes later. Nearly all Americans borrow to buy their homes, and most automobiles are bought on time. Add to this the credit card balances, finance company loans, department store debts, and debts to individuals, and you begin to get an idea of the pervasiveness of household debt (about $5.5 trillion in late 1997). We "sign and travel" for vacations, charge the wife's birthday present, and put the health club membership on plastic. About one-third of the nation's population describe themselves as either heavily or moderately in financial debt, one-third report being slightly in debt, and only one-third report no financial (that is, excluding home mort-gage) debts at all. As I write these words, the fraction of Americans' disposable income that goes toward debt servicing continues to rise; it has now reached 18 percent. The total amount of debt held by the average household has increased relentlessly for decades, and it now equals just about what that household makes in any given year.

The rise in indebtedness is in large part due to credit cards. Between 1990 and 1996, credit card debt doubled. Credit cards, with interest rates reaching nearly 20 percent, are a remarkably lucrative part of the loan business. Debtors pay an average of $1,000 a year in interest and fees alone. And the companies look increas-ingly like "credit pushers," soliciting heavily and beyond their traditional creditwor-thy base. Using subtle tactics to encourage borrowing, the recent onslaught has led consumers to hold more cards, to borrow more, and to fork over an increasing fraction of their incomes to the companies. If you don't borrow, the company may cancel your card, since it isn't making money on you. . . .

See-want-borrow-and-buy is a comparative process; desire is structured by what we see around us. Even as we differentiate ourselves through fashion or cul-ture, we are located within, and look for validation to, a particular social space.

For most of us, that social space begins with relatives, friends, and coworkers. These are the people whose spending patterns we know and care most about. They are the people against whom we judge our own material lifestyles, and with whom we try to keep up. They are the groups that spur our consumer desires. . . . [However,] for many Americans, it's imaginary buddies who provide the prompts. . . .

While television has long been suspected as a promoter of consumer desire, there has been little hard evidence to support that view, at least for adult spending. After all, there's not an obvious connection. Many of the products advertised on television are everyday low-cost items such as aspirin, laundry detergent, and deodorant. Those TV ads are hardly a spur to excessive consumerism. Leaving aside other kinds of ads for the moment (for cars, diamonds, perfume), there's another counter to the argument that television causes consumerism: TV is a *substitute* for spending. One of the few remaining free activities, TV is a popular alternative to costly recreational spending such as movies, concerts, and restaurants. If it causes us to spend, that effect must be powerful enough to overcome its propensity to save us money.

Apparently it is. My research shows that the more TV a person watches, the more he or she spends. The likely explanation for the link between television and spending is that what we see on TV inflates our sense of what's normal. The lifestyles depicted on television are far different from the average American's: with a few exceptions, TV characters are upper-middle-class, or even rich.

Studies by the consumer researchers Thomas O'Guinn and L. J. Shrum confirm 15 this upward distortion. The more people watch television, the more they think American households have tennis courts, private planes, convertibles, car telephones, maids, and swimming pools. Heavy watchers also overestimate the portion of the population who are millionaires, have had cosmetic surgery, and belong to a private gym, as well as those suffering from dandruff, bladder control problems, gingivitis, athlete's foot, and hemorrhoids (the effect of all those ads for everyday products). What one watches also matters. Dramatic shows—both daytime soap operas and prime-time drama series—have a stronger impact on viewer perceptions than other kinds of programs (say news, sports, or weather).

Heavy watchers are not the only ones, however, who tend to overestimate standards of living. Almost everyone does. (And almost everyone watches TV.) In one study, ownership rates for twenty-two of twenty-seven consumer products were generally overstated. Your own financial position also matters. Television inflates standards for lower-, average-, and above-average-income students, but it does the reverse for really wealthy ones. (Among those raised in a financially rarefied atmosphere, TV is almost a reality check.) Social theories of consumption hold that the inflated sense of consumer norms promulgated by the media raises people's aspirations and leads them to buy more. In the words of one Los Angeles resident, commenting on this media tendency, "They try to portray that an upper-class lifestyle is normal and typical and that we should all have it."

Television also affects norms by giving us real information about how other people live and what they have. It allows us to be voyeurs, opening the door to the "private world" inside the homes and lives of others. There was a time when we didn't need television to get such information. In the past, homes, possessions, and habits were much more open to view and fully part of what Erving Goffman has called the system of "impression management." But as we have gotten richer, we have become more private. Much more private. We may not surface between the garage and the house. We rarely linger on the street. We build a deck instead of a front porch. We almost never hang out in our front yards. Indeed, as I unpacked a box in my front yard the other day, so I could keep an eye on the kids, a drive-by shopper stopped for my "yard sale." (Apparently the only thing we use our front yards for now is to sell the junk we can't fit inside.) As O'Guinn and Shrum note, television has replaced personal contact as our source of information about "what members of other social classes have and how they consume, even behind their closed doors."

Another piece of evidence for the TV-spending link is the apparent correlation between debt and excessive TV viewing. In the Merck Family Fund poll, the fraction responding that they "watch too much TV" rose steadily with indebtedness. More than half (56 percent) of all those who reported themselves "heavily" in debt also said they watched too much TV.

It is partly because of television that the top 20 percent of the income distribution, and even the top 5 percent within it, has become so important in setting and escalating consumption standards for more than just the people immediately below them. Television lets *everyone* see what these folks have and allows viewers to want it in concrete, product-specific ways. . . .

Of course, the TV effect is hard to prove. My results do not unravel what is undoubtedly a complex link between watching a program and ending up at the cash register. One difficulty with pinning down the impact of television is that almost everyone watches TV, and most people watch a lot. So it's difficult to find individuals who are not affected by it. However, the fact that different types of programming have different effects provides one piece of evidence. . . . TV and social pressure in one's daily life are interchangeable sources of consumer upscaling. . . . [20]

The fact that people pay extra money for status, or replicate the lifestyles of their friends, is not in itself an insurmountable problem. If we aped the guy in the corner office once and that was the end of it, it would be a relatively minor issue. The difficulty is the dynamic aspect of keeping up: the emulation process never ends. Growth is built into the very structure of our economy. Manufacturers strive for continuous productivity improvements. Retailers count on higher sales volume each year. Investors demand that their capital increase each quarter. The market imperative is bigger, better, more. Consumers have not escaped this escalation mentality. We expect our standard of living to rise annually, and throughout our working lives. Indeed, the rising standard is a national icon, firmly rooted in the political discourse. It is progress.

The commitment to rising incomes can be seen in a variety of public opinion polls. The standard answer to the amount of money a family of four needs to live in "reasonable comfort" has been $1,000 to $2,000 more than whatever the median family income happens to be. In 1978, $19,600, or $1,960 more than the national median, was thought to be necessary for "reasonable comfort." In 1985 reasonable comfort cost $30,600 (compared to median income of $27,734). By 1994 the reasonable-comfort level had risen to $40,000. Rising standards are also evident in our changing attitudes to necessities and luxuries. A wide range of consumer

The Upgrading of a "Comfortable Life"

Question: *In order to live in reasonable comfort around here, how much income per year do you think a family of four needs today?*

	Median Response	Median Income
1978	$19,600	$17,640
1981	$24,800	$22,388
1983	$28,400	$24,673
1985	$30,600	$27,734
1987	$32,500	$30,970
1990	$36,800	$35,353
1992	$38,000	$35,939
1994	$40,000	$38,782

SOURCE: Reasonable Comfort from Roper Center, University of Connecticut; Median Income from Council of Economic Advisers 1996. Table B-29, p. 314.

products considered luxuries in the 1970s are deemed necessities today. The luxuries of 1998 will be the necessities of the early twenty-first century.

The Merck Family Fund poll revealed another way in which having more is hardwired into our psyches. We are not satisfied with whatever level we have. When asked to define their own economic situation on a scale of 1–10 (with 10 representing the wealthiest people in the country), respondents on average chose 5.1, almost smack in the middle, as we would expect. Asked to define the *lowest* number at which they would feel satisfied with their economic situation, the average response was higher—5.4. Apparently, we still don't feel we have enough. In [a] sample [of high earners] (almost no one earned below $25,000 annually, and 35 percent earned above $55,000), 28 percent of those surveyed expressed dissatisfaction with their incomes, and 54 percent said they were only "somewhat satisfied." Of those, about one-third said they'd need 20 percent more income to be satisfied, and one-quarter said they'd need twice as much or more to reach satisfaction.

What drives the escalation of standards? Why do we never seem to have enough? There are cultural reasons, of course. But the economic structure itself is also to blame. As I argued in *The Overworked American,* the nation has become enmeshed in a cycle of work and spend. Employers, rather than employees, choose hours of work, and they typically choose long hours. Firms' annual productivity increases—courtesy of technological change or a better-educated workforce—cannot be used by employees to reduce hours of work but is passed on as income (if it *is* passed on).

Once they have it, employees spend their additional income. The imperatives 25 to spend in consumer society are numerous, and the incentives to save are weak. But there is another reason, unique to the work-and-spend dynamic. Rising incomes create social pressures to spend. A more leisured, lower-spending lifestyle does not emerge. Instead, people get more money and put in long hours on the job. As long as a few fashion-minded or highly consumerist households take on the role of innovators, spending their increased income on new, better, or more consumer items, the impact of their consumption ripples through the system. Marketing and advertising accelerate the process. Smiths emulate Joneses, and in turn are emulated by Bernsteins, Vitellis, and O'Rourkes. When the Chens don't want to go along, they are relatively alone—not only alone, but left behind.

There is an important irrationality in the system, and it is not hard to see: if we measure our satisfaction by how well we are doing compared to others, general increases in affluence do not raise our personal satisfaction (as mounting evidence shows). Then why do we participate? Why don't we learn after a few rounds of keeping up? Because, besides psychological factors, other powerful forces, both social and economic, keep us in the system.

For professionals, managers, salespeople, and many of the self-employed—people whose stock in trade is their "human capital"—maintaining a certain standard is important for success in the market. Consumption is taken as a signal of their skills and talents. They have to dress, drive, even eat the part. The lawyer in a cheesy suit, the psychiatrist with a seedy office, and the salesman in a twelve-year-old car all project failure.

In some jobs, image can be all-important. A wardrobe is as necessary as a diploma, as my interviewees repeatedly stressed. Makeup, accessories, and jewelry are de rigueur. Indeed, attractiveness itself affects market success. Economists have found that people who are more physically attractive gain better jobs and higher wages. Advertising firms with better-looking executives have higher revenues. And physical attractiveness is often created with the help of consumer products—cosmetics, beauty shops, tanning salons, health clubs, exercise equipment. Even male executives, downsized, or downsizable, are getting blepharoplasty (to reduce droopy skin around the eyes) and other cosmetic surgeries to make themselves more marketable in a world where youth counts for everything. For Lauren Vandermeer, moving up the corporate ladder necessitated more spending, on clothes and other accessories. "Now, maybe not to the extent of a Rolex watch. We're in the nineties, and the Rolex is no longer cool. But definitely, a Tissot watch from Switzerland. I got this in the Cayman Islands on vacation. It was important to have. Because when I would extend my hand to present something, they would see that, and that meant I was somebody to reckon with." While we need not go all the way with the claim of Oxxford Clothes (purveyor of $1,500 suits) that "business is war—never underestimate the importance of your uniform," the clothier does have a point. Keeping up is good business. . . .

The social dimensions of technological change also keep us on the consumer escalator. When the telephone was introduced, life without one posed no problems. But as phones became widely disseminated throughout the population, practical difficulties arose. Alternative forms of interpersonal communication declined. (Remember the private couriers so common in nineteenth- and early-twentieth-century novels?) Paying a social visit without an advance phone call became less acceptable among the middle classes. Today rotary phones, already inadequate for accessing certain services, have become nearly obsolete. Callers get annoyed if you don't have an answering machine. In business, voice mail, faxes, and mobile phones are standard, and they are becoming so in private life. As more and more people buy these items, substitutes disappear and life without them becomes more vexing.

Of course, technology also raises a host of daily paradoxes for us, as David 30
Mick and Susan Fournier have argued. New products promise freedom but often
feel enslaving. They promise to save us time but may not. And, of course, they
come with their own keeping-up dynamic. As one of their informants noted about
the laptop computer he had purchased just six weeks before, it "is not outmoded
[yet], but in another six months it will be. I know I'm going to be envious of what's
out there." . . .

Upscaling transforms the consumer market itself. Once new products are diffused throughout the population, the items they replaced disappear. Where are the
manual typewriters, houses without closets, and monochrome computer monitors?
When the old appliances break, parts are no longer available. Indeed, there is a
general bias in our economy against repair and in favor of buying new. (One reason this bias can prevail is that new products do not pay their true environmental
costs.) For those who don't want to change what they have and are comfortable
with a static lifestyle, the market offers limited choices. It is geared to newer and
more expensive products. It is perpetually upshifting. . . .

However rational it may be for individuals to keep up with the upscaling of
consumer standards, it can be deeply irrational for society as a whole. Or, as one
Chicago woman put it, "We'd all be better off if we cared less about what someone's wearing and what kind of a car they're driving or where they're living." Like
standing up in a crowd to get a better view, it stops working once others do it
too. In the end, the view is the same, but everyone's legs are tired. The more our
consumer satisfaction is tied into social comparisons—whether upscaling, just keeping up, or not falling too far behind—the less we achieve when consumption grows,
because the people we compare ourselves to are also experiencing rising consumption. Our relative position does not change. Jones's delight at being able to afford
the Honda Accord is dampened when he sees Smith's new Camry. Both must put
in long hours to make the payments, suffer with congested highways and dirty air,
and have less in the bank at the end of the day. And both remain frustrated when
they think about the Land Cruiser down the street.

Of course, relative positions do change. Some people get promotions or pay
raises that place them higher up in the hierarchy. Others fall behind. But these
random changes cancel each other out. Of more interest is how the broad social
groupings that make up the major comparison groups fare. From the end of the
Second World War until the mid-1970s, growth was relatively equally distributed.
The rough doubling in living standards was experienced by most Americans, including the poor. In fact, the income distribution was even compressed, as people at
the bottom gained some ground relative to those at the top. Since then, however,
and particularly since the 1980s, the income groups have diverged, as I noted in
the introduction.

Middle-class Americans began to experience themselves falling behind as their
slow-growing wages and salaries lagged behind those of the groups above them.
Their anxiety grew, and it became a commonplace that it was no longer possible
to achieve a middle-class standard of living on one salary. At the same time, increasing numbers began to lose completely the respectability that defined their class.

Below them, a segment of downwardly mobile working people found that their reduced job prospects and declining wages had placed them in the ranks of the working poor. And the nonemployed poor fell even further as their numbers grew and their average income fell.

Thus, relative position has worsened for most people, making it increasingly 35 difficult to keep up. The excitement, convenience, or joy that households may have experienced through the billions in additional spending between 1979 and the present seems to have been overshadowed by feelings of deprivation. Among the upper echelons, all those personal computers, steam showers, Caribbean vacations, and piano lessons have not been sufficient to offset the anxieties inherent in a rapidly upscaling society.

The current mood has led to nostalgia about the older, simpler version of the American dream. There is a palpable sense of unease, a yearning for the less expansive, and less expensive, aspirations of our parents. In the words of one young man, "My dream is to build my own house. When my parents grew up, they weren't so much 'I want this, I've got to have that.' They just wanted to be comfortable. Now we're more—I know I am—'I need this.' And it's not really a need."

The greater the weight people place on the social comparison aspect of their consumption, relative to other aspects like function, aesthetics, or convenience, the greater the social irrationality of upscaling. If, as some have argued, these social aspects become more important as basic needs are met and we grow more affluent, then the system takes on an increasingly perverse character. The problem is not just that more consumption doesn't yield more satisfaction (as in the extreme case where all satisfaction comes from relative position), but that it always has a cost. The extra hours we have to work to earn the money cut into personal and family time. *Whatever* we consume has an ecological impact, whether it's the rain forests cleared to graze the cattle which become Big Macs, the toxins collecting in our bodies from the plastics that now dominate our material environment, or the pesticides used to grow the cotton for our T-shirts. Americans increasingly resent paying taxes to buy public goods like parks, schools, the arts, or support for the poor because taxes are perceived as subtracting from the private consumption they deem absolutely necessary. We find ourselves skimping on invisibles such as insurance, college funds, and retirement savings as the visible commodities somehow become indispensable. In the process, we are threatening our temporal, social, and biological infrastructures. We are impoverishing ourselves in pursuit of a consumption goal that is inherently unachievable. In the words of one focus-group participant, we "just don't know when to stop and draw the line."

The Grill-Buying Guy

DAVID BROOKS

> David Brooks, a graduate of University of Chicago, is a regular columnist for the
> *New York Times,* writing with what he describes as a "Hamiltonian or Giuliani"
> conservative viewpoint. His two books of social commentary are *Bobos in Paradise:*
> *The New Upper Class and How They Got There* (Touchstone, 2000) and *On Paradise*
> *Drive: How We Live Now (And Always Have) in the Future Tense* (Simon & Schuster,
> 2004). Although he pokes fun at consumers' behavior, Brooks reveals a deep
> appreciation for Americans' work ethic, ingenuity, and tireless pursuit of their
> dreams. This selection is from *On Paradise Drive.*

I don't know if you've ever seen the expression of a man who is about to buy a
first-class barbecue grill. He walks into Home Depot or Lowe's or one of the other
mega-hardware complexes, and his eyes are glistening with a faraway visionary
zeal, like one of those old prophets gazing into the promised land. His lips are
parted and twitching slightly.

Inside the megastore, the man adopts the stride American men fall into when
in the presence of large amounts of lumber. He heads over to the barbecue grills,
just past the racks of affordable house-plan books, in the yard-machinery section.
They are arrayed magnificently next to the vehicles that used to be known as riding
mowers but are now known as lawn tractors, because to call them riding mowers
doesn't fully convey the steroidized M1 tank power of the things. The man approaches
the barbecue grills with a trancelike expression suggesting that he has cast aside all
the pains and imperfections of this world and is approaching the gateway to a higher
dimension. In front of him is a scattering of massive steel-coated reactors with names
like Broilmaster P3, Thermidor, and the Weber Genesis, because in America it seems
perfectly normal to name a backyard barbecue grill after a book of the Bible.

The items in this cooking arsenal flaunt enough metal to survive a direct
nuclear assault. Patio Man goes from machine to machine comparing their various
features—the cast-iron/porcelain-coated cooking surfaces, the 328,000-BTU heat-
generating capacities, the 2,000-degree tolerance linings, multiple warming racks,
lava-rock containment dishes, or built-in electrical meat thermometers. Certain profound questions flow through his mind. Is a 542-cubic-inch grilling surface enough,
considering he might someday get the urge to roast a bison? Can he handle the
TEC Sterling II grill, which can hit temperatures of 1,600 degrees, thereby causing
his dinner to spontaneously combust? Though the matte-steel overcoat resists
scratching, doesn't he want a polished steel surface so he can glance down and
admire his reflection while performing the suburban manliness rituals such as brushing tangy teriyaki sauce on meat slabs with his right hand while clutching a beer
can in an NFL foam insulator in his left?

Pretty soon a large salesperson in an orange vest—looking like an SUV in
human form—comes up to him and says, "Howyadoin'," which is "May I help

you?" in Home Depot talk. Patio Man, who has so much lust in his heart, it is all he can do to keep from climbing up on one of these machines and whooping rodeo-style with joy, still manages to respond appropriately. He grunts inarticulately and nods toward the machines. Careful not to make eye contact at any point, the two manly suburban men have a brief exchange of pseudo-scientific grill argot that neither of them understands, and pretty soon Patio Man comes to the reasoned conclusion that it would make sense to pay a little extra for a grill with V-shaped metal baffles, ceramic rods, and a side-mounted smoker box.

But none of this talk matters. The guy will end up buying the grill with the 5 best cup holders. All major purchases of consumer durable goods these days ultimately come down to which model has the most impressive cup holders.

Having selected his joy machine, Patio Man heads for the cash register, Visa card trembling in his hand. All up and down the line are tough ex-football-playing guys who are used to working outdoors. They hang pagers and cell phones from their belts (in case a power line goes down somewhere) and wear NASCAR sunglasses, mullet haircuts, and faded T-shirts that they have ripped the sleeves off of to keep their arm muscles exposed and their armpit hair fully ventilated. Here and there are a few innately Office Depot guys who are trying to blend in with their more manly Home Depot brethren, and not ask Home Depot inappropriate questions, such as "Does this tool belt make my butt look fat?"

At the checkout, Patio Man is told that some minion will forklift the grill over to the loading dock around back. He is once again glad that he's driving that Yukon XL so he can approach the loading-dock guys as a co-equal in the manly fraternity of Those Who Haul Things.

As he signs the credit-card slip, with its massive total price, his confidence suddenly collapses, but it is revived as wonderful grill fantasies dance in his imagination:

There he is atop the uppermost tier of his multilevel backyard dining and recreational area. This is the kind of deck Louis XIV would have had if Sun Gods had had decks. In his mind's eye, Patio Man can see himself coolly flipping the garlic-and-pepper T-bones on the front acreage of his new grill while carefully testing the citrus-tarragon trout filets simmering fragrantly on the rear. On the lawn below, his kids Haley and Cody frolick on the weedless community lawn that is mowed twice weekly courtesy of the people who run Monument Crowne Preserve, his townhome community.

Haley, the fourteen-year-old daughter, is a Travel-Team Girl who spends her 10 weekends playing midfield against similarly ponytailed, strongly calved soccer marvels such as herself. Cody, ten, is a Buzz-Cut Boy whose naturally blond hair has been cut to lawnlike stubble, and the little that's left is highlighted an almost phosphorescent white. Cody's wardrobe is entirely derivative of fashions he has seen watching the X Games. Patio Man can see the kids playing with child-safe lawn darts alongside a gaggle of their cul-de-sac friends, a happy gathering of Haleys and Codys and Corys and Britneys. It's a brightly colored scene—Abercrombie & Fitch pink spaghetti-strap tops on the girls and ankle-length canvas shorts and laceless Nikes on the boys. Patio Man notes somewhat uncomfortably that in America today the average square yardage of boyswear grows and grows, while the square inches in the girls' outfits shrinks and shrinks. The boys carry so much fabric they look like skateboarding Bedouins, and the girls look like preppy prostitutes.

Nonetheless, Patio Man envisions a Saturday-evening party—his adult softball-team buddies lounging on his immaculate deck furniture, watching him with a certain moist envy as he mans the grill. They are moderately fit, sockless men in Docksiders, chinos, and Tommy Bahama muted Hawaiian shirts. Their wives, trim Jennifer Aniston lookalikes, wear capris and sleeveless tops, which look great on them owing to their countless hours on the weight machines at Spa Lady. . . .

They are wonderful people. Patio Man can envision his own wife, Cindy, the Real-tor Mom, circulating among them serving drinks, telling parent-teacher-conference stories and generally stirring up the hospitality; he, Patio Man, masterfully wields his extra-wide fish spatula while absorbing the aroma of imported hickory chips—again, to the silent admiration of all. The sun is shining. The people are friendly. The men are no more than twenty-five pounds overweight, which is the socially acceptable male-paunch level in upwardly mobile America, and the children are well adjusted. This vision of domestic bliss is what Patio Man has been shooting for all his life.

SUGGESTIONS FOR WRITING

For Inquiry and Convincing (or Mediating)

James Twitchell and Alex Kotlowitz have contrasting views about whether buying similar brands and products is a unifying force in society. Does poor people's desire for high-end products bring them into mainstream culture, or does it offer them a false sense of belonging? Make your own case for the viewpoint you think holds the most truth, or write a mediatory essay showing how each writer's position holds some truth. You may want to do additional research, such as, How fluid is the economic status of the poor population in America? What causes people to remain in conditions such as Kotlowitz describes?

For Convincing

Juliet Schor mentions that consumer societies put a great deal of value on individual privacy. Why do you think this happens? What do you think the effects of this are? For example, how has the privacy of a consumer society affected family life or life on your college campus? Arrive at a specific claim about this aspect of consumer societies and defend it through firsthand observations as well as additional research.

For Inquiry and Persuasion

Although Virginia Postrel and James Twitchell do not mention the impact of consumer spending on the environment, Juliet Schor does bring up this issue both directly and indirectly in several passages. Find some of these passages, and after discussing them in class, look into some particular aspect of the consumer society to determine its impact on the Earth's environment. If you can see a need for people to reduce their consumption in some area that is not often discussed in the media, write a persuasive essay to raise people's awareness and move them to change their spending.

SECTION 2: THE MESSAGES OF ADVERTISING
Overview

In the first section of this chapter, writers talked about the meaning of products in a consumer society. Consumers buy a product for its meaning, for what it says to them and about them. And much of the meaning of products comes from advertising, the focus of the readings in this section. Advertisements these days tell us very little about the product itself; instead, they associate the product with a targeted audience's values, emotions, and aspirations. Some people deny the power of advertising, saying they are not influenced by it, but evidence of its power is undeniable. In the United States, over $150 billion is spent on advertising each year, as much as the total national expenditure on higher education. Corporations would not put that kind of money into wasted efforts. Advertising works.

One issue connected with advertising in a consumer society is the question "Does advertising manipulate people into buying things against their better judgment?" It uses emotional appeals, suggesting that a product will help us find love, success, and personal fulfillment, even—as Jean Kilbourne argues in "Jesus Is a Brand of Jeans"—a transcendental or spiritual promise. But what happens when people buy the product and find that the ads made false promises? Critics such as Kilbourne argue that repeatedly discovering the broken promises of advertising, people become depressed and cynical. But the power of advertising is so great that they keep on believing. Says Kilbourne, "In the history of the world there has never been a propaganda effort to match that of advertising in the past 50 years." The only one that was parallel, she implies, was that of Nazi Germany.

James B. Twitchell, whom we met in Section One as a defender of luxury spending, agrees in this section about the power of advertising but not about whether consumers are duped by it. He believes ads sell us our dreams, and savvy consumers willingly and knowingly buy the promises, as he did when an ad caused him to buy his red Miata.

Another issue addressed in this section is the collateral effects of advertising on people's values and behavior. Besides showing us products, ads show us images of the good life. Some would argue that those images simply reflect values already present in a society; others would argue that the images affect the society, influencing people to accept the values implied in the ads. Juliet Schor made this case in Section One when she explained that middle-class people emulate the lifestyles seen on TV. Jean Kilbourne, in the second of her two essays in this section, argues that advertising both reflects and affects dangerous attitudes toward girls and women, leading to mental health problems and eating disorders. But men are no longer immune from media-induced body-image dissatisfaction. Now they compare themselves to the buff guys in commercial messages and engage in their own risky behavior to achieve perfection, the topic of Alissa Quart's essay "X-Large Boys."

How I Bought My Red Miata

JAMES B. TWITCHELL

You have already met James Twitchell if you read the preceding section of this casebook where his essay "Needing the Unnecessary" appears. If you haven't already, read the headnote about Twitchell on page 337. The following selection comes from another of his books, *Lead Us into Temptation: The Triumph of American Materialism* (Columbia University Press, 1999).

All our wants, beyond those which a very moderate income will supply, are purely imaginary.

—Henry St. John, 1743

Things, as such, become goods as soon as the human mind recognizes them as means suitable for the promotion of human purposes.

—Carl Menger, 1871

. . . When my daughters were little they would go with me to the grocery store. We would start as friends, and before a few aisles had passed we would be at each other's throats. "Gimme this, I want that, can we have these?"—it would go on and on until, by the vegetables, I would lose control and things would degenerate into Kmart Khaos. "No, no, a thousand nos," I would yell at them. "No, you can't have that. No, I won't buy you that." This didn't work, and by the time we had reached the checkout line, they had gotten much of what they had sought.

To stop the demoralizing defeat I tried to teach them about consumption. I developed The Nerminological Laws of Consumption, and I drilled these so-called laws into them so that I could later say, "What Nerminological law have you just broken?" whenever they asked for anything.

Here are the rules. First, isolate the need. Do you need this thing or do you just want it? Don't let *needs* be confused with *wants*. Next, shop around. Check out the competition. Do your research. Third, can you afford this? Check current and anticipated cash flow. And last, once you have decided, can you read the instructions on how to use it properly? Why buy a toy you can't assemble? The success of such a system was not so much that it was logical but that it took so long to go through that once they had come to the instruction part, we were out the door. I would live to regret my explanation of what goes on in the Land of the Nermies ruled by the inexorable Nerminological Laws.

It happened about ten years ago. I bought a Mazda Miata. This is a snappy little red sports car that twelve-year-old boys really like, but chubby, balding fifty-year-olds usually buy. My daughters like driving it, but better, they like asking me which of the Nerminological Laws I followed when I bought it. Did I need a car when I biked to work? Did I need a car that seats only two? Did I really shop around? Could I afford it on my schoolteacher salary? Did I even know how to drive it properly? If so, why did I brake during cornering instead of accelerating? Could I fix it? Did I even know where the battery was hidden? Clearly, they enjoyed seeing me hoisted by my own petard.

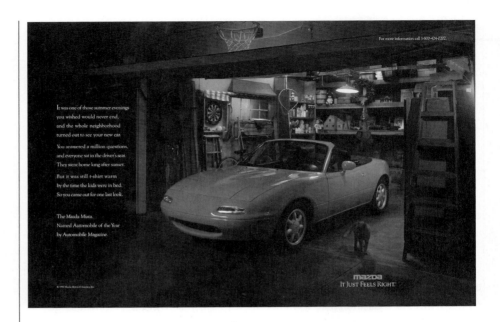

Although this car has given me much pleasure, I still can't figure out exactly 5 why I bought it. I know how to buy stuff. I'm fully mature. I have a 401(k) plan. When I was growing up my parents subscribed to *Consumer Reports,* and I learned how to read all the little bulls-eye symbols telling you if this was a good deal or a so-so one. So what happened?

I bought the car because of an advertisement. The ad itself is not complex. In fact, it is the standard "product as hero" ad that we have all seen a thousand times. There stage center, lit from behind like a haloed angel, is this thing in your garage. If you are middle-aged, the garage is clearly from your early ado- lescence, when you were moving out of your room and mixing your toys with the stuff of your parents. But wait! That stuff in the pictured garage is not your dad's stuff—those are not his toys, they are yours. Dad didn't grow up with a whiffle ball, a dart board, the teddy bear, the metronome (aargh!), the dollhouse, that bike.

The maudlin text below the icon makes it clear. All this is/was yours:

> It was one of those summer evenings you wished would never end, and the whole neighborhood turned out to see your new car. You answered a million questions, and everyone sat in the driver's seat. They went home long after sunset.

In an interesting kind of temporal dislocation the "you" is in the past tense. This is the "you" of your childhood, the you who rushed downtown each September to see what the new cars looked like, the you who dreamed about getting an MG, an Austin Healey 3000, or maybe a Triumph. It would be red, or maybe English racing green. When someone had a car like that what could you do but just stand there and look at it? There was really nothing you could say.[1]

The last line in the copy pulls the plug. "But it was still T-shirt warm by the time the kids were in bed. So you came out for one last look." The "you" as observer has become the "you" as owner. It's yours now. This missing part of your past, this thing that always belonged to someone else, is yours. Little wonder the car is positioned and lit like a holy relic. It's coming at you. All you have to do is grasp it.

What separates this ad from the usual automotive pitch is its claim on memory. 10 The more usual claim for sports cars is sexual: Get this car, get that girl. So the sports car is usually photographed out in the rugged countryside, the sport himself is young and virile, and the chick by his side just can't stop looking at him. In advertising lingo this is called the aspirational sell: use the product and everyone will see what a real man you are.

What is important about the Miata ad is that there is no one at the wheel and no dreamy chick flapping her lashes at him. This driver's seat is vacant. You've always wanted to sit there. Now you can. Here as my colleagues might say, is nostalgic onanism.[2]

Although I had "new-car fever" (a common enough strain of affluenza), the object was difficult to consume. Here's why. I teach school. I wear khaki pants. I had a green book bag in graduate school. I am a company man. I buy my cars from Volvo or Saab, not because I like these cars—I don't. They are built to be ugly and are no fun. But they are part of the uniform. They are from Sweden, for goodness' sake, the Valhalla of academic liberalism. If I bought the Miata I was not just going to lose my afficiation with my PRIZM group. I was going over to a different group, to a group I abhorred. If I bought this car I was going to become . . . a yuppie!

At the time I was making my decision, yuppies were the group du jour of marketers and the group de résistance for all the rest of us. Yuppies were disgusting. What made them disgusting was their lack of reticence in the displaying of commercial badges. More interesting still was that no one ever would admit to being one of them. In fact, in retrospect, the real sign of being a yuppie

---

[1] I still remember being in the parking lot in Stowe, Vermont at the base of Mt. Mansfield after a day of skiing. Someone from New York City had left his Aston Martin idling while he was in the warming hut. There must have been fifteen teenage boys who stopped in their tracks and just listened to that car. No one dared get near it. It was as holy as any object I had ever seen. Later at Christmas I remember thinking that I could understand how the wise men felt as they beheld the Christ child in Bethlehem. I knew it was sacrilegious to make such a comparison but I also knew it was true.

[2] Larry Kapold, executive creative director of Foote, Cone & Belding in Los Angeles, which made the ad, has a slightly different explanation. He says he was able to tease this ad from various focus groups.

> Early on, whenever we'd show a picture of the car to anyone, we'd get one of two reactions. Either, it's beautiful or you know what it reminds me of. . . . We wanted to tap that feeling of a car evoking warm memories without hitting people over the head with something like a 1950s sock-hop. (Goldrich 6)

was that you tried hard to disassociate from them while all along displaying their badges.[3]

Yuppies were unique in that they were the first consumption community that I can think of known *only* by their badges. No one came forward like Marlon Brando, Abbie Hoffman, John Wayne, or Elton John to personify the group. Richard Gere laying out his clothes on the bed in the movie *American Gigolo* might have been the yuppie archetype, but he seemed a little too moody about his stuff. Still, rather like Eagle Scouts, yuppies had no distinct personality other than their merit (or demerit, it's up to you) badges worn almost Pancho Villa style around their vacuous lifestyles.

Here are just a few of the yuppie badges: yellow ties and red suspenders, 15 Merlot, marinated salmon steaks, green-bottle beer, Club Med vacations, stuff with ducks on it, Gaggenau stoves, Sub-Zero refrigerators, latte, clothing from Ann Taylor or Ralph Lauren, designer water, Filofax binders, Cuisinarts, kiwi fruit, Ben & Jerry's ice cream, ventless Italian suits, pasta makers, bread makers, espresso-cappuccino makers, cellphones, home fax machines, air and water cleaners, laptop computers, exercise machines, massage tables, and remote controls for the television, the VCR, the CD player, the stereo receiver, the garage door, the child. More than anything, of course, the car—especially the BMW, the infamous beemer—was the yuppie badge nonpareil.

The yuppie and his German or Japanese car were academic anathema. If a colleague were to see me in such a car he would surely think I had gone over to the other side. My cousin with the pricy condo, the Jenn-Air gas grill, Biggest Bertha Ever golf club, and the Suburban could be a yuppie. But not me. I only bought just the things I absolutely needed . . . like a red Miata? And that, of course, was precisely my problem. When I bought this car, I became one of them.

I dilate on my Miata decision because it shows the dynamic of pressures in the commercial world. Two generations ago maybe choosing what denomination of the Congregational church to attend would have caused me such distress. Do I dare be seen with Unitarians? At the turn of this century what musical instrument you played would have been important. "They laughed when I sat down at the piano, but when I started to play!" describes a Horatio Alger experience we have trouble understanding. Maybe status would have been derived from what I read. Could I be seen reading Walt Whitman? What about what I ate? Our grandparents read etiquette books detailing the shame you should feel if you ordered the same meal too often. "Again she orders—A chicken salad, please!" is the headline of an ad for such an etiquette book. It is presumably spoken by an exasperated young man about his date. What if I coughed? Would that be a social blunder? Perhaps

---

[3]The original definition was a young urban professional, but at some point this became corrupted to young upwardly mobile professional. From there meaning spread to define an entire generation of afflu-ent and selfish twenty-somethings who were hot on the heels of us baby boomers. Demographically, yuppies were part of the 76 million people born between 1946 and 1964. Their number was small (the only definitive estimate of the yuppie population found just four million of them, representing a mere 5 percent of late baby boomers [see "The Big Chill Revisited," and entire issue of *American Demographics,* September 1985]), but their impact on the rest of us was huge—reverse magnetism.

what I wore. Could I be seen wearing a gold stickpin in my tie? The way we live now, I worry that I might be mistaken for a yuppie.

While I certainly went through the modern version of the "agonies of the damned" buying a Japanese internal-combustion engine advertised through nostalgia and wrapped in red plastic, I never once was duped, misled, waylaid, or reified. In fact, I loved the process. They offered me my dream and I gladly bought it. I never liked that dreary Volvo to begin with. Now I'm wondering about a Jaguar, perhaps something from the early '80s, not too ostentatious but still flashy, if you know what I mean.

Let's face it, the idea that consumerism creates artificial desires rests on a wistful ignorance of history and human nature, on the hazy, romantic feeling that there existed some halcyon era of noble savages with purely natural needs. Once fed and sheltered, our needs have always been cultural, not natural. Until there is some other system to codify and satisfy those needs and yearnings, capitalism—and the culture it carries with it—will continue not just to thrive but to triumph.

In the way we live now, it is simply impossible to consume objects without 20 consuming meaning. Meaning is pumped *and* drawn everywhere throughout the modern commercial world, into the farthest reaches of space and into the smallest divisions of time. Commercialism is the water we all swim in, the air we breathe, our sunlight and shade. Currents of desire flow around objects like smoke in a wind tunnel. The complications of my Miata purchase are the norm. . . .

To some degree, the triumph of consumerism is the triumph of the popular will. You may not like what is manufactured, advertised, packaged, branded, and broadcast, but it is far closer to what most people want most of the time than at any other period of modern history. . . .

We have not been led into this world of material closeness against our better judgment. For many of us, especially when young, consumerism is our better judgment. And this is true regardless of class or culture. We have not just asked to go this way, we have demanded. Now most of the world is lining up, pushing and shoving, eager to elbow into the mall. Woe to the government or religion that says no.

Getting and spending has been the most passionate, and often the most imaginative, endeavor of modern life. We have done more than acknowledge that the good life starts with the material life, as the ancients did. We have made stuff the dominant prerequisite of organized society. Things "R" Us. Consumption has become production. While this is dreary and depressing to some, as doubtless it should be, it is liberating and democratic to many more.

REFERENCE

Gobrich, Robert. "Go West, Creatives . . . ." *Back Stage,* August 11, 1989, p. 6B.

Jesus Is a Brand of Jeans

JEAN KILBOURNE

Jean Kilbourne is a renowned lecturer, documentary filmmaker, and writer on the subject of advertising. Her works reveal the destructive power of many images in advertising, particularly the damage images do to women's mental and physical health. She is best known for her award-winning book *Deadly Persuasion: Why Women and Girls Must Fight the Addictive Power of Advertising* (1999) and her film *Killing Us Softly: Advertising's Image of Women.* She has a BA in English from Wellesley and a PhD in education from Boston University. She has been a visiting research scholar at the Wellesley Centers for Women as well as a member of numerous government and social agencies. The essay below originally appeared in *New Internationalist,* September 2006.

A recent ad for Thule car-rack systems features a child in the backseat of a car, seatbelt on. Next to the child, assorted sporting gear is carefully strapped into a child's carseat. The headline says: "We Know What Matters to You." In case one misses the point, further copy adds: "Your gear is a priority."

Another ad features an attractive young couple in bed. The man is on top of the woman, presumably making love to her. However, her face is completely covered by a magazine, open to a double-page photo of a car. The man is gazing passionately at the car. The copy reads, "The ultimate attraction."

These ads are meant to be funny. Taken individually, I suppose they might seem amusing or, at worst, tasteless. As someone who has studied ads for a long time, however, I see them as part of a pattern: just two of many ads that state or imply that products are more important than people. Ads have long promised us a better relationship via a product: *buy this and you will be loved.* But more recently they have gone beyond that proposition to promise us a relationship with the product itself: *buy this and it will love you.* The product is not so much the means to an end, as the end itself.

After all, it is easier to love a product than a person. Relationships with human beings are messy, unpredictable, sometimes dangerous. "When was the last time you felt this comfortable in a relationship?" asks an ad for shoes. Our shoes never ask us to wash the dishes or tell us we're getting fat. Even more important, products don't betray us. "You can love it without getting your heart broken," proclaims a car ad. One certainly can't say that about loving a human being, as love without vulnerability is impossible.

We are surrounded by hundreds, thousands of messages every day that link 5 our deepest emotions to products, that objectify people and trivialize our most heartfelt moments and relationships. Every emotion is used to sell us something. Our wish to protect our children is leveraged to make us buy an expensive car. A long marriage simply provides the occasion for a diamond necklace. A painful reunion between a father and his estranged daughter is dramatized to sell us a phone system. Everything in the world—nature, animals, people—is just so much stuff to be consumed or to be used to sell us something.

The problem with advertising isn't that it creates artificial needs, but that it exploits our very real and human desires. Advertising promotes a bankrupt concept of *relationship*. Most of us yearn for committed relationships that will last. We are not stupid: we know that buying a certain brand of cereal won't bring us one inch closer to that goal. But we are surrounded by advertising that yokes our needs with products and promises us that *things* will deliver what in fact they never can. In the world of advertising, lovers are things and things are lovers.

It may be that there is no other way to depict relationships when the ultimate goal is to sell products. But this apparently bottomless consumerism not only depletes the world's resources, it also depletes our inner resources. It leads inevitably to narcissism and solipsism. It becomes difficult to imagine a way of relating that isn't objectifying and exploitative.

TUNED IN

Most people feel that advertising is not something to take seriously. Other aspects of the media are serious—the violent films, the trashy talk shows, the bowdlerization of the news. But not advertising! Although much more attention has been paid to the cultural impact of advertising in recent years than ever before, just about everyone still feels personally exempt from its influence. What I hear more than anything else at my lectures is: "I don't pay attention to ads . . . I just tune them out . . . they have no effect on me." I hear this most from people wearing clothes emblazoned with logos. In truth, we are all influenced. There is no way to tune out this much information, especially when it is designed to break through the "tuning out" process. As advertising critic Sut Jhally put it: "To not be influenced by advertising would be to live outside of culture. No human being lives outside of culture."

Much of advertising's power comes from this belief that it does not affect us. As Joseph Goebbels said: "This is the secret of propaganda: those who are to be persuaded by it should be completely immersed in the ideas of the propaganda, without ever noticing that they are being immersed in it." Because we think advertising is trivial, we are less on guard, less critical, than we might otherwise be. While we're laughing, sometimes sneering, the commercial does its work.

Taken individually, ads are silly, sometimes funny, certainly nothing to worry 10 about. But cumulatively they create a climate of cynicism that is poisonous to relationships. Ad after ad portrays our real lives as dull and ordinary, commitment to human beings as something to be avoided. Because of the pervasiveness of this kind of message, we learn from childhood that it is far safer to make a commitment to a product than to a person, far easier to be loyal to a brand. Many end up feeling romantic about material objects yet deeply cynical about other human beings. . . .

Some argue that advertising simply reflects societal values rather than affecting them. Far from being a passive mirror of society, however, advertising is a pervasive medium of influence and persuasion. Its influence is cumulative, often subtle and primarily unconscious. A former editor-in-chief of *Advertising Age,* the leading advertising publication in North America, once claimed: "Only eight per cent of an ad's message is received by the conscious mind. The rest is worked and re-worked deep within, in the recesses of the brain."

Advertising performs much the same function in industrial society as myth did in ancient societies. It is both a creator and perpetuator of the dominant values of the culture, the social norms by which most people govern their behaviour. At the very least, advertising helps to create a climate in which certain values flourish and others are not reflected at all.

Advertising is not only our physical environment, it is increasingly our spiritual environment as well. By definition, however, it is only interested in materialistic values. When spiritual values show up in ads, it is only in order to sell us something. Eternity is a perfume by Calvin Klein. Infiniti is an automobile, and Hydra Zen a moisturizer. Jesus is a brand of jeans.

Sometimes the allusion is more subtle, as in the countless alcohol ads featuring the bottle surrounded by a halo of light. Indeed products such as jewellery shining in a store window are often displayed as if they were sacred objects. Advertising co-opts our sacred symbols in order to evoke an immediate emotional response. Media critic Neil Postman referred to this as "cultural rape."

It is commonplace to observe that consumerism has become the religion of 15 our time (with advertising its holy text), but the criticism usually stops short of what is at the heart of the comparison. Both advertising and religion share a belief in transformation, but most religions believe that this requires sacrifice. In the world of advertising, enlightenment is achieved instantly by purchasing material goods. An ad for a watch says, "It's not your handbag. It's not your neighbourhood. It's not your boyfriend. It's your watch that tells most about who you are." Of course, this cheapens authentic spirituality and transcendence. This junk food for the soul leaves us hungry, empty, malnourished.

SUBSTITUTE STORIES

Human beings used to be influenced primarily by the stories of our particular tribe or community, not by stories that are mass-produced and market-driven. As George Gerbner, one of the world's most respected researchers on the influence of the media, said: "For the first time in human history, most of the stories about people, life and values are told not by parents, schools, churches, or others in the community who have something to tell, but by a group of distant conglomerates that have something to sell."

Although it is virtually impossible to measure the influence of advertising on a culture, we can learn something by looking at cultures only recently exposed to it. In 1980 the Gwich'in tribe of Alaska got television, and therefore massive advertising, for the first time. Satellite dishes, video games and VCRs were not far behind. Before this, the Gwich'in lived much the way their ancestors had for generations. Within 10 years, the young members of the tribe were so drawn by television they no longer had time to learn ancient hunting methods, their parents' language or their oral history. Legends told around campfires could not compete with Beverly Hills 90210. Beaded moccasins gave way to Nike sneakers, and "tundra tea" to Folger's instant coffee.

As multinational chains replace local character, we end up in a world in which everyone is Gapped and Starbucked. Shopping malls kill vibrant downtown centers locally and create a universe of uniformity internationally. We end up in a world ruled by, in John Maynard Keynes's phrase, the values of the casino. On this deeper level, rampant commercialism undermines our physical and psychological health, our environment and our civic life, and creates a toxic society.

Advertising creates a world view that is based upon cynicism, dissatisfaction and craving. Advertisers aren't evil. They are just doing their job, which is to sell a product; but the consequences, usually unintended, are often destructive. In the history of the world there has never been a propaganda effort to match that of advertising in the past 50 years. More thought, more effort, more money goes into advertising than has gone into any other campaign to change social consciousness. The story that advertising tells is that the way to be happy, to find satisfaction—and the path to political freedom, as well—is through the consumption of material objects. And the major motivating force for social change throughout the world today is this belief that happiness comes from the market.

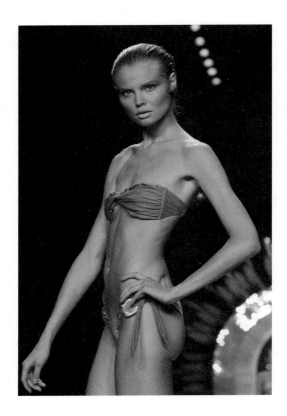

A model at the Spring 2007 Fashion Week in New York.

Cutting Girls Down to Size

JEAN KILBOURNE

For information about Jean Kilbourne, see the headnote to the preceding selection (page 370), which is also by Kilbourne. This selection comes from an anthology titled *Psychology and Consumer Culture: The Struggle for a Good Life in a Materialistic World* (American Psychological Association, 2004). Find out more about Kilbourne at <http://www.jeankilbourne.com/bio.html>.

At no time are we more vulnerable to the seductive power of advertising than during adolescence. Adolescents are relatively new and inexperienced consumers and, as such, prime targets. They are in the process of learning their values and roles and of developing their self-concepts. Most teenagers are sensitive to peer pressure and find it difficult to resist or even to question the dominant cultural messages perpetuated and reinforced by the media. Mass communication has made possible a kind of national peer pressure that erodes private and individual values and standards, as well as community values and standards. As Margaret Mead

(1977) once said, today our children are not brought up by parents; they are brought up by the mass media.

Advertisers are aware of their power and do not hesitate to take advantage of the insecurities and anxieties of young people, usually in the guise of offering solutions. A cigarette provides a symbol of independence. Designer jeans or sneakers convey status. The right perfume or beer resolves doubts about femininity or masculinity. Most young people are vulnerable to these messages. Adolescence is a time of doubt and insecurity for most young people, but a particular kind of insecurity afflicts adolescent girls.

As most of us know so well by now, when a girl enters adolescence, she faces a series of losses—loss of self-confidence, loss of a sense of efficacy and ambition, and the loss of her "voice," the sense of being a unique and powerful self that she had in childhood. Girls who were active, confident, and feisty at the ages of 8 and 9 and 10 often become hesitant, insecure, and self-doubting by 11. Their self-esteem plummets. As Carol Gilligan (1982), Mary Pipher (1994), and other social critics and psychologists (e.g., Sadker & Sadker, 1994) have pointed out in recent years, adolescent girls in America are afflicted with a range of problems, including low self-esteem, eating disorders, binge drinking, date rape and other dating violence, teen pregnancy, and cigarette use. Teenage women today are engaging in far riskier health behavior in greater numbers than any prior generation (Roan, 1993).

According to a 1998 status report by a consortium of universities and research centers, girls have closed the gap with boys in math performance and are coming close in science (Vobejda & Perlstein, 1998). However, they are also now smoking, drinking, and using drugs as often as boys their own age. Although girls are not nearly as violent as boys, they are committing more crimes than ever before and are far more often physically attacking each other.

It is important to understand that these problems go far beyond individual 5 psychological development and pathology. Even girls who are raised in loving homes by supportive parents grow up in a toxic cultural environment, at risk for self-mutilation, eating disorders, and addictions. The culture, both reflected and reinforced by advertising, urges girls to adopt a false self, to bury alive their real selves, to become *feminine,* which means to be nice and kind and sweet, to compete with other girls for the attention of boys, and to value romantic relationships with boys above all else. Girls are put into a terrible double bind. They are supposed to repress their power, their anger, and their exuberance and be simply "nice," although they also eventually must compete with men in the business world and be successful. They must be overtly sexy and attractive but essentially passive and virginal. It is not surprising that most girls experience adolescence as painful and confusing, especially if they are unconscious of these conflicting demands (Gilligan, 1982; Pipher, 1994). . . .

Girls try to make sense of the contradictory expectations of themselves in a culture dominated by advertising. Advertising is one of the most potent messengers in a culture that can be toxic for girls' self-esteem. Indeed if we look only at advertising images, this would be a bleak world for girls and women. Girls are a favorite target of advertisers because they are new consumers, are beginning to have significant disposable income, and are developing brand loyalty that might last a lifetime. Teenage girls spend more than $4 billion annually on cosmetics alone (J. D. Brown, Greenberg, & Buerkel-Rothfuss, 1993). . . .

Primarily girls are told by advertisers that what is most important about them is their perfume, their clothing, their bodies, and their beauty. Their "essence" is their underwear. "He says the first thing he noticed about you is your great personality," says an ad featuring a very young woman in tight jeans. The copy continues, "He lies." Even very little girls are offered makeup and toys like Special Night Barbie, which shows them how to dress up for a night out. Girls of all ages get the message that they must be flawlessly beautiful and, above all these days, they must be thin.

Even more destructively, they get the message that this is possible and that, with enough effort and self-sacrifice, they can achieve this ideal. Thus many girls spend enormous amounts of time and energy attempting to achieve something that is not only trivial but also completely unattainable. The glossy images of flawlessly beautiful and extremely thin women that surround us would not have the impact they do if we did not live in a culture that encourages women to believe that they can and should remake their bodies into perfect commodities. These images play into the American belief of transformation and ever-new possibilities, no longer through hard work but through the purchase of the right products. This belief is by no means universal. People in many other cultures may admire a particular body shape without seeking to emulate it.

Women are especially vulnerable because our bodies have been objectified and commodified for so long. Young women are the most vulnerable, especially those who have experienced early deprivation, sexual abuse, family violence, or other trauma (Smith, Fairburn, & Cowen, 1999; Thompson, 1994). Cultivating a thinner body offers some hope of control and success to a young woman with a poor self-image, overwhelming personal problems, and no easy solutions.

Although troubled young women are especially vulnerable, these messages 10 affect all girls. Researchers at Brigham and Women's Hospital in Boston found that the more frequently girls read magazines, the more likely they were to diet and to feel that magazines influence their ideal body shape (Field et al., 1999). Nearly half reported wanting to lose weight because of a magazine picture, even though only 29% were actually overweight. Studies at Stanford University and the University of Massachusetts found that about 70% of college women say they feel worse about their own looks after reading women's magazines (Richins, 1991; Then, 1992). Another study of young men and women found that a preoccupation with one's appearance takes a toll on mental health (Fredrickson, Roberts, Noll, Quinn, & Twenge, 1998). Women scored much higher than men on what the researchers called "self-objectification." This tendency to view one's body from the outside in—regarding physical attractiveness, sex appeal, measurements, and weight as more central to one's physical identity than health, strength, energy level, coordination, or fitness—has many harmful effects, including diminished mental performance, increased feelings of shame and anxiety, depression, sexual dysfunction, and the development of eating disorders. . . .

Advertising clearly does not cause eating problems any more than it causes alcoholism. Anorexia in particular is a disease with a complicated etiology, and media images probably do not play a major role. However, these images certainly contribute to the body-hatred so many young women feel and to some of the resulting eating problems, which range from bulimia to compulsive overeating to simply being obsessed with controlling one's appetite. Advertising does promote abusive and abnormal attitudes about eating, drinking, and thinness. It thus provides fertile soil for these obsessions to take root in and creates a climate of denial in which these diseases flourish.

The influence of the media is strikingly illustrated in a recent study (Becker & Burwell, 1999) that found a sharp rise in eating disorders among young women in Fiji soon after the introduction of television to the culture. Before television was available, there was little talk of dieting in Fiji. "You've gained weight" was a traditional compliment and "going thin" the sign of a problem. In 1995 television came to the island. Within 3 years, the number of teenagers at risk for eating disorders more than doubled: 74% of the teens in the study said they felt "too big or too fat" and 62% said they had dieted in the past month. This does not prove a direct causal link between television and eating disorders; Fiji is a culture in transition in many ways. However, it seems more than coincidental that the Fijian girls who were heavy viewers of television were 50% more likely to describe themselves as fat and 30% more likely to diet than those girls who watched television less frequently. As Ellen Goodman (1999) wrote, "The big success story of our entertainment industry is our ability to export insecurity: We can make any woman anywhere feel perfectly rotten about her shape" (p. A23).

Not everything is intentional on the part of advertisers. Some advertising is intended to arouse anxiety and affect women's self-esteem. However, some simply reflects the unconscious attitudes and beliefs of the individual advertisers, as well as what Carl Jung referred to as the "collective unconscious." Advertisers are members of the culture, too, and have been as thoroughly conditioned as anyone else. The magazines and the ads deliberately create and intensify anxiety about weight because it is so profitable to do so. On a deeper level, however, they reflect cultural concerns and conflicts about women's power (Faludi, 1991; Kilbourne, 1986). Real freedom for women would change the very basis of our male-dominated society. It is not surprising that many men (and women, to be sure) fear this.

This fear is reflected in an ad that ran in several women's and teens' magazines in 1997 with the headline, "The more you subtract, the more you add." Surprisingly, it is an ad for clothing, not for a diet product. Overtly, it is a statement about minimalism in fashion. However, the fact that the girl in the ad is very young and very thin reinforces another message, a message that an adolescent girl constantly gets from advertising and throughout the popular culture: the message that she should diminish herself, that she should be less than she is.

On the most obvious and familiar level, this refers to her body. However, the loss, the subtraction, the cutting down to size also refers, albeit indirectly, to her sense of her self, her sexuality, her need for authentic connection, and her longing for power and freedom. I certainly do not think that the creators of this particular ad had all this in mind. They are simply selling expensive clothing in an unoriginal way, by using a very young and very thin woman and an unfortunate tagline. It would not be important at all were there not so many other ads that reinforce this message and did it not coincide with a cultural crisis taking place now for adolescent girls.

"We cut Judy down to size," says an ad for a health club. "Soon, you'll both be taking up less space," says an ad for a collapsible treadmill, referring both to the product and the young woman exercising on it. The obsession with thinness is most deeply about cutting girls and women down to size. It is only a symbol, albeit a very powerful and destructive one, of tremendous fear of female power (Faludi, 1991; Kilbourne, 1986). Powerful women are seen by many people (women as well as men) as inherently destructive and dangerous. Some argue that it is men's awareness of just how powerful women can be that has created the attempts to keep women small. Indeed, thinness as an ideal has always accompanied periods of greater freedom for women: As soon as women got the vote, boyish flapper bodies came into vogue. No wonder there is such pressure on young women today to be thin, to shrink, to be like little girls, not to take up too much space, literally or figuratively. . . .

Many ads feature girls and young women in very passive poses, limp, doll-like, sometimes acting like little girls, playing with dolls and wearing bows in their hair. One ad uses a pacifier to sell lipstick and another the image of a baby to sell BabyDoll Blush Highlight. As Erving Goffman (1978) pointed out in *Gender Advertisements,* we learn a great deal about the disparate power of male and female individuals simply through the body language and poses of advertising. Women, especially young women, are generally subservient to men in ads, both in size and position.

A double-paged spread for Calvin Klein's clothing for kids conveys a world of information about the relative power of boys and girls. One of the boys seems to be in the act of speaking, expressing himself, whereas the girl has her hand over her mouth. Boys are generally shown in ads as active and rambunctious, whereas girls are more often passive and focused on their appearance. The exception to the rule involves African American children, male and female, who are often shown in advertising as passive observers of their White playmates (Seiter, 1993).

Girls are often shown as playful clowns in ads, perpetuating the attitude that girls and women are childish and cannot be taken seriously, whereas even very young men are generally portrayed as secure, powerful and serious. People in control of their lives stand upright, alert and ready to meet the world. In contrast, female individuals often appear off-balance, insecure, and weak. Often women's body parts are bent, conveying unpreparedness, submissiveness, and appeasement. Women exhibit what Goffman (1978) called *licensed withdrawal,* the appearance of being psychologically removed, disoriented, defenseless, or spaced out.

Female individuals touch people and things delicately and caressingly, whereas 20 male individuals grip, clench, and grasp. Girls and women cover their faces with their hair or hands, conveying shame or embarrassment, and no matter what happens, they keep on smiling. "Just smiling the bothers away," as one ad says. This ad is particularly disturbing because the model is a young African American woman, a member of a group that has long been encouraged to just keep smiling, no matter what. She's even wearing a kerchief, like Aunt Jemima. The cultural fear of angry women is intensified dramatically when the women are African American (Nelson, 1997).

As girls come of age sexually, the culture gives them impossibly contradictory messages. As the *Seventeen* ad says, "She wants to be outrageous. And accepted." Advertising slogans such as "Because innocence is sexier than you think," "Purity, yes. Innocence, never," and "Nothing so sensual was ever so innocent" place them in a double bind. Somehow girls are supposed to be both innocent and seductive, virginal and experienced, all at the same time. As they quickly learn, this is tricky.

Women have long been divided into virgins and whores. What is new is that girls are now supposed to embody both within themselves. This is symbolic of the central contradiction of the culture—women must work hard and produce and achieve success and yet, at the same time, they are encouraged to live impulsively, spend a lot of money, and be constantly and immediately gratified. This tension is reflected in women's attitudes toward many things, including sex and eating. Girls are promised fulfillment both through being thin and through eating rich foods, just as they are promised fulfillment through being innocent and virginal and through wild and impulsive sex. . . .

The emphasis for girls and women is always on being desirable, not on experiencing desire. Girls who want to be sexually active instead of simply being the objects of male desire are given only one model to follow, that of exploitive male sexuality. It seems that advertisers cannot conceive of a kind of power that is not manipulative and exploitive or a way that women can be actively sexual without being like traditional men.

Women who are "powerful" in advertising are uncommitted. They treat men like sex objects: "If I want a man to see my bra, I take him home," says an androgynous young woman. They are elusive and distant: "She's the first woman who refused to take your phone calls," says one ad, as if it were a good thing to be rude and inconsiderate. Why should any of us, male or female, be interested in someone who will not take our phone calls, who either cares so little for us or is so manipulative?

Mostly, however, girls are not supposed to have sexual agency. They are 25 supposed to be passive, swept away, overpowered. "See where it takes you," says a perfume ad featuring a couple passionately embracing. "Unleash your fantasies," says another. This contributes to the strange and damaging concept of the "good girl" as the one who is swept away, unprepared for sex, versus the "bad girl" as the one who plans for sex, uses contraception, and is generally responsible. A young woman can manage to have sex and yet in some sense maintain her virginity by being "out of control," drunk, or deep in denial about the entire experience. . . .

Adolescent girls are told that they have to give up much of what they know about relationships and intimacy if they want to attract men. Most tragically, they are told they have to give up each other. The truth is that one of the most powerful antidotes to destructive cultural messages is close and supportive female friendships. Unfortunately, girls are often encouraged by the culture to sacrifice their relationships with one another and to enter into hostile competition for the attention of boys and men. "What the bitch who's about to steal your man wears," says one ad. Many ads feature women fighting or glaring at each other.

Some girls do resist and rebel. Some are encouraged (by someone, perhaps a loving parent or a supportive teacher) to see the cultural contradictions clearly and to break free in a healthy and positive way. Others rebel in ways that damage themselves. A young woman seems to have only two choices: She can bury her sexual self, be a "good girl," give in to what L. M. Brown and Gilligan (1992) called "the tyranny of nice and kind" (p. 53)—and numb the pain by overeating or starving or cutting herself or drinking heavily. Or she can become a rebel, flout her sexuality, seduce inappropriate partners, smoke, drink flamboyantly, and use other drugs. Both of these responses are self-destructive, but they begin as an attempt to survive, not to self-destruct. . . .

Few healthy alternatives are available for girls who want to truly rebel against restrictive gender roles and stereotypes. . . . Girls who want to escape the stereotypes are viewed with glee by advertisers, who rush to offer them, as always, power through products. The emphasis in the ads is always on their sexuality, which is exploited to sell them makeup and clothes and shoes. A trio of extremely thin African American women brandish hair appliances and products as if they were weapons—and the brand is 911. A cosmetics company has a line of products called "Bad Gal." In one ad, eyeliner is shown in cartoon version as a girl, who is holding a dog saying, "grrrr. . . ," surely a reference to "grrrrls," a symbol these days of "girl power." Unfortunately, girl power doesn't mean much if girls do not have the tools to achieve it. Without reproductive freedom and freedom from violence, girl power is nothing but a marketing slogan. . . .

Other ads go further and offer products as a way to rebel, to be a real individual. "Live outside the lines," says a clothing ad featuring a young woman walking out of a men's room. This kind of rebellion is not going to rock the world. Not surprisingly, the young woman is very thin and conventionally pretty. Another pretty young woman sells a brand of jeans called "Revolt." "Don't just change . . . revolt," says the copy, but the young woman is passive, slight, her eyes averted.

"Nude with attitude" features an African American woman in a powerful pose, 30 completely undercut by the brevity of her dress and the focus on her long legs. Her "attitude" is nothing to fear—she's just another sex object. Good thing, given the fear many people have of powerful African American women (Nelson, 1997).

Some ads do feature women who seem really angry and rebellious, but the final message always is the same. "Today, I indulge my dark side," says an ad featuring a fierce young woman tearing at what seems to be a net. "Got a problem with that?" The slogan is "be extraordinary not ordinary." The product that promises to free this girl from the net that imprisons her? Black nail polish.

Nail polish. Such a trivial solution to such an enormous dilemma. But such triviality and superficiality is common in advertising. How could it be otherwise? The solution to any problem always has to be a product. Change (transformation) is thus inevitably shallow and moronic, rather than meaningful and transcendent.

These days self-improvement seems to have more to do with calories than with character, with abdomens rather than absolutes, with nail polish than with ethics.

It has not always been so. Joan Jacobs Brumberg (1997) described this vividly in *The Body Project: An Intimate History of American Girls*:

> When girls in the nineteenth century thought about ways to improve themselves, they almost always focused on their internal character and how it was reflected in outward behavior. In 1892, the personal agenda of an adolescent diarist read: "Resolved, not to talk about myself or feelings. To think before speaking. To work seriously. . . . To be dignified. Interest myself more in others."
>
> A century later, in the 1990s, American girls think very differently. In a New Year's resolution written in 1982, a girl wrote: "I will try to make myself better in every way I possibly can with the help of my budget and baby-sitting money. I will lose weight, get new lenses, already got new haircut, good makeup, new clothes and accessories." (p. xxi)

Not that girls didn't have plenty of problems in the 19th century. Surely by now we should have come much further. This relentless trivialization of a girl's hopes and dreams, her expectations for herself, cuts to the quick of her soul. Just as she is entering womanhood, eager to spread her wings, to become more sexual, more empowered, and more independent, the culture moves in to cut her down to size.

REFERENCES

Becker, A. E., & Burwell, R. A. (1999, May). *Acculturation and disordered eating in Fiji.* Poster presented at the annual meeting of the American Psychiatric Association, Washington, DC.

Brown, J. D., Greenberg, B. S., & Buerkel-Rothfuss, N. L. (1993). Mass media, sex and sexuality. In V. C. Strasburger & G. A. Comstock (Eds.), *Adolescent medicine: Adolescents and the media* (pp. 511–525). Philadelphia: Hanley & Belfus.

Brown, L. M., & Gilligan, C. (1992). *Meeting at the crossroads: Women's psychology and girls' development.* New York: Ballantine Books.

Brumberg, J. J. (1997). *The body project: An intimate history of American girls.* New York: Random House.

Faludi, S. (1991). *Backlash.* New York: Crown.

Field, A. E., Cheung, L., Wolf, A. M., Herzog, D. B., Gortmaker, S. L., & Colditz, G. A. (1999). Exposure to the mass media and weight concerns among girls. *Pediatrics, 103,* 36–41.

Fredrickson, B. L., Roberts, T. A., Noll, S. M., Quinn, D. M., & Twenge, J. M. (1998). That swimsuit becomes you: Sex differences in self-objectification, restrained eating, and math performance. *Journal of Personality and Social Psychology, 75,* 269–284.

Gilligan, C. (1982). *In a different voice.* Cambridge, MA: Harvard University Press.

Goffman, E. (1978). *Gender advertisements.* Cambridge, MA: Harvard University Press.

Goodman, E. (1999, May 27). The culture of thin bites Fiji teens. *Boston Globe,* p. A23.

Kilbourne, J. (1986). The child as sex object: Images of children in the media. In M. Nelson & K. Clark (Eds.), *The educator's guide to preventing child sexual abuse* (pp. 40–46). Santa Cruz, CA: Network Publications.

Nelson, J. (1997, July/August). Accepting rage. Ms., pp. 92–95.

Pipher, M. (1994). *Reviving Ophelia. Saving the selves of adolescent girls.* New York: G.P. Putnam's.

Richins, M. L. (1991). Social comparison and idealized images of advertising. *Journal of Consumer Research, 18,* 71–83.

Roan, S. (1993, June 8). Painting a bleak picture for teen girls. *Los Angeles Times,* p. 28.

Sadker, M., & Sadker, D. (1994). *Failing at fairness: How our schools cheat girls.* New York: Simon & Schuster.

Anorexia Victims: Models Ana Carolina Reston (left) *and Luisel Ramos died in 2006. Their deaths led to bans on super-thin models in fashion shows in Spain and Italy.*

Seiter, E. (1993). *Sold separately: Children and parents in consumer culture.* Winchester, MA: Unwin Hyman.

Smith, K. A., Fairburn, C. G., & Cowen, P. J. (1999). Symptomatic relapse in bulimia nervosa following acute tryptophan depletion. *Journal of the American Medical Association, 56,* 171–176.

Then, D. (1992, August). *Women's magazines: Messages they convey about looks, men and careers.* Paper presented at the 100th Annual Convention of the American Psychological Association, Washington, DC.

Thompson, B. W. (1994). *A hunger so wide and so deep.* Minneapolis: University of Minnesota Press.

Vobejda, B., & Perlstein, L. (1998, June 17). Girls closing gap with boys, but not always for the best. *Boston Globe,* p. A3.

Calvin Klein
underwear

X-Large Boys

ALISSA QUART

Alissa Quart, a graduate of Columbia School of Journalism, has written two critically acclaimed books: *Branded: The Buying and Selling of Teenagers* (Basic Books, 2003), from which the selection below is excerpted, and *Hothouse Kids: The Dilemma of the Gifted Child* (Penguin, 2006). She also writes for the *New York Times* and *Atlantic Monthly*.

"Supersize your superset" proclaims one teen weightlifter, echoing female teens' urges to augment their breasts.

The term *superset* refers to an extraordinary number of exercises, or weightlifting sets, performed with little or no rest between them. The hope for the boys who do supersets is to grow big—bigger than their classmates, as big as male models, professional wrestlers, and bodybuilders. In a sense, teen superset obsessions result from branding efforts . . .—the selling of nutritional-supplement companies and preppy clothing manufacturers such as Abercrombie & Fitch. In just five years, these firms have created a greater sense of inadequacy among boys about their bodies than ever before. Not so coincidentally, this has produced a whole new market for underwear and powdered drinks that teen boys now buy in an attempt to end this inadequacy. An astronomical and younger-than-ever use of steroids accompanies it all, along with a trade in dubious, over-the-counter nutritional supplements. The drive to grow big, like the drive for youthful plastic surgery, goes beyond becoming big or becoming perfect; it's the sort of self-construction that Generation Y understands. It's self-branding as an emotional palliative.

According to a Blue Cross-Blue Shield 2001 survey of ten-to-seventeen-year-olds, half of the 785 children interviewed said they were "aware" of sports supplements and drugs, and one in five take them. Forty-two percent did it to build muscle and 16 percent just to look better (i.e., "built"). These numbers are way up: In contrast, the 1999 BCBS survey found that no sample of kids under fourteen had taken products.

The push began in 1999 with the emergence of products such as Teen Advantage Creatine Serum, which made appearances on the shelves of vitamin chain stores. The marketing shows a kind of malignant genius: The formula was developed, according to the label, "especially for young aspiring athletes 8–19 years of age." (It also carries the necessary but misleadingly low-key caveat that excess dosage of creatine is not a "wise decision.") Not surprisingly, the products took off; there's nothing like a new teen-specific product that claims to alleviate a new teen-specific pathology.

The campaign worked so well that 52 percent of young users of performance-enhancing supplements said they had tried creatine (only 18 percent of adults surveyed used these supplements). Other supplements popular with kids—kids as young as ten—include ephedrine (which ostensibly increases endurance) and "andro," or androstenedione, an over-the-counter alternative to anabolic steroids (like steroids, androstenedione increases testosterone in the body—in fact, it also increases production of estrogen). These supplements, experts agree, range from suspect to dangerous, and even deadly, as ephedra turned out to be. In fact, some of these supplements, says Charles Yesalis, author of *The Steroids Game,* are permitted to be called supplements only because of legal loopholes and are in fact drugs that are virtually unregulated by the FDA.

All this supplement use does not, unfortunately, mean that kids are staying away from steroids: In the 2001 Monitoring the Future study, 2.8 percent of eighth graders, 3.5 percent of tenth graders, and 3.7 percent of twelfth graders said they had taken steroids, meaning they had "cycled" on the drugs from eight to twelve weeks at least once (only 1.7 percent of high school sophomores had taken steroids in 1992). Why? Because steroids change body fat by adding muscle and thus decrease body fat proportionally. The possible side effects of steroids include stunted bone growth, liver damage, and shrunken testicles. A cycle is also costly, ranging from a few hundred to a few thousand dollars. But, as happens with a new wardrobe or a new pair of breasts, that's not seen as much of a price for looking more attractive. Allowances are up, working hours are up; kids can afford to juice. In such an environment, the decision not to use steroids but to depend instead on supplements can seem both cautious and economical. The no-worries attitude toward supplements, and dependence on them, can be seen in Sam, a thoughtful, quiet, dedicated prep school sophomore. Sam is also a prize-winning sixteen-year-old bodybuilder who writes for teen bodybuilding sites on which he proudly posts photos of his rippling and massive physique. Every day, Sam takes ephedrine mixed with caffeine along with 5 milligrams of creatine. He's been lifting weights since he was seven, and his punishing regimen now takes two hours of lifting daily.

Sam's passion for weightlifting started when he was exploring a hotel where he was staying with his family and he saw an adult lifting in the weight room. This weightlifter was his version of Edgar Allan Poe's Annabel Lee—he would never forget the image of the strong older man lifting the barbells. As soon as he got home, he bought some weights at a discount store and began working on getting big. Sam is not alone in starting so early. It's a trend that echoes the other ways in which kids are getting older younger in the market economy: Thirty-five percent of 60,000 weightlifting injuries in 1998 were for those aged from fifteen to twenty-four, and 12 percent were suffered by *children* aged from five to fourteen.

Today, he weighs 225 pounds, and has 6 percent body fat. He says that lifting helps him "stay healthy, look good, and feel confident," but acknowledges that for some of his peers, "exposed to weightlifting at first by popular culture," the reasons for their passions are not as hale and hearty. Some use steroids, for instance. (His own practice of taking ephedrine—an herbal supplement that can lead to heart attacks, seizures, psychoses, and death—to lose weight is arguably not such a great way of "staying healthy" either.) "There is definitely undue pressure on teen boys to look good and be big," Sam says. There is also undue pressure not to be fat given the commercial pressure to eat and the rising rates of obesity spurred on by commercials for fattening and sugary foods. In the stories of adolescents, childhood and teen obesity is a recurring theme. "The fat child is more abused than the muscled one; look at Piggy in *Lord of the Flies,*" explains Sam. "The big boy with the glasses—nobody listens to him. Teens now start lifting because they are overweight."

For sure, teen male body culture is a response to the now ubiquitous overweight childhoods of American boys; a fat child may put a hard body between the self that was ostracized and emasculated flesh and his new adolescent self. The teen muscle boys, like the breast augmentation girls, exchange one supersized consumerism for another: They trade family-sized packages of branded food bought in bulk at discount stores for giant, branded adult-male-looking bodies and large vats of powdered supplements.

Juan, a Cuban American sixteen-year-old bodybuilder who lives in New Jersey, 10 used weightlifting to go from 225 pounds to 165 pounds in one year. He says he started weightlifting because he "got a lot of prejudice" when he was fat. "That's why I did it [weightlifting], so they wouldn't make fun of me." Now his classmates respect him, he says, and girls talk to him, although he doesn't care about girls; he's more interested in the company of other high school weightlifters. "I want to get big, really big, but natural. I wanna be feared," Juan says. Like Sam, Juan doesn't consider the supplements unnatural—he takes from 5 to 10 milligrams of creatine a day, as well as whey for protein and glutamine for joint strength.

The desire of adolescents to leave behind the scrawny or husky teaseable boy for the hard, well-packaged man is not a new one, of course. The virtues of the well-developed man are extolled in the writings of the Greeks and in Shakespeare's *Measure for Measure*: "O, it is excellent / To have a giant's strength; but it is tyrannous / To use it like a giant." The wish to become big in puberty, for reasons of both dominance over one's peers and of display, can be seen in the twentieth-century in the fifty years of Charles Atlas magazine advertisements. The Atlas ads famously promised pubescents bodybuilding courses that would "make you a new man in just 15 minutes a day," that could "'RE-BUILD' skinny rundown weaklings" into creatures with "a coat of muscle straight across your stomach." In addition, bodybuilding magazines aimed at boys have a long history (and so do complementary homoerotic physique magazines). The 1977 film *Pumping Iron* also gave encouragement to boys to build themselves up.

However, the omnipresent gymmed-out, almost-naked male body began to make the rounds only in the late 1980s. A big force for this was a new advertising culture—the giant billboards for Calvin Klein underwear flaunting well-built models, the denuded male torsos in that same designer's perfume ads, helped to change the shape of men, literally. It is no coincidence that this was a period when the teen members of Generation Y were toddlers.

"When you hear girls gawking at Abercrombie & Fitch about how hot the guy is on the bag—that makes an impression," one teen bodybuilder told the *New York Times Magazine* in 1999. One of Abercrombie's countless bare-chested and buff youths had clearly been seared on that teen's mind; perhaps he still thinks of him every time he makes yet another andro shake.

The rise of teen male bigoriexa, as media wags have called it, has also been spurred on by a new strain of magazines as well. There's the abdomen-mania of the men's magazines that these boys have grown up with, from *Men's Health* to *GQ*. In 2000, for instance, *Men's Health* even launched a magazine in celebration of the teen male abdomen called *MH-17*. According to its initial press release, *MH-17* was "aimed at the 'rapidly growing' market of male teenagers in the United States."

MH-17 and its ideology of male teen "fitness" (read: male bodily self-hatred) 15 flopped. But the tyranny of taut, ripped, and dieted teen male bodies on screen and in advertisements still rules. Teen films, for example, almost entirely lack the sloppy, scrawny, or plumpish boys of yesteryear, boys who were blissfully oblivious of the body obsession of their female counterparts. Now even those who play geeks, actors such as Jason Biggs of *American Pie 2,* are forced to have washboard stomachs or "six-packs" and to bare them constantly.

To achieve the required body, teen boys are willing to put in time and painful effort that many of their fathers couldn't have imagined—becoming a branded boy body takes just as much labor and pain as becoming a branded girl body. For instance, teen boy bodybuilders tend to engage in spartan, highly structured eating patterns. On the teenbodybuilder.com Web site, one boy describes the ten austere meals on his daily menu for the months when he prepares for competition. The meals are austere, obsessively observed, and protein-filled fare, one consisting of one scoop of egg white protein, one scoop of casein, half a scoop of Optimum's whey, four slices of turkey, and two pieces of whole wheat bread.

In their urge to build themselves into commercially approved hypermasculine specimens, the boys of Generation Y are in solidarity with their long-suffering female peers. Once there was a hope among feminists that girls could be taught to escape their oppressive body project. This has not occurred. Now, boys partake in it as well. Weightlifting, enthusiasts say, is a form of self-construction. For the teen weightlifters, however—boys shooting steroids and eating egg whites for breakfast; shaving their chests and backs and legs—the line between self-betterment and a morphic pathology is a blurry one.

QUESTIONS FOR DISCUSSION

1. James Twitchell admits that he bought his Miata because of an advertisement (paragraph 6). What was the promise of the ad, as he describes it in paragraphs 6–11? As the ad's creator describes it in footnote 2? Why does Twitchell not see the ad as manipulative or exploitative (see paragraphs 18 and 19)? Compare his thinking with Jean Kilbourne's points in "Jesus Is a Brand of Jeans" about how advertising appeals to people's desires (paragraph 6) and about ads as propaganda (paragraph 9). Who do you think has the better interpretation of what is really going on?

2. Both James Twitchell and Jean Kilbourne discuss the possibility that consumer objects and values have become the religion of our day. For example, Twitchell describes the Miata as pictured "like a haloed angel" (paragraph 6), and Kilbourne notes that advertisements associate spiritual meanings with products. What else do these authors have to say on the question of how consumerism has become similar to a religion? For more on Twitchell's view of spirituality in a consumer society, look at page 342, paragraphs 34 and 36.

3. In telling the story of his Miata purchase, James Twitchell discusses his own struggle with what he calls the "dynamic of pressures in the commercial world" (paragraph 17). The Miata was not one of the brands of his consumption community, "liberal academics." If you read his description in the Section One essay, "Needing the Unnecessary," of college students' knowledge of clusters that form around brands (paragraphs 7–12), were you surprised that professors have a branded niche as well? How does Twitchell describe it? What products are badges of the "liberal academic" group? Why is a Miata not acceptable to the "liberal academic" group? Have you experienced similar conflicts when considering a purchase your friends might disapprove of?

4. Alissa Quart discusses the pressure on boys to conform to commercial messages about supersized male bodies, and Jean Kilbourne, in "Cutting Girls Down to Size," discusses the pressures on girls to be small. Both

writers suggest that commercial messages exploit teens' insecurities about values, roles, and identity. What do advertisements tell teenagers about gender roles? What is harmful about these images of masculinity and femininity? In what ways does advertising undermine girls' development as women? What are boys learning about masculinity? Men used to think it was effeminate to be too concerned about looks. Is the image of the "new man" liberating or entrapping?

5. Read Virginia Postrel's definition of aesthetics in paragraphs 6–9 in "The Aesthetic Imperative" (Section One, pages 333–336). Why is aesthetic communication "emotional" rather than "cognitive"? In one issue of any magazine, examine the ads. Would you say that ads themselves have been affected by what Postrel calls "the aesthetic imperative"? If so, how might that affect the ways that ads appeal to their target audiences?

SUGGESTIONS FOR WRITING

For Persuasion and Visual Rhetoric

Look at advertisements aimed at you and your peers. Do you see the same kinds of messages that either Jean Kilbourne (regarding females) or Alissa Quart (regarding males) sees? Or do you see other harmful messages about values or gender roles? One of the writers in Section Three of this casebook, John F. Schumaker, suggests that the economic interests of consumer societies are best served by making citizens feel anxious and inadequate. If you see evidence of this, select representative ads to illustrate a persuasive essay helping readers to understand how the ads are harmful to them.

For Convincing

Research the debate over legislation in some countries to ban super-thin models from fashion shows, which began in Spain and Italy in the fall of 2006 after the death of South American model Luisel Ramos. What has been the response of the fashion industry? If you agree that super-thin modeling needs to stop, argue for the best course of action for stopping it. If you think a ban or policy against it is unnecessary, argue why.

For Convincing with Visual Rhetoric

James Twitchell analyzes the rhetoric of the Miata ad that persuaded him to buy his red Miata. He claims that the ad "worked" on his memories of childhood, but did not manipulate him. Read Chapter 4 of this text on visual arguments, especially the material on advertising on pages 63–64. Then choose an advertisement that you find persuasive and that makes you want to buy the advertised product. Write an analysis of the rhetoric of the ad and make a case as to whether the ad manipulates or does not manipulate.

SECTION 3: THE PURSUIT OF HAPPINESS
Overview

The readings in this section all deal with the question of how happy people are in consumer societies. A problem arises, first of all, with the key term *happiness*. What is happiness? If you look up *happy* in a dictionary, the definitions range all the way from "lucky" to "cheerful" to "showing joy," and even to "having enthusiasm" for something. Social scientists often use a testing instrument called the "Satisfaction with Life Scale," developed by Ed Diner in 1985. The test asks people to respond to items like these:

In most ways my life is close to my ideal.

The conditions of my life are excellent.

I am satisfied with my life.

So far I have gotten the important things I want in life.

If I could live my life over, I would change almost nothing.

Our first reading in this section reports on the efforts of a Dutch sociologist to measure the relationship between a country's per capita income and its happiness in terms of life satisfaction. The results of his surveys have been positive: People report being happy more than you might expect. The surprise in his findings is that after a certain level of income stability and life comforts, satisfaction with life does not increase with more income.

However, clinical psychologist John F. Schumaker, in his essay "The Happiness Conspiracy: What Does It Mean to Be Happy in a Modern Consumer Society?" questions the measurement and definition of happiness in terms of self-satisfaction. Schumaker points out that this scale "mirrors the supreme value that consumer culture attaches to the romancing of desire and the satiation of the self." Therefore, although they may claim to be happy, people in consumer societies suffer more depression and other mental health problems. Schumaker suggests that we would be healthier if we thought of happiness in less self-centered and materialistic ways.

In the next essay, psychologist Mihaly Czikszentmihalyi offers "Enjoyment as an Alternative to Materialism." Although shopping may give us pleasure, he suggests that a more lasting satisfaction comes from being so involved in a challenging and outwardly directed activity that you lose awareness of self. To balance the picture, however, we end this section, and the casebook itself, with another selection from David Brooks in which he defends shopping as a pleasurable activity deeply connected with Americans' aspirations for the ever more perfect life.

Does Money Buy Happiness?

DON PECK AND ROSS DOUTHAT

In the following selection, which appeared originally in the *Atlantic Monthly* (January/February 2003), Peck and Douthat report on research into the connection between per capita income and self-reported happiness in various countries around the world. Some of the findings may surprise you.

Historically the province of philosophers and theologians, the relationship between wealth and happiness has recently been taken up by a cadre of social scientists seeking to quantify and compare levels of well-being worldwide.

The results of their research, thus far, are clear: money does buy happiness— but only to a point. Study after study shows that the inhabitants of richer countries are, on average, significantly happier than those of poorer ones. This is true even controlling for other variables that rise with income and that may influence personal happiness: education, political freedom, women's rights, and so forth. National income appears to be one of the best single predictors of overall well-being, explaining perhaps 40 percent of the difference in contentment among nations. For individual countries, with few exceptions, self-reported happiness has increased as incomes have risen.

The chart on pages 392–393 shows survey data on happiness for fifty-four countries, compiled throughout the 1990s by the Dutch sociologist Ruut Veenhoven.

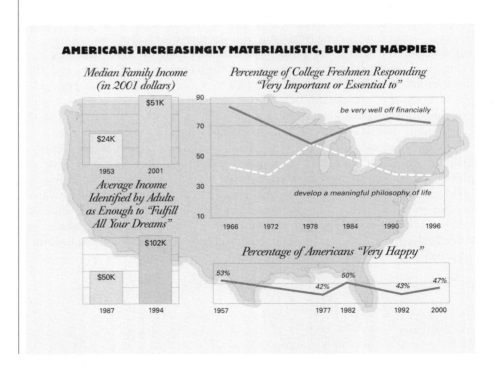

AMERICANS INCREASINGLY MATERIALISTIC, BUT NOT HAPPIER

Median Family Income (in 2001 dollars)

$51K

$24K

1953 2001

Average Income Identified by Adults as Enough to "Fulfill All Your Dreams"

$102K

$50K

1987 1994

Percentage of College Freshmen Responding "Very Important or Essential to"

be very well off financially

develop a meaningful philosophy of life

1966 1972 1978 1984 1990 1996

Percentage of Americans "Very Happy"

53% 50% 47%
42% 43%

1957 1977 1982 1992 2000

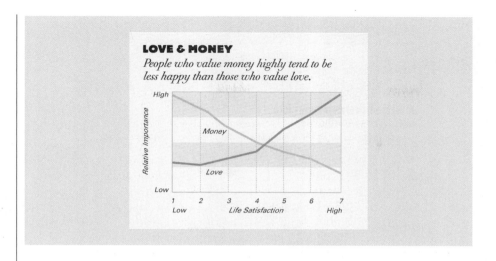

LOVE & MONEY

People who value money highly tend to be less happy than those who value love.

These data indicate a robust, if inexact, relationship between per capita income and "life satisfaction." Veenhoven's findings provide an unexpectedly sunny view. First, they indicate that most people worldwide say they are fairly happy. It is debatable whether most people have ever viewed life as nasty, brutish, and short; but on balance, they don't now. (Even citizens of impoverished or politically star-crossed countries, such as the Philippines and Romania, or of countries with high levels of income inequality, such as Brazil and the United States, report being at least somewhat happy on average.) Moreover, though the fact that richer countries are in general happier than poorer ones may not seem terribly surprising, it does suggest that continuing economic development will generate rising happiness worldwide.

That said, there are clear limits to what money can buy. Although improvements in income produce large improvements in happiness for poor countries—gains that continue to rise with income well above the level where basic food, shelter, and sanitation needs have been met—the law of diminishing returns takes effect at higher income levels. Above about $20,000 per capita, increases in wealth yield at best minimal increases in happiness. This effect takes place at both the individual and the societal level. In poor societies those at the top of the socioeconomic ladder are significantly happier than those at the bottom; in highly developed societies there is little class difference in happiness. (In fact, oddly, in wealthy nations both those in the top 10 percent of the socioeconomic spectrum and those in the bottom 50 percent appear to be slightly happier, on average, than those in between.)

Robert E. Lane, a political scientist at Yale, argues that the leveling off of hap- 5 piness in wealthy societies reflects more than just diminishing returns. Lane suggests that happiness is derived largely from two sources—material comfort, and social and familial intimacy—that are often incompatible. Economic development increases material comfort, but it systematically weakens social and familial ties by encouraging mobility, commercializing relationships, and attenuating the bonds of both the extended and the nuclear family. In less developed countries, where social ties are

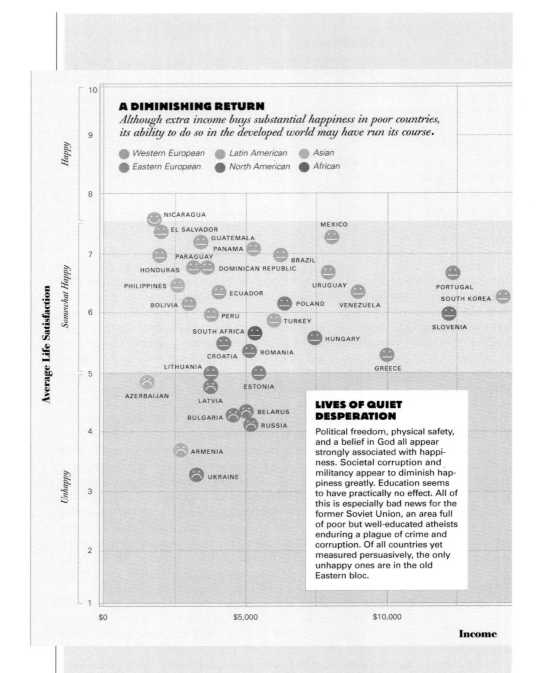

A DIMINISHING RETURN

Although extra income buys substantial happiness in poor countries, its ability to do so in the developed world may have run its course.

Western European   Latin American   Asian
Eastern European   North American   African

LIVES OF QUIET DESPERATION

Political freedom, physical safety, and a belief in God all appear strongly associated with happiness. Societal corruption and militancy appear to diminish happiness greatly. Education seems to have practically no effect. All of this is especially bad news for the former Soviet Union, an area full of poor but well-educated atheists enduring a plague of crime and corruption. Of all countries yet measured persuasively, the only unhappy ones are in the old Eastern bloc.

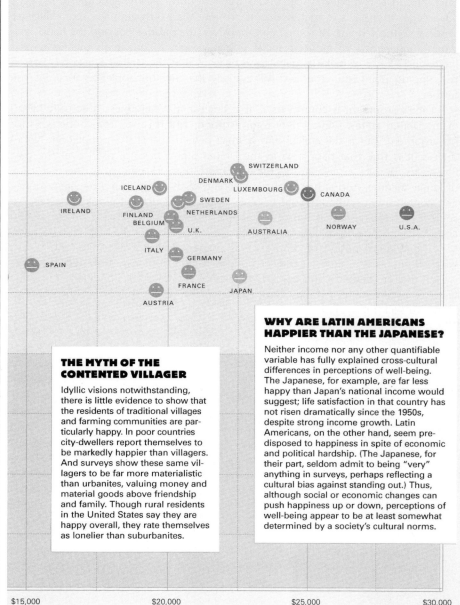

SWITZERLAND

DENMARK

ICELAND   LUXEMBOURG

SWEDEN   CANADA

NETHERLANDS

IRELAND

FINLAND

BELGIUM

U.K.   AUSTRALIA

NORWAY   U.S.A.

ITALY

GERMANY

SPAIN

FRANCE

JAPAN

AUSTRIA

THE MYTH OF THE CONTENTED VILLAGER

Idyllic visions notwithstanding, there is little evidence to show that the residents of traditional villages and farming communities are particularly happy. In poor countries city-dwellers report themselves to be markedly happier than villagers. And surveys show these same villagers to be far more materialistic than urbanites, valuing money and material goods above friendship and family. Though rural residents in the United States say they are happy overall, they rate themselves as lonelier than suburbanites.

WHY ARE LATIN AMERICANS HAPPIER THAN THE JAPANESE?

Neither income nor any other quantifiable variable has fully explained cross-cultural differences in perceptions of well-being. The Japanese, for example, are far less happy than Japan's national income would suggest; life satisfaction in that country has not risen dramatically since the 1950s, despite strong income growth. Latin Americans, on the other hand, seem predisposed to happiness in spite of economic and political hardship. (The Japanese, for their part, seldom admit to being "very" anything in surveys, perhaps reflecting a cultural bias against standing out.) Thus, although social or economic changes can push happiness up or down, perceptions of well-being appear to be at least somewhat determined by a society's cultural norms.

$15,000 $20,000 $25,000 $30,000

Per Person

often strong and money is scarce, this tradeoff works overwhelmingly to society's advantage—the gains in material comfort more than outweigh the slight declines in social connectedness. At some point, however, the balance tips and the happiness-diminishing effects of reduced social stability begin to outweigh the happiness-increasing effects of material gain. Lane believes that the United States has passed this tipping point, and that we will actually become unhappier as incomes rise further.

Lane's argument is controversial. It is unclear that happiness is actually falling in the United States. Clinical depression is rising, which Lane cites as one basis for his argument, but it still afflicts only a small percentage of the population. Nonetheless, it is true that happiness in the United States has not risen over the past fifty years, despite an average increase of more than 85 percent in the real value of family income. And although the weakening of the relationship between money and contentment perhaps ought to have induced Americans to look elsewhere for sources of happiness, that hasn't happened. Indeed, as the graphs on pages 390 and 391 show, Americans have become *more* materialistic over the past three decades.

The Western notion of progress was shaped during a centuries-long period when rising wealth almost certainly bought rising happiness. Only recently have we left that era behind—and our society has not yet adjusted. Conditioned to value financial achievement, we may cling to materialism even as it makes the contentment we seek more elusive.

clinique happy heart.
the new floral heart.
clinique happy
heart.
get happy news at
www.clinique.com

The Happiness Conspiracy: What Does It Mean to Be Happy in a Modern Consumer Society?

JOHN F. SCHUMAKER

John F. Schumaker, a clinical psychologist, was born in Wisconsin but now lives and practices in New Zealand. He has published nine books and many articles on culture and mental health. His most recent book is *In Search of Happiness: Understanding an Endangered State of Mind* (Penguin, 2006). Schumaker's essay "The Happiness Conspiracy" appeared in the magazine *New Internationalist,* July 2006.

"The trouble with normal is it always gets worse," sang the Canadian guitarist Bruce Cockburn back in 1983. Seems he was on to something. Normal doesn't seem to be working any longer. The new Holy Grail is happiness. At every turn are "how-to" happiness books, articles, TV and radio programs, videos, and websites. There are happiness institutes, camps, clubs, classes, cruises, workshops, and retreats. Universities are adding courses in Happiness Studies. Fast-growing professions include happiness counseling, happiness coaching, "life-lift" coaching, "joyology," and happiness science. Personal happiness is big business and everyone is selling it.

Being positive is mandatory, even with the planet in meltdown. Cynics and pessimists are running for cover while the cheerleaders are policing the game with an iron fist. Only the bravest are not being bullied into cheering up or at least shutting up.

But a society of "happichondriacs" isn't necessarily a healthy sign. No one is less able to sustain happiness than someone obsessed with feeling only happiness. A happy and meaningful existence depends on the ability to feel emotions other than happiness, as well as ones that compete with happiness.

"Happiness never appeared to me as an absolute aim," said Einstein. "I am even inclined to compare such moral aims to the ambitions of a pig. The ideals that have lighted my way are Kindness, Beauty and Truth."

If we've become pigs at the happiness trough, it's understandable. As higher 5 systems of meaning have withered, life purpose has dwindled to feeling good. Innocence, the lifeblood of happiness, is obsolete. We live on cultural soil perfectly suited for depression.

Other happiness blockers include materialism, perpetual discontent, overcomplication, hypercompetition, stress, rage, boredom, loneliness, and existential confusion. We're removed from nature, married to work, adrift from family and friends, spiritually starved, sleep deprived, physically unfit, dumbed down, and enslaved to debt.

Health professionals face new epidemics of "hurry sickness," "toxic success syndrome," the "frantic family," the "over-commercialized child," and "pleonexia" or out-of-control greed.

Too much is no longer enough. Many are stretching themselves so far that they have difficulty feeling anything at all. At its heart the happiness boom is a metaphor for the modern struggle for meaning.

We laugh only a third as often as we did 50 years ago—hence the huge popularity of laughter clubs and laughter therapy. We make love less frequently and enjoy it less, even though sex is now largely deregulated and available in endless guilt-free varieties. Yet we're the least happy society in history if we measure happiness in terms of mental health, personal growth, or general sense of aliveness.

A society's dominant value system dictates how happiness is measured. The 10 native Navajos in the southwest of the U.S. saw happiness as the attainment of universal beauty, or what they called Hozho. Their counterpart of "Have a nice day" was "May you walk in beauty."

Personal satisfaction is the most common way of measuring happiness today (via something called the Life Satisfaction Scale). This mirrors the supreme value that consumer culture attaches to the romancing of desire and the satiation of the self. When measured this way, almost everyone seems pretty happy—even if it's primarily false needs being satisfied. A high percentage of depressed people even end up happy when "personal satisfaction" is the yardstick.

By the middle of the 19th century, social critics were already noticing how happiness was losing its social, spiritual, moral, and intellectual anchors and becoming a form of emotional masturbation. In his classic 1863 work, *Utilitarianism,* John Stuart Mill scorned this trend: "Better to be Socrates dissatisfied than a fool satisfied," he opined.

Total satisfaction can actually be a major obstacle to happiness. Artist Salvador Dali lamented: "There are days when I think I'm going to die from an overdose of satisfaction." To preserve the "rarity value" of life one must resist wrapping heaven around oneself. Keeping paradise at a distance, yet within reach, is a much better way of staying alive. People who have it all must learn the art of flirting with deprivation.

The highest forms of happiness have always been experienced and expressed as love. But happiness is being wooed in increasingly autistic ways that lack this vital dimension. In a recent survey only one per cent of people indicated "true love" as what they wanted most in life. Our standard of living has increased but our standard of loving has plummeted.

The backlash against today's narcissistic happiness is rekindling interest in 15 the ancient Greek philosophers who equated happiness with virtue. Especially celebrated by them were loyalty, friendship, moderation, honesty, compassion, and trust. Research shows that all these traits are in steep decline today—despite being happiness boosters. Like true love and true happiness, they have become uneconomic.

When author John Updike warned, "America is a vast conspiracy to make you happy," he was referring to the superficial mass happiness that prevails when economics successfully conspires to define our existence. I profit, therefore I am. To be happy, gulp something. Pay later.

Novelist J. D. Salinger was so unnerved by the happiness conspiracy that he confessed: "I'm a kind of paranoiac in reverse. I suspect people are plotting to make one happy." The wrong type of happiness is worse than no happiness at all.

Governments are the biggest players in the happiness conspiracy. Any political action aimed at a more people-friendly or planet-friendly happiness is certain to be met with fierce resistance. The best consumers are itchy narcissists who hop, skip, and jump from one fleeting desire to the next, never deeply satisfied, but always in the process of satisfying themselves. Our entire socioeconomic system is designed to spew out this type of "ideal citizen." Contentment is the single greatest threat to the economics of greed and consumer happiness.

Our ignorance of happiness is revealed by the question on everyone's lips: "Does money make us happy?" The head of a U.S. aid agency in Kenya commented recently that volunteers are predictably dumbstruck and confused by the zest and jubilance of the Africans. It's become a cliché for them to say: "The people are so poor, they have nothing—and yet they have so much joy and seem so happy."

I never knew how measly my own happiness was until one day in 1978 when 20 I found myself stranded in a remote western Tanzanian village. I saw real happiness for the first time—since then I have learned that it has vastly more to do with cultural factors than genetics or the trendy notion of personal "choice."

So it didn't surprise me that an African nation, Nigeria, was found recently to be the world's happiest country. The study of "happy societies" is awakening us to the importance of social connectedness, spirituality, simplicity, modesty of expectations, gratitude, patience, touch, music, movement, play, and "down time."

The small Himalayan nation of Ladakh is one of the best-documented examples of a "happy society." As Helena Norberg-Hodge writes in *Ancient Future,* Ladakhis were a remarkably joyous and vibrant people who lived in harmony with their harsh environment. Their culture generated mutual respect, community-mindedness, an eagerness to share, reverence for nature, thankfulness, and love of life. Their value system bred tenderness, empathy, politeness, spiritual awareness, and environmental conservation. Violence, discrimination, avarice, and abuse of power were non-existent while depressed, burned-out people were nowhere to be found.

But in 1980 consumer capitalism came knocking with its usual bounty of raised hopes and social diseases. The following year, Ladakh's freshly appointed Development Commissioner announced: "If Ladakh is ever going to be developed, we have to figure out how to make these people more greedy." The developers triumphed, and a greed economy took root. The issues nowadays are declining mental health, family breakdown, crime, land degradation, unemployment, a widening gap between rich and poor, pollution, and sprawl.

Writer Ted Trainer says before 1980 the people of Ladakh were "notoriously happy." He sees in their tragic story a sobering lesson about our cherished goals of development, growth, and progress. For the most part these are convenient myths that are much better at producing happy economies than happy people.

When normality fails, as it has today, happiness becomes a form of protest. Some 25 disillusioned folks are resorting to "culture jamming" and "subvertisements" to expose the hollow core of commercial society. Others are seeking refuge in various forms of primitivism and eco-primitivism. Spurring this on is intriguing evidence from the field of cognitive archaeology suggesting that our Paleolithic ancestors were probably happier and far more alive than people today. The shift toward "Paleo" and "Stone Age" diets also reflects the belief that they had happier bodies.

There is an exquisite line by the philosopher Friedrich Nietsche which touches on one of the keys to happiness: the need to appreciate "the least, the softest, lightest, a lizard's rustling, a breath, a moment." Paradoxically, happiness is closer when we kneel than when we soar. Our own nothingness can be a great source of joy.

We usually hitch our emotional wagons to ego, ambition, personal power, and the spectacular. But all of these are surprising flops when it comes to happiness. Today's "success" has become a blueprint for failure.

Visionaries tell us that the only happiness that makes sense at this perilous juncture in Earth's history is "sustainable happiness." All worthwhile happiness is life-supporting. But so much of what makes us happy in the age of consumerism is dependent upon the destruction and over-exploitation of nature. A sustainable happiness implies that we take responsibility for the wider contexts in which we live and for the well-being of future generations.

Sustainable happiness harks back to the classical Greek philosophies in viewing ethical living as a legitimate vehicle for human happiness. Compassion in particular plays a central role. In part it rests on the truth that we can be happy in planting the seeds of happiness, even if we might miss the harvest.

Some argue that as a society we are too programmed to selfishness and over- 30 consumption for a sustainable happiness to take root. Democracy itself is a problem when the majority itches for the wrong things. But if we manage to take the first few steps, we may rediscover that happiness resonates most deeply when it has a price.

The greatest irony in the search for happiness is that it is never strictly personal. For happiness to be mature and heartfelt, it must be shared—whether by those around us or by tomorrow's children. If not, happiness can be downright depressing.

*"I didn't do anything on my summer vacation—
should I write about what I bought?"*

Enjoyment as an Alternative to Materialism

MIHALY CSIKSZENTMIHALYI

> Mihaly Csikszentmihalyi is the C. S. and D. J. Davidson Professor of Psychology at Claremont Graduate University. He is also the director of the Quality of Life Research Center at Claremont's Peter F. Drucker and Masatoshi Ito Graduate School of Management. Through his research and writing on the experience of "flow" as a state of mind, Csikszentmihalyi has earned recognition in the fields of education, business, and positive psychology. An extended version of the selection below appeared in the collection *Psychology and Consumer Culture: The Struggle for a Good Life in a Materialistic World,* edited by Tim Kasser and Allen D. Kramer (APA, 2004).

Evolution has built two contradictory motivations into our nervous system: *pleasure,* which is the well-being we feel when eating, resting, and procreating; and *enjoyment,* which is the exhilarating sensation we feel when going beyond the requirements of survival (Csikszentmihalyi, 1993; Ryan & Deci, 2000; Waterman, 1993). Pleasure is a powerful source of motivation, but it does not produce change; it is a conservative force that makes us want to satisfy existing needs and to achieve comfort and relaxation. It is the motivation that makes us look for material resources to improve the quality of life—after all, these are scarce and everyone wants them, so they must be valuable. The concreteness of material goals also makes them seem more real than more complex goals. However, the improvement that money,

physical sensations—me looking at a perfect kitchen in a glossy magazine—and it blends a fantasy landscape, me with my perfect family in the perfect kitchen and the dishes are clean and the meal was relaxed yet perfect.

Imagination is slippery. It lives halfway in the world of physical reality and half 5 in the realm of what isn't, what could be or never could be. In the realm of the imagination, it is very hard to draw a sensible distinction between the material and the nonmaterial. When we confront a new house, or a new car, or a new blouse, we see the physical object, but our imagination is racing ahead, concocting future pleasures and possibilities.

Each of us has little templates in our minds, cognitive scientists have found, influenced by culture, genetics, and individual will, so certain products or goods set off those light shows in the imagination, while other products leave us cold. You may be aroused by the aroma of a certain wine or perhaps the sight of a certain powerboat, depending on your background and tastes. But when a product or an image in a magazine hits the right ignition button, it is like July Fourth in the brain. The imagination goes wild. The longing begins.

These glossy magazines are nutrition for the imagination. It's common to say that they're like pornography. *Food & Wine* is pornography for food. *Auto Week* is pornography for cars. *Condé Nast Traveler* is pornography for beaches, and *House Beautiful* is pornography for Italian-made truffle shavers. *Playboy* and *Penthouse* have the same kind of lavish photo spreads, the same glistening perfections, the same fantasies and lusts, just for different things.

For millions of people, the ridiculously perfect images—the worlds in which every breast is round and firm, every house is immaculate, every vacation destination is uncrowded, and every thigh is firm—are the images that arouse the imagination most powerfully. Why else would so many men spend billions of dollars a year looking at pictures of women who are nothing like real women, let alone the women they are likely to sleep with? Why else would so many people subscribe to *Architectural Digest* and pore over flawless interiors that no human beings could actually live in and that few could ever afford? Why is it that the magazines that sell best off the racks are the ones with bright photos of smiling celebrities on the cover—stunning movie stars, rock stars, royalty, and athletes who are far better-looking than the people we know, far richer than anybody around us, and are depicted living in a social stratosphere far removed from the realm most of us inhabit?

In short, why do we torture ourselves with things we don't have and aren't likely to get? Why do we eagerly seek out images of lives we are unlikely to lead?

It is precisely because fantasy, imagination, and dreaming play a far more 10 significant role in our psychological makeup than we are accustomed to acknowledging. We are influenced, far more than most of us admit, by some longing for completion, some impulse to heaven. The magazine images are not really about hedonism, about enjoying some pleasure that fits into our life here and now. They're not even mainly about conspicuous consumption, finding the right item that will help us show off and look richer and more sophisticated than our friends and neighbors. These magazines are about aspiration.

What they offer is the possibility of a magical conversion process. By mastering the skills described in the magazines, cultivating the tastes, building the sorts of environment, wearing the right fashions, adopting this or that diet, I will be able to transform my present caterpillar self into the shimmering butterfly that is the future me. The magazines show us the avenue to this infinity, and they fill in, in concrete detail, the substance of our vague longings for contentment. . . .

If you study people as they shop, you quickly perceive that the economists' model of human behavior—in which rational actors calculate costs and benefits—doesn't explain the crucial choices. (Why do some people fall in love with Jaguars but not Corvettes?) Nor does Thorstein Veblen's model, in which consumers are involved in a status race to keep up with the Joneses. (Do you really think that's how you select your purchases? And if you don't, what makes you think everyone else is more shallow and status-crazed than you are? Furthermore, in a decentralizing world, which Joneses are you supposed to keep up with, anyway?)

The key to consumption is not calculation or emulation, it's aspiration. Shopping, at least for non-necessities, is a form of daydreaming. People wander through stores browsing for dream kindling. They are looking for things that inspire them to tell fantasy tales about themselves. That apple corer at Crate and Barrel can help you make those pies you've always savored; you can imagine the aromas and the smiles when you bring them out for dessert. That drill from Sears can help you build a utility closet; you can imagine the organized garage and the satisfaction of having everything in its place. That necklace is just what your wife would love; you can imagine the joy she will feel when you give it to her.

Often the pleasure that shoppers get from anticipating an object is greater than the pleasure they get from owning it. Once an item ceases to fire their imagination—when it no longer inspires a story about some brighter future—then they lose interest in it, and their imagination goes off in search of new and exciting things to dream about and buy. (Kids can go through this process with dispiriting speed, as anybody can tell you on a Christmas afternoon.)

People might browse through things they cannot possibly afford, simply 15 because the pleasure they get from daydreaming in a luxury showroom compensates for the frustration of not being able to buy anything. The shoppers may play a distinctly modern game: They know that Gatorade won't make them jocks, that Nike sneakers won't make them jump like Mike. At the same time, they enjoy the fantasies and are happy to play along.

Sometimes shopping sets off a dream or a sensation that is actually revealing and true. In Virginia Woolf's short story "The New Dress," a woman tries on a dress:

> Suffused with light, she sprang into existence. Rid of cares and wrinkles, what she had dreamed of herself was there—a beautiful woman. Just for a second . . . there looked at her, framed in the scrolloping mahogany, a gray-white, mysteriously smiling, charming girl, the core of herself, the soul of herself; and it was not true vanity only, not only self-love that made her think it good, tender and true.

Woolf beautifully captured the way the woman's vision has both the quality of hallucination—it exists for a moment, the woman's cares and wrinkles vanish—but also the quality of truth, because in this moment, the woman sees her truest and best self, which does exist deep down.

People tend to buy things that set off light shows in their imaginations, which fit into the daydreams. For many people, shopping is its own joy, a way of envisioning a better life to come. . . .

The magazine stand, the department store, and the mall are all arenas for fantasy. The more upscale you go, the more imaginatively evocative the stores become. Cartier is less utilitarian than Dollar General. Lamborghini is more fantasy-oriented than Ford. People with money flock toward things that don't only serve a purpose but stir the heart. They are drawn by their imagination to move and improve and chase their fantasy visions of their own private heaven. The cash register is a gateway to paradise.

QUESTIONS FOR DISCUSSION

1. From the article "Does Money Buy Happiness?" paraphrase Robert Lane's explanation of why happiness "levels off" as incomes rise (paragraph 5). What can you find in John Schumaker's argument about the "happiness conspiracy" that corroborates Lane's interpretation?

2. According to Mihaly Csikszentmihalyi, what is the difference between pleasure and enjoyment? What is wrong with choosing TV or shopping to occupy free time? What are some activities that he labels enjoyment? What are the benefits of the more challenging activities?

3. According to Mihaly Csikszentmihalyi, why do people turn to shopping when they are depressed? What is causing the depression in the first place? (See paragraphs 16–20.) Compare his views on the kinds of satisfactions people get from shopping with David Brooks's analysis of what is really happening when people go shopping (see paragraphs 12–16). Which explanation seems more plausible to you?

4. There is some overlap in this section with an important theme in some of the earlier sections: the comparison between spiritual and material routes to happiness. James Twitchell claims (paragraph 34, page 342) that people today find their happiness through consumer goods because it is our nature to be materialistic, not spiritual; "spiritualism is more likely a substitute when objects are scarce," he writes. Jean Kilbourne, in "Jesus Is a Brand of Jeans," argues that advertising co-opts the promises of religion in the service of selling stuff (paragraph 13, page 372). What contribution to this question does David Brooks offer in the selection "Shopping for Paradise"? What is the happiness Brooks describes as "paradise"? In what ways is it parallel to notions of heaven?

SUGGESTIONS FOR WRITING

For Exploration

Compare what David Brooks and Jean Kilbourne say about advertisements as promising people some kind of transformation. What is that transformation for

Brooks? What is positive about it? What is it for Kilbourne? What is dangerous about it? Evaluate the two arguments and decide which holds more truth.

For Analysis and Convincing

Jean Kilbourne argues that advertising "performs much the same function in industrial society as myth did in ancient societies. It is both a creator and perpetuator of the dominant values of the culture, the social norms by which most people govern their behavior. At the very least, advertising helps create a climate in which certain values flourish and others are not reflected at all" (paragraph 12). John Schumaker gives examples of other cultures, such as the Navajo and the ancient Greeks, whose values contrast with those of modern consumer society. Examine some popular advertising campaigns aimed at young people today. What values are displayed in advertising? Do you agree with Schumaker that the values of consumer culture, as depicted in advertising, are not compatible with mental well-being? Arrive at a claim on the issue and defend it in an argument to convince.

For Persuasion

Because of the stress of college life, students often choose the kinds of leisure activities that Mihaly Csikszentmihalyi describes as pleasure rather than enjoyment. What sorts of activities do you choose? If you have known the benefits of "enjoyment" over "pleasure," write an argument to persuade other students that enjoyment is worth the effort. If you have experienced the "flow" state, you could describe that experience as part of your evidence.

For Convincing

Using John Schumaker and Mihaly Csikszentmihalyi as sources but adding any additional reasons and evidence you wish, make a case against the commonly held idea of happiness in mainstream American society. Be sure to define happiness as your readers would see it; then give reasons and evidence why they should not seek it.

For Mediation

Drawing from readings in all three sections of this casebook, sum up some of the major objections to the consumer society. Sum up some of the benefits. Propose suggestions for living meaningfully and well in a materialistic culture.

FOR FURTHER READING AND RESEARCH

Berger, Arthur Asa. *Shop 'Til You Drop.* Lanham, MD: Rowman & Littlefield, 2005.

Brooks, David. *On Paradise Drive: How We Live Now (And Always Have) in the Future Tense.* New York: Simon & Schuster, 2004.

Csikszentmihalyi, Mihaly. "If We Are So Rich, Why Aren't We Happy?" *American Psychologist* Oct. 1999:821–27.

Easterbrook, Gregg. *The Progress Paradox: How Life Gets Better While People Feel Worse.* New York: Random House, 2004.

———. "The Real Truth about Money." *Time* 17 Jan. 2005:32–34.

Ebsco Academic Host. Dallas, TX, Fondren Library, Southern Methodist University.

Milner, Murray, Jr. *Freaks, Geeks, and Cool Kids: American Teenagers, Schools, and the Culture of Consumption.* New York: Routledge, 2004.

Rosenblatt, Roger, ed. *Consuming Desires: Consumption, Culture, and the Pursuit of Happiness.* Washington, D.C.: Island Press, 1999.

Schor, Juliet. *Born to Buy: The Commercialized Child and the New Consumer Culture.* New York: Scribner, 2004.

———. *The Overspent American: Why We Want What We Don't Need.* Basic Books, 1992.

———. *The Overworked American. The Unexpected Decline of Leisure.* HarperPerennial, 1998.

Schumaker, John F. *In Search of Happiness: Understanding an Endangered State of Mind.* Auckland: Penguin New Zealand, 2006.

———. "Dead Zone." *New Internationalist* July 2001.

Twitchell, James B. *Adcult USA: The Triumph of Advertising in American Culture.* New York: Columbia, 1997.

———. *Lead Us Into Temptation: The Triumph of American Materialism.* New York: Columbia, 1999.

———. *Living It Up: America's Love Affair with Luxury.* New York: Simon & Schuster, 2003.

CHAPTER 12

Romantic Relationships: Sex, Love, and Maybe Marriage

GENERAL INTRODUCTION: LOVE TODAY

In the twenty-first century, there is no decline in the patterns and habits that make us less connected as a society: families see each other less because of the demands of school and jobs; neighbors move in and out without our knowing much about them; marriages continue to break up at the rate of about 50%; more and more people live alone; and our churches and schools are so large that individuals may feel like just another number. The pursuit of individual happiness means that we go our own ways rather than adhering to traditional institutions that once connected us to family, friends, and neighbors. But one connection persists—the romantic relationship based in love. Our love lives are often the defining factor in personal happiness today.

Whether you call the person a husband or wife, girlfriend or boyfriend, partner, significant other, or something else, we seem highly invested in finding love. Surveys of college freshmen show that interest in marriage and raising a family is among their highest goals; surveys of young adults indicate the desire to find a soul mate and stay married for life. While some people resist conventional marriage, the vast majority still seek lifelong commitment.

And yet none of this comes easily. Although marriage is still the goal, the percentage of unmarried people is at an all-time high. The process of finding a mate, making a commitment to marry, and remaining married is more and more defined in terms of work, not pleasure. Books, magazines, reality TV, Dr. Phil, E. Jean, Dear Abby, therapists and counselors—all offer advice about how to obtain, maintain, and recover from personal relationships. Because of its importance, the personal relationship seems a source of insecurity and anxiety. Why are Americans having so much trouble with the personal relationships they claim to value so much?

The writers who appear in this casebook describe Americans trying to navigate in a sea of conflicting ideas and social pressures:

1. We have unrealistic ideas about what love is. Popular culture depicts love as romantic infatuation between beautiful people, usually young. We don't see many portrayals of love as long-term attachment between real-life, mature couples.

2. We have high expectations for what we want in a mate. According to evolutionary psychologists, nature made us fussy. We look for a partner with good genes and reproductive potential. But our culture exaggerates the youth, beauty, wealth, and status that an ideal mate should possess. Other expectations are just as high. Whoever invented the term "soul mate" hit a chord with people's needs today; both sexes want deep emotional intimacy with their partner. We want mates who will anticipate and satisfy all our needs.

3. We want intimacy, and yet we fear it. College students go out in groups because they want to protect themselves from intimacy. But avoiding personal relationships for years makes the search for the right partner more serious than fun. Dating services and publishers of advice books feed off

of people's anxiety about finding the right partner and women's fears that it will not happen in time for them to bear children.

4. Marriage has gone from a public institution to a private one. Family and community used to be more involved when marriages were arranged, or at least when courtship took place in the family home; marriages were seen as joining two families, not just two individuals. Economic factors also make us more independent than when women depended on a husband for financial support and when men depended on a wife for domestic services. These and many other factors have made personal relationships less stable.

SECTION 1: ATTRACTING AND CHOOSING A MATE
Overview

When people are powerfully attracted to one another, they talk about having "chemistry," which turns out to be not only a metaphor. The research Lauren Slater discusses in the first selection shows that certain powerful chemicals in our bodies, especially dopamine, serotonin, and oxytocin, stimulate both the "high" of early romance and the less exciting but more stable feelings of long-term attachment. It also shows something else we could predict: that certain parts of our brains are involved much more than others in passionate attraction. Our brains began to evolve for mating hundreds of millions of years ago, when animals started reproducing sexually. In short, it's hardly surprising that desire and devotion have deep and complicated biological foundations, strong enough to take over and drive our behavior. We sometimes say that being in love is like addiction to a drug. And so it is—more than we realize.

But the chemistry of love helps us understand only a little of the mystery of love—basically why people are drawn to other people and why love can be so overwhelming. It doesn't help us grasp why we are attracted to some people and not to others. The second selection, from Helen Fisher's influential book, *Why We Love,* exposes the largely unconscious motivations involved. Many of these evidently developed to ensure that people would mate with genetically appropriate partners, produce many and healthy children, and tie parents together long enough to raise their offspring.

So, is romantic love in the final analysis all genetics, chemistry, brain structures, and evolution? Are we learning more about love only to take the wonderful mystery out of it? No, on both counts. As Slater and Fisher both recognize in different ways, human love is as much cultural as it is biological. When our species originated in Africa about 150,000 years ago, we were already tool-users with complex social arrangements. Our behavior has always been a combination of nature and nurture, biology and culture. So intertwined are the two that we can't disentangle them. As far as the mystery of love is concerned, we'll never understand everything involved in one person loving another, much less everything the relationship reveals to two people who love each other. But perhaps we can grow wiser, learn to love better, and free ourselves from delusions that lead to disappointment.

Love: The Chemical Reaction

LAUREN SLATER

> Lauren Slater is a freelance writer. The following article appeared in *National Geographic* in February 2006.

My husband and I got married at eight in the morning. It was winter, freezing, the trees encased in ice and a few lone blackbirds balancing on telephone wires. We were in our early 30s, considered ourselves hip and cynical, the types who decried the institution of marriage even as we sought its status. During our wedding brunch we put out a big suggestion box and asked people to slip us advice on how to avoid divorce; we thought it was a funny, clear-eyed, grounded sort of thing to do, although the suggestions were mostly foolish: Screw the toothpaste cap on tight. After the guests left, the house got quiet. There were flowers everywhere: puckered red roses and fragile ferns. "What can we do that's really romantic?" I asked. . . . Benjamin suggested we take a bath. I didn't want a bath. He suggested a lunch of chilled white wine and salmon. I was sick of salmon.

What can we do that's really romantic? The wedding was over, the silence seemed suffocating, and I felt the familiar disappointment after a longed-for event has come and gone. We were married. Hip, hip, hooray. I decided to take a walk. . . . I came to our town's tattoo parlor. Now I am not a tattoo type person, but for some reason, on that cold silent Sunday, I decided to walk in. "Can I help you?" a woman asked.

"Is there a kind of tattoo I can get that won't be permanent?" I asked.

"Henna tattoos," she said.

She explained that they lasted for six weeks, were used at Indian weddings, 5 were stark and beautiful and all brown. She showed me pictures of Indian women with jewels in their noses, their arms scrolled and laced with the henna markings. Indeed they were beautiful, sharing none of the gaudy comic strip quality of the tattoos we see in the United States. . . . And because I had just gotten married, and because I was feeling a post wedding letdown, and because I wanted something really romantic to sail me through the night, I decided to get one.

"Where?" she asked.

"Here," I said. I laid my hands over my breasts and belly.

She raised her eyebrows. "Sure," she said.

I am a modest person. But I took off my shirt, lay on the table, heard her in the back room mixing powders and paints. She came to me carrying a small black-bellied pot inside of which was a rich red mush, slightly glittering. She adorned me. She gave me vines and flowers. She turned my body into a stake supporting whole new gardens of growth, and then, low around my hips, she painted a delicate chain-linked chastity belt. An hour later, the paint dry, I put my clothes back on, went home to find [Benjamin]. This, I knew, was my gift to him, the kind of present you offer only once in your lifetime. I let him undress me.

"Wow," he said, standing back.   10

I blushed, and we began.

We are no longer beginning. . . . This does not surprise me. Even back then, wearing the decor of desire, the serpentining tattoos, I knew they would fade, their red-clay color bleaching out until they were gone. On my wedding day I didn't care.

I do now. Eight years later, pale as a pillowcase, here I sit, with all the extra pounds and baggage time brings. And the questions have only grown more insistent. Does passion necessarily diminish over time? How reliable is romantic love, really, as a means of choosing one's mate? . . .

In the Western world we have for centuries concocted poems and stories and plays about the cycles of love, the way it morphs and changes over time, the way passion grabs us . . . and then leaves us for something saner. . . . We have relied on stories to explain the complexities of love, tales of jealous gods and arrows. Now, however, these stories—so much a part of every civilization—may be changing as science steps in to explain what we have always felt to be myth, to be magic. For the first time, new research has begun to illuminate where love lies in the brain, the particulars of its chemical components.

Anthropologist Helen Fisher may be the closest we've ever come to having a 15 doyenne of desire. . . . She has devoted much of her career to studying the biochemical pathways of love in all its manifestations: lust, romance, attachment, the way they wax and wane. . . . "A woman unconsciously uses orgasms as a way of deciding whether or not a man is good for her. If he's impatient and rough, and she doesn't have the orgasm, she may instinctively feel he's less likely to be a good husband and father. Scientists think the fickle female orgasm may have evolved to help women distinguish Mr. Right from Mr. Wrong."

One of Fisher's central pursuits in the past decade has been looking at love, quite literally, with the aid of an MRI machine. Fisher and her colleagues Arthur Aron and Lucy Brown recruited subjects who had been "madly in love" for an average of seven months. Once inside the MRI machine, subjects were shown two photographs, one neutral, the other of their loved one.

What Fisher saw fascinated her. When each subject looked at his or her loved one, the parts of the brain linked to reward and pleasure—the ventral tegmental area and the caudate nucleus—lit up. What excited Fisher most was not so much finding a location, an address, for love as tracing its specific chemical pathways. Love lights up the caudate nucleus because it is home to a dense spread of receptors for a neurotransmitter called dopamine. . . . In the right proportions, dopamine creates intense energy, exhilaration, focused attention, and motivation to win rewards. It is why, when you are newly in love, you can stay up all night, watch the sun rise, run a race, ski fast down a slope ordinarily too steep for your skill. . . .

I first fell in love when I was only 12, with a teacher. His name was Mr. McArthur, and he wore open-toed sandals and sported a beard. I had never had a male teacher before, and I thought it terribly exotic. Mr. McArthur did things no other teacher dared to do. He explained to us the physics of farting. He demonstrated how to make an egg explode. He smoked cigarettes at recess, leaning languidly against the side of the school building, the ash growing longer and longer until he casually tapped it off with his finger. . . .

Sound familiar?. . . Donatella Marazziti is a professor of psychiatry at the University of Pisa in Italy who has studied the biochemistry of lovesickness. Having

"I'd do anything for you," whispers Blair Witherspoon to girlfriend Erica Hoskey. . . . Sweet talk and gifts fuel romantic passion. But biochemists say this feverish stage of love typically burns out after a few years. Why? Perhaps the brain can't maintain the intense neural activity of infatuation.

been in love twice herself and felt its awful power, Marazziti became interested in exploring the similarities between love and obsessive-compulsive disorder.

She and her colleagues measured serotonin levels in the blood of 24 subjects 20 who had fallen in love within the past six months and obsessed about this love object for at least four hours every day. Serotonin is, perhaps, our star neurotransmitter, altered by our star psychiatric medications: Prozac and Zoloft and Paxil, among others. Researchers have long hypothesized that people with obsessive-compulsive disorder (OCD) have a serotonin "imbalance." Drugs like Prozac seem to alleviate OCD by increasing the amount of this neurotransmitter available at the juncture between neurons.

Marazziti compared the lovers' serotonin levels with those of a group of people suffering from OCD and another group who were free from both passion and mental illness. Levels of serotonin in both the obsessives' blood and the lovers' blood were 40 percent lower than those in her normal subjects. Translation: Love and obsessive-compulsive disorder could have a similar chemical profile. Translation: Love and mental illness may be difficult to tell apart. Translation: Don't be a fool. Stay away.

Of course that's a mandate none of us can follow. We do fall in love, sometimes over and over again, subjecting ourselves, each time, to a very sick state of mind. There is hope, however, for those caught in the grip of runaway passion—Prozac. There's nothing like that bicolored bullet for damping down the sex drive. . . . Helen Fisher believes that the ingestion of drugs like Prozac jeopardizes one's ability to fall in love—and stay in love. By dulling the keen edge of love and its associated libido, relationships go stale. Says Fisher, "I know of one couple on the edge of divorce. The wife was on an antidepressant. Then she went off it, started having orgasms once more, felt the renewal of sexual attraction for her husband, and they're now in love all over again.". . .

Psychiatrists such as Thomas Lewis from the University of California at San Francisco's School of Medicine hypothesize that romantic love is rooted in our earliest infantile experiences with intimacy, how we felt at the breast, our mother's face, these things of pure unconflicted comfort that get engraved in our brain and that we ceaselessly try to recapture as adults. According to this theory we love whom we love not so much because of the future we hope to build but because of the past we hope to reclaim. Love is reactive, not proactive, it arches us backward, which may be why a certain person just "feels right." Or "feels familiar." He or she is familiar. He or she has a certain look or smell or sound or touch that activates buried memories.

When I first met my husband, I believed this psychological theory was more or less correct. My husband has red hair and a soft voice. A chemist, he is whimsical and odd. One day before we married he dunked a rose in liquid nitrogen so it froze, whereupon he flung it against the wall, spectacularly shattering it. That's when I fell in love with him. My father, too, has red hair, a soft voice, and many eccentricities. He was prone to bursting into song, prompted by something we never saw.

However, it turns out my theories about why I came to love my husband may be just so much hogwash. Evolutionary psychology has said good riddance to Freud and the Oedipal complex and all that other transcendent stuff and hello to simple survival skills. . . . It hypothesizes that we tend to see as attractive, and thereby choose as mates, people who look healthy. . . .

It all seems too good to be true, that we are so hardwired and yet unconscious of the wiring. . . . We say, "I married him (or her) because he's intelligent, she's beautiful, he's witty, she's compassionate." But we may just be as deluded about love as we are when we're in love. . . .

Why doesn't passionate love last? How is it possible to see a person as beautiful on Monday, and 364 days later, on another Monday, to see that beauty as bland? Surely the object of your affection could not have changed that much. She still has the same shaped eyes. Her voice has always had that husky sound, but now it grates on you—she sounds like she needs an antibiotic. Or maybe you're the one who needs an antibiotic, because the partner you once loved and cherished and saw as though saturated with starlight now feels more like a low-level infection, tiring you, sapping all your strength.

Studies around the world confirm that, indeed, passion usually ends. Its conclusion is as common as its initial flare. No wonder some cultures think selecting a lifelong mate based on something so fleeting is folly. Helen Fisher has suggested that relationships frequently break up after four years because that's about how long it takes to raise a child through infancy. Passion, that wild, prismatic insane feeling, turns out to be practical after all. We . . . need enough passion to start breeding, and then feelings of attachment take over as the partners bond to raise a helpless human infant. . . .

Biologically speaking, the reasons romantic love fades may be found in the way our brains respond to the surge and pulse of dopamine that accompanies passion and makes us fly. . . . Maybe it's a good thing that romance fizzles. Would we have railroads, bridges, planes, faxes, vaccines, and television if we were all always besotted? In place of the ever evolving technology that has marked human culture from its earliest tool use, we would have instead only bonbons, bouquets, and birth control. More seriously, if the chemically altered state induced by romantic love is akin to a mental illness or a drug-induced euphoria, exposing yourself for too long could result in psychological damage. . . .

Once upon a time, in India, a boy and a girl fell in love without their parents' 30 permission. They were from different castes, their relationship radical and unsanctioned. Picture it: the sparkling sari, the boy in white linen, the clandestine meetings on tiled terraces with a fat, white moon floating overhead. Who could deny these lovers their pleasure, or condemn the force of their attraction?

Their parents could. In one recent incident a boy and girl from different castes were hanged at the hands of their parents as hundreds of villagers watched. A couple who eloped were stripped and beaten. Yet another couple committed suicide after their parents forbade them to marry.

Anthropologists used to think that romance was a Western construct, a bourgeois by-product of the Middle Ages. Romance was for the sophisticated, took place in cafes, with coffees and Cabernets, or on silk sheets, or in rooms with a flickering fire. It was assumed that non-Westerners, with their broad familial and social obligations, were spread too thin for particular passions. How could a collectivist culture celebrate or in any way sanction the obsession with one individual that defines new love? Could a lice-ridden peasant really feel passion?

Easily, as it turns out. Scientists now believe that romance is panhuman, embedded in our brains since Pleistocene times. In a study of 166 cultures, anthropologists William Jankowiak and Edward Fischer observed evidence of passionate love in 147 of them. In another study men and women from Europe, Japan, and the Philippines were asked to fill out a survey to measure their experiences of passionate love. All three groups professed feeling passion with the same searing intensity.

But though romantic love may be universal, its cultural expression is not. To the Fulbe tribe of northern Cameroon, poise matters more than passion. Men who spend too much time with their wives are taunted, and those who are weak-kneed are thought to have fallen under a dangerous spell. Love may be inevitable, but for the Fulbe its manifestations are shameful, equated with sickness and social impairment.

In India romantic love has traditionally been seen as dangerous, a threat to a 35 well-crafted caste system in which marriages are arranged as a means of preserving lineage and bloodlines. Thus the gruesome tales, the warnings embedded in fables about what happens when one's wayward impulses take over. Today love marriages appear to be on the rise in India, often in defiance of parents' wishes.

The triumph of romantic love is celebrated in Bollywood films. Yet most Indians still believe arranged marriages are more likely to succeed than love marriages. In one survey of Indian college students, 76 percent said they'd marry someone with all the right qualities even if they weren't in love with the person (compared with only 14 percent of Americans). Marriage is considered too important a step to leave to chance.

Renu Dinakaran is a striking 45-year-old woman who lives in Bangalore, India. . . . [She] was born into a traditional Indian family where an arranged marriage was expected. She was not an arranged kind of person, though, emerging from her earliest days as a fierce tennis player, too sweaty for saris, and smarter than many of the men around her. Nevertheless at the age of 17 she was married off to a first cousin, a man she barely knew, a man she wanted to learn to love, but couldn't. Renu considers many arranged marriages to be acts of "state-sanctioned rape."

Renu hoped to fall in love with her husband, but the more years that passed, the less love she felt, until, at the end, she was shrunken, bitter, hiding behind the curtains of her in-laws' bungalow, looking with longing at the couple on the balcony across from theirs. "It was so obvious to me that couple had married for love, and I envied them. I really did. It hurt me so much to see how they stood together, how they went shopping for bread and eggs."

Exhausted from being forced into confinement, from being swaddled in saris that made it difficult to move, from resisting the pressure to eat off her husband's plate, Renu did what traditional Indian culture forbids one to do. She left. By this time she had had two children. She took them with her. In her mind was an old movie she'd seen on TV, a movie so strange and enticing to her, so utterly confounding and comforting at the same time, that she couldn't get it out of her head. It was 1986. The movie was *Love Story.* "Before I saw movies like *Love Story,* I didn't realize the power that love can have," she says.

Renu was lucky in the end. In Mumbai she met a man named Anil, and it was 40 then, for the first time, that she felt passion. "When I first met Anil, it was like nothing I'd ever experienced. He was the first man I ever had an orgasm with. I was high, just high, all the time. And I knew it wouldn't last, couldn't last, and so that infused it with a sweet sense of longing, almost as though we were watching the end approach while we were also discovering each other."

When Renu speaks of the end, she does not, to be sure, mean the end of her relationship with Anil; she means the end of a certain stage. The two are still happily married, companionable, loving if not "in love," with a playful black dachshund they bought together. Their relationship, once so full of fire, now seems to simmer along at an even temperature, enough to keep them well fed and warm. They are grateful.

"Would I want all that passion back?" Renu asks. "Sometimes, yes. But to tell you the truth, it was exhausting."

From a physiological point of view, this couple has moved from the dopamine-drenched state of romantic love to the relative quiet of an oxytocin-induced attachment. Oxytocin is a hormone that promotes a feeling of connection, bonding. It is released when we hug our long-term spouses, or our children. It is released when a mother nurses her infant. . . . In long-term relationships that work—like Renu and Anil's—oxytocin is believed to be abundant in both partners. In long-term relationships that never get off the ground, like Renu and her first husband's, or that crumble once the high is gone, chances are the couple has not found a way to stimulate or sustain oxytocin production.

"But there are things you can do to help it along," says Helen Fisher. "Massage. Make love. These things trigger oxytocin and thus make you feel much closer to your partner."

Well, I suppose that's good advice, but it's based on the assumption that you 45 still want to have sex with that boring windbag of a husband. Should you fake-it-till-you-make-it?

"Yes," says Fisher. "Assuming a fairly healthy relationship, if you have enough orgasms with your partner, you may become attached to him or her. You will stimulate oxytocin.". . .

Arthur Aron, a psychologist at Stony Brook University in New York, conducted an experiment that illuminates some of the mechanisms by which people become and stay attracted. He recruited a group of men and women and put opposite sex pairs in rooms together, instructing each pair to perform a series of tasks, which included telling each other personal details about themselves. He then asked each couple to stare into each other's eyes for two minutes. After this encounter, Aron found most of the couples, previously strangers to each other, reported feelings of attraction. In fact, one couple went on to marry.

Fisher says this exercise works wonders for some couples. Aron and Fisher also suggest doing novel things together, because novelty triggers dopamine in the brain, which can stimulate feelings of attraction. In other words, if your heart flutters in his presence, you might decide it's not because you're anxious but because you love him. Carrying this a step further, Aron and others have found that even if you just jog in place and then meet someone, you're more likely to think they're attractive. So first dates that involve a nerve-racking activity, like riding a roller coaster, are more likely to lead to second and third dates. That's a strategy worthy of posting on Match.com. Play some squash. And in times of stress—natural disasters, blackouts, predators on the prowl—lock up tight and hold your partner.

In Somerville, Massachusetts, where I live with my husband, our predators are primarily mosquitoes. That needn't stop us from trying to enter the windows of each other's soul. When I propose this to Benjamin, he raises an eyebrow.

"Why don't we just go out for Cambodian food?" he says.   50

"Because that's not how the experiment happened."

As a scientist, my husband is always up for an experiment. But our lives are so busy that, in order to do this, we have to make a plan. We will meet next Wednesday at lunchtime and try the experiment in our car.

On the Tuesday night before our rendezvous, I have to make an unplanned trip to New York. My husband is more than happy to forget our date. I, however, am not. That night, from my hotel room, I call him.

"We can do it on the phone," I say.

"What am I supposed to stare into?" he asks. "The keypad?"   55

"There's a picture of me hanging in the hall. Look at that for two minutes. I'll look at a picture I have of you in my wallet."

"Come on," he says.

"Be a sport," I say. "It's better than nothing."

Maybe not. Two minutes seems like a long time to stare at someone's picture with a receiver pressed to your ear. My husband sneezes, and I try to imagine his picture sneezing right along with him, and this makes me laugh.

Another 15 seconds pass, slowly, each second stretched to its limit so I can   60 almost hear time, feel time, its taffy-like texture, the pop it makes when it's done. Pop pop pop. I stare and stare at my husband's picture. It doesn't produce any sense of startling intimacy, and I feel defeated.

Still, I keep on. I can hear him breathing on the other end. The photograph before me was taken a year or so ago, cut to fit my wallet, his strawberry blond hair pulled back in a ponytail. I have never really studied it before. And I realize that in this picture my husband is not looking straight back at me, but his pale blue eyes are cast sideways, off to the left, looking at something I can't see. I touch his eyes. I peer close, and then still closer, at his averted face. Is there something sad in his expression, something sad in the way he gazes off?

I look toward the side of the photo, to find what it is he's looking at, and then I see it: a tiny turtle coming toward him. Now I remember how he caught it after the camera snapped, how he held it gently in his hands, showed it to our kids, stroked its shell, his forefinger moving over the scaly dome, how he held the animal out toward me, a love offering. I took it, and together we sent it back to the sea.

Cartoon

SAM GROSS

"I don't care if she is a tape dispenser. I love her."

For Discussion

The love-struck snail knows that the object of his affection is a tape dispenser but believes, like many people, that the only thing that matters is love. Discuss the idea that the power of love can overcome significant differences between partners.

"That First Fine Careless Rapture": Who We Choose

HELEN FISHER

Helen Fisher is a research professor in anthropology at Rutgers. The following selection comes from her celebrated book, *Why We Love: The Nature and Chemistry of Romantic Love* (Henry Holt, 2004).

Love can be triggered when you least expect it—by pure chance. The perfect partner can sit right next to you at a party and you might not notice him or her if you are exceptionally busy at work or school, enmeshed in another relationship, or otherwise emotionally preoccupied.

But if you just entered college or moved to a new city by yourself, recently recovered from an unsatisfactory love affair, began to make enough money to raise a family, are lonely or suffering through a difficult experience, or have too much spare time, you are ripe to fall in love.[1] In fact, people who are emotionally aroused, be it by joy, sadness, anxiety, fear, curiosity, or *any* other feeling, are more likely to be vulnerable to this passion.[2]

I suspect this is because all agitated mental states are associated with arousal mechanisms in the brain, as well as with elevated levels of stress hormones. Both systems elevate levels of dopamine—thus setting up the chemistry for romantic passion. . . .

Many other hidden forces play a role in whom you choose. Among them: mystery.

MYSTERY

Both sexes are often attracted to those they find mysterious. As Baudelaire wrote, 5 "We love women in proportion to their degree of strangeness to us." The sense that one has a slippery grip on an elusive, improbable treasure can trigger romantic passion.

The reverse is also true. Familiarity can deaden thoughts of romantic love—as life on one Israeli kibbutz has shown. Here children grew up together in a common house where they lived, slept, and bathed with other youths of all ages. Boys and girls touched and lay together playfully. By age twelve, however, they became tense with one another. Then as teenagers, they developed strong brother-sister bonds. But none of those who started life in this common cradle married a fellow kibbutznik.[3] So scientists now think that at a critical time in childhood, sometime between ages three and six, boys and girls who live in close proximity and get to know each other well lose the ability to fall in love with one another. . . .

You and I inherited this natural repulsion for copulation with close family members and other individuals we know well, a distaste that undoubtedly evolved to discourage in-breeding—the destructive act of mixing one's DNA with close kin. As a result, we are more likely to become attracted to someone from outside our family or the group in which we were raised—someone with a touch of mystery. . . .

DO OPPOSITES ATTRACT?

Nevertheless, "that first fine careless rapture," as Robert Browning called romantic love, is generally directed toward someone much like one's self. Most people around the world do feel that amorous chemistry for unfamiliar individuals of the *same* ethnic, social, religious, educational, and economic background, who have a similar amount of physical attractiveness, a comparable intelligence, and similar attitudes, expectations, values, interests, and social and communication skills.[4]

In fact, in a new study of mate selection in America, evolutionary biologists Peter Buston and Stephen Emlen report that young men and women think of themselves as particular types of marriage partners and choose people with the same traits, ranging from financial and physical assets to intricacies of personality.[5] If a woman is blessed with a trust fund, for example, she seeks another from the upper class. Handsome men seek beautiful women. And those devoted to family and sexual fidelity select someone with these attributes. . . . Men and women also gravitate to lovers who share their sense of humor, to those with similar social and political values, and to individuals with much the same beliefs about life in general.[6] . . .

SYMMETRY: THE "GOLDEN MEAN"

Another biological taste we have inherited from the animal kingdom is our tendency to choose well-proportioned mates. . . . Almost twenty-five hundred years ago Aristotle maintained that there were some universal standards of physical beauty. One, he believed, was balanced bodily proportions, including symmetry. This accorded with his high respect for what he called the golden mean, or moderation between extremes.

Modern science supports Aristotle's notion. Symmetry is beautiful—to insects, birds, mammals, all of the primates, and people around the world.[7] Female scorpion flies seek mates with uniform wings. Barn swallows like partners with well-proportioned tails. Monkeys are partial to consorts with symmetrical teeth. If you walk into a village in New Guinea and point to the most beautiful man or woman sitting around the campfire, the natives will agree with you.[8] And when researchers used computers to blend many faces into a composite "average" face, both men and women liked the average face better than any of the individual ones.[9] It was more balanced. Even two-month-old infants gaze longer at more symmetrical faces.[10] . . .

The beauty of symmetry does tell a basic truth. Creatures with balanced, well-proportioned ears, eyes, teeth, and jaws, with symmetrical elbows, knees, and breasts, have been able to repel bacteria, viruses, and other minute predators that can cause bodily irregularities. By displaying symmetry, animals advertise their superior genetic ability to combat diseases.[11]

So our human attraction to symmetrical suitors is a primitive animal mechanism designed to guide us to select genetically sturdy mating partners.[12]

And nature has taken no chances; the brain naturally responds to a beautiful face. When scientists recorded the brain activity of heterosexual men ages twenty-one to thirty-five as they looked at women with beautiful faces, the ventral tegmental area (VTA) "lit up."[13] A similar response occurred in our scanning

10

study: those subjects who gazed at photos of better-looking partners showed more activity in the VTA. And the VTA is rich with dopamine—the neurotransmitter that provides the energy, elation, focussed attention, and motivation to win a reward. . . .

Because symmetry enhances one's choices in the mating game, women go to 15 extraordinary lengths to achieve it or at least a semblance of it. With powders they make the two sides of the face more similar. With mascara and eyeliner, they make their eyes appear more alike. With lipstick they enhance one lip to match the other. And with plastic surgery, exercise, belts, bras, and tight jeans and shirts, they mold their forms to create the symmetrical proportions men prefer.

Nature helps. Scientists have found that women's hands and ears are more symmetrical during monthly ovulation—a time when it is reproductively important to attract a man.[14] Women's breasts become more symmetrical during ovulation too.[15] Moreover, young men and young women are often quite symmetrical; we become more and more lopsided as we age.

"WAIST TO HIP" RATIO

The golden mean of balance also applies to other bodily proportions. To a group of American men, psychologist Devendra Singh displayed an array of line drawings of young women and asked which body types they found most attractive.[16] Most chose women whose waist circumference was about 70 percent of their hips. This experiment was then redone in Britain, Germany, Australia, India, Uganda, and several other countries. Responses varied, but many informants favored this same general waist-to-hip ratio.

When Singh measured the waist-to-hip ratio of 286 ancient sculptures from several African tribes, as well as from ancient India, Egypt, Greece, and Rome, he found that all favored a ratio that was smaller for women than for men. And in a study of 330 artworks of Europe, Asia, the Americas, and Africa, some of which date back thirty-two thousand years, scientists found that most women were depicted with a waist-to-hip ratio of these same general proportions.[17] Interestingly, *Playboy* centerfolds display these proportions, too, as do American "supermodels.". . .

A woman's waist-to-hip ratio is largely inherited; it is produced by genes. Moreover, although it clearly varies from one woman to the next, this ratio adjusts during ovulation to come closer to 70 percent. Why has nature gone to such extraordinary lengths to produce curvaceous women? And why do men around the world appreciate this particular waist-to-hip ratio in women?

Most likely for an evolutionary reason. Women with a waist-to-hip ratio of around 20 70 percent are more likely to bear babies, Singh reports. They possess the right amount of fat in the right places—due to high levels of bodily estrogen in relation to testosterone. Women who vary substantially from these proportions find it harder to get pregnant; they conceive later in life; and they have more miscarriages. . . .

So Singh theorizes that male attraction to a specific female waist-to-hip ratio is a natural preference for healthy, fertile partners. . . . Of course, men prefer other things in women, too.

WHO MEN CHOOSE

In a classic study of some ten thousand people in thirty-seven societies, scientists asked men and women to rank eighteen characteristics in order of their importance in choosing a spouse.[18] Both sexes ranked love or mutual attraction first. A dependable character came next, followed by emotional stability and maturity, and a pleasing disposition. Both men and women also said they would choose someone who was kind, smart, educated, sociable, healthy, and interested in home and family.

But this study also showed a distinct gender difference in romantic tastes. When it came to sizing up potential romantic partners, men were more likely to choose women who displayed *visual* signs of youth and beauty.

These masculine predilections are documented across millennia and cultures.[19] Osiris, the legendary ruler of predynastic Egypt, was overwhelmed by the physical beauty of his beloved wife, Isis. As he wrote over four thousand years ago, "Isis has cast her net, / and ensnared me / in the noose of her hair / I am held by her eyes / curbed by her necklace / imprisoned by the scent of her skin."[20]

A Tiv tribesman of Nigeria was swept away by the shapeliness of a woman, 25 exclaiming, "When I saw her dance she took my life away and I knew I must follow her."[21]

American men who place courtship ads in newspapers and magazines are three times more likely than women to mention that they seek beauty in a partner.[22]

And on average, men around the world marry women who are three years younger than themselves.[23] In the United States, men who remarry usually choose a woman about five years younger; if they wed a third time, they often take a bride about eight years their junior.[24]

When asked why people desire physical beauty, Aristotle replied: "No one that is not blind could ask that question." Men unquestionably find good-looking women aesthetically pleasing to look at. They also like to impress friends and colleagues with their dazzling girlfriends or trophy wives. In fact, people in general tend to regard beautiful women (and good-looking men) as warm, smart, strong, giving, friendly, polite, sexy, interesting, financially secure, and socially popular.[25]

But evolutionary psychologists now believe that men subconsciously also prefer youth and beauty because it gives them reproductive payoffs.[26] Young women with smooth skin, snow-white teeth, sparkling eyes, gleaming hair, taut muscles, a lithe body, and a lively personality are more likely to be healthy and energetic—good qualities for bearing and rearing babies. Smooth, clear skin and babylike facial features also signal elevated levels of estrogen that can aid in reproduction. . . .

THE MALE BRAIN IN LOVE

Our fMRI study on the brain circuitry of people in love turned up some unexpected 30 results: we found several gender differences.[27] These findings were complex and varied. Men did not fit neatly in one category and women in another. . . . But there were statistically significant differences between the sexes. No one knows exactly what these findings mean. But I will speculate about men for the moment and theorize about women later.

In our sample, men tended to show more activity than women in brain regions associated with *visual* processing, particularly of the face.

Could this have evolved to enhance men's ability to fall in love when they *saw* a woman who was young, symmetrical, and a good reproductive bet? Maybe. This brain activity could also help explain why men generally fall in love faster than women.[28] When the time is right and a man *sees* an attractive woman, he is anatomically equipped to rapidly associate attractive *visual* features with feelings of romantic passion. What an effective courtship device.

Indeed, we found another gender difference that could have evolved to help men court efficiently. . . . When our subjects looked at their beloveds, men tended to show more positive activity in a brain region associated with penile erection. . . . This male response directly links romantic passion with a brain region associated with sexual arousal.

Although this may be far-fetched, this male brain response may also shed light on why men so avidly support the worldwide trade in *visual* pornography; why women are more likely than men to regard their personal appearance as an important component of their self-esteem;[29] and why women go to such extraordinary lengths to advertise their assets *visually,* with all manner of clothing, makeup, and ornaments. . . .

MALE "MATING EFFORT"

Another male penchant interests me because it also comes, I think, directly from deep history. Psychologists report that men want to help women, to solve their problems, to be useful by *doing* something.[30] Men feel manly when they rescue a damsel in distress.

No doubt millions of years of protecting and providing for women has bred into the male brain this tendency to choose women they feel they need to save. In fact, the male brain is well built to assist women. Men are, on average, more skilled at all sorts of mechanical and spatial tasks than women are. Men are problem solvers.[31] And many of men's particular skills are fashioned in the womb by high levels of fetal testosterone. Perhaps men evolved this biological machinery, at least in part, to attract, assist, and save women.

Men are also more single-minded than women when they love. Only 40 percent of the young women in my survey agreed with the statement: "Having a good relationship with _____ is more important than having a good relationship with my family," whereas a solid 60 percent of young men reported that their love relationship came first. Moreover, although most people think women are the ones who wait by the phone, change their schedules, and hang around the office or the gym to be available to a beloved, my questionnaire showed that American men reorder their priorities more frequently than women do. . . .

This male penchant may be due to the fact that men have fewer intimate connections with their natal families and friends than women. But deep evolutionary forces probably contribute. Women are custodians of the egg—a valuable commodity. And women expend much more time rearing infants and small children, a vital job. For millions of years men needed to make themselves available to potential mating partners, even risk their lives to save these precious reproductive vessels. . . .

THE FEMALE BRAIN IN LOVE

Much of the psychological literature reports that both sexes feel passionate romantic love with roughly the same intensity.[32] I suspect this is true; their responses are just somewhat different. For example, my questionnaire on this passion showed that more American and Japanese women than men reported feeling "lighter than air" when they were certain their beloved felt passionately about them. Women also experienced slightly more obsessive thinking about an amor.

Our fMRI experiment also showed several ways in which our female subjects 40 responded differently than our male participants. When women looked at the photo of their beloved, they tended to show *more* activity in the body of the caudate nucleus and the septum—brain regions associated with motivation and attention. Parts of the septum are also associated with the processing of emotion. Women also showed activity in some different brain regions, including one associated with retrieval and recall of memories and some associated with attention and emotion.[33]

Once again, no one knows what these results mean. But as you recall memories and register your emotions, you inform yourself about your feelings[34] and assemble information into patterns; both activities help you make decisions. And for millions of years, women needed to make appropriate decisions about a potential mating partner. If an ancestral woman became pregnant during a romance, she was obliged to incubate the embryo for nine months, then deliver the child. These were (and remain) metabolically costly, time-consuming, uncomfortable, and physically dangerous tasks. Moreover, a woman had to raise her helpless infant through a long childhood and adolescence.

While a man can *see* many of a woman's assets for bearing and rearing babies, a woman cannot see a man's "mate value" just by looking. She must compute a partner's ability to protect and provide. And these gender differences suggest that when a woman gazes at her lover, natural selection has given her specific brain responses that enable her to recall the details and emotions she needs to assess her man.

"Heredity is nothing but stored environment," wrote the great botanist Luther Burbank. The vicissitudes of rearing helpless infants in a hostile ancestral environment have unquestionably bred into women other mechanisms they use to choose a mate.

WHO WOMEN CHOOSE

In a survey of eight hundred personal advertisements placed in newspapers and magazines, American women sought partners who offered financial security twice as frequently as men did.[35] Many female doctors, lawyers, and very wealthy women are interested in men with even more money and status than themselves.[36] In fact, women everywhere in the world are more attracted to partners with education, ambition, wealth, respect, status, and position—the kinds of assets their prehistoric predecessors needed in a parenting partner. As scientists sum this up: men look for sex objects and women look for success objects.

Women are also attracted to tall men, perhaps because towering men are 45 more likely to acquire prestige in business and politics and provide more bodily defense.[37] Women like men who sit in a carefree position, a sign of dominance, as well as men who are self-confident and assertive. Women are somewhat more likely to choose a long-term partner who is smart.[38] And women respond to men who are well-coordinated, strong, and courageous—as world literature and legend attest. . . .

No wonder a man's self-respect is more tightly linked to his general status at work and in the community.[39] No wonder men are also more likely to jeopardize their health, safety, and spare time to achieve rank. . . .

Women also prefer men with distinctive cheekbones and a strong jaw—for another unconscious reason. Masculine cheekbones and a rugged jawline are built with testosterone—and testosterone suppresses the immune system. Only exceedingly healthy teenage boys can tolerate the effects of this and build a rugged face.[40] Not surprisingly, around the time of monthly ovulation women become even more interested in men with these signs of testosterone. Now they can get pregnant, so they unconsciously seek males with superior genes. . . .

CASUAL PASSION

The sexes become more flexible in their romantic choices when they are looking for short-term love, such as when they are on vacation or seeking a temporary romance while pursuing other interests.

Historically, women looking for short-term passion choose free-spending men with resources—bestowers of gifts, lavish vacations, fancy dinners, and social or political connections.[41] Frugality was not acceptable to a woman on a fling. But today's women are wealthier and more independent than in the historical past and those pursuing casual passion are somewhat more eager to choose tall, symmetrical men with chiseled cheekbones and rugged jaws, men who are likely to have sturdy genes.[42]

Some of these women are testing their own mate value—seeing what kind of 50 man they can attract.[43] Others use a casual relationship as a form of insurance policy; they want a backup in case their own mate defects or becomes ill and dies. But many women also use casual sex to "try out" a particular person for a longer relationship.

Psychologists know this because women are less enthusiastic than men about engaging in a one-night stand with someone who is married or involved in another love relationship. Not only is this lover unavailable but his resources are directed elsewhere. And since he is cheating on his established partner, he is likely to be unfaithful to her as well. Most women don't lower their standards for brief love affairs either. They still seek a partner who is healthy, stable, funny, kind, and generous. For women, casual sex is often not as casual as it is for men.[44] . . .

"Tell me where is fancy bred, / Or in the heart, or in the head? / How begot, how nourished? / Reply, reply."[45] We can answer much of Shakespeare's question. A taste for symmetry; men's love of youthfulness and beauty and their need to help women in distress; women's attraction to men's wealth and status: these biological predilections can potentially trigger the brain circuitry for romantic love. An element of mystery, along with similarities of background, education, and beliefs, guide our tastes. Chance, timing, and proximity can also play a part in who we choose.

But of all the forces that guide your mate selection, I think the most important is your personal history, the myriad childhood, teenage, and adult experiences that have shaped and reshaped your likes and dislikes throughout your life. All these combine to create your largely unconscious psychological chart, what is called your "love map."

LOVE MAPS

We grow up in a sea of moments that slowly sculpt our romantic choices. Your mother's wit and way with words; your father's zest for politics and tennis; your uncle's love of boats and hiking; your sister's interests in training dogs; how people in your household use silence, express intimacy and anger; how those around you handle money; the amount of laughter at the dinner table; what your older brother finds challenging; your religious education and intellectual pursuits; the pastimes of your school chums; what your grandmother finds polite; how the community you live in views honor, justice, loyalty, gratitude, and kindness; what teachers admire and deplore; what you see on television and in the movies: these and thousands of other subtle forces build our individual interests, values, and beliefs. So by the teenage years, each of us has constructed a catalogue of aptitudes and mannerisms we are looking for in a mate.

This chart is unique. Even identical twins, who have similar interests and life-   55
styles, as well as similar religious, political, and social values, tend to develop different styles of loving and choose different types of partners.[46] Subtle differences in their experiences have shaped their romantic tastes.

This idiosyncratic psychological chart is also enormously complex. Some people seek a partner who will agree with what they say; others like a spirited debate. Some love a prank; others want predictability, order, or flamboyance. Some want to be amused; others wish to be intellectually excited. Many need a partner who will support their causes, quell their fears, or share their goals. And some choose a partner for the lifestyle they wish to lead. Søren Kierkegaard, the Danish philosopher, felt that love must be unselfish, filled with devotion for the beloved. But some are uncomfortable with a doting mate. Instead, they want a partner to challenge them to grow intellectually or spiritually.

Love maps are subtle and difficult to read. A good example is a friend of mine who grew up with an alcoholic father. She acclimated to the unpredictability around the house. But she resolved she would never marry a man like dear ol' dad. Indeed, she didn't. She married an unpredictable, chaotic artist instead—a match that suited her largely unconscious love map.

"Love looks not with the eyes, but the mind, / And therefore is winged Cupid painted blind," wrote Shakespeare.[47] This is probably why it is so difficult to introduce single friends to one another and why Internet dating services often fail:

matchmakers don't know the intricacies of their clients' love templates. Often men and women don't know their own love map either. . . .

THE LOVER'S PSYCHE

. . . Individual "love maps" probably begin to develop in infancy as we adjust to countless environmental forces that influence our feelings and ideas. As Maurice Sendak wisely noted, childhood is "damned serious business." Then as we enter school and make new friends, we engage in infatuations that further mold our likes and dislikes. As we develop more durable love affairs as teenagers, we continue to expand this personal psychological chart. And as we ride the waves of life—and experience a few romantic disasters—we trim and enrich this mental template.

So as you walk into a room of potential mating partners, you carry within your 60 brain an extraordinary sum of infinitesimal, mostly unconscious biological and cultural preferences that can spoil or spark romantic passion.

To make matters even more complex, our suitors are, themselves, enormously varied. Do you know any two people who are alike? I don't. The variety of human personalities is remarkable. Some are brilliant musicians; others can write a touching poem, build a bridge, make the perfect golf shot, perform Shakespearean roles from memory, deliver witticisms to thousands from a bandstand, philosophize coherently about the universe, preach effectively on God or duty, predict economic patterns, or charismatically lead soldiers into battle. And that's just the beginning. Nature has provided us with a seemingly infinite variety of individuals to choose from—even within our social, economic, and intellectual milieu.

And here is the focal point of this chapter. It is my belief that along with the evolution of humanity's outstanding variety came the fundamental mechanism with which we choose a mate—the brain circuitry for human romantic love.

THE MATING MIND

Why are we all so different from one another? My thinking on this matter stems from Charles Darwin's fascinating idea of sexual selection.

Darwin was annoyed by all the ornaments he saw in nature.[48] Crimson ruffs, blue penises, pendulous breasts, whirling dances, melodious trills, particularly the peacock's cumbersome tail feathers: he felt these seemingly superfluous decorations undermined his theory that all traits evolved for a purpose. . . .

But with time Darwin came to believe that all these flashy embellishments 65 evolved for an important purpose: to attract mates. Those with the finest courtship displays, he reasoned, attracted more and better mating partners; these dandies disproportionately bred—and passed along to their descendants these seemingly useless decorations. He called this process sexual selection.

In a highly original book, *The Mating Mind,* psychologist Geoffrey Miller adds to Darwin's theory of sexual selection. He proposes that human beings have also evolved extravagant traits to impress potential mating partners.

As Miller reasons, our human intelligence, linguistic talent, and musical ability, our drive to create visual arts, stories, myths, comedies, and dramas, our taste for all kinds of sports, our curiosity, our ability to solve complex math problems, our moral virtue, our religious fervor, our impulse for charitable giving, our political convictions, sense of humor, need to gossip, creativity, even our courage, pugnacity, perseverance, and kindness are all far too ornate and metabolically expensive to have evolved solely to survive another day.[49] Had our forebears needed these advanced aptitudes simply to live, chimpanzees would have developed these abilities as well. They didn't.

Miller believes, therefore, that all these marvelous human capacities evolved to win the mating game. We are "courtship machines," Miller writes.[50] Those ancestors who could speak poetically, draw deftly, dance nimbly, or deliver fiery moral speeches were regarded as more attractive. These talented men and women produced more babies. And gradually these human capacities became inscribed in our genetic code. Moreover, to distinguish themselves, our forebears specialized—creating the tremendous variety in human personalities seen today.

Miller acknowledges that in their simple forms, many of these traits were also useful in order to survive on the grasslands of ancient Africa; these talents had *many* purposes. But these aptitudes, he believes, became more and more complex because the opposite sex *liked* them and chose to mate with verbal, musical, or otherwise talented men and women. . . .

But Miller offers no concrete suggestion as to what actually enables the display 70 chooser to choose one wooing tactic rather than another, saying only that it is something like "a big pleasure meter" in the brain and that endorphins (the brain's natural painkillers) might be involved.

I propose that this pleasure meter is the brain circuitry for romantic love—orchestrated largely by dopamine networks through the caudate nucleus and other reward pathways in the brain. As ancestral men and women sifted through their array of mating opportunities, the primordial brain circuitry for animal attraction evolved into human romantic love—to help the chooser choose a specific mating partner, pursue this beloved avidly, and devote his/her courtship time and energy to this reproductive prize.

NOTES

1. Hatfield 1988, p. 204.
2. Walster and Berscheid 1971; Dutton and Aron 1974; Hatfield and Sprecher 1986; Aron et al. 1989.
3. Shepher 1971.
4. Galton 1884; Rushton 1989; Laumann et al. 1994; Pines 1999.
5. Buston and Emlen 2003.
6. Byrne, Clore, and Smeaton 1986; Cappella and Palmer 1990.
7. Gangestad and Thornhill 1997.
8. Gangestad, Thornhill, and Yeo 1994; Jones and Hill 1993.
9. Langlois and Roggman 1990.
10. Langlois et al. 1987.
11. Hamilton and Zuk 1982; Thornhill and Gangestad 1993.

12. Gangestad and Thornhill 1997.
13. Aharon et al. 2001.
14. Manning and Scutt 1996.
15. Manning et al. 1996.
16. Singh 1993.
17. Singh 2002.
18. Buss et al. 1990.
19. Ford and Beach 1951; Ellis 1992.
20. Wolkstein 1991, pp. 6–7.
21. Jankowiak 1995, p. 10.
22. Harrison and Saeed 1977.
23. Buss 1994.
24. Guttentag and Secord 1983; Low 1991.
25. Dion, Berscheid, and Walster 1972.
26. Johnston 1999.
27. H. Fisher et al. 2003; Aron et al., in preparation.
28. Kanin, Davidson, and Scheck 1970; Dion and Dion 1985; Peplau and Gordon 1985.
29. Berscheid et al. 1971; Lerner and Karabenick 1974.
30. Tannen 1990; Tavris 1992.
31. Baron-Cohen 2003.
32. Hatfield and Rapson 1996; Tennov 1979.
33. H. Fisher et al. 2003; Aron et al., in preparation.
34. Damasio 1999.
35. Harrison and Saeed 1977.
36. Ellis 1992; Buss 1994.
37. Ellis 1992; Buss 1994.
38. Kenrick et al. 1990.
39. Lerner and Karabenick 1974.
40. Buss 2003, p. 242.
41. Buss 1994.
42. Buss and Schmitt 1993; Kenrick et al. 1993; Gangestad and Thornhill 1997.
43. Buss 2003; Cristiani 2003.
44. Buss 2003.
45. Shakespeare 1936, *The Merchant of Venice,* act III, scene ii, line 63.
46. Waller and Shaver 1994.
47. Shakespeare 1936, *A Midsummer Night's Dream,* act I, scene i, lines 241–42.
48. Darwin (1859/1978, 1871/n.d.). Darwin (1871/n.d.) distinguished between two types of sexual selection: *intra*sexual selection, by which members of one sex evolve traits that enable them to compete directly with one another to win mating opportunities; and *inter*sexual selection or "mate choice," by which individuals of one sex evolve traits because the opposite sex prefers them. The antlers on the male moose are a good example of Darwin's first principle. This appendage developed to enable its wearer to intimidate other males during the breeding season. It is Darwin's second form of sexual selection that is central to this book: mate choice. Human female breasts are a good example. Unlike female teats, these fleshy appendages have no purpose in reproduction; they probably evolved primarily because ancestral males *liked* them. In fact, scientists now call these adornments that evolved by mate choice "fitness indicators," precisely because they are extreme, striking, metabolically expensive, hard to fake, and useless in the daily struggle to survive (Fisher 1915; Zahavi 1975; Miller 2000). Because these traits are "handicaps," only the fittest can build and maintain them (Zahavi 1975). For this reason alone, these traits impress.
49. Miller 2000, p. 35.
50. Ibid., pp. 3, 29.

REFERENCES

Aharon et al. 2001. Beautiful faces have variable reward value: fMRI and behavioral evidence. *Neuron* 32(3):537–51.

Aron, A., D. G. Dutton, E. N. Aron, and A. Iverson. 1989. Experiences of falling in love. *Journal of Social and Personal Relationships* 6:243–57.

Baron-Cohen, S. 2003. *The Essential Difference: The Truth about the Male and Female Brain.* New York: Basic Books.

Berscheid, E., K. K. Dion, E. Walster, and G. W. Walster. 1971. Physical attractiveness and dating choice: a test of the matching hypothesis. *Journal of Experimental Social Psychology* 7:173–89.

Buss, D. M. 1994. *The Evolution of Desire: Strategies of Human Mating.* New York: Basic Books.

———. 2003. *The Evolution of Desire: Strategies of Human Mating.* Rev. and exp. ed. New York: Basic Books.

Buss, D. M., and D. P. Schmitt. 1993. Sexual strategies theory: an evolutionary perspective on human mating. *Psychological Review* 100:204–32.

Buss, D. M., et al. 1990. International preferences in selecting mates: A study of 37 cultures. *Journal of Cross-Cultural Psychology* 21:5–47.

Buston, P. M., and S. T. Emlen. 2003. Cognitive processes underlying human mate choice: the relationship between self-perception and mate preference in Western society. *Proceedings of the National Academy of Sciences* 100(15):8805–10.

Byrne, D., G. L. Clore, and G. Smeaton. 1986. The attraction hypothesis: do similar attitudes affect anything? *Journal of Personality and Social Psychology* 51:1167–70.

Cappella, J. N., and M. T. Palmer. 1990. Attitude similarity, relational history, and attraction: the mediating effects of kinesic and vocal behaviors. *Communication Monographs* 57: 161–83.

Cristiani, M. 2003. A life history perspective on dating and courtship among Albuquerque adolescents. Ph.D. dissertation, Dept. of Anthropology, University of New Mexico.

Damasio, A. R. 1999. *The Feeling of What Happens: Body and Emotion in the Making of Consciousness.* New York: Harcourt Brace.

Darwin, C. 1859/1978. *The Origins of Species by Means of Natural Selection.* Franklin Center, Pa.: Franklin Library.

———. 1871/n.d. *The Descent of Man and Selection in Relation to Sex.* New York: The Modern Library/Random House.

Dion K. K., E. Berscheid, and E. Walster. 1972. What is beautiful is good. *Journal of Personality and Social Psychology* 24:285–90.

Dion, K. L., and K. K. Dion. 1985. Romantic love: Individual and cultural perspectives. In *The Psychology of Love,* ed. R. J. Sternberg and M. L. Barnes. New Haven: Yale University Press.

Dutton, D. G., and A. P. Aron. 1974. Some evidence of heightened sexual attraction under conditions of high anxiety. *Journal of Personality and Social Psychology* 30(4):510–17.

Ellis, B. J. 1992. The evolution of sexual attraction: evaluative mechanisms in women. In *The Adapted Mind: Evolutionary Psychology and the Generation of Culture,* ed. J. H. Barkow, L. Cosmides, and J. Tooby. New York: Oxford University Press.

Fisher, H., A. Aron, D. Mashek, G. Strong, H. Li, and L. L. Brown. 2003. Early stage intense romantic love activates cortical-basal-ganglia reward/motivation, emotion and attention systems: An fMRI study of a dynamic network that varies with relationship length, passion intensity and gender. Poster presented at the Annual Meeting of the Society for Neuroscience, New Orleans, November 11.

Fisher, R. A. 1915. The evolution of sexual preference. *Eugenics Review* 7:184–92.

Ford, C. S., and F. A. Beach. 1951. *Patterns of Sexual Behavior.* New York: Harper and Row.

Galton, F. 1884. The measurement of character. *Fortnightly Review* 36:179–85.

Gangestad, S. W., and R. Thornhill. 1997. The evolutionary psychology of extra-pair sex: the role of fluctuating asymmetry. *Evolution and Human Behavior* 18(2):69–88.

Gangestad, S. W., R. Thornhill, and R. A. Yeo. 1994. Facial attractiveness, developmental stability, and fluctuating asymmetry. *Ethology and Sociobiology* 15:73–85.

Guttentag, M., and P. F. Secord. 1983. *Too Many Women: The Sex Ratio Question.* Beverly Hills, Calif.: Sage Publications.

Hamilton, W. D., and M. Zuk. 1982. Heritable true fitness and bright birds: A role for parasites? *Science* 218:384–87.

Harrison, A. A., and L. Saeed. 1977. Let's make a deal: An analysis of revelations and stipulations in lonely hearts advertisements. *Journal of Personality and Social Psychology* 35:257–64.

Hatfield, E. 1988. Passionate and companionate love. In *The Psychology of Love,* ed. R. J. Sternberg and M. L. Barnes. New Haven: Yale University Press.

Hatfield, E., and R. Rapson. 1996. *Love and Sex: Cross-Cultural Perspectives.* Needham Heights, Mass.: Allyn and Bacon.

Hatfield, E., and S. Sprecher. 1986. *Mirror, Mirror: The Importance of Looks in Everyday Life.* Albany, N.Y.: State University of New York Press.

Jankowiak, W. 1995. Introduction. In *Romantic Passion: A Universal Experience?,* ed. W. Jankowiak. New York: Columbia University Press.

Johnston, V.S. 1999. *Why We Feel: The Science of Human Emotions.* Cambridge, Mass.: Perseus Books.

Jones, E., and K. Hill. 1993. Criteria of facial attractiveness in five populations. *Human Nature* 4:271–96.

Kanin, E. J., K. R. Davidson, and S. R. Scheck. 1970. A research note on male-female differentials in the experience of heterosexual love. *Journal of Sex Research* 6(1):64–72.

Kenrick, D. T., G. E. Groth, M. R. Trost, and E. K. Sadalla. 1993. Integrating evolutionary and social exchange perspectives on relationships: Effects of gender, self-appraisal, and involvement level on mate selection. *Journal of Personality and Social Psychology* 64:951–69.

Kenrick, D. T., E. K. Sadalla, G. E. Groth, and M. R. Trost. 1990. Evolution, traits and the states of human courtship: Qualifying the parental investment model. *Journal of Personality* 58(1):97–116.

Langlois, J. H., and L. A. Roggman. 1990. Attractive faces are only average. *Psychological Science* 1:115–21.

Langlois, J. H., L. A. Roggman, R. J. Casey, J. M. Ritter, L. A. Rieser-Danner, and V. Y. Jenkins. 1987. Infant preferences for attractive faces: Rudiments of a stereotype. *Developmental Psychology* 23:363–69.

Laumann, E. O., J. H. Gagnon, R. T. Michael, and S. Michaels. 1994. *The Social Organization of Sexuality: Sexual Practices in the United States.* Chicago: University of Chicago Press.

Lerner, R. M., and S. A. Karabenick. 1974. Physical attractiveness, body attitudes, and self-concept in late adolescents. *Journal of Youth and Adolescence* 3:307–16.

Low, B. S. 1991. Reproductive life in nineteenth-century Sweden: An evolutionary perspective on demographic phenomena. *Ethology and Sociobiology* 12:411–48.

Manning, J. T., and D. Scutt. 1996. Symmetry and ovulation in women. *Human Reproduction* 11:2477–80.

Manning, J. T., D. Scutt, G. H. Whitehouse, S. J. Leinster, and J. H. Walton. 1996. Asymmetry and menstrual cycle in women. *Ethology and Sociobiology* 17:129–43.

Miller, G. F. 2000. *The Mating Mind: How Sexual Choice Shaped the Evolution of Human Nature.* New York: Doubleday.

Peplau, L., and S. Gordon. 1985. Women and men in love: Gender differences in close heterosexual relationships. In *Women, Gender and Social Psychology,* ed. V. O'Leary, R. Unger, and B. Wallston. Hillsdale, N.J.: Erlbaum.

Pines, A. M. 1999. *Falling in Love: Why We Choose the Lovers We Choose.* New York: Routledge.

Rushton, J. P. 1989. Epigenesis and social preference. *Behavioral and Brain Sciences* 12:31–32.

Shakespeare, W. 1936. *The Complete Works of William Shakespeare: The Cambridge Edition Text,* ed. W. A. Wright. New York: Doubleday.

Shepher, J. 1971. Mate selection among second-generation kibbutz adolescents and adults: Incest avoidance and negative imprinting. *Archives of Sexual Behavior* 1:293–307.

Singh, D. 1993. Adaptive significance of waist-to-hip ratio and female physical attractive-ness. *Journal of Personality and Social Psychology* 65:293–307.

———. 2002. Female mate value at a glance: Relationship of waist-to-hip ratio to health, fecundity and attractiveness. *Neuroendocrinology Letters* 23(suppl 4):81–91.

Tannen, D. 1990. *You Just Don't Understand: Women and Men in Conversation.* New York: Ballantine Books.

Tavris, C. 1992. *The Mismeasure of Woman.* New York: Simon and Schuster, pp. 15–25.

Tennov, D. 1979. *Love and Limerence: The Experience of Being in Love.* New York: Stein and Day.

Thornhill, R., and S. W. Gangestad. 1993. Human facial beauty. *Human Nature* 4(3):237–69.

Waller, N., and P. Shaver. 1994. The importance of nongenetic influences on romantic love styles: a twin-family study. *Psychological Science* 5(5):268–74.

Walster, E., and E. Berscheid. 1971. Adrenaline makes the heart grow fonder. *Psychology Today,* June, 47–62.

Wolkstein, D. 1991. *The First Love Stories.* New York: HarperPerennial.

Zahavi, A. 1975. Mate selection: A selection for a handicap. *Journal of Theoratical Biology* 53:205–14.

QUESTIONS FOR DISCUSSION

1. Lauren Slater's article begins with an amusing anecdote about getting a henna tattoo. How does her act connect with the chemistry of love she discusses later? The tattoo is also a metaphor—for what? How would Helen Fisher explain Slater's unusual choice of a way to be romantic? That is, what does it have to do with what men find appealing and how they are aroused?

2. Clearly love and sexual desire are not just "socially constructed," as some people claim. Biochemistry and the evolution of attraction show that love is not just "made up" by each human society. Furthermore, most people in most cultures experience passionate love and in much the same way. Yet, Lauren Slater calls attention to how culture strongly shapes passionate love. How does she insist on the importance of culture? Moreover, she calls attention to one way that human desire is fundamentally different from even our closest living relatives, the higher apes. We respond to sym-bols, to language, as no other animal does. How do symbols figure in Slater's understanding of attraction and attachment?

3. At least since Freud, most students of human motivation have stressed the role of the unconscious. What does Helen Fisher reveal about attraction that you weren't aware of before? What does she discuss that you more or less understood already, but understood more clearly after reading her article? If your pattern of attraction doesn't conform to what's common— say, you are a heterosexual woman who isn't drawn to tall or successful men—how do you account for "the type" you like?

4. Few people have the "total package" for being attractive as lovers and potential mates. Why, then, is Helen Fisher's discussion of Geoffrey Miller's *The Mating Mind* especially important for understanding how, for instance, a man compensates for not having a jutting jaw or a woman for not having a waist that's 70% the size of her hips? To what extent does the human cultivation of certain talents and abilities make Darwin's notion of sexual selection too simple to account for human mating?

5. The essays by Slater and Fisher give us many ways to think about attraction and desire—as the chemistry of the body, as preferences that developed over thousands of years of evolution, as cultural variation, as love maps, as the cultivation of talents and abilities that attract lovers, and so on. As a result of your own experience and observation, which of these seem strongest to you?

SUGGESTIONS FOR WRITING

For Convincing

It's not hard to see why some people are disturbed by what Lauren Slater and Helen Fisher say. We may resist or refuse to believe that the chemistry of attraction has so much power. Must long-term sexual love eventually lose most of its passion? Or we may feel that a formula such as "men look for sex objects and women look for success objects" is too simple or is insulting to both sexes. Consider both articles in terms of what people are likely to resist or dispute and select a point or several related points that interest you most.

Using additional research or your own experience and knowledge (or both), defend the point or set of related points you've selected. Convince your readers that they should accept the basic truth of the claim (or claims) you're defending. Of course, you can recognize exceptions or situations where the claim may not apply.

For Inquiry

In the selections you have read, neither Lauren Slater nor Helen Fisher has much to say about current ways that men and women relate. Some selections in Section Two, such as the ones by Grimes, Watters, Twenge, and Wartik, open up such matters for discussion. Furthermore, Chapter 14, Twenty-Something: Issues Facing Young Adults, offers more to consider, especially the impact of economics on love and marriage.

As a class, list and discuss current ways men and women relate. You might consider, for instance, how financial independence for women, which was not common just fifty years ago, has affected mating choices. Or you might ponder the implications of the decline of traditional dating. Or you could investigate how both men and women are now often breaking out of traditional gender roles and attitudes. There's much to talk about, because current conditions are in many ways quite different from those in even the recent past.

After the discussion, select one way that men and women relate now that is clearly new and that you find especially interesting. Write an exploratory essay that poses and attempts to answer this question: To what extent do the Slater and Fisher selections shed light on what's going on now? Have conditions changed so much that what they have to say doesn't help you understand your own behavior? If they help some, what insights did you gain? What don't you understand that Slater and Fisher fail to illuminate? Of that which is left in the dark, what suggestions do you have for understanding what's going on better?

SECTION 2: GETTING TOGETHER
Overview

It's hard to appreciate how much things have changed in only the last one hundred years. A century ago few people went to college, and the United States was still predominantly rural. Most people were born, lived, and died in the same place, surrounded by friends and relatives. The local community is what mattered to them and what they knew—no television, movies, or Internet. In 1900 the average age at death in the United States was just under fifty.

Many marriages were arranged or were between two people who had known each other from childhood, raised in the same small community. Men and women married much younger—middle to late teens. Once married, they rarely divorced. Women had many children, partly because they were useful for farm work, partly because infant and child mortality rates were much higher, partly because reliable birth control—the pill—would not come into use for another sixty years.

Now, except that people still want relationships, what hasn't changed? Probably the biggest change is more years of education, with college almost assumed for middle-class young adults. Consequently, most people aren't in a position to marry until at least their middle twenties. Couple this with the earlier onset of puberty, because of improved nutrition, and clearly there can be fifteen years or more between the beginning of sexual development and marriage. Toss in a sex-obsessed media and our urban-centered, intensely competitive, fast-paced economy and you have all the basic ingredients for change in love relationships. It's no wonder that people don't get together in ways common even a generation ago. Traditional dating, for instance, is apparently the exception rather than the rule.

This section focuses on how young adults get together now. There's Jack Grimes on "hooking up," Nancy Wartik on living together, also known as cohabitation, and Ethan Watters on "urban tribes," large bands of friends hanging out together, now a common practice among young singles. There's even a selection, by Jean Twenge, on what happens when young adults fail to get together or get together in relationships that don't last— loneliness, isolation, sometimes depression, and even suicide.

Sculpture

ANTONIO CANOVA

Psyche Revived by Eros' Kiss

For Discussion

The beautiful and sensual sculpture *Psyche Revived by Eros' Kiss,* by Antonio Canova, is displayed at the Louvre in Paris. The photo of it can't capture what you see in three dimensions, but still conveys its power. How would you describe its appeal or impact? What are the implications of Eros (passionate love) reviving Psyche (spirit or mind)?

Photograph

ROBERT DOISNEAU

"Kiss at the Hotel de Ville"

For Discussion

The photograph "Kiss at the Hotel de Ville" was taken by Robert Doisneau in Paris in 1950. Doisneau was shooting a pseudo-documentary series for *Life* magazine on young lovers in the spring. He used models and posed them in various locations around Paris. The photograph became an iconic image of love, ubiquitous as a poster in the 1980s. What message about love does this art photograph convey? Does knowing that it was posed affect your interpretation of it? What does it say about love?

Hook-Up Culture

JACK GRIMES

Jack Grimes was a senior at Tufts when he wrote this opinion column for the school paper, the *Tufts Daily*. It appeared March 30, 2004.

Whatever happened to dating? College students have been asking that question for years. Every once in a while, even a newspaper will pick up the question and interview a few co-eds. The reporter finds dating's departure mostly blamed on what is universally called "the hook-up culture." While there are no (as of yet) proposals for the [student] Senate to take on a Hook-up Culture Rep, I do not think many would deny that the culture is here and thriving at Tufts. But where did it come from? And is it here to stay?

The hook-up culture is simply an environment that expects casual sexual encounters that do not necessarily lead to anything further. Common sense would say that people hook-up for basic physical needs. They do not want to get involved in a relationship, but they do have intense desires for a sexual partner. In a word, they are horny. So they hook-up—either with a friend or a stranger. But something makes me think folks hook-up for something more than just the raging hormones.

What makes me think horniness cannot fully explain the hook-up culture is this question: Would you hook-up with someone who was fast asleep—totally unresponsive? You could kiss them, touch them, make them touch you, whatever you would like. But they would remain completely oblivious to you and just lay there dead to the world. Not exactly appealing, is it? A bit like eating cold oatmeal. All the physical parts are there, all the same sensations, but something is missing—an energy, a spark, a life. There must then be a pleasure that is not strictly physical. What makes a hook-up more desirable than any pornography or anything you could do to yourself is the one pleasure neither of those could ever provide—the consent of a partner.

A lively, animated partner is lively and animated for you and (for the moment at least) you alone. You are special. What your partner does not let the world see, she lets you see. Personal space that is ordinarily walled off from the outside world becomes open to you alone. You are being let in, given privileged access. You become, for a few moments, the center of his attention. The real thrill of a hook-up is not simply what you do with a partner, but the fact that your partner wants to be doing it with you! It is not just "She's so hot," but "She's so hot and she wants me!" Not just "He's so cute," but "He's so cute and he likes me!"

The physical pleasure does not, and cannot, exist by itself. It is inextricably tied 5 up with the emotional. The body and soul are one. To give someone your body is to give them all of yourself. A sexual encounter is in its essence an act of deepest intimacy, and so to be considered worthy of that intimacy is powerfully affirming and very exciting. Everyone wants to be loved that much. Consensual sex is an affirmation so powerful that the porno fiend fabricates it and the rapist steals it. It is a feeling of acceptance so intoxicating that it gets pursued weekend after weekend in frat after frat.

Is it being found there? Well, how could it be? How can you find love and intimacy in a system that presupposes the meaninglessness of sex? If sex is simply handed out to anyone, then sexual intimacy becomes no big deal. Even if it happens to get handed over to you, you are no longer special. You are just a fling. The premise of the hook-up culture is to receive pleasure without commitment. But the pleasure really being sought can only come from commitment, from someone saying "Yes, I want to give my all to you and no one else." But hooking-up is all about holding back, not giving all of one's self, not committing. The more that commitment gets detached from sex, the less sex means anything. The less it means anything, the less enjoyable it becomes, and so the more hook-ups are made to get the old thrill. And on it goes, spiraling down. Trying to find intimate fulfillment by hooking-up is like trying to dig your way out of a hole in the ground.

Some people claim that they are not at all bothered by emotional needs. They get a thrill from the display of independence and sexual virility that serial hook-ups can give. Now this used to be said mostly by men. They do not talk like this much anymore (at least in public), as it seems to hinder their ability to get much play.

Appeals to self-determination and sexual empowerment to support hook-ups are now given by women. And this I find strange. I wonder what is so empowering about being, in essence, an unpaid prostitute. The boys may politely clap and publicly congratulate the women for liberating their sexuality and owning their miniskirt and so on, but privately they are having a good laugh and passing the word on who is the easy lay. A woman who embraces the hook-up culture is simply making it easier for guys to treat her as a sex object. Is this women's liberation? Both sexes can use a partner for their own selfish gratification, but more often than not, it is the woman whose hopes of a relationship get tossed in the trash. The real sexual power a woman has is to refuse to give away sex until the man has proved his commitment to her.

The hook-up culture is very deceptive. Hooking-up promises to be liberating and strengthening. Yet people find themselves needing more and more "liquid courage" to even make the first move. Hooking-up promises fun and fulfillment and no regrets, but when morning comes it delivers the "walk of shame." The hook-up culture has tricked us. It has led us to believe that our emotions are disconnected from our bodies, that love is divorced from sex.

What can we do about it? Well, a culture only lasts as long as people are willing to live it. If we refuse to believe its false promises, then we can build a new culture that says sex is just too good to be thrown around. We can bring back some middle ground between random hook-ups and being joined-at-the-hip. We can bring dating back to life. Or not. We can also make the break between love and sex complete and final. We can become dead to the ache within for intimacy. We can consider ourselves simply people with assets: he has what she wants, she has what he wants. Just a mutual exchange. Just business. Cold, soulless, heartless, loveless business. 10

Photographs: Couples Past vs. Present

A 1950s couple

A couple on Sex and the City

For Discussion

In the 1950s, the most popular venue for dating was the soda shop, and a standard "couple" photo showed them drinking ice cream sodas, heads together. In contrast, media images today often show the couple in a bar, as in the scene from the popular show *Sex and the City*. What messages about love or "romance" do these two images send?

In My Tribe

ETHAN WATTERS

Ethan Watters is a writer whose book *Urban Tribes* (2003), from which this essay is excerpted, describes his own life prior to marriage, as part of a circle of good friends similar to those depicted in television shows like *Seinfeld* and *Friends*.

You may be like me: between the ages of 25 and 39, single, a college-educated city dweller. If so, you may have also had the unpleasant experience of discovering that you have been identified (by the U.S. Census Bureau, no less) as one of the fastest-growing groups in America—the "never marrieds." In less than 30 years, the number of never-marrieds has more than doubled, apparently pushing back the median age of marriage to the oldest it has been in our country's history—about 25 years for women and 27 for men.

As if the connotation of "never married" weren't negative enough, the vilification of our group has been swift and shrill. These statistics prove a "titanic loss of family values," according to *The Washington Times*. An article in *Time* magazine asked whether "picky" women were "denying themselves and society the benefits of marriage" and in the process kicking off "an outbreak of 'Sex and the City' promiscuity." In a study on marriage conducted at Rutgers University, researchers say the "social glue" of the family is at stake, adding ominously that "crime rates . . . are highly correlated with a large percentage of unmarried young males."

Although I never planned it, I can tell you how I became a never-married. Thirteen years ago, I moved to San Francisco for what I assumed was a brief transition period between college and marriage. The problem was, I wasn't just looking for an appropriate spouse. To use the language of the Rutgers researchers [see pages 469–473], I was "soul-mate searching." Like 94 percent of never-marrieds from 20 to 29, I, too, agree with the statement "When you marry, you want your spouse to be your soul mate first and foremost." This *über*-romantic view is something new. In a 1965 survey, fully three out of four college women said they'd marry a man they didn't love if he fit their criteria in every other way. I discovered along with my friends that finding that soul mate wasn't easy. Girlfriends came and went, as did jobs and apartments. The constant in my life—by default, not by plan—became a loose group of friends. After a few years, that group's membership and routines began to solidify. We met weekly for dinner at a neighborhood restaurant. We traveled together, moved one another's furniture, painted one another's apartments, cheered one another on at sporting events and open-mike nights. One day I discovered that the transition period I thought I was living wasn't a transition period at all. Something real and important had grown there. I belonged to an urban tribe.

I use the word "tribe" quite literally here: this is a tight group, with unspoken roles and hierarchies, whose members think of each other as "us" and the rest of the world as "them." This bond is clearest in times of trouble. After earthquakes (or the recent terrorist strikes), my instinct to huddle with and protect my group is no different from what I'd feel for my family.

Ethan Watters, center, with his tribe in San Francisco

Once I identified this in my own life, I began to see tribes everywhere I looked: 5 a house of ex-sorority women in Philadelphia, a team of ultimate-frisbee players in Boston and groups of musicians in Austin, Tex. Cities, I've come to believe, aren't emotional wastelands where fragile individuals with arrested development mope around self-indulgently searching for true love. There are rich landscapes filled with urban tribes.

So what does it mean that we've quietly added the tribe years as a developmental stage to adulthood? Because our friends in the tribe hold us responsible for our actions, I doubt it will mean a wild swing toward promiscuity or crime. Tribal behavior does not prove a loss of "family values." It is a fresh expression of them.

It is true, though, that marriage and the tribe are at odds. As many ex-girlfriends will ruefully tell you, loyalty to the tribe can wreak havoc on romantic relationships. Not surprisingly, marriage usually signals the beginning of the end of tribal membership. From inside the group, marriage can seem like a risky gambit. When members of our tribe choose to get married, the rest of us talk about them with grave concern, as if they've joined a religion that requires them to live in a guarded compound.

But we also know that the urban tribe can't exist forever. Those of us who have entered our mid-30's find ourselves feeling vaguely as if we're living in the latter episodes of *Seinfeld* or *Friends,* as if the plot lines of our lives have begun to wear thin.

So, although tribe membership may delay marriage, that is where most of us are still heading. And it turns out there may be some good news when we get there. Divorce rates have leveled off. Tim Heaton, a sociologist at Brigham Young University, says he believes he knows why. In a paper to be published next year, he argues that it is because people are getting married later.

Could it be that we who have been biding our time in happy tribes are now 10 actually grown up enough to understand what we need in a mate? What a fantastic twist—we "never marrieds" may end up revitalizing the very institution we've supposedly been undermining.

And there's another dynamic worth considering. Those of us who find it so hard to leave our tribes will not choose marriage blithely, as if it is the inevitable next step in our lives, the way middle-class high-school kids choose college. When we go to the altar, we will be sacrificing something precious. In that sacrifice, we may begin to learn to treat our marriages with the reverence they need to survive.

Web Page

eHARMONY

Reprinted with permission.

For Discussion

Computer dating services claim that by studying the personalities and tastes of clients, they can find good matches more effectively and efficiently than people can find for themselves through ads, friends, and the more traditional ways of finding a partner. After reading "Who Wants to Marry a Soul Mate?" (pages 469–473), discuss the eHarmony ad (above) and the service itself. (You may want to log in and take the free personality profile.) How do the ad and service appeal to people looking for a soul mate?

Loneliness and Isolation

JEAN M. TWENGE

Jean M. Twenge is an associate professor of psychology at San Diego State. The following selection comes from *Generation Me: Why Today's Young Americans Are More Confident, Assertive, and Entitled—and More Miserable Than Ever Before* (Free Press, 2006).

My friend Peter moved to an apartment on the North Side of Chicago after graduating from college. He did not seem happy when I visited him that fall. He had several hellish stories about going out on dates through personal ads, including one woman who told him outright that he was not good-looking enough. His friends from college were either still living near campus or had scattered to graduate schools around the country. In his apartment, he showed me the feature on his cable TV that allowed him to buy movies. "This is what I do most weekends," he said, a sad smile on his face.

He's not the only one. More than four times as many Americans describe themselves as lonely now than in 1957. In *Bowling Alone*, Robert Putnam documents the steep decline in all kinds of social connections: we're less likely to belong to clubs and community organizations, less likely to have friends over for dinner, and less likely to visit our neighbors. Our social contacts are slight compared to those enjoyed by earlier generations.

It's almost as if we are starving for affection. "There is a kind of famine of warm interpersonal relations, of easy-to-reach neighbors, of encircling, inclusive memberships, and of solid family life," argues political scientist Robert Lane. To take the analogy a little further, we're malnourished from eating a junk-food diet of instant messages, e-mail, and phone calls, rather than the healthy food of live, in-person interaction.

It helps explain a new kind of get-together that's popping up in cities around the country: cuddle parties. It's a deliberately nonsexual (though usually coed) gathering where pajama-clad people can enjoy the hugs and touch of others, overseen by a "cuddle lifeguard on duty" who keeps things friendly and non-threatening. One 26-year-old participant called it "rehab for lonely people.". . .

For many in GenMe, the instability in close relationships began at an early age 5 with their parents' divorce. In *Prozac Nation,* her memoir of adolescent depression, Elizabeth Wertzel describes her father's departure from her life and her mother's subsequent struggle to raise her. When Wertzel told her therapists about her background, they would say, "No wonder you're so depressed." She was not as sure. "They react as if my family situation was particularly alarming and troublesome," she writes, "as opposed to what it actually is in this day and age: perfectly normal." And she's right: almost half of GenMe has seen their parents divorce, or have never known their father at all. . . .

GenMe's own romantic relationships often don't go much better. Although a little extreme, the situations faced by the four characters on *Sex and the City* are right on the mark; the young women I know describe similar dating pitfalls of strange behavior and dashed hopes. Even when the date goes well and becomes a relationship, there is no guarantee it will last. The cycle of meeting someone, falling in love, and breaking up is a formula for anxiety and depression. . . . In college, many people find that their romantic relationships are a lifeline in an otherwise lonely place—until the relationship ends. Leslie, 20, went through a breakup a month ago. "He was basically my whole life besides school and family," she says. "Now I am very lonely and depressed because I don't have many friends and the friends I do have are all away at their colleges."

The situation is so dire that some young people think there has to be a better way. One day in a graduate class on cultural differences, I was surprised when the students—almost all Americans from the Midwest and West—expressed their approval of arranged marriage. Two women in their mid-twenties were particularly adamant: they hated dating, living alone sucked, and they wanted to settle down. The men in the class agreed. Arranged marriage is probably not the solution, but the students' attraction to the idea is telling—young people clearly feel that something is missing in the current dating scene. . . .

Dating websites are one recent development that has made it easier to meet people, though they, too, can often lead to anxiety. You write a profile, post your picture, and wait. About half the time, no one e-mails you; often the people who do e-mail are not your type. If you e-mail other people, most of them don't write back—some as a passive form of rejection, but many others because they have let their accounts lapse. My own two months of Internet dating were fraught with worry about what I must be doing wrong and will-he-write-me-back-please-let-him-write-me-back high anxiety. I have never checked my e-mail so obsessively in my life. Fortunately, my story has a happy ending: the man who would become my husband e-mailed me on match.com (asking me, in a particularly deft generational move, what my favorite John Hughes movie was). We went out on our first date two weeks later, and married two years after that. A month later, his best friend married a woman he had met on eharmony.com.

Typical for our generation, both men were in their early thirties by this time. GenMe marries later than any other previous generation. Though later marriage has some advantages, it also means that many in GenMe spend their twenties (and sometimes thirties) in pointless dating, uncertain relationships, and painful breakups. Many relationships last several years and/or involve living together, so the breakups resemble divorces rather than run-of-the-mill heartbreak (as if there were such a thing). . . . Divorce after only a few years of marriage has become so common that Pamela Paul wrote a book called *The Starter Marriage*. It is the rare member of GenMe who has not experienced the breakup of a serious romantic relationship (or two, or five, or ten).

Many people think of single women when they imagine lonely young peo- 10 ple. . . . But there are plenty of lonely guys out there, too. There are actually thousands more single young *men* than women—between the ages of 25 and 39, for every 1 unmarried woman there are 1.2 unmarried men. Even when you look only between the ages of 35 and 39, there are thousands more unmarried men. I can hear women immediately yelling that all of the good ones are taken, but the truth is that it's single men who should be anxious and complaining. Men get lonely too, though we rarely see that addressed on TV or in the movies. For a noteworthy exception, check out the great movie *Swingers,* which features a fairly realistic look at young men talking about loneliness and their anxiety around dating. For GenMe, loneliness is an equal-opportunity experience.

As a result of modern dating, later marriage, and the higher divorce rate, a lot of people spend a great deal of time living alone. Twice as many 15-to-24-year-olds are in one-person households now compared to 1970, as are almost three times more 25-to-34-year-olds. More than 1 out of 3 people aged 25 to 29 lives alone or with roommates. . . .

Not only is GenMe single for longer, but we often don't stay in one place long enough to make friends. More than 1 out of 4 people aged 25 to 29 moved between 2002 and 2003. It is shocking to consider the number of professions that require frequent moves for advancement. This is definitely true in academia: I have lived in six states, my friend Kathleen has lived in all four North American time zones, and few of my friends live within 500 miles of where they grew up. . . .

Even if you stay in the same place, just having *time* to date and make friends is difficult. With the workweek expanding from relatively sane 9-to-5 hours into countless evenings and weekends, it's often impossible to find the time and energy to be with other people. . . . Seventy-five percent of women aged 25 to 35 say that their work lives interfere with their personal lives, and 35% say that the conflict is extreme. This goes for men as well—my brother works so many hours that it's no coincidence he met both his first New York girlfriend and his wife at work. . . .

Friends of mine who are lawyers and accountants often find it difficult to spare the time for a movie, a phone call to a long-distance friend, or a casual chat with a neighbor. In *The Costs of Living,* Barry Schwartz describes a former student who says his friendships "were not that *close.* Everyone was too busy. He thought twice about burdening friends with his life and his problems because he knew how consumed they were with their own, and what a sacrifice it would entail for them to spend the time required to listen to him and to help him out.". . .

Isolation and loneliness readily lead to anxiety and depression. A mountain of   15 scientific evidence links loneliness (and being alone) with negative mental health outcomes. Single and divorced people are significantly more likely to become depressed or suffer other mental health problems. Even people in unhappy marriages are happier than those who divorce. Of course, in many situations divorce is necessary and best in the long run, but even then it is painful and can lead to depression. When you consider the loneliness felt by many young people today, it's surprising that more of us aren't depressed. I often feel that many of us are one breakup or one move away from depression—our roots are not deep enough, our support systems too shallow.

The sadness of being alone is often the flip side of freedom and putting ourselves first. When we pursue our own dreams and make our own choices, that pursuit often takes us away from friends and family. An independence-minded society such as ours would never accept rules that encouraged arranged marriage or multigenerational households. Even marriage before a certain age—these days, around 25—is viewed as unwise and overly restricting. There is nothing wrong with individual freedom, of course; this is the advantage of the social change of the last few decades. But there are consequences, and loneliness is often one of them. . . .

One of the strangest things about modern life is the expectation that we will stand alone, negotiating breakups, moves, divorces, and all manner of heartbreak that previous generations were careful to avoid. This may be the key to the low rate of depression among older generations: despite all the deprivation and war they experienced, they could always count on each other. People had strong feelings of community; they knew the same people all their lives; and they married young and stayed married. It may not have been exciting, and it stymied the dreams of many, but it was a stable life that avoided the melancholy that is so common now.

NOTES

454 *More than four times as many:* Easterbrook, Gregg. 2003. *The Progress Paradox.* New York: Random House; p. 180.

454 *"There is a kind of famine:* Lane, Robert E. 2000. *The Loss of Happiness in Market Democracies.* New Haven, CT: Yale University Press; p. 9.

454 *One 26-year-old participant called it: "Group Hug." People,* September 27, 2004.

454 *In Prozac Nation, her memoir:* Wertzel, Elizabeth. 1994. *Prozac Nation: Young and Depressed in America.* New York: Riverhead Books; p. 33.

455 *There are actually thousands more: Statistical Abstract of the United States,* 2004 and earlier years. Available online at http://www.census.gov/prod/www/abs/statab.html.

456 *Twice as many 15-to-24-year-olds:* New Strategist Editors. 2004 *Generation X: Americans Born 1965 to 1976.* 4th ed. Ithaca, NY: New Strategist Publications; p. 172.

456 *More than 1 out of 4 people aged 25 to 29:* New Strategist Editors. 2004. *Generation X: Americans Born 1965 to 1976.* 4th ed. Ithaca, NY: New Strategist Publications; p. 84.

456 *Seventy-five percent of women aged 25 to 35:* The Next Generation: Today's Professionals, Tomorrow's Leaders. 2001. New York: Catalyst. www.catalystwomen.org.

456 *In* The Costs of Living, *Barry Schwartz describes:* Schwartz, Barry. 1994. *The Costs of Living.* New York: Norton; p. 18.

456 *A mountain of scientific evidence links:* Williams, D. R.; Takeuchi, D. T.; and Adair, R. K. 1992. Marital Status and Psychiatric Disorders Among Blacks and Whites. *Journal of Health and Social Behavior,* 33: 140–157; Robins, Lee, and Reiger, Darrel. 1991. *Psychiatric Disorders in America.* New York: Free Press; Baumeister, R. F., and Leary, M. R. 1995. The Need to Belong: Desire for Interpersonal Attachments as a Fundamental Human Motivation. *Psychological Bulletin,* 117: 497–529; and Myers, David. 2000. *The American Paradox.* New Haven: Yale University Press; chap. 3.

The Perils of Playing House

NANCY WARTIK

> Nancy Wartik is a freelance writer. The following article appeared in *Psychology Today* (August 2005).

Forget undying love or shared hopes and dreams—my boyfriend and I moved in together, a year after meeting, because of a potential subway strike. He lived in Manhattan, and I across the river in Brooklyn. Given New York City taxi rates, we'd have been separated for who knows how long. And so, the day before the threatened strike, he picked me up along with two yowling cats and drove us home. Six years, one wedding and one daughter later, we still haven't left.

Actually, if the strike threat hadn't spurred us to set up housekeeping, something else would have. By then, we were 99 percent sure we'd marry some day—just not without living together first. I couldn't imagine getting hitched to anyone I hadn't taken on a test-spin as a roommate. Conjoin with someone before sharing a bathroom? Not likely!

With our decision to cohabit, we joined the mushrooming ranks of Americans who choose at some point in their lives to inhabit a gray zone—more than dating, less than marriage, largely without legal protections. Thirty or 40 years ago, cohabitation was relatively rare, mainly the province of artists and other questionable types, and still thought of as "living in sin." In 1970 only about 500,000 couples lived together in unwedded bliss.

Now, nearly 5 million opposite-sex couples in the United States live together outside of marriage; millions more have done it at some point. Some couples do choose to live together as a permanent alternative to marriage, but their numbers are only a tiny fraction: More than 50 percent of couples who marry today have lived together beforehand. (At least 600,000 same-sex couples also cohabit, but their situation is different, since most don't have the choice to marry.)

"It's not this bad little thing only a few people are doing," says University of 5 Michigan sociologist Pamela Smock. "It's not going away. It's going to become part of our normal, typical life course—it already is for younger people. They think it would be idiotic not to live with someone before marriage. They don't want to end up the way their parents or older relatives did, which is divorced."

In my and my husband's case, the pre-matrimonial experiment seems to have worked out well. But according to recent research, our year of shacking up could have doomed our relationship. Couples who move in together before marriage have up to two times the odds of divorce, as compared with couples who marry before living together. Moreover, married couples who have lived together before exchanging vows tend to have poorer-quality marriages than couples who moved in after the wedding. Those who cohabited first report less satisfaction, more arguing, poorer communication and lower levels of commitment.

Many researchers now argue that our penchant for combining households before taking vows is undermining our ability to commit. Meaning, the precautions we take to ensure marriage is right for us may wind up working against us.

FROM TOOTHBRUSH TO REGISTRY

Why would something that seems so sensible potentially be so damaging? Probably the reigning explanation is the inertia hypothesis, the idea that many of us slide into marriage without ever making an explicit decision to commit. We move in together, we get comfortable, and pretty soon marriage starts to seem like the path of least resistance. Even if the relationship is only tolerable, the next stage starts to seem inevitable.

Because we have different standards for living partners than for life partners, we may end up married to someone we never would have originally considered for the long haul. "People are much fussier about whom they marry than whom they cohabitate with," explains Paul Amato, a sociologist at Penn State University and one of the theory's originators. "A lot of people cohabit because it seems like a good idea to share expenses and have some security and companionship, without a lot of commitment."

Couples may wind up living together almost by accident. "People move in 10 their toothbrush, their underwear, pretty soon a whole dresser," says Marshall Miller, coauthor with his partner, Dorian Solot, of *Unmarried to Each Other: The Essential Guide to Living Together as an Unmarried Couple*. "Then someone's lease is up and since they're spending all their time together anyhow.". . .

"There's an inevitable pressure that creates momentum toward marriage," says Amato. "I've talked to so many cohabiting couples, and they'll say, 'My mother was so unhappy until I told her we were getting married—then she was so relieved.'" On top of the social pressure, Amato points out, couples naturally start making investments together: a couch, a pet—even a kid. Accidental pregnancies are more common among cohabiting couples than among couples who don't live together.

Once their lives are thoroughly entangled, some couples may decide to wed more out of guilt or fear than love. "I know a lot of men who've been living with women for a couple of years, and they're very ambivalent about marrying them," says John Jacobs, a New York City psychiatrist and author of *All You Need Is Love and Other Lies About Marriage*. "What sways them is a feeling they owe it to her. She'll be back on the market and she's older. He's taken up a lot of her time." Women in particular may be afraid to leave an unhappy cohabiting relationship and confront the dating game at an older age. "If you're 36, it's hard to take the risk of going back into the single world to look for another relationship," says Jacobs. . . .

Some evidence indicates that women have less control over the progress of the cohabiting relationship. She may assume they're on the road to marriage, but he may think they're just saving on rent and enjoying each other's company. Research by sociologist Susan Brown at Bowling Green State University in Ohio has shown there's a greater chance cohabiting couples will marry if the man wants to do so. The woman's feelings don't have as much influence, she found: "The guy has got to be on board. What the woman wants seems to be less pivotal.". . .

THE COHABITING TYPE

The inertia theory is not the only way to explain why couples who move in before marriage are less likely to stick it out for the long haul. There may also be something specific about the experience that actually changes people's minds about marriage, making it seem less sacrosanct. "A couple of studies show that when couples cohabit, they tend to adopt less conventional beliefs about marriage and divorce, and it tends to make them less religious," says Amato. That could translate, once married, to a greater willingness to consider options that are traditionally frowned upon—like saying "so long" to an ailing marriage.

Nonetheless, there's a heated debate among social scientists about whether the 15 research to date has been interpreted properly or overplayed to some extent. Having a family income below $25,000, for example, is a stronger predictor of divorce in the first 15 years of marriage than having shared a premarital address. "Having money, a sense of an economically stable future, good communication skills, living in a safe community—all of those things are more important," says Smock.

Because it's impossible to directly compare the effects of marriage and cohabitation, there's just no way to prove cohabiters' higher divorce rates aren't a side effect of their other characteristics, says psychologist William Pinsof, president of the Family Institute at Northwestern University. They may just be less traditional people—less likely to stay in an unhappy marriage in observance of religious beliefs or for the sake of appearances. "Those who choose to live together before getting married have a different attitude about marriage to begin with. I think cohabiting is a reflection of that, not a cause of higher divorce rates," he says. . . .

In short, not everyone buys the idea that cohabitation itself is hazardous to your relationship. For some couples, it may serve a useful purpose—even when it lacks a happy ending. About half of all cohabiters split up rather than marry, and many of those splits save the parties involved from rocky marriages, miserable divorces or both. . . .

The debate over cohabitation is partly a rehash of the values and morals conflicts that tend to become political footballs in America today. But on one point, virtually all researchers agree: We need to understand the effects of cohabitation on children. Some 40 percent of all cohabiting households include kids—that's somewhere close to 3.5 million children living in homes with two unmarried opposite-sex grown-ups.

Cohabiting relationships, by their nature, appear to be less fulfilling than marital relationships. People who cohabit say they are less satisfied and more likely to feel depressed, Susan Brown has found. While the precarious finances of many cohabiters has something to do with it, Brown also points to the inherent lack of stability. Long-term cohabitation is rare: most couples either break up or marry within five years. "Cohabiters are uncertain about the future of their relationship and that's distressing to them," she says.

As a result, cohabitation is not an ideal living arrangement for children. Emo- 20 tionally or academically, the children of cohabiters just don't do as well, on average, as those with two married parents, and money doesn't fully explain the difference. The stress of parenting in a shakier living situation may be part of the problem, says Brown. "Stability matters. It matters for the well-being of children and adults alike," she adds. "We're better off with commitment, a sense that we're in it for the long haul."

THE MUST-HAVE DISCUSSION

Cohabitation rates may be skyrocketing, but Americans are still entirely enchanted with marriage. That's a sharp contrast with some Western societies—Sweden, France or the Canadian province of Quebec, for example—where cohabitation is beginning to replace marriage. In the United States, 90 percent of young people are still expected to tie the knot at some point.

Since most Americans are destined for marriage—and a majority will live together beforehand—how can we protect against the potentially undermining effects of cohabitation? Follow the lead of one subgroup of cohabiters: Those who make a permanent commitment to each other first. One study that tracked 136 couples through the initial months of marriage found that early intentions seem to make a big difference. About 60 of the couples in the study lived together before getting engaged, while the rest waited either until after they were engaged or after they were married to set up housekeeping. Ten months after the wedding, the group that had cohabited before being engaged had more negative interactions, less confidence about the relationship and weaker feelings of commitment than the other two groups. But the marriages of couples who had moved in together after getting engaged seemed just as strong as those who had moved in together after marrying.

Miller and Solot don't advise against cohabitation for couples without immediate plans to marry. But they do believe each partner needs to understand clearly what the other is thinking. "The most important thing is for people to treat moving in together as a serious decision, a major life choice," Miller says. "What does it mean to you both for the long and short term? If one person thinks living together means a quick path towards marriage and the other thinks it's just saving on rent and having a friend with benefits, there could be trouble. The important thing is to be on the same page."

QUESTIONS FOR DISCUSSION

1. Do you think Jack Grimes's rejection of hooking up (pages 448–449) raises *moral* objections? If so, what are they? If not, on what grounds does Grimes object?

2. "The sadness of being alone," Jean Twenge observes, "is often the flip side of freedom and putting ourselves first" (paragraph 16). If this is so, how do you explain the "urban tribes" Ethan Watters discusses (pages 451–452)? Are these rather loose but apparently loyal associations of friends the result of not being as free and self-centered? Or do the people Twenge talks about have different motives from Watters's friends? Watters says that the tribe resists any of its members getting married (paragraph 7). Why is that? Is marriage the end of freedom and self-centeredness? Do you think other motives are involved?

3. In "The Perils of Playing House," Nancy Wartik cites Pamela Smock, a sociologist who is one of the leading experts on cohabitation. According to Smock, living together is "going to become . . . normal . . . it already is for younger people" (paragraph 5) She explains it as motivated by a desire to avoid divorce. What other motives does Wartik say enter into it? Based

on your own experience or that of young adults you know who live together, what motives not discussed by Wartik might be involved? Considering all the motivations that might be involved, is cohabitation an option you would consider? If you have lived with someone or do so now, what's your assessment of the experience?

SUGGESTIONS FOR WRITING

For Research and Mediation

Jack Grimes is hardly the only person to argue against the practice of "hooking up" and to advocate a return to traditional dating. But traditional dating requires two things that many young adults, especially those attending college, lack: time and money. And dating may sometimes have been just a different way of hooking up that only seems more respectable.

Find what you can about hooking up from research done on it. Supplement knowledge from research with interviews of people who have experience with it. Whether you find hooking up acceptable or not, what arguments can you find or invent in defense of the practice?

Then write an essay that mediates between those who, like Grimes, reject hooking up, and those who practice it without seriously considering the potential emotional emptiness. Hooking up is a common practice and likely to continue, given the circumstances of young, single, college-attending adults. So coming up with an approach to it that would make it both morally acceptable and not unhealthy or destructive is important.

For Research and Inquiry

The selection by Jean Twenge deals with a serious problem in our society, one not restricted to young, single adults—loneliness, isolation. About one in four Americans now live alone. Read or reread her piece, noting all the explanation she offers for the problem being especially acute among young adults.

There's a large amount of research, mainly in psychology, on the sometimes devastating effects of being alone and feeling bereft of meaningful human companionship. Read some of this research to gain more insight and detailed knowledge than you can get from Twenge alone.

Then write a paper that both explores the causes of loneliness in American society and offers some tentative suggestions for solving the problem. Bear in mind that many college students feel isolated and alienated even on campuses famed for being "party schools." You need to look beneath the surface to understand some of what is going on.

SECTION 3: ATTACHMENT AND MARRIAGE
Overview

Most of us have romantic relationships, or perhaps the relationships have us. To begin to understand them, we should start as we did in the first section, with attraction. That's how it usually gets under way. But attraction is not enough. People have to get together somehow—hence the focus in Section Two on hooking up, urban tribes, and living together. Attraction has deep biological foundations, an evolutionary history, and depends on something as natural as brain chemistry. How we get together, however, is largely cultural, varying a great deal from place to place and from era to era. Once we had a dating culture; now we don't.

Most people also want to attach, to form a permanent relationship with one person. Of course, living together is one way of doing this, but in our culture few people choose it *instead* of marriage; for the overwhelming majority, living together is a prelude to marriage. And so this section deals with attachment and marriage, with norms typical of not only our culture but most human cultures in all places and times. As we have seen, marriage has biological and chemical roots: the need for parents to bond long enough to raise children, the stable comforts of couples bound more by oxytocin than driven by the passions of dopamine (see Lauren Slater selection, pages 420–427). But, despite its near universality, marriage is largely a social construction. How we think about marriage now was not typical one hundred or even fifty years ago in the United States, and how Americans have always thought of marriage differs significantly from how others around the world think of it. Marriage, like most human arrangements, fuses biology and culture.

We begin with the crucial question, What is love? The first selection, by Robert and Lisa Firestone, two clinical psychologists who specialize in intimate relationships, explores the general question insightfully. Then, in the second selection, Barbara Dafoe Whitehead and David Popenoe address the question in a more specific context—the common distinction between people we might have sex with and people we might marry. Presumably, part of the difference is love, love developed over time in a sustained relationship. The question is crucial because our culture routinely tends to equate romance and love, which most cultures, past and present, do not. We need to consider carefully what love is, especially in marriage. And so three reflections on marital love are offered against the backdrop of the attitudes of young adults toward marriage gathered and interpreted by Whitehead and Popenoe in "Who Wants to Marry a Soul Mate?" The ideal encounters the reality, but not with discouraging results. What Joan Konner calls "grown-up love" cannot be the same as the all-consuming fire and elation of new relationships, but the satisfactions can also run deep. We see it in Eve LaPlante's successful marriage, despite being the child of divorce, and in Helen Fremont's marriage to Donna, made legal in 2004 in Massachusetts. No one thinks love and marriage necessarily go together, but they aren't necessarily incompatible either, which offers some basis for hope even in a culture where about 50% of all marriages end in divorce.

What Is Love?

ROBERT W. FIRESTONE, LISA A. FIRESTONE, AND JOYCE CATLETT

Robert Firestone and Lisa Firestone are prominent clinical psychologists who specialize in treating intimacy problems. Joyce Catlett is an author and lecturer who often collaborates with the Firestones. The following selection is from *Sex and Love in Intimate Relationships* (American Psychological Association, 2006).

The great aim of every human being is to understand the meaning of total love. Love is not to be found in someone else, but in ourselves; we simply awaken it. But in order to do that, we need the other person. The universe only makes sense when we have someone to share our feelings with.

—Paulo Coelho, *Eleven Minutes*, 2004

Volumes have been written about the nature of love and how love is manifested in an intimate relationship. The philosopher Singer (2001), in *Sex: A Philosophical Primer,* asserted that

There is no single entity, no discernible sensation or emotion, that is love. . . . Love is a form of life, though often short-lived, a disposition, a tendency to respond in a great variety of ways, many overlapping but none that is necessary and sufficient. . . . (pp. 84–85)

In *The Four Loves,* [C. S.] Lewis (1960) wrote about Eros (or what many refer to as passion), describing it as "that state which we call 'being in love'" (p. 91). He observed that "the lover desires the Beloved herself, not the pleasure she can give" (p. 94).

Without Eros sexual desire, like every other desire, is a fact about ourselves. Within Eros it is rather about the Beloved. . . . [It is] entirely a mode of expression. It . . . [is] something outside us, in the real world. . . . One of the first things Eros does is to obliterate the distinction between giving and receiving. (pp. 95–96)

In *You Can't Go Home Again,* [Thomas] Wolfe (1934) gave "love" great significance when he eloquently described the basic nature of human beings:

Man loves life, and loving life, hates death, and because of this he is great, he is glorious, he is beautiful, and his beauty is everlasting. He lives below the senseless stars and writes his meanings in them. . . . Thus it is impossible to scorn this creature. For out of his strong belief in life, this puny man made love. At his best, he *is* love. Without him there can be no love . . . no desire. (p. 411)

In a conversation with Arnold Toynbee (Gage, 1976), Daisaku Ikeda, former president of Soka Gakkai International, a Buddhist organization, described a version of the Buddhist conception of love:

The word *love* has been highly conceptualized and made very abstract. . . . I believe that the Buddhist concept of compassion . . . defined as removing sorrow and bringing happiness to others . . . gives love substantial meaning. . . .

Yoraku—the second component of compassion in the Buddhist sense—means the giving of pleasure. . . . It is the joy of living . . . the ecstacy of life. It includes both material and spiritual pleasure. Without the deep feelings of fulfillment and the ecstacy generated by the emotions of life, pleasure in the truest sense is impossible. (pp. 357–358)

There are also many Judeo-Christian conceptualizations of love. Perhaps the most familiar are the statements attributed to the apostle Paul in I Corinthians 13 (World English Bible):

Love is patient and is kind; love doesn't envy. Love doesn't brag, is not proud, doesn't behave itself inappropriately, doesn't seek its own way, is not provoked, takes no account of evil; doesn't rejoice in unrighteousness, but rejoices with the truth; bears all things, believes all things, hopes all things, endures all things. Love never fails. . . . But now faith, hope, and love remain—these three. The greatest of these is love. (vv. 4–13)

OUR VIEW OF LOVE

But what is love, really? What does it mean to love someone? . . . In *Altruism and Altruistic Love,* Post, Underwood, Schloss, and Hurlbut (2002) raised an important question: "What is at the very core of human altruistic love?" Their answer was that love might be conceptualized as "affirmative affection."

We all know what it feels like to be valued in this way, and we remember loving persons who conveyed this affective affirmation through tone of voice, facial expression, a hand on the shoulder in time of grief, and a desire to be with us. . . . Love implies benevolence, care, compassion, and *action.* (p. 4) [italics added]

In our view, actions that fit the description of a loving relationship are expressions of affection, both physical and emotional; a wish to offer pleasure and satisfaction to one's mate; tenderness, compassion, and sensitivity to the needs of the other; a desire for shared activities and pursuits; an appropriate level of sharing of one's possessions; an ongoing, honest exchange of personal feelings; and the process of offering concern, comfort, and outward assistance for the love object's aspirations. . . .

Our thinking regarding the nature of love is congenial with the words written by Fromm (1956) in *The Art of Loving.* Fromm observed that "There is only one proof for the presence of love: the depth of the relationship, and the aliveness and strength in each person concerned; this is the fruit by which love is recognized" (p. 87). These manifestations of love [are described in] one man's feelings for his wife after 25 years of marriage:

When I first met Annette, I thought that she was attractive and she appeared to be a very nice person. At the time, however, I wasn't especially drawn to her; in fact, she seemed a little boring. Yet for some bizarre reason, a crazy thought came into my mind and it came up repeatedly: "You're going to marry this girl." It was so odd and out of character to the way I usually think that I told my friends about it and we all laughed. . . .

Later on, Annette became involved in my social circle and we actually became friends. One day, on our way to meet friends for a day sail, Annette and I found ourselves alone together. . . . While we were driving to the marina, I suggested that we stop for a moment to look at the ocean conditions. Parked by the break-water, I leaned toward her and we kissed. From that moment on we were in love.

In our love, a remarkable transformation took place in both of our lives. For one thing, her looks changed radically; indeed, in love, she developed into an exceptionally beautiful woman and I wasn't the only one who noticed the difference. All of our friends commented on it. Now it's close to thirty years later since we first met and she's still beautiful, but it's not just her physical beauty.

For me, my life changed radically. We did get married, my friendships expanded, and I was inspired in my work. I had the courage to forge ahead in many new and creative endeavors.

Annette is an incredibly sensitive, psychologically sophisticated and sweet person, very affectionate and naturally responsive sexually. . . . I love her body and her responsiveness. I know that it's hard to believe, but after all of these years, I'm still as sexually attracted as I was originally.

There are many other qualities in Annette that I discovered as our relationship unfolded. Annette is exceptionally intelligent, free-thinking, creative, and has an incredible sense of humor. She can turn an unfortunate or embarrassing situation into something poignant and special. . . .

In our relationship there has always been a sense of equality and mutual respect. We fully believe in the personal freedom of each other and pose no limits on each other's development. This has been a guiding principle for us even when it caused us inconvenience or pain. I think that's why our relationship is still fresh and exciting. In that respect, we feel different from what we see in so many other couples. They appear to be so much more possessive and intrusive on each other and act different in each other's company than otherwise. I find the company of most couples . . . boring. They seem to cancel out each other's sexuality and appear deadened in each other's presence.

From what I have said, you might think that life for us has always been happy. It has certainly been good overall, but we have had our bad times. When I first suggested that we have children together, Annette became emotionally distraught, even hostile. I had never seen her like that before and it shocked her as well. She had never been defensive and caught on that something was radically wrong with her response. But that didn't change things. We had trouble for months after that. Her feelings were all over the place and it practically ruined us. Luckily she got help and worked out her fears about having children. The result was that we now have four grown daughters who have turned out well.

And the trouble about having children wasn't our only problem. Whenever the issue of death came up—a movie, something on the news or information about the tragedy of someone we knew—she would become cold and unaffectionate. I would be hurt at those times and it was difficult for both of us. . . .

There were occasions when I was shaken up, too, because I had never been so vulnerable in a relationship. But eventually we sweated out these difficult times together because we really cared deeply for one another. To this day, we are lovers and the best of friends, rely on each other for support and companionship, and are a vital part of each other's lives. I know that she knows me and loves me and that I make her happy. She says that her life would be impossibly dull without me. I can barely imagine the horror of living life without her.

The relationship between this man and woman was inspirational to all of their friends and acquaintances and was illustrative of what we conceive to be the essence of a loving style of relating. Both parties were kind, generous with one another, independent, self-reliant, warm, respectful, sexually responsive, not restrictive or intrusive, and nondefensive. Although this example illustrates love between a couple, many of the same qualities apply to love between friends and family members and can be extended to a love for humanity.

WHAT GENUINE LOVE IS NOT

To better understand what genuine love is, perhaps we should also describe what 10 it is not. Love is not what we mean when one is told by a family member that "mommy or daddy really loves you but he/she just doesn't know how to show it." Love is not selfish, possessive, or demanding, or a proprietary right over the other. Love is never submission or dominance, emotional coercion, or manipulation. Love is not the desperate attempt to deny aloneness or the search for security that many couples manifest in their desire for a fused identity.

Lawrence (1920) stressed this theme in his work:

> Why should we consider ourselves, men and women, as broken fragments of one whole? It is not true. We are not broken fragments of one whole. (p. 271)

> Fusion, fusion, this horrible fusion of two beings, which every woman and most men insisted on, was it not nauseous and horrible anyhow, whether it was a fusion of the spirit or of the emotional body? Why could they not remain individuals, limited by their own limits? Why this dreadful all-comprehensiveness, this hateful tyranny? Why not leave the other being free, why try to absorb, or melt, or merge? One might abandon oneself utterly to the *moments,* but not to any other being. (p. 391)

Love is not to be confused with emotional hunger, that is, a desperate, immature need for dependence on another that drains the other person's vitality. Nor is it to be confused with a deep longing to find total confirmation of oneself in the other. In *The Denial of Death,* Becker (1973/1997) described the results of finding such an "ideal" love:

> If you find the ideal love and try to make it the sole judge of good and bad in yourself, the measure of your strivings, you become simply the reflex of another person. You lose yourself in the other, just as obedient children lose themselves in the family. . . . When you confuse personal love and cosmic heroism you are bound to fail in both spheres. . . . How can a human being be a god-like "everything" to another? (p. 166)

We have found that many people fail to reach a level of emotional maturity that would allow them to be capable of offering love, and they are also afraid of accepting or receiving love. In working with couples in initial intake sessions, we have observed that one or the other will outline a number of objections that amount to a fairly extensive annihilation of the other's character, only to be followed by an equally denigrating attack by the other partner. As the session progresses, we often notice their mistreatment of one another firsthand and tend to agree with both parties' assessment of each other, as these negative behaviors become more obvious. In other words, they have described each other fairly accurately, as it turns out, and manifest considerable hostility. Yet when we ask these warring couples why they stay together when they find each other so objectionable, they typically respond by saying, "Because we love each other." However, the destructive behaviors these people manifest toward one another do not fit any acceptable definition of the word love. Why call it "love" when the behavior toward the love object is neither affectionate nor respectful, lacks communication and companionship, violates the personal boundaries of the other, and is often insensitive or outright hostile or abusive? . . .

CONCLUSION

Learning to love wholeheartedly is a most worthwhile endeavor but requires considerable devotion, time, and energy. As Rilke (1908/1984) observed,

> It is also good to love: because love is difficult. For one human being to love another human being: that is perhaps the most difficult task that has been entrusted to us, the ultimate task, the final test and proof, the work for which all other work is merely preparation. (p. 68)

    . . . [W]hen people have been hurt in the past, they are reluctant to trust and 15 be open to being hurt again. They feel self-protective and fear being vulnerable and open to emotional pain. In describing this learning process, Coelho (2004) wrote

> Everyone knows how to love, because we are all born with that gift. Some people have a natural talent for it, but the majority of us have to re-learn, to remember how to love, and everyone, without exception, needs to burn on the bonfire of past emotions, to relive certain joys and griefs, certain ups and downs, until they can see the connecting thread that exists behind each new encounter; because there is a connecting thread. (p. 139)

    A person who overcomes self-limiting defenses and learns to give and receive love experiences the most satisfaction in life. . . . When love is sincere and real, it reaches spiritual proportions that give value and meaning to life.

REFERENCES

Becker, E. *The denial of death.* New York: Free Press. (Original work published 1973).

Coelho, P. (2004). *Eleven minutes* (M. J. Costa, Trans.). New York: HarperCollins.

Fromm, E. (1956). *The art of loving.* New York: Bantam Books.

Gage, R. L. (Ed). (1976). *Choose life: A dialogue: Arnold Toynbee and Daisaku Ikeda.* Oxford, England: Oxford University Press.

Lawrence, D. H. (1920). *Women in love.* London: Penguin Books.

Lewis, C. S. (1960). *The four loves.* New York: Harcourt Brace.

Post, S. G., Underwood, L. G., Schloss, J. P., & Hurlbut, W. B. (2002). General introduction. In S. G. Post, L. G. Underwood, J. P. Schloss, & W. B. Hurlbut (Eds.), *Altruism and altruistic love: Science, philosophy and religion in dialogue* (pp. 3–12). New York: Oxford University Press.

Rilke, R. M. (1984). *Letters to a young poet* (S. Mitchell, Trans.). New York: Vintage Books. (Original work published 1908).

Singer, I. (2001). *Sex: A philosophical primer.* Lanham, MD: Rowman & Littlefield.

Wolfe, T. (1934). *You can't go home again.* New York: Harper and Row.

Who Wants to Marry a Soul Mate?

BARBARA DAFOE WHITEHEAD AND DAVID POPENOE

The Rutgers National Marriage Project (http://marriage.rutgers.edu/about.htm), headed by Rutgers sociology professors David Popenoe and Barbara Dafoe Whitehead, aims to study the institution of marriage in America and, from a conservative perspective, educate the public about their concerns over the apparent decline of marriage as the foundation for family life. Each year the Project focuses on a different question. In 2001, the Project sociologists surveyed young people on their preferences for choosing a mate.

[Who wants to marry a soul mate?] Practically all young adults, according to a national survey of men and women conducted for the National Marriage Project by the Gallup Organization—the first large-scale study to look at attitudes about dating and marriage among married and single people, ages 20–29.

Young adults today are searching for a deep emotional and spiritual connection with one person for life. The overwhelming majority (94%) of never-married singles agree that "when you marry you want your spouse to be your soul mate, first and foremost." There is no significant gender gap in this response; similarly high proportions of men and women agree that they want to marry a soul mate. In another measure of the strength of the soul-mate ideal, over 80% of all women, married and single, agree it is more important to them to have a husband who can communicate about his deepest feelings than to have a husband who makes a good living.

Among single men and women, a large majority (88%) also agree that "there is a special person, a soul mate, waiting for you somewhere out there." And never-married singles are highly confident that they will be successful in locating that soul mate; a substantial majority (87%) agree that they will find that special someone when they are ready to get married.

Along with their ambitions for a spouse who meets their needs for emotional closeness and intimacy, these twentysomething singles also aspire to a marriage that lasts a lifetime. Seventy-eight percent agree that a couple should not get married unless they are prepared to stay together for life. In addition, they are reasonably confident that their own future marriages will be long lasting. Only 6% say it is unlikely that they will stay married to the same person for life.

Although young adults are confident that they will be successful in achieving 5 a soul-mate marriage for themselves, they are less confident about the state of marriage in general. A substantial majority (68%) agree that it is more difficult to have a good marriage today than in their parents' generation, and slightly more than half (52%) agree that one sees so few good or happy marriages that one questions it as a way of life. Women, and those with a high-school education or less, are more likely than others to agree that there are very few people who have really good or happy marriages.

As one might expect, the generation that grew up in the midst of the divorce revolution also worries about the risks of divorce. Slightly more than half of all single adults (52%)—and an even higher percentage of those in their late twenties

(60%)—agree that one of their biggest concerns about getting married is the possibility it will end in divorce.

The high aspirations for a soul mate may be one reason why so many young adults are cohabiting before they take the plunge into marriage. Among the young adults surveyed, 44% had at some time lived with an opposite sex partner outside of marriage. As we reported in *The State of Our Unions, 2000,* single men and women in their twenties see cohabitation as a way to investigate a prospective partner's character, habits and capacity for fidelity before marriage. Many believe that living together yields more useful information about a partner than simply dating for a period of time. . . .

FROM SOCIAL INSTITUTION TO SOUL-MATE RELATIONSHIP

Although young adults express high aspirations for the marital relationship, they see a diminished role for marriage in other domains. Many of the larger social, economic, religious and public purposes once associated with marriage are receding or missing altogether from their portrait of marriage.

Most noteworthy is the weakened link between marriage and child rearing. Only 16% of young adults agree that the main purpose of marriage these days is to have children. The idea that marriage is the principal pathway into parenthood is changing as well. A clear majority of young men (62%) agree that, while it may not be ideal, it's okay for an adult woman to have a child on her own if she has not found the right man to marry. More than four out of ten describe adults who choose to raise a child out of wedlock as "doing their own thing."

The survey also points to some evidence of the declining importance of marriage as an economic institution. Although two-thirds (65%) of singles say that they believe that marriage will improve their economic situation, an even higher percentage say it is extremely important to be economically "set" as individuals before they marry. It is especially noteworthy that young women are as likely as young men to agree that it is important for them to be economically "set" before marriage. 10

Indeed, this attitude represents a dramatic shift for women. In earlier generations, most women saw marriage as a stepping-stone to achieving economic independence from parents and to gaining economic security. Today, however, women are more likely to look to themselves and to their own educational and career achievements as a source of economic independence and security.

Partly this shift is due to changing patterns of education and work during the young adult years. More women are going on to higher education—now outranking men among college graduates—and also spending more years as working singles before marriage. During this expanded period of early adult singlehood, they acquire credit ratings, debts and assets on their own. For this reason, they tend to think about their economic lives and fortunes in individual terms.

But the shift is also due to fears of the high risk of divorce. Because marriages break up at a high rate, young adults—and especially young women—no longer trust marriage as a reliable economic partnership. A large majority (82%) agree it is unwise for a woman to rely on marriage for financial security. For this reason, young women may prefer to invest in portable assets, like education and career development, rather than to place all their trust and self-investment in marriage. This pattern may also explain why young women say that they are less interested in having a spouse who makes a good living than in having a spouse who is a soul mate. . . .

Along with the diminished importance assigned to marriage as a parental and economic partnership, the role of marriage as a religious institution seems to be fading. Although young adults seek a deep spiritual connection through marriage, they are not necessarily looking to marry someone who shares their own religion. Among singles, less than half (42%) agree that it is important to find a spouse who shares their own religious faith. Indeed, the popular soul-mate ideal may be a substitute for more traditional religious understandings of marriage. In a secular society, where sex has lost its connection to marriage and also its sense of mystery, young people may be attracted to the soul-mate ideal because it endows intimate relationships with a higher spiritual, though not explicitly religious, significance. . . .

Taken together, these findings paint a portrait of marriage as emotionally deep 15 but socially shallow. While marriage is losing much of its broad public and institutional character, it is gaining popularity as a SuperRelationship, an intensely private spiritualized union, combining sexual fidelity, romantic love, emotional intimacy and togetherness. Indeed, this intimate couple relationship pretty much defines the sum total of marriage. Other bases for the marital relationship, such as an economic partnership or parental partnership, have receded in importance or disappeared altogether.

SOUL-MATE MARRIAGE IN A HIGH-DIVORCE SOCIETY

There is nothing historically new in the desire for lasting friendship in marriage. Indeed, the notion of combining friendship, romantic love and sexual fidelity in marriage is one of the distinctive features, and perhaps most daring experiments, in the Western marriage tradition. (Most societies, past and present, still prefer marriages arranged by kin or parents, and many adhere to the sexual double standard "she's faithful, he's not.") However, the findings in this survey suggest that today's young adults may be reaching even higher in their expectations for marriage. The centuries-old ideal of friendship in marriage, or what sociologists call companionate marriage, may be evolving into a more exalted and demanding standard of a spiritualized union of souls.

This development is understandable. Amid the dislocations of today's mobile society, dynamic economy, and frantic pace of life, it is difficult to sustain deep and lasting attachments. What's more, the desire for loving and lasting relationships may be especially strong among members of a generation that has come of age during the divorce revolution. It is not surprising, therefore, that young adults look to a soul mate for the steady emotional support and comfort that may be missing in other parts of their life. And, indeed, this is not an unworthy aspiration. For those who achieve it, a soul-mate relationship can be personally rewarding and deeply satisfying.

However, as today's young adults seem to realize, a soul-mate marriage in a high divorce society is difficult to sustain. Perhaps that is why a high percentage (86%) indicate that marriage is hard work and a full-time job. Over eight in ten young adults (86%) agree that one reason for divorce is too much focus on expectations for happiness and not enough hard work needed for a successful marriage. Women and college-educated young adults are more likely than men and those with fewer years of formal education to agree that marriage is hard work. . . .

IMPLICATIONS FOR CHILDREN

The emphasis on marriage as an intimate couples relationship rather than as a child-rearing partnership has profound implications for children. For one thing, it means that marriages with children are likely to remain at high risk of breakdown and breakup. The soul-mate ideal intensifies the natural tension between adult desires and children's needs. When children arrive, some couples may find it difficult to make the transition between couplehood and parenthood and may become disappointed and estranged from one another during the child-rearing years. This is not to say that couples should neglect each other while they are in the intensive child-rearing years, but it is to suggest that the soul-mate ideal of marriage may create unrealistic expectations that, if unfulfilled, may lead to marital discontent and perhaps a search for a new soul mate.

Moreover, the high expectations for marriage as a couples relationship may 20 also cause parents to leave marriages at a lower threshold of unhappiness than in the past. Indeed, in 1994, a nationally representative survey found only 15% of the population agreeing that "when there are children in the family, parents should stay together even if they don't get along." And, according to one recent study, the meaning of "not getting along" is being defined down. It's been estimated that more than half of recent divorces occur, not because of high conflict, but because of "softer" forms of psychological distress and unhappiness. Unfortunately, these are the marriages that might improve over time and with help. As it turns out, people do change their minds about the level of marital contentment. One recent large-scale study indicates that 86% of people who said they were unhappily married in the late 1980s but stayed married, indicated that they were happier when interviewed five years later. Indeed, three-fifths of the formerly unhappily married couples rated their marriages as either "very happy" or "quite happy."

The central importance assigned to the soul-mate relationship also means that unwed parenthood is likely to remain at high levels. As the survey indicates, a high percentage of young adults, who are in the peak years of fertility, tend to separate sex and parenthood, on the one hand, from marriage, on the other. Put another way, people are pickier about the person they choose for a soul-mate relationship than they are about the people they choose as sexual partners, or as biological parents of their children. This is consistent with findings in other recent surveys. For example, a 1994 survey of University of California undergraduates found both men and women agreeing that a man is financially responsible for his child but not responsible to marry his pregnant girlfriend.

However, these speculations could be wrong. Perhaps today's young adults will be able to reconcile their aspirations for emotional closeness with the realities of parenthood and domestic life. Clearly, they are more strongly committed to avoiding parental divorce than the Baby Boom generation. Indeed, while only 15% of adults in the general population agree that parents should stay together for the sake of the children, 40% of young adults in the National Marriage Project survey agree. Moreover, our survey indicates that young adults are not cavalier about marriage or marital permanence. They are committed to lifelong marriage and to the idea that it takes constant effort to sustain a happy marriage. These attitudes may offer some glimmer of hope for their future marriages and for the future of marriage itself.

Cartoon

TOM CHENEY

"And do you, Rebecca, promise to make love only to Richard, month after month, year after year, and decade after decade, until one of you is dead?"

For Discussion

The cartoon gets its humor from its rewording of the standard wedding vows—and the expressions of the couple at the altar, who have apparently never thought of their lifelong monogamous commitment as the preacher's words describe it. The serious point, of course, is that monogamy *does* mean making love to the same person, "month after month, year after year . . . until one of you is dead." You probably have attitudes toward monogamy in long-term relationships. What are they? After reading the Lauren Slater article (pages 420–427) on the chemistry of love, does your view of monogamy change? Why or why not?

18,260 Breakfasts

EVE LAPLANTE

Eve LaPlante is the author of *Salem Witch Judge: The Life and Repentance of Samuel Sewall* (2007), *American Jezebel: The Uncommon Life of Anne Hutchinson, the Woman Who Defied the Puritan* (2004), and *Seized: Temporal Lobe Epilepsy as a Medical, Historical, and Artistic Phenomenon* (1993). She has written for *The Atlantic, The New York Times,* and many other publications. The following essay appeared in *Why I'm Still Married,* a collection of articles by women, edited by Karen Propp and Jean Trounstein (Hudson Street Press, 2006).

"That's not Daddy," my daughter Charlotte, who is eight, informs me, pointing to the wedding photo on my dresser. "He doesn't have a beard." In the photo, David and I stand, hand in hand, on a granite headland in bright sunlight. Visible behind us are brambles, the ocean, and a stone pier. Our smiles look frozen. Fear—panic—plays on our faces.

At our wedding, a third of our lifetimes ago, David was clean-shaven. The David in the photograph is practically a stranger to me, too, as is the younger-looking version of myself, a blushing innocent who looks more like Charlotte than like me now, at middle age.

In fifteen years of marriage, David and I have changed in the usual ways. We've braided together our lives, sharing a bed and tax and mortgage payments, raising children, and, lately, watching our gums start to recede. Every evening after the kids are upstairs, David and I talk together over what have become ritual cups of tea. . . .

"So who *is* that guy in the photo?" I ask Charlotte, who ignores me. She doesn't linger over the photo, which is what I would have done as a child. She doesn't need to linger over photos of us, I suppose, because she actually has her father and me.

My parents' wedding photos were not displayed when I was a child, nor did 5 anyone ever show them to me. I was three when Mom and Dad separated and five at their divorce, so by Charlotte's age I had no conscious awareness of them as a couple. To me, their interactions consisted of hot exchanges at the door of Mom's apartment, where I lived, before and after my occasional weekend with Dad. So their wedding photos, when I eventually discovered them, became an obsession.

I must have been eight when I found the packet of photos tucked away inside the cover of Mom's photograph album. Black and white, with the silvery brilliance of old photographs, they were windows on a past that seemed unreal. Mom and Dad were radiant, shining, glowing with expectation. I pored over their images, my heart pounding, searching for a clue as to who I was. But the photos never helped: I couldn't find myself in them. A few years later, while visting my maternal grandparents, I found some of the same images pasted into a family album with jagged holes replacing my father's face. . . .

As a child of divorce, I yearned for marriage, yet the path . . . was a mystery to me. Had I dared to think what marriage really meant, I'd have had to say, marriage is dangerous. It means being embattled and apart, like my parents. The very thing I longed for seemed out of my reach. This quandary was behind some of the panic that still, in the wedding photo, plays on my face.

Fifteen years later, I know [the fulfillment of marriage]. There's the abiding warmth of waking up each morning beside David, confident that he'll be there to encourage, critique, and even tease me. There's the exhilaration of knowing another person, deeply and without pretense, and similarly being known. . . . As ordinary as it may seem, David's and my ability to jointly—rather than separately—raise our children thrills me. I savor family life more than I might have if I'd known it as a child. I appreciate special occasions doubly, once because they're fun, and again because they represent the stability I missed. Simply gathering for regular meals as a gang, crowded around the kitchen table, is a delightful contrast to the solitary meals I ate as a girl with Mom or Dad. "Staying together is more important to those of us who come from divorce," a friend in her forties explains. "You really want to work things out."

"The ability to be grateful for comparative happiness," as she puts it, comes up often in conversations with adult children of divorce, who comprise a growing segment of the population. The great wave of divorce in the United States began around 1960, the year before my parents split up. A generation later, during the final decade of the twentieth century, a striking social shift occurred: the number of Americans living in single- or stepparent families surpassed the number in traditional families. Today, one in two new marriages includes at least one child of divorce.

Like many offspring of divorce, I grew up with a poignant sense of loss. Besides 10 the trauma of the breakup and its aftermath, there's the prolonged pain of missing one parent and the security of an intact family. During my teens, I dreamed of a future happy family, but believed my chances of ever attaining one were infinitesimal. I felt inadequate as a potential marital partner; my parents' divorce served as a scar. As a college senior, with little sense of my prospects or of myself, I watched, amazed, as classmates planned weddings as well as careers.

Several years later, I had a series of blind dates that almost turned me off marriage forever. At some point, in hopes of short-circuiting this process, I began trying to figure out what I was looking for in a potential mate. . . . Some time passed before I came up with just one question, the answer to which could determine whether to proceed to a second date. That question is: Can you conceive of wanting to wake up every morning and chat with this person over breakfast for fifty years? The time frame arose from the fact that a couple that weds around age thirty can probably look forward to a half century of mornings together. I assumed that the breakfasts my husband and I would consume through the decades would be neither solitary nor silent; this was my hope. I didn't do the math then, but I have now: a fifty-year marriage entails 18,260 breakfasts.

In devising this scheme I was behaving, I believe, like a typical child of divorce. Based on my lengthy if unscientific survey of my peers, we are unlike the children of stable marriages in that we plan for, or rather anticipate, divorce even as we marry. Having learned firsthand that marriage is difficult and precious, we approach commitment with unusual thoughtfulness and practicality.

My scheme may not have been romantic, but it was discriminating. It shrank the number of my dates. Once I met David it allowed us a second date. So far we've been together only fifteen years—that's 5,478 breakfasts—but I remain intrigued by what he may come up with tomorrow over a bowl of cereal and a cup of coffee.

Our marriage is not always easy, of course. We find each other exasperating from time to time, and some of our fights get nasty. Early in our marriage we chose to spend several nights apart, one of us at a hotel, and a few times considered divorce. In our early battles of wills, we kept score, brought up old conflicts, and generally played dirty, as many new couples do. To me, our first few years of marriage felt oddly like reenacting the same years of my parents' lives, during which I was not even present. I became uncharacteristically anxious. I could hear my parents' voices slicing the air and see the worn threshold of the kitchen doorway where I huddled as a toddler to escape their rage. I cannot say where I got this material, for it was certainly not in conscious awareness, but I was somehow compelled to replay scenes from their marriage, perhaps in an effort to defuse their emotional power. It was an odd personal challenge: Can I endure marital conflicts like those of my parents and resolve them in a new way?

For David and me, marriage gets better every year. . . . The pleasures it brings 15 mitigate the frustrations. On Saturday mornings when David and I would like nothing more than to make love, we are blocked by a four-year-old in snowman pajamas, his limbs splayed between us. He, a result of our having made love, is sweet, too, and warm. A few years ago David surprised me by taking up insight meditation, a Buddhist practice. Seeing its calming effect, I began a practice of Christian meditation based on the writings of Saint Ignatius of Loyola. In our tandem journeys, our differences draw us closer.

Marriage is good for my body as well as my soul. I like my physical self more than I did before. David finds me beautiful, which helps me feel beautiful. To be known by him is part of the pleasure: we have nothing to hide. I find every human detail of him delightful, no less so as we age. . . .

Even with four children, marriage is good for my work. I recall that when I was single and childless, each day stretched out before me. With few obligations to anyone, I often didn't begin writing until the sun was setting. What did I do all day? I have no idea. Now, with my workweek limited to the hours when my children are at school (which has included preschool and part-time family day care), I get much more accomplished. My first book, composed before I had kids, took years to write. My most recent book, begun when our fourth child was less than two years old, emerged in just nine months. During that period, I should add, David did almost all the child care on weekends so that I could write.

This may be the keystone of our marriage: David and I share the work. While he makes more money and works longer hours, we divide the chores. I do more child care during the week, when he has a full-time office job, and he does more child care on the weekend. We divide minor chores by preference: he writes checks; I take care of our cars; he plants in the garden; I rake . . .

The really crucial split involved the two big chores besides child care. David cooks. I clean. That is, David shops for and prepares twenty-one meals each week, while I wash, dry, and put away our clothes, occasionally visit the dry cleaner, and twice a month write a check to a housecleaning crew.

You may think I've got the better deal. I would agree. Producing twenty-five 20 bag lunches weekly, which is only part of David's chore, seems herculean to me. But David would disagree. He actually chose the cooking, back when we first divided the household chores, and I—with an eye to the future—was accommodating enough to agree to clean. He enjoys preparing food, and even when it feels onerous, as it can, he believes eating together at home is healthy and economical. An inventive chef, he scans the Food and Dining pages and keeps a growing list of favorite recipes in a loose-leaf binder he shares with the kids. . . .

Our arrangement may sound complicated, but it feels simple. One reason it's sustainable is that we each have a separate realm of duty. I never fret about preparing dinner, while David never feels the tug of the stuffed laundry hamper. Dividing the labor is an essential ingredient of our marriage. If I find myself resenting David because he has shirked some chore or other, I remind myself of the delicious meals he routinely prepares. I may even taste one in the midst of my resentment, which might prompt me to do the chore myself. . . .

A happy marriage, it seems to me, is filled with compromises of one sort or another. Now and then, one of us is offered a business trip to someplace wonderful like Ireland or Hawaii. We usually try to bring the whole family along. But if a family trip is not feasible, financially or otherwise, David or I go solo. . . .

Not long ago, I had business in England. David urged me to go alone, knowing I'd get more work done. Then, to my amazement, he requested that I travel during February school vacation, the sort of week I admit I dread because of the unrelenting family time. Unlike me, who enjoys combining part-time work with part-time child care, David said that in my absence he would rather go whole hog, spending all day every day with the kids. Naturally, I agreed.

Thick snowflakes were falling on the morning of my flight to London. Taking a trip unnerves me, which may be another legacy of divorce. As a child I hated the long car or, later, bus ride between my parents' homes. Traveling without my family also arouses a certain amount of guilt. While I finished packing, David baked chocolate zucchini bread with the children. As we ate lunch, the five of them discussed all the places they could go and things they could do during the week. . . .

I listened quietly as David and our children planned their week without me, 25 feeling myself relax. When the time came to depart for the airport, everyone boarded the minivan to take me to the trolley station near our house. There I kissed each of them, hoisted my bag, and walked across the tracks. I watched the van drive away, David at the wheel, and our children's hands waving in the windows.

Alone in the falling snow, awaiting the trolley that would take me to the airport, I was conscious of having left behind the fear I felt on our wedding day, the fear that persists in the photograph on my dresser. Neither did I feel any guilt about leaving our children at home with David. They would all eagerly await my return. In the meantime, they would be well fed.

Photograph

KIMBERLY WHITE

For Discussion

Officials in California and other states have married same-sex couples in defiance of state laws forbidding such marriages. The photograph shows Joy Galloway and Keltie Jones's ceremony in San Francisco's City Hall in February 2004. What was your first reaction to the photo? What attitude do you have toward lesbians and gays marrying? What in your background or experience helps to explain your attitude?

First Person Plural

HELEN FREMONT

> Helen Fremont wrote the national best seller *After Long Silence*. She works as a public defender. The following essay appeared in the same collection as the previous essay, *Why I Am Still Married* (2006).

COMMITMENT

Our marriage is based on a fundamental, irrefutable fact: neither of us can bear the trauma of dating. Our own courtship was excruciatingly long. The general rule of thumb in lesbian relationships is that on the second date you move in together. Donna and I held off cohabitation for nearly two months, which is something like a record in the gay community. Having accomplished this feat together, we are not about to venture out on our own again. This basic fear lies at the heart of our relationship, and offers us a sense of stability and security. We are bound to each other because neither of us has the courage to start over again.

THE DANGERS OF MARRIAGE

Getting married is a little like sticking your feet in cement: it feels sublimely gooey and sensual now, but you know that it's going to feel constricting in time—stabilizing, yes, but dangerously . . . well . . . *permanent.*

And let's face it: marriage is an act of pure arrogance. You are pretending to lay claim to the future, which is a risky business at best. The gods may not like it. They might feel obliged to prove that *they*'re in charge, not you. Common ways for gods to get their point across would be to kill your spouse for no good reason at all—by introducing a drunk driver into your lane, or a suicide bomber, or a grade IV glioblastoma. Something like this happens every day, and I think it is a pretty simple matter for the gods to arrange for it to happen to you.

And then, of course, there's a statistical reason not to get married: marriage, as any lawyer will tell you, is the first step to divorce.

THE ILLEGAL MARRIAGE

So my wife and I were cautious, and we took both of our weddings seriously. Our 5 first marriage—the illegal one—took place in 1996 in our living room. . . . The illegal marriage was the one that really mattered to us. We bought similar white linen dresses and had rings made by a local goldsmith. I wrote our vows, and Donna planned and cooked an elaborate menu for our guests. We got nervous and drank champagne afterward.

HISTORY LESSON

My wife had been married before—she was what she called a serial monogamist, having been married to a man for ten years (during her twenties), and then having lived with a woman for the next ten years (there went her thirties). These relationships had ended badly and therefore she was hardly interested in starting a new one. My history of love was not exactly confidence-inspiring. Until the age of thirty-seven, when I met Donna in my backyard, I had never set up house with anyone. In my twenties, I had gone through the motions of sleeping with boys because that seemed to be what girls did. I had been passionately in love with several of my college and law school roommates, but they were all women, and the Amazing Force of Denial kept me clueless for years. I could not imagine that I might be a pervert or a deviant, so my worshipful feelings must be what all roommates feel for each other. I certainly wasn't queer. My love for these drop-dead gorgeous, sharp-witted women was pure, platonic, and agonizing.

After losing roommate after roommate to their fiancés, I finally decided to get my own fiancé in law school. He was adorable. I'd known him since high school, when we'd flirted and played endurance Ping-Pong for hours, progressing over the years to bicycling and distance running, winter camping and ski mountaineering.

Now, in my third year of law school, we added sex and big American-style breakfasts to our repertoire of activities and accomplishments. I was crazy about him, and he loved me anyway. We announced our engagement to our parents, and then I backed out of the marriage a few weeks later. I had doubts. What, exactly, was love? And why was my sexual attention span so short? I was no longer keen on being a lawyer, either, and I suspected other surprises lurking in my subconscious—that strange corridor where so many of my feelings have permanent lockers.

Sure enough, good old-fashioned introspection (coupled with expensive psychotherapy) led me, within a year, to the epiphany that I was, in fact, a lesbian. For an additional charge, I learned that this was okay. It would take me another five years before I actually tested out my new hunch of homosexuality in the field—I have never been particularly impulsive. And it would be another ten years before I fell for Donna.

COURTSHIP

Donna and I were set up by my neighbors, a gang of opera singers who knew 10 Donna from their day jobs in the health-care industry, where Donna worked. These boys decided to throw a Memorial Day barbecue in my backyard. It was supposed to be a team effort, but they had songs to sing and boys to see, so I ended up doing all the cleaning, grocery shopping, preparing, and cooking, and they invited fifty of their closest friends. One of them was Donna. She walked into my backyard Monday afternoon bearing twenty pounds of potato salad. She was wearing an Indian-print skirt and a little black tank top; her toes were painted a honking red. I was wearing my ratty college crew shirt and a pair of giant industrial-strength canary-yellow rubber gloves, because I was carrying the mildewed grill from the backyard to the kitchen sink.

"Hi," I said, my hands full of greasy grill.

"Hi," she said, tipping the bowl of potato salad in greeting.

I was in love. Immediately after washing the grill I went upstairs and changed into a nicer T-shirt.

The next day I called her for a date and we went out to dinner. She invited me home afterward to meet her cat—an auspicious start, I thought. Her cat was a used cat; Donna had gotten him from the local shelter a few months before. He had already broken every lamp in her apartment. He looked at me with suspicion, but I must have passed the test because Donna accepted my invitation to see the Mark Morris Dance Group the following week. She seemed depressed, however, and cried throughout the performance, so I believed my chances might be dwindling.

But I soldiered on. On the advice of my romance counselors (a couple of friends 15 who had met Donna at the barbecue), I asked her over for dinner. Soon after, she asked me to bring my dog to meet her cat. Fortunately, the two seemed to get along, if not in temperament, at least in color. They're both redheads.

In July, we had dinner at a little jazz restaurant. I cried over the loss of my last girlfriend to cancer; she cried over the loss of her last girlfriend to a younger woman. We shared a container of pocket tissues. Within a month my dog and I moved in with her and her cat. I proposed marriage almost immediately. Two years later, she agreed.

MARRIAGE, LEGAL-STYLE

In 2004, everyone was running down to City Hall to register; Massachusetts had legalized same-sex marriages. All our friends were planning their ceremonies, ordering invitations and flowers and dresses and cakes and caterers and musicians. Time was of the essence. There was movement afoot to amend the Constitution to ban same-sex marriages, and our chance to get state recognition was shrinking.

This was both annoying and exhilarating. After all, Donna and I had been married for eight years already, without an ounce of help from the state. Now, in 2004, we had a chance to make our bond legal, albeit at tremendous psychic cost to millions of decent, God-fearing Americans, who considered the sanctity of their own marriages suddenly at risk.

In September, Donna and I went on vacation to Provincetown for a week, and we decided to get married there. Unlike our first marriage at the dinner table, this marriage was a cold, calculated legal move. The week before vacation, we went to get our blood drawn for the medical certificate. It turned out that neither of us had syphilis, and our doctors pronounced us eligible for marriage. We drove to the Cape, checked into our beach cottage, and went to town hall to fill out the application for marriage. The town clerk congratulated us and gave us a list of justices of the peace. We had to wait three days, the legally required cooling-off period, before scheduling the wedding. For a justice of the peace, our innkeeper recommended a friend of his, a Provincetown old-timer who needed the business. I called her up. Judge Millie, as I will call her, was on disability and asked that we pay her in cash, so as not to confuse the authorities. She also pointed out that she was desperately in debt, and that the state-set fees for justices of the peace (seventy-five dollars) didn't begin to cut it. We should feel free to pay whatever additional "donation" we could for her services. We agreed on a time and place. She already had a five o'clock marriage scheduled, but would squeeze us in at four at the rotary in the West End of town, overlooking the marshes. She encouraged us to exchange vows, but very *short ones*.

The wedding was exactly what we'd hoped for. It took less than fifteen min- 20 utes. . . . Donna and I exchanged two-sentence vows, including promises to be honest with each other, to fail, and to keep trying—goals we believed we could fulfill. There were no witnesses (none are required in Massachusetts), and Judge Millie pronounced us married. . . .

THE CERTAINTY OF ABANDONMENT AND LOSS

Throughout our ten-year relationship, Donna and I have been certain that each will be abandoned by the other. Consequently, we remain ever vigilant and . . . well, frankly . . . paranoid.

Perhaps due to a failure of imagination, each of us anticipates the other's betrayal according to a precise transcript of what happened in our previous relationships. Donna's former lover left her for a younger woman, so Donna believes I will inevitably do the same. Never mind that I am not the Babe Magnet that her former lover was. . . . Donna does not confine her fears to the rational.

Neither do I, of course, but I have good reason for my paranoia. My previous lover died of cancer, so I am convinced that Donna will do the same. To prove my theory, Donna came into our relationship with a solid track record of previous bouts of cancer, three abdominal surgeries, six weeks of radiation, and a year of chemotherapy. And sure enough . . . six years into our relationship, Donna had a recurrence. As I had done with my previous lover, I now went to the hospital with Donna, wrung my hands waiting for the surgeon's report, slept in the chair at her bedside for a week, disobeyed the nurses, ate her food, brought her take-out from McDonald's, and planned to kill myself after she died.

For the next ten months, I took Donna to chemotherapy every Monday morning, and we'd cap the day off with a matinee at the multiplex cinema next to the health center. The movies produced in late 2000 and early 2001, by and large, sucked. But we were living our own melodrama, and despite the fact that Donna survived this ordeal, I remain convinced that she will die on me. I believe I'm carcinogenic.

This was the year that made our marriage four-dimensional. It had weight and 25 shape and depth, and now *time.*

LOSS, CONTINUED

My wife and I are middle-aged. It is our season of mothers and fathers dying. They are dropping like flies, left and right. They ruled our lives, and now—poof—they're gone.

In the last three years Donna and I have gone to several funerals: her mother's, my father's, her father's. And we have mourned another sort of death—my own. (Just before dying, my father signed a codicil to his will, disowning me and declaring me dead. This had nothing to do with Donna, whom he had liked, or with our relationship, which seemed to amuse him. It had to do with my having written a memoir revealing my Jewish heritage—an identity far more complicated than lesbianism.)

Families are proof that love and loss go hand in hand, but marriage can be a sort of compensation. Donna and I collect our losses and grow closer, like two stitches pulled more tightly together. We fill the gaps for each other, growing into the holes left behind. . . .

THE MARITAL BED

Our lily pad. It sits in the middle of the room, facing the sun. We spend sleepless nights plotting revenge here. We spend hours wondering what went wrong, and then more hours making love, and then more hours floating in our bodies. She tells me her dreams in the morning. We make new ones each night. We snore into each other's ears here, and toss the covers and yank the covers and flop around in the stupidity of sleep. We are most married with our arms and legs flung across each other, unselfconscious, unconscious.

We wash the sheets and make the bed, and now that we are Old Marrieds, 30 we sleep less and spend more time watching the years vanish. The city sizzles outside the window, and we wait until it's safe to wake. We are madly in love, and only the solidity of the days that stretch before and behind us give lie to our sense that we are suspended in midair, that all our intentions amount to nothing but ideas, thin and permeable.

THE DAILY GRIND

My wife and I snap to attention at the buzz of the alarm. We take turns with the hair dryer, the nail clipper, the cuticle scissors. We reach for the nylons and rub lotion on our elbows and begin the day, and then the next day, and the next, and the next. We share a calendar. We share a tube of toothpaste, a bottle of wine, a cold. We share a joke, a fight, a bank account, an apartment, a dog and a cat who consider us divisible. We share doubts about the dog and cat.

She goes to her office, I to mine. And then we call each other in the middle of the day. What's your day like? What are you doing? I miss you. What shall we eat? Who will call the plumber? Who will call our friends? I miss you. Hours go by when we do not think of each other. It happens. I'm sure it happens.

MARRIAGE, THE CREATURE

Ten years in, you realize that marriage is a breathing organism that grows with you. Regardless of what you thought you were raising, you now have a preteen on your hands, a restless, rambunctious ten-year-old marriage that thinks it knows everything, but that still has a lot of surprises left. We're watching this kid grow, and it's got a zillion things up its sleeve, delights and disappointments, and every so often, we feel like slapping it around and taking it to Disneyland. Well, maybe not Disneyland, but Provincetown. Or St. Thomas. Or Pitigliano. Sometimes we are sorry. You never know when you travel with a ten-year-old marriage. Sometimes it gets cranky, but it can be so easily distracted!

THE LONG HAUL

We don't answer the phone. Who goes there? We pull the covers over our heads and wait it out together. We hibernate.

Months go by. Years. We crawl out of bed to see what's new in the world. We 35 double-park and return all the videos and library books and pay all the late fees. We forgive ourselves our trespasses. We eat our daily bread and chocolate. We pray and hold hands. For ever and ever.

Grown-Up Love

JOAN KONNER

Joan Konner is a professor and dean emerita of the Columbia University Graduate School of Journalism. She has written and produced over fifty documentary films and has received twelve Emmys. This essay appeared originally in *O, The Oprah Magazine,* in February 2003.

I have been researching the subject of love all my life. First, unsystematically, as a girl, trying to follow the programmed prescription—seeking "the one" and living happily ever after. Next I divorced and researched love as a woman, more systematically, confronting fantasies and failures, possibilities and disappointments, false starts, and at last, beginning 24 years ago, a love that's enduring and nourishing—at least for the moment (I've learned never to take the gift of love for granted).

Now I am on the case as a professional, a journalist who rebels against almost everything I see, hear, and read about love in the popular media. Every story insults my experience of love. Every story offers a ridiculous scenario that results in half-baked romance and scorched lives. There's the tragic version: Love, Obstacle, Separation, Loss (*Romeo and Juliet, Tristan and Isolde,* Erich Segal's *Love Story*). And there's the fairy-tale version: Love, Obstacle, Triumph, Happily Ever After (*Cinderella, My Big Fat Greek Wedding*). The obstacles—class, clan, race, work, conflicting dreams—provide the dramatic tension.

In America we live in a culture that glorifies passionate, romantic love. Our friends are in love, dreaming or daydreaming of it, waiting and dating to fall into it. Women and men begin new lives in love. Romantic love is our inspiration, our motivation—our reason to be. Romance is a cultural obsession, an imperial ideal. We believe that love can be found, here and now and forever, in an instant, across a crowded room—or tomorrow, just around the corner.

It can—but rarely. In reality, romance is more fleeting and more dangerous than we are told, more complicated than we could have imagined, more elusive than we've been led to believe. Love is a promise made every day only to be broken tomorrow.

As the Jungian analyst Robert Johnson wrote in *We: Understanding the Psychology of Romantic Love,* "The fact that we say 'romance' when we mean 'love' shows us that underneath our language there is a psychological muddle. . . . We are confusing two great psychological systems within us, and this has a devastating effect on our lives and our relationships."

In a documentary I'm researching and developing for television, I want to distinguish love from romance, to explore the ideal of true love, or real love, as Johnson describes it. Talking to Johnson, I told him that it seems to me that love, not romance, is the love we seek, the love we need, the love that enriches life and has the potential to make us happy. That's the story I want to tell, I said—a different story of love—and show its appeal to our deeper desires and nature.

"Good luck!" Johnson said. "In this society, nobody wants to hear about it. Even if it is the truth."

He may be right. Even our language undermines that story. [We] use words like *settle* and *settle down* when we marry or accept a more stable relationship. We "compromise" for a mate who is flesh and blood if not quite the prince we imagined. Johnson calls the love he's talking about oatmeal love. Isn't there a tastier image? The very vocabulary advertises that the champagne of true love is flat.

If we care or dare to look at what those who have thought deeply about love have written, we could learn that romance is potentially transformational but never lasting. Research conducted by social scientists suggests that "romance" lasts 18 months to three years. (Isolde's love potion worked for three years before it wore off.) We could learn that sexual union is only one expression of transcendent passion and human connection. More often sex is neither. We could learn that although the chemistry of connection can occur in an instant, the passage of time—along with friendship and respect—is a crucial element of grown-up love, what might be called enlightened love.

"The passion of romance is always directed at our own projections, our own 10 expectations, our own fantasies," Johnson writes. "It is a love not of another person, but of ourselves."

On the other hand, "Love is the one power that awakens the ego to the existence of something outside itself, outside its empire, outside its security."

Love, in other words, is transcending the ego to connect with another.

Johnson writes: "The task of salvaging love from the swamps of romance begins with a shift of vision. . . . Real relatedness between two people is experienced in the small tasks they do together: the quiet conversation when the day's upheavals are at rest, the soft word of understanding, the daily companionship, the encouragement offered in a difficult moment, the small gift when least expected, the spontaneous gesture of love."

Enlightened love is the connective tissue of existence—a state of being that exists regardless of our opinions of what it ought to be. We live for this kind of love. We work for this kind of love.

The noted psychoanalyst Ethel Person wrote in *Dreams of Love and Fateful* 15 *Encounters:* "Love is an act of the imagination." She says, "Most of us are not originators of stories. Most of us pull our ideas of love from the culture, from the poets and artists who bring this form of desire and gratification together into one script, one scenario. Only then does the average individual try to change the imaginary act into a lived life." In other words: Me, Meg Ryan; you, Tom Hanks—even in New Jersey, maybe especially in New Jersey.

So love is a story we tell ourselves. Except the familiar love stories have gone stale. Today Cinderella's sisters hold jobs, and her stepmother has a support group. The prince buys Viagra on the Internet, and the king opens his castle to the public to make ends meet, if he's not trafficking in insider trading. Romance has been degraded into a sexual how-to. We need a new story or a new telling of the old story. We need a *Star Wars* of the heart—an epic, with heroes and heroines, huge challenges and glorious victories.

Here's a personal story:

It was our first vacation together now 24 years ago. We were rafting on the Rio Grande in central Colorado. Just the two of us, in a small rubber raft. No guide, as two inexperienced rafters probably should have had. The gray water was swift and turbulent. Rocks jutted out everywhere, jagged knives, sentries of slime, poised to rip our flimsy float. We twisted and spun in the flow. Now I was in front, then he, then I. Hoarse with fear, I shouted over the roar of the river: Paddle this way! Paddle that! I resurrected strokes from long-gone memories of summer camp. Pull the paddle! Push the paddle! (No time for feathering now.) We traveled like smoke in a breeze, for miles it seemed, when abruptly the river veered right and a tall wall of rock appeared directly in our path. "Back, back," I screamed. "Stroke! Back!" Though he must have heard, he did not heed me. He'd gone to camp, too—Boy Scout camp. He did what he had to do, issued orders of his own—not that I could see or hear beyond myself at that moment. Miraculously, we cleared the wall and headed into a lull in the river. In frustration and fatigue, I announced: "We have conceptual differences!" To which he answered: "Shut up and paddle." Not exactly what I might have dreamed of. But we were safe after all, and in relief and disillusion, we laughed and kept paddling down the canyon.

What is a story if not a metaphor, a myth in the making?

Love is a raft in a swiftly moving river, scant protection against rapids and 20 rocks, a private place of smells and tastes, eloquent looks and intimate touch, a cache of common dreams and accumulated history. We seek its secret, but it is as individual as one's own face, hidden even from ourselves. Me, Joan; you, Al. We have conceptual differences. We are conceptual differences. We don't even pull into the driveway the same way. But isn't that where love begins, in the difference—the otherness—that makes love possible, and necessary?

Love is the mystery of union, the distance to be transcended, the fuel to cross an infinity. . . . As Robert Heinlein told us in his 1961 novel *Stranger in a Strange Land:* "Love is that condition in which the happiness of another person is essential to your own." So simple—the happiness of the other is essential to our own. Practice it for homework. That's a how-to that bears repeating, on a daily basis. As one wise woman, who outlived three happy husbands, advised: "Find out what he doesn't like, and don't do it."

That's a love story I'd like to report, a story missing in the popular media. As Johnson said: It takes a shift of vision.

QUESTIONS FOR DISCUSSION

1. As the many definitions of love in "What Is Love?" imply, it's evidently hard to say what love is and easier to say what it isn't. The authors say that "love is not selfish, possessive, and demanding," never involves "submission or dominance, emotional coercion, or manipulation," and is "not the desperate attempt to deny aloneness or the search for security that many couples manifest in their desire for a fused identity." Do you agree with these descriptions? Would you say your past or present romantic relationships avoid the negatives entirely? Is it realistic to think that most

romantic relationships can avoid them entirely? It seems to us that many people confuse love with what it isn't—would you agree? If so, why is there so much confusion about the nature of love?

2. Barbara Dafoe Whitehead and David Popenoe propose that "the popular soul-mate ideal may be a substitute for more traditional religious under-standings of marriage" (paragraph 14). They go on to claim that "sex has lost its connection to marriage and also its sense of mystery," and there-fore we need the soul-mate notion as a kind of spiritual compensation. What do you think? Is the traditional religious understanding of marriage at odds with, or even markedly different from, the soul-mate ideal? If so, how? Has sex lost its connection with marriage for you? Has sex lost its mystery? If romantic love has a spiritual dimension for you, how would you characterize it?

3. The accounts of married love in Eve LaPlante's "18,260 Breakfasts" and Helen Fremont's "First Person Plural" are obviously different, and some of the differences surely are due to differences in heterosexual and homosexual relationships. Yet, the love described in both pieces has much in common. In what ways is the love depicted the same or similar? Would you say that the relationships described avoid or overcome what the Firestones say love is not? (see question 1). Would you say that the people involved are soul mates as you understand that concept?

4. "In America," Joan Konner complains, "we live in a culture that glorifies passionate, romantic love." She goes on to agree with Robert Johnson, author of *We: Understanding the Psychology of Romantic Love,* that we confuse "romance" with "love." The passion of romance, Johnson contends, is nothing more than love of self, a projection of our own fantasies, while real love is, as Konner understands Johnson, a "transcending [of] the ego to connect with another." It seems indisput-able that our culture glorifies passionate, romantic love. But do you think that romantic love is only or mainly self-love or fantasy projec-tion? Would you consider married love that lacks or has lost all passion but nevertheless involves genuine companionship satisfactory? Read or reread the account of one man's love for his wife in "What Is Love?" (paragraph 8). Would you say he's describing romance or love as Johnson defines them?

5. No doubt there are die-hard romantics among us, people who can only be satisfied with that state of affairs we call being "in love." But most people just want a reasonably happy long-term relationship that works, where the two people involved love each other and manage to cope with life together. Is this what Joan Konner means by "grown-up love"? Is this what the Firestones have in mind in their effort to depict love? We often say that married love means "settling" for something less than what we really want. In your experience, would you say that realistic compromise is an accurate and fair description of long-term love?

SUGGESTIONS FOR WRITING

For Persuasion

The specter of divorce hangs over marriage today. Marriages end in divorce too often. Many young adults today are children of failed marriages and understandably fear repeating the mistakes of their parents.

It's not surprising, then, that many proposals have been offered to make divorce more difficult by changing the legal grounds for obtaining one. Many people think that only adultery and perhaps spousal or child abuse or extreme emotional cruelty should qualify—otherwise, there should be no legal remedy for an unhappy marriage. Instead of thinking about changing the law, consider reducing divorce from another angle: the private agreement the couple reaches *before* they marry. Decide what you think a couple should recognize as grounds for splitting up, regardless of whether the split ends in permanent separation or divorce. Write an essay persuading your peers to adopt your view of what justifies ending a marriage and making it part of what couples promise each other before they marry.

For Inquiry and Convincing

We encounter different explanations for the problems with marriage today in Part Three's selections. Let's focus attention on two of them. Barbara Dafoe Whitehead and David Popenoe see in the views of young adults "a portrait of marriage as emotionally deep but socially shallow." In other words, couples today are conceiving marriage as an intensely private matter between soul mates, without much connection with the social network that used to help sustain married couples—family, faith and church, friends, and so on. Joan Konner sees confusion between romance and love in a culture that glorifies sexual passion. As she sees it, an unrealistic, distorted view of love is the culprit, making us dissatisfied with marriages that aren't, can't, and shouldn't be based in passionate, romantic love.

The two views are obviously related, but also different especially in their implied programs for action. Whitehead and Popenoe require us to change our idea of marriage. Konner requires us to change our idea of love. Discuss these two explanations and trace their implications in class discussion or in small groups. Which do you find more convincing as a diagnosis? Which do you think offers the more practical route for change?

Write an essay addressed to your peers supporting and developing either Whitehead and Popenoe's view or Konner's. Draw on your own experience or observation of couples in long-term relationships. Examine the attitudes you had before reading the selections and the attitudes you hear other adults express. If relevant, consider the forces that push couples toward being almost entirely on their own. If relevant, consider how the media and other aspects of our culture glorify romantic love.

FOR FURTHER READING AND RESEARCH

Ackerman, Diane. *The Natural History of Love.* New York: Random House, 1994.

Buss, David M. *The Evolution of Desire: Strategies of Human Mating.* New York: Basic Books, 1994.

Firestone, Robert W., Lisa A. Firestone, and Joyce Catlett. *Sex and Love in Intimate Relation-ships.* Washington, D.C.: American Psychological Association, 2006.

Fisher, Helen. *Why We Love: The Nature and Chemistry of Romantic Love.* New York: Holt, 2004.

Kipnis, Laura. *Against Love: A Polemic.* New York: Pantheon, 2005.

Mitchell, Stephen A. *Can Love Last? The Fate of Romance over Time.* New York: Norton, 2002.

Propp, Karen, and Jean Trounstein, eds. *Why I'm Still Married: Women Write Their Hearts Out on Love, Loss, Sex, and Who Does the Dishes.* New York: Hudson Street Press, 2006.

Trimberger, E. Kay. *The New Single Woman.* Boston: Beacon Press, 2005.

Whitehead, Barbara Defoe, and David Popenoe. See the annual reports of the Rutgers Marriage Project at <http://www.marriage.rutgers.edu>.

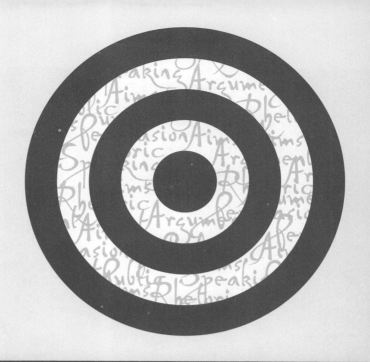

Readings:
Issues and Arguments

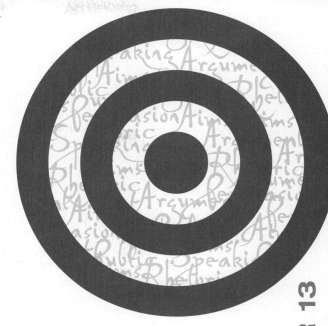

Global Warming: What Should Be Done?

There's no issue quite like global warming. As the first article in this chapter shows, a strong consensus exists among scientists that the Earth is warming up at an alarming rate. Natural processes are involved, but most of the warming is caused by human activities, especially the burning of fossil fuels, mainly coal and oil. If something is not done and done soon—within the next decade or two—we face a long list of trouble: rising sea levels that will threaten coastal cities, droughts that will make farming difficult or impossible, increasingly destructive weather (such as the hurricane that devastated New Orleans), complete loss of the already stressed coral reefs, widespread extinction of species in the ocean and on land, and so on.

Yet, despite the repeated warnings from scientists, often reported in the press and television news, the American public as a whole lacks a sense of urgency. Many people seem to believe either that global warming isn't happening or that, if it is, human behavior couldn't be its primary cause. Others accept the fact of warming and the human role in causing it but believe that the warming is a good thing. In short, the scientific consensus, backed by overwhelming evidence, is not having the impact it should, and too many people think questions that have been answered with a high degree of probability are still matters of serious dispute. This chapter attempts to engage the genuine issues, as summed up in its title, What should be done?

Many people who understand and accept what science is telling us feel that global warming is such an overwhelming problem that nothing can be done about it. They have surrendered to indifference or despair. That's understandable but, as this chapter shows, not warranted. We have the technology to reduce greenhouse gases like carbon dioxide to tolerable levels, and more technological ideas are under development all the time. The measures that would save our planet from catastrophic warming need not reduce our standard of living nor damage our economy—in fact, some offer the potential for economic growth as well as other advantages, such as freedom from reliance on foreign crude oil. What we need is greater public awareness and concern, which will in turn lead to the political will to take appropriate action.

What are the real issues? Some are technological. We have many "green" sources of power—wind, solar, ethanol produced from corn, biodiesel, and so on. Which should we use and in what combination? We have a 200-year supply of coal—can we use some of it while making the transition to cleaner power sources without producing the current huge discharge of carbon dioxide (CO_2) into our atmosphere? These and many other technological issues are certainly arguable. Other questions are economic. What approach to reducing greenhouse gases will prove least expensive to consumers and most profitable for industry and investors, many of whom are increasingly aware of both the wisdom and the money in going green? It's not obvious where economic commitments should be. Then there are political questions. What will persuade our energy companies to think beyond fossil fuels? How can we secure the cooperation of countries like Saudi Arabia, whose wealth is too dependent on oil exports? While reducing our own greenhouse gas emissions, how can we help developing countries, like China, from becoming polluters as bad as or worse than the United States and Europe currently are? Again, the best political course of action is far from settled.

This chapter explores many facets of the global warming problem, but not all of them, and many solutions, but not all of them. It's meant to encourage you to explore both problem and solutions in greater depth. We think learning to live in harmony with our planet may be *the* most important issue we face.

A Climate Repair Manual

GARY STIX

> The September 2006 issue of *Scientific American* focuses on global warming and the various technologies for reducing greenhouse gas emissions. The eight articles that constitute "Energy's Future: Beyond Carbon" are well worth reading and careful study. Gary Stix, the Special Projects Editor for *Scientific American*, wrote the introduction to this set of articles.

Explorers attempted and mostly failed over the centuries to establish a pathway from the Atlantic to the Pacific through the icebound North, a quest often punctuated by starvation and scurvy. Yet within just 40 years, and maybe many fewer, an ascending thermometer will likely mean that the maritime dream of Sir Francis Drake and Captain James Cook will turn into an actual route of commerce that competes with the Panama Canal.

The term "glacial change" has taken on a meaning opposite to its common usage. Yet in reality, Arctic shipping lanes would count as one of the more benign effects of accelerated climate change. The repercussions of melting glaciers, disruptions in the Gulf Stream and record heat waves edge toward the apocalyptic: floods, pestilence, hurricanes, droughts—even itchier cases of poison ivy. Month after month, reports mount of the deleterious effects of rising carbon levels. One recent study chronicled threats to coral and other marine organisms, another a big upswing in major wildfires in the western U.S. that have resulted because of warming.

The debate on global warming is over. Present levels of carbon dioxide—nearing 400 parts per million (ppm) in the earth's atmosphere—are higher than they have been at any time in the past 650,000 years and could easily surpass 500 ppm by the year 2050 without radical intervention.

The earth requires greenhouse gases, including water vapor, carbon dioxide and methane, to prevent some of the heat from the received solar radiation from escaping back into space, thus keeping the planet hospitable for protozoa, Shetland ponies and Lindsay Lohan. But too much of a good thing—in particular, carbon dioxide from SUVs and local coal-fired utilities—is causing a steady uptick in the thermometer. Almost all of the 20 hottest years on record have occurred since the 1980s.

No one knows exactly what will happen if things are left unchecked—the 5 exact date when a polar ice sheet will complete a phase change from solid to liquid cannot be foreseen with precision, which is why the Bush administration and warming-skeptical public-interest groups still carry on about the uncertainties of climate change. But no climatologist wants to test what will arise if carbon dioxide levels drift much higher than 500 ppm.

A LEAGUE OF RATIONS

Preventing the transformation of the earth's atmosphere from greenhouse to unconstrained hothouse represents arguably the most imposing scientific and technical challenge that humanity has ever faced. Sustained marshaling of cross-border engineering

THE HEAT IS ON

A U.S. senator has called global warming the "greatest hoax" ever foisted on the American people. But despite persistently strident rhetoric, skeptics are having an ever harder time making their arguments: scientific support for warming continues to grow.

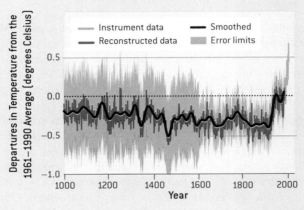

This "hockey stick graph," from one of many studies showing a recent sharp increase in average temperatures, received criticism from warming skeptics, who questioned the underlying data. A report released in June by the National Research Council lends new credence to the sticklike trend line that traces an upward path of temperatures during the 20th century.

A line of SUVs symbolizes high per-capita U.S. energy consumption. But rising expectations pervade the developing world. Many Chinese dream of trading a bicycle for a car.

GREENHOUSE EFFECT

A prerequisite for life on earth, the greenhouse effect occurs when infrared radiation (heat) is retained within the atmosphere.

| 1 Most solar energy reaching the earth is absorbed at the surface | 2 The warmed surface emits infrared radiation | 3 Like a blanket, atmospheric greenhouse gases absorb and reradiate the heat in all directions, including back to the earth | 4 Human activity has increased the amount of greenhouse gas in the atmosphere and thus the amount of heat returned to the surface. In consequence, global temperatures have risen |

and political resources over the course of a century or more to check the rise of carbon emissions makes a moon mission or a Manhattan Project appear comparatively straightforward.

Climate change compels a massive restructuring of the world's energy economy. Worries over fossil-fuel supplies reach crisis proportions only when safeguarding the climate is taken into account. Even if oil production peaks soon—a debatable contention given Canada's oil sands, Venezuela's heavy oil and other reserves—coal and its derivatives could tide the earth over for more than a century. But fossil fuels, which account for 80 percent of the world's energy usage, become a liability if a global carbon budget has to be set.

Translation of scientific consensus on climate change into a consensus on what should be done about it carries the debate into the type of political minefield that has often undercut attempts at international governance since the League of

Nations.[1] The U.S. holds less than 5 percent of the world's population but produces nearly 25 percent of carbon emissions and has played the role of saboteur by failing to ratify the Kyoto Protocol[2] and commit to reducing greenhouse gas emissions to 7 percent below 1990 levels.

Yet one of the main sticking points for the U.S.—the absence from that accord of a requirement that developing countries agree to firm emission limits—looms as even more of an obstacle as a successor agreement is contemplated to take effect when Kyoto expires in 2012. The torrid economic growth of China and India will elicit calls from industrial nations for restraints on emissions, which will again be met by even more adamant retorts that citizens of Shenzhen and Hyderabad should have the same opportunities to build their economies that those of Detroit and Frankfurt once did.

Kyoto may have been a necessary first step, if only because it lit up the pitted 10 road that lies ahead. But stabilization of carbon emissions will require a more tangible blueprint for nurturing further economic growth while building a decarbonized energy infrastructure. An oil company's "Beyond Petroleum" slogans will not suffice.

Industry groups advocating nuclear power and clean coal have stepped forward to offer single-solution visions of clean energy. But too much devoted too early to any one technology could yield the wrong fix and derail momentum toward a sustainable agenda for decarbonization. Portfolio diversification underlies a plan laid out by Robert H. Socolow and Stephen W. Pacala in this single-topic edition of *Scientific American*. The two Princeton University professors describe how deployment of a basket of technologies and strategies can stabilize carbon emissions by midcentury.

Perhaps a solar cell breakthrough will usher in the photovoltaic age, allowing both a steel plant and a cell phone user to derive all needed watts from a single source. But if that does not happen—and it probably won't—many technologies (biofuels, solar, hydrogen and nuclear) will be required to achieve a low-carbon energy supply. All these approaches are profiled by leading experts in this special issue, as are more radical ideas, such as solar power plants in outer space and fusion generators, which may come into play should today's seers prove myopic 50 years hence.

NO MORE BUSINESS AS USUAL

Planning in 50- or 100-year increments is perhaps an impossible dream. The slim hope for keeping atmospheric carbon below 500 ppm hinges on aggressive programs of energy efficiency instituted by national governments. To go beyond what climate specialists call the "business as usual" scenario, the U.S. must follow Europe and even some of its own state governments in instituting new policies that affix a price on carbon—whether in the form of a tax on emissions or in a cap-and-trade system (emission allowances that are capped in aggregate at a certain level and then traded in open markets). These steps can furnish the breathing space to estab-

[1]The League of Nations was established after World War I, but failed in its mission to prevent further conflicts. The U.S. did not join the League, despite the role of President Woodrow Wilson in establishing it.

[2]The Kyoto Protocol was a 1997 international agreement to limit greenhouse gas emissions. The U.S. Senate rejected the agreement by a 95–0 vote.

Then and now: Sunset Glacier in Alaska's Denali National Park, shown covering a mountainside in August 1939, had all but vanished 65 years later when photographed during the same month.

lish the defense-scale research programs needed to cultivate fossil fuel alternatives. The current federal policy vacuum has prompted a group of eastern states to develop their own cap-and-trade program under the banner of the Regional Greenhouse Gas Initiative.

Fifty-year time frames are planning horizons for futurists, not pragmatic policymakers. Maybe a miraculous new energy technology will simultaneously solve our energy and climate problems during that time, but another scenario is at least as likely: a perceived failure of Kyoto or international bickering over climate questions could foster the burning of abundant coal for electricity and synthetic fuels for transportation, both without meaningful checks on carbon emissions.

A steady chorus of skeptics continues to cast doubt on the massive peer- 15 reviewed scientific literature that forms the cornerstone for a consensus on global warming. "They call it pollution; we call it life," intones a Competitive Enterprise Institute advertisement on the merits of carbon dioxide. Uncertainties about the extent and pace of warming will undoubtedly persist. But the consequences of inaction could be worse than the feared economic damage that has bred overcaution. If we wait for an ice cap to vanish, it will simply be too late.

FOR DISCUSSION

1. "The debate on global warming is over," the author says. What does he think is certain, beyond debate? What can't science tell us with a high degree of reliability? In your view, how important are the questions we can't answer right now? What effect should they have on taking action?

2. The author has much to say about "translat[ing] scientific consensus on climate change into a consensus on what should be done." What are the barriers to action as he depicts them? Which seem most important to you? Why?

3. Energy efficiency is certainly part of the solution to global warming. One approach is the cap-and-trade approach the author mentions. What does cap-and-trade involve? How might it contribute to both energy efficiency and the development of alternate energy sources (nonfossil fuels)?

FOR RESEARCH, INQUIRY, AND CONVINCING

The Kyoto Protocol is an international agreement to limit greenhouse gases. President Clinton played a major role in negotiating the agreement, but the U.S Senate rejected it by a 95–0 vote. As a class project, investigate Kyoto, paying special attention to why countries like the United States and Australia never ratified it.

What can we learn from Kyoto that might make international agreements on action to counter global warming work better? How much effort should go into crafting such agreements? That is, what role can we reasonably expect international agreements to play in climate control?

After discussing these questions, write a short paper stating your view. Justify it by evidence from research on the Kyoto Protocol.

15 Ways to Make a Wedge

SCIENTIFIC AMERICAN

This chart comes from the same issue of *Scientific American* as the previous article. It's helpful as a way of envisioning the many routes to reducing global warming and as a reminder that only a multifaceted approach will yield satisfactory results. Read the chart counterclockwise, starting at the top, and pay special attention to the five major divisions in the overall carbon reduction strategy, displayed on the outer edge of the circle. Do note that one wedge is left blank, symbolizing other means at hand or in development that are not represented in this chart.

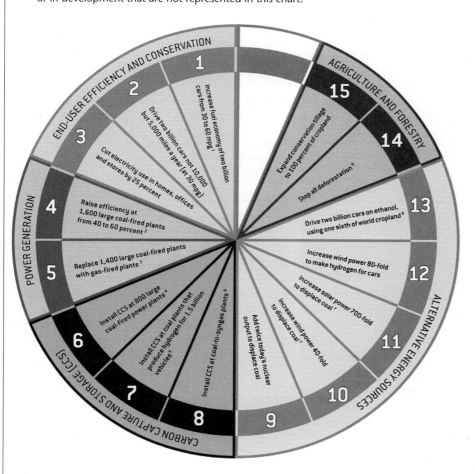

An overall carbon strategy for the next half a century produces seven wedges' worth of emissions reductions. Here are 15 technologies from which those seven can be chosen. Each of these measures, when phased in over 50 years, prevents the release of 26 billion tons of carbon. Leaving one wedge blank symbolizes that this is by no means exhaustive.

NOTES

[1] World fleet size in 2056 could well be two billon cars. Assume they average 10,000 miles a year.

[2] "Large" is one gigawatt (GW) capacity. Plants run 90 percent of the time.

[3] Here and below, assume coal plants run 90 percent of the time at 50 percent efficiency. Present coal power output is equivalent to 800 such plants.

[4] Assume 90 percent of CO_2 is captured.

[5] Assume a car (10,000 miles a year, 60 miles per gallon equivalent) requires 170 kilograms of hydrogen a year.

[6] Assume 30 million barrels of synfuels a day, about a third of today's total oil production. Assume half of carbon originally in the coal is captured.

[7] Assume wind and solar produce, on average, 30 percent of peak power. Thus replace 2,100 GW of 90-percent-time coal power with 2,100 GW (peak) wind or solar plus 1,400 GW of load-following coal power, for net displacement of 700 GW.

[8] Assume 60-mpg cars, 10,000 miles a year, biomass yield of 15 tons a hectare, and negligible fossil-fuel inputs. World cropland is 1,500 million hectares.

[9] Carbon emissions from deforestation are currently about two billion tons a year. Assume that by 2056 the rate falls by half in the business-as-usual projection and to zero in the flat path.

Illustration by Janet Chao from Robert H. Socolow and Stephen W. Pacala, "A Plan to Keep Carbon on Track," *Scientific American,* September 2006. Reprinted by permission of Janet Chao.

FOR DISCUSSION AND RESEARCH

Some of the fifteen wedges are clear enough, such as increasing fuel economy in cars and trucks. The less gasoline and diesel we burn, the less carbon dioxide escapes from exhaust tailpipes into the air. Others may not be so clear, such as carbon capture and storage. In class, discuss all the wedges, listing the ones that are unfamiliar and the ones that are familiar but not understood.

Using the September 2006 issue of *Scientific American* and other quality sources, individuals or groups in the class should find out more about any of the wedges the class knows little about or doesn't understand. Short oral reports to the class will help bring everyone up to speed on all the existing and developing methods for reducing carbon dioxide emissions.

Another approach is to divide the class into five groups and assign them one of the categories on the outer edge of the circle. Each group should investigate its category in depth and report to the class. The advantage of this approach is that even familiar technologies, such as solar power, are in constant development and need to be grasped in considerable detail to appreciate their potential and limitations.

Contributions to Global Warming

AL GORE

If you want a popular and largely visual argument for taking global warming seriously and doing something about it, see *An Inconvenient Truth* (Rodale, 2006), available at almost any bookstore. Al Gore, of course, was vice president when Bill Clinton was president and was the Democratic presidential candidate in 2000. His commitment to environmental causes goes back many years and has made him the best-known major American politician to raise public awareness about ecology in general and about global warming in particular.

The graphic on the following two pages, from *An Inconvenient Truth* (pp. 250–251), represents the relative amounts of carbon dioxide emissions contributed from various parts of the world.

FOR DISCUSSION

1. What is the principle behind the scale used to represent the various parts of the world? What point does it imply? Is the graphic effective? If so, in what way or ways?

2. The United States and Europe account for almost 60% of estimated CO_2 emissions worldwide. Clearly, relative prosperity correlates with greenhouse gas generation. But the graphic misleads in some ways. For example, Southeast Asia, China, and India may now contribute only 12.2% of the total, but their share, especially that of China and India, is on the rise. What other aspects of this graphic might mislead?

3. Note the source of the information used to create the graphic—the U.S. Department of Energy. How much credence and authority do you allot to federal government agencies?

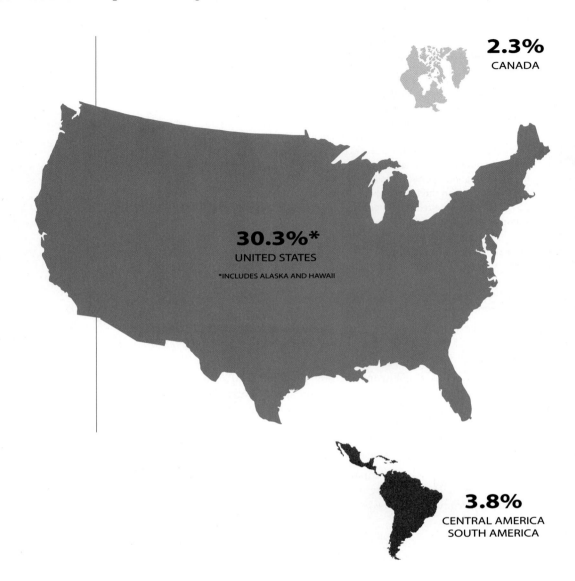

2.3%
CANADA

30.3%*
UNITED STATES
*INCLUDES ALASKA AND HAWAII

3.8%
CENTRAL AMERICA
SOUTH AMERICA

CONTRIBUTIONS TO GLOBAL WARMING

■ United States   ■ Other industrialized nations ■ Developing nations

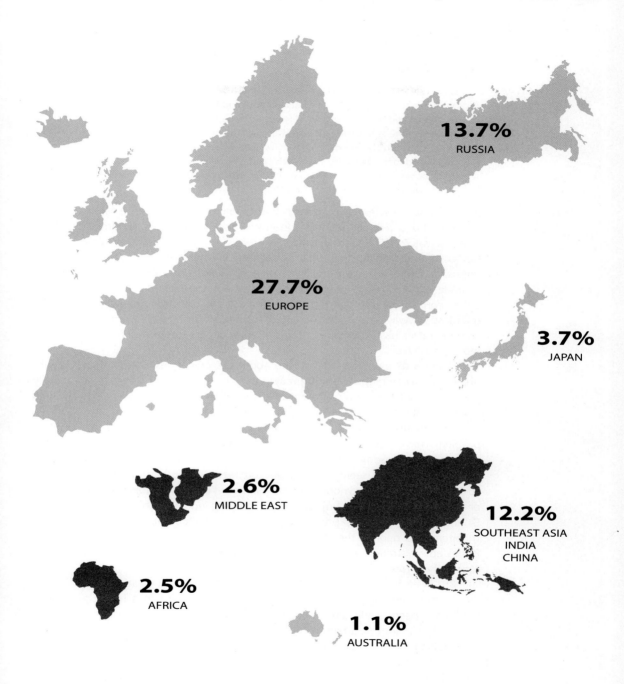

SOURCE: U.S. DEPARTMENT OF ENERGY, ENERGY INFORMATION ADMINISTRATION, CARBON DIOXIDE
INFORMATION ANALYSIS CENTER

Some Convenient Truths

GREGG EASTERBROOK

> Obviously playing off the title of Al Gore's controversial book, Gregg Easterbrook
> argues that both advocates of climate control and those who oppose it are guilty
> of "gloom and doom" attitudes. A few enlightened government policies that
> encourage the entrepreneurial spirit will solve the problem, he believes.
>
> Easterbrook is a prominent journalist who writes often about scientific subjects.
> He is an editor for both *Atlantic Monthly* and *New Republic* and the author of
> many books, including *The Progress Paradox*. The following article came from the
> September 2006 issue of *Atlantic Monthly*.

If there is now a scientific consensus that global warming must be taken seriously, there is also a related political consensus: that the issue is Gloom City. In *An Inconvenient Truth,* Al Gore warns of sea levels rising to engulf New York and San Francisco and implies that only wrenching lifestyle sacrifice can save us. The opposing view is just as glum. Even mild restrictions on greenhouse gases could "cripple our economy," Republican Senator Kit Bond of Missouri said in 2003. Other conservatives suggest that greenhouse-gas rules for Americans would be pointless anyway, owing to increased fossil-fuel use in China and India. When commentators hash this issue out, it's often a contest to see which side can sound more pessimistic.

Here's a different way of thinking about the greenhouse effect: that action to prevent runaway global warming may prove cheap, practical, effective, and totally consistent with economic growth. Which makes a body wonder: Why is such environmental optimism absent from American political debate?

Greenhouse gases are an air-pollution problem—and all previous air-pollution problems have been reduced faster and more cheaply than predicted, without economic harm. Some of these problems once seemed scary and intractable, just as greenhouse gases seem today. About forty years ago urban smog was increasing so fast that President Lyndon Johnson warned, "Either we stop poisoning our air or we become a nation [in] gas masks groping our way through dying cities." During Ronald Reagan's presidency, emissions of chlorofluorocarbons, or CFCs, threatened to deplete the stratospheric ozone layer. As recently as George H. W. Bush's administration, acid rain was said to threaten a "new silent spring" of dead Appalachian forests.

But in each case, strong regulations were enacted, and what happened? Since 1970, smog-forming air pollution has declined by a third to a half. Emissions of CFCs have been nearly eliminated, and studies suggest that ozone-layer replenishment is beginning. Acid rain, meanwhile, has declined by a third since 1990, while Appalachian forest health has improved sharply.

Most progress against air pollution has been cheaper than expected. Smog 5 controls on automobiles, for example, were predicted to cost thousands of dollars for each vehicle. Today's new cars emit less than 2 percent as much smog-forming pollution as the cars of 1970, and the cars are still as affordable today as they were then. Acid-rain control has cost about 10 percent of what was predicted in 1990, when Congress enacted new rules. At that time, opponents said the regulations would cause a "clean-air recession"; instead, the economy boomed.

Greenhouse gases, being global, are the biggest air-pollution problem ever faced. And because widespread fossil-fuel use is inevitable for some time to come, the best-case scenario for the next few decades may be a slowing of the rate of greenhouse-gas buildup, to prevent runaway climate change. Still, the basic pattern observed in all other forms of air-pollution control—rapid progress at low cost—should repeat for greenhouse-gas controls.

Yet a paralyzing negativism dominates global-warming politics. Environmentalists depict climate change as nearly unstoppable; skeptics speak of the problem as either imaginary (the "greatest hoax ever perpetrated," in the words of Senator James Inhofe, chairman of the Senate's environment committee) or ruinously expensive to address.

Even conscientious politicians may struggle for views that aren't dismal. Mandy Grunwald, a Democratic political consultant, says, "When political candidates talk about new energy sources, they use a positive, can-do vocabulary. Voters have personal experience with energy use, so they can relate to discussion of solutions. If you say a car can use a new kind of fuel, this makes intuitive sense to people. But global warming is of such scale and magnitude, people don't have any commonsense way to grasp what the solutions would be. So political candidates tend to talk about the greenhouse effect in a depressing way."

One reason the global-warming problem seems so daunting is that the success of previous antipollution efforts remains something of a secret. Polls show that Americans think the air is getting dirtier, not cleaner, perhaps because media coverage of the environment rarely if ever mentions improvements. For instance, did you know that smog and acid rain have continued to diminish throughout George W. Bush's presidency?

One might expect Democrats to trumpet the decline of air pollution, which 10 stands as one of government's leading postwar achievements. But just as Republicans have found they can bash Democrats by falsely accusing them of being soft on defense, Democrats have found they can bash Republicans by falsely accusing them of destroying the environment. If that's your argument, you might skip over the evidence that many environmental trends are positive. One might also expect Republicans to trumpet the reduction of air pollution, since it signifies responsible behavior by industry. But to acknowledge that air pollution has declined would require Republicans to say the words, "The regulations worked."

Does it matter that so many in politics seem so pessimistic about the prospect of addressing global warming? Absolutely. Making the problem appear unsolvable encourages a sort of listless fatalism, blunting the drive to take first steps toward a solution. Historically, first steps against air pollution have often led to pleasant surprises. When Congress, in 1970, mandated major reductions in smog caused by automobiles, even many supporters of the rule feared it would be hugely expensive. But the catalytic converter was not practical then; soon it was perfected, and suddenly, major reductions in smog became affordable. Even a small step by the United States against greenhouse gases could lead to a similar breakthrough.

And to those who worry that any greenhouse-gas reductions in the United States will be swamped by new emissions from China and India, here's a final reason to be optimistic: technology can move across borders with considerable speed. Today it's not clear that American inventors or entrepreneurs can make money by reducing greenhouse gases, so relatively few are trying. But suppose the United States regulated greenhouse gases, using its own domestic program, not the cumbersome Kyoto Protocol; then America's formidable entrepreneurial and engineering communities would fully engage the problem. Innovations pioneered here could spread throughout the world, and suddenly rapid global warming would not seem inevitable.

The two big technical advances against smog—the catalytic converter and the chemical engineering that removes pollutants from gasoline at the refinery stage—were invented in the United States. The big economic advance against acid rain—a credit-trading system that gives power-plant managers a profit incentive to reduce pollution—was pioneered here as well. These advances are now spreading globally. Smog and acid rain are still increasing in some parts of the world, but the trend lines suggest that both will decline fairly soon, even in developing nations. For instance, two decades ago urban smog was rising at a dangerous rate in Mexico; today it is diminishing there, though the country's population continues to grow. A short time ago declining smog and acid rain in developing nations seemed an impossibility; today declining greenhouse gases seem an impossibility. The history of air-pollution control says otherwise.

Americans love challenges, and preventing artificial climate change is just the sort of technological and economic challenge at which this nation excels. It only remains for the right politician to recast the challenge in practical, optimistic tones. Gore seldom has, and Bush seems to have no interest in trying. But cheap and fast improvement is not a pipe dream; it is the pattern of previous efforts against air pollution. The only reason runaway global warming seems unstoppable is that we have not yet tried to stop it.

FOR DISCUSSION

1. What reasons are offered to explain the negativism about solving the greenhouse gas problem? Do you find them convincing? Why or why not? Can you think of other reasons why the problem is not being addressed in more positive terms?

2. The author bases his optimism on previous successes with smog, CFCs, and acid rain, arguing that CO_2 emissions are just another air pollution problem, larger in scale but not fundamentally different. Do you agree? How much does the size and global extent of the problem matter?

3. Easterbrook clearly doesn't put much stock in international agreements such as Kyoto, preferring instead national policies to encourage innovation, which he thinks will rapidly cross national borders. "Americans love challenges," he says. Do you find this approach appealing? Why or why not?

FOR PERSUASION

"Some Convenient Truths" is a good model for writing persuasively about environmental problems such as global warming. Using Easterbrook's essay as your inspiration, write an article of similar length for your local or college paper advocating measures ordinary citizens can take to reduce their contribution to greenhouse gases. You may want to look at later articles in this chapter or read about green movements currently under way on many college campuses. Whatever you choose to talk about, remember that taking action depends on believing that action is worthwhile. Overcoming what Easterbrook calls "listless fatalism" is essential.

The Coal Paradox

TIM APPENZELLER

> Electricity is clean by the time we use it in homes, offices, and industry but not, at present, in the power plants that generate it. Many of them are coal-powered, and every ton of coal burned produces four tons of CO_2. Yet coal is abundant and relatively cheap—hence the paradox Tim Appenzeller explores in the following *National Geographic* (March 2006) article. We can't seem to do without coal, but using it contributes significantly to global warming and many other problems, such as the destruction of land where the coal is mined.
>
> Appenzeller is the science editor for *National Geographic* and a winner of the Walter Sullivan Award for Excellence in Science Journalism.

On a scorching August day in southwestern Indiana, the giant Gibson generating station is running flat out. Its five 180-foot-high boilers are gulping 25 tons of coal each minute, sending thousand-degree steam blasting through turbines that churn out more than 3,000 mega-watts of electric power, 50 percent more than Hoover Dam. The plant's cooling system is struggling to keep up, and in the control room warnings chirp as the exhaust temperature rises.

But there's no backing off on a day like this, with air conditioners humming across the Midwest and electricity demand close to record levels. Gibson, one of the biggest power plants in the country, is a mainstay of the region's electricity supply, pumping enough power into the grid for three million people. Stepping from the sweltering plant into the air-conditioned offices, Angeline Protogere of Cinergy, the Cincinnati-based utility that owns Gibson, says gratefully, "This is why we're making all that power."

Next time you turn up the AC or pop in a DVD, spare a thought for places like Gibson and for the grimy fuel it devours at the rate of three 100-car trainloads a day. Coal-burning power plants like this one supply the United States with half its electricity. They also emit a stew of damaging substances, including sulfur dioxide—a major cause of acid rain—and mercury. And they gush as much climate-warming carbon dioxide as America's cars, trucks, buses, and planes combined.

Here and there, in small demonstration projects, engineers are exploring technologies that could turn coal into power without these environmental costs. Yet unless utilities start building such plants soon—and lots of them—the future is likely to hold many more traditional stations like Gibson.

Last summer's voracious electricity use was just a preview. Americans' taste for 5 bigger houses, along with population growth in the West and air-conditioning-dependent Southeast, will help push up the U.S. appetite for power by a third over the next 20 years, according to the Department of Energy. And in the developing world, especially China, electricity needs will rise even faster as factories burgeon and hundreds of millions of people buy their first refrigerators and TVs. Much of that demand is likely to be met with coal.

For the past 15 years U.S. utilities needing to add power have mainly built plants that burn natural gas, a relatively clean fuel. But a near tripling of natural gas prices in the past seven years has idled many gas-fired plants and put a damper on new construction. Neither nuclear energy nor alternative sources such as wind and solar seem likely to meet the demand for electricity.

Meanwhile, more than a quarter trillion tons of coal lie underfoot, from the Appalachians through the Illinois Basin to the Rocky Mountains—enough to last 250 years at today's consumption rate. You hear it again and again: The U.S. is the Saudi Arabia of coal. About 40 coal-burning power plants are now being designed or built in the U.S. China, also rich in coal, could build several hundred by 2025.

Mining enough coal to satisfy this growing appetite will take a toll on lands and communities. Of all fossil fuels, coal puts out the most carbon dioxide per unit of evergy, so burning it poses a further threat to global climate, already warming alarmingly. With much government prodding, coal-burning utilities have cut pollutants such as sulfur dioxide and nitrogen oxides by installing equipment like the building-size scrubbers and catalytic units crowded behind the Gibson plant. But the carbon dioxide that drives global warming simply goes up the stacks—nearly two billion tons of it each year from U.S. coal plants. Within the next two decades that amount could rise by a third.

There's no easy way to capture all the carbon dioxide from a traditional coal-burning station. "Right now, if you took a plant and slapped a carbon-capture device on it, you'd lose 25 percent of the energy," says Julio Friedmann, who studies carbon dioxide management at Lawrence Livermore National Laboratory. But a new kind of power station could change that.

A hundred miles up the Wabash River from the Gibson plant is a small power 10 station that looks nothing like Gibson's mammoth boilers and steam turbines. This one resembles an oil refinery, all tanks and silvery tubes. Instead of burning coal, the Wabash River plant chemically transforms it in a process called coal gasification.

The Wabash plant mixes coal or petroleum coke, a coal-like residue from oil refineries, with water and pure oxygen and pumps it into a tall tank, where a fiery reaction turns the mixture into a flammable gas. Other equipment removes sulfur and other contaminants from the syngas, as it's called, before it's burned in a gas turbine to produce electricity.

Cleaning the unburned syngas is cheaper and more effective than trying to sieve pollutants from power plant exhaust, as the scrubbers at a plant like Gibson do. "This has been called the cleanest coal-fired power plant in the world," says Steven Vick, general manager of the Wabash facility. "We're pretty proud of that distinction."

The syngas can even be processed to strip out the carbon dioxide. The Wabash plant doesn't take this step, but future plants could. Coal gasification, Vick says, "is a technology that's set up for total CO_2 removal." The carbon dioxide could be pumped deep underground into depleted oil fields, old coal seams, or fluid-filled rock, sealed away from the atmosphere. And as a bonus, taking carbon dioxide out of the syngas can leave pure hydrogen, which could fuel a new generation of nonpolluting cars as well as generate electric power.

The Wabash plant and a similar one near Tampa, Florida, were built or refurbished with government money in the mid-1990s to demonstrate that gasification is a viable electricity source. Projects in North Dakota, Canada, the North Sea, and

FACTS ABOUT COAL

WHO HAS COAL?
The world has more than a trillion tons of readily available coal. The U.S. has the largest share, but other energy-hungry countries, such as China and India, are richly endowed as well.

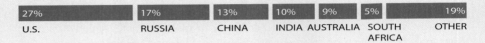

27%	17%	13%	10%	9%	5%	19%
U.S.	RUSSIA	CHINA	INDIA	AUSTRALIA	SOUTH AFRICA	OTHER

WHO USES COAL NOW?
Global coal consumption is roughly five billion tons a year, with China burning the most. Western Europe has cut coal use by 36 percent since 1990 by using available natural gas from the North Sea and Russia.

MILLIONS OF TONS

1,531	1,117	1,094	431	251	1,016
CHINA	EUROPE*	U.S.	INDIA	RUSSIA	OTHER

WHO WILL USE IT TOMORROW?
China's coal needs will more than double by 2025 to satisfy factories and consumers. The country also plans to convert coal to liquid motor fuels. Worldwide, consumption will rise by 56 percent.

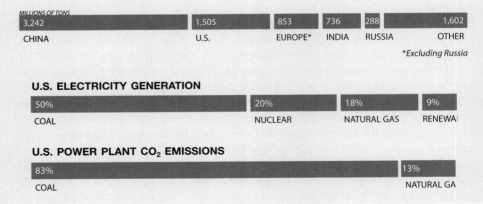

MILLIONS OF TONS

3,242	1,505	853	736	288	1,602
CHINA	U.S.	EUROPE*	INDIA	RUSSIA	OTHER

*Excluding Russia

U.S. ELECTRICITY GENERATION

50%	20%	18%	9%
COAL	NUCLEAR	NATURAL GAS	RENEWA

U.S. POWER PLANT CO$_2$ EMISSIONS

83%	13%
COAL	NATURAL GA

elsewhere have tested the other parts of the equation: capturing carbon dioxide and sequestering it underground. Researchers say they need to know more about how buried carbon dioxide behaves to be sure it won't leak back out—a potential threat to climate or even people. But Friedmann says, "For a first cut, we have enough information to say, 'It's a no-brainer. We know how to do this.'"

WHAT'S IN COAL SMOKE?

Sulfur Dioxide

The sulfur in coal forms this gas, which gives rise to acid rain when it reacts with water in clouds. Many plants control sulfur emissions by burnling low-sulfur coal and passing the exhaust through scrubbers, which capture sulfur dioxide.

Nitrogen Oxides

The heat of power-plant burners turns nitrogen from the air into nitrogen oxides, which can contribute to acid rain and ground-level ozone. Pollution controls on many plants limit nitrogen oxide emissions.

Mercury

The traces of mercury in coal escape in power-plant exhaust. Falling hundreds of miles away in rain or snow, the mercury builds up in fish, making some species unsafe for children and pregnant women to eat.

Carbon Dioxide

Coal produces more CO_2 per energy unit than any other fossil fuel. CO_2 is a green-house gas, affecting climate by trapping heat that would otherwise escape to space. Power plants today release all their CO_2 into the atmosphere.

Particulates

Particles from coal-burning plants can harm people who have heart and breathing disorders. Soot and ash are captured before they go up the stacks, but finer particles can form later, from oxides of sulfur and nitrogen.

Yet that's no guarantee utilities will embrace the gasification technology. "The fact that it's proved in Indiana and Florida doesn't mean executives are going to make a billion-dollar bet on it," says William Rosenberg of Harvard's Kennedy School of Government. The two gasification power plants in the U.S. are half the size of most commercial generating stations and have proved less reliable than traditional plants. The technology also costs as much as 20 percent more. Most important, there's little incentive for a company to take on the extra risk and expense of cleaner technology: For now U.S. utilities are free to emit as much carbon dioxide as they like. 15

Cinergy CEO James Rogers, the man in charge of Gibson and eight other carbon-spewing plants, says he expects that to change. "I do believe we'll have regulation of carbon in this country," he says, and he wants his company to be ready. "The sooner we get to work, the better. I believe it's very important that we develop the ability to do carbon sequestration." Rogers says he intends to build a commercial-scale gasification power plant, able to capture its carbon dioxide, and several other companies have announced similar plans.

The energy bill passed last July by the U.S. Congress offers help in the form of loan guarantees and tax credits for gasification projects. This should jump-start things," says Rosenberg, who advocated these measures in testimony to Congress. The experience of building and running the first few plants should lower costs and improve reliability. And sooner or later, says Rogers, new environmental laws that put a price on carbon dioxide emissions will make clean technology look far more attractive. "If the cost of carbon is 30 bucks a ton, it's amazing the kinds of technologies that will evolve to allow you to produce more electricity with less emissions."

If he's right, we may one day be able to cool our houses without turning up the thermostat on the entire planet.

FOR DISCUSSION

1. According to Tim Appenzeller, why is coal the choice of so many power-generating plants? Though still producing significant amounts of CO_2, natural gas is a cleaner alternative—why is it falling out of use?

2. What are the advantages of coal gasification? What are the disadvantages?

3. Neither conventional nor coal gasification plants currently capture and sequester the CO_2 they produce, though we're told in the article that research projects have tested this technology. In essence in this process, the gas is liquefied, pumped underground, and stored in such places as played-out oil fields. What is your reaction to such a method of pollution control?

FOR RESEARCH AND CONVINCING

Let's suppose that carbon sequestration will work and that economic and political forces allow it to come into widespread use. Because coal is a fossil fuel, we still have the problem that the supplies will eventually run out. Furthermore, the damage done by strip-mining will be even greater than it is now. Clearly, we need to find alternatives to coal, and natural gas isn't satisfactory because it is in shorter supply, pollutes significantly, and is needed for other industrial processes besides power generation.

There are basically two ways to approach the problem. The first way is to continue to build massive power-generating plants but to power them with something that's cleaner—such as nuclear energy. The other way is to encourage what is already being done in Japan and elsewhere on a significant scale—to have each home and business generate its own power via solar or wind energy. Of course, the two ways can be combined. When the sun is shining or the wind is blowing, a home or business can go off the grid and use its own power, resorting to the centrally generated source only when necessary.

Explore these two approaches. There is much information on both. Then write a paper proposing and defending the approach or combination of approaches that you think will work best in your area.

Existing Technologies for Reducing CO_2 Emissions

AL GORE

We need to remind ourselves often that powerful technologies exist for reducing carbon dioxide emissions. The ones pictured here, from *An Inconvenient Truth,* are only a few of many.

Fuel-Cell Hybrid Buses

Green Roof

Hybrid Car

Compact Fluorescent Lightbulbs

Solar Panels

Electric Car Powered by Hydrogen Fuel Cell

Geothermal Power Station

FOR DISCUSSION

In the short term, we need energy conservation, ways to reduce pollution from cars and power-generating plants, and increasing use of power sources that are renewable and clean. Such measures will buy us time for more radical and permanent solutions. In the long term, we need to cease using fossil fuels as an energy source entirely, replacing them with wind, solar, tidal, hydrogen, fusion, and other potentially inexhaustible and nonpolluting sources of energy. As a class, brainstorm the possibilities both short and long term. Don't worry too much about how practical the suggestions are. After the class completes the brainstorming, examine what you've generated. Which suggestions appeal the most? Why?

How America Can Free Itself of Oil—Profitably

AMORY LOVINS

> Emissions from our vehicles are responsible for about one-third of the CO2 released in the United States. Some experts believe that we are close to exhausting crude oil supplies, that shortly oil will become scarce and therefore even more expensive. Oil is essential for certain products we can't easily do without, such as plastics. Yet we are burning up our supply, and the demand for more is driving U.S. foreign policy too much. For these and many other reasons, we eventually have to free ourselves from oil dependency.
>
> Amory Lovins, who directs the Rocky Mountain Institute, offers a detailed plan in the following article from Fortune (October 4, 2004).

Enough about the oil problem; now there's an oil solution. Within the next few decades the U.S. can end its oil dependence.

On Sept. 20, my team of scientists, engineers, economists, and consultants at Rocky Mountain Institute published a fully elaborated plan for an oil-free America— an independent peer-reviewed synthesis that the Pentagon co-sponsored. This is the first strategy for displacing the black stuff not incrementally but radically, not at a cost to the economy but at a net gain, and in ways that will appeal to diverse business and political leaders. If we use our heads to build the right playing field, the markets will do the rest. America's shift from oil can be led profitably by business at a net savings to the economy of $70 billion a year by 2025.

By applying the past two decades of often unnoticed technological progress, it will cost less to displace all the oil that the U.S. will need than to buy that oil. Oil's market price leaves out many of its true economic, military, and environmental costs, but even if those "externalized" burdens were zero, completely displacing oil would still be profitable for the U.S. economy (and other economies too) starting now.

How do we achieve it? The solution is to save half the oil America uses and substitute cheaper alternatives for the other half. Getting there requires four integrated steps:

- Double the efficiency of using oil. The U.S. today wrings twice as much work from each barrel of oil as it did in 1975. Proven techniques can redouble oil productivity. The U.S. Energy Administration forecasts that in 2005 oil will cost $26 a barrel (in 2000 dollars); but the investment needed to deliver the same or better services with just half the oil is far less: It averages $12 a barrel.

  Inefficient light trucks and cars, which consume 40% of our oil, are at the center of our oil habit. And ultralight and ultrastrong materials for vehicles are the No. 1 enabling technology for changing that. Advanced composites like carbon fiber, backstopped by lightweight steels, can nearly double the efficiency of cars and light trucks and improve both safety and performance. The new materials will cost about the same per vehicle as today's metals, in part because manufacturing will become simpler and the system needed to propel the vehicle smaller and lighter.

  If we use ultralight materials to engineer advanced versions of vehicles like today's Toyota Prius hybrid, we'll go a long way toward realizing the gains. A Prius costs a few thousand dollars more than a comparable nonhybrid but uses just half the gasoline. At the cost Toyota expects to reach in 2007, the fuel savings will repay the added cost in about five years. Building an ultralight version of the Prius would save 71% of the fuel, cutting the payback time to three years.

- Coordinate public policies and business strategies to speed the adoption not just of superefficient light vehicles, but also of superefficient heavy trucks and airplanes. The necessary technologies exist here too—innovations like aircraft composites and wide-based single truck tires to replace double ones. Combined with more-efficient buildings and factories, efficient vehicles can cut the forecast total U.S. oil use by 29% by 2025 and another 23 percentage points soon thereafter—52% in all. At the same time, the shift can revitalize strategic industrial sectors that will make the key oil-saving technologies, including auto manufacturing, aerospace, advanced materials, and more.

- Turn to modern biofuels to replace another 20% of U.S. oil needs. New ways to convert woody plants like switchgrass and poplar into ethanol can yield twice as much fuel as today's corn-into-ethanol processes, yet cost less in both capital and energy. Replacing fossil fuels with these plant-derived carbohydrates will strengthen rural America too: it will boost net farm income by tens of billions of dollars a year and create 750,000 jobs.

- Use established, highly profitable efficiency techniques to save half the projected 2025 use of natural gas. Simply by using electricity efficiently, especially at periods of peak demand, the U.S. can save eight trillion cubic feet of gas a year. Gas efficiency will make this fuel abundant and affordable again, cut gas and power bills by $55 billion a year—and free 10 trillion cubic feet a year to substitute for oil. The most profitable option is to convert the saved gas into hydrogen, whose superefficient use can then displace most or all of the remaining oil.

I don't want to minimize the management challenge of what we propose. 5 These four shifts are fundamentally disruptive to current business models. But companies quick to adopt new models will be the winners of the 21st century; those that deny and resist change will join the dead from the last millennium.

What policies are needed? Jump-starting the 21st-century energy economy will take a cohesive strategy, bold leadership, and federal, or at least state, action. If we don't move aggressively, we will face a costly, chaotic, 100-year transition in which change will be forced by the intolerable pressure of wars, shortages, and other awful events. But if we act, we can exchange this chaos for a profitable, orderly 30-year transition on our terms. Our report, Winning the Oil Endgame, charts practical policies—market-oriented without taxes, and innovation-driven without mandates, supporting rather than distorting business logic—to speed that transition.

The most important innovation is "feebates" for new cars and light trucks. Feebates combine fees on inefficient vehicles with rebates on efficient ones, to influence consumer choice. The rebates need be no bigger than automakers' current sales incentives, which range as high as $5,000. But rather than drain automakers' margins, the new rebates would be paid for by fees on inefficient models.

Feebates would be much more consumer-friendly than gas-guzzler taxes; they'd apply separately within each vehicle size class. That way, you won't be penalized for buying an SUV; instead, you'll be rewarded for choosing an efficient one. By encouraging customers to invest as if they're counting fuel savings over the vehicle's whole life, feebates will pull superefficient vehicles from the drawing-board into the showroom more quickly, expanding choice.

America also needs to get its polluting, gas-guzzling junkers off the road. A far-sighted solution would be a national scrap-and-replace program. It would lease or sell superefficient cars to low-income people—with payments and fuel bills they can afford—while scrapping clunkers. That would quickly create a profitable million-car-a-year market for advanced-technology vehicles, and help clean our cities' air. As a bonus, it would boost job opportunity by helping breadwinners get to work reliably.

Smart government financing can also accelerate oil independence. Temporary federal loan guarantees can encourage automakers to retool and airlines to buy efficient airplanes while scrapping inefficient ones. Farm subsidies can be trimmed as profit-making biofuels and biomaterials supplant loss-making crops. Within a few years farm net income could triple.

Oil industry giants like Shell and BP are already preparing to move beyond oil 10 by transforming themselves into energy companies. Done right, this shift will enable them to redeploy their skills and assets profitably rather than lose market share. Biofuels are a major new product line that leverages existing distribution and retail infrastructure and that can, we estimate, attract $90 billion in new investment from the private sector.

The total investment needed for the moves I've outlined is $180 billion in industrial capacity over the next decade. The amount sounds massive, but consider: Every time the price of oil goes up $1 a barrel, Americans export $7 billion a year, with zero return at home. Ending dependency can save $133 billion every year by 2025, assuming $26 oil. This saving, equivalent to a large, permanent tax cut, can replace today's $120-billion-a-year oil imports with reinvestments in ourselves: $40 billion flows as revenue to farmers producing biofuels, while the rest returns to the nation's communities and businesses. By 2015 the early steps in the transition will have saved as much oil as the U.S. now gets each year from the Persian Gulf. By 2040, oil imports could be gone. By 2050, the U.S. economy could be flourishing with no oil at all.

In the process, more than a million high-wage automotive and related jobs can be saved, and a million net new jobs added. U.S. car, truck, and airplane makers can again lead the world. A more efficient and effective military can refocus on protecting American citizens, not foreign oil supplies. Carbon dioxide emissions will shrink by one-fourth. Federal deficits will decrease slightly, and trade deficits dramatically. Countries with oil will no longer require special treatment. The U.S., no longer suspected of having oil as a motive, could restore its world stature as a moral leader and regain its clarity of purpose.

How do we start? Astute business leaders can turn innovation from a threat to a friend. Military leaders can support advanced-materials R&D and procure super-efficient platforms. Political leaders can craft policies that stimulate demand for efficient vehicles, reduce investment risks, and purge perverse incentives. Citizens must play a role too—a big role—because their choices guide the markets, enforce account-ability, and spur social innovation. The surprise popularity of Toyota's Prius, Honda's Civic hybrid, and Ford's Escape hybrid SUV suggests that consumers welcome efficient designs if they're appealing.

America's energy future is choice, not fate. Oil dependence is a problem we needn't have, and it's cheaper not to. When the U.S. last paid attention to oil efficiency, between 1977 and 1985, oil use fell 17% while GDP grew 27%. During those eight years, oil imports fell 50% and imports from the Persian Gulf fell by 87%. That exercise of market muscle—from the demand side—broke OPEC's pric-ing power for a decade. Today we can rerun that play even more decisively, at a big profit. What are we waiting for? We can end oil dependence forever.

FOR DISCUSSION

1. "Oil's market price leaves out many of its true economic, military, and environmental costs," writes Lovins. What does he have in mind? Who winds up paying for these hidden costs?

2. Summarize in your own words the proposals offered in paragraph 4. How will each contribute to freeing us from oil dependency? Suppose that we did what Lovins proposes. Would we eliminate our need for oil or only significantly reduce the demand?

3. Explain the concept of "feebates" (paragraph 7). Do you think such an approach will produce better consumer choices? If not, what do you think would work better?

4. Lovins has much to say about the purely economic advantages of his pro-posal. Are you convinced that the advantages are as great as he thinks? Why or why not?

5. What does Lovins mean by the "management challenges" his scheme entails? In your view, are the challenges greater than he admits they are?

FOR RESEARCH AND INQUIRY

Leadership to reduce global warming, including action to reduce our dependence on oil, has not come from Washington in recent years. Rather, state and local governments, certain businesses, and environmental groups have provided most of it. Find out what you can about actions taken and initiatives promoted. Who's doing what and with what outcomes, actual and potential?

Then write a paper exploring the question "Can we reduce our carbon footprint without significant involvement by the federal government?" If you think we can, whose leadership should we heed the most? If not, what must the federal government do to complement the efforts, both public and private, cur-rently under way?

Selling the Wind

MICHELLE NIJHUIS

> The dream is an inexhaustible, inexpensive, and nonpolluting source of energy—a dream right now because, for instance, about 80% of the electricity generated in the United States comes from fossil fuels, but also a reality because of the many kinds of alternate energy sources already in use here and abroad. Many of these are old power sources, such as the wind, revolutionized by new technology. In the following piece from *Audubon*, the freelance writer Michelle Nijhuis discusses some of the pluses and minuses of wind power.

On the Emick family ranch in far southeastern Colorado, a row of antique windmills adorn the entrance road, their delicate wooden blades stilled for the moment. These windmills, some more than a century old, once helped prairie homesteaders pump water out of the ground, sustaining both families and farms. Throughout the Great Plains, such windmills are still a proud symbol of survival—of pioneer persistence in a land often too hot or too cold, too dry or too windy.

Today a very different sort of windmill is helping the Emick family survive on the blustery western edge of the Great Plains. In every direction, lines of cylindrical steel towers rise from the landscape, each white column topped by three sleek, swooping blades. These modern wind turbines, which measure more than 300 feet from their base to the tips of their blades, are more than 10 times taller than the frontier-era windmills at their feet.

The 108 turbines in this neighborhood comprise the Colorado Green project, the largest wind farm in Colorado and among the 10 largest in the nation. The project, a joint venture of Shell Wind Energy and PPM Energy (a subsidiary of Scottish-Power), produces roughly enough electricity each year to supply more than 52,000 average homes.

Though the Emicks and other families who lease land to wind-power companies can't divulge the details of their agreements, typical payments range from $3,000 to $6,000 per turbine per year, and generally allow farmers to continue raising crops and livestock among the towers. For agricultural families, which face the vagaries of rainfall and commodity prices, the reliable additional income is welcome. It can help them keep their farms afloat—and keep land relatively undeveloped, in some cases preserving both wildlife habitat and open vistas.

Small farmers are far from the only fans of wind energy. Wind farms in the 5 United States now have a combined capacity of more than 9,000 megawatts, generating enough electricity to power approximately 2.3 million homes. . . . While wind currently provides less than 1 percent of the country's total energy needs, many states are looking to increase their supplies of renewable energy, helping to make wind the nation's second-fastest-growing source of electricity (natural gas is tops).

Multinationals continue to make significant investments in wind power. GE Energy built well more than half of the new turbines in the United States last year, and Goldman Sachs, one of the world's largest investment banking firms, recently purchased a wind-power development company now called Horizon Wind Energy.

Meanwhile, the U.S. Department of Energy has set a goal of helping at least 30 states increase their wind-power generating capacity to 100 megawatts each by 2010.

While consumers have long paid a premium for wind power, high natural gas and coal prices are enhancing wind's appeal. Last year in Colorado and in Austin, Texas, the price of wind power dipped below the price of traditional energy sources, and utility customers of all political stripes flocked to sign up for it.

If wind power dilutes our diet of coal and other fossil fuels, it will reduce air pollution, and even cushion the devastating, and increasingly apparent, effects of global warming. "It's critical to have a sense of urgency about dealing with global climate challenge in general, and about displacing coal in particular," says Ralph Cavanagh, an expert on renewable energy at the Natural Resources Defense Council (NRDC). "Wind is a very important part of that equation."

For many conservationists, however, wind power remains an uncomfortable subject. It's well known that wind turbines kill both birds and bats, though exactly how often—and why—these deaths occur remains poorly understood. Wildlife advocates hope they can push for more research, better planning, and more stringent oversight of wind farms without sabotaging the industry's hard-won momentum.

Much of the current controversy over wind power and wildlife stems from a 10 place called Altamont Pass, a line of golden, oak-studded hills on the eastern outskirts of the San Francisco Bay Area. The Altamont Wind Resource Area, established in the early 1980s, was one of the first modern wind farms in the nation, and a visit to Altamont is a one-stop tour of the history of wind power.

On one grassy hillside stands a row of closely spaced "eggbeater" turbines, each with three busily spinning blades mounted on a latticed steel tower. Arrayed on another slope are the smooth, solid towers of newer turbines, much like those on the Emick family ranch in Colorado. Although the blades of these turbines turn more slowly than those of their smaller predecessors, each enormous turbine can generate 1.5 megawatts of power, more than twice that produced by older models. In all, more than 5,000 turbines crowd into Altamont Pass, generating enough electricity to serve some 100,000 homes.

But these turbines are believed to kill more birds of prey than any other wind farm in the world. Beginning in the late 1980s biologists reported that large numbers of golden eagles, hawks, and other raptors were flying into the spinning blades at Altamont, and dying as a result. Wind-energy companies tried many measures to limit the damage, such as installing chicken wire on the latticed towers to discourage perching. But a recent five-year study by the California Energy Commission estimated that every year up to 1,300 raptors are killed at Altamont, including more than a hundred golden eagles. . . .

The farms and ranches of the West and Midwest are now favored homes for wind turbines, and so far they seem to be relatively safe for both raptors and songbirds. "The bird mortality we're seeing is lower than what's been seen at Altamont," says Tim Cullinan, director of science and bird conservation for Audubon Washington and a wildlife biologist. Cullinan is working with the U.S. Fish and Wildlife Service and other stakeholders such as the American Wind Energy Association and the International Association of Fish and Wildlife Agencies to strengthen siting standards for wind facilities nationwide. . . .

Even if biologists underestimate the number of birds killed by turbines, the damage is surely smaller, in orders of magnitude, than the numbers killed in other ways. While a 2001 study surmised that some 10,000 to 40,000 birds die in wind turbines each year, the U.S. Fish and Wildlife Service contends that these numbers are out of date and that the true mortality figures are much higher. Still, an estimated 100 million birds are killed a year by hunting housecats, and as many as 60 million die from collisions with cars and trucks.

Yet if the wind industry continues to boom, turbine numbers multiply, and the 15 gaps in research persist, it is possible that collisions with turbines—and construction associated with wind farms—will become a more widespread and substantial threat, particularly for threatened and endangered species. "The fear is that with all the new wind farms rolling out, there is a new Altamont being created today," says Greg Butcher, National Audubon's director of bird conservation. "But because we don't have the data, we just don't know about it."

When wildlife researchers have looked closely at wind farms, disturbing numbers have emerged. One 2003 study spent seven months compiling bat fatalities at a wind-power site in the West Virginia mountains. Researchers found, to their surprise, that the 44 turbines killed as many as 4,000 migratory bats. Similarly grim findings have since been reported at wind farms in Pennsylvania and Tennessee, raising the possibility that significant bat kills are a regional or even national phenomenon.

The three wind farms in question stand on forested Appalachian ridges, and Ed Arnett, a conservation scientist for Bat Conservation International, speculates that tree-roosting bats hunt insects in the clearings around the turbines. But because the wind industry has only a handful of bat studies to draw on, the reasons for the kills are unclear, the number of species involved uncertain, and no one is sure how to mitigate the impacts at existing or future sites. "There's a huge dearth of research," Arnett says. "What we do know is that these are long-lived species with low reproductive rates, so a new source of mortality could drive them into serious declines very quickly."

Other researchers are concerned that proliferating wind turbines will take a heavy toll on night-migrating songbirds or ground-nesting birds. A 2004 study, led by Robert Robel, a biology professor at Kansas State University, found that roads and other infrastructure disturb ground-nesting species such as the lesser-prairie chicken, a candidate for federal listing as an endangered species. Again, though, the questions far outnumber the answers.

In a 2005 Government Accountability Office report to Congress summarizing the research on wind farms and wildlife impacts, the authors describe "significant gaps in the literature" that "make it difficult for scientists to draw conclusions about wind power's impact on wildlife in general.". . .

So conservationists find themselves in a tough spot. How can they support and 20 encourage the rapid spread of wind power—our most promising source of clean, renewable energy—while ensuring that the industry minimizes its damage to birds and other wildlife?

"We can't lose sight of the larger benefits of wind," says Audubon Washington's Tim Cullinan. "The direct environmental impacts of wind get a lot of attention, because there are dead bodies on the ground. But nobody ever finds the bodies of the birds killed by global warming, or by oil drilling on the North Slope of Alaska. They're out there, but we don't see them.". . .

The solution to this dilemma, say many conservationists, begins with early, consistent involvement in project planning. "Once those turbines go in," says biologist Pete Bloom, "they don't come down." To encourage early consideration of wildlife, environmental groups have developed guidelines and policies for wind development. Audubon Washington's guidelines, for instance, call for several seasons of bird surveys and other in-depth wildlife studies at proposed wind-power sites, and support statewide or multi-state planning efforts for wind facilities. . . .

By asking the right questions at the right time, conservationists can help wind power continue its growth and fulfill its promise. They can also share in the building enthusiasm for wind's wide-ranging benefits. Farmer and rancher Greg Emick, who grew up on his family's land, guesses that his ancestors—immigrants from Germany who arrived in Colorado nearly 100 years ago—would be pleased by the towering wind turbines that rise from the land they once homesteaded. "They always thought the prairie would be good for more than just raising cattle and growing a little bit of crop," says Emick, as he listens to the steady swoosh of the gigantic turbine blades above his head. "But I don't think they ever imagined we could sell the wind."

FOR DISCUSSION

1. As the author emphasizes, wind energy has developed far past the old windmill on the family farm and become big business. What positive signs do you detect in the significant economic incentives for wind power?

2. When we compare 40,000 birds killed annually by wind turbines with the 100 million that cats kill or the 60 million lost to being hit by vehicles, we may be tempted to dismiss the damage done by the turbines. But other details in the article show that bird and bat mortality may be more significant than the raw numbers indicate. What details indicate this? How can we best reduce this problem to a minimum?

3. Because the author is writing for conservationists whose concern is wind power's impact on wildlife and habitats, she says little about the main objection to wind turbines: many people consider them unsightly and take the NIMBY (not in my backyard) position. In view of the obvious pluses to wind power, how serious do you feel this objection is?

FOR RESEARCH AND CONVINCING

As "Selling the Wind" shows, no form of energy is without drawbacks, and some of the negatives can be quite serious, such as the radioactive waste from nuclear power plants. Nevertheless, we must give up or greatly reduce our dependence on fossil fuels. For this to happen, the general public must strongly support alternate energy sources.

Choose one of the many alternate sources—wind, water, geothermal, nuclear, hydrogen, biodiesel, ethanol, and so on—and do enough research to understand the advantages and disadvantages. Then write an editorial for your local or school newspaper urging support for the energy source. Be sure to deal with the negatives honestly, arguing either that they must be tolerated or that measures can be taken to remedy or reduce them.

FOR MEDIATION

In practical terms, no way of reducing global warming can work without negotiation among conflicting interests. Even at the personal and private level, individuals have to balance money and convenience against environmental concerns. At the public level are situations like the one Nijhuis discusses—the value of wind power vs. the concerns for species loss and aesthetics. The various interests have to be fitted together somehow.

Imagine you are an advocate for wind power and that you are addressing an audience of conservationists and ordinary citizens who oppose wind turbines in their community. Compose the text of a speech that mediates—that firmly advocates increased use of wind power but does so in a way that respects and accommodates, as much as possible, the concerns of your audience. You may need to do research on wind power to find the information and lines of argument you need.

Ten Personal Solutions

UNION OF CONCERNED SCIENTISTS

> We tend to think of global warming as a large-scale problem involving public issues such as the generation of electric power. But much of the solution is personal and small-scale, a matter of what you and I choose to do or not do in our daily lives. The suggestions in the following article (see www.ucsusa.org) are only a few of the many choices we can make.

Individual choices can have an impact on global climate change. Reducing your family's heat-trapping emissions does not mean forgoing modern conveniences; it means making smart choices and using energy-efficient products, which may require an additional investment up front, but often pay you back in energy savings within a couple of years.

Since Americans' per capita emissions of heat-trapping gases is 5.6 tons—more than double the amount of western Europeans—we can all make choices that will greatly reduce our families' global warming impact.

1. **The car you drive: the most important personal climate decision.** When you buy your next car, look for the one with the best fuel economy in its class. Each gallon of gas you use releases 25 pounds of heat-trapping carbon dioxide (CO_2) into the atmosphere. Better gas mileage not only reduces global warming, but will also save you thousands of dollars at the pump over the life of the vehicle. Compare the fuel economy of the cars you're considering and look for new technologies like hybrid engines.

2. **Choose clean power.** More than half the electricity in the United States comes from polluting coal-fired power plants. And power plants are the single largest source of heat-trapping gas. None of us can live without electricity, but in some states, you can switch to electricity companies that provide 50 to 100 percent renewable energy. (For more information go to Green-e.org.)

3. **Look for Energy Star.** When it comes time to replace appliances, look for the Energy Star label on new appliances (refrigerators, freezers, furnaces, air conditioners, and water heaters use the most energy). These items may cost a bit more initially, but the energy savings will pay back the extra investment within a couple of years. Household energy savings really can make a difference: If each household in the United States replaced its existing appliances with the most efficient models available, we would save $15 billion in energy costs and eliminate 175 million tons of heat-trapping gases.

4. **Unplug a freezer.** One of the quickest ways to reduce your global warming impact is to unplug the extra refrigerator or freezer you rarely use (except when you need it for holidays and parties). This can reduce the typical family's carbon dioxide emissions by nearly 10 percent.

5. **Get a home energy audit.** Take advantage of the free home energy audits offered by many utilities. Simple measures, such as installing a programmable

thermostat to replace your old dial unit or sealing and insulating heating and cooling ducts, can each reduce a typical family's carbon dioxide emissions by about 5 percent.

6. **Light bulbs matter.** If every household in the United States replaced one regular light bulb with an energy-saving model, we could reduce global warming pollution by more than 90 billion pounds over the life of the bulbs; the same as taking 6.3 million cars off the road. So, replace your incandescent bulbs with more efficient compact fluorescents, which now come in all shapes and sizes. You'll be doing your share to cut back on heat-trapping pollution and you'll save money on your electric bills and light bulbs.

7. **Think before you drive.** If you own more than one vehicle, use the less fuel-efficient one only when you can fill it with passengers. Driving a full minivan may be kinder to the environment than two midsize cars. Whenever possible, join a carpool or take mass transit.

8. **Buy good wood.** When buying wood products, check for labels that indicate the source of the timber. Supporting forests that are managed in a sustainable fashion makes sense for biodiversity, and it may make sense for the climate too. Forests that are well managed are more likely to store carbon effectively because more trees are left standing and carbon-storing soils are less disturbed.

9. **Plant a tree.** You can also make a difference in your own backyard. Get a group in your neighborhood together and contact your local arborist or urban forester about planting trees on private property and public land. In addition to storing carbon, trees planted in and around urban areas and residences can provide much-needed shade in the summer, reducing energy bills and fossil fuel use.

10. **Let policymakers know you are concerned about global warming.** Our elected officials and business leaders need to hear from concerned citizens.

FOR DISCUSSION

1. The piece claims that each American produces 5.6 tons of greenhouse gas emissions each year—double the European amount. In your view, how much of this difference is a matter of circumstances, such as the size of the United States, and how much is the result of lifestyle choices that could be changed?

2. What action have you taken to reduce your personal carbon footprint? What in the list of ten suggestions appeals to you most? What has the least appeal? Do you have resistance to any of the ten items? If there are changes you don't want to make, such as the car you drive, what could you do to reduce carbon emissions in other ways?

FOR INQUIRY AND CONVINCING

Besides taking action at the personal and home or family level, each of us can urge greater concern for the environment in local institutions and workplaces. Universities and colleges, for instance, are not always models of efficient energy use. A growing student movement in the United States aims to address this problem.

As a class project, find out what your university or college is doing and plans to do to use energy more efficiently. As part of this research, walk around campus and tour the buildings. Is the level of heating and cooling appropriate? Are lights left on in rooms that are empty? Take note of anything that seems wasteful to you.

Discuss the results of your research and work together as a class to create a document to present to the central administration, urging whatever improvements the class thinks might make a difference.

Consuming Earth's Gifts

WILLIAM F. RUDDIMAN

Global warming has gotten so much attention recently that we are apt to forget that it is only one of many environmental problems. William Ruddiman, retired professor of environmental science at the University of Virginia, reminds us of another big problem—exhaustion of the Earth's resources, including water and topsoil. The following essay comes from his very influential book, *Plows, Plagues, and Petroleum* (Princeton UP, 2005), which traces human impact on climate back to the invention of agriculture, about 10,000 years ago.

Even though I have made the case that future climate change is likely to be large . . . , I do not rank the oncoming global warming as the greatest environmental problem of our time. Other environmental issues seem to me far more immediate and pressing, and in the future I suspect our concerns will focus heavily on the eventual depletion of key resources.

. . . Humankind has been steadily transforming Earth's surface for some 8,000 years, initially in Eurasia and later on all continents. Initially, we caused these transformations by clearing land for farming; later, other aspects of civilized life joined farming as important causes of this transformation. Well before the industrial era, the cumulative result over many millennia was an enormous loss of what had been "natural" on this planet.

During the 1800s and 1900s, human population increased from 1 billion to 6 billion, an explosion unprecedented in human history. This rise came about because new sanitary standards and medicines reduced the incidence of disease and because human ingenuity led to innovations in agriculture that fed ever-larger numbers of people. As a result, our already sizable impact on Earth's surface increased at a much faster rate. . . .

By most estimates, the explosive population increase still under way will end near AD 2050 as global population levels out at some 9–10 billion people, or roughly 50 percent more people than now. A major reason for the predicted stabilization will be the increase in affluence that has historically resulted in fewer children per family. . . .

On the other hand, as affluence and technology continue to spread, increased 5 pressures on the environment will occur for that reason alone. If a billion or more people in China and India begin to live the way Americans and Europeans do now, their additional use of Earth's resources will be enormous. Even without population increases, humanity will continue to alter the environment in new ways.

The cumulative impact of so many millennia of transforming Earth's surface has inevitably come at a cost to nature. Many of the problems our actions have created have been described elsewhere by ecologists and others knowledgeable about the environment. In the process of transforming Earth's surface, we have fragmented the space that ecosystems require, transported species from the places they belong to regions where their presence is invasive to existing flora and fauna, and caused the extinction of species in numbers that no one really knows. . . .

Those with environmental concerns have in recent decades added a new argument to their side of this battle. Ecologists have coined the term "ecosystem services" to describe processes that nature provides for free and that have real economic value. For example, trees and other vegetation on hill slopes trap rainfall that would otherwise flow away and erode soils. As the retained water passes into subsurface layers, the soils slowly filter it and transform it into clean, drinkable water that can be retrieved from wells or springs. Some of the water flows into wetlands and is further cleansed there. Nature gives us a large supply of clean water.

But when the trees are cut or the wetlands are filled in, these free services are lost, and society must pick up the cost of doing nature's job. . . . The loss of nature's subsurface cleansing of water requires municipal water treatment plants and home water filters, but these remedies rarely return water of the quality nature once provided. So we buy bottled water shipped from other regions or even other continents. All in all, we pay an economic price to replace ecosystem services. Ecologists rightly argue that the costs incurred from losing ecosystem services must be included in complete "economic" analyses of land-use decisions. . . .

Probably as a result of my long interest in Earth's climate history, my own concerns about the future tend to focus on a related set of longer-term problems—"gifts" that nature has provided us through slow-acting processes that took place well back in Earth's past and that cannot be replaced once they are consumed.

My concern about these gifts is simple: When these resources run low or 10 run out, how will we find comparably inexpensive replacements? . . . We live today in an era of remarkably cheap oil, gas, and coal. It took nature hundreds of millions of years to create the world's supply of these resources, by burying organic carbon in swamps and inland seas and shallow coastal areas, and by cooking the carbon at just the right temperature and pressure. We only began using these resources in significant amounts in the middle 1800s, and yet the first signs are already at hand that the world will reach the year of peak oil production and consumption in just one or two decades, if not sooner. World supplies of natural gas will last a bit longer, and coal for a few centuries. I wonder whether we will ever find a substitute even remotely as inexpensive as these carbon gifts. We are investigating alternative sources of energy, but as of now none of them seems likely to be as widely available and as inexpensive as the solar energy stored in carbon-based fuels.

At some point early in the current century, gradual depletion of this vital commodity will presumably become a major economic issue. Once world oil production begins to decline by 1 percent or so per year, it seems likely to add a measurable cost to the functioning of the global economy, in effect adding a new form of built-in "inflation" on top of the normal kind. Fuel for cars and trucks is not the only concern; a vast array of products made from petrochemicals has become part of the basic fabric of our lives. All of them will cost more.

I also wonder about the long-term supply of water. With more than half of the supply of water from surface run-off already in use for irrigation and human consumption, we have for years been pumping water from aquifers deep in the ground, especially in arid and semi-arid regions into which many people are now moving. The water stored in the deep aquifers of the American West was put there tens to hundreds of thousands of years ago by melt water flowing southward from the margins of the great ice sheets, and by snow and rain water that fell during climatic conditions much wetter than today. In recent decades, the level of those aquifers has been falling as we extract water from depths where it cannot be quickly replenished by nature.

Pumping ever deeper will require more carbon fuel, which in turn will become more expensive. Gradually, the water from greater depths will contain ever-larger concentrations of dissolved salts that will be left on irrigated fields, making agriculture more difficult. Eventually, we will exhaust the useable water in these underground reservoirs. Little by little, agriculture will probably retreat from the arid high-plains regions of the West back toward the midcontinent regions nearer the Mississippi River, where natural rainfall supports agriculture. The same retreat will occur in other regions of extensive groundwater use across the globe.

I have no idea when these groundwater limits will be reached in each region, but new reports suggest the start of the problem may be close at hand in some regions. To conserve water, the municipal government of Santa Fe, New Mexico, recently began requiring home builders to retrofit six existing houses for improved water economy to offset the added water use in each new house built. In the Oklahoma-Texas panhandle region, oilman and investor T. Boone Pickens has been buying up the rights to groundwater in the glacial-age Ogallala aquifer. When municipal governments put extra burdens on local builders, and when wealthy oil tycoons invest in underground water as a scarce commodity, problems must be looming. . . .

I also wonder about topsoil. The most productive farms in the American Mid- 15 west can thank the ice sheets for their topsoil. Ice repeatedly gouged bedrock and scraped older soils in north-central Canada and pushed the eroded debris south, where streams of glacial melt water carried it into river valleys, and winds blew it across the western prairies. During the 1800s, farmers began breaking up the tough top layer of prairie sod, which had been held in place by extremely deep-rooted plants, and farming began at a scale the world had never seen. The midwestern American agricultural miracle has been one of the great success stories in human history.

But this great success came at a price. Repeated tilling exposed the rich prairie soils to decades of dry winds and floods. Estimates are that half of the original topsoil layer in the American Midwest has been lost, most of it flowing down the Mississippi River to the Gulf of Mexico. In the late 1900s, farmers began adapting new techniques that have reduced, but not stopped, the rapid removal of this precious gift. These methods and other conservation efforts will keep us from losing soil as rapidly as before, but slower rates of loss will continue to deplete soils that no longer have the natural protection provided by prairie vegetation.

Farmers and farm corporations now spend enormous sums of money every year on manufactured fertilizers to replenish nutrients lost to crop production and natural erosion. These fertilizers are produced from petrochemical (petroleum) products, which again brings us back to the gradual depletion (and increased expense) of carbon-based products in the coming decades. Once again, it will be a very long wait indeed until nature gets around to making more topsoil, probably 50,000 to 100,000 years until the next ice sheet bulldozes the next rich load southward. . . .

With no wish to be alarmist about the slow depletion of these many gifts, especially carbon-based energy sources, I still wonder: What will humankind do when they grow scarce? Will our resourcefulness as a species open up new avenues? Or will the depletion be a true loss? I have no clue what answers to these vital questions the distant future will bring.

FOR DISCUSSION

1. In your own words, describe what Ruddiman means by "ecosystem services." He points to the economic costs when technology has to replace what nature once provided freely, as "gifts" to us. What other costs are involved?

2. One of the author's concerns is depletion of fossil fuels or prohibitively expensive supplies. He understands the role of such sources of energy in global warming, so why is he concerned?

3. Water is another of nature's "gifts." Why, according to the author, should we be worried about it?

4. Why is topsoil erosion a problem? Are there other ecological problems connected with it? What, for instance, happens when topsoil is washed down a river and deposited in the ocean?

FOR RESEARCH, DISCUSSION, AND PERSUASION

Environmental problems seldom have a single cause. We're losing coral reefs, for example, through a combination of forces: ocean warming, ocean acidification (caused by CO_2 from the atmosphere turning into carbonic acid), topsoil erosion (the soil smothers the reefs), pollution from many other sources, and the carelessness of boaters and divers.

Do research on coral reefs—or on rain forests, which are also in deep trouble. Investigate all the causes of their destruction or degradation, including but not limited to global warming. Then write an article aiming to raise awareness of the value of what we are losing, the complex causes, and the necessity of taking immediate action. Address your U.S. congressperson or senator.

FOR FURTHER READING

Flannery, Tim. *The Weather Makers: How Man Is Changing the Climate and What It Means for Life on Earth*. New York: Atlantic Monthly P, 2005.

Gore, Al. *An Inconvenient Truth*. Emmaus, PA: Rodale, 2006.

Houghton, John. *Global Warming: The Complete Briefing*. Cambridge: Cambridge UP, 1997.

Linden, Eugene. *The Winds of Change: Climate, Weather, and the Destruction of Civilizations*. New York: Simon and Schuster, 2006.

National Aeronautics and Space Administration (NASA) Web site: www.nasa.gov

Newell, Peter. *Climate for Change: Non-State Actors and the Global Politics of the Greenhouse.* Cambridge: Cambridge UP, 2000.

National Oceanic and Atmospheric Administration Web site: www.noaa.gov

Ruddiman, William F. *Plows, Plagues, and Petroleum: How Humans Took Control of Climate.* Princeton: Princeton UP, 2005.

Union of Concerned Scientists Web site: www.ucsusa.org

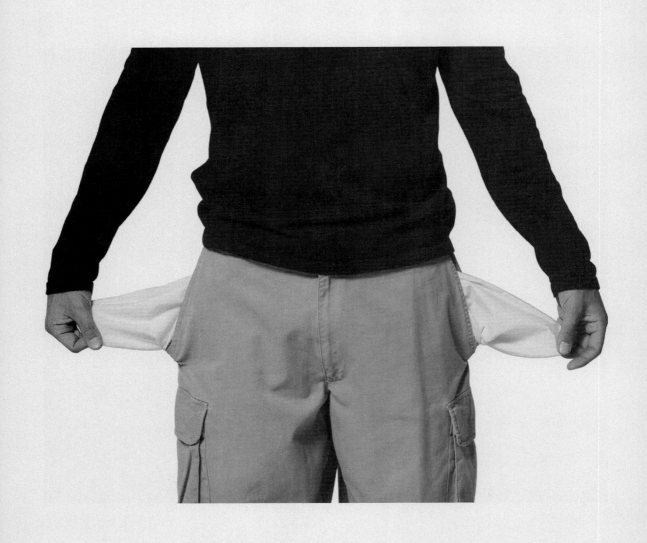

Twenty-Something: Issues Facing Young Adults

About ten years ago, young adults were called Generation X, after the title of a novel whose main characters wanted to distance themselves from society in order to focus on developing their own identity. For no reason other than alphabetical order, young people today are known as Generation Y. But other labels have also been attached to people now in their late teens and twenties, and these labels are more descriptive of behavior patterns characteristic of the group. In news articles, they have been referred to "twixters," "adultes-cents," "kidults," and "boomerang kids." These terms describe an awkward combination of child and adult; "boomerang kids" implies parents' resent-ment toward adult children who return home when they should be on their own. Social scientists offer up gentler characterizations, such as "emerging adults," but just the fact that so much research is devoted to young adults implies that there is a problem. Is there something wrong with people 18 to about 30 now? What exactly is going on?

What's going on is clear and indisputable. A generation ago, eighteen was the beginning of adulthood, and the average woman married at about twenty-one and had a child by about twenty-two. The average for both is now five years later, and the trend is toward later still. It's true that more and more adults in their twenties are living with their parents, in many cases after college is behind them—twice as many as were living at home thirty years ago. And there are many other signs that full adulthood occurs significantly later than it used to.

But is this a problem? If it is, what should be done?

Our first article was the cover story for an issue of *Time* magazine, which shows how much popular concern there is about young adults not growing up. The author sees "twixters" as a problem and blames it on a culture that presents adulthood as a grind, with crushing responsibilities and no opportunity for fun. The next two authors likewise see a problem, but blame it on economics. Basically, young adults want to grow up but can't because of the high cost of college, which often leaves them deeply in debt; no jobs or bad jobs with low salaries and no benefits; the high cost of rent and of buying a first home; and so on. Both authors think that young adults need a powerful organization, a political action group as potent as AARP is to retired people.

The economic situation *is* grim, as no one needs to tell young adults who have been "out there" at all. It may make sense, then, as many experts contend, for parents who can afford it to welcome even college-educated children to return home until they can develop the financial means for independence. Furthermore, because opportunity depends often now on advanced degrees, education won't be over for many until at least the middle twenties anyway.

Growing up, of course, has never been easy, and people don't mature at the same rate or in every dimension at the same time. You surely know middle-aged or even older people whom no one would consider less than an adult but who are immature in one or several ways. The issues, then, are many and not always what they appear to be on the surface. Nor do all the numbers you'll encounter tell the whole story. There are many facets of growing up that can't be quantified. In any case, what *adulthood* and *maturity* mean are worth pondering at any age and regardless of any particular set of circumstances. "What do you want to be when you grow up?" is not a question that can be answered just by naming an occupation. It involves everything we are and strive to become.

Grow Up? Not So Fast: Meet the Twixters

LEV GROSSMAN[1]

As most popular journalism does, this piece from *Time* (January 24, 2005) plays to the prejudices of its readers—that is, to an older generation's point of view. It depicts the situation of many young adults better than it understands it. Yet the author does point to sources that grasp current conditions better and calls attention to something we can't ignore, the role of culture, especially popular culture, in shaping attitudes toward growing up. He also draws attention to the big commercial stake in the young adult market, also important in understanding the present state of affairs.

All in all, then, the article is worth reading, and reveals how young adults are viewed by many older people today, including their own parents.

Michele, Ellen, Nathan, Corinne, Marcus and Jennie are friends. All of them live in Chicago. They go out three nights a week, sometimes more. Each of them has had several jobs since college; Ellen is on her 17th, counting internships, since 1996. They don't own homes. They change apartments frequently. None of them are married, none have children. All of them are from 24 to 28 years old.

Thirty years ago, people like Michele, Ellen, Nathan, Corinne, Marcus and Jennie didn't exist, statistically speaking. Back then, the median age for an American woman to get married was 21. She had her first child at 22. Now it all takes longer. It's 25 for the wedding and 25 for baby. It appears to take young people longer to graduate from college, settle into careers and buy their first homes. What are they waiting for? Who are these permanent adolescents, these twentysomething Peter Pans? And why can't they grow up?

Everybody knows a few of them—full-grown men and women who still live with their parents, who dress and talk and party as they did in their teens, hopping from job to job and date to date, having fun but seemingly going nowhere. Ten years ago, we might have called them Generation X, or slackers, but those labels don't quite fit anymore. This isn't just a trend, a temporary fad or a generational hiccup. This is a much larger phenomenon, of a different kind and a different order.

Social scientists are starting to realize that a permanent shift has taken place in the way we live our lives. In the past, people moved from childhood to adolescence and from adolescence to adulthood, but today there is a new, intermediate phase along the way. The years from 18 until 25 and even beyond have become a distinct and separate life stage, a strange, transitional never-never land between adolescence and adulthood in which people stall for a few extra years, putting off the iron cage of adult responsibility that constantly threatens to crash down on them. They're betwixt and between. You could call them twixters.

Where did the twixters come from? And what's taking them so long to get 5 where they're going? Some of the sociologists, psychologists and demographers who study this new life stage see it as a good thing. The twixters aren't lazy, the argument goes, they're reaping the fruit of decades of American affluence and social liberation. This new period is a chance for young people to savor the pleasures of irresponsibility, search their souls and choose their life paths. But more

[1]With reporting by Nadia Mustafa; Deirdre van Dyk/New York; Kristin Kloberdanz/Chicago; Marc Schultz/Atlanta

historically and economically minded scholars see it differently. They are worried that twixters aren't growing up because they can't. Those researchers fear that whatever cultural machinery used to turn kids into grownups has broken down, that society no longer provides young people with the moral backbone and the financial wherewithal to take their rightful places in the adult world. Could growing up be harder than it used to be?

The sociologists, psychologists, economists and others who study this age group have many names for this new phase of life—"youthhood," "adultescence"—and they call people in their 20s "kidults" and "boomerang kids," none of which have quite stuck. Terri Apter, a psychologist at the University of Cambridge in England and the author of *The Myth of Maturity,* calls them "thresholders."

Apter became interested in the phenomenon in 1994, when she noticed her students struggling and flailing more than usual after college. Parents were baffled when their expensively educated, otherwise well-adjusted 23-year-old children wound up sobbing in their old bedrooms, paralyzed by indecision. "Legally, they're adults, but they're on the threshold, the doorway to adulthood, and they're not going through it," Apter says. The percentage of 26-year-olds living with their parents has nearly doubled since 1970, from 11% to 20%, according to Bob Schoeni, a professor of economics and public policy at the University of Michigan.

Jeffrey Arnett, a developmental psychologist at the University of Maryland, favors "emerging adulthood" to describe this new demographic group, and the term is the title of his new book on the subject. His theme is that the twixters are misunderstood. It's too easy to write them off as overgrown children, he argues. Rather, he suggests, they're doing important work to get themselves ready for adulthood. "This is the one time of their lives when they're not responsible for anyone else or to anyone else," Arnett says. "So they have this wonderful freedom to really focus on their own lives and work on becoming the kind of person they want to be." In his view, what looks like incessant, hedonistic play is the twixters' way of trying on jobs and partners and personalities and making sure that when they do settle down, they do it the right way, their way. It's not that they don't take adulthood seriously; they take it so seriously, they're spending years carefully choosing the right path into it.

But is that all there is to it? Take a giant step backward, look at the history and the context that led up to the rise of the twixters, and you start to wonder, Is it that they don't want to grow up, or is it that the rest of society won't let them?

SCHOOL DAZE

Matt Swann is 27. He took 6 ½ years to graduate from the University of Georgia. 10 When he finally finished, he had a brand-spanking-new degree in cognitive science, which he describes as a wide-ranging interdisciplinary field that covers cognition, problem solving, artificial intelligence, linguistics, psychology, philosophy and anthropology. All of which is pretty cool, but its value in today's job market is not clear. "Before the 90s maybe, it seemed like a smart guy could do a lot of things," Swann says. "Kids used to go to college to get educated. That's what I did, which I think now was a bit naive. Being smart after college doesn't really mean anything. 'Oh, good, you're smart. Unfortunately your productivity's s——, so we're going to have to fire you.'"

College is the institution most of us entrust to watch over the transition to adulthood, but somewhere along the line that transition has slowed to a crawl. In a TIME poll of people ages 18 to 29, only 32% of those who attended college left school by age 21. In fact, the average college student takes five years to finish. The era of the four-year college degree is all but over.

Swann graduated in 2002 as a newly minted cognitive scientist, but the job he finally got a few months later was as a waiter in Atlanta. He waited tables for the next year and a half. It proved to be a blessing in disguise. Swann says he learned more real-world skills working in restaurants than he ever did in school. "It taught me how to deal with people. What you learn as a waiter is how to treat people fairly, especially when they're in a bad situation." That's especially valuable in his current job as an insurance-claims examiner.

There are several lessons about twixters to be learned from Swann's tale. One is that most colleges are seriously out of step with the real world in getting students ready to become workers in the postcollege world. Vocational schools like DeVry and Strayer, which focus on teaching practical skills, are seeing a mini-boom. Their enrollment grew 48% from 1996 to 2000. More traditional schools are scrambling to give their courses a practical spin. In the fall, Hendrix College in Conway, Ark., will introduce a program called the Odyssey project, which the school says will encourage students to "think outside the book" in areas like "professional and leadership development" and "service to the world." Dozens of other schools have set up similar initiatives.

As colleges struggle to get their students ready for real-world jobs, they are charging more for what they deliver. The resulting debt is a major factor in keeping twixters from moving on and growing up. Thirty years ago, most financial aid came in the form of grants, but now the emphasis is on lending, not on giving. Recent college graduates owe 85% more in student loans than their counterparts of a decade ago, according to the Center for Economic and Policy Research. In TIME's poll, 66% of those surveyed owed more than $10,000 when they graduated, and 5% owed more than $100,000. (And this says nothing about the credit-card companies that bombard freshmen with offers for cards that students then cheerfully abuse. Demos, a public-policy group, says credit-card debt for Americans 18 to 24 more than doubled from 1992 to 2001.) The longer it takes to pay off those loans, the longer it takes twixters to achieve the financial independence that's crucial to attaining an adult identity, not to mention the means to get out of their parents' house.

Meanwhile, those expensive, time-sucking college diplomas have become worth 15 less than ever. So many more people go to college now—a 53% increase since 1970—that the value of a degree on the job market has been diluted. The advantage in wages for college-degree holders hasn't risen significantly since the late 1990s, according to the Bureau of Labor Statistics. To compensate, a lot of twixters go back to school for graduate and professional degrees. Swann, for example, is planning to head back to business school to better his chances in the insurance game. But piling on extra degrees costs precious time and money and pushes adulthood even further into the future.

WORK IN PROGRESS

Kate Galantha, 29, spent seven years working her way through college, transferring three times. After she finally graduated from Columbia College in Chicago (major: undeclared) in 2001, she moved to Portland, Ore., and went to work as a nanny and as an assistant to a wedding photographer. A year later she jumped back to Chicago, where she got a job in a flower shop. It was a full-time position with real benefits, but she soon burned out and headed for the territories, a.k.a. Madison, Wis. "I was really busy but not accomplishing anything," she says. "I didn't want to stay just for a job."

She had no job offers in Madison, and the only person she knew there was her older sister, but she had nothing tying her to Chicago (her boyfriend had moved to Europe) and she needed a change. The risk paid off. She got a position as an assistant at a photo studio, and she loves it. "I decided it was more important to figure out what to do and to be in a new environment," Galantha says. "It's exciting, and I'm in a place where I can accomplish everything. But starting over is the worst."

Galantha's frenetic hopping from school to school, job to job and city to city may look like aimless wandering. (She has moved six times since 1999. Her father calls her and her sister gypsies.) But *Emerging Adulthood*'s Arnett—and Galantha—see it differently. To them, the period from 18 to 25 is a kind of sandbox, a chance to build castles and knock them down, experiment with different careers, knowing that none of it really counts. After all, this is a world of overwhelming choice: there are 40 kinds of coffee beans at Whole Foods Market, 205 channels on DirecTV, 15 million personal ads on Match.com and 800,000 jobs on Monster.com. Can you blame Galantha for wanting to try them all? She doesn't want to play just the hand she has been dealt. She wants to look through the whole deck. "My problem is I'm really overstimulated by everything," Galantha says. "I feel there's too much information out there at all times. There are too many doors, too many people, too much competition."

Twixters expect to jump laterally from job to job and place to place until they find what they're looking for. The stable, quasi-parental bond between employer and employee is a thing of the past, and neither feels much obligation to make the relationship permanent. "They're well aware of the fact that they will not work for the same company for the rest of their life," says Bill Frey, a demographer with the Brookings Institution, a think tank based in Washington. "They don't think long-term about health care or Social Security. They're concerned about their careers and immediate gratification."

Twixters expect a lot more from a job than a paycheck. Maybe it's a reaction 20 to the greed-is-good 1980s or to the whatever-is-whatever apathy of the early 1990s. More likely, it's the way they were raised, by parents who came of age in the 1960s as the first generation determined to follow its bliss, who want their children to change the world the way they did. Maybe it has to do with advances in medicine. Twixters can reasonably expect to live into their 80s and beyond, so their working lives will be extended accordingly and when they choose a career, they know they'll be there for a while. But whatever the cause, twixters are looking for a sense of purpose and importance in their work, something that will add meaning to their lives, and many don't want to rest until they find it. "They're not just looking for a job," Arnett says. "They want something that's more like a calling, that's going to be an expression of their identity." Hedonistic nomads, the twixters may seem, but there's a serious core of idealism in them.

Still, self-actualization is a luxury not everybody can afford, and looking at middle- and upper-class twixters gives only part of the picture. Twixters change jobs often, but they don't all do it for the same reasons, and one twixter's playful experimentation is another's desperate hustling. James Côté is a sociologist at the University of Western Ontario and the author of several books about twixters, including *Generation on Hold* and *Arrested Adulthood.* He believes that the economic bedrock that used to support adolescents on their journey into adulthood has shifted alarmingly. "What we're looking at really began with the collapse of the youth labor market, dating back to the late 70s and early 80s, which made it more difficult for people to get a foothold in terms of financial independence," Côté says. "You need a college degree now just to be where blue-collar people the same age were 20 or 30 years ago, and if you don't have it, then you're way behind." In other words, it's not that twixters don't want to become adults. They just can't afford to.

One way society defines an adult is as a person who is financially independent, with a family and a home. But families and homes cost money, and people in their late teens and early 20s don't make as much as they used to. The current crop of twixters grew up in the 1990s, when the dotcom boom made Internet millions seem just a business proposal away, but in reality they're worse off than the generation that preceded them. Annual earnings among men 25 to 34 with full-time jobs dropped 17% from 1971 to 2002, according to the National Center for Education Statistics. Timothy Smeeding, a professor of economics at Syracuse University, found that only half of Americans in their mid-20s earn enough to support a family, and in TIME'S poll only half of those ages 18 to 29 consider themselves financially independent. Michigan's Schoeni says Americans ages 25 and 26 get an average of $2,323 a year in financial support from their parents.

The transition to adulthood gets tougher the lower you go on the economic and educational ladder. Sheldon Danziger, a public-policy professor at the University of Michigan, found that for male workers ages 25 to 29 with only a high school diploma, the average wage declined 11% from 1975 to 2002. "When I graduated from high school, my classmates who didn't want to go to college could go to the Goodyear plant and buy a house and support a wife and family," says Steve Hamilton of Cornell University's Youth and Work Program. "That doesn't happen anymore." Instead, high school grads are more likely to end up in retail jobs with low pay and minimal benefits, if any. From this end of the social pyramid, Arnett's vision of emerging adulthood as a playground of self-discovery seems a little rosy. The rules have changed, and not in the twixters' favor.

WEDDINGS CAN WAIT

With everything else that's going on—careers to be found, debts to be paid, bars to be hopped—love is somewhat secondary in the lives of the twixters. But that doesn't mean they're cynical about it. Au contraire: among our friends from Chicago— Michele, Ellen, Nathan, Corinne, Marcus and Jennie—all six say they are not ready for marriage yet but do want it someday, preferably with kids. Naturally, all that is comfortably situated in the eternally receding future. Thirty is no longer the looming deadline it once was. In fact, five of the Chicago six see marriage as a decidedly post-30 milestone.

"It's a long way down the road," says Marcus Jones, 28, a comedian who works 25 at Banana Republic by day. "I'm too self-involved. I don't want to bring that into a relationship now." He expects to get married in his mid- to late 30s. "My wife is currently a sophomore in high school," he jokes.

"I want to get married but not soon," says Jennie Jiang, 26, a sixth-grade teacher. "I'm enjoying myself. There's a lot I want to do by myself still."

"I have my career, and I'm too young," says Michele Steele, 26, a TV producer. "It's commitment and sacrifice, and I think it's a hindrance. Lo and behold, people have come to the conclusion that it's not much fun to get married and have kids right out of college."

That attitude is new, but it didn't come out of nowhere. Certainly, the spectacle of the previous generation's mass divorces has something to do with the healthy skepticism shown by the twixters. They will spend a few years looking before they leap, thank you very much. "I fantasize more about sharing a place with someone than about my wedding day," says Galantha, whose parents split when she was 18. "I haven't seen a lot of good marriages."

But if twixters are getting married later, they are missing out on some of the social-support networks that come with having families of their own. To make up for it, they have a special gift for friendship, documented in books like Sasha Cagen's *Quirkyalone* and Ethan Watters' *Urban Tribes,* which asks the not entirely rhetorical question Are friends the new family? They throw cocktail parties and dinner parties. They hold poker nights. They form book groups. They stay in touch constantly and in real time, through social-networking technologies like cell phones, instant messaging, text messaging and online communities like Friendster. They're also close to their parents. TIME's poll showed that almost half of Americans ages 18 to 29 talk to their parents every day.

Marrying late also means that twixters tend to have more sexual partners than 30 previous generations. The situation is analogous to their promiscuous job-hopping behavior—like Goldilocks, they want to find the one that's just right—but it can give them a cynical, promiscuous vibe too. Arnett is worried that if anything, twixters are too romantic. In their universe, romance is totally detached from pragmatic concerns and societal pressures, so when twixters finally do marry, they're going to do it for Love with a capital L and no other reason. "Everybody wants to find their soul mate now," Arnett says, "whereas I think, for my parents' generation—I'm 47—they looked at it much more practically. I think a lot of people are going to end up being disappointed with the person that's snoring next to them by the time they've been married for a few years and they realize it doesn't work that way."

TWIXTER CULTURE

When it comes to social change, pop culture is the most sensitive of seismometers, and it was faster to pick up on the twixters than the cloistered social scientists. Look at the Broadway musical *Avenue Q,* in which puppets dramatize the vagaries of life after graduation. ("I wish I could go back to college," a character sings. "Life was so simple back then.") Look at that little TV show called *Friends,* about six people who put off marriage well into their 30s. Even twice-married Britney Spears fits the profile. For a succinct, albeit cheesy summation of the twixter predicament, you couldn't do much better than her 2001 hit "I'm Not a Girl, Not Yet a Woman."

The producing duo Edward Zwick and Marshall Herskovitz, who created the legendarily zeitgeisty TV series *thirtysomething* and *My So-Called Life,* now have a pilot with ABC called *1/4life,* about a houseful of people in their mid-20s who can't seem to settle down. "When you talk about this period of transition being extended, it's not what people intended to do," Herskovitz says, "but it's a result of the world not being particularly welcoming when they come into it. Lots of people have a difficult time dealing with it, and they try to stay kids as long as they can because they don't know how to make sense of all this. We're interested in this process of finding courage and one's self."

As for movies, a lot of twixters cite *Garden State* as one that really nails their predicament. "I feel like my generation is waiting longer and longer to get married," says Zach Braff, 29, who wrote, directed and starred in the film about a twentysomething actor who comes home for the first time in nine years. "In the past, people got married and got a job and had kids, but now there's a new 10 years that people are using to try and find out what kind of life they want to lead. For a lot of people, the weight of all the possibility is overwhelming."

Pop culture may reflect the changes in our lives, but it also plays its part in shaping them. Marketers have picked up on the fact that twixters on their personal voyages of discovery tend to buy lots of stuff along the way. "They are the optimum market to be going after for consumer electronics, Game Boys, flat-screen TVs, iPods, couture fashion, exotic vacations and so forth," says David Morrison, president of Twentysomething Inc., a marketing consultancy based in Philadelphia. "Most of their needs are taken care of by Mom and Dad, so their income is largely discretionary. [Many twentysomethings] are living at home, but if you look, you'll see flat-screen TVs in their bedrooms and brand-new cars in the driveway." Some twixters may want to grow up, but corporations and advertisers have a real stake in keeping them in a tractable, exploitable, pre-adult state—living at home, spending their money on toys.

LIVING WITH PETER PAN

Maybe the twixters are in denial about growing up, but the rest of society is equally 35 in denial about the twixters. Nobody wants to admit they're here to stay, but that's where all the evidence points. Tom Smith, director of the General Social Survey, a large sociological data-gathering project run by the National Opinion Research Center, found that most people believe that the transition to adulthood should be completed by the age of 26, on average, and he thinks that number is only going up. "In another 10 or 20 years, we're not going to be talking about this as a delay. We're going to be talking about this as a normal trajectory," Smith says. "And we're going to think about those people getting married at 18 and forming families at 19 or 20 as an odd historical pattern."

There may even be a biological basis to all this. The human brain continues to grow and change into the early 20s, according to Abigail Baird, who runs the Laboratory for Adolescent Studies at Dartmouth. "We as a society deem an individual at the age of 18 ready for adult responsibility," Baird points out. "Yet recent evidence suggests that our neuropsychological development is many years from being complete. There's no reason to think 18 is a magic number." How can the twixters be expected to settle down when their gray matter hasn't?

A new life stage is a major change, and the rest of society will have to change to make room for it. One response to this very new phenomenon is extremely old-fashioned: medieval-style apprenticeship programs that give high school graduates a cheaper and more practical alternative to college. In 1996 Jack Smith, then CEO of General Motors, started Automotive Youth Educational Systems (AYES), a program that puts high school kids in shops alongside seasoned car mechanics. More than 7,800 students have tried it, and 98% of them have ended up working at the business where they apprenticed. "I knew this was my best way to get into a dealership," says Chris Rolando, 20, an AYES graduate who works at one in Detroit. "My friends are still at pizza-place jobs and have no idea what to do for a living. I just bought my own house and have a career."

But success stories like Rolando's are rare. Child welfare, the juvenile-justice system, special-education and support programs for young mothers usually cut off at age 18, and most kids in foster care get kicked out at 18 with virtually no safety net. "Age limits are like the time limits for welfare recipients," says Frank Furstenberg, a sociologist who heads a research consortium called the MacArthur Network on Transitions to Adulthood. "They're pushing people off the rolls, but they're not necessarily able to transition into supportive services or connections to other systems." And programs for the poor aren't the only ones that need to grow up with the times. Only 54% of respondents in the TIME poll were insured through their employers. That's a reality that affects all levels of society, and policymakers need to strengthen that safety net.

Most of the problems that twixters face are hard to see, and that makes it harder to help them. Twixters may look as if they have been overindulged, but they could use some judicious support. Apter's research at Cambridge suggests that the more parents sympathize with their twixter children, the more parents take time to discuss their twixters' life goals, the more aid and shelter they offer them, the easier the transition becomes. "Young people know that their material life will not be better than their parents'," Apter says. "They don't expect a safer life than their parents had. They don't expect more secure employment or finances. They have to put in a lot of work just to remain O.K." Tough love may look like the answer, but it's not what twixters need.

The real heavy lifting may ultimately have to happen on the level of the culture 40 itself. There was a time when people looked forward to taking on the mantle of adulthood. That time is past. Now our culture trains young people to fear it. "I don't ever want a lawn," says Swann. "I don't ever want to drive two hours to get to work. I do not want to be a parent. I mean, hell, why would I? There's so much fun to be had while you're young." He does have a point. Twixters have all the privileges of grownups now but only some of the responsibilities. From the point of view of the twixters, upstairs in their childhood bedrooms, snuggled up under their Star Wars comforters, it can look all downhill.

If twixters are ever going to grow up, they need the means to do it—and they will have to want to. There are joys and satisfactions that come with assuming adult responsibility, though you won't see them on *The Real World.* To go to the movies or turn on the TV is to see a world where life ends at 30; these days, every movie is *Logan's Run.* There are few road maps in the popular culture—and to most twixters, this is the only culture—to get twixters where they need to go. If those who are 30 and older want the rest of the world to grow up, they'll have to show the twixters that it's worth their while. "I went to a Poster Children concert, and there were 40-year-olds still rocking," says Jennie Jiang. "It gave me hope."

Lev Grossman, "Grow Up? Not So Fast: Meet the Twixters," *Time,* January 24, 2005. Copyright TIME Inc. Reprinted by permission. TIME is a registered trademark of Time Inc. All rights reserved.

FOR DISCUSSION

1. In paragraph 8 Grossman mentions the developmental psychologist Jeffrey Arnett. In his book *Emerging Adulthood,* Arnett celebrates the "wonderful freedom" of the as-yet-unattached "emerging adults." If you are in your mid-twenties, would you characterize your life as wonderfully free? Why or why not? If you are not there yet, do you look forward to a time "when you can really focus on your own life"? If you're older, and have made the usual commitments of an adult, what was this earlier period in your life like? Do you agree with Arnett's view or not?

2. Grossman points to something we must not forget—that many young people don't go to college or don't complete an undergraduate degree and are therefore dealing with circumstances quite different from those of college graduates. Do you know people your age who are trying to make it with only a high school diploma or less? How are they doing? What are their prospects? Who seems to be making it relatively well? Who isn't? Why?

3. In paragraph 34, Grossman cites David Morrison, who offers a certain picture of the twenty-something market for consumer goods. In your experience, is Morrison's view accurate? Do you agree with Grossman that "corporations and advertisers have a real stake in keeping [young adults] . . . tractable, exploitable, . . . living at home, spending their money on toys"?

FOR ANALYSIS AND PERSUASION

According to Grossman, "to go to the movies or turn on the TV is to see a world where life ends at 30." Test his assertion by watching a movie or a TV show that centers on the world of young adults. Analyze how life is depicted—is Grossman right, wrong, or perhaps to some extent both right and wrong?

Based on your analysis, write an essay persuading a readership of your peers to watch the movie or the show the way you do—as a false and misleading depiction of young adult life or as insightful and valuable in some or all respects, or as a mix of both. Be specific about what you like or dislike and why—and whether your piece of popular culture is working with or against the interests and values of young adults.

Survey: Becoming an Adult

TIME

> The following survey appeared in the same issue of *Time* (January 24, 2005) as the previous article. SRBI Public Affairs conducted the telephone poll of 601 Americans from 18 to 29. The margin of error is ± 4 points. The margin of error is higher for subgroups. The "not sure" response has been left out for some questions.

Becoming an Adult

The markers of adulthood haven't changed for people ages 18 to 29 . . .

What makes you an adult?

Having first child	22%
Moving out of parents' home	22%
Getting a good job with benefits	19%
Getting married	14%
Finishing school	10%

. . . yet over a third of twixters don't consider themselves grown up . . .

How would you describe yourself?

An adult	61%
Entering adulthood	29%
Not there yet	10%

. . . and they cite a variety of reasons for their delayed entry into adulthood

What is the main reason that you do not consider yourself an adult?

Just enjoying life the way it is	35%
Not financially independent yet	33%
Not out of school	13%

Getting an Education

College is traditionally the institution that serves as a transition to adulthood, but students are taking longer to leave . . .

23% say they were 24 or older when they finished

. . . and when they do get out of college, many find themselves in debt

29% say paying for their education is a major financial concern
52% say they owed money when they finished school
66% owe over $10,000
23% owe over $30,000
5% owe over $100,000

Earning Money

Even though 43% worry about paying bills, they're big spenders . . .

Percentage who say they spend more than most people do on:

Eating out	32%
Clothes	26%

- Rob and Laura, a white couple now in their mid-thirties, are further along in their journey to adulthood. When they first got married, they thought they were on sound financial footing. Though neither finished college, Rob became trained as a heating and air-conditioning technician while Laura got a job working in the accounts-receivable department at the local plastics plant. They made $50,000 between them, which enabled them to live comfortably, but not extravagantly. When Laura became pregnant with their first child, Rob's parents gave them the down payment to buy a house. Their "first child" turned out to be twins—and, overnight, comfortable became very uncomfortable. Without the option of affordable child care, Laura had little choice but to quit her job and take care of the twins. Just then her husband's business took a dive. With their savings dwindling, credit cards went from occasional aids to lifelines. Today, the couple have three young children and $40,000 in credit card debt. They never dreamed that starting a family would plunge them into such deep financial and emotional straits.

- Wanda and Jerome seem like the quintessential middle-class African American couple who have captured the American dream. Both aged thirty-two, they are a dynamic duo with multiple college degrees. Wanda has a master's in human relations and Jerome has an M.B.A. Getting these credentials also got them $30,000 in student loan debt. Thankfully the couple resides in Montgomery, Alabama, where the cost of living is low. But with a five-month-old baby, a six-year-old son, and a twelve-year-old daughter, this family of five is living paycheck to paycheck. They are unable to afford child care, so Wanda's mother has been living with them for five months, and they don't know what they'll do when she leaves. After Jerome was laid off from his account-manager position at a Fortune 100 company, they ran up a couple of thousand dollars in credit card debt. His layoff was an especially bitter pill, since it was this job that brought them to Alabama in the first place. They would like to move out of Montgomery because the educational system is poor, but right now they're biding their time and trying to pay down their debts.

The lives of Cecilia, Rob and Laura, and Wanda and Jerome are at once strik- 5 ingly different and fundamentally similar. Three different backgrounds. Three different classes. Three different life experiences. They did all the right things, but they're all struggling to make ends meet. And they're not alone. All across the country young adults are sinking economically. The question is, why?

Behind each of these individual stories is a broader tale of economic and political changes that have occurred over the last three decades. For our parents, who grew up during the 1950s and early 1960s, establishing oneself as an adult was a fairly straightforward process. Moving out of your parents' house, getting a job, and starting a family—the three major markers of adulthood—unfolded in a rather swift and orderly fashion. There was little time between graduation, landing a well-paying job, getting married, and having kids. But in the late 1960s, the baby boomers, then in their twenties, began charting a different course to adulthood. Driven by social, economic, and political forces, young adults began delaying definitive "adult" behaviors such as getting married and having kids. As college and career opportunities expanded for women and minorities, more young adults began going to college instead of directly into the labor market after high school. The transition to adulthood was becoming less rigid and more ill defined. A generation later, these trends became more exacerbated. The path to adulthood for today's young adults is a full-blown obstacle course of loop-de-loop turns and jagged-edged hurdles.

When our parents were starting out, three factors helped smooth the transition to adulthood. The first was the fact that there were jobs that provided good wages even for high school graduates. A college degree wasn't necessary to earn a decent living. But even if you wanted to go to college, it wasn't that expensive and grants were widely available. The second was a robust economy that lifted all boats, with productivity gains shared by workers and CEOs alike. The result was a massive growth of the middle class, which provided security and stability for families. Third, a range of public policies helped facilitate this economic mobility and opportunity: a strong minimum wage, grants for low-income students to go to college, a generous unemployment insurance system, major incentives for home ownership, and a solid safety net for those falling on hard times. Simply put, government had your back.

This world no longer exists. The story of what happened is well known. The nation shifted to a service- and knowledge-based economy, dramatically changing the way we lived and worked. Relationships between employers and employees became more tenuous as corporations faced global competitors and quarterly bottom-line pressures from Wall Street. Increasingly, benefits such as health care and pension plans were provided only to well-paid workers. Wages rose quickly for educated workers and declined for those with only high school diplomas, resulting in new demands for college credentials. As most families saw their incomes stagnate or decline, they increasingly needed two full-time incomes just to stay afloat, which created new demands and pressures on working parents. Getting into the middle class now required a four-year college degree, and even that was no guarantee of achieving the American dream.

Although adults of all ages have endured the economic and social changes wrought by the postindustrial era, today's young adults are the first to experience its full weight as they try to start their adult lives. But the challenges facing young adults also reflect the failure of public policy to address the changing realities of building a life in the twenty-first century. Government no longer has our back. . . .

COLLEGE: A LUXURY-PRICED NECESSITY

College students today are graduating on average with close to $20,000 in debt. 10 Those who take the plunge into graduate school can plan on carrying about $45,000 in combined student loan debt.[1] Those who want to be lawyers or doctors will be lucky to escape with less than $100,000 in debt. Back in the 1970s, before college became essential to securing a middle-class lifestyle, our government did a great job of helping students pay for school. Students from modest economic backgrounds received almost free tuition through Pell grants, and middle-class households could still afford to pay for their kids' college.

That was before tuition began to spiral ever upward and student aid fossilized. Inflation-adjusted tuition at public universities has nearly tripled since 1980, up from $1,758 in 1980 to $5,132 in 2004.[2] To be fair, the federal government is spending more money than ever before on student aid, over $81 billion in the 2003–04 school year. But 70 percent of this aid is in the form of loans, while grant aid only makes up 21 percent and tax credits the remaining 9 percent.[3] Federal grant funding hasn't kept up with rising enrollments, so what little grant aid is available gets spread more thinly across a greater number of students.

As a result of soaring college costs and dwindling financial aid, in 2001 half a million high school graduates who were college-ready either downscaled their dreams by enrolling in community college or skipped college altogether. Congress has responded to this crisis in educational opportunity by merely tinkering with grant and student loan amounts—a bit like the fire department pulling up to a five-alarm fire with a garden hose. Case in point: The maximum Pell Grant award— the nation's premier government program for helping low-income students pay for college—covers about 40 percent of the costs of a four-year college today. It covered nearly three quarters in the 1970s.[4]

Thirty years ago, in 1976–77, the average cost of attending a *private* college was $12,837 annually, in inflation-adjusted dollars. Today, the average cost of attending a *public* college is $11,354—which means the burden of affording a state college today is equivalent to that of paying for a private college in the 1970s.[5] These figures include tuition, fees, and room and board. While tuition at four-year public colleges has soared, tuition at private colleges has entered the stratosphere, costing an average of $27,000 per year. Adding to the financial pressures is the new credential craze that all but mandates a master's degree to get out of the entry-level track in business, marketing, social work, teaching, and many other professions. Already in the hole for a bachelor's degree, many young adults find that the demand to get even more education leaves them up against the ropes. They want the better jobs but can't take the risk of going even deeper into debt.

Young adults have been given the signal loud and clear that getting a degree is now the only way into the middle class. As the burden of paying for college has shifted to the individual, more students are going into debt, dropping out, or not enrolling at all.

THE REAL "NEW" ECONOMY

What does the . . . job market for young adults look like? In a word, depressing. 15 Compared to older workers, young adults are more likely to be unemployed, hold part-time jobs, or work as temps. Almost half of temp agency workers are in the 18-to-34 age group. That's half a million young adults stuck in the temp system, and another 2.2 million who are independent contractors. These job arrangements rarely offer health care or other benefits, such as pensions.

For college grads who land a job with an actual firm, it's still far from sure that they'll be offered health or retirement benefits. One out of three young adults—a full 17.9 million 18-to-34-year-olds—don't have health insurance, making this the age group with the largest percentage of uninsured. They're not going without health-care coverage out of some sense of invincibility either; in fact, only 3 percent of young workers are uninsured because they declined available coverage.

In addition to often working in a benefit-free zone, moving up the wage or career ladder in the new economy is more difficult than it was a generation ago. The well-paying middle-management jobs that characterized the workforce up to the late 1970s have been eviscerated. Corporate downsizing in the 1980s and 1990s slashed positions in the middle of the wage distribution, and now outsourcing threatens to take thousands more. Instead of becoming more financially secure with each passing year, many young adults in their late twenties and early thirties find themselves struggling ever harder as they start having children and taking on mortgages. What they're experiencing is paycheck paralysis.

Today, America's economy looks like an hourglass. Job growth is concentrated at the top and bottom, while the middle is increasingly whittled away. According to the Bureau of Labor Statistics, jobs requiring a bachelor's degree or higher will account for 29 percent of total job growth from 2000 to 2010. Many of these new jobs are what we think of as "hot jobs"—those clustered in the tech and computer sector. The *largest* job growth, accounting for 58 percent of new jobs, will be those requiring only work-related training. These jobs are primarily in the low-wage retail and food sector, including such jobs as sales associates, food preparation, cashiers, and waitstaff.

Young adults who came of age in the mall culture are still trolling the malls—only this time they're looking for work.

As the job market has changed, so have the paychecks. Young adults across 20 the board are earning less today than they would have twenty or even thirty years ago. In 1972, the typical earnings for males 25 to 34 years old with a high school diploma was $42,630 (in 2002 dollars). In 2002, the typical earnings for high school grads had dropped to $29,647. Typical earnings for young males with a bachelor's degree or higher have also declined, from $52,087 in 1972 to $48,955 in 2002.[6]

Living paycheck to paycheck is the new norm for young adults. College grads may have a better shot of slowly digging their way out of the insecurity, but it most likely will not happen until they hit their forties. Today's paycheck paralysis makes it almost impossible for most young adults to get ahead. Dwindling salaries and rising costs mean less leftover money to put into savings, less to contribute to a 401(k), and less to put into their own kids' college funds. And all the while, they're racking up credit card debt to pay for any additional expenses, like going to the dentist or fixing the car, at exorbitant interest rates that rob them of even more money.

NOTES

1. Sandy Baum and Marie O'Malley, "College on Credit: How Borrowers Perceive Their Education Debt: Results of the 2002 National Student Loan Survey," Nellie Mae Corporation, February 6, 2003, available at http://www.nelliemae.com/library/research_10.html.

2. College Board, "Trends in College Pricing 2004," available at http://www.collegeboard.com/prod_downloads/press/cost04/041264TrendsPricing2004_FINAL.pdf.
3. College Board, "Trends in Student Aid 2004," available at http://www.collegeboard.com/prod_downloads/press/cost04/TrendsinStudentAid2004.pdf.
4. Lawrence E. Gladieux, "Low-Income Students and the Affordability of Higher Education," in Richard D. Kahlenberg, ed., *America's Untapped Resource: Low-Income Students in Higher Education* (New York: Century Foundation Press, 2004), p. 29.
5. College Board, "Trends in College Pricing 2004."
6. U.S. Department of Education, National Center for Education Statistics, *The Condition of Education 2004,* indicator 14, table 14-1, available at http://nces.gov//programs/coe/2004/pdf/14_2004.pdf.

FOR DISCUSSION

1. It's important to realize that the debt and job problems Draut discusses are widely distributed in the young adult group. How does she establish that the economic crunch is not restricted to an unfortunate few or a particular social class? Are you facing or have you seen similar drastic circumstances among your friends and acquaintances?

2. One of Draut's key points is that things have changed significantly since the 1950s and 1960s. What exactly has changed? Why have these changes had a greater impact on today's young adults than on their parents' generation? In your view, what changes must just be accepted, lived with somehow, and what changes can be coped with better by government policy designed to help young adults?

3. A college degree, almost any degree in any major, was once virtually a guarantee of economic opportunity, and certainly college graduates still earn more on average over a lifetime than high school graduates do. However, the college degree is not the passport to success it once was. As Draut describes the situation, why isn't it? What have you observed about the financial value of a college degree from people you know who have graduated recently?

FOR RESEARCH AND CONVINCING

The high cost of college is beyond dispute. As Draut points out, a public university now costs as much as a private one did thirty years ago. People tend to accept it without asking why, as if escalating costs were inevitable. Are they? Find out why college expenses have increased faster than inflation over the last few decades. What causes almost yearly tuition hikes?

Based on what you learn from research, make a case defending what you think will best contain runaway college costs. Address it to an audience of your peers and their parents, who need to understand what's driving the rising cost of higher education before they can hope to do anything about it.

Waking Up and Taking Charge

ANYA KAMENETZ

It is one thing to know we have a problem, quite another to do something to solve it, even when we understand it reasonably well. In the following excerpt from *Generation Debt: Why Now Is a Terrible Time to Be Young* (Riverside Press, 2006), Anya Kamenetz proposes action to promote needed change.

Like Tamara Draut, who offers similar proposals in *Strapped* (see the previous selection), Kamenetz, despite being a recent Yale graduate, has struggled herself with difficult economic conditions. And like Draut, she's helping to lead young adults toward becoming a potent political force.

We aren't particularly interested in "rocking the vote." . . . We're here to represent our generation because decisions are made by the people who show up.

—Virginia21, *the first student-led state political action committee, 2004*

If you're like me, you're a little impatient with the political sphere of action. Spend months and years supporting local candidates? Send blast faxes to your congresspeople? Actually read those endless e-mail alerts?

Well, look, if 35 million people over fifty can band together to demand respect from Congress, so can we. Unless we're willing to continue being typecast as passive "adultescents," unless we really want to get "rolled over by greedy middle-aged and older people who have been expropriating our earnings for generations," as the economist Laurence Kotlikoff says, it's the only way. Young people urgently need a strong national generational movement—for higher education funding, fairer credit laws, a better-designed school-to-work system, justice system reform, worker protections, a living wage, health care, saving programs, support for young families and homeowners, entitlement reform, and a million other issues.

As college gets ever more out of reach, there are signs of a nascent movement. At my alma mater on a freezing day in February 2005, fifteen students sat in at the admissions office until removed by police. The undergraduates were demanding changes to Yale's financial aid policy to bring it in line with several other Ivies, including Harvard, Princeton, and Brown. In the past few years, these schools have all dipped into their multimillion-dollar endowments to make it easier for families to afford college without heavy loans. One week after the sit-in, Yale, too, announced that it would no longer expect any tuition contribution at all from families earning less than $45,000 a year.

By all accounts, the financial aid reform issue galvanized the campus. One in five Yalies signed on to the reform platform, including the president of the Yale College Republicans and other campus conservatives. "This is self-interested organizing in a positive way," Phoebe Rounds, a sophomore on financial aid who organized for six months leading up to the sit-in, told me. "The campaign has made people realize the extent to which their individual struggles are shared by a large number of students."

The Yale action also demonstrates, however, that without a unified voice, individual protests can make only small ripples. Tuition discounting is possible only at 5 a tiny percentage of well-endowed private schools serving a tiny percentage of students. At selective colleges in 2004, only 10 percent of students came from the bottom half of the income scale.

An effective student movement should be organized state by state, to pressure the governors who make decisions about public schools where the vast majority of students are enrolled. When it comes to the broader problems facing young people, only national political organizing will do.

The student loan debt explosion could potentially be more amenable to lobbying than any of the other problems facing Generation Debt. The federal government gives out most student financial aid. They say how much you can borrow in guaranteed student loans and how high an interest rate the banks can charge. Given a true reordering of our national priorities—a big given—a few amendments to the Higher Education Act could immediately bring student borrowing down to a manageable level and lower the barriers to access. Increasing the maximum Pell Grant, and making the grant an entitlement that rises automatically from year to year, are obvious first steps. In the words of the National Association of Student Financial Aid Administrators, "If we are serious about reducing student loan debt . . . making the Pell Grant Program a true entitlement, divorced from the vagaries of the appropriations process, is the only way."

As this book is going to press, the eighth reauthorization of the Higher Education Act is finally getting under way, a few years overdue. The Bush administration assigned the lion's share of spending cuts for the purpose of deficit reduction to the House and Senate Education committees, and they turned around and passed the pain on to student aid, with $15 billion in cuts and new fees—the biggest cuts since HEA programs were created.

Even if legislative reform is years in coming, a vocal activist campaign about the dangers of student loans could accomplish a lot. After all, excessive student debt is not measured by a fixed number of dollars. It's a function of each person's income, other debts, financial management skills, ability to persist in college, and expectations about the value of a diploma. Raising awareness about the long-term dangers of high debt could help all those kids who "just sign on the dotted line as an eighteen-year-old and you don't know what you're getting into," as one interviewee put it.

Youth activism could effectively address credit card debt, too. It would be great 10 to reinstate usury laws nationwide and end 29 percent annual interest rates, so that twenty-somethings earning $12,000 a year are no longer profitable customers for $10,000 lines of credit. That would require a morally high-fiber Congress willing to take on one of the fastest-growing profit areas in financial services. Failing that, returning to the norms of the 1980s, when college students without incomes needed a parental cosigner for a card, would keep eighteen-year-olds from charging down that path before they realize the consequences.

With credit card debt, just as with student loans, a vocal activist movement could bring the problem out into the open, making kids think twice before signing up for the free Frisbees and key chains. Universities have a role to play, too, in limiting their students' exposure to credit card marketing. Just as Stella, [a] thirty-one-year-old debtor . . . , says, the next time you see the Discover Card table, RUN the other way!

Where is our national student antidebt crusade? Over the past four decades, college students have gained a reputation as the most engaged political activists in the country—except on issues directly affecting them. Each year, for example, *Mother Jones* magazine recognizes the top ten activist campuses in the nation. From 2001 to 2005, the list featured left-wing campaigns on free speech, the war in Iraq, AIDS, the drug war, and living wages. Missing were bipartisan student issues like mounting debt burden, aggressive credit card marketing, the lack of health insurance, and the dearth of solid entry-level jobs.

Standing up for world peace is utterly admirable, but the social safety net in this country was woven by people lobbying for their own lives, not fighting for causes a world away. American college students need to experience that "click" moment, as the feminists of the 1970s called it, and realize that our personal problems are also political. If we young people don't march on our own behalf, who will march for us?

In other countries, students get it. Many EU and Latin American countries have overwhelmingly public, centralized university systems, making organizing easier (and education cheaper). Around the world, national undergraduate student unions have lobbied forcefully for decades. They address issues like diversity and date rape, along with tuition, books, housing, health care, debt, and jobs. They win battles for their constituencies, keeping young people on the social agenda.

The UK's National Union of Students claims 5 million members, nearly all the 15 country's higher education students. In October 2003, an estimated 31,000 of them rallied in London against higher school fees.

After huge national budget cuts in the '90s, Canadians' student loans are comparable to Americans', at an average $22,520 ($19,143 U.S.) in 2001. Educational access is worsening for lower-income Canadians, although not quite as badly as in the United States.

Canada's two national student lobbying organizations boast combined memberships of 750,000, nearly half the nation's college students. James Kusie, a 2002 university grad from Manitoba, served from 2003 to 2005 as the elected national director of the Canadian Alliance of Student Associations (CASA). His group, founded in 1995, represents 300,000 students at nineteen universities across Canada. Member associations fund CASA's full-time staff of five, which drafts policy in the nation's capital and builds relationships with lawmakers, both elected representatives and bureaucrats. "You can be rallying outside and shouting through the window, and that's an important piece of building public support," Kusie says. "But you also need to be at the table with them, engaging them on the issues."

Each year, the presidents and vice presidents of each student council in CASA come to the national capital, Ottawa, and meet in person with their elected representatives. They also hold media stunts. In November 2003, they built a 120-foot Wall of Debt out of foam blocks, bearing the signatures of 20,000 students along with the debt burdens of each.

Throughout the 1990s, Canadian student organizations won tuition freezes and even cuts in several provinces. Kusie glows as he describes the accomplishments of his term as CASA's chair. In 2004, the federal government adopted their proposal for a new grant to low-income students, up to $3,000, modeled on the Pell Grant. They also changed the formulas for expected parental contributions, making up to 50,000 more students eligible for financial aid. These victories came during comparatively good economic times for Canada, but after more than a decade of deep budget cuts that shrank the size of the federal government by a third and while the country was experiencing the same increases in health care and pension costs as in the United States. CASA and the Canadian Federation of Students work to ensure that a government tending to the needs of an aging population does not forget young people.

"When Parliament begins a new session following an election, the government 20 gives a 'throne speech,' setting out its priorities for the legislative session," Kusie says. "When it came to the section on education, chunks of it seemed to have come word for word from our pre-budget submission. . . . We were very happy to see that our work had paid off."

The United States Student Association, this nation's oldest and largest student organization, contrasts poorly with the muscle flexed abroad. Its exact membership is not available on its seldom updated website. Most students have never heard of it, and the media tend to pass it over. Its lobbying clout is dwarfed by that of the big student loan companies—it spent just $20,000 on lobbying in 2000, compared with $1.5 million spent by Sallie Mae.

The 80 percent of students who attend public schools are pitted against the immovable object of state budgets. In the past few years, community college and state university students from California and New York demonstrated against big tuition hikes coupled with budget cuts. Ten thousand students from California's community colleges marched to Sacramento in 2003 to protest a 120 percent rise in fees and budget cuts in the hundreds of millions. They carried paper effigies representing an estimated 200,000 students priced out of the community college system. Public college students backed by the New York Public Interest Research Group rallied strongly against tuition hikes throughout the '90s, marching 561 miles across New York State in 2003. In both cases, despite temporary responses, the budget cuts and tuition increases continued.

There is a model here in America of what students could be doing to focus legislators' attention on education. A state political action committee, as powerful and well organized as the student unions in other countries, has taken root in, of all places, placid suburban Virginia.

In 2002, students at the public College of William and Mary formed Students PAC to help pass a $900 million state bond issue for higher education. In the summer of 2003, the coalition, now called Virginia21, went statewide. It now boasts over 14,500 members at all fifteen public four-year colleges and universities in the Commonwealth.

VA21, the first student-led state PAC, addresses voters between eighteen and 25 twenty-four on economic issues like tuition, book costs, and education budget cuts. They reject the popular approach of relying on mass media or celebrity to sell young voters on civic involvement. Jesse Ferguson, the twenty-four-year-old executive director, notes that voters of all ages tend to be motivated by concrete self-interest, not abstract ideals.

"We're trying to find a way to support mainstream, bipartisan, middle-of-the-road issues that affect all of us on a day-to-day basis," Ferguson says. He cofounded Students of Virginia PAC as a college student. Now he and a small staff work full-time in Virginia's capital to drive home their message about budget priorities. At their website, you can check the status of all the legislation they're working on, from cutting textbook prices, to increasing student financial aid, to reforming absentee voting so college students have an easier time getting to the ballot box. Their rhetoric strikes a determined but not angry note; they remind legislators that education is an investment in Virginia, and they remind students that they don't deserve to be priced out. In June 2004, Virginia21 celebrated passage of a state budget with $275 million more for higher education than the year before, the first such increase in years.

VA21 draws on its members for letter-writing campaigns, e-mail blasts, and rallies. They collected and trucked 200,000 pennies to the state capitol in 2004 in support of a one-cent sales tax for education. Meanwhile, Ferguson and his team haunted the halls of the capitol during their first legislative session just as all the other power players did.

In a bow to the realities of American politics, VA21, unlike the Canadian groups, depends on corporate contributions. Their 2003–2004 budget was $100,000. Donors included America Online, Bank of America, and Philip Morris's corporate owner. With this backing, it's hard to imagine VA21 addressing issues like unfair credit card marketing. Still, they're getting results, and lawmakers are taking them seriously.

Jesse Ferguson says he would seize the chance to take VA21 national if offered the funding. He calls his group a young, wired equivalent of the AARP, for its focus on issues that affect everyone of a certain age, and for its pragmatic, even insider, approach. "There's a change you can see in recent years in eighteen- to twenty-four-year-olds—they would rather have a seat at the table than a rally outside," Ferguson told me, echoing James Kusie of CASA. "It's got to be not just student activism but effective student activism."

FOR DISCUSSION

1. A common charge, which Kamenetz indirectly acknowledges, is that young adults are alienated from politics, too passive in accepting whatever older adults dish out. In your experience, is there any truth in this criticism? If you pay little or no attention to politics and don't vote, how do you explain or justify your behavior?

2. Kamenetz presents VA21 in terms obviously designed to make political action attractive. Do you find the idea for a college student–young adult PAC (political action committee) appealing? Why or why not? If you had a chance to take a role in such a group, would you? Why or why not?

3. Unfortunately, there's too much in American culture that encourages young adults to think that the sky's the limit, that you can achieve anything you

want to achieve—"chase your dreams" is an American credo. What's good about such an outlook? How much do you think the credo contributes to college students and their parents taking on too much debt for college expenses? What do you think should be done to encourage young adults to assess themselves and their financial situation with greater realism and practicality?

FOR RESEARCH AND INQUIRY

The great model for an age-specific PAC is AARP. Find out all you can about its membership, how it's organized, what it does to create a sense of group identity and purpose, and why it's effective with the political establishment.

Then write a paper exploring the possibility of creating a similar group for young adults, a group that would embrace college students and college graduates as well as the majority of young adults who don't go to or don't finish college. In what ways could such a group follow the AARP model? In what ways should it depart from it? What do you think needs to be done to make young adults a political force to be reckoned with by politicians at all levels of government?

An alternative is to research VA21 instead, the student-led PAC in Virginia that won important concessions from state government. If you take this route, ponder what VA21 accomplished and exactly why and how they managed to get things done. Would a similar PAC work in your state? Would it be better to go national—form a group that takes in all college students—or remain more local, working state by state instead?

FOR FURTHER READING

Apter, Terri. *The Myth of Maturity: What Teenagers Need from Parents to Become Adults.* New York: Norton, 2001.

Arnett, Jeffrey Jensen. *Emerging Adulthood: The Winding Road from the Late Teens through the Twenties.* New York: Oxford UP, 2004.

Draut, Tamara. *Strapped: Why America's 20- and 30-Somethings Can't Get Ahead.* New York: Doubleday, 2005.

Kamenetz, Anya. *Generation Debt: Why Now Is a Terrible Time to Be Young.* New York: Riverside Books, 2006.

Twenge, Jean M. *Generation Me: Why Today's Young Americans Are More Confident, Assertive, Entitled—and More Miserable Than Ever Before.* New York: Free Press, 2006.

A couple scales the wall near Douglas, Arizona, 2006.

CHAPTER 15

Immigration Revisited: A New Look at a Permanent Issue

About a decade ago, we had a chapter on immigration in the second edition
of this book. In many important ways, little has changed:

- About 1.2 million immigrants come to the United States each year, the
  vast majority of whom are Hispanics and Asians.

- Many of them are undocumented aliens.

- Our border with Mexico remains leaky, with perhaps about half a million people crossing it illegally each year since 2000.

- All measures to control the border and significantly reduce illegal immigration have failed.
- Immigrants, both legal and illegal, contribute significantly to our economy while also imposing significant costs, especially on state and local governments.

We could extend this list, but you get the point: as the French proverb says, "The more things change, the more they stay the same."

Yet things have changed. Many recent legal immigrants come from regions and countries that supplied few willing residents in the past—from Africa and India, for instance. In the past, most immigrants were confined to coastal or gateway cities and the Southwest. That's less and less the case; states such as North Carolina and Iowa now receive many new immigrants.

Furthermore, 9/11 led Americans to worry about the country's porous borders more than before. More recently, immigration has been discussed extensively in the news, on talk radio, and on thousands of Web sites, raising awareness of the issue to heights not seen since the 1920s and resulting in efforts to pass new legislation in Congress. Hardly anyone doubts that new laws will eventually pass—but what they will be no one knows for sure, and the actual impact they will have is anyone's guess.

Few issues confronting us are more poorly understood, more emotional, and more up in the air than immigration. Consequently, we need to focus on certain fundamental questions of long-term importance:

- There are now more than 300 million Americans. How long can we continue to absorb so many new people? From the standpoint of population control and ecology, *should we want to reduce the immigration rate?*
- Measures to control immigration are often both ineffective and produce unintended results, some of them clearly negative. Supposing that we want to, *can we reduce the immigration rate?* Economic forces drive immigration; perhaps we should let market forces control it. If not, what measures would really work, without producing intolerably bad side effects?
- All data indicates that without immigrants many millions of jobs would go unfilled. Even assuming we'd like to reduce immigration and can actually do so, *can we afford to reduce the immigration rate?*
- Finally, until recently, the pressure on new immigrants to "become Americans" was unrelenting and almost unquestioned. But now assimilation itself is an issue. *Do we really want immigrants to lose all sense of connection to their culture of origin?* If, as many people believe, the whole idea of the melting pot belongs to the past, *how much assimilation is desirable?*

The following selections address these questions directly and by implication. How we answer them will determine the nature and future of our country.

Historical Images: Our Contradictory Attitudes toward Immigration

The following posters were printed in popular publications about one hundred years ago, when immigration was highest, as measured by percentage of the total U.S. population. We think they capture in dramatic fashion the conflicting attitudes Americans have always had toward new arrivals. These and several similar drawings appeared in the magazine *Reason,* August–September 2006.

THE TRIUMPHAL ARCH.

The caption beneath the poster's title, "The Triumphal Arch," reads, "All those who enter here leave despair behind."

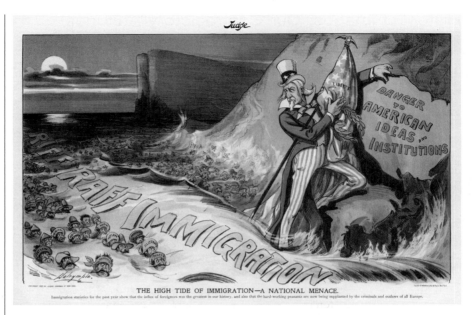

THE HIGH TIDE OF IMMIGRATION—A NATIONAL MENACE.
Immigration statistics for the past year show that the influx of foreigners was the greatest in our history, and also that the hard-working peasants are now being supplanted by the criminals and outlaws of all Europe.

The caption beneath the poster's title, "The High Tide of Immigration . . .," reads, "Imigration statistics for the past year show that the influx of foreigners was the greatest in history, and also that the hard-working peasants are now being supplanted by the criminals and outlaws of all Europe."

FOR DISCUSSION

Look carefully at the details in these two posters. What "assertions" are they making by implication? In your view, how do they reflect reality? How do they distort it?

FOR RESEARCH, ANALYSIS, AND INQUIRY

As a class project, collect recent images connected with attitudes toward immigration—photographs, cartoons, anything pictorial. Discuss each image in class, exploring both its conscious and unconscious impact, and comparing it with the posters from a century ago. How much has changed? How much remains the same?

Select two or three recent images you find particularly interesting and write an essay about the attitudes they express. Do they capture your own ideals and fears? If so, how?

The New Immigrants and the Issue of Assimilation

TAMAR JACOBY

> One of the better books published on immigration recently is a collection of essays
> called *Reinventing the Melting Pot: The New Immigrant and What It Means to Be American*
> (New York: Basic Books, 2004). The following selection is an excerpt from the first
> two chapters, both written by Tamar Jacoby, the editor of the volume and a senior
> researcher at the Manhattan Institute. She provides basic information on the current
> wave of immigrants and poses the issue of assimilation as we wrestle with it now.

THE BIG PICTURE

The immigrant influx of the last forty years is a demographic shift of historic proportions. The percentage of the population that was born abroad is slightly lower than
it was when the last great wave of immigrants arrived, at the beginning of the
twentieth century: 11 percent now compared to 15 percent then. But the absolute
number of newcomers living in the United States today is the highest it has ever
been: some 31 million. Roughly 1.2 million arrive on our shores every year. One in
nine Americans is an immigrant. And half the laborers entering the American workforce in the 1990s were foreign-born. Add in their families and extended families and
the picture grows more dramatic still. Together, immigrants and their children now
account for one in five Americans. Hispanics, at nearly 14 percent of the population,
are already the largest minority, outnumbering blacks. Asian-Americans are still a
relatively small share of the nation—at only 4 percent. But despite their numbers,
they, too, are going to play a major part in the country's future: already, they make
up between 15 and 20 percent of the students at most Ivy League colleges.

Where do these new arrivals come from? Just over half the foreign-born are
Hispanic and a little more than a quarter are Asian. They hail from all the corners of
the globe, though more from some countries than from others. Mexicans, by far the
largest category, account for roughly one in three first-generation immigrants—almost
ten times more than any other nationality. The next largest groups are Filipinos and
Indians, followed by Chinese, Vietnamese, Koreans, Cubans and Salvadorans—but
none of these account for more than 3 or 4 percent of the total.

What do the newcomers do for a living? They tend to be clustered at both
the top and the bottom of the job ladder. A large percentage work in dirty,
demeaning, low-paid jobs that native-born Americans no longer want to do: bus-
boys, chambermaids, farmhands, nurses' aides, sweatshop workers, on the assembly-
line in meatpacking plants. But a large number also work at the top of the job
pyramid: as scientists, engineers, nurses, high-tech entrepreneurs and the like. Two
of the statistics that paint this picture most vividly are the percentage of U.S.
farmhands who are foreign-born (an astonishing 80 percent) and the percentage
of patents that are held by foreigners (an equally astonishing 26 percent). Social
scientists call this a "barbell pattern," and it has some predictable corollaries. Not
surprisingly, today's newcomers are either quite rich or quite poor, and they are
either very well educated or hardly educated at all. Roughly a quarter have less
than nine years of schooling, while an equal percentage have university

degrees—a much larger share than the proportion of native-born Americans who have stayed in school that long.

Where in the United States do most immigrants settle? Until about ten years ago, they were concentrated in what demographers call "gateway cities": New York, Los Angeles, Miami, Houston, Chicago. But this is changing dramatically and with profound consequences for the country. States such as New York and California and New Jersey are still home to the largest numbers. But the states with the fastest growing immigrant populations are places like North Carolina, Georgia, Arkansas and Tennessee. Even Iowa more than doubled its share in the 1990s. The cities where the immigrant population expanded the most in the past decade are equally surprising: Greensboro, N.C., Charlotte, N.C., Raleigh, N.C., Atlanta and Las Vegas. Still more of a departure, while some of today's new arrivals still gravitate to urban areas, many head straight for the suburbs, and roughly half of all Asians and Latinos now live outside the center city. . . .

Most foreigners, whether they arrive legally or illegally, come to the United 5 States to work. Most do not come in the expectation of living on welfare: most are not entitled to most kinds of benefits for at least five years. Thanks to modern technology, they generally know from other immigrants who have preceded them from their regions whether or not work is available. And in economic downturns, when there are fewer jobs to be had, fewer immigrants seem to make the trip. . . .

Of course, however hard they work, many poor, ill-educated immigrants who start at the bottom of the ladder remain there throughout their lives. This is not particularly surprising, and it may seem to vindicate those who claim that the United States today is importing a new lower class. But that's part of the point of our immigration policy: America no longer has this kind of working class, and it turns out that we need one. And even this does not necessarily mean the newcomers will not be absorbed into the economy or do well by it. Indeed while most brand-new arrivals make considerably less than the native-born, by the time they have been in the United States for ten or fifteen years, they are usually making more. (Mexicans seem to be an exception—and a troubling one—but despite their overwhelming numbers and the way this weights any statistical measure, the overall immigrant average is still a success story.) By the time they've been in the country for fifteen to twenty years, immigrants are also less likely than the native-born to be living in poverty.

The trajectory of high-end immigrants—those who come with some money or an education—is even more impressive. Immigrant entrepreneurship is nothing short of astonishing—in the first and second generation and beyond. Asian and Latino business start-up rates were four times the average American rate in the 1990s. Most of these minority-owned firms were small, and most had no paid employees—but that was also true of the businesses owned by native-born Americans. . . .

In some cases, immigrants are not merely assimilating into a regional economy: they dominate it. In Silicon Valley in the 1990s, foreign-born scientists accounted for a third of the scientific workforce, and Chinese and Indian entrepreneurs ran a quarter of the high-tech companies. In New York, by one estimate, Korean immigrants own 70 percent of the independent groceries, 80 percent of the nail salons and 60 percent of the dry cleaners. In Los Angeles, an increasing share of the banks are Asian-owned, and newcomers—whether from the Middle East, North Africa or Korea—control most of the $22 billion fashion industry. Whatever one calls it, there can be little question, immigrants are finding their place—and generally a productive place—in the American economy. . . .

THE TENSIONS OF ASSIMILATION

Like many Asian-Americans of his generation, Eddie Liu* isn't quite sure how to place or describe himself. Born in Taiwan to professional parents who moved to the United States when he was two years old, Eddie grew up in a California suburb, speaking mostly English and absorbing the manners and morals he saw on television, hardly aware of any differences between himself and his mostly Anglo school friends. Going to college changed all that: by the mid–1990s, identity politics had taken over his University of California campus, and Eddie quickly learned to see himself as an Asian-American. He took courses in Asian-American studies, joined several Chinese-American organizations, decided he could date only Asian women and grew more and more skeptical about the United States—the typical trajectory of a young, hyphenated American in the age of multiculturalism.

By the time I met him, he was twenty-five, and his life reflected both of these 10 younger selves. He lived in a comfortable Los Angeles suburb, drove an expensive late-model car, dated both Asian and white women and, though he worked for an internet company that targeted Asian-Americans, knew more about American popular culture than I did. A bright and engaging young man, he grew thoughtful and a little tentative when our conversation turned to ethnic identity. Asked whether he saw himself as an excluded minority or a "person of color," he laughed good-naturedly. "Hardly," he said. And yet, when asked about the word "assimilation," he was plainly uncomfortable. "I don't know," he mused, "not if it's a one-way street. Not if you're asking me to give up who I am and fit into some 1950s 'Leave It To Beaver' America. Of course, I'm American. But I'm not sure I'm assimilated—or want to be."

Eddie's ambivalence is far from unique. Like most immigrants in the past, the overwhelming majority of today's brand-new arrivals know why they have come to the United States: to make a better life for themselves and their children by becoming American. These newcomers struggle against all odds to fit in—finding jobs, learning the system, picking up the rudiments of the language. And with the exception of a few community leaders who draw their status and livelihood from their separate ethnicity, first-generation immigrants have no trouble with the word "assimilation." "I don't see why people would not want to assimilate," a Chinese-American newcomer said to me recently with a certainty typical of those born in another country.

But the second generation, be it Asian or Latino or some other group, is often far less clear about its relationship to the new place. Like Eddie, they know what they don't want. None seek to lose themselves and their cultural heritage in a bland, homogenized America—assimilation as defined by the conformist, lily-white suburban neighborhoods of 1950s television and advertising. Multiculturalism com-

*That isn't his real name.

bined with the sheer number of newcomers arriving today has laid that dream—if it ever really was anyone's dream—to rest forever. But nor do most voice the oppositional attitudes and color-coded divisiveness associated with identity politics. They are keen to make it in America, yet reject the metaphor of the melting pot—and desperately need a way to understand just who they are and how they fit it. . . .

MAKING IT INTO THE MAINSTREAM—AS HARD IF NOT HARDER THAN EVER

The story of immigrant absorption is as old as America, but the new arrivals and the country they are settling in are very different today than in the past. Yesterday's newcomers were ethnically more similar to the nation they were joining: like the native born, virtually all were of European stock. In contrast, today, most immigrants hail from the developing world, more than half of them from Latin-America and a quarter from Asia. Today's newcomers include skilled, middle-class people, but many are poor and uneducated and woefully unprepared to join the knowledge economy. (Some 60 percent of those from India, for example, have completed four years of college, but only 6 percent of refugees from Cambodia have, and the average Mexican arrives with 7.6 years of schooling.) Together, immigrants and their children account for more than 60 million people, or a fifth of all U.S. residents. And by 2050, if today's projections are borne out, a third of all Americans will be either Asian or Latino.

The America they come to is also different: at once more prosperous and unequal economically than it was a century ago, often making it harder for newcomers to assimilate into the middle class. The gap between rich and poor is wider than ever, creating what some social scientists call an "hourglass economy." In many cities, well-paid factory jobs have been replaced by service-sector work, and for some time now, real wages at the bottom of the pay scale have been declining rather than growing. On top of this, many newcomers settle in impoverished inner cities, where crime, drugs, gangs and broken families conspire to hinder their climb up the economic ladder. Getting an education—the most critical step in assimilating into the knowledge economy—is no easy matter in the barrios of, say, south central Los Angeles. . . .

Some immigrant enclaves are better off: many Asian-Americans in California, 15 for example, live in leafy, upscale suburbs. But pleasant as they are, these neighborhoods can be as insular as any ghetto: their ethnic shopping malls, ethnic restaurants and groceries, in-language newspapers, one-country Rotary Clubs, community banks, ethnic movie theaters and other amenities often make it unnecessary to have much contact with the integrated mainstream. The more newcomers arrive from the old country, the larger and more all-encompassing these enclaves—both rich and poor—grow, reducing incentives to make the difficult transition to a mixed neighborhood. Meanwhile, geographic proximity and cheap air travel allow newcomers to shuttle back and forth to their home countries and, in some cases, to maintain dual citizenship and even vote in both places.

Then there are the cultural factors that conspire against assimilation: everything from the internet and niche advertising to color-coded identity politics. The attacks of September 11, 2001, have sparked new patriotism and a new confidence in what brings us together as Americans. Some forty years after the Black Power movement and the ethnic revival it sparked among people of all backgrounds, the excesses of group chauvinism seem finally to be fading a bit. But no mere swing of the cultural pendulum is going to repeal multiculturalism or erase the profound effect it has had on the way most Americans live and view the world. From the relativism that now reigns in intellectual circles to the way Congress divides up into monolithic ethnic caucuses, multiculturalism has become the civil religion of the United States. . . .

The drumbeat of ethnocentric messages can be constant and unavoidable. In an inner city high school, native-born minority classmates tease you for listening and doing your homework—both widely condemned by poor blacks and Latinos as "acting white" or "selling out." If this doesn't deter you, if and when you get to college, you'll be assailed by campus ethnic activists pressing you to question why you want to join the mainstream, racist and exploitative as it is seen to be. By the time you've finished your education, according to one study, you'll be far less likely to consider yourself an American, or even a hyphenated American, than you were as a young teenager. In many cases, by then, you'll see yourself simply as an aggrieved minority or as what some are now calling "ampersand Americans"— as in "Mexican & American." . . .

We shouldn't exaggerate the threat. Today, as before in our history when the immigrant tide was rising, nativists peddle a frightening array of grim scenarios: balkanization, civil strife, economic ruin and worse. Very few of these nightmare visions are based in fact, and all are unlikely. . . . The nation is steadily absorbing tens of millions of newcomers: people of all ages and backgrounds who are finding work, learning English, making their way through school and up into more comfortable circumstances than they knew at home or when they first arrived in America. Still, like any wholesale social shift or personal transformation of this magnitude, the integration of today's influx needs watching—and occasional tending. . . .

A NEW INTELLECTUAL CURRENT

What about Eddie Liu and his doubts? Is what we as a nation want to encourage really *assimilation*? The very notion is almost a dirty word today. Some who oppose it are plainly extremists: people so taken with multiculturalism that they see being absorbed into a larger America as so much cultural "genocide." Yet Eddie is no activist, and concerns like his are widely felt, particularly in his generation. To young people like him, "assimilation" implies a forced conformity. They feel that it would require them to give up what makes them special, and they dread being reduced to what they see as the lowest common denominator of what it means to be American. As for the melting pot, if anything, that seems even more threatening: who wants to be melted down, after all—for the sake of national unity or anything else?

Meanwhile, at the other end of the political spectrum are those who think 20 that, desirable as it is, assimilation is no longer possible in America. Some in this camp are driven by racial concerns: they view today's immigrants as simply too different ethnically ever to fit in in the United States. Others believe that the obstacles are cultural: that America has a distinct national ethos that cannot be grasped by any but a few newcomers—the better educated, perhaps, or those from Christian Europe. Still others feel that the problem lies less in the foreign influx than in ourselves: that in the wake of multiculturalism and the upheavals of the 1960s, we as a nation have lost the confidence to assert who we are and what we believe in. But whatever their reasoning, all three kinds of pessimists have gained a wider hearing in the wake of 9/11 as the nation has grown ever more anxious about what many imagine are the unassimilated in our midst. And together, these two groups—those who believe assimilation is impossible and those who fear it—have come to dominate most discussion of the issue, leaving little room for those in the middle who take a more positive view. . . .

Hemmed in on both sides, hardly heard in the din of an often emotional debate, in fact, many of the thinkers who have thought longest and hardest about immigration believe that assimilation is still possible and indeed desirable, if not inevitable, today. They don't all like or use that word—for some of the same reasons that Eddie has trouble with it. Very few imagine that it should look as it looked in the 1950s: that it requires newcomers to forget their roots or abandon their inherited loyalties. And fewer still believe that it happens automatically—that it needs no tending or attention from the nation as a whole. Still, whatever word they use, these thinkers maintain that we as a nation not only can but must continue to absorb those who arrive on our shores: absorb them economically, culturally, politically and, perhaps most important, give them a sense that they belong.

FOR DISCUSSION

1. Of all the facts about immigration Jacoby provides, which ones surprised you the most? Which seem most important? Why?

2. Recent immigrants cluster at either the top or the bottom of our society—the "barbell effect" the author refers to. In terms of actual numbers, however, most arrive poor and stay poor for some time. Given what Jacoby tells us and what you know about immigrants in general, is it accurate and fair to say we are importing a new lower class?

3. Summarize the complex view of assimilation Jacoby presents, being sure to include the opinions she characterizes as extreme and between which she seeks a middle ground. Where would you locate your own opinion in this spectrum of outlooks? How did you acquire your opinion?

FOR INQUIRY AND PERSUASION

"As for the melting pot . . . ," Jacoby asks, "who wants to be melted down . . . , for the sake of national unity or anything else?" Find out as much as you can about your own background. Where did your family originate? How much of your culture of origin does your family preserve? How much is fading away or lost?

Write an essay defending the proposition that being American ought not to imply loss of our sense of origins and family cultural traditions.

One Nation, Out of Many: Why "Americanization" of Newcomers Is Still Important

SAMUEL HUNTINGTON

> A professor of political science at Harvard, Samuel Huntington has been a leading intellectual voice for neoconservative views for many years. In the following article he argues that "Anglo Protestant culture, values, [and] institutions" formed America and must be preserved amid a large influx of immigrants from other traditions, especially from Mexico. Without stronger efforts to "Americanize" this latest wave of immigrants, we are in danger, he believes, of becoming two nations instead of one.
>
> The following article appeared in *The American Enterprise* (September 2004). It's an excerpt from his book *Who Are We? The Challenges to America's National Identity* (Simon and Schuster, 2004).

America's core culture has primarily been the culture of the seventeenth and eighteenth century settlers who founded our nation. The central elements of that culture are the Christian religion; Protestant values, including individualism, the work ethic, and moralism; the English language; British traditions of law, justice, and limits on government power; and a legacy of European art, literature, and philosophy. Out of this culture the early settlers formulated the American Creed, with its principles of liberty, equality, human rights, representative government, and private property. Subsequent generations of immigrants were assimilated into the culture of the founding settlers and modified it, but did not change it fundamentally. It was, after all, Anglo Protestant culture, values, institutions, and the opportunities they created that attracted more immigrants to America than to all the rest of the world. . . .

One has only to ask: Would America be the America it is today if in the seventeenth and eighteenth centuries it had been settled not by British Protestants but by French, Spanish, or Portuguese Catholics? The answer is no. It would not be America; it would be Quebec, Mexico, or Brazil. . . .

During the decades before World War I, the huge wave of immigrants flooding into America generated a major social movement devoted to Americanizing these new arrivals. It involved local, state, and national governments, private organizations, and businesses. Americanization became a key element in the Progressive phase of American politics, and was promoted by Theodore Roosevelt, Woodrow Wilson, and other leaders. . . .

The central institution for Americanization was the public school system. Indeed, public schools had been created in the nineteenth century and shaped in considerable part by the perceived need to Americanize and Protestantize immigrants. "People looked to education as the best way to transmit Anglo-American Protestant values and to prevent the collapse of republican institutions," summarizes historian Carl Kaestle. In 1921–22, as many as a thousand communities conducted "special public school programs to Americanize the foreign-born." Between 1915 and 1922, more than 1 million immigrants enrolled in such programs. School systems "saw public education as an instrument to create a unified society out of the multiplying diversity created by immigration," reports Reed Ueda.

Without these Americanizing activities starting in the early 1890s, America's dra- 5 matic 1924 reduction in immigration would in all likelihood have been imposed much earlier. Americanization made immigration acceptable to Americans. The success of the movement was manifest when the immigrants and their children rallied to the colors and marched off to fight their country's wars. In World War II in particular, racial, ethnic, and class identities were subordinated to national loyalty, and the identification of Americans with their country reached its highest point in history.

National identity then began to fade. In 1994, 19 scholars of American history and politics were asked to evaluate the level of American unity in 1930, 1950, 1970, and 1990. The year 1950, according to these experts, was the "zenith of American national integration." Since then "cultural and political fragmentation has increased" and "conflict emanating from intensified ethnic and religious conscious-ness poses the main current challenge to the American nation."

Fanning all of this was the new popularity among liberal elites of the doctrines of "multiculturalism" and "diversity," which elevate subnational, racial, ethnic, cul-tural, gender, and other identities over national identity, and encourage immigrants to maintain dual identities, loyalties, and citizenships. Multiculturalism is basically an anti-Western ideology. Multiculturalists argue that white Anglo America has sup-pressed other cultural alternatives, and that America in the future should not be a society with a single pervasive national culture, but instead should become a "tossed salad" of many starkly different ingredients.

In sharp contrast to their predecessors, American political leaders have recently promoted measures consciously designed to weaken America's cultural identity and strengthen racial, ethnic, and other identities. President Clinton called for a "great revolution" to liberate Americans from their dominant European culture. Vice Presi-dent Gore interpreted the nation's motto, *E pluribus unum* (Out of many, one), to mean "out of one, many." By 1992, even some liberals like Arthur Schlesinger, Jr. were warning that the "ethnic upsurge" which had begun "as a gesture of protest against the Anglocentric culture" had become "a cult, and today it threatens to become a counterrevolution against the original theory of America as 'one people,' a common culture, a single nation."

These efforts by members of government to deconstruct the nation they led are, quite possibly, without precedent in human history. And important parts of academia, the media, business, and the professions joined them in the effort. A study by Paul Vitz of 22 school texts published in the 1970s and 1980s for grades three and six found that only five out of 670 stories and articles in these readers had "any patriotic theme." All five dealt with the American Revolution; none had "anything to do with American history since 1780." In four of the five stories the principal person is a girl, in three the same girl, Sybil Ludington. The 22 books lack any story "featuring Nathan Hale, Patrick Henry, Daniel Boone, or Paul Revere's ride." "Patriotism," Vitz concludes, "is close to nonexistent" in these readers.

The deconstructionist coalition, however, does not include most Americans. In 10 poll after poll, majorities of Americans reject ideas and measures that would lessen national identity and promote subnational identities. Everyday Americans remain deeply patriotic, nationalistic in their outlook, and committed to their national culture, creed, and identity. A major gap has thus developed between portions of our elite and the bulk of our populace over what America is and should be. . . .

The current wave of immigration to the U.S. has increased with each decade. During the 1960s, 3 million people entered the country. During the 1980s, 7 million people did. In the 1990s it was over 9 million. The foreign born percentage of the American population, which was a bit above 5 percent in 1960, more than doubled to close to 12 percent in 2002.

The United States thus appears to face something new in its history: persistent high levels of immigration. The two earlier waves of heavy immigration (1840s and 50s; and 1880s to 1924) subsided as a result of world events. But absent a serious war or economic collapse, over 1 million immigrants are likely to enter the United States each year for the indefinite future. This may cause assimilation to be slower and less complete than it was for past waves of immigration.

That seems to be happening with today's immigration from Latin America, especially from Mexico. Mexican immigration is leading toward a demographic "reconquista" of areas Americans took from Mexico by force in the 1830s and 1840s. Mexican immigration is very different from immigration from other sources, due to its sheer size, its illegality, and its other special qualities.

One reason Mexican immigration is special is simply because there are now so very many arrivals (legal and illegal) from that one country. Thanks to heavy Mexican inflows, for the very first time in history a majority of U.S. immigrants now speak a single non-English language, Spanish. The impact of today's large flow of Mexican immigrants is reinforced by other factors: the proximity of their country of origin; their geographical concentration within the U.S.; the improbability of their inflow ending or being significantly reduced; the decline of the assimilation movement; and the new enthusiasm of many American elites for multiculturalism, bilingualism, affirmative action, and cultural diversity instead of cultural unity. In addition, the Mexican government now actively promotes the export of its people to the United States while encouraging them to maintain their Mexican culture, identity, and nationality. President Vicente Fox regularly refers to himself as the president of 123 million Mexicans, 100 million in Mexico, 23 million in the United States. The net result is that Mexican immigrants and their progeny have not assimilated into American society as other immigrants did in the past, or as many other immigrants are doing now. . . .

Problems in digesting Mexican immigrants would be less urgent if Mexicans 15 were just one group among many. But because legal and illegal Mexicans comprise such a large proportion of our current immigrant flow, any assimilation problems arising within their ranks shape our immigrant experience. The overwhelming influence of Mexicans on America's immigration flow becomes clearly visible if one poses a thought experiment. What if Mexican immigration to the U.S. somehow abruptly stopped, while other immigration continued as at present? In such a case, illegal entries in particular would diminish dramatically. Agriculture and other businesses in the southwest would be disrupted, but the wages of low-income Americans would rise. Debates over the use of Spanish, and whether English should be made the official language of state and national governments, would fade away. Bilingual education and the controversies it spawns would decline. So also would controversies over welfare and other benefits for immigrants. The debate over whether immigrants are an economic burden on state and federal governments would be decisively resolved in the negative. The average education and skills of the immigrants coming to America would rise to levels unprecedented in American history. Our inflow of immigrants would again become highly diverse, which would increase incentives for all immigrants to learn English and absorb American culture. The possibility of a split between a predominantly Spanish-speaking America and English-speaking America would disappear, and with it a major potential threat to the cultural and possibly political integrity of the United States.

A glimpse of what a splintering of America into English- and Spanish-speaking camps might look like can be found in current day Miami. Since the 1960s, first Cuban and then other Latin American immigrants have converted Miami from a fairly normal American city into a heavily Hispanic city. By 2000 Spanish was not just the language spoken in most homes in Miami, it was also the principal language of commerce, business, and politics. The local media and communications are increasingly Hispanic. In 1998, a Spanish language television station became the number one station watched by Miamians–the first time a foreign-language station achieved that rating in a major American city. . . .

Is Miami the future for Los Angeles and the southwest generally? In the end, the results could be similar: the creation of a large, distinct, Spanish-speaking community with economic and political resources sufficient to sustain its own Hispanic identity apart from the national identity of other Americans, and also sufficient to significantly influence American politics, government, and society. The process by which this might come about, however, is different. The Hispanization of Miami has been led from the top down by successful Cuban and other Central and South American immigrants. In the southwest, the overwhelming bulk of Spanish-speaking immigrants are Mexican, and have been poor, unskilled, and poorly educated. It appears that many of their offspring are likely to be similar. The pressures toward Hispanization in the southwest thus come from below, whereas those in South Florida came from above. . . .

The continuation of high levels of Mexican and Hispanic immigration and low rates of assimilation of these immigrants into American society and culture could eventually change America into a country of two languages, two cultures, and two peoples. This will not only transform America. It will also have deep consequences for Hispanics—who will be in America but not of the America that has existed for centuries.

FOR DISCUSSION

1. In the previous selection, Tamar Jacoby characterized one view of immigration as based on the assumption or fear that many of the new immigrants can't be "Americanized"—that is, assimilated. Is that Huntington's view? What is the problem with "Americanization" as Huntington sees it?

2. According to Huntington, patriotic values are not being taught much in our schools. Based on your own experience as a high school student or as a parent of high school children, would you agree? If you do, should this change?

3. We all have what Huntington calls "subnational" aspects of identity, dimensions of what we are based on race, ethnicity, culture, class, and gender, among other differences. He believes that these subnational aspects have become too important, even more important than loyalty to the United States. Is he right? That is, do you recognize such attitudes in your own life? In other people you know well?

FOR RESEARCH, DISCUSSION, AND CONVINCING

As a class project, find out all you can about Hispanic immigration in general and immigration from Mexico in particular. Discuss the implications of the various points of view and the information you discover.

Then write an essay that addresses the question Huntington raises: Are we on the way to becoming two countries? Does the large influx of Hispanics pose a serious, long-term threat to U.S. national identity?

Cartoon: Playing POLITICS with the Border

JEFF KOTERBA

Like most political cartoons, this one makes a simple point forcefully: Politics may be the real barrier to handling illegal immigration intelligently.

Jeff Koterba. © North American Syndicate.

FOR DISCUSSION

1. Most of us get impatient with politics at least sometimes, and the accusation of "playing politics" with some serious issue is a frequent criticism. But in what way are our impatience and that accusation misdirected?

The Border

ROSS DOUTHAT AND JENNY WOODSON

> This compact, fact-filled article and graphic appeared in *The Atlantic Monthly* (January–February 2006).

More than 1.3 million people were caught trying to enter the United States illegally from Mexico in 2004. Nearly 200,000 were attempting to cross, often concealed in vehicles, at one of the twenty-five U.S.-Mexican Customs stations; most of the rest—those indicated on the map [map on pages 580–581]—were apprehended by the U.S. Border Patrol, while making their way across the Rio Grande or the Sonora Desert or through the fences and other barriers separating Tijuana from southern California.

The Border Patrol has become much larger and more sophisticated in recent decades. Since the current wave of illegal Mexican immigration began, in the mid-1970s, the number of agents along the southern U.S. border has risen from 2,000 to 11,000. Roadways have been extended into remote areas to give agents better access to smuggling routes; floodlights, motion sensors, and remote video cameras have been installed; and agents have started patrolling in aircraft as well as on the ground. Last year the Border Patrol deployed a "Predator B" unmanned aerial vehicle—the first American UAV put to civilian use. It provides real-time bird's-eye views of previously inaccessible areas, transmitting images that are quickly relayed to agents on the ground.

But, of course, the migrants keep slipping through. The Border Patrol will not speculate about how many evade capture and enter the United States; the Pew Hispanic Center recently estimated that, on average, 485,000 Mexicans have crossed the border illegally every year since 2000, and that more illegal than legal aliens have entered the country altogether since 1995.

Immigration pressure from Mexico is unlikely to abate anytime soon. Nearly half of all Mexicans asked by Pew said they would come to the United States immediately if they had "the means and opportunity." Twenty-one percent said they would do so even if they had to come illegally. Indeed, many Mexicans seem to have a sense of entitlement regarding the United States: 58 percent surveyed in a 2002 Zogby poll believe that "the territory of the United States' Southwest rightfully belongs to Mexico."

Americans are unhappy about this state of affairs: according to recent polls, [5] most favor beefing up the enforcement of immigration laws and using troops to police the border. A majority even voiced support for the Minuteman Project, a group of civilian vigilantes who have begun patrolling the border themselves.

However, political leaders in both parties (along with many business organizations, media outlets, and bipartisan interest groups) see the issue differently, believing that restricting immigration is not economically desirable. The immigration proposals currently circulating in Washington seem unlikely to reduce the influx from the south. They are aimed instead at regularizing it, by creating a temporary-visa program for migrant laborers. Although such a "guest worker" program might be paired with legislation to tighten border security and curb the hiring of illegal

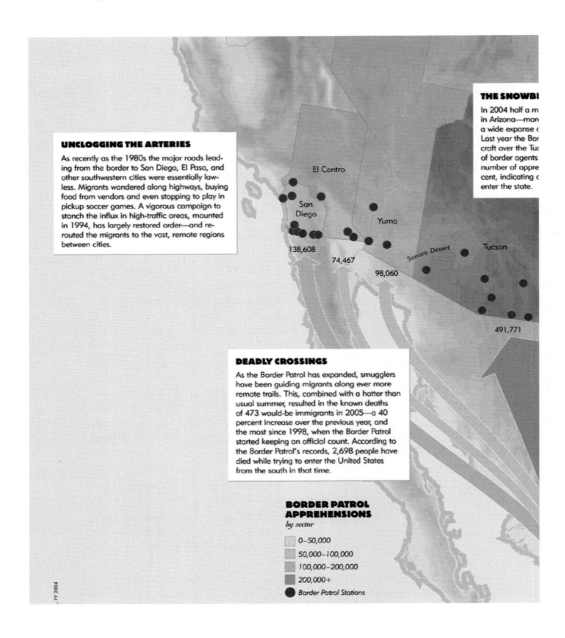

UNCLOGGING THE ARTERIES

As recently as the 1980s the major roads leading from the border to San Diego, El Paso, and other southwestern cities were essentially lawless. Migrants wandered along highways, buying food from vendors and even stopping to play in pickup soccer games. A vigorous campaign to stanch the influx in high-traffic areas, mounted in 1994, has largely restored order—and rerouted the migrants to the vast, remote regions between cities.

THE SNOWB

In 2004 half a m in Arizona—mon a wide expanse c Last year the Bor craft over the Tuc of border agents number of appre cent, indicating c enter the state.

El Centro

San Diego

Yuma

138,608

74,467

98,060

Sonora Desert

Tucson

491,771

DEADLY CROSSINGS

As the Border Patrol has expanded, smugglers have been guiding migrants along ever more remote trails. This, combined with a hotter than usual summer, resulted in the known deaths of 473 would-be immigrants in 2005—a 40 percent increase over the previous year, and the most since 1998, when the Border Patrol started keeping an official count. According to the Border Patrol's records, 2,698 people have died while trying to enter the United States from the south in that time.

BORDER PATROL APPREHENSIONS
by sector

- 0–50,000
- 50,000–100,000
- 100,000–200,000
- 200,000+
- ● Border Patrol Stations

immigrants, as President Bush suggested in a November policy speech, there's reason to doubt that serious restrictions would actually result. The last major immigration reform, in 1986, was supposed to provide a similar tradeoff—an amnesty program for illegal aliens already in the United States was joined to commitment to crack down on employers of illegal immigrants. The amnesty was implemented; the crackdown fizzled out. And in December of 2004 Congress authorized the

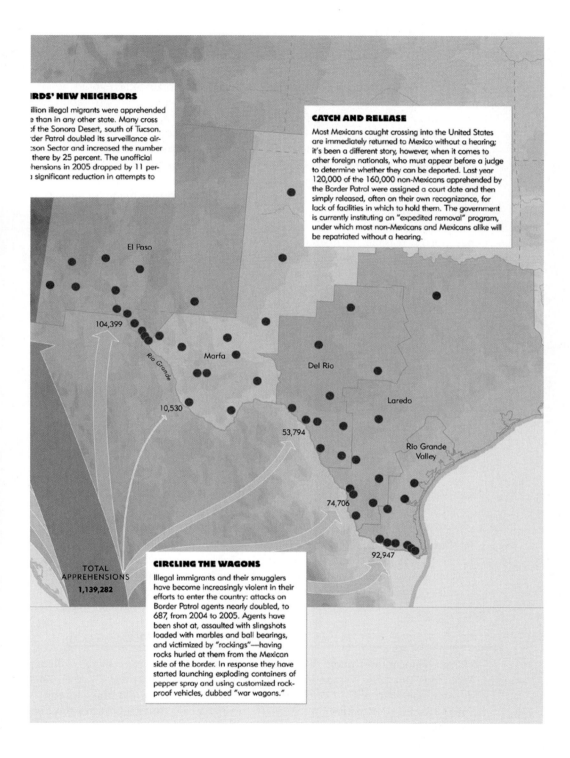

IRDS' NEW NEIGHBORS

illion illegal migrants were apprehended
e than in any other state. Many cross
f the Sonora Desert, south of Tucson.
der Patrol doubled its surveillance air-
:son Sector and increased the number
there by 25 percent. The unofficial
hensions in 2005 dropped by 11 per-
a significant reduction in attempts to

CATCH AND RELEASE

Most Mexicans caught crossing into the United States
are immediately returned to Mexico without a hearing;
it's been a different story, however, when it comes to
other foreign nationals, who must appear before a judge
to determine whether they can be deported. Last year
120,000 of the 160,000 non-Mexicans apprehended by
the Border Patrol were assigned a court date and then
simply released, often on their own recognizance, for
lack of facilities in which to hold them. The government
is currently instituting an "expedited removal" program,
under which most non-Mexicans and Mexicans alike will
be repatriated without a hearing.

El Paso

104,399

Rio Grande

Marfa

Del Rio

Laredo

10,530

53,794

Rio Grande
Valley

74,706

92,947

TOTAL
APPREHENSIONS
1,139,282

CIRCLING THE WAGONS

Illegal immigrants and their smugglers
have become increasingly violent in their
efforts to enter the country: attacks on
Border Patrol agents nearly doubled, to
687, from 2004 to 2005. Agents have
been shot at, assaulted with slingshots
loaded with marbles and ball bearings,
and victimized by "rockings"—having
rocks hurled at them from the Mexican
side of the border. In response they have
started launching exploding containers of
pepper spray and using customized rock-
proof vehicles, dubbed "war wagons."

addition of 10,000 Border Patrol agents over a five-year period beginning in 2006—but only 210 new positions were funded for this year.

This gap between popular and elite opinion means that the porousness of 5 the border is becoming a potent issue, especially for working-class voters, whose jobs may be vulnerable to guest-worker programs. Tom Tancredo, a Republican congressman from Colorado, has threatened to make an insurgent run for the 2008 GOP presidential nomination if no other candidate comes out strongly against illegal immigration, and observers speculate that Democrats might use the issue to try to outflank the GOP on the right. (Last year the governors of New Mexico and Arizona, both Democrats, declared states of emergency because of the influx of illegal immigrants, blaming the federal government for failing to secure the border.)

Nativist politics hasn't fared well in recent decades. And securing the border may not be feasible no matter what the public wants—at least absent a heavy military presence and the sorts of barriers used in Cold War Berlin and the Korean DMZ. (Spending on border security rose dramatically during the 1990s, but so did the number of illegal immigrants.) However, unless the gap on this issue between America's leaders and its citizenry is somehow narrowed, whether by stringent reform or by rising economic optimism on Main Street, a populist backlash could ensue—against both illegal immigrants themselves and those many see as their enablers in Washington.

FOR DISCUSSION

1. This article is an example of one kind of slightly disguised argument. It seems to be informative and, of course, is. But the information implies conclusions, arguable contentions, some spelled out, some not. What conclusions both explicit and implicit do you find?

2. What information were you unaware of? What surprised you the most? What conclusions do you draw from the information you now have? Are any of your conclusions different from the viewpoint of the authors?

3. Border control is a topic of much casual, often heated discussion. The graphic depicts the magnitude of the problem well and mentions the vast amount of manpower and money devoted to apprehending undocumented aliens. In your view, is the effort worthwhile?

FOR RESEARCH, DISCUSSION, AND MEDIATION

Many commentators point to the gap between the opinions of many ordinary Americans and those of the so-called elite concerning immigration. All the articles so far allude to it, and "The Border" highlights it. Basically, the popular view is generally anti-immigration and strongly for increased efforts to control the border with Mexico. Elite opinion—professors who study immigration, big business concerns, and many politicians—tend to be more pro-immigration and skeptical of efforts to control the border.

Do research on this rift in opinion, including current legislative proposals in Congress, which reflect the sharp contrast. Discuss the implications of what you turn up, being sure to reflect on *why* popular opinion moves one way and elite opinion another.

Then write an essay proposing an approach to border control designed to give both sides some of what they want. Defend it as a practical, middle-of-the-road way of better coping with this difficult problem.

The Realities of Immigration

LINDA CHAVEZ

Chairperson of the Center for Equal Opportunity in Washington, D.C., and author of *Out of the Barrio* (1991), Linda Chavez is a frequent and perceptive commentator on immigration. She argues here that large-scale immigration from Mexico does not pose the threat some make it out to be, but we need a guest-worker program coupled with other measures to bring our border under greater control.

Her article appeared in *Commentary* (July–August 2006).

What to do about immigration—both legal and illegal—has become one of the most controversial public-policy debates in recent memory. But why it has occurred at this particular moment is something of a mystery. The rate of immigration into the U.S., although high, is still below what it was even a few years ago, the peak having been reached in the late 1990's. President Bush first talked about comprehensive immigration reform almost immediately after assuming office, but he put the plan on hold after 9/11 and only reintroduced the idea in 2004. Why the current flap?

By far the biggest factor shaping the popular mood seems to have been the almost daily drumbeat on the issue from political talk-show hosts, most prominently CNN's Lou Dobbs and the Fox News Channel's Bill O'Reilly and Sean Hannity (both of whom also have popular radio shows), syndicated radio hosts Rush Limbaugh, Laura Ingraham, Michael Savage, and G. Gordon Liddy, and a plethora of local hosts reaching tens of millions of listeners each week. Stories about immigration have become a staple of cable news, with sensational footage of illegal crossings featured virtually every day.

Media saturation has led, in turn, to the emergence of immigration as a wedge issue in the . . . 2008 presidential campaign. Several aspiring Republican candidates—former House Speaker Newt Gingrich, Senate Majority Leader Bill Frist, and Senator George Allen—have worked to burnish their "get tough" credentials, while, on the other side of the issue, Senator John McCain has come forward as the lead sponsor of a bill to allow most illegal aliens to earn legal status. For their part, potential Democratic candidates have remained largely mum, unsure how the issue plays with their various constituencies.

And then there are the immigrants themselves, who have shown surprising political muscle, especially in response to legislation passed by the House that would turn the illegal aliens among them into felons. Millions of mostly Hispanic protesters have taken to the streets in our big cities in recent months, waving American flags and (more controversially) their own national flags while demanding recognition and better treatment. Though Hispanic leaders and pro-immigrant advocates point to the protests as evidence of a powerful new civil-rights movement, many other Americans see the demonstrators as proof of an alien invasion—and a looming threat to the country's prosperity and unity.

In short, it is hard to recall a time when there has been so much talk about 5 immigration and immigration reform—or when so much of the talk has been misinformed, misleading, and ahistorical. Before policy-makers can decide what to do about immigration, the problem itself needs to be better defined, not just in terms of costs and benefits but in relation to America's deepest values.

Contrary to popular myth, immigrants have never been particularly welcome in the United States. Americans have always tended to romanticize the immigrants of their grandparents' generation while casting a skeptical eye on contemporary newcomers. In the first decades of the 20th century, descendants of Northern European immigrants resisted the arrival of Southern and Eastern Europeans, and today the descendants of those once unwanted Italians, Greeks, and Poles are deeply distrustful of current immigrants from Latin America. Congressman Tom Tancredo, a Republican from Colorado and an outspoken advocate of tighter restrictions, is fond of invoking the memory of his Italian immigrant grandfather to argue that he is not anti-immigrant, just anti-*illegal* immigration. He fails to mention that at the time his grandfather arrived, immigrants simply had to show up on American shores (or walk across the border) to gain legal entry. . . .

The modern immigration era commenced in 1965 with the passage of the Immigration and Nationality Act, which abolished all national-origin quotas, gave preference to close relatives of American citizens, refugees, and individuals with certain skills, and allowed for immigrants from the Western hemisphere on a first-come, first-served basis. The act's passage drew a huge wave, much of it from Latin America and Asia. From 1970 to 2000, the United States admitted more than 20 million persons as permanent residents.

By 2000, some 3 million of these new residents were formerly illegal aliens who had gained amnesty as part of the 1986 Immigration Reform and Control Act (IRCA). This, Congress's first serious attempt to stem the flow of illegal immigration, forced employers to determine the status of their workers and imposed heavy penalties on those hiring illegal entrants. But from the beginning, the law was fraught with problems. It created huge bureaucratic burdens, even for private individuals wanting to hire someone to cut their lawn or care for their children, and spawned a vast new document-fraud industry for immigrants eager to get hold of the necessary paperwork. The law has been a monumental failure. Today, some 11.5 million illegal aliens reside in the U.S.—quadruple the population of two decades ago, when IRCA was enacted—and the number is growing by an estimated 500,000 a year. . . .

The real question is not whether the U.S. has the means to stop illegal immigration—no doubt, with sufficient resources, we could mostly do so—but whether we would be better off as a nation without these workers. Restrictionists claim that large-scale immigration—legal and illegal—has depressed wages, burdened government resources, and acted as a net drain on the economy. The Federation for American Immigration Reform (FAIR), the most prominent of the pressure groups on the issue, argues that, because of this influx, hourly earnings among American males have not increased appreciably in 30 years. As the restrictionists see it, if the U.S. got serious about defending its borders, there would be plenty of Americans willing to do the jobs now performed by workers from abroad. . . .

Despite the presence in our workforce of millions of illegal immigrants, the U.S. 10 is currently creating slightly more than two million jobs a year and boasts an unemployment rate of 4.7 percent, which is lower than the average in each of the past four decades. More to the point perhaps, when the National Research Council (NRC) of the National Academy of Sciences evaluated the economic impact of immigration in its landmark 1997 study *The New Americans: Economic, Demographic, and Fiscal Effects of Immigration,* it found only a small negative impact on the earnings of Americans, and even then, only for workers at lower skill and education levels.

Moreover, the participation of immigrants in the labor force has had obvious positive effects. The NRC estimated that roughly 5 percent of household expenditures in the U.S. went to goods and services produced by immigrant labor—labor whose relative cheapness translated into lower prices for everything from chicken to new homes. These price advantages, the study found, were "spread quite uniformly across most types of domestic consumers," with a slightly greater benefit for higher-income households.

Many restrictionists argue that if Americans would simply cut their own lawns, clean their own houses, and care for their own children, there would be no need for immigrant labor. But even if this were true, the overall economy would hardly benefit from having fewer workers. If American women were unable to rely on immigrants to perform some household duties, more of them would be forced to stay home. A smaller labor force would also have devastating consequences when it comes to dealing with the national debt and government-funded entitlements like Social Security and Medicare, a point repeatedly made by former Federal Reserve Board Chairman Alan Greenspan. As he told a Senate committee in 2003, "short of a major increase in immigration, economic growth cannot be safely counted upon to eliminate deficits and the difficult choices that will be required to restore fiscal discipline." The following year, Greenspan noted that offsetting the fiscal effects of our own declining birthrate would require a level of immigration "much larger than almost all current projections assume."

The contributions that immigrants make to the economy must be weighed, of course, against the burdens they impose. FAIR and other restrictionist groups contend that immigrants are a huge drain on society because of the cost of providing public services to them—some $67 to $87 billion a year, according to one commonly cited study. Drawing on numbers from the NRC's 1997 report, FAIR argues that "the net fiscal drain on American taxpayers [from immigration] is between $166 and $226 a year per native household."

There is something to these assertions, though less than may at first appear. Much of the anxiety and resentment generated by immigrants is, indeed, a result of the very real costs they impose on state and local governments, especially in border states like California and Arizona. Providing education and health care to the children of immigrants is particularly expensive, and the federal government picks up only a fraction of the expense. But, again, there are countervailing factors. Illegal immigrants are hardly free-riders. An estimated three-quarters of them paid federal taxes in 2002, amounting to $7 billion in Social Security contributions and $1.5 billion in Medicare taxes, plus withholding for income taxes. They also pay state and local sales taxes and (as homeowners and renters) property taxes.

Moreover, FAIR and its ilk have a penchant for playing fast and loose with 15 numbers. To support its assessment of immigration's overall fiscal burden, for instance, FAIR ignores the explicit cautions in a later NRC report about cross-sectional analyses that exclude the "concurrent descendants" of immigrants—that is, their adult children. These, overwhelmingly, are productive members of the workforce. As the NRC notes, when this more complete picture is taken into account, immigrants have "a positive federal impact of about $1,260 [per capita], exceeding their net cost [$680 per capita on average] at the state and local levels." Restrictionists also argue that fewer immigrants would mean more opportunities for low-skilled native workers. Of late, groups like the Minuteman Project have even taken to presenting themselves as champions of unemployed American blacks (a curious tactic, to say the least, considering the views on race and ethnicity of many in the anti-immigrant camp*).

But here, too, the factual evidence is mixed. Wages for American workers who have less than a high-school education have probably been adversely affected by large-scale immigration; the economist George Borjas estimates a reduction of 8 percent in hourly wages for native-born males in that category. But price competition is not the only reason that many employers favor immigrants over poorly educated natives. Human capital includes motivation, and there could hardly be two more disparately motivated groups than U.S.-born high-school drop-outs and their foreign-born rivals in the labor market. Young American men usually leave high school because they become involved with drugs or crime, have difficulty with authority, cannot maintain regular hours, or struggle with learning. Immigrants, on the other hand, have demonstrated enormous initiative, reflecting, in the words of President Reagan, "a special kind of courage that enabled them to leave their own land, leave their friends and their countrymen, and come to this new and strange land."

Just as important, they possess a strong desire to work. Legal immigrants have an 86-percent rate of participation in the labor force; illegal immigrant males have a 94-percent rate. By contrast, among white males with less than a high-school education, the participation rate is 46 percent, while among blacks it is 40 percent. If all immigrants, or even only illegal aliens, disappeared from the American work-force, can anyone truly believe that poorly skilled whites and blacks would fill the gap? To the contrary, productivity would likely decline, and employers in many sectors would simply move their operations to countries like Mexico, China, and the Philippines, where many of our immigrants come from in the first place.

Of equal weight among foes of immigration are the cultural changes wrought by today's newcomers, especially those from Mexico. In his book *Who Are We? The Challenges to National Identity* (2004), the eminent political scientist Samuel P. Huntington warns that "Mexican immigration is leading toward the demographic *reconquista* of areas Americans took from Mexico by force in the 1830's and 1840's." . . .

---

*As the author and anti-immigration activist Peter Brimelow wrote in his 1995 book *Alien Nation,* "Americans have a legitimate interest in their country's racial balance . . . [and] a right to insist that their government stop shifting it." Himself an immigrant from England, Brimelow wants "more immigrants who look like me."

Does it not seem likely that today's immigrants—because of their numbers, the constant flow of even more newcomers, and their proximity to their countries of origin—will be unable or unwilling to assimilate as previous ethnic groups have done?

There is no question that some public policies in the U.S. have actively dis- 20 couraged assimilation. Bilingual education, the dominant method of instruction of Hispanic immigrant children for some 30 years, is the most obvious culprit, with its emphasis on retaining Spanish. But bilingual education is on the wane, having been challenged by statewide initiatives in California (1998), Arizona (2000), and Massachusetts (2004), and by policy shifts in several major cities and at the federal level. States that have moved to English-immersion instruction have seen test scores for Hispanic youngsters rise, in some cases substantially.

Evidence from the culture at large is also encouraging. On most measures of social and economic integration, Hispanic immigrants and their descendants have made steady strides up the ladder. English is the preferred language of virtually all U.S.-born Hispanics; indeed, according to a 2002 national survey by the Pew Hispanic Center and the Kaiser Family Foundation, 78 percent of third-generation Mexican-Americans cannot speak Spanish at all. In education, 86 percent of U.S.-born Hispanics complete high school, compared with 92 percent of non-Hispanic whites, and the drop-out rate among immigrant children who enroll in high school after they come here is no higher than for the native-born. . . .

As for the effect of Hispanic immigrants on the country's social fabric, the NRC found that they are more likely than other Americans to live with their immediate relatives: 88.6 percent of Mexican immigrant households are made up of families, compared with 69.5 percent of non-Hispanic whites and 68.3 percent of blacks. These differences are partially attributable to the age structure of the Hispanic population, which is younger on average than the white or black population. But even after adjusting for age and immigrant generation, U.S. residents of Hispanic origin—and especially those from Mexico—are much more likely to live in family households. Despite increased out-of-wedlock births among Hispanics, about 67 percent of American children of Mexican origin live in two-parent families, as compared with 77 percent of white children but only 37 percent of black children.

Perhaps the strongest indicator of Hispanic integration into American life is the population's high rate of intermarriage. About a quarter of all Hispanics marry outside their ethnic group, almost exclusively to non-Hispanic white spouses, a rate that has remained virtually unchanged since 1980. And here a significant fact has been noted in a 2005 study by the Population Reference Bureau—namely, that "the majority of inter-Hispanic children are reported as Hispanic." Such intermarriages themselves, the study goes on, "may have been a factor in the phenomenal growth of the U.S. Hispanic population in recent years."

It has been widely predicted that, by mid-century, Hispanics will represent fully a quarter of the U.S. population. Such predictions fail to take into account that increasing numbers of these "Hispanics" will have only one grandparent or great-grandparent of Hispanic heritage. By that point, Hispanic ethnicity may well mean neither more nor less than German, Italian, or Irish ethnicity means today.

How, then, to proceed? Congress is under growing pressure to strengthen 25 border control, but unless it also reaches some agreement on more comprehensive reforms, stauncher enforcement is unlikely to have much of an effect. With a growing economy and more jobs than our own population can readily absorb, the U.S. will continue to need immigrants. Illegal immigration already responds reasonably well to market forces. It has increased during boom times like the late 1990's and decreased again when jobs disappear, as in the latest recession. Trying to determine an ideal number makes no more sense than trying to predict how much steel or how many textiles we ought to import; government quotas can never match the efficiency of simple supply and demand. As President Bush has argued—and as the Senate has now agreed—a guest-worker program is the way to go.

Does this mean the U.S. should just open its borders to anyone who wants to come? Hardly. We still need an orderly process, one that includes background checks to insure that terrorists and criminals are not being admitted. It also makes sense to require that immigrants have at least a basic knowledge of English and to give preference to those who have advanced skills or needed talents.

Moreover, immigrants themselves have to take more responsibility for their status. Illegal aliens from Mexico now pay significant sums of money to "coyotes" who sneak them across the border. If they could come legally as guest workers, that same money might be put up as a surety bond to guarantee their return at the end of their employment contract, or perhaps to pay for health insurance. Nor is it good policy to allow immigrants to become welfare recipients or to benefit from affirmative action: restrictions on both sorts of programs have to be written into law and stringently applied.

A market-driven guest-worker program might be arranged in any number of ways. A proposal devised by the Vernon K. Krieble Foundation, a policy group based in Colorado, suggests that government-licensed, private-sector employment agencies be put in charge of administering the effort, setting up offices in other countries to process applicants and perform background checks. Workers would be issued tamper-proof identity cards only after signing agreements that would allow for deportation if they violated the terms of their contract or committed crimes in the U.S. Although the Krieble plan would offer no path to citizenship, workers who wanted to change their status could still apply for permanent residency and, ultimately, citizenship through the normal, lengthy process.

Do such schemes stand a chance politically? A poll commissioned by the Krieble Foundation found that most Americans (except those with less than a high-school education) consider an "efficient system for handling guest workers" to be more important than expanded law enforcement in strengthening the country's border. Similarly, a CNN tracking poll in May found that 81 percent of respondents favored legislation permitting illegal immigrants who have been in the U.S. more than five years to stay here and apply for citizenship, provided they had jobs and paid back taxes. True, other polls have contradicted these results, suggesting public ambivalence on the issue—and an openness to persuasion.

Regardless of what Congress does or does not do—the odds in favor of an 30 agreement between the Senate and House on final legislation are still no better than 50-50—immigration is likely to continue at high levels for the foreseeable future. Barring a recession or another terrorist attack, the U.S. economy is likely to need some 1.5 to 2 million immigrants a year for some time to come. It would be far better for all concerned if those who wanted to work in the U.S. and had jobs waiting for them here could do so legally, in the light of day and with the full approval of the American people.

FOR DISCUSSION

1. Chavez thinks that media attention and politics are responsible for the current spotlight on immigration—implying that the issue is hyped, over-blown. Based on what you've read in this section and your own knowledge, would you agree? Why or why not?

2. Chavez makes a strong case for the economic necessity of immigrant workers. Summarize her position, including her effort to refute viewpoints such as FAIR's. Do you find her case convincing? Why or why not? If you agree, what implications does your assent have for immigration policy? If you disagree, what implications does your dissent have?

3. Compare Chavez's view of the assimilation of Mexican immigrants with Samuel Huntington's in his selection in this chapter. Who makes the stronger case? If you think Chavez does, what points does Huntington make that must be taken into account? If Huntington does, what does Chavez say that merits attention?

FOR RESEARCH AND CONVINCING

There's a great deal of resentment toward illegal immigration on the level of local government, both state and city. It's not hard to see why—local government bears much of the cost of services required for undocumented workers. Investigate this problem and then write a paper urging the federal government to take on more of the costs of illegal immigration.

The Border Patrol State

LESLIE MARMON SILKO

Whenever illegal immigration is discussed, someone asserts that we have lost control of our borders. The contention is typically accepted as a fact rather than thought about seriously. This classic article examines this notion seriously, while calling attention to violations of the civil rights of American citizens by Border Patrol agents.

Leslie Marmon Silko is a celebrated Native American writer. Her article appeared originally in The Nation *(17 October 1994).*

I used to travel the highways of New Mexico and Arizona with a wonderful sensation of absolute freedom as I cruised down the open road and across the vast desert plateaus. On the Laguna Pueblo reservation where I was raised, the people were patriotic despite the way the U.S. government had treated Native Americans. As proud citizens, we grew up believing the freedom to travel was our inalienable right, a right that some Native Americans had been denied in the early twentieth century. Our cousin, old Bill Pratt, used to ride his horse 300 miles overland from Laguna, New Mexico, to Prescott, Arizona, every summer to work as a fire lookout.

In school in the 1950s, we were taught that our right to travel from state to state without special papers or threat of detainment was a right that citizens under communist and totalitarian governments did not possess. That wide open highway told us we were U.S. citizens; we were free. . . .

Not so long ago, my companion Gus and I were driving south from Albuquerque, returning to Tucson after a book promotion for the paperback edition of my novel *Almanac of the Dead.* I had settled back and gone to sleep while Gus drove; but I was awakened when I felt the car slowing to a stop. It was nearly midnight on New Mexico State Road 26, a dark, lonely stretch of two-lane highway between Hatch and Deming. When I sat up, I saw the headlights and emergency flashers of six vehicles—Border Patrol cars and a van were blocking both lanes of the highway. Gus stopped the car and rolled down the window to ask what was wrong. But the closest Border Patrolman and his companion did not reply; instead, the first agent ordered us to "step out of the car." Gus asked why, but his question seemed to set them off. Two more Border Patrol agents immediately approached our car, and one of them snapped, "Are you looking for trouble?" as if he would relish it.

I will never forget that night beside the highway. There was an awful feeling of menace and violence straining to break loose. It was clear that the uniformed men would be only too happy to drag us out of the car if we did not speedily comply with their request (asking a question is tantamount to resistance, it seems). So we stepped out of the car and they motioned for us to stand on the shoulder of the road. The night was very dark, and no other traffic had come down the road since we had been stopped. All I could think about was a book I had read—*Nunca Mas*—the official report of a human rights commission that investigated and certified more than 12,000 "disappearances" during Argentina's "dirty war" in the late 1970s.

The weird anger of these Border Patrolmen made me think about descriptions 5
in the report of Argentine police and military officers who became addicted to
interrogation, torture and the murder that followed. When the military and police
ran out of political suspects to torture and kill, they resorted to the random abduction of citizens off the streets. I thought how easy it would be for the Border Patrol
to shoot us and leave our bodies and car beside the highway, like so many bodies
found in these parts and ascribed to "drug runners."

Two other Border Patrolmen stood by the white van. The one who had asked
if we were looking for trouble ordered his partner to "get the dog," and from the
back of the van another patrolman brought a small female German shepherd on
a leash. The dog apparently did not heel well enough to suit him, and the handler
jerked the leash. They opened the doors of our car and pulled the dog's head into
it, but I saw immediately from the expression in her eyes that the dog hated them,
and that she would not serve them. When she showed no interest in the inside of
the car, they brought her around back to the trunk, near where we were standing.
They half-dragged her up into the trunk, but still she did not indicate any stowed-
away human beings or illegal drugs.

The mood got uglier; the officers seemed outraged that the dog could not
find any contraband, and they dragged her over to us and commanded her to
sniff our legs and feet. To my relief, the strange violence the Border Patrol agents
had focused on us now seemed shifted to the dog. I no longer felt so strongly
that we would be murdered. We exchanged looks—the dog and I. She was afraid
of what they might do, just as I was. The dog's handler jerked the leash sharply
as she sniffed us, as if to make her perform better, but the dog refused to accuse
us: She had an innate dignity that did not permit her to serve the murderous
impulses of those men. I can't forget the expression in the dog's eyes; it was as
if she were embarrassed to be associated with them. I had a small amount of
medicinal marijuana in my purse that night, but she refused to expose me. I am
not partial to dogs, but I will always remember the small German shepherd that
night.

Unfortunately, what happened to me is an everyday occurrence here now. . . .

I was [also] detained once at Truth or Consequences, despite my and my
companion's Arizona driver's licenses. Two men, both Chicanos, were detained at
the same time, despite the fact that they too presented ID and spoke English without the thick Texas accents of the Border Patrol agents. While we were stopped,
we watched as other vehicles—whose occupants were white—were waved through
the checkpoint. White people traveling with brown people, however, can expect
to be stopped on suspicion they work with the sanctuary movement, which shelters
refugees. White people who appear to be clergy, those who wear ethnic clothing
or jewelry and women with very long hair or very short hair (they could be nuns)
are also frequently detained; white men with beards or men with long hair are
likely to be detained, too, because Border Patrol agents have "profiles" of "those
sorts" of white people who may help political refugees. (Most of the political refugees from Guatemala and El Salvador are Native American or mestizo because the
indigenous people of the Americas have continued to resist efforts by invaders to

displace them from their ancestral lands.) Alleged increases in illegal immigration by people of Asian ancestry means that the Border Patrol now routinely detains anyone who appears to be Asian or part Asian, as well.

Once your car is diverted from the Interstate Highway into the checkpoint area, 10 you are under the control of the Border Patrol, which in practical terms exercises a power that no highway patrol or city patrolman possesses: They are willing to detain anyone, for no apparent reason. Other law-enforcement officers need a shred of probable cause in order to detain someone. On the books, so does the Border Patrol; but on the road, it's another matter. They'll order you to stop your car and step out; then they'll ask you to open the trunk. If you ask why or request a search warrant, you'll be told that they'll have to have a dog sniff the car before they can request a search warrant, and the dog might not get there for two or three hours. The search warrant might require an hour or two past that. They make it clear that if you force them to obtain a search warrant for the car, they will make you submit to a strip search as well. . . .

This is the police state that has developed in the southwestern United States since the 1980s. No person, no citizen, is free to travel without the scrutiny of the Border Patrol. In the city of South Tucson, where 80 percent of the respondents were Chicano or Mexicano, a joint research project by the University of Wisconsin and the University of Arizona recently concluded that one out of every five people there had been detained, mistreated verbally or nonverbally, or questioned by I.N.S. [Immigration and Naturalization Service] agents in the past two years.

Manifest Destiny may lack its old grandeur of theft and blood—"lock the door" is what it means now, with racism a trump card to be played again and again, shamelessly, by both major political parties. "Immigration," like "street crime" and "welfare fraud," is a political euphemism that refers to people of color. Politicians and media people talk about "illegal aliens" to dehumanize and demonize undocumented immigrants, who are for the most part people of color. Even in the days of Spanish and Mexican rule, no attempts were made to interfere with the flow of people and goods from south to north and north to south. It is the U.S. government that has continually attempted to sever contact between the tribal people north of the border and those to the south.[1]

Now that the "Iron Curtain" is gone, it is ironic that the U.S. government and its Border Patrol are constructing a steel wall ten feet high to span sections of the border with Mexico. . . . Like the pathetic multimillion-dollar "antidrug" border surveillance balloons that where continually deflated by high winds and made only a couple of meager interceptions before they blew away, the fence along the border is a theatrical prop, a bit of pork for contractors. Border entrepreneurs have already used blowtorches to cut passageways through the fence to collect "tolls," and are doing a brisk business. . . .

[1]The Treaty of Guadalupe Hidalgo, signed in 1848, recognizes the right of the Tohano O'Odom (Papago) people to move freely across the U.S.–Mexico border without documents. A treaty with Canada guarantees similar rights to those of the Iroquois nation in traversing the U.S.–Canada border. [Author's note]

It is no use; borders haven't worked, and they won't work, not now, as the indigenous people of the Americas reassert their kinship and solidarity with one another. A mass migration is already under way; its roots are not simply economic. The Uto-Aztecan languages are spoken as far north as Taos Pueblo near the Colorado border, all the way south to Mexico City. Before the arrival of the Europeans, the indigenous communities throughout this region not only conducted commerce, the people shared cosmologies, and oral narratives about the Maize Mothers, the Twin Brothers and their Grandmother, Spider Woman, as well as Quetzalcoatl the benevolent snake. The great human migration within the Americas cannot be stopped; human beings are natural forces of the Earth, just as rivers and winds are natural forces. . . .

One evening at sundown, we were stopped in traffic at a railroad crossing in   15 downtown Tucson while a freight train passed us, slowly gaining speed as it headed north to Phoenix. In the twilight I saw the most amazing sight: Dozens of human beings, mostly young men, were riding the train; everywhere, on flat cars, inside open boxcars, perched on top of boxcars, hanging off ladders on tank cars and between boxcars. I couldn't count fast enough, but I saw fifty or sixty people headed north. They were dark young men, Indian and mestizo; they were smiling and a few of them waved at us in our cars. I was reminded of the ancient story of Aztlán, told by the Aztecs but known in other Uto-Aztecan communities as well. Aztlán is the beautiful land to the north, the origin place of the Aztec people. I don't remember how or why the people left Aztlán to journey farther south, but the old story says that one day, they will return.

FOR DISCUSSION

1. Silko refers to the "weird anger" (paragraph 5) of the Border Patrol officers. Why does she call it "weird"? What might explain their anger?

2. "Immigration," like "street crime" and "welfare fraud," Silko claims, "is a political euphemism that refers to people of color." Is she right? What do these terms make you think of? How do such associations distort clear thinking about immigration, legal or illegal?

3. Originally "The Border Patrol State" appeared under the caption "America's Iron Curtain," an allusion to the Berlin Wall, one of the great symbols of tyranny for Americans of Silko's generation. Thus, the editors of *The Nation* magazine compare our border walls to the Berlin Wall, torn down only a few years before Silko's article appeared. How apt is the analogy?

FOR RESEARCH, DISCUSSION, AND MEDIATION

Silko reminds us of how short-sighted views of immigration can be—they tend to focus on the current situation without much awareness of the history, for example, of peoples moving back and forth along the U.S. border with Mexico. Find out all you can about the movement of peoples along our southern border, being sure to go all the way back to when there was no border and the region was populated by Native Americans only. Answer these questions: What does the history tell us about cultural ties among the people who live on both sides of the current border? How much should what we know from history influence our thinking now about border control and immigration?

Write an essay proposing an approach to border control based on your new knowledge of history. Use your knowledge to propose a solution in between the current extremes: shutting off illegal immigration entirely and creating completely open borders.

FOR FURTHER READING

Huntington, Samuel P. *Who Are We? The Challenges to America's Identity.* New York: Simon and Schuster, 2004.

Jacoby, Tamar, ed., *Reinventing the Melting Pot: The New Immigrants and What It Means to Be American.* Basic Books, 2004.

Reason (August–September 2006). A series of provocative articles in a special section of the issue. See especially Carolyn Lockheed, "The Unexpected Consequences of Immigration Reform."

Wilson Quarterly (Summer 2006). Some interesting pieces on recent immigration trends, including legal immigration from Africa.

Zollberg, Aristide R. *A Nation by Design: Immigration Policy in the Fashioning of America.* Boston: Harvard UP, 2004.

Marines around a fire in Iraq between patrols (2006).

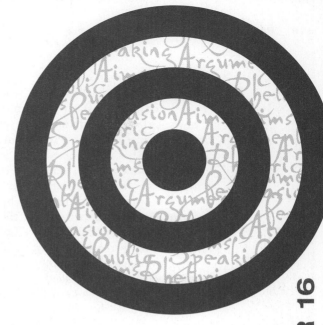

Countering Terrorism: Where to from Here?

We are writing shortly after the fifth anniversary of 9/11. The good news is that we've suffered no major terrorist attack since that horrific day five years ago. The bad news is that American combat deaths outnumber the people lost on 9/11, and there's no end in sight to the insurgencies in both Afghanistan and Iraq. Over 20,000 American soldiers have been wounded in Iraq alone. The good news is that two tyrannical regimes have fallen as a result of our military actions: the Taliban in Afghanistan and Saddam Hussein in Iraq. The bad news is that the governments which have replaced them are weak, unlikely to survive without the support of American troops. The good news is that al Qaeda has been seriously degraded and dispersed and is today nothing like the center for Islamic militants that it was five years ago. The bad news is that al Qaeda has survived, that new recruits continue to join the *jihad* movement, and that the view of the United States among most Muslims in the Middle East has gotten much more negative.

Good news, bad news: It's hard to assess where we are. The vast majority of terrorism experts think the general situation has either not improved or gotten worse. Furthermore, virtually all agree that we remain highly vulnerable to terrorist activity within the United States. It's only a matter of time, they say, until another major attack occurs. But why hasn't it occurred already? Because al Qaeda has been disrupted? Because there are so many American targets close at hand in Afghanistan and Iraq? Because the authorities now take the possibility of another 9/11 so seriously? Because . . . So many explanations have been offered. We just don't know.

Amid all the uncertainty, however, we can say this without fear of contradiction: The focus of attention is the Bush administration's foreign policy meant to counter terrorism. Consequently, we have selected articles and organized this chapter around it.

The first essay is "Trends in Global Terrorism," an assessment by U.S. intelligence agencies of the situation in 2006 and trends for the immediate future. Nothing in the four (out of thirty) pages President Bush declassified and released is especially surprising, but the report does help to answer two important questions: Where are we in the struggle with terrorism? What might we expect in the near future?

We move from there to two important articles that supply background information. "The Protean Enemy" explains why al Qaeda remains the greatest threat of any single terrorist group; "Freedom and Justice in the Modern Middle East" examines the prospects for democracy in Muslim countries, relevant because establishing democratic regimes is a Bush policy cornerstone.

Three policy arguments follow. "All the Same Fight" urges us to link Afghanistan with Iraq and "stay the course," fight on until the new governments in these countries are able to stand on their own. "It's What We Do" argues that we are targets of terrorism because of American foreign policy, not because Islamic militants hate what we are or what we represent; consequently, we must alter what we do, including withdrawing our military forces from the Middle East. "The Wrong Strategy against the Next Generation" supports most of the goals of our current military efforts but not the means. Instead of maintaining military forces on Islamic soil, which the author thinks provokes terrorism, we should rely on an offshore military force instead.

We conclude with two articles that draw attention to relatively new developments. "Jihad Wired" addresses the increasing terrorist reliance on the World Wide Web. "Mother. Daughter. Sister. Bomber." focuses on the now-common practice of women carrying out suicide attacks.

Declassified Key Judgments of the National Intelligence Estimate "Trends in Global Terrorism: Implications for the United States"

OFFICE OF THE DIRECTOR OF NATIONAL INTELLIGENCE

> Whatever doubts we may have about the U.S. intelligence community, the following excerpt from its April 2006 report merits our attention. No other group of people has as much information, much of it classified, at their disposal, and their conclusions influence decision-makers at all levels of government.
>
> Authorship of the document is not known. It was surely a committee effort involving many hands.

United States-led counterterrorism efforts have seriously damaged the leadership of al-Qa'ida and disrupted its operations; however, . . . al-Qa'ida will continue to pose the greatest threat to the Homeland and US interests abroad by a single terrorist organization. . . . [T]he global jihadist movement—which includes al-Qa'ida, affiliated and independent terrorist groups, and emerging networks and cells—is spreading and adapting to counterterrorism efforts.

- Although we cannot measure the extent of the spread with precision, a large body of all-source reporting indicates that activists identifying themselves as jihadists, although a small percentage of Muslims, are increasing in both number and geographic dispersion.

- If this trend continues, threats to US interests at home and abroad will become more diverse, leading to increasing attacks worldwide.

- Greater pluralism and more responsive political systems in Muslim majority nations would alleviate some of the grievances jihadists exploit. Over time, such progress, together with sustained, multifaceted programs targeting the vulnerabilities of the jihadist movement and continued pressure on al-Qa'ida, could erode support for the jihadists.

. . . [T]he global jihadist movement is decentralized, lacks a coherent global strategy, and is becoming more diffuse. New jihadist networks and cells, with anti-American agendas, are increasingly likely to emerge. The confluence of shared purpose and dispersed actors will make it harder to find and undermine jihadist groups.

- . . . [T]he operational threat from self-radicalized cells will grow in importance to US counterterrorism efforts, particularly abroad but also in the Homeland.

- The jihadists regard Europe as an important venue for attacking Western interests. Extremist networks inside the extensive Muslim diasporas in Europe facilitate recruitment and staging for urban attacks, as illustrated by the 2004 Madrid and 2005 London bombings.

. . . [T]he Iraq jihad is shaping a new generation of terrorist leaders and operatives; perceived jihadist success there would inspire more fighters to continue the struggle elsewhere.

- The Iraq conflict has become the "cause celebre" for jihadists, breeding a deep resentment of US involvement in the Muslim world and cultivating supporters for the global jihadist movement. Should jihadists leaving Iraq perceive themselves, and be perceived, to have failed, . . . fewer fighters will be inspired to carry on the fight.

. . . [T]he underlying factors fueling the spread of the movement outweigh its vulnerabilities. . . .

- Four underlying factors are fueling the spread of the jihadist movement: (1) Entrenched grievances, such as corruption, injustice, and fear of Western domination, leading to anger, humiliation, and a sense of powerlessness; (2) the Iraq "jihad;" (3) the slow pace of real and sustained economic, social, and political reforms in many Muslim majority nations; and (4) pervasive anti-US sentiment among most Muslims—all of which jihadists exploit.

. . . [V]ulnerabilities in the jihadist movement have emerged that, if fully exposed and exploited, could begin to slow the spread of the movement. They include dependence on the continuation of Muslim-related conflicts, the limited appeal of the jihadists' radical ideology, the emergence of respected voices of moderation, and criticism of the violent tactics employed against mostly Muslim citizens.

- The jihadists' greatest vulnerability is that their ultimate political solution—an ultra-conservative interpretation of *shari'a*-based governance spanning the Muslim world—is unpopular with the vast majority of Muslims. Exposing the religious and political straitjacket that is implied by the jihadists' propaganda would help to divide them from the audiences they seek to persuade.

- Recent condemnations of violence and extremist religious interpretations by a few notable Muslim clerics signal a trend that could facilitate the growth of a constructive alternative to jihadist ideology: peaceful political activism. This also could lead to the consistent and dynamic participation of broader Muslim communities in rejecting violence, reducing the ability of radicals to capitalize on passive community support. In this way, the Muslim mainstream emerges as the most powerful weapon in the war on terror.

- Countering the spread of the jihadist movement will require coordinated multilateral efforts that go well beyond operations to capture or kill terrorist leaders.

If democratic reform efforts in Muslim majority nations progress over the next five years, political participation probably would drive a wedge between intransigent extremists and groups willing to use the political process to achieve their local objectives. Nonetheless, attendant reforms and potentially destabilizing transitions will create new opportunities for jihadists to exploit.

Al-Qa'ida, now merged with Abu Mus'ab al-Zarqawi's network, is exploiting 5 the situation in Iraq to attract new recruits and donors and to maintain its leadership role.

- The loss of key leaders, particularly Usama Bin Ladin, Ayman al-Zawahiri, and al-Zarqawi, in rapid succession, probably would cause the group to fracture into smaller groups. . . . [T]he resulting splinter groups would, at least for a time, pose a less serious threat to US interests than does al-Qa'ida.

- Should al-Zarqawi continue to evade capture and scale back attacks against Muslims, . . . he could broaden his popular appeal and present a global threat.

- The increased role of Iraqis in managing the operations of al-Qa'ida in Iraq might lead veteran foreign jihadists to focus their efforts on external operations.

Other affiliated Sunni extremist organizations, such as Jemaah Islamiya, Ansar al-Sunnah, and several North African groups, unless countered, are likely to expand their reach and become more capable of multiple and/or mass-casualty attacks outside their traditional areas of operations.

- . . . [S]uch groups pose less of a danger to the Homeland than does al-Qa'ida but will pose varying degrees of threat to our allies and to US interests abroad. The focus of their attacks is likely to ebb and flow between local regime targets and regional or global ones.

. . . [M]ost jihadist groups—both well-known and newly formed—will use improvised explosive devices and suicide attacks focused primarily on soft targets to implement their asymmetric warfare strategy, and . . . they will attempt to conduct sustained terrorist attacks in urban environments. Fighters with experience in Iraq are a potential source of leadership for jihadists pursuing these tactics.

- CBRN [Chemical, Biological, Radiological, and Nuclear] capabilities will continue to be sought by jihadist groups.

While Iran, and to a lesser extent Syria, remain the most active state sponsors of terrorism, many other states will be unable to prevent territory or resources from being exploited by terrorists.

Anti-US and anti-globalization sentiment is on the rise and fueling other radical ideologies. This could prompt some leftist, nationalist, or separatist groups to adopt terrorist methods to attack US interests. The radicalization process is occurring more quickly, more widely, and more anonymously in the Internet age, raising the likelihood of surprise attacks by unknown groups whose members and supporters may be difficult to pinpoint.

- . . . [G]roups of all stripes will increasingly use the Internet to communicate, propagandize, recruit, train, and obtain logistical and financial support.

FOR DISCUSSION

1. In class, list the major conclusions of the report. Which seem most important to you? Why do you think so?

2. "Most jihadist groups . . . will focus on soft targets to implement their asymmetric warfare strategy [in] . . . urban environments." What are "soft

targets"? What does "asymmetric warfare strategy" mean? Why are urban environments the preferred setting for terrorist activity?

3. "The Iraq conflict has become the 'cause celebre' for jihadists." This statement has drawn the most commentary so far. It's been commonly interpreted as implying that our efforts in Iraq have encouraged the *growth* of terrorism rather than reducing its appeal. Do you agree? Why or why not?

FOR RESEARCH AND CONVINCING

We helped to overthrow the Taliban in Afghanistan because they allowed al Qaeda to maintain a base of operation in their country. One of the justifications for removing Saddam Hussein from power in Iraq was his support for terrorist groups. Yet the report tells us that "Iran, and to a lesser extent Syria, remain the most active state sponsors of terrorism." Find out what Iran and Syria are doing and why. What are we and our allies doing to prevent these countries from supporting terrorists? How effective are the actions taken so far?

Write an essay either defending current policy toward Iran and Syria or arguing for other measures to discourage their support for terrorism.

The Protean Enemy

JESSICA STERN

> Understanding the kind of organization al Qaeda is poses a major challenge for
> most people, as does its frustrating resilience in the face of determined efforts to
> destroy it. Jessica Stern, a long-term and much-respected scholar of Islamic militant
> movements, helps us grasp both in the following article from *Foreign Affairs* (2003).
> She teaches at Harvard's John F. Kennedy School of Government and is the author of
> *The Ultimate Terrorists* and *Terror in the Name of God: Why Religious Militants Kill*.

Having suffered the destruction of its sanctuary in Afghanistan . . . , al-Qaeda's
already decentralized organization has become more decentralized still. The group's
leaders have largely dispersed to Pakistan, Iran, Iraq, and elsewhere around the
world (only a few still remain in Afghanistan's lawless border regions). And with
many of the planet's intelligence agencies now focusing on destroying its network,
al Qaeda's ability to carry out large-scale attacks has been degraded.

Yet despite these setbacks, al Qaeda and its affiliates remain among the most
significant threats to U.S. national security today. . . . What accounts for al Qaeda's
ongoing effectiveness in the face of an unprecedented onslaught? The answer lies
in the organization's remarkably protean nature. Over its life span, al Qaeda has
constantly evolved and shown a surprising willingness to adapt its mission. This
capacity for change has consistently made the group more appealing to recruits,
attracted surprising new allies, and—most worrisome from a Western perspective—
made it harder to detect and destroy. Unless Washington and its allies show a
similar adaptability, the war on terrorism won't be won anytime soon, and the
death toll is likely to mount.

MALLEABLE MISSIONS

Why do religious terrorists kill? In interviews over the last five years, many terrorists
and their supporters have suggested to me that people first join such groups to
make the world a better place—at least for the particular populations they aim to
serve. Over time, however, militants have told me, terrorism can become a career
as much as a passion. Leaders harness humiliation and anomie [lawlessness] and
turn them into weapons. Jihad becomes addictive, militants report, and with some
individuals or groups—the "professional" terrorists—grievances can evolve into
greed: for money, political power, status, or attention.

In such "professional" terrorist groups, simply perpetuating their cadres
becomes a central goal, and what started out as a moral crusade becomes a
sophisticated organization. Ensuring the survival of the group demands flexibility
in many areas, but especially in terms of mission. Objectives thus evolve in a
variety of ways. Some groups find a new cause once their first one is achieved. . . .
Other groups broaden their goals in order to attract a wider variety of recruits.
Still other organizations transform themselves into profit-driven organized criminals, or form alliances with groups that have ideologies different from their own,
forcing both to adapt. Some terrorist groups hold fast to their original missions.
But only the spry survive.

Consider, for example, Egyptian Islamic Jihad (EIJ). EIJ's original objective was 5 to fight the oppressive, secular rulers of Egypt and turn the country into an Islamic state. But the group fell on hard times after its leader, Sheikh Omar Abdel Rahman, was imprisoned in the United States and other EIJ leaders were killed or forced into exile. Thus in the early 1990s, Ayman al-Zawahiri decided to shift the group's sights from its "near enemy"—the secular rulers of Egypt—to the "far enemy," namely the United States and other Western countries. Switching goals in this way allowed the group to align itself with another terrorist aiming to attack the West and able to provide a significant influx of cash: Osama bin Laden. In return for bin Laden's financial assistance, Zawahiri provided some 200 loyal, disciplined, and well-trained followers, who became the core of al Qaeda's leadership. . . .

Even Osama bin Laden himself has changed his objectives over time. The Saudi terrorist inherited an organization devoted to fighting Soviet forces in Afghanistan. But he turned it into a flexible group of ruthless warriors ready to fight on behalf of multiple causes. His first call to holy war, issued in 1992, urged believers to kill American soldiers in Saudi Arabia and the Horn of Africa but barely mentioned Palestine. The second, issued in 1996, was a 40-page document listing atrocities and injustices committed against Muslims, mainly by Western powers. With the release of his third manifesto in February 1998, however, bin Laden began urging his followers to start deliberately targeting American civilians, rather than soldiers. . . . Although this third declaration mentioned the Palestinian struggle, it was still only one among a litany of grievances. Only in bin Laden's fourth call to arms— issued to the al Jazeera network on October 7, 2001, to coincide with the U.S. aerial bombardment of Afghanistan—did he emphasize Israel's occupation of Pal- estinian lands and the suffering of Iraqi children under UN sanctions, concerns broadly shared in the Islamic world. By extending his appeal, bin Laden sought to turn the war on terrorism into a war between all of Islam and the West. The events of September 11, he charged, split the world into two camps—believers and infi- dels—and the time had come for "every Muslim to defend his religion." . . .

FRIENDS OF CONVENIENCE

Apart from the flexibility of its mission, another explanation for al Qaeda's remark- able staying power is its willingness to forge broad—and sometimes unlikely—alli- ances. In an effort to expand his network, bin Laden created the International Islamic Front for Jihad Against the Jews and Crusaders (IIF) in February 1998. In addition to bin Laden and EIJ's Zawahiri, members included the head of Egypt's Gama'a al Islamiya, the secretary-general of the Pakistani religious party known as the Jamiat- ul-Ulema-e-Islam (JUI), and the head of Bangladesh's Jihad Movement. Later, the IIF was expanded to include the Pakistani jihadi organizations Lashkar-e-Taiba, Harkat- ul-Mujahideen, and Sipah-e-Sahaba Pakistan, the last an anti-Shi'a sectarian party. Senior al Qaeda lieutenant Abu Zubaydah was captured at a Lashkar-e-Taiba's safe house in Faisalabad in March 2002, suggesting that some of Lashkar-e-Taiba's mem- bers are facilitating and assisting the movement of al Qaeda members in Pakistan. And Indian sources claim that Lashkar-e-Taiba is now trying to play a role similar to that once played by al Qaeda itself, coordinating and in some cases funding pro–bin Laden networks, especially in Southeast Asia and the Persian Gulf.

In addition to its formal alliances through the IIF, bin Laden's organization has also nurtured ties and now works closely with a variety of still other groups around the world, including Ansar al Islam, based mainly in Iraq and Europe; Jemaah Islamiah in Southeast Asia; Abu Sayyaf and the Moro Islamic Liberation Front in the Philippines; and many Pakistani jihadi groups. In some cases, al Qaeda has provided these allies with funding and direction. In others, the groups have shared camps, operatives, and logistics. Some "franchise groups," such as Jemaah Islamiah, have raised money for joint operations with al Qaeda.

Perhaps most surprising (and alarming) is the increasing evidence that al Qaeda, a Sunni organization, is now cooperating with the Shi'a group Hezbollah, considered to be the most sophisticated terrorist group in the world. Hezbollah, which enjoys backing from Syria and Iran, is based in southern Lebanon and in the lawless "triborder" region of South America, where Paraguay, Brazil, and Argentina meet. . . . Although low-level cooperation between al Qaeda and Hezbollah has been evident for some time . . . , the two groups have formed a much closer relationship since al Qaeda was evicted from its base in Afghanistan. Representatives of the two groups have lately met up in Lebanon, Paraguay, and an unidentified African country. According to a report in Israel's *Ha'aretz* newspaper, Imad Mughniyah, who directs Hezbollah in the triborder area, has also been appointed by Iran to coordinate the group's activities with Hamas and Palestinian Islamic Jihad.

The triborder region of South America has become the world's new Libya, a   10
place where terrorists with widely disparate ideologies—Marxist Colombian rebels, American white supremacists, Hamas, Hezbollah, and others—meet to swap tradecraft. Authorities now worry that the more sophisticated groups will invite the American radicals to help them. Moneys raised for terrorist organizations in the United States are often funneled through Latin America, which has also become an important stopover point for operatives entering the United States. Reports that Venezuela's President Hugo Chavez is allowing Colombian rebels and militant Islamist groups to operate in his country are meanwhile becoming more credible, as are claims that Venezuela's Margarita Island has become a terrorist haven. . . .

NEW-STYLE NETWORKS

Al Qaeda seems to have learned that in order to evade detection in the West, it must adopt some of the qualities of a "virtual network": a style of organization used by American right-wing extremists for operating in environments (such as the United States) that have effective law enforcement agencies. American antigovernment groups refer to this style as "leaderless resistance." The idea was popularized by Louis Beam, the self-described ambassador-at-large, staff propagandist, and "computer terrorist to the Chosen" for Aryan Nations, an American neo-Nazi group. Beam writes that hierarchical organization is extremely dangerous for insurgents, especially in "technologically advanced societies where electronic surveillance can often penetrate the structure, revealing its chain of command." In leaderless organizations, however, "individuals and groups operate independently of each other, and never report to a central headquarters or single leader for direction or instruction, as would those who belong to a typical pyramid organization." Leaders do not issue orders or pay operatives; instead, they inspire small cells or individuals to take action on their own initiative. . . .

Already the effects of these leaderless cells have been felt. In February 2002, Ahmed Omar Saeed Sheikh, the British national who was recently sentenced to death for his involvement in the abduction and murder of *Wall Street Journal* reporter Daniel Pearl, warned his Pakistani interrogators that they would soon confront the threat of small cells, working independently of the known organizations that Pakistani President Pervez Musharraf had vowed to shut down. Sure enough, soon after Omar Sheikh made this threat, unidentified terrorists killed 5 people in an Islamabad church known to be frequented by U.S. embassy personnel, and another group killed 11 French military personnel in Karachi in May. And in July, still other unidentified terrorists detonated a truck bomb at the entrance of the U.S. consulate in Karachi, killing 12 Pakistanis.

JOINING THE FAMILY

Virtual links are only part of the problem; terrorists, including members of bin Laden's IIF, have also started to forge ties with traditional organized crime groups, especially in India. One particularly troubling example is the relationship established between Omar Sheikh and an ambitious Indian gangster named Aftab Ansari. Asif Reza Khan, the "chief executive" for Ansari's Indian operations, told interrogators that he received military training at a camp in Khost, Afghanistan, belonging to Lashkar-e-Taiba, and that "leaders of different militant outfits in Pakistan were trying to use his network for the purpose of jihad, whereas [Ansari] was trying to use the militants' networks for underworld operations."

Khan told his interrogators that the don provided money and hideouts to his new partners, in one case transferring $100,000 to Omar Sheikh—money that Omar Sheikh, in turn, wired to Muhammad Atta, the lead hijacker in the September 11 attacks. According to Khan, Ansari viewed the $100,000 gift as an "investment" in a valuable relationship.

Still another set of unlikely links has sprung up in American prisons, where Saudi charities now fund organizations that preach radical Islam. According to Warith Deen Umar, who hired most of the Muslim chaplains currently active in New York State prisons, prisoners who are recent Muslim converts are natural recruits for Islamist organizations. Umar, incidentally, told *The Wall Street Journal* that the September 11 hijackers should be honored as martyrs, and he traveled to Saudi Arabia twice as part of an outreach program designed to spread Salafism (a radical Muslim movement) in U.S. prisons. . . .

Still another surprising source of al Qaeda recruits is Tablighi Jamaat (TJ), a revivalist organization that aims at creating better Muslims through "spiritual jihad": good deeds, contemplation, and proselytizing. According to the historian Barbara Metcalf, TJ has traditionally functioned as a self-help group, much like Alcoholics Anonymous, and most specialists claim that it is no more prone to violence than are the Seventh-Day Adventists, with whom TJ is frequently compared. But several Americans known to have trained in al Qaeda camps were brought to Southwest Asia by TJ and appear to have been recruited into jihadi organizations while traveling under TJ auspices. For example, Jose Padilla (an American now being held as an "enemy combatant" for planning to set off a "dirty" radiological bomb in the United States) was a member of TJ, as were Richard Reid and John Walker Lindh (the so-called American Taliban). According to prosecutors, the "Lackawanna Six" group (an alleged al Qaeda sleeper cell from a Buffalo, New York, suburb) similarly first went to Pakistan to receive TJ religious training before proceeding to the al Farooq training camp in Afghanistan. A Pakistani TJ member told me that jihadi groups openly recruit at the organization's central headquarters in Raiwind, Pakistan, including at the mosque. And TJ members in Boston say that a lot of Muslims end up treating the group, which is now active in American inner cities and prisons, as a gateway to jihadi organizations. . . .

Totalitarian Islamist revivalism has become the ideology of the dystopian new world order. In an earlier era, radicals might have described their grievances through other ideological lenses, perhaps anarchism, Marxism, or Nazism. Today they choose extreme Islamism.

Radical transnational Islam, divorced from its countries of origin, appeals to some jobless youths in depressed parts of Europe and the United States. As the French scholar Olivier Roy points out, leaders of radical Islamic groups often come from the middle classes, many of them having trained in technical fields, but their followers tend to be working-class dropouts. . . .

FOR DISCUSSION

1. Flexibility in mission or objectives is one of the hallmarks of professional jihad groups. How has bin Laden changed his? What did he gain in doing so?

2. As the daily news from Iraq shows, Sunni and Shiite Muslims are often in conflict. Yet the Sunni al Qaeda may be cooperating with the Lebanese Hezbollah, a Shiite group. Stern calls this development "alarming." Why? How does it threaten the interests of the United States and Europe?

3. Explain the concept of "virtual network." How does such a mode of organization work to the advantage of a group like al Qaeda?

FOR RESEARCH AND PERSUASION

One thing is beyond doubt where countering terrorism is concerned—we can't destroy or neutralize an enemy we don't understand. As a class research project, pull together all the information you can find on how al Qaeda, Hezbollah, and other prominent Islamic militant organizations operate. Besides Stern's books, another excellent source is a book by Rohan Gunaratna, *Inside Al Qaeda: Global Network of Terror.*

Write an essay directed at other students at your college that both tells them what they need to know about such groups and advocates ways to combat them effectively. Be sure to relate what you're advocating to current national administration policies.

Freedom and Justice in the Modern Middle East

BERNARD LEWIS

What is the Islamic understanding of government? Why have so many Muslim countries succumbed to authoritarian tyrannies? What are the prospects for democracy in such countries? Bernard Lewis, a renowned Middle Eastern historian, attempts to answer these questions in a *Foreign Affairs* article (May–June 2005).

Lewis is professor emeritus of Near Eastern Studies at Princeton. His many books include *Islam and the West* and *The Shaping of the Modern Middle East.*

[T]he traditional Islamic ideal of good government is expressed in the term "justice." This is represented by several different words in Arabic and other Islamic languages. The most usual, *adl,* means "justice according to the law" (with "law" defined as God's law, the *sharia,* as revealed to the Prophet and to the Muslim community). But what is the converse of justice? What is a regime that does not meet the standards of justice? If a ruler is to qualify as just, as defined in the traditional Islamic system of rules and ideas, he must meet two requirements: he must have acquired power rightfully, and he must exercise it rightfully. In other words, he must be neither a usurper nor a tyrant. It is of course possible to be either one without the other, although the normal experience was to be both at the same time.

The Islamic notion of justice is well documented and goes back to the time of the Prophet. The life of the Prophet Muhammad, as related in his biography and reflected in revelation and tradition, falls into two main phases. In the first phase he is still living in his native town of Mecca and opposing its regime. He is preaching a new religion, a new doctrine that challenges the pagan oligarchy that rules Mecca. The verses in the Koran, and also relevant passages in the prophetic traditions and biography, dating from the Meccan period, carry a message of opposition—of rebellion, one might even say of revolution, against the existing order.

Then comes the famous migration, the *hijra* from Mecca to Medina, where Muhammad becomes a wielder, not a victim, of authority. Muhammad, during his lifetime, becomes a head of state and does what heads of state do. He promulgates and enforces laws, he raises taxes, he makes war, he makes peace; in a word, he governs. The political tradition, the political maxims, and the political guidance of this period do not focus on how to resist or oppose the government, as in the Meccan period, but on how to conduct government. So from the very beginning of Muslim scripture, jurisprudence, and political culture, there have been two distinct traditions: one, dating from the Meccan period, might be called activist; the other, dating from the Medina period, quietist [conformist]. . . .

These two traditions, the one quietist and the other activist, continue right through the recorded history of Islamic states and Islamic political thought and practice. Muslims have been interested from the very beginning in the problems of politics and government: the acquisition and exercise of power, succession, legitimacy, and—especially relevant here—the limits of authority. . . .

In the course of time, the quietist, or authoritarian, trend grew stronger, and 5 it became more difficult to maintain those limitations on the autocracy of the ruler that had been prescribed by holy scripture and holy law. And so the literature places increasing stress on the need for order. A word used very frequently in the discussions is *fitna,* an Arabic term that can be translated as "sedition," "disorder," "disturbance," and even "anarchy" in certain contexts. The point is made again and again, with obvious anguish and urgency: tyranny is better than anarchy. Some writers even go so far as to say that an hour—or even a moment—of anarchy is worse than a hundred years of tyranny. That is one point of view—but not the only one. In some times and places within the Muslim world, it has been dominant; in other times and places, it has been emphatically rejected.

THEORY VERSUS HISTORY

The Islamic tradition insists very strongly on two points concerning the conduct of government by the ruler. One is the need for consultation. This is explicitly recommended in the Koran. It is also mentioned very frequently in the traditions of the Prophet. The converse is despotism; in Arabic *istibdad,* "despotism" is a technical term with very negative connotations. It is regarded as something evil and sinful, and to accuse a ruler of *istibdad* is practically a call to depose him. . . .

Consultation is a central part of the traditional Islamic order, but it is not the only element that can check the ruler's authority. The traditional system of Islamic government is both consensual and contractual. The manuals of holy law generally assert that the new caliph—the head of the Islamic community and state—is to be "chosen." The Arabic term used is sometimes translated as "elected," but it does not connote a general or even sectional election. Rather, it refers to a small group of suitable, competent people choosing the ruler's successor. In principle, hereditary succession is rejected by the juristic tradition. Yet in practice, succession was always hereditary, except when broken by insurrection or civil war; it was—and in most places still is—common for a ruler, royal or otherwise, to designate his successor.

But the element of consent is still important. In theory, at times even in practice, the ruler's power—both gaining it and maintaining it—depends on the consent of the ruled. The basis of the ruler's authority is described in the classical texts by the Arabic word *bay'a,* a term usually translated as "homage," as in the subjects paying homage to their new ruler. But a more accurate translation of *bay'a*—which comes from a verb meaning "to buy and to sell"—would be "deal," in other words, a contract between the ruler and the ruled in which both have obligations.

Some critics may point out that regardless of theory, in reality a pattern of arbitrary, tyrannical, despotic government marks the entire Middle East and other parts of the Islamic world. Some go further, saying, "That is how Muslims are, that is how Muslims have always been, and there is nothing the West can do about it." That is a misreading of history. . . .

Since 1940 and again after the arrival of the Soviets, the Middle East has basi- 10 cally imported European models of rule: fascist, Nazi, and communist. But to speak of dictatorship as being the immemorial way of doing things in that part of the world is simply untrue. It shows ignorance of the Arab past, contempt for the Arab present, and unconcern for the Arab future. The type of regime that was maintained by Saddam Hussein—and that continues to be maintained by some other rulers in the Muslim world—is modern, indeed recent, and very alien to the foundations of Islamic civilization. There are older rules and traditions on which the peoples of the Middle East can build.

CHUTES AND LADDERS

There are, of course, several obvious hindrances to the development of democratic institutions in the Middle East. The first and most obvious is the pattern of auto-cratic and despotic rule currently embedded there. Such rule is alien, with no roots in either the classical Arab or the Islamic past, but it is by now a couple of centu-ries old and is well entrenched, constituting a serious obstacle.

Another, more traditional hurdle is the absence in classical Islamic political thought and practice of the notion of citizenship, in the sense of being a free and participating member of a civic entity. This notion, with roots going back to the Greek [*polis*] . . . has been central in Western civilization from antiquity to the present day. It, and the idea of the people participating not just in the choice of a ruler but in the conduct of government, is not part of traditional Islam. . . . To this day, there is no word in Arabic corresponding to "citizen." The word normally used on passports and other documents is *muwatin,* the literal meaning of which is "compatriot." With a lack of citizenship went a lack of civic representation. Although different social groups did choose their own leaders during the classical period, the concept of choosing individuals to represent the citizenry in a corporate body or assembly was alien to Muslims' experience and practice.

Yet, other positive elements of Islamic history and thought could help in the development of democracy. Notably, the idea of consensual, contractual, and lim-ited government is again becoming an issue today. The traditional rejection of despotism, of *istibdad,* has gained a new force and new urgency: Europe may have disseminated the ideology of dictatorship, but it also spread a corresponding ideol-ogy of popular revolt against dictatorship.

The rejection of despotism, familiar in both traditional and, increasingly, modern writings, is already having a powerful impact. Muslims are again rais-ing—and in some cases practicing—the related idea of consultation. For the pious, these developments are based on holy law and tradition, with an impres-sive series of precedents in the Islamic past. One sees this revival particularly in Afghanistan, whose people underwent rather less modernization and are there-fore finding it easier to resurrect the better traditions of the past, notably con-sultation by the government with various entrenched interests and loyalty groups. This is the purpose of the Loya Jirga, the "grand council" that consists of a wide range of different groups—ethnic, tribal, religious, regional, professional, and others. There are signs of a tentative movement toward inclusiveness in the Middle East as well.

There are also other positive influences at work, sometimes in surprising forms. 15 Perhaps the single most important development is the adoption of modern com-munications. The printing press and the newspaper, the telegraph, the radio, and the television have all transformed the Middle East. Initially, communications technology was an instrument of tyranny, giving the state an effective new weapon for propaganda and control.

But this trend could not last indefinitely. More recently, particularly with the rise of the Internet, television satellites, and cell phones, communications technology has begun to have the opposite effect. It is becoming increasingly clear that one of the main reasons for the collapse of the Soviet Union was the information revolution. The old Soviet system depended in large measure on control of the production, distribution, and exchange of information and ideas; as modern communications developed, this became no longer possible. . . .

A parallel process is already beginning in the Islamic countries of the Middle East. Even some of the intensely and unscrupulously propagandist television programs that now infest the airwaves contribute to this process, indirectly and unintentionally, by offering a diversity of lies that arouse suspicion and questioning. Television also brings to the peoples of the Middle East a previously unknown spectacle—that of lively and vigorous public disagreement and debate. In some places, young people even watch Israeli television. In addition to seeing well-known Israeli public figures "banging the table and screaming at each other" (as one Arab viewer described it with wonderment), they sometimes see even Israeli Arabs arguing in the Knesset, denouncing Israeli ministers and policies—on Israeli television. The spectacle of a lively, vibrant, rowdy democracy at work, notably the unfamiliar sight of unconstrained, uninhibited, but orderly argument between conflicting ideas and interests, is having an impact.

Modern communications have also had another effect, in making Middle Eastern Muslims more painfully aware of how badly things have gone wrong. In the past, they were not really conscious of the differences between their world and the rest. They did not realize how far they were falling behind not only the advanced West, but also the advancing East—first Japan, then China, India, South Korea, and Southeast Asia—and practically everywhere else in terms of standard of living, achievement, and, more generally, human and cultural development. Even more painful than these differences are the disparities between groups of people in the Middle East itself.

Right now, the question of democracy is more pertinent to Iraq than perhaps to any other Middle Eastern country. In addition to the general factors, Iraq may benefit from two characteristics specific to its circumstances. One relates to infrastructure and education. Of all the countries profiting from oil revenues in the past decades, pre-Saddam Iraq probably made the best use of its revenues. Its leaders developed the country's roads, bridges, and utilities, and particularly a network of schools and universities of a higher standard than in most other places in the region. These, like everything else in Iraq, were devastated by Saddam's rule. But even in the worst of conditions, an educated middle class will somehow contrive to educate its children, and the results of this can be seen in the Iraqi people today.

The other advantage is the position of women, which is far better than in most 20 places in the Islamic world. They do not enjoy greater rights—"rights" being a word without meaning in that context—but rather access and opportunity. Under Saddam's predecessors, women had access to education, including higher education, and therefore to careers, with few parallels in the Muslim world. In the West, women's relative freedom has been a major reason for the advance of the greater society; women would certainly be an important, indeed essential, part of a democratic future in the Middle East.

FUNDAMENTAL DANGERS

The main threat to the development of democracy in Iraq and ultimately in other Arab and Muslim countries lies not in any inherent social quality or characteristic, but in the very determined efforts that are being made to ensure democracy's failure. The opponents of democracy in the Muslim world come from very different sources, with sharply contrasting ideologies. An alliance of expediency exists between different groups with divergent interests. . . .

Most dangerous are the so-called Islamic fundamentalists, those for whom democracy is part of the greater evil emanating from the West, whether in the old-fashioned form of imperial domination or in the more modern form of cultural penetration. Satan, in the Koran, is "the insidious tempter who whispers in men's hearts." The modernizers, with their appeal to women and more generally to the young, are seen to strike at the very heart of the Islamic order—the state, the schoolroom, the market, and even the family. The fundamentalists view the Westerners and their dupes and disciples, the Westernizers, as not only impeding the predestined advance of Islam to final triumph in the world, but even endangering it in its homelands. Unlike reformers, fundamentalists perceive the problem of the Muslim world to be not insufficient modernization, but an excess of modernization—and even modernization itself. For them, democracy is an alien and infidel intrusion, part of the larger and more pernicious influence of the Great Satan and his cohorts.

The fundamentalist response to Western rule and still more to Western social and cultural influence has been gathering force for a long time. . . . Political Islam first became a major international factor with the Iranian Revolution of 1979. . . . [W]hat happened in Iran was a genuine revolution, a major change with a very significant ideological challenge, a shift in the basis of society that had an immense impact on the whole Islamic world, intellectually, morally, and politically. The process that began in Iran in 1979 was a revolution in the same sense as the French and the Russian revolutions were. . . .

The theocratic regime in Iran swept to power on a wave of popular support nourished by resentment against the old regime, its policies, and its associations. Since then, the regime has become increasingly unpopular as the ruling mullahs have shown themselves to be just as corrupt and oppressive as the ruling cliques in other countries in the region. There are many indications in Iran of a rising tide of discontent. Some seek radical change in the form of a return to the past; others, by far the larger number, place their hopes in the coming of true democracy. The rulers of Iran are thus very apprehensive of democratic change in Iraq, the more so as a majority of Iraqis are Shiites, like the Iranians. By its mere existence, a Shiite democracy on Iran's western frontier would pose a challenge, indeed a mortal threat, to the regime of the mullahs, so they are doing what they can to prevent or deflect it.

Of far greater importance at the present are the Sunni fundamentalists. An important element in the Sunni holy war is the rise and spread—and in some areas dominance—of Wahhabism. Wahhabism is a school of Islam that arose in Nejd, in central Arabia, in the eighteenth century. It caused some trouble to the rulers of the Muslim world at the time but was eventually repressed and contained. It reappeared in the twentieth century and acquired new importance when the House of Saud, the local tribal chiefs committed to Wahhabism, conquered the holy cities of Mecca and Medina and created the Saudi monarchy. This brought together two factors of the highest importance. One, the Wahhabi Saudis now ruled the holy cities and therefore controlled the annual Muslim pilgrimage, which gave them immense prestige and influence in the Islamic world. Two, the discovery and exploitation of oil placed immense wealth at their disposal. What would otherwise have been an extremist fringe in a marginal country thus had a worldwide impact. Now the forces that were nourished, nurtured, and unleashed threaten even the House of Saud itself.

The first great triumph of the Sunni fundamentalists was the collapse of the Soviet Union, which they saw—not unreasonably—as their victory. For them the Soviet Union was defeated not in the Cold War waged by the West, but in the Islamic jihad waged by the guerrilla fighters in Afghanistan. As Osama bin Laden and his cohorts have put it, they destroyed one of the two last great infidel superpowers—the more difficult and the more dangerous of the two. Dealing with the pampered and degenerate Americans would, so they believed, be much easier. American actions and discourse have at times weakened and at times strengthened this belief.

In a genuinely free election, fundamentalists would have several substantial advantages over moderates and reformers. One is that they speak a language familiar to Muslims. Democratic parties promote an ideology and use a terminology mostly strange to the "Muslim street." The fundamentalist parties, on the other hand, employ familiar words and evoke familiar values both to criticize the existing secularist, authoritarian order and to offer an alternative. To broadcast this message, the fundamentalists utilize an enormously effective network that meets and communicates in the mosque and speaks from the pulpit. None of the secular parties has access to anything comparable. Religious revolutionaries, and even terrorists, also gain support because of their frequently genuine efforts to alleviate the suffering of the common people. This concern often stands in marked contrast with the callous and greedy unconcern of the current wielders of power and influence in the Middle East. The example of the Iranian Revolution would seem to indicate that once in power these religious militants are no better, and are sometimes even worse, than those they overthrow and replace. But until then, both the current perceptions and the future hopes of the people can work in their favor.

Finally, perhaps most important of all, democratic parties are ideologically bound to allow fundamentalists freedom of action. The fundamentalists suffer from no such disability; on the contrary, it is their mission when in power to suppress sedition and unbelief.

Despite these difficulties, there are signs of hope, notably the Iraqi general election in January. Millions of Iraqis went to polling stations, stood in line, and cast their votes, knowing that they were risking their lives at every moment of the process. It was a truly momentous achievement, and its impact can already be seen in neighboring Arab and other countries. Arab democracy has won a battle, not a war, and still faces many dangers, both from ruthless and resolute enemies and from hesitant and unreliable friends. But it was a major battle, and the Iraqi election may prove a turning point in Middle Eastern history. . . .

FEAR ITSELF

The creation of a democratic political and social order in Iraq or elsewhere in the 30 Middle East will not be easy. But it is possible, and there are increasing signs that it has already begun. At the present time there are two fears concerning the possibility of establishing a democracy in Iraq. One is the fear that it will not work, a fear expressed by many in the United States and one that is almost a dogma in Europe; the other fear, much more urgent in ruling circles in the Middle East, is that it will work. Clearly, a genuinely free society in Iraq would constitute a mortal threat to many of the governments of the region, including both Washington's enemies and some of those seen as Washington's allies.

The end of World War II opened the way for democracy in the former Axis powers. The end of the Cold War brought a measure of freedom and a movement toward democracy in much of the former Soviet domains. With steadfastness and patience, it may now be possible at last to bring both justice and freedom to the long-tormented peoples of the Middle East.

FOR DISCUSSION

1. Lewis strongly rejects the common opinion that Muslim countries are just by nature caught "in . . . a pattern of arbitrary, tyrannical, despotic government." He calls this view "a misreading of history." What evidence does he offer to refute it?

2. Lewis obviously doesn't want the United States—or the Western powers generally—to give up on the possibility for a better future for Muslim-dominated countries in the Middle East. Yet he calls attention to the significant forces working against democracy in the region. What are they? What advantages do they have in working against democratic institutions?

3. What hopeful signs for democracy does Lewis see both in Islamic tradition and in recent events? In your view, do these signs warrant his view that "creation of a democratic political and social order . . . will not be easy but is possible"?

FOR RESEARCH AND INQUIRY

Too often news reporting and discussions of current events lack historical knowledge or perspective. We see only what is going on now, without any sense of the past, without which we cannot adequately understand the present.

Going back at least as far as World War I, find out as much as you can about the histories of Afghanistan and Iraq, and try to see what's happened in these countries in the context of historical forces in the region generally. Then write an essay exploring the insights you've gained. How have they changed your understanding of what's going on in Afghanistan and Iraq now? What implications do your new insights have for current and future U.S. policy?

All the Same Fight

RICH LOWRY AND DAVID RIVKIN, JR.

Whatever anyone thinks about the wisdom of overthrowing the Taliban in Afghanistan and deposing Saddam Hussein in Iraq, these actions cannot be undone and they have had consequences that can't be denied. So the fundamental question is, What now? In this and the next two articles, we encounter three quite different proposals. This one asserts a strong linkage between Afghanistan and Iraq and urges "staying the course"—or risk ceding both countries to Islamic insurgents.

Rich Lowry is editor of the *National Review* and David Rivkin is a lawyer who served under both Ronald Reagan and George H. W. Bush. Their editorial appeared in the *Dallas Morning News* on October 2, 2006.

To critics of the Bush administration, the war in Afghanistan is the "good" counterinsurgency. Their calls for troop reductions or a timetable to end the "bad war" in Iraq are matched by demands for more resources and perseverance in Afghanistan. However, this preference is senseless, driven either by sentimentality or partisanship.

There is no sound strategic reason to favor the Afghan war over the war in Iraq. In fact, the fates of Baghdad and Kabul are intertwined.

The two wars began differently, of course. The Afghan war has always been much less controversial. No one has ever denied that the Taliban's harboring of al-Qaeda was a legitimate *casus belli*. The Iraq war had much more opposition from the beginning and one of its chief rationales—that Saddam Hussein was harboring stockpiles of weapons of mass destruction—seemed to collapse after the U.S. invasion.

But if you put aside how the wars began—and we realize that many opponents of the Iraq war will never be able to do that—there is little to differentiate them.

In Iraq, we face a vicious insurgency that will take years to defeat; the same 5 is true in Afghanistan. In Iraq, the insurgency is made more difficult by the overlay of sectarian violence (Sunni vs. Shiite); the same is true in Afghanistan (Pashtun vs everyone else). In Iraq, the insurgents are aided by infiltration from neighboring countries (Syria, Iran); the same is true in Afghanistan (Pakistan). In both countries, we are trying to rebuild the army and the police—with fitful progress—and fostering a fragile central government.

Of course, at least today, the difficulties in the two countries are not of equal severity. In Iraq, the violence is worse, American casualties are much higher and the capital city—the center of gravity of the country—is besieged by insurgents and murderous sectarians. Compared to that, Afghanistan is doing quite well. But it has deep problems of its own—namely the risk that it will become a lawless narco-state.

Pessimists about Iraq say the country is in the midst of a civil war. By most definitions, it certainly is, but this needn't be cause for despair. Indeed, in Afghanistan, the U.S. success driving out the Taliban regime was greatly aided by the fact that the country was in the midst of a civil war and that we allied ourselves with one side. Likewise, there is no reason that the U.S. cannot successfully navigate the shoals of communal violence in Iraq.

A helicopter carries the body of an Italian soldier killed south of Kabul, Afghanistan, on Tuesday [9/26/06].

The most important similarity between the Iraq and Afghan wars is that in both we are fighting al-Qaeda. Leaving aside the issue of how and when al-Qaeda came to be in Iraq, it is there now, and it considers Iraq a central battlefield. What we are fighting to prevent in Iraq—a country established as a terrorist base—is exactly what we fought to destroy in Afghanistan immediately after 9/11 and are fighting to prevent from re-emerging there now.

Insurgents in both countries share the jihadi battle against the U.S., and tactics such as the use of improvised explosive devices and suicide car-bombings have migrated from Iraq to Afghanistan.

At the strategic level, the more Iraqi insurgents seem to be succeeding, the more 10 emboldened insurgents in Afghanistan become. As the just-declassified portions of the National Intelligence Estimate put it, "Perceived jihadist success (in Iraq) would inspire more fighters to continue the struggle elsewhere."

The costs of the Iraq war are higher to the U.S. in terms of blood and treasure. But the stakes are higher as well. If the terrorists capture Iraq, they would win a country much more strategically located than Afghanistan, and they would control the world's fourth-biggest oil reserves.

There is no doubt, as the intelligence estimate noted, that the Iraq war is a recruiting tool for terrorists. But Iraq war opponents should not fool themselves; so are Afghanistan and dozens of other Muslim grievances.

The Afghan war was launched in a brief period of national unity, while the Iraq war helped stoke our current period of political enmity. But one war will not be won without the other.

FOR DISCUSSION

1. Afghanistan has almost been forgotten because news coverage has centered on Iraq in the last few years. Furthermore, the two arenas of conflict are usually discussed as if they are entirely different and distinct. Lowry and Rivkin want us to see them as "all the same fight." What reasons do they offer for understanding them this way? Are you persuaded by their view? Why or why not?

2. Lowry and Rivkin concede that "by most definitions" Iraq is "in the midst of a civil war." Why are they not discouraged by this state of affairs?

3. Lowry and Rivkin point to something no one can ignore in thinking about Iraq: It is "strategically located" and has a huge reserve of crude oil—neither of which is true of Afghanistan. In your view, can the United States afford to withdraw troops from Iraq without first securing our interests there? That is, are Lowry and Rivkin right to say that the stakes are too high to abandon the struggle in Iraq?

FOR DISCUSSION AND CONVINCING

Lowry and Rivkin point to the National Intelligence Estimate about trends in global terrorism, the first selection in this chapter, which said that "perceived jihadist success" in Iraq "would inspire more fighters to continue the struggle elsewhere." But that document also said that Iraq has become a "cause celebre" for the jihadists, helping them to recruit still more people to their cause. It appears, then, that we can't win; the jihadists have us caught on the horns of a dilemma.

Discuss this state of affairs in class. Then write an essay advocating an approach for dealing with it. That is, if the jihadist cause profits no matter what we do, how can we best minimize its gain?

It's What We Do

IVAN ELAND

> Why is the United States one of the prime targets of terrorism? What should we do
> to remove the target from our back? Eland argues that American foreign policy is
> the cause and that changing it radically is the only solution.
>   His article appeared in *American Prospect* (January 2006). He is a senior fellow and
> director of the Center for Peace and Liberty at the Independent Institute.

George W. Bush, in his global war on terror, has specifically avoided the clash of civilizations hypothesis, holding that the United States is not waging a war against the religion of Islam. However, the president has backed into the hypothesis by saying that terrorists "hate us because we are free." The president, that is, has essentially made the argument that they hate America for "what it is." We are not, Bush once said, "facing a set of grievances that can be soothed or addressed." After September 11, this argument proved extremely seductive to the American political classes, media, and public, all of whom perceived that American values were under attack by the alien and villainous values of the Islamists. The argument has provided, for four years, the entire philosophical basis for how the U.S. government is fighting terrorism.

Yet the argument is wrong. Had people bothered to scratch below the surface, they would have seen warning signs that Bush's aphorism was false and even dangerous. To start with, public opinion polls in Islamic nations repeatedly show that people in those countries actually admire America's political and economic freedom. They also admire American wealth, technology, and even culture. So some other factor must be generating anti-U.S. hatred in these parts of the world.

Furthermore, Bush's grand plan to reduce terrorism by spreading freedom and democracy to Islamic nations—thereby eliminating the hatred of such values—is not based on any empirical evidence that oppression causes terrorism. Spreading democracy doesn't reduce terrorism and, if anything, actually may make it worse. F. Gregory Gause III, a political scientist at the University of Vermont who reviewed terrorism statistics and the academic literature, noted that the State Department's own statistics from 2000 to 2003 reported 269 major terrorist incidents in countries Freedom House classifies as "free," 119 in "partially free" nations, and 138 in "not free" countries. These data corroborate an earlier well-known study by William Eubank and Leonard Weinberg, professors at the University of Nevada, Reno, which found that most terrorist attacks happen in democracies—with both the victims and the attackers usually being citizens of democracies. Gause also notes that recent elections and public opinion polls in Arab countries indicate that the advent of democracy would probably generate Islamic governments that would be much less likely to cooperate with the United States than their authoritarian predecessors. Those Islamic governments might also be more likely to sponsor terrorism.

Iraq provides a current example of democratization leading to more terrorism. During the authoritarian reign of Saddam Hussein, Iraq provided some limited assistance to selected Palestinian groups attacking Israel, but did not fund groups that focused their attacks on the United States. Terrorism now runs rampant in a more democratic Iraq, which, according to the U.S. intelligence community, threatens to become an even more significant training ground for worldwide Islamist jihad than Afghanistan during the Soviet occupation.

Finally, and most importantly, the evidence is startlingly clear that Bush's war 5 on terror has actually made things worse. According to the State Department's data, the number of major terrorist incidents worldwide increased from 121 in 2001 to 175 in 2003, a 21-year high. Then, in 2004, the number skyrocketed to 655 significant attacks. Richard Clarke, the chief counterterrorism advisor to both Presidents Bill Clinton and Bush, has noted that terrorism in the three years after 9/11 exceeded that during the three years preceding it.

If evidence indicates that Bush's broadly constructed war on terror is counterproductive, what can be done to get better results? To respond adequately to terrorism, the U.S. government and American people need to know why the terrorists are motivated to give up their time, money, and sometimes even their lives to attack the targets of a faraway land. To deny or delude ourselves about the true causes of such terrorism is dangerous. And the facts about terrorism lead us to the conclusion, controversial and difficult to accept as it may be, that the terrorists don't hate the United States for "what it is." They hate the United States for what it does.

Let's take another look at those public opinion polls in Islamic countries. Although people in most of those nations admire U.S. political and economic freedoms, wealth, technology, and culture, the poll numbers plummet when respondents are asked if they approve of U.S. foreign policy toward the Arabic and Islamic world. A recent poll conducted by Zogby International and the University of Maryland asked 3,617 respondents in six Arab nations: "Would you say that your attitudes toward the United States are based more on American values or on American policy in the Middle East?" More than 75 percent of respondents specified policies, while just 11 percent objected more to American values.

Empirical evidence indicates that a primary cause of terrorism is the U.S. government's foreign policy. In a 1998 report entitled "Does U.S. Intervention Overseas Breed Terrorism?: The Historical Record," I cataloged more than 60 terrorist attacks against U.S. targets; all were perpetrated in retaliation for U.S. foreign policy. For example, since the 1970s, terrorists have struck U.S. targets in retaliation for, among other things, support and aid for the Shah of Iran and for Israel; aid and military advisors sent to the Salvadoran government; our military presence in Honduras, Panama, Japan, the Philippines, and the Persian Gulf; hostile actions toward Libya; involvement in the civil wars in Lebanon, Bosnia, Kosovo, and Somalia; and prosecution of the first Gulf War and the use of Turkish bases to do so. . . .

During the Persian Gulf War, from mid-January to mid-February 1991, anti-U.S. attacks spiked around the world. During that war, the attacks numbered 120, compared to 17 during the same period in 1990. In 1993, a group of Iraqis was arrested in Kuwait and charged with an Iraqi government plot to assassinate former President George H. W. Bush. A large car bomb and weapons were confiscated. Saddam Hussein had vowed to assassinate Bush for his prosecution of the war.

In early 1993, Islamic extremists attempted to kill 250,000 people by toppling 10 the twin towers of the World Trade Center in New York City. Ramzi Yousef, the leader of the group, claimed that the intent was to cause casualties on the order of the atomic bomb blast at Hiroshima in order to punish the United States for its support and aid for Israel. . . .

In 1996, Hezbollah of Saudi Arabia (which differs from Hezbollah of Lebanon) attacked the U.S. military apartment complex at Khobar Towers near Dhahran, Saudi Arabia. The attack killed 19 U.S. airmen and wounded 515 people. The perpetrators, rather than despising America per se, had a very specific . . . goal: They wanted to compel the withdrawal of the U.S. military from Saudi Arabia.

Also, in October 2003, a U.S. diplomatic convoy was attacked in Gaza. Three U.S. security guards were killed. A day earlier, Israel had arrested suspects from a rogue Palestinian militant group. A senior U.S. official believed the attack on the convoy was motivated by growing anti-American resentment in Palestinian areas caused, in part, by U.S. policy in the region.

My report also described several al-Qaeda-related attacks. In late 1993, Osama bin Laden's al-Qaeda fighters trained Somalis who conducted an ambush of U.S. forces in Somalia. The ambush caused the downing of two helicopters, the deaths of 19 U.S. soldiers, and eventually a U.S. withdrawal from Somalia. A criminal indictment of bin Laden's followers noted that al-Qaeda believed that the "infidel" United States planned to occupy Islamic countries, as shown by its involvement in Somalia and the first Gulf War.

Al-Qaeda has also been implicated in bombing attacks against a U.S. military complex in Riyadh, Saudi Arabia, in 1995 and the U.S. embassies in Kenya and Tanzania in 1998, which caused more than 200 deaths. The attacks on U.S. military facilities in Saudi Arabia were designed to compel the withdrawal of non-Islamic U.S. forces from the nation containing Islam's holiest shrines. . . .

U.S. leaders would prefer to muddle bin Laden's motives for attacking the 15 United States. Yet if they want to know why bin Laden has dedicated his life to killing Americans and their allies, they don't even need to ask him. He has written many manifestos and has done interviews with Western media. From these writings and interviews, one can conclude only that bin Laden's major grievance is with U.S. foreign policy. According to Peter Bergen, one of the few Western journalists to interview him, bin Laden rarely condemns permissive U.S. culture. Also, he rarely speaks of the evils of democracy as such. Instead, he is especially incensed by U.S. support for corrupt regimes in the Islamic world and the U.S. military presence in the Islamic lands of the Persian Gulf, a presence he would like to dislodge. A lesser issue is his opposition to U.S. support and aid for Israel. Recently, al-Qaeda also has attacked U.S. allies, but only to drive a wedge between them and the United States in order to stymie U.S. overseas intervention—especially in Iraq. . . .

[M]ere logic should indicate that the United States is usually not attacked for "what it is." Like the United States, many nations are wealthy, have corporations with a global business presence, export their technology and culture along with their products, and allow political, economic, and religious freedoms, but they are not prime targets for terrorists. The United States' use of a dominant military and a covert action arm (the CIA) to intervene in the affairs of other nations all over the world is its unique attribute. If logic is not enough, on October 29, 2004, bin

Laden—frustrated with Bush's allegation that al-Qaeda strikes the United States because of its freedom—created a videotape specifically mentioning as the reasons for his attacks U.S. meddling in Muslim lands and supporting corrupt rulers there:

> Contrary to Bush's claim that we hate freedom . . . why don't we strike Sweden? . . . We want to restore freedom to our nation . . . Bush is still engaged in distortion, deception and hiding from you the real causes . . . The events that effected my soul in a direct way started in 1982 when America permitted the Israelis to invade Lebanon. And the American Sixth Fleet helped them do that . . . And as I looked at those demolished towers in Lebanon, it entered my mind that we should punish the oppressor in kind—and that we should destroy the towers in America in order that they taste some of what we tasted, and so that they be deterred from killing our women and children. We found it difficult to deal with the Bush administration, in light of the resemblance it bears to the regimes in our countries, half of which are ruled by the military and the other half of which are ruled by the sons of kings and presidents . . . Your security is in your own hands. And every state that does not play with our security will automatically guarantee its own security.

Paradoxically, the larger and more capable the U.S. military becomes (as a result of recent defense budget increases) and the more the U.S. "defense" perimeter is expanded, the less secure Americans will be. In other words, empire does not equal security and, in fact, undermines it. . . .

A more restrained foreign policy is crucial because improved intelligence and homeland security can only do so much. Officials in the intelligence community agree that intelligence is not perfect (the understatement of the decade, after the failure to detect the 9/11 plot and Iraq's lack of significant nuclear, biological, and chemical weapons and programs), and that future successful terrorist attacks are likely. The United States is a large, wealthy, free country with porous borders and many lucrative targets to hit—for example, skyscrapers, ports, schools, sports stadiums, and chemical and nuclear plants. Furthermore, the recent reorganizations of government intelligence and homeland structures added bureaucracy that may actually impede the government's ability to counter small, agile terrorist groups, which don't have to fill out piles of forms to accomplish their mission. Given the vulnerability of the country to terrorism and the government's inability to protect everything, reducing the motivation for terrorists to attack the United States is crucial. Using military force only as a last resort in times of genuine peril to the nation would reduce the size of the bull's eye that the U.S. government has painted on the backs of its people.

If doubt exists that a change in policy toward more restraint would have the desired result, history shows that Hezbollah of Lebanon drastically curtailed its attacks on U.S. targets after the United States withdrew military forces from there, and that Libya's anti-U.S. attacks tapered off after the Reagan administration and its provocations of Quaddafi ended. . . .

Does attributing the primary cause of anti-U.S. terrorism to U.S. foreign policy and advocating military restraint overseas implicitly blame the victim for the attack and indicate that we should appease terrorists? Neither is the case. The terrorists' killing of innocent civilians is heinous, and the short-term U.S. policy should be to punish terrorist groups that attack the United States, whether apprehending their members by using intelligence and law enforcement methods or killing them with the quiet and surgical use of military force (to avoid inflaming anti-U.S. hatred as much as possible). Thus, a policy of swift punishment meted out to anti-U.S. terrorist groups, especially al-Qaeda, cannot be misconstrued as appeasement.

But in the long-term, Americans must realize that although the terrorists are wrong for killing innocents, their own government bears some of the blame for creating the underlying grievances motivating terrorists to attack in the first place. Over the longer horizon, the U.S. government should quietly narrow its conception of vital interests and adopt a policy of military restraint. Also, a more restrained foreign policy, by changing how Arabs think about America, could dramatically lessen whatever popular support terrorists have in Islamic countries.

A more humble U.S. foreign policy would include removing U.S. support for despotic Arabic governments, such as those in Egypt, Jordan, Saudi Arabia, and other Persian Gulf countries; eliminating the U.S. military presence in the Persian Gulf; terminating the more than $3 billion in aid given to the wealthy state of Israel and adopting a more neutral policy toward the Israeli-Palestinian dispute; and avoiding antagonistic—overt or covert—behavior toward groups that don't focus their attacks on the United States, such as Hezbollah, Hamas, and Palestinian Islamic Jihad, all of which concentrate on striking Israel. Although these significant departures from existing U.S. policy may be difficult to achieve soon, Americans should realize that adopting them would dramatically reduce terrorists' motives to attack the United States. If Americans want to continue such policies anyway, they should at least be aware of the high cost.

Far from appeasement, these policy changes would benefit the United States whether or not anti-U.S. terrorists launch attacks. Costs in U.S. lives and money would be reduced dramatically, the U.S. military would not be in its currently overstretched condition, and imperial overextension would be eliminated—all reducing the likelihood of American decline as a great power. Furthermore, resisting the urge to strike groups and countries that aren't attacking the United States is more in keeping with the values of a republic (rather than those of an empire).

A policy of military restraint overseas merely goes back to the traditional U.S. foreign policy adopted by George Washington, Thomas Jefferson, and the other founders and followed (with sporadic deviations) until after World War II. The founders realized that the United States had intrinsic security because of separation by two great oceans from the world's centers of conflict. Despite advances in transportation and communications, the U.S. is still relatively immune from conventional attack or invasion, especially with the deterrent effect of our modern nuclear weapons. The only threat that such distances and military capability cannot defeat or deter is the terrorist threat. Because the intrinsically good U.S. security situation has always allowed the United States the option of staying out of most foreign conflicts, the age of catastrophic terrorism now makes imperative that course of action.

The founders also realized what many modern-day politicians have forgotten: Constant warfare undermines the republic. As Rome's territory grew, power passed from the assembly to the aristocratic Senate to the dictator to the emperor. Similarly, in the United States, the aberrant post–World War II interventionism overseas has concentrated power in an imperial president and is undermining the nation's civil liberties. U.S. interventionism provokes terrorist attacks, which in turn lead to the constriction of civil liberties—for example, the USA PATRIOT Act and unconstitutional executive actions by the Bush administration. A more restrained U.S. foreign policy would eliminate the security–civil liberties trade-off—America could have both. So as advantageous as lower costs and lower casualties (to U.S. troops and indigenous peoples overseas and American civilians at home) of a more humble foreign policy would be, the greatest benefit would accrue to our cherished and unique constitutional system. The U.S. empire threatens the American republic itself.

FOR DISCUSSION

1. Eland challenges the notion that attempting to establish democracies in the Middle East will reduce terrorism. What evidence does he offer that democratic regimes, even if they can be created and sustained, may not help? Do you find his argument convincing? Why or why not?

2. Eland cites Peter Bergen, "one of the few Western journalists to interview" bin Laden, to establish the motivation for al Qaeda's attacks on the United States and its allies. What are the motives Bergen describes? Which, if any, could we abandon or change fundamentally without jeopardizing our interests in the Middle East?

3. Eland contends that he does not advocate appeasing terrorists. What does he say to support this contention? Can we punish the terrorists, as Eland advocates, and also "adopt a policy of military restraint," which he also advocates? What do you think "military restraint" means to Eland?

FOR RESEARCH, DISCUSSION, AND MEDIATION

One response to Eland's argument would be to say, "Of course it's American foreign policy that makes us a terrorist target. But how much can we change what we do and still maintain our vital interests in the Middle East?"

As a class, do research to establish both what our vital interests are and what current policy does in pursuit of those interests. Then, as a way to mediate between current policy and its critics, write an essay suggesting ways, as Eland puts it, to "quietly narrow [our government's] conception of vital interests" in the Middle East. That is, are some of our perceived interests not really vital, or even counter to our interests? Can some policies be modified a lot or a little 5 while not retreating from our vital interests and also reducing terrorist motivation to attack us at home and abroad?

The Wrong Strategy against the Next Generation

ROBERT A. PAPE

> In the previous selection, Ivan Eland blamed American foreign policy in general for increasing the threat of terrorism since 9/11. In this selection, Pape contends that the cause is much more specific—American troops stationed in or fighting in Islamic countries, or both. Consequently, he advocates what he calls "off-shore balancing," maintaining a military force on ships in the region to respond to crises rapidly but without constant or sustained forces on the ground.
>
> The following selection comes from *Dying to Win: The Strategic Logic of Suicide Terrorism* (Random House, 2005). Pape is a professor of political science at the University of Chicago and directs the Chicago Project on Suicide Terrorism.

Since September 11, 2001, the United States has responded to the growing threat of suicide terrorism by embarking on a policy to conquer Muslim countries—not simply rooting out existing havens for terrorists in Afghanistan but going further, to remake Muslim societies in the Persian Gulf. Proponents claim that Islamic fundamentalism is the principal cause of suicide terrorism and that this radical ideology is spreading through Muslim societies, dramatically increasing the prospects for a new, larger generation of anti-American terrorists in the future. Hence, the United States should install new governments in Muslim countries in order to transform and diminish the role of radical Islam in their societies. This logic led to widespread support for the conquest of Iraq and is promoted as the principal reason for regime change in Iran, Saudi Arabia, and other Persian Gulf states in the future.

The goal of this strategy is correct, but its premise is faulty. American security depends critically on diminishing the next generation of anti-American Muslim terrorists. However, Islamic fundamentalism is not the main cause of suicide terrorism, and conquering Muslim countries to transform their societies is likely to increase the number coming at us.

Spokesmen for the "Muslim transformation" strategy present a sweeping case. Although these arguments are sometimes vague and incomplete, they all center on the presumption that Islamic fundamentalism is the driving force behind the growing threat of suicide terrorism. According to David Frum and Richard Perle, "The terrorists kill and will accept death for a cause with which no accommodation is possible. That cause is militant Islam." Moreover, these beliefs are not really confined to a radical fringe, but infect even ordinary Muslims: "And though it is comforting to deny it, all the available evidence indicates that militant Islam commands wide support, and even wider sympathy, among Muslims worldwide, including Muslim minorities in the West." For Frum and Perle, "the roots of Muslim rage are to be found in Islam itself. . . . The Islamic world has lagged further and further behind the Christian West." While there are multiple terrorist groups, the common element of Islam makes the threat monolithic: "The distinction between Islamic terrorism against Israel, on the one hand, and Islamic terrorism against the United States and Europe, on the other, cannot be sustained. . . . Worse, the ideology that justifies the terrible crimes of Hamas and Hezbollah is the same ideology that justifies the crimes of al-Qaeda." The result is an unlimited threat to dominate the world: "This strain seeks to overthrow our civilization and remake the nations of the West into Islamic societies, imposing on the whole world its religion and its law." The solution, Perle and Frum contend, is regime change: "We must move boldly against [Iran] and against all the other sponsors of terrorism as well: Syria, Libya, and Saudi Arabia."[1]

This argument is fatally flawed. First, al-Qaeda's suicide terrorists have not come from the most populous Islamic fundamentalist populations in the world, but mainly from the Muslim countries with heavy American combat presence. From 1995 through 2003, there have been a total of seventy-one al-Qaeda suicide terrorists. Only 6 percent (4 of 71) have come from the five countries with the world's largest Islamic fundamentalist populations—Pakistan (149 million), Bangladesh (114 million), Iran (63 million), Egypt (62 million), and Nigeria (37 million). By contrast, 55 percent of al-Qaeda's suicide terrorists (39 of 71) have come from Saudi Arabia and other Persian Gulf countries, a region whose population totals less than 30 million, but where the United States has stationed heavy combat troops more or less continuously since 1990.

This comparison of the relative weight of American military presence and 5 Islamic fundamentalism is important. If Islamic fundamentalism is driving al-Qaeda's suicide terrorism, then we would expect a close relationship between the world's largest Islamic fundamentalist populations and the nationality of al-Qaeda's suicide terrorists. However, this is not the case. The world's five largest Islamic fundamentalist populations without American military presence have produced al-Qaeda suicide terrorists on the order of 1 per 71 million people, while the Persian Gulf countries with American military presence have produced al-Qaeda suicide terrorists at a rate of 1 per million, or 70 times more often. Further, even if we narrow our definition of Islamic fundamentalism to Salafism, the specific form associated with Osama bin Laden but not with Iran or even many Sunnis, American military presence remains the pivotal factor driving al-Qaeda's suicide terrorists. The stationing of tens of thousands of American combat troops on the Arabian Peninsula from 1990 to 2001 probably made al-Qaeda suicide attacks against Americans, including the horrible crimes committed on September 11, 2001, from five to twenty times more likely. Hence, the longer American troops remain in Iraq and in the Persian Gulf in general, the greater the risk of the next September 11.

Second, Islamic fundamentalism has not created a monolithic terrorism threat against the United States or other Western countries. Islamic fundamentalism does not lead suicide terrorist organizations to cooperate with each other in the ways that matter most—the sharing of suicide terrorists across groups, or one group conducting a suicide terrorist campaign on behalf of another. Hezbollah and Hamas have each waged numerous suicide terrorist campaigns against Israel, but never for each other and never at the same time. Al-Qaeda has never attacked Israel at all, while Hamas has never attacked the United States, and Hezbollah has attacked only Americans in Lebanon. When one studies the various suicide terrorist campaigns by Hezbollah, Hamas, and al-Qaeda what stands out is not that these groups share military resources or act in concert, like a monolithic movement. Instead, what stands out is that each is driven by essentially nationalist goals to compel target democracies to withdraw military forces from their *particular* homeland.

Third, the idea that all Muslims around the world are quietly anti-American because Islam encourages hatred for American values for democracy and free markets does not square with the facts. Indeed, robust evidence shows that American military policies, not revulsion against Western political and economic values, are driving anti-Americanism among Muslims.

Our best information on Muslim attitudes comes from the Pew Global Attitudes surveys. Since 2000, approval of the United States has been declining sharply among Muslims from across a broad cross section of countries—among both Muslims who were initially highly favorable to the United States and those who were not. Even with the slight rise in 2004, America's image even among our closest Muslim allies is now a pale reflection of where it was four years ago.

Table 1 Muslims with a Favorable View of the United States

	Percentage of Population			
	2000	**2002**	**2003**	**2004**
Turkey	52	30	15	30
Morocco	77	na	27	27
Pakistan	23	10	13	21
Jordan	na	25	1	5

SOURCE: Pew Global Attitudes Project, "Global Opinion: The Spread of Anti-Americanism" (Washington, D.C.: Pew Research Center, January 2005).

The underlying reason is not discontent with Western political or economic 10 values, which are supported by majorities or near majorities in these countries.

Table 2 Muslim Attitudes on Western Economic and Political Values

	Percentage Favorable		
	World Trade	**Free Markets**	**Democracy**
Turkey	82	60	57
Morocco	na	na	na
Pakistan	78	50	42
Jordan	52	47	47

SOURCE: Pew Global Attitudes Project, "Views of a Changing World" (Washington, D.C.: Pew Research Center, June 2003).

Rather, the taproot is American military policy. Overwhelming majorities across a range of Muslim countries believe that the United States conquered Iraq to control its oil or to help Israel rather than to end terrorism or promote democracy, and fear that their country might be next.[2]

Table 3 Muslim Views of U.S. Motives for Iraq and Future Threat

	Percentage of Population				
	Control Oil	Support Israel	Stop Terrorism	Promote Democracy	U.S. Military Threat to Your Country
Pakistan	54	44	6	5	73
Turkey	64	45	20	9	71
Morocco	63	54	17	15	na
Jordan	71	70	11	7	56

SOURCE: Pew Global Attitudes Project, "Views of a Changing World" (Washington, D.C.: Pew Research Center, June 2003 and March 2004).

Fourth, the idea that Islamic fundamentalism is on the verge of world domination and poses a realistic threat to impose Islamic laws in the United States and Europe is pure fantasy. Some radicals may harbor such delusions. Some fearmongers may use such delusions to whip up hysteria. But these are delusions nonetheless. The United States and Europe are overwhelmingly Christian countries and, short of physical conquest, will remain so.[3]

Fifth, and most important, an attempt to transform Muslim societies through regime change is likely to dramatically increase the threat we face. The root cause of suicide terrorism is foreign occupation and the threat that foreign military presence poses to the local community's way of life. Hence, any policy that seeks to conquer Muslim societies in order, deliberately, to transform their culture is folly. Even if our intentions are good, anti-American terrorism would likely grow, and grow rapidly.

Consider Iraq. Proponents of Muslim transformation were staunch advocates of the invasion of Iraq in March 2003, fully expecting that American forces would be greeted as liberators rather than as conquerors. The projected resistance was thought to be so light that the number of American troops would be reduced to 30,000 just six months later. Muslims around the world would come to support this policy, because the war would demonstrate America's commitment to democracy and freedom. Two years later, things have not turned out this way.

The resistance to American occupation has grown steadily from April 2003 to the present. Even though the United States kills an average of 2,000 insurgents every month, the size of the insurgency has grown from approximately 5,000 fighters in April 2003 to 18,000 in January 2005. The overwhelming number of these fighters are local Iraqis and their numbers have risen along with popular support for American withdrawal. Foreign fighters make up less than 5 percent, as estimated by U.S. intelligence.

Moreover, suicide terrorism has been a prime weapon. Prior to April 2003, Iraq 15 had never experienced even a single suicide terrorist attack in its history. Since then, the trajectory has been rising, with twenty suicide terrorist attacks in 2003 and more than fifty in 2004. The number is on pace in the first months of 2005 to set a new record for the year. The main targets have been American troops, Iraqi troops, and political leaders thought to be working with the Americans.

Table 4 Resistance of U.S. Occupation of Iraq, 2003–2005

	July 2003	January 2004	July 2004	January 2005
Percent of Iraqis favoring near-term U.S. withdrawal	30	30	65	82
Estimated insurgents/foreign fighters	5,000/300	5,000/300	20,000/400	18,000/600
Foreign Coalition troops (U.S./other)	149,000/21,000	122,000/26,000	140,000/22,000	150,000/25,000

SOURCE: Adriana Lins de Albuquerque and Michael O'Hanlon, "The State of Iraq," *New York Times* (February 21, 2005). Numbers of insurgents and foreign fighters are based on official U.S. estimates.

The identities of the Iraqi suicide attackers are now murky. This is not unusual in the early years of a suicide terrorist campaign. Hezbollah did not publish many of the biographies and last testaments of its suicide attackers until after the suicide operations had ended, a pattern adopted by the Tamil Tigers in Sri Lanka as well. At the moment, our best information is that the attackers are from two main sources, Sunni Iraqis and foreign fighters, principally from Saudi Arabia. If so, this would mean that the two main sources of suicide terrorists in Iraq—Iraqis and Saudis—are from the countries whose societies are most vulnerable to transformation by the presence of American combat troops. This picture is fully consistent with the theory of suicide terrorism presented in this book [*Dying to Win*].

Democracy is a source of peace. However, spreading democracy at the barrel of a gun in the Persian Gulf is not likely to lead to a lasting solution against suicide terrorism. Just as al-Qaeda's suicide terrorism campaign began against American troops on the Arabian Peninsula and then escalated to the United States, we should recognize that the longer that American forces remain in Iraq, the greater the threat of the next September 11 from groups who have not targeted us before. Even if our intentions are good, the United States cannot depend on democratic governments in the region to dampen the risk of suicide terrorism so long as American forces are stationed there.

NOTES

1. David Frum and Richard Perle, *An End to Evil: How to Win the War on Terror* (New York: Random House, 2003), pp. 34, 35, 40, 83, and 106. Frum and Perle also call for regime change in North Korea, although how this is related to their definition of the threat as Islamic fundamentalism is unclear.
2. For extensive evaluation of the growing resentment of American policies in numerous areas around the world, see Stephen M. Walt, *Taming American Power: The Global Response to U.S. Primacy* (New York: W. W. Norton, 2005). For analysis of the consequences of U.S. policy toward Israel, see Stephen Van Evera, "Why the U.S. Needs Mideast Peace," *The American Conservative* (March 14, 2005), pp. 7–10.
3. On the similarity with myths guiding past empires, see Jack Snyder, "Imperial Temptations," *National Interest,* no. 71 (Spring 2003), pp. 29–41; and idem, *Myths of Empire: Domestic Politics and International Ambition* (Ithaca, N.Y.: Cornell University Press, 1991).

FOR DISCUSSION

1. In the opening paragraphs, Pape describes the thinking that has led to our current policy to combat terrorism in the Middle East. He says, "The goal of this strategy is correct, but its premise is faulty." What does he mean? What does he think the correct premise would be?

2. The enemy, we are told over and over, is not Islam or Muslims in general, but rather "Islamic fundamentalism" or "Islamic militants." But Pape contends that the American military presence more than anything else motivates suicide terrorism. What evidence does he supply to confirm his contention? Is it compelling? Why or why not?

3. Pape grants that "the identities of the Iraqi suicide attackers are now murky." Why does he care who they are? That is, what bearing on his argument does the question of identity have?

FOR STUDY, DISCUSSION, AND MEDIATION

It may surprise you that Pape is a prominent *conservative* voice in the terrorism debate. But it's easy to confirm by looking into the sources he cites in endnotes 2 and 3 in his article. The policy he advocates differs from Ivan Eland's in the previous selection, whose view most would call "liberal." And yet in some ways their outlooks converge.

Read and study both selections carefully. How *exactly* do they differ? In what ways are they alike or similar? Write an essay attempting to bring the two positions closer together, an effort to find common ground among positions labeled "conservative" and "liberal." Advocate your approach as a consensus position for countering terrorism.

Jihad Wired

DANIEL BENJAMIN AND STEVEN SIMON

> Use of the Internet by jihadist groups is not new, but the scope and sophistication of it in recent years is, and for anyone concerned with the struggle to influence the thinking of Muslim people throughout the world, it is a prime concern. It's often said that we are losing this struggle—if we are, the Internet is a major factor.
>
> The following excerpt comes from *The Next Attack* (Henry Holt, 2005). Daniel Benjamin served on the National Security Council (NSC) staff as a director for counterterrorism, 1994–1999. Steven Simon also served on the NSC after a career in the State Department as a specialist in Middle Eastern security affairs.

The link between advances in communications technology and social change is a well-mined historical theme. Just as writing allowed the priesthoods of the great religions to eclipse local cults and the printed book enabled people to think beyond tribal boundaries and conceive of themselves as nations, the Internet has spawned a universe of new communities. The early prophets of the World Wide Web, certain that it would promote American-style free markets, predicted that its spread would lead to the riotous bloom of democracy and "the creation of a new civilization, founded in the eternal truths of the American Idea," as Newt Gingrich's Progress and Freedom Foundation put it in 1994.[1]

Information technology may be revolutionizing modern life, but American values and free marketeers have hardly been the only beneficiaries. For individual Muslims, the Internet has provided the means to transcend their surroundings and participate in the new *umma.* It is the delivery vehicle par excellence for a set of powerful ideas, which now ricochet around the world with light speed. Sermons from Saudi Arabia, communiqués from the jihad, instruction on proper Islamic behavior, history lessons, Quranic exegesis—all these flicker onto millions of computer screens or land in e-mail in-boxes daily. Where there are few computers, adherents wait their turn in the Internet café or print the message and circulate it that way. Without the Internet, bin Laden still could have taken his jihad global—videotapes and compact discs were already spreading the word before Netscape—but its growth would be at a comparative snail's pace. In fact, the Internet is driving the creation of the new transnational Muslim identity and, with it, a hatred of America.

For those who wish to deepen their devotion, the Islamist Web provides a 10 slippery slope that may easily lead to the embrace of violent jihad. There is an abundance of sites that provide religious guidance in the form of sermons given in Saudi mosques, fatwas issued by important and not so important clerics, and question-and-answer-format Web pages on every conceivable issue of religious observance. But these sites typically include content related to the plight of Muslims in Palestine, Chechnya, Kashmir, and Iraq and exhortations about the duties these travails impose on all Muslims. Indeed, if someone looking for guidance on an issue of observance regarding food or dress follows one link or another, he will soon be confronted with the imperative of jihad in terms like those posted on Islahi.net in a scolding letter from a Saudi sheikh: "You who shirk Jihad. . . . How can you enjoy life and comfort while your noble sisters are being raped and their honor is defiled in the Abu Ghraib prison. . . . You who shirk jihad, what excuse can you give Allah while your brethren in the prisons of Abu Ghraib and Guantanamo and ar-Ruways and al-Ha'ir [prisons in Saudi Arabia] are stripped naked? [W]hat are you waiting for?"

In just a few years, the radical Islamist Web has exploded in size. According to Gabriel Weimann of Haifa University in Israel, the number of Web sites related to terrorist groups—including non-Muslim ones, which are a small fraction of the total—has grown from twelve in 1998 to about 4,400 today. Countless other sites espouse radical Islamist views without being associated with particular violent groups. Many of the sites have flashy graphics, compelling content, and frequent updates. Chat rooms serve to establish personal contacts and provide space for views that are too extreme for posting to the site itself.

To grab the attention of children, some sites present cartoons, interactive games, 5 fables, adventure stories—as well as images of children with real weapons playacting as terrorists. For adolescents, there are rap videos, like Sheikh Terra's *Dirty Kuffar* (infidel), which flashes images of Marines cheering as one of them shoots an Iraqi on the floor; a rolling list of the fifty-six countries that are said to have been the victims of American aggression since World War II; a Russian soldier being blasted by a Chechen guerrilla with an AK-47; and pictures of Colin Powell and Condoleezza Rice with the words "still slaves" superimposed on them. As the heavy beat goes on, the rappers guffaw in the background while on the screen the destruction of the Twin Towers is replayed. For those a little older, there are applications for recruitment accompanied by background "investigation" forms, job listings, and links to stores where books and pamphlets that glamorize jihad can be bought.

To grasp the impact the Internet is having, it is worth recalling how a different medium revolutionized attitudes in another time and place. In the America of the 1960s and 1970s, television brought the Vietnam War, as it was so often said, into the nation's living rooms. The images and reportage caused an unprecedented revulsion in a population accustomed to trusting its government and supporting its armed forces. It was a war that President Lyndon Johnson said was over when he heard that the anchorman Walter Cronkite had come out in opposition. The pictures removed the heroic sheen from the fighting and helped create a bond of opposition to the war. Without the coverage, it is hard to imagine the antiwar movement gathering strength or the chain of events that ultimately led to the U.S. pullout from Indochina. Certainly no other war in American history was brought to an end—and closed in defeat—because of public opinion.

For many Muslims who are experiencing events in Iraq as a virtual war, the experience is the inverse: Instead of a tragedy, the scenes are part of a heroic epic. A new video is posted every few days, if not more frequently. The clips tend to be relatively short—most a few minutes—though compilations are made by both the jihadists in the field and the home audience. The scenes are more varied and often more kinetic than those filmed by the embedded American crews that operated with the U.S. military in Iraq in 2003. Indeed, the filming is an integral part of the overall operation—the footage is dramatic precisely because the cameraman is part of the combat unit, there to document a planned attack or execution, not a journalist waiting for something to happen nearby. The effect they strive for is exaltation, not disenchantment. What, after all, was the tape of four American contractors being trampled and hacked to death in Fallujah in April 2004 but a downmarket version of Hector being dragged before the gates of Troy?

The most common subject is the rocketing of Humvees, but scenes that have been posted include: mujahedin shooting down a helicopter with a shoulder-fired missile and then dispatching the one surviving passenger with a bullet; a clump of men, purportedly American soldiers, who have emerged from their damaged vehicle only to be blown up, presumably by a rocket-propelled grenade; car bombings near buildings or against other vehicles, presumably with Coalition or "converter"—Iraqis who support the occupation or work in the new Iraqi regime—personnel inside; the suicide attack on the U.S. base in Mosul in December 2004, which caused the greatest single-day death toll among American forces. The clips almost invariably begin with the logo of the group responsible—Ansar al-Sunnah's calligraphy-with-rocket-propelled-grenade; al Qaeda's Iraqi assault rifle emerging from an open book (presumably a Quran) superimposed on a globe; the Islamic Army's Kalashnikov and a jihadist's face framed by the map of Iraq—as though they were team insignia to spark the fan's sense of belonging.

For most viewers, the videos are a dramatic change from what they are accustomed to. A longtime jihadist sympathizer is likely to have seen videos that show mujahedin in Afghanistan running through an obstacle course and firing weapons, with perhaps a shot of the damaged U.S.S. *Cole* as a closing image. If the individual is someone who ordinarily sticks to Arab television or Muslim news sites, then he is probably used to images of defeat and horror—for example, the iconic picture of Muhammad al-Durra, the young boy who was shot and killed, allegedly by Israeli forces, while cowering at the Netzarim junction with his father at the outset of the second intifada in 2000. After decades in which Muslim armies were routinely humiliated—in the Middle East repeatedly, in Iraq, even in South Asia, where Pakistan has lost four wars to India—these new images of Muslims destroying military targets and enjoying dominance over their captives must be inspiring. In some of the compilation videos, the images of retribution and of an enemy rendered powerless are juxtaposed with images of the humiliation of Muslims and the killing of children like al-Durra.

There may not be any focus group data on the strengths and weaknesses of 10 jihadist Web sites, but we can get some idea of what is going on in the minds of some members of the new *umma* by looking at the most popular—and grisly—of the downloads. Nothing else has lit up the Web like the videos of beheadings, and nothing else demonstrates how an archaic practice has taken on the aspect of a public sacrament with the help of modern technology.

The appeal of decapitation is grounded in its earliest connection with Islam: "When you encounter the unbelievers on the battlefield, strike off their heads until you have crushed them completely; then bind the prisoners tightly" is an injunction delivered in a discussion of the laws of war in the forty-seventh Sura of the Quran. According to Ibn Ishaq, the Prophet's earliest biographer, Muhammad ordered the decapitation of 700 men of the Jewish Banu Qurayza tribe in Medina for plotting against him, and as a result the practice has had the aura of authenticity for centuries. Beheading has been the culmination of many a tale of Muslim warfare, and it remains a form of capital punishment in Saudi Arabia to this day. Along with its variant throat-slitting, decapitation has also been used in modern times in the Algerian war of liberation in the 1960s, when it was the punishment for informers and collaborators. The practice reached gruesome proportions in the 1990s again in Algeria, when it became the signature method of killing for the radical Islamists, who murdered thousands of their countrymen with a justification—apostasy—much like the one bin Laden cites for killing Muslims who collaborate with the West. In 1994, Egypt's Nobel laureate novelist Naguib Mahfouz was stabbed in the throat by extremists who sought to punish him for his writings. In the late 1990s, Chechen rebels began to cut throats, too.

When a terrorist kills today by slitting the throat or cutting off the head of his victim, it underscores his identity as a jihadist and acts as a kind of sacrament, a way of making the violence holy. This has been clear since the discovery of the document that was found in the baggage of several of the 9/11 hijackers, often called "The Last Will and Testament of Muhammad Atta." The document describes how in the course of taking over the airplanes, the hijackers will slaughter those who get in their way. The Arabic word used is the same one for the ear-to-ear cutting of a sheep that reenacts the biblical sacrifice of Isaac on the Muslim holiday of Eid al-Adha. Severing the infidel's head from his body thus becomes an act redolent with the sense of sacrifice and the literal execution of God's law, which to the jihadist means death for infidels and apostates.

To seize their aircraft on September 11, the hijackers carried out their instructions and killed members of the flight crew by slitting their throats. Ever since, the practice has been spreading. The abduction and murder of *Wall Street Journal* reporter Daniel Pearl in January 2002 made decapitation virtually de rigueur in jihadist killings of individuals or small groups. Pearl's murder was videotaped, copies were widely sold, and it was posted on the Internet. The market for such carnage has exploded since then. When the American civilian contractor Nicholas Berg was kidnapped and beheaded in Iraq in May 2004, so many people tried to download the file that it had to be posted on dozens of different sites to prevent servers from crashing.

According to MIT's *Technology Review*, demand for the beheading videos has been overwhelming. Dan Klinker, webmaster of Ogrish.com, a non-jihadist site that specializes in gore and posts the videos, says that each beheading video has been downloaded from his site several million times; the Berg video was downloaded 15 million times from his site alone.[2] Undoubtedly, plenty of the hits come from non-Muslim devotees of snuff films, but these videos are also posted on numerous Arab language sites as well. These sites have a habit of either crashing from overuse or being shut down because of their terrorist content, and as result, it seems likely that some who are clicking on Ogrish.com are doing so because of their jihadist sympathies. "During certain events (beheadings, etc.) the servers can barely handle the insane bandwidths—sometimes 50,000 to 60,000 visitors an hour," Klinker says. An Associated Press report in September 2004 observed that decapitation videos were outselling pornography in Baghdad.[3] Berg was the first of three Americans to be decapitated in Iraq; the number of Iraqis who have been killed this way is unknown but certainly exponentially larger.

Jihadist message boards attest to the delight of those who watch the behead- 15 ings. At one point in 2004 during a lull in the killing, one writer posted a message urging the insurgents on, saying that they were not only making history but helping their supporters' physical health.

> O Mujahideen! . . . You have marked our faces with joy after they had forgotten laughter. You have lifted up heads that were covered with humiliation. . . . Yes, by Allah, you are the men of the era. You are the protectors of the religion and the guards of the ideology. . . . We used to start our day by watching a slaughter [beheading] scene, for it is no secret to the knowledgeable that it stimulates and appeases the contents of the chests. . . . By Allah, many of those who suffer from high blood pressure and diabetes, have complained about the cease of these operations, for they were tranquilizing them. . . . Someone even told me, and I believe he speaks the truth, that he does not eat his food until he has watched a beheading scene, even if it were replayed or old.[4]

For some who download the decapitations, these are not just spectacles for ogling; they are a kind of participatory event that binds the distant Web surfer with the triumphant killers. One well-known case involved a series of executions: The insurgents had captured two American contractors and a Briton. After American Eugene Armstrong was beheaded in September 2004, someone posted a message on a jihadist message board suggesting that the most dramatic way to proceed would be to place the British hostage, Kenneth Bigley, next to the second American, Jack Hensley, and to film his horrified reaction during the beheading. The captors accepted the suggestion. It was the Web at its most interactive.

NOTES

1. Esther Dyson, George Gilder, George Keyworth, and Alvin Toffler, "Cyberspace and the American Dream: A Magna Carta for the Knowledge Age," *Progress and Freedom Foundations,* Release 1.2, August 22, 1994. The introduction notes that "this statement represents the cumulative wisdom and innovation of many dozens of people. It is based primarily on the thoughts of four 'co-authors': Ms. Esther Dyson; Mr. George Gilder; Dr. George Keyworth; and Dr. Alvin Toffler." http://www.pff.org/issues-pubs/futureinsights/f11.2magnacarta.html.
2. David Talbot, "Terror's Server," *Technology Review,* February 2005.
3. Hamza Hendawi, "Real-life Horror Replaces Porn as Traumatized City's Preferred TV Viewing," Associated Press, September 26, 2004.
4. SITE Institute, trans., "Do Not Stop Slaughters for They Are Cure for the Hearts," December 22, 2004.

FOR DISCUSSION

1. "Without the Internet, bin Laden still could have taken his jihad global"— and did, in fact, in Afghanistan, where Islamic guerilla fighters defeated the Soviet Union about two decades ago. So what difference has the Internet made? Is it just another way to spread a message?

2. Why don't we just shut down the Web sites espousing jihad? common sense might ask. Why is such a measure almost impossible? By our own principles, can we object to sites that offer "sermons from Saudi Arabia, . . . instructions on proper Islamic behavior, history lessons, Quranic exegesis [interpretations]"?

3. Benjamin and Simon describe at length the content of some of the Web sites. Imagine that you are a devout Muslim living in the Middle East—what would you find most persuasive? As an American, what do you find most alarming in the content and tactics used to promote jihad?

FOR READING, DISCUSSION, AND CONVINCING

Gabriel Weimann's book, *Terror on the Internet* (United States Institute of Peace Press, 2006) is the current authority on the issue of "jihad wired." Read, study, and discuss this book at length as a class project, and then write an essay proposing and defending a way of coping with this dimension of the terrorist threat more effectively. Because we can't and shouldn't prevent the free exchange of ideas via the Internet, how might we make our ideas more appealing to those currently being influenced by the jihadist sites?

Mother. Daughter. Sister. Bomber.

MIA BLOOM

> Not long ago, Islamic suicide terrorism was rare and was never carried out by
> women. Now, suicide terrorism is in the news almost every day, and women often
> carry out the attacks, especially by Hamas and the Lebanese Hezbollah in their
> struggle with Israel. The following article examines and explains this relatively new
> and some would say surprising development.
>
> Mia Bloom is a professor of political science at the University of Cincinnati and
> author of *Dying to Kill: The Allure of Suicide Terror* (2005).

The woman known as Dhanu stood waiting for former Indian Prime Minister Rajiv
Gandhi. It was May 21, 1991. She wore thick glasses that obscured her face and
clutched a sandalwood garland; the bulge beneath her orange *salwar kameez*
(a traditional Hindu dress) bespoke her apparent pregnancy. As Gandhi strode
toward the podium at the political rally where he was to speak, he acknowledged
well-wishers lined along the red carpet. He clasped Dhanu's hand, and she respect-
fully kneeled before him. With her right hand she activated an explosive device
strapped to her belly with a denim belt and embedded with 10,000 steel pellets.
Gandhi, his assassin, and 16 others were killed.

Later it was revealed that a policewoman had attempted to prevent Dhanu—
an assassin allegedly dispatched by the Liberation Tigers of Tamil Eelam (LTTE)—
from reaching the prime minister. But Gandhi had intervened, saying something
like, "Relax, baby"—quite possibly the last words he ever spoke.[1]

Gandhi may have been blinded by gender, but if so, he was not the first, nor
the last. Even the security-conscious United States, post–9/11, failed to include
women among an official profile of potential terrorists developed by the Department of Homeland Security to scrutinize visa seekers.[2] Traditionally, women have
been perceived as victims of violence rather than as perpetrators. Yet they are now
taking a leading role in conflicts by becoming terrorists and, specifically, suicide
bombers—using their bodies as human detonators.

The female suicide bomber is a phenomenon that predates the Rajiv Gandhi
assassination. The Syrian Socialist National Party (SSNP), a secular, pro-Syrian, Lebanese organization, sent the first such bomber, a 17-year-old Lebanese girl named
Sana'a Mehaydali, to blow herself up near an Israeli convoy in Lebanon in 1985.
Out of 12 suicide attacks conducted by the SSNP, women took part in five of them.
After Lebanon in the 1980s, female bombers spread to other parts of the globe,
including Sri Lanka, Turkey, Chechnya, and Israel. Worldwide, approximately 17
groups have started using the tactical innovation of suicide bombing, with women
operatives accounting for 15 percent of those attacks.[3] According to terror expert
Rohan Gunaratna, almost 30 percent of suicide attackers are women.[4] Most have
belonged to secular separatist organizations, such as LTTE and the Kurdistan Workers' Party (PKK). But recent years have witnessed the worrisome emergence of
women suicide bombers in religious organizations.

Historically, to the extent that women have been involved in conflict, they have   5
served supporting roles. Their primary contribution to war has been to give birth

Ten-year-old Suwar Abu Salem wears a necklace with a portrait of her sister Zainab, who blew herself up at a hitchhiking post in Jerusalem on September 22, 2004. Suicide bombers Wafi Idris and Reem Riashi with her children.

to fighters and raise them in a revolutionary environment. The advent of women suicide bombers has not so much annulled that identity as it has transformed it. Even as martyrs, they may be portrayed as the chaste wives and mothers of revolution. When Wafa Idris became the first female Palestinian suicide bomber to strike Israel in January 2002, an Egyptian newspaper eulogized: "The bride of Heaven preferred death to the pleasures of life, so as to convey a powerful message to the Arab nation."[5] Another editorial noted, "From Mary's womb issued a Child who eliminated oppression, while the body of Wafa became shrapnel that eliminated despair and aroused hope."[6]

To complicate the notions of femininity and motherhood, the female bomber's improvised explosive device (IED) is often disguised under her clothing to make it appear as if she is pregnant and thus beyond suspicion or reproach. Police reports in Turkey have emphasized caution approaching Kurdish women who may appear pregnant; several female PKK fighters disguised themselves this way in order to penetrate crowds of people more effectively and to avoid detection, assuming correctly that they would not be frisked or subjected to intense scrutiny. Israel learned this lesson as well. Hanadi Jaradat, a law student from Jenin who killed 19 civilians in a crowded Haifa restaurant in 2003, wore an explosive belt around her waist in order to feign pregnancy.

Moreover, according to a British security source, "The terrorists know there are sensitivities about making intimate body searches of women, particularly Muslim women, and thus you can see why some groups might be planning to use a female suicide bomber. Hiding explosives in an intimate part of the body means even less chance of detection."[7] The report said a woman could conceal up to 12 pounds of plastic explosives inside her body. The detonator and other components, which can be hidden in a watch, cell phone, or electrical device, could easily be taken past security checkpoints.

The use of the least-likely suspect is the most-likely tactical adaptation for a terrorist group under scrutiny. A growing number of insurgent organizations have adopted suicide bombing not only because of its tactical superiority to traditional guerrilla warfare, but also because suicide bombing, especially when perpetrated by women and girls, garners significant media attention both domestically and abroad.

The recruitment of women by insurgent organizations can mobilize greater numbers of operatives by shaming men into participating. This tactic has parallels to right-wing Hindu women who goad men into action through speeches saying, "Don't be a bunch of eunuchs."[8] This point is underscored by the bombers themselves. A propaganda slogan in Chechnya reads: "Women's courage is a disgrace to that of modern men."[9] Before Ayat Akras blew herself up in Israel in April 2002, she taped her martyrdom video and stated, "I am going to fight instead of the sleeping Arab armies who are watching Palestinian girls fighting alone," in an apparent dig at Arab leaders for not being sufficiently proactive or aggressive against the Israeli enemy.[10]

But why do these women become suicide bombers? The defining characteristics of a suicide bomber, in general, are elusive. Contrary to popular perception, 10 they are not unbalanced sociopaths prone to self-destructive tendencies. Nor are they poor, uneducated religious fanatics. "The profile of a suicide terrorist resembles that of a politically conscious individual who might join a grassroots movement more than it does the stereotypical murderer, religious cult member, or everyday suicide," notes Robert Pape of the University of Chicago.[11]

Additionally, they may feel a sense of alienation from their surrounding societies, or be seeking retribution for humiliation. (Eyad El-Sarraj, the founder and director of the Gaza Community Mental Health Program, has found that Palestinian suicide bombers share childhood traumas—notably, the humiliation of their fathers by Israeli soldiers.)[12] Suicide bombers tend to emerge in societies that extol the virtues of self-sacrifice. And, crucially, suicide bombers rarely act on their own. They are recruited and indoctrinated by organizations that might exploit their desire for a sense of belonging and that may act as surrogate families.

These same characteristics apply to women suicide bombers—albeit through the unique prism of their experiences and status. In Sri Lanka, Mangalika Silva, the coordinator of Women for Peace in Colombo, observes that, "The self-sacrifice of the female bombers is almost an extension of the idea of motherhood in the Tamil culture. In this strongly patriarchal society, Tamil mothers make great sacrifices for their sons on a daily basis; feeding them before themselves or the girl children, serving on them and so on."[13] Anecdotal evidence suggests that many women bombers have been raped or sexually abused either by representatives of the state or by insurgents—thereby contributing to a sense of humiliation and powerlessness, made only worse by stigmatization within their own societies. They may be avenging the loss of a family member or seeking to redeem the family name. And these women, not content to play the designated roles of passive observer or supportive nurturer, may seek to prove to their own societies that they are no less capable than their male counterparts to be vital contributors to the cause. Clara Beyer, a researcher for the International Policy Institute for Counter-Terrorism in Israel, astutely observes that, "When women become human bombs, their intent is to make a statement not only in the name of a country, a religion, a leader, but also in the name of their gender."[14]

DAUGHTERS OF REVOLUTION

Insurgent and terrorist organizations have long provided women a potential avenue for advancement beyond what their traditional societies could offer. Women in radical secular organizations have engaged in anticolonial and revolutionary struggles in the developing world and elsewhere since the 1960s. They have played vital support roles in the Algerian revolution (1958–1962), the Iranian Revolution (1979), the war in Lebanon (1982), the first Palestinian Intifada (1987–1991), and the Al Aqsa Intifada (since 2000).[15]

Female terrorists have come from all parts of the globe: Italy's Red Brigades, Germany's Baader-Meinhof faction, America's Black Panthers, and the Japanese Red Army—occasionally emerging as leaders. Women have even been on the front lines of combat, demonstrating that their revolutionary and military zeal is no less than that of men. (The Tamil Tigers have units exclusively for women.) There also have been a handful of notorious Palestinian women militants. In 1970, Leila Khaled was caught after attempting to hijack an El Al flight to London. Khaled, as journalist Eileen Macdonald puts it, "shattered a million and one taboos overnight and she revolutionized the thinking of hundreds of other angry young women around the world."[16]

Khaled explained her rationale: "Violence was a way of leveling the patriarchal society through revolutionary zeal—the women would demonstrate that their commitment was no less than those of their brothers, sons, or husbands. Strategically, women are able to gain access to areas where men had greater difficulty because the other side assumed that the women were second-class citizens in their own society—dumb, illiterate perhaps, and incapable of planning an operation."[17]

More recently, the idea of violence empowering women has spread throughout the West Bank and the Gaza Strip. This militant involvement by women has had an extreme effect on the existing norms of Palestinian society, which has long had a cultural set of rules that describe and limit gender roles. These norms have dictated the separation of the sexes and prescribed that women restrict themselves to the private space of the home.

Through violence, however, women have placed themselves on the front lines, in public, alongside men to whom they are not related. This results in a double trajectory for militant women—convincing society of their valid contributions while at the same time reconstructing the normative ideals of their society.[18] "Palestinian women have torn the gender classification out of their birth certificates, declaring that sacrifice for the Palestinian homeland would not be for men alone," declared female columnist Samiya Sa'ad Al Din in the Egyptian newspaper *Al-Akhbar*. "On the contrary, all Palestinian women will write the history of the liberation with their blood, and will become time bombs in the face of the Israeli enemy. They will not settle for being mothers of martyrs."[19]

The first wave of Palestinian women who became *shahidas* (female martyrs) had varied backgrounds: one ambulance worker, one seamstress, two in college, one in high school, one law school graduate, and one mother of two who left relatives stricken and shocked.[20] Some analysts have suggested a shared characteristic among them, that they were misfits or outcasts—young women who found themselves, for various reasons, "in acute emotional distress due to social stigmatization."[21] Journalist Barbara Victor corroborated this hypothesis when she determined that the first four female Palestinian suicide bombers were in situations where the act of martyrdom was seen as their sole chance to reclaim the "family honor" that had been lost by their own actions or the actions of other family members.[22] Allegations abound that the first female Hamas suicide bomber, Reem Riashi, a mother of two, was coerced by both her husband and lover as a way of saving face after an extramarital affair.[23]

Elsewhere in the world, sexual violence against women—and the ensuing social stigma associated with rape in patriarchal societies—appears to be a common motivating factor for suicide attackers. Kurdish women allegedly raped in Turkey by the military have joined the PKK, while Tamil women allegedly raped by the Sinhalese security services and military join the LTTE. Gandhi's assassin, Dhanu, is alleged to have been raped, although this issue remains one of intense debate and contro-versy. (By some accounts, it was her mother who was raped by Indian peacekeep-ers who occupied Sri Lanka from 1987 to 1990.) According to the Hindu faith, once a woman is sexually violated she cannot get married or have children. Fight-ing for Tamil freedom might have been seen as the only way for such a woman to redeem herself.

For Dhanu, the conflict had another personal dimension: The peacekeepers in 20 Sri Lanka had killed her brother, a well-known cadre for the Tamil Tigers. In that regard, she shared an experience common in conflict-ridden societies—the loss of loved ones. Most of the Chechen attacks against Russia in 2004 involved "Black Widows" reportedly wishing to avenge the deaths of family members in Russia's conflict in Chechnya.

Female bombers have participated in more than 18 major attacks since the outbreak of the second Chechen War in 1999 and have developed into an increasingly serious threat since 2000. Previous acts of violence took place in the Northern Caucasus and were primarily aimed at military targets. They did not aim to kill large numbers of Russian civilians. The attacks by female suicide bomb-ers have reversed these patterns. Imran Yezhiyev, of the Chechen-Russian Friend-ship Society in Ingushetia, observes: "Suicide attacks were an inevitable response to the 'most crude, the most terrible' crimes Russian forces had committed against Chechen civilians during the war. When Russian soldiers kill children and civilians and demand payment for their return, many in Chechnya are outraged and vow revenge. One woman, Elvira, whose 15-year-old son had been killed by Russian troops who demanded $500 to return his corpse, stated, 'Oh, yes, I want to kill them. Kill Russians, kill their children. I want them to know what it is like.'"[24]

DIVINE INTERVENTION

Islamic leaders initially opposed women's activism and banned women from becom-ing suicide bombers on their behalf; only a handful of clerics endorsed such oper-ations. The Saudi High Islamic Council gave the go-ahead to women suicide bombers in August 2001, after a 23-year-old Palestinian mother of two was seized by Israeli security as she brought explosives to Tel Aviv's central bus station. Reli-gious leaders in Palestine disagreed, and a theological debate rages as to whether women should or could be martyrs.[25]

Hamas's former spiritual leader, Sheikh Ahmad Yassin, argued that a woman's appropriate role in the conflict was to support the fighters (that is, the men). According to Yassin, "In our Palestinian society, there is a flow of women toward jihad and martyrdom, exactly like the young men. But the woman has uniqueness. Islam sets some restrictions for her, and if she goes out to wage jihad and fight, she must be accompanied by a male chaperon." Sheikh Yassin further rationalized his reservations—not because of *Shariah* (Islamic religious law), but because women martyrs were deemed unnecessary: "At the present stage, we do not need women to bear this burden of jihad and martyrdom. The Islamic Movement cannot accept all the Palestinian males demanding to participate in jihad and in martyrdom operations, because they are so numerous. Our means are limited, and we cannot absorb all those who desire to confront the enemy."[26]

This situation is alarmingly true. Most of the militant organizations in Palestine cannot fill positions for martyrdom operations fast enough.[27] After Wafa Idris blew herself up in downtown Jerusalem in January 2002, Yassin categorically renounced the use of women as suicide bombers or assailants. Yet, sensing the increasing support for women martyrs and bowing to public pressure and demands, Yassin amended his position, saying that a woman waging jihad must be accompanied by a male chaperon "if she is to be gone for a day and a night. If her absence is shorter, she does not need a chaperon." In a second statement, Yassin granted a woman's right to launch a suicide attack alone only if it does not take her more than 24 hours to be away from home—an ironic position, since she would be gone for longer if she succeeded in her mission.[28]

While Yassin pointed out that it was Hamas's armed wing that decided where 25 and when attacks would take place, his comments included quotes from the videotape that Riashi, Hamas's first female bomber, recorded before carrying out her January 2004 attack, about how she hoped her "organs would be scattered in the air and her soul would reach paradise." Yassin added: "The fact that a woman took part for the first time in a Hamas operation marks a significant evolution. . . . The male fighters face many obstacles on their way to operations, and this is a new development in our fight against the enemy. The holy war is an imperative for all Muslim men and women, and this operation proves that the armed resistance will continue until the enemy is driven from our land. This is revenge for all the fatalities sustained by the armed resistance."[29]

Among Islamic groups, the trend toward women suicide bombers appears to be contagious, as religious authorities are making exceptions and finding legal precedent to permit women's participation. Groups affiliated with Al Qaeda have begun to employ women bombers. An indication of this ideological shift was the capture of two young women in Rabat, Morocco, on their way to target a liquor store in a preempted suicide attack. Within weeks of the U.S. invasion of Iraq, on March 29, 2003, two women (one of whom was pregnant) perpetrated suicide attacks against Coalition forces. Al Jazeera television reported on April 4 that the two Iraqi women had videotaped their intentions: "We say to our leader and holy war comrade, the hero commander Saddam Hussein, that you have sisters that you and history will boast about."[30]

Also in March 2003, *Al-Sharq Al-Awsat* published an interview with a woman calling herself "Um Osama," the alleged leader of the women Mujahideen of Al Qaeda. The Al Qaeda cell claimed to have set up squads of female suicide bombers under orders from Osama bin Laden to target the United States. The women bombers purportedly include Afghans, Arabs, Chechens, and other nationalities. "We are preparing for the new strike announced by our leaders, and I declare that it will make America forget . . . the September 11 attacks," she said. "The idea came from the success of martyr operations carried out by young Palestinian women in the occupied territories. Our organization is open to all Muslim women wanting to serve the [Islamic] nation . . . particularly in this very critical phase."[31]

Yet another measure of Al Qaeda's growing interest in recruiting women was the publication in August 2004 of the online magazine *Al Khansaa*. Published by the group's self-described Arabian Peninsula Women's Information Bureau, the magazine's first issue calls upon women to participate in jihad in a variety of ways. Reflecting the evolving duality of women's proscribed role in armed struggle, the magazine emphasized first and foremost that the "woman in the family is a mother, wife, sister, and daughter. In society she is an educator, propagator, and preacher of Islam, and a female jihad warrior. Just as she defends her family from any possible aggression, she defends society from destructive thoughts and from ideological and moral deterioration, and she is the soldier who bears [the man's] pack and weapon on his back in preparation for the military offensive." However, the article added, "When jihad becomes a personal obligation, then the woman is summoned like a man, and need ask permission neither from her husband nor from her guardian, because she is obligated, and none need to ask permission in order to carry out a commandment that everyone must carry out."[32]

Indeed, some see female suicide bombers as a crucial blow against the decadent influences of Western culture—an act of defiance that does not redefine women's traditional roles, but reaffirms them. A columnist in the Jordanian newspaper *Al-Dustour* noted, "The Arab woman has taken her place and her dignity. It is the women's rights activists in the West who robbed women of their right to be human, and viewed them as bodies without souls. . . . Wafa [Idris] did not carry makeup in her suitcase, but enough explosives to fill the enemies with horror. . . . Wasn't it the West that kept demanding that the Eastern woman become equal to the man? Well, this is how we understand equality—this is how the martyr Wafa understood equality."[33]

Yet, the women who seek empowerment and equality by turning themselves into human bombs merely reinforce the inequalities of their societies, rather than confront them and explode the myths from within. Traditional societies have a well-scripted set of rules in which women sacrifice themselves—the ideal of motherhood, in particular, is one of self-denial and self-effacement. The women who choose the role of martyrs do not enhance their status, but give up their sense of self as they contribute to this ultimate, albeit twisted, fulfillment of patriarchal values.

For their part, terrorist groups will continue to find recruits as long as they can offer women a way out of their societies, a chance to participate as full members in the struggle. As such, increasing women's roles in peaceful activities, addressing their needs during times of peace and during conflict, and protecting and promoting their rights cannot be an afterthought in foreign policy. The best way to fight the war on terror is to make the terrorist organizations less appealing—to men and to women.

NOTES

1. "Lady with the Poison Flowers," *Outlook India,* August 29, 2005.
2. Jessica Stern, "When Bombers Are Women," *Washington Post,* December 18, 2003.
3. Yoram Schweitzer, "Suicide Terrorism: Historical Background and Risks for the Future," June 18, 2004 (pbs.org).

4. Rohan Gunaratna, "Suicide Terrorism—A Global Threat," *Jane's Intelligence Review,* October 20, 2000.

5. *Al-Wafd,* February 1, 2002, as cited in *Al-Quds Al-Arabi,* February 2, 2002 (memri.org).

6. Adel Sadeq, *Hadith Al-Medina,* February 5, 2002, as cited in *Al-Quds Al-Arabi,* February 6, 2002 (memri.org).

7. Daniel McGrory, "'She-Bomber' Fears Over Plot for Woman to Blow Up Plane," Times Online, February 21, 2004.

8. Amrita Basu, "Hindu Women's Activism and the Questions It Raises," in Amrita Basu and Patricia Jeffrey (eds.), *Appropriating Gender: Women's Activism and Politicized Religion in South Asia* (London: Routledge, 1997).

9. Dimitri Sudakov, "Shamil Besaev Trains Female Suicide Bombers," *Pravda,* May 15, 2003.

10. Libby Copeland, "Female Suicide Bombers: The New Factor in Mideast's Deadly Equation," *Washington Post,* April 27, 2002.

11. Cited in Cameron Stewart, "Enemy Within," *Australian,* July 16, 2005.

12. Michael Bond, "The Making of a Suicide Bomber," *New Scientist,* May 15, 2004.

13. Quoted in Ana Cutter, "Tamil Tigresses," *Slant: The Magazine of Columbia University's School of International and Public Affairs,* Spring 1998.

14. Clara Beyer, "Messengers of Death: Female Suicide Bombers," February 12, 2003 (ict.org.il/articles/articledet.cfm?articleid=470).

15. After the Iranian Revolution, the clerical regime created informal cadres of women to fight the war, though the Islamic republic could not bring itself to employ women martyrs. Reuel Marc Gerecht, "They Live to Die," *Wall Street Journal,* April 8, 2002.

16. Eileen Macdonald, *Shoot the Women First* (New York: Random House, 1992).

17. Leila Khaled, *My People Shall Live: The Autobiography of a Revolutionary* (London: Hodder and Stoughton, 1973).

18. Lucy Frazier, "Abandon Weeping for Weapons," *Online Journal of Education, Media, and Health: Issue on Terrorism,* August 6, 2002 (nyu.edu/classes/keefer/joe/frazier.html).

19. Samiya Sa'ad Al-Din, *Al-Akhbar,* February 1, 2002.

20. Israel's security forces are aware of more than 20 cases in which women were involved in sabotage activity against Israeli targets. "The Role of Palestinian Women in Suicide Terrorism," January 2003 (mfa.gov.il/mfa/go.asp?MFAH0n210); Copeland, "Female Suicide Bombers."

21. Israeli Security Sources, "Blackmailing Young Women into Suicide Terrorism," February 12, 2002 (mfa.gov.il/mfa/go.asp?MFAH0n2a0).

22. Barbara Victor, *Army of Roses: Inside the World of Palestinian Suicide Bombers* (New York: Rodale Press, 2003).

23. Chris McGreal, "Palestinians Shocked at Use of Suicide Mother," *Guardian,* January 27, 2004.

24. Cited by Owen Matthews, "So Warped by Hate, They Will Kill Anyone to Take Revenge Against Russia," *Daily Mail,* September 4, 2004.

25. Peter Beaumont, "Woman Suicide Bomber Strikes," *Guardian,* January 28, 2002.

26. *Al-Sharq Al-Awsat,* January 31, 2002.

27. Nasra Hassan observed this fact years ago in her article, "An Arsenal of Believers," *New Yorker,* November 2001.

28. *Al-Sharq Al-Awsat,* January 31, 2002; February 2, 2002.

29. Arnon Regular, "Mother of Two Becomes First Female Suicide Bomber for Hamas," *Ha'aretz,* January 15, 2004.

30. Cited by Roman Kupchinsky, in "Smart Bombs with Souls," in *Organized Crime and Terrorism Watch,* April 17, 2003.

31. "Bin Laden Has Set Up Female Suicide Squads: Report," *Arab News,* Dubai, March 13, 2003.

32. Middle East Media Research Institute, "Al-Qa'ida Women's Magazine: Women Must Participate in Jihad," *Special Dispatch Series,* September 7, 2004.

33. *Al-Dustour,* February 5, 2002.

FOR DISCUSSION

1. Perhaps nothing terrorists do is more incomprehensible and alienating to most people in the West than suicide attacks. How does Bloom lead us to understand them? Do you see suicide terror as largely explicable in cultural or situational terms? That is, is there "something about Islam" that encourages it?—or instead in the desperate conditions in the Middle East generally?

2. Bloom points out that the motives of women suicide attackers are different from those of men. How exactly? In what ways do their motives resemble what you know about violence by women in Western countries?

3. It's obvious that women suicide bombers would offer a temporary tactical advantage to terrorists—the element of surprise. It's also obvious that the surprise factor no longer exists. Why then are women still being used? What "message" do such attacks send to Muslims and the rest of the world?

FOR RESEARCH AND INQUIRY

Suicide bombers, Mia Bloom claims, "are not unbalanced sociopaths prone to self-destructive tendencies" and not "poor, uneducated religious fanatics," but rather, as Robert Pape maintains, "politically conscious individual[s] who might join a grassroots movement." In other words, they are not people we can "write off" as deranged deviants whose emotional or psychological problems explain what they do.

Profiles of suicide attackers exist, and much has been written about nearly every aspect of their background and motives. Find out all you can about them. Then write an essay exploring what you've learned directed at your fellow students. The purpose of the essay is to promote understanding, although not, of course, approval of what they do.

FOR FURTHER READING

Benjamin, David, and Steven Simon. *The Next Attack: The Failure of the War on Terror and a Strategy for Getting It Right.* New York: Holt, 2005.

Bloom, Mia. *Dying to Kill: The Allure of Suicide Terror.* New York: Columbia UP, 2005.

Clarke, Richard A. *Against All Enemies: Inside America's War on Terror.* New York: Free Press, 2004.

Lewis, Bernard. *Islam in History: Ideas, People, and Events in the Middle East.* Chicago: Open Court, 1993.

Nacos, Brigitte L. *Terrorism and Counterterrorism: Understanding Threats and Responses in the Post–9/11 World.* New York: Pearson-Longman, 2006.

Pape, Robert A. *Dying to Win: The Strategic Logic of Suicide Terrorism.* New York: Random House, 2005.

Shanahan, Timothy, ed. *Philosophy 9/11: Thinking about the War on Terrorism.* Chicago: Open Court, 2005.

Weimann, Gabriel. *Terror on the Internet: The New Arena, the New Challenges.* Washington, D.C.: U.S. Institute of Peace Press, 2006.

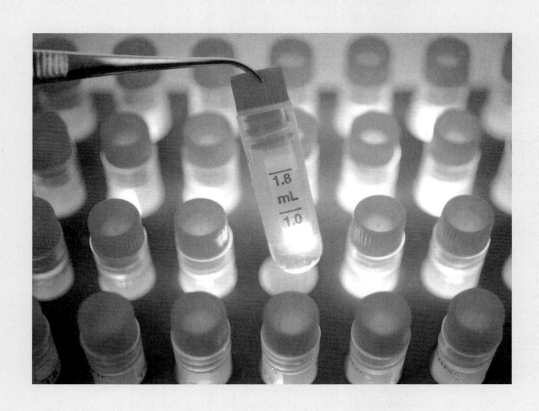

Genetics and Enhancement: Better Than Human?

Human beings have always found ways to enhance life by improving on what nature provides. That's what technology is all about, from the first primitive stone tools to today's computers and cell phones. Now technology can improve not just how we live but also who we are through genetic engineering. The question is *How far should we go in using genetics to enhance human life?*

Some people object entirely to gene manipulation on the grounds that it's unnatural or playing God. But human beings aren't natural. Other species live in environments; we create our own. Our lives are artificial in the sense of *artifice*—we depend on things we've made. The alternative is naked existence in caves. As for "playing God": That happens every time a doctor cures a disease that would otherwise kill someone. It happens when desperately ill people are placed on or removed from life support. "Playing God" is an everyday occurrence.

So, is genetic engineering just another human artifice, another technology? Is it any different fundamentally from all the other ways we enhance ourselves?

When someone gets a "nose job," for instance, only the person with the nose he or she doesn't like is directly affected. Because genetics can alter germ cells, human sperm and eggs, it's possible to alter not only one person but also his or her children, the children's children, and so on. With a nose job, the person knows or should know the possible outcomes that may be less than ideal. Because genes interact with other genes in ways too complex for complete understanding or prediction, it's hard to know exactly what the outcome might be. We might change a person's genes to eliminate, say, colon cancer that runs in her or his family but, in doing so, increase the person's likelihood of contracting some other deadly disease. But the side effect may not turn up for years, maybe not for several generations.

Clearly, then, genetic enhancement is different from plastic surgery. Its power to transform is far greater. Genetic engineering has the potential to cure devastating diseases, like Alzheimer's, and to repair tissue damaged from accidents that otherwise won't regenerate. People who are wheelchair-bound from spinal-cord injuries could walk again. Stem cells, which have the unique capacity to develop into any tissue in the body, might well be used to repair a diseased brain or restore damaged nerves in a spinal cord.

But stem cells are harvested either from aborted fetuses or from embryos created in laboratories for that purpose. This disturbs enough people that President Bush severely restricted stem cell research. He also formed the President's Council on Bioethics to advise him on all matters relating to genetic engineering.

The ethical problems are hardly limited to what we have mentioned so far. We already can screen embryos to give a couple a boy rather than a girl, or vice versa—why not a child who is unusually pretty or handsome, gifted athletically or musically, and so on? All of this sounds wonderful. But do we really want to do this? Do we want to be *responsible* for what our children are to a degree that far exceeds the obligation to raise them as best we can?

We've only touched here on the extraordinary potential of genetic enhancement and the equally extraordinary ethical problems it raises. The articles in this section will take us further and deeper. We need to examine the issues because, like the physics of the atom and the digital revolution, genetic engineering is a major development that must be confronted squarely. Most of the crucial decisions have yet to be made. We need to be prepared to help make them. Nothing less than the meaning of "being human" is at stake.

Stem Cell Stumping

ANNE APPLEBAUM

> This article reminds us of some basic points to keep in mind as we read all the selections in this chapter: that politics is in the middle of the controversy; that, consequently, extravagant and simplistic claims are made both for and against genetic engineering; that, to see clearly past the hype, what we need is a solid grasp of the facts.
>
> Applebaum is a political columnist for *The Washington Post.* Her book, *Gulag,* won the 2004 Pulitzer Prize for general nonfiction.

"We also—we also need to lift the ban on stem cell research—(cheers, applause) and find cures that will help millions of Americans (applause continues)."

Applause continues. That's a direct quote from the transcript of the speech that Sen. Hillary Rodham Clinton gave at the Democratic convention last week. Unexpectedly, the applause continued all week long, for anyone who spoke about stem cell research. Sen. John Kerry got some for asking, "What if we have a president who believes in science, so we can unleash the wonders of discovery—like stem cell research—and treat illness for millions of lives?" Ron Reagan, son of the late president, who mistakenly imagined he was being cheered merely for what he said rather than who his father was, hit an even higher rhetorical note: "Sound like magic? Welcome to the future of medicine."

Listening to all these speeches, you might have come away with the impression that stem cell research is illegal in this country, and that if our recalcitrant, medieval, anti-science fundamentalist president would only "lift the ban," or lose the election, there would be "magic" cures for old people with Alzheimer's and children with diabetes. . . .

As it happens, I do think we should liberalize our national policy on stem cell research. But before we do that, it's important to be pretty clear about what that national policy actually is, and how it got to be that way. Stem cell research is not, in fact, either illegal or unfunded: The federal budget in 2003 included $24.8 million for human embryonic stem cell research—up from zero in 2000. Private funding of stem cell research, which is unlimited, runs into the tens and possibly hundreds of millions of dollars. The current, admittedly hairsplitting policy came about because Congress in 1995 passed a ban on federal (but not private) funding for any form of research that involved the destruction of human embryos, because it is a form of research many American voters dislike and don't want to pay for. After some important (privately funded) breakthroughs, the Clinton administration began looking for legal ways to bypass the ban, but never got around to paying for any actual research.

The Bush administration thought about it, too, and came up with a solution: 5 Federal funding could be used for research on stem cell lines already in existence. In practice, this means scientists who get their funding from the government are restricted in which materials they can use. Although this compromise will soon become a real obstacle to research, for the moment the irritant is largely philosophical. "What hampers people is the concept that there is a lack of freedom to operate," one scientist told me.

If all of that sounds a little long-winded and complicated, that's because it is. The question now is whether we want, as a nation, to continue to have long-winded and complicated debates about complicated issues, or whether we want to resort to slogans such as "lift the ban" and "unleash the wonders of discovery." The question is also whether Americans and their political representatives are allowed to think twice about the implications of brand-new science—a prerequisite for public support, one would think—or whether the patients' groups and pollsters behind last week's rhetoric always get the last word. . . .

But simplifying the argument must work as a political tactic or the Kerry campaign wouldn't have let so many people do it. Perhaps it's because "stem cell research" makes a more attractive cultural buzzword than "abortion," and a more unifying cultural issue than gay marriage. Perhaps it's because it is so easy to use personal anecdotes—Ron Reagan spoke of a 13-year-old girl who decorates her insulin pump with rhinestones—to turn a dry scientific subject into an emotional one. Or perhaps it's because the discussion taps into an old and familiar metaphor—Galileo vs. the pope, Voltaire vs. the clerics, progress vs. religion—which helps people feel more comfortable about choosing sides. Call me antediluvian, but I'd still like it better if debates about science began with facts.

FOR DISCUSSION

1. In paragraph 4, Applebaum tells us about the current state of national policy on and funding of stem cell research. Summarize what she says. What didn't you know before reading this essay? What seems most important to you? Why?

2. We all know how politics tends to turn complex issues into simple slogans. But is it realistic to expect "long-winded and complicated debates about complicated issues" (paragraph 6) in the context of political campaigns? What works against such debates? In what contexts and circumstances should such debates go on?

FOR RESEARCH AND CONVINCING

Stem cell research is only one aspect of genetic enhancement, but a good place to begin overcoming lack of basic knowledge. As a class project, collect articles and book chapters about it that concentrate on "the facts," current knowledge about stem cells and possible therapies based on it. What do the facts imply about the potential of stem cell research? Make this question the center of class discussion.

Write an essay taking a stance on how much money and talent should be devoted to stem cell research. That is: in your view, how important is it as one among many avenues for scientific research? Conceive your essay as an opinion piece for your campus or local newspaper.

In Defense of Nature, Human and Non-Human

FRANCIS FUKUYAMA

In recent decades we've gained a renewed respect for nature's blind, trial-and-error approach to genetic diversity, the process we call evolution. We've also learned to appreciate the intricate interactions of life forms in ecosystems and how easily rain forests and coral reefs can be damaged and destroyed by human interventions.

Francis Fukuyama, author of *Our Posthuman Future,* argues for strict regulation of bioengineering. He is a professor at the Johns Hopkins School of Advanced International Studies. His article appeared in *World Watch* (July-August 2002).

People who have not been paying close attention to the debate on human biotechnology might think that the chief issue in this debate is about abortion, since the most outspoken opponents of cloning to date have been right-to-lifers who oppose the destruction of embryos. But there are important reasons why cloning and the genetic technologies that will follow upon it should be of concern to all people, religious or secular, and above all to those who are concerned with protecting the natural environment. For the attempt to master human nature through biotechnology will be even more dangerous and consequential than the efforts of industrial societies to master non-human nature through earlier generations of technology.

If there is one thing that the environmental movement has taught us in the past couple of generations, it is that nature is a complex whole. The different parts of an ecosystem are mutually interdependent in ways that we often fail to understand; human efforts to manipulate certain parts of it will produce a host of unintended consequences that will come back to haunt us.

Watching one of the movies made in the 1930s about the construction of Hoover Dam or the Tennessee Valley Authority is today a strange experience: the films are at the same time naive and vaguely Stalinist, celebrating the human conquest of nature and boasting of the replacement of natural spaces with steel, concrete, and electricity. . . .

If the problem of unintended consequences is severe in the case of non-human ecosystems, it will be far worse in the realm of human genetics. The human genome has in fact been likened to an ecosystem in the complex way that genes interact and influence one another. It is now estimated that there are only about 30,000 genes in the human genome, far fewer than the 100,000 believed to exist until recently. This is not terribly many more than the 14,000 in a fruitfly or the 19,000 in a nematode, and indicates that many higher human capabilities and behaviors are controlled by the complex interworking of multiple genes. A single gene will have multiple effects, while in other cases several genes need to work together to produce a single effect, along causal pathways that will be extremely difficult to untangle.

The first targets of genetic therapy will be relatively simple single gene disorders 5 like Huntington's disease or Tay Sachs disease. Many geneticists believe that the genetic causality of higher-order behaviors and characteristics like personality, intelligence, or even height is so complex that we will never be able to manipulate it. But this is precisely where the danger lies: we will be constantly tempted to think that we understand this causality better than we really do, and will face even nastier surprises than we did when we tried to conquer the non-human natural environment. In this case, the victim of a failed experiment will not be an ecosystem, but a human child whose parents, seeking to give her greater intelligence, will saddle her with a greater propensity for cancer, or prolonged debility in old age, or some other completely unexpected side effect that may emerge only after the experimenters have passed from the scene.

Listening to people in the biotech industry talk about the opportunities opening up with the completion of the sequencing of the human genome is eerily like watching those propaganda films about Hoover Dam: there is a hubristic confidence that biotechnology and scientific cleverness will correct the defects of human nature, abolish disease, and perhaps even allow human beings to achieve immortality some day. We will come out the other end a superior species because we understand how imperfect and limited our nature is.

I believe that human beings are, to an even greater degree than ecosystems, complex, coherent natural wholes, whose evolutionary provenance we do not even begin to understand. More than that, we possess human rights because of that specifically human nature: as Thomas Jefferson said at the end of his life, Americans enjoy equal political rights because nature has not arranged for certain human beings to be born with saddles on their backs, ready to be ridden by their betters. A biotechnology that seeks to manipulate human nature not only risks unforeseen consequences, but can undermine the very basis of equal democratic rights as well.

So how do we defend human nature? The tools are essentially the same as in the case of protecting non-human nature: we try to shape norms through discussion and dialogue, and we use the power of the state to regulate the way in which technology is developed and deployed by the private sector and the scientific research community. Biomedicine is, of course, heavily regulated today, but there are huge gaps in the jurisdiction of those federal agencies with authority over biotechnology. The U.S. Food and Drug Administration can only regulate food, drugs, and medical products on the basis of safety and efficacy. It is enjoined from making decisions on the basis of ethical considerations, and it has weak to nonexistent jurisdiction over medical procedures like cloning, preimplantation genetic diagnosis (where embryos are screened for genetic characteristics before being implanted in a womb), and germline engineering (where an embryo's genes are manipulated in ways that are inherited by future generations). The National Institutes of Health (NIH) make numerous rules covering human experimentation and other aspects of scientific research, but their authority extends only to federally funded research and leaves unregulated the private biotech industry. The latter, in U.S. biotech firms alone, spends over $10 billion annually on research, and employs some 150,000 people.

Other countries are striving to put legislation in place to regulate human biotechnology. One of the oldest legislative arrangements is that of Britain, which established the Human Fertilisation and Embryology Agency more than ten years ago to regulate experimentation with embryos. Twenty-four countries have banned reproductive cloning, including Germany, France, India, Japan, Argentina, Brazil, South Africa, and the United Kingdom. In 1998, the Council of Europe approved an Additional Protocol to its Convention on Human Rights and Dignity With Regard to Biomedicine banning human reproductive cloning, a document that has been signed by 24 of the council's

43 member states. Germany and France have proposed that the United Nations draft a global convention to ban reproductive cloning. . . .

Anyone who feels strongly about defending non-human nature from technological 10 manipulation should feel equally strongly about defending human nature as well. In Europe, the environmental movement is more firmly opposed to biotechnology than is its counterpart in the United States, and has managed to stop the proliferation of genetically modified foods there dead in its tracks. But genetically modified organisms are ultimately only an opening shot in a longer revolution, and far less consequential than the human biotechnologies now coming on line. Some people believe that, given the depredations of humans on non-human nature, the latter deserves more vigilant protection. But in the end, they are part of the same whole. Altering the genes of plants affects only what we eat and grow; altering our own genes affects who we are. Nature—both the natural environment around us, and our own—deserves an approach based on respect and stewardship, not domination and mastery.

FOR DISCUSSION

1. Although some religious viewpoints deny it, much evidence indicates that human beings did evolve from other life forms. But we also developed culture, on which we depend at least as much as on nature. What does the vast influence of culture do to Fukuyama's contention that human beings are "complex, coherent natural wholes"?

2. Fukuyama cites Thomas Jefferson's statement that equal rights depend on people "[not] be[ing] born with saddles on their backs." There's a deep irony here, for Jefferson was a slave owner, a system that depended on the proposition that some people were born "to be ridden by their betters." Do equal rights really depend on the natural equality of human beings? If not, from what does the notion of equality derive?

3. Fukuyama points to Europe's success in preventing the growth of genetically modified foods. So far, however, no demonstrable harm has come to humans who consume such food items—and we need to remember that almost everything we eat has been modified by developing strains and breeds through, for example, selective breeding. In your opinion, does Fukuyama offer any evidence that further regulation of bioengineering is justified?

FOR RESEARCH AND CONVINCING

Fukuyama points to the largely unregulated private biotech industry in the United States, which he says "spends over $10 billion annually on research, and employs some 150,000 people." Find out more about such firms. What are they researching? How are they doing it? What practical applications have resulted? What possible applications are on the way? Do you see any reason to impose federal regulation on private biotech firms? Write an essay arguing for or against federal oversight. If you support regulation, indicate what you think ought to be controlled.

Cartoon: Gene-Splicing as Big Business

LARRY GONICK AND MARK WHEELIS

If you want to learn about genetics and have fun at the same time, read *The Cartoon Guide to Genetics* (HarperCollins, 1991), from which the following satire comes.

From *The Cartoon Guide* to Genetics by Larry Gonick and Mark Wheelis. © Larry Gonick and Mark Wheelis. All rights reserved. Reprinted with permission.

FOR DISCUSSION

There's been a great deal of concern about the alliance between business and American colleges in recent years. So the questions raised by the appalled academics in the cartoon are serious questions, even if the economic incentives for turning discoveries into profits are so great that they tend to overwhelm them. What do you think about the issues raised, especially as they bear on business applications of genetic engineering?

5

Choosing Our Genes

GREGORY STOCK

> Gregory Stock is director of the Program on Medicine, Technology, and Society at UCLA and author of the best-seller *Redesigning Humans*. In his book and the following article from *The Futurist* (July-August 2002), he offers a detailed discussion of what's likely to happen soon in applying genetics to enhance human beings.

Technologies giving us control over our genetic destiny will be developed, whether they are banned or not. But clumsy regulatory efforts could greatly impede our progress toward improving the future health and well-being of our descendants.

What is causing all the fuss are technologies that will give parents the ability to make conscious choices about the genetics and traits of their children. For the foreseeable future, genetically altering adults is not in the cards, other than for treating a handful of specific diseases like cystic fibrosis. Changing the genes of an adult is far too daunting, and there are simpler, safer, and more effective ways of intervening to restore or enhance adult function.

Germinal choice technology refers to a whole realm of technologies by which parents influence the genetic constitutions of their children at the time of their conception. The simplest such intervention would be to correct genes. It is not a particularly radical departure, since it would have exactly the same effect as could be accomplished by screening multiple embryos and picking one with the desired genes. In fact, such embryo screening is being done now in preimplantation genetic diagnosis. Such technology has been in use for more than a decade, but what can be tested for is going to become increasingly sophisticated in the next 5 to 10 years. And as these technologies mature, the kinds of decisions that parents can make will become much more complex.

Farther into the future will be germline interventions—alterations to the egg, sperm, or more likely the first cell of an embryo. These procedures are being done already in animal systems, but using approaches that don't have the safety or reliability that would be required in human beings. . . .

GOALS OF GERMINAL CHOICE

The prevention of disease will likely be the initial goal of germinal choice. And the 5 possibilities may soon move well beyond the correction of aberrant genes. Recent studies suggest, for example, that children who have Down syndrome have close to a 90% reduction in the incidence of many cancers. It is possible that trisomy 21—i.e., having a third copy of chromosome 21, with increased gene expression levels that lead to the retardation and other symptoms of Down syndrome—may be protective against cancer. What if we could identify which of the genes on that chromosome are responsible for this protection from cancer? Geneticists might take a set of those genes and place them on an artificial chromosome, then add it to an embryo to reduce the incidence of cancer to the levels seen with Down syndrome, but without all the problems brought by the duplication of the other genes on chromosome 21. Many other similar possibilities will no doubt emerge, and some will almost certainly prove beneficial.

The use of artificial chromosomes might work quite well, particularly because the chromosomes themselves could be tested within the laboratory environment before any human use. They could be tested on animals, validated, and used in humans in essentially the same state they were tested in. Today, each gene therapy is done anew, so it is impossible to gain that kind of reliability. . . .

All sorts of ideas will occur to future gene therapists, who will then test them out to see if they are possible. If they are, then we will not forgo them. Reducing the incidence of cancer and heart disease, for example, or retarding aging are health enhancements that will be seen as very, very desirable.

GENETICALLY EXTENDING LIFESPANS

Antiaging will be an especially significant area of research because such interventions seem so plausible and are so strongly desired by large numbers of people. If it turns out that there are interventions that could—through our unraveling of the underlying process of aging—allow us to develop pharmaceutical and other interventions that are effective in adults, then that is what everybody would want. . . .

But embryo engineering will likely be easier and more effective than gene therapy in an adult. This is because genes placed in an embryo are copied into every single cell in the body and could be given tissue-specific control elements. So there may well be interventions to an embryo that are infeasible in an adult. And in this case, parents will likely look at conception as their one chance to give their child significant health advantages—a chance that will never again be available.

A "cure for aging" might be greatly accelerated by an infusion of funds into 10 research on the biology of aging. Right now, the area is rather underfunded. Much more money is being spent to find treatments for diseases of aging than to understand the underlying process that may be responsible for a wide variety of age-related diseases, such as cancer, heart disease, Alzheimer's, arthritis, and diabetes. . . .

Antiaging—offering one's children longer lifespans—will probably be a key goal of germline interventions, but not the only one. To do what is best for our children is a very human response. In fact, international polls have shown that in every country polled there is at least a significant minority who are interested in enhancing the physical or mental well-being of their children. They are thinking not of simple therapy to avoid particular diseases, but interventions aimed at actually improving (at least in their eyes) a child's beauty, intelligence, strength, altruism, and other qualities.

AN UNWELCOME CHOICE?

Society may not welcome some parents' choices. Sex selection is legal in the United States, but illegal in Britain and a number of other countries. And quite a few people think the procedure should be illegal in the United States as well, despite the fact that in the West, where no serious gender imbalances arise, it is hard to see who is injured by such choices. Another immediate decision will be whether parents screen for broad numbers of genetic diseases, some of which may not be terribly serious.

And soon, parents will likely be able to make choices about the height or IQ of their children, or other aspects of temperament and personality—predispositions and vulnerabilities that may soon be rather obvious in each of our genetic readouts.

The first wave of possibilities from germinal choice technology will be in genetic testing and screening, choosing one embryo instead of another. Initially, it will be very difficult for a lot of people to accept this, but it will be almost impossible to regulate, since any such embryo could have arrived completely naturally. These choices may prove agonizing, but they won't be dangerous, and I suspect they will bring us more benefits than problems.

Some people worry about a loss of diversity, but I think a more wrenching issue may be parents who decide to specifically select an embryo that would result in a child with a serious health condition. Should parents be allowed to make such choices?

In the deaf community, for instance, there is a whole movement that is very 15 opposed to the use of cochlear implants, because it hurts deaf culture and treats deafness like a disability. This is exactly the way most hearing people view it. And there are deaf parents who say that they would use germinal choice technology to ensure that their children were deaf. That is not to say they would take an embryo and damage it, but they would select an embryo that would develop into a deaf child.

That becomes a real issue for society when, for example, such health problems have medical costs that society must bear. If we feel that parents do have the right to make such choices and that there is no reason to value the birth of a healthy individual any more than someone with serious health challenges, then we won't regulate such choices. But if we decide there is a problem, and really want to come to grips with it, we may find it very challenging.

FRIGHTENING OURSELVES TO DEATH

Shortly after reports were heard of the first pregnancy resulting from a human cloning program (reports that most scientists believe are a total fabrication), U.S. President George W. Bush voiced his support for a Senate bill that would outlaw all forms of human cloning, including biomedical research aimed at creating embryonic stem cells that would not be rejected when transplanted, so-called therapeutic cloning.

I believe such a ban is premature, futile, extremely misguided, and just plain wrong. It would not significantly delay the arrival of reproductive cloning, which in my view is almost certain to occur within this decade somewhere in the world. It would inject politics, religion, and philosophy into the workings of basic research and inquiry, which would be a dangerous precedent. It would legislate greater concern for a microscopic dot of cells than for real people with real diseases and real suffering. And it would threaten embryo researchers with criminal penalties so extreme (10 years in prison) that they are almost unbelievable in the United States, a country where women during their first trimester have the right to an abortion for any reason whatsoever.

U.S. restraints on embryo research have already had an impact on the development of biomedical technologies directed toward regenerative medicine. Those restraints have slowed progress in this realm in the United States, which has the most powerful biomedical research effort in the world. Such research has now moved to Britain and other countries, such as Singapore, which is funding a huge program to explore embryonic stem cells. But such delays are very unfortunate because of the might-have-beens that still are not. For most people, a delay of a decade or two is not a big problem, but this is not so for people like actor Michael J. Fox and others who are undergoing progressive decline from serious diseases like Parkinson's or Alzheimer's. . . .

No matter how much it disturbs us, human germinal choice is inevitable. 20 Embryo selection is already here, cloning is on the way, and even direct germline engineering in humans will arrive. Such technology is inevitable because many people see it as beneficial, because it will be feasible in thousands of labs all over the world, and, most importantly, because it will be a mere spin-off of mainstream biomedical research to decipher our biology. . . .

A DEMOCRATIZING TECHNOLOGY?

The effort to block these new reproductive technologies renders them extremely divisive socially, because it will guarantee that they are only available to the wealthy who are able to circumvent any kinds of restrictions rather easily, either by traveling to other locations or by simply paying money to get black-market services.

At their core, germinal choice technologies—if handled properly—could be very democratizing, because the kinds of interventions that will be available initially are going to compensate for deficits. It will be much easier to lift someone with an IQ of 70 up to 100 (the population average) than to raise someone's IQ from 150 (the top fraction of a percent of the population) up to 160. And the same will be true in selecting the predispositions of future children. . . .

The genetic lottery can be very, very cruel. Ask anybody who is very slow or has a genetic disease of one sort or another. They don't believe in some abstract principle of how wonderful the genetic lottery is. They would like to be healthier or have more talent in one way or another. The broad availability of these technologies would thus level the playing field in many ways, because it would give opportunities to those who otherwise would be genetically disadvantaged.

Another point is that these technologies, as do any technologies, evolve rather rapidly. The differences will not so much be between the wealthy and the poor in one generation (although obviously there will be more things available to those who have more resources), but between one generation and the next. Today, even a Bill Gates could not obtain the genetic enhancements or services for his child that will seem primitive compared with what any middle-class person is going to have access to in 25 years. . . .

LOSING OUR HUMANITY—OR CONTROLLING IT?

Another misplaced fear is that, by tampering with our biology, we risk losing our 25 humanity. But does "humanity" have to do with very narrow aspects of our biology, or does it have to do with the whole process of engaging the world and with our interactions with one another? For instance, if our lifespan were to double, would that make us "not human" in some sense? It would certainly change the trajectory of our lives, the way we interact with one another, our institutions, our sense of family, and our attitudes about education. But we would still be human, and I daresay we would soon adjust to these changes and wonder how we could ever have lived without them. . . .

Humans now are just in the very early stages of their evolution—early adolescence at most. A thousand years from now, when future humans look back at this era, they're going to see it as a primitive, difficult, and challenging time. They will also see it as an extraordinary, rather glorious moment when we laid down the foundations of their lives. It is hard to imagine what human life will be like even a hundred years from now, but I suspect that the reworking of our own biology will figure heavily in our future.

FOR DISCUSSION

1. According to Stock, why is genetic alteration of adults "not in the cards" for the most part?

2. "Correcting genes" in embryos would not be, Stock claims, "a particularly radical departure" from current practices used in in-vitro fertilization. Why does he say this? How does it differ from what he calls "preimplantation genetic diagnosis"?

3. Stock points to an interesting "side effect" of Down syndrome—that children afflicted by it also "have close to a 90% reduction in the incidence of many cancers" (paragraph 5). How does he propose that such knowledge could be used to reduce cancer in the general population?

4. "Society may not welcome some parents' choices," Stock admits. He points out that some deaf parents will want deaf children as an example. What other choices might society find troubling?

5. Stock argues that genetic manipulation of human embryos could be a democratizing technology. What does he offer to support his view? Compare his argument to Francis Fukuyama's, which takes exactly the opposite position. Who makes the better case?

6. How does Stock view the question of what makes human beings human? Do you agree that gene manipulation will not fundamentally change what it means to be human?

FOR RESEARCH AND DISCUSSION

"The genetic lottery can be very, very cruel," Stock observes, and to verify that all you need to do is visit the cancer ward at a children's hospital or encounter an example or two of other congenital diseases. It's difficult to extol natural processes when about 2% of all live births result in genetically impaired children.

Compile a list of diseases linked to genetic defects. Individually or in groups, select a disease, then find out about symptoms and current, nongenetic treatment, including what it costs. Give a short, informative presentation about each disease.

Then discuss this question in class: Can there be any reasonable objection to genetic research designed to prevent such diseases either through screening embryos or through altering germ cells that produce or can produce genetic illnesses?

FOR CONVINCING

Stock points to the area of greatest controversy where applications of genetic knowledge are concerned—enhancing human traits a culture considers desirable. It's one thing to cure disease, the common argument goes, quite another to extend lifetimes or raise IQs or design children to be more attractive or less susceptible to depression.

Suppose that we have the knowledge and the means to select the traits our children will have. Suppose also that it's affordable and that conception would be the result of sexual intercourse only—no petri dishes and artificial means of insemination. In a short essay, make a case for using or not using that technology.

Why Designer Babies Won't Happen Soon

STEVEN PINKER

> Steven Pinker is a cognitive scientist at Harvard and best-selling author of many
> books, most recently *The Blank Slate.* The following selection came from a talk
> before the President's Council on Bioethics, "Human Nature and Its Future,"
> delivered March 6, 2003. We have taken a section from Pinker's much longer talk
> and assigned the title above to it.

I'm going to talk about the ability to change human nature that's of . . . direct
interest to the members of this committee [President's Council on Bioethics,]
namely, voluntary genetic engineering, popularly known as designer babies, and
that will be the topic of the rest of my presentation.

I don't have to remind you that this is ethically fraught, and there are vociferous voices arguing that this would be a bad thing or that it would be a good thing.
I'm going to address a common assumption both of people who are alarmed and
people who welcome genetic enhancement.

The assumption [is] that this is inevitable, that science has reached the point
where it's only a matter of time before genetic enhancement is routine and possibly the human species will change unless we intervene and regulate the science
and practice now.

I'm going to present a skeptical argument about designer babies to give you
an overview. I'm going to suggest that genetic enhancement of human nature is
not inevitable. Indeed, I would be willing to venture that it's highly unlikely in our
lifetimes.

Why? First of all, because of the fallibility of predictions about complex technol- 5
ogy in general.

Secondly, impediments to genetic enhancement from what we know about
the human behavioral genetics.

And, third, impediments from human nature itself.

Well, let me begin with the frailty of technological predictions in general.
There's a wonderful book called *The Experts Speak* by Victor Navasky and Christopher Cerf, which has some delicious quotations about what is inevitable in our
future, such as the following one. "Fifty years hence we shall escape the absurdity
of growing a whole chicken in order to eat the breast or wing by growing these
parts separately under a suitable medium"—Winston Churchill in 1932. That should
have happened by 1982, and we're still waiting.

Nuclear-powered vacuum cleaners will probably be a reality within ten years,
a prediction made in 1955 by a manufacturer of vacuum cleaners. A few other
predictions that I remember from my childhood, and in fact, from newspapers of
just a few years ago. Dome cities, jet pack commuting, mile-high buildings, routine
artificial organs, routine consumer space flights, such as the Pan Am shuttle to the
moon featured in 2001, interactive television, the paperless office, and the dot-com
revolution and the end of bricks-and-mortar retail. All of these predictions we know
to be false, and a number of them . . . we can say with a fair amount of confidence
never will happen.

We're not going to have domed cities, at least not in the future that's worth 10 worrying about.

Now, why are technological predictions so often wrong? First, there's a habit of assuming that technological progress can be linearly extrapolated. If there's a little bit of progress now, there will be proportional progress as we multiply the number of years out.

Engineers sometimes refer to this as the fallacy of thinking that we can get to the moon by climbing trees. A little bit of progress now can be extended indefinitely.

Secondly, there's a tendency to underestimate the number of things that have to go exactly right for a given scenario to take place. Most technological changes don't depend on a single discovery, but rather on an enormous number of factors, scores or even hundreds, all of which have to fall into place exactly right. . . .

Third, there's a widespread failure of futurologists to consider the costs of new technologies, as well as the benefits, whereas in reality the actual users faced with a particular technology consider both the benefits and the costs.

Finally, there is an incentive structure to futurology. Someone who predicts 15 a future that's radically different from our own, either to hype it or to raise an alarm against it, will get the attention of the press and the public. The chances are the *New York Times* won't call you up if you say either that the future is going to be pretty similar to the present or we haven't a clue as to what the future will be.

The second part of my talk, reasons for skepticism about designer babies, is that there's a considerably bracing splash of cold water on the possibility of designer babies from what we know about behavioral genetics and neural development today. There's a widespread assumption that we have discovered or soon will discover individual genes for talents such as mathematical giftedness, musical talent, athletic prowess, and so on.

But the reality is considerably different, and I think an Achilles' heel of genetic enhancement will be the rarity of single genes with consistent beneficial psychological effects. I think there's a myth that such genes have been discovered or inevitably will be discovered, but it isn't necessarily so.

Indeed, I would say that the science of behavioral genetics at present faces something of a paradox. We know that tens of thousands of genes working together have a large effect on the mind. We know that from twin studies that show that identical twins are far more similar than fraternal twins who, in turn, are more similar than unrelated individuals, and from adoption studies that show that children resemble their biological parents more than their adopted parents.

But these are effects of sharing an entire genome or half of a genome or a quarter of a genome. It's very different from the existence of single genes that have a consistent effect on the mind, which have been few and far between.

Anyone who has kept up with the literature on behavioral genetics has noticed 20 that there's been a widespread failure to find single genes for schizophrenia, autism, obsessive-compulsive disorder, and so on. And those, by the way, are the areas where we're most likely to find a single gene simply because it's easier to disrupt a complex system with a single defective part than it is to install an entire complex ability with a single gene. The failure to find a gene with consistent effect on, say, schizophrenia means that it's even less likely that we will find a gene for something as complex as musical talent or likability.

And though there have been highly publicized discoveries of single genes for syndromes such as bipolar illness, sexual orientation, or in perhaps the most promising case, a gene that appeared to correlate with four IQ points in gifted individuals; all of those discoveries have been withdrawn in recent years, including the four-point IQ gene withdrawn just last month.

Now, it's really not such a paradox when you think about what we know about biological development in general. The human brain is not a bag of traits with one gene for each trait. That's just not the way genetics works.

Neural development is a staggeringly complex process which we are only beginning to get the first clues about. It involves many genes interacting in complex feedback loops. . . .

The pattern of expression of genes is often as important as which genes are present, and therefore, it's a good idea not to hold your breath for the discovery of the musical talent gene or any other single gene or small number of genes with a large, consistent effect on cognitive functioning or personality. . . .

I think there are other genetic impediments to the possibility of genetic 25 enhancement. One is that the genes, even acting across an entire genome, have effects that are, at best, probabilistic. A sobering discovery is that monozygotic twins reared together who share all of their genes and most of their environment are imperfectly correlated. When it comes to personality measures, such as extroversion or neuroticism, correlations are in the range of 5.

Now, that's much, much bigger than correlations among non-identical twins or, let alone, unrelated individuals, but it's much less than one, and what that tells us is that there is an enormous and generally unacknowledged role for chance in the development of a human being.

Secondly, . . . most genes have multiple effects, and in general, evolution selects for the best compromise among the positive and negative effects that come from an individual gene.

A vivid example of this is . . . the . . . mice reported two years ago that were given extra MNDA receptors, receptors that are critical to learning and memory. These were artificially engineered mice that had an enhanced ability to learn mazes.

[But] it was later discovered that these mice were hypersensitive to inflammatory pain. So a genetic change had both positive and negative effects.

Because of this, . . . there are ethical impediments to research on human 30 enhancement, namely, how can you get there from here? Are there experiments that a typical human subjects committee would approve of, given the likelihood that any given gene will have negative effects on a child, in addition to the positive ones?

Finally, most human traits are desirable at intermediate values. Wallis Simpson [the duchess of Windsor] famously said that you can't be too rich or too thin, and it may be true that you can't be too smart, but for most other traits, you really can have too much of a good thing.

Most parents don't want their child to be not assertive enough, to be a punching bag or a door mat. [However,] most parents would also not want their child to be Jack the Ripper.

You want your child to have some degree of risk taking, not to sit at home cowering out of fear of negative consequences. [But] you don't want a self-destructive maniac either.

So if a given gene, even if it did have as its effect an enhancement, say, of risk taking, put it in a child and you'll have ten extra points on the risk taking scale; the crucial question is: what are the other 29,999 genes doing? Would they be placing your child on the left-hand side of the Bell curve, in which case an extra dose of assertiveness would be a good thing, or have they already put your child on the right-hand side of the Bell curve so that an extra dose of assertiveness is the last thing that you would want?

The third part of the argument is I think there are impediments in human 35 nature to enhancing human nature. Now, one feature of parental psychology that is often invoked in these discussions is the desire of parents to give their children whatever boost is possible, and lurking in all of these discussions is the stereotype of the Yuppie parent who plays Mozart to the mother's belly while the mother is pregnant, bombards the baby with flash cards, has them taking violin lessons at the age of three, and so on. And the assumption is that parents would stop at nothing to enhance their children's ability, including genetic engineering.

Well, that obviously is a feature of parental psychology, but there's a second feature of parental psychology that also has to be factored in, namely, the aversion to harm your children. Most parents know that even if they are not sure whether playing Mozart to a pregnant woman's belly will help their child, they have reasonable belief that it couldn't harm the child. Likewise the flash cards, the violin lessons, and so on.

If it came to genetic enhancement where this was unknown, it's not so clear that parents would opt for the risk of doing their children genuine harm for the promise of a possibility of doing them good.

Also, one ubiquitous feature of human nature is intuitions about naturalness and contamination, sometimes referred to by cognitive psychologists as psychological essentialism, the folk belief that living things have an essence which can be contaminated by pollutants from without.

This has been an impediment to the acceptance of other technologies. Famous examples are nuclear power, which is notoriously aversive to large segments of the population. As you all know, there hasn't been a new nuclear power plant built in this country for several decades, despite the possibility that it could be an effective solution to global warming.

In Europe and in large segments of this country, there is a widespread repug- 40 nance to genetically modified foods for reasons that are probably more irrational than rational, but nonetheless cannot be gainsaid. If people have a horror about genetically modified soybeans, it's not so clear that they would rush to welcome genetically modified children.

Finally, anyone who knows someone who has undergone IVF knows that this is a traumatic, painful, and rather unpleasant procedure, especially in comparison to sex. . . . There is reason to believe that this would not necessarily catch on in the population as a whole.

So the choice that parents would face in a hypothetical future . . . would not be the one that's popularly portrayed, namely, would you opt for a procedure that would give you a happier and more talented child?

When you put it like that, well, who would say no to that question?

More realistically, the question that parents would face would be something like this. Would you opt for a traumatic and expensive procedure that might give you a very slightly happier and more talented child, might give you a less happy, less talented child, might give you a deformed child, and probably would do nothing?

We don't know the probabilities of those four outcomes. I think this is a more 45 realistic way of thinking about the choices that parents might face.

For genetic enhancement to change human nature or to lead to a post human future, not a few, but billions of people would have to answer yes to this question.

So, to sum up, changing human nature by a voluntary genetic enhance-ment . . . is not inevitable because [of] the complexity of neural development and the rarity or absence of single genes with large, consistent, beneficial effects, and because of the tradeoff of risks and benefits enhancement that will inevitably be faced by researchers and by parents.

The conclusions that I would draw are the following. I am not arguing that genetic enhancement will never happen. If there's anything more foolish than say-ing that some technological development is inevitable, it's saying that some tech-nological development is impossible.

And corresponding to the silly predictions about the inevitable future of domed cities and jet packed commuters, one can find equally silly quotes from people who said things like we will never reach the moon.

So it's not that I am arguing that genetic enhancement is impossible. Rather, 50 it's an argument that bioethics policy should acknowledge the frailty of long-term technological predictions which have a very spotty track record at best. The bioeth-ics policy should be based on fact, not fantasy. Both our positive and our negative fantasies are unlikely to come true, and policies predicated on the inevitability of genetic enhancement should be rethought.

FOR DISCUSSION

1. Like Francis Fukuyama, Pinker emphasizes the complex interaction of genes, each of which may have multiple functions in relation to other genes. But whereas Fukuyama takes the extreme complexity of genetics as warning number one about how genetic alterations can go wrong, Pinker sees it as a good reason to doubt that designer babies will happen in the next few decades or so. Whose view seems more convincing? Why?

2. Pinker emphasizes a point no other author in this section seems to be aware of—that "genes . . . have effects that are, at best, probabilistic." That is, even identical twins, who share exactly the same genetic makeup, 5 do not behave in exactly the same way. It would seem that somehow environment or chance is playing a big role beyond the behavioral impact of genes. What does this mean for the likelihood that engineered children will happen soon?

3. Pinker admits that some parents can go to extraordinary lengths to enhance their children's development and chances for success in life, but he pits this against another parental motivation, "the aversion to harm your children." Think about nongenetic means of enhancement you've seen parents resort to. Did they do any harm? Was the potential for harm understood and did it play a role in choosing and pursuing the enhancement sought? Based on your experience, which motive seems the stronger, the desire to enhance or the desire to not cause harm?

4. Pinker makes the amusing point that not many couples will prefer the joy of IVF (in vitro fertilization) to the joy of sex as a way of conceiving children. This is good common sense. What then would have to happen to make designer babies a practical option?

FOR PERSUASION

Pinker throws cold water on Gregory Stock's vision of human genetic enhancement. However, they agree on one crucial point: "The bioethics policy should be based on fact, not fantasy." In other words, both take the position that we should not regulate until genuine problems emerge—facts we must confront, not hypotheticals that may never materialize.

After studying carefully the arguments of Stock and Pinker, write an essay addressed to your senator or congressperson arguing that genetic engineering should not be regulated until demonstrated dangers or irresponsible use of the technology emerge. Urge oversight but not government action.

Making Babies?

SONDRA WHEELER

Sondra Wheeler is a professor of Christian ethics at Wesley Theological Seminary, Washington, D.C. The following article appeared in *Sojourners* (May 1999).

   Science and religion have always had, to put it mildly, an uneasy relationship. But the fact is that ethics does matter in scientific research and in technological applications of scientific knowledge. Ethics in turn cannot be divorced from religion, and so science and religion will continue to dance somewhat awkwardly together in human affairs.

One of the obvious but decisive facts about parenting is that prior to embarking upon the relationship, we don't know who is coming. We receive and live out our responsibilities toward our children, whoever they turn out to be, simply because they are ours and we are theirs, and most of the time that is enough to bring us to welcome and cherish and protect them. We do it whether they are beautiful or homely, brilliant or ordinary, cheerful or fretful. Even when they grow into adolescents with strange haircuts who, it seems, can hardly stand us, by and large and with varying degrees of struggle, we continue to welcome and cherish and care for them. Parenting is the most routine and the most socially essential form of welcoming the stranger.

   It is this unreserved and uncalculated commitment to accept and love the children we are given that makes the relationship between parent and child so central a metaphor for our relation to God, who welcomes and receives and cares for us, whoever we are. In this most fundamental and natural of all social relationships, we see the nearest analogue for the divine charity which loves each of us in her or his particularity, but universally and without conditions.

   It now seems likely, due to certain recent advances in scientific technique, that soon we will develop the capacity to make changes in the genetic makeup of human beings, including changes that they will pass to their descendants. The challenge this presents is, how much should we try to determine about our offspring?

   The possibilities go all the way from that offered by cloning—which would allow us to select a complete genome (the total complement of chromosomes of a species) as long as we had an existing "template" to reproduce—to much more modest alterations in a single gene designed to prevent the development and transmission of a particular genetic disease.

   Among the myriad questions forming around these technologies is a fairly 5 broad and basic one: What will it mean if we move from a social practice of welcoming the children who are born to us to a practice of selecting them and their characteristics, either by cloning or by modifying the genome in vitro before implantation? In particular, it is important to address what for Christians and Jews (at least) defines and limits the senses in which human beings may be said to belong to each other, and what this suggests about the terms on which we ought to intervene in the genetic makeup of another human being.

   What all this highlights is the very different moral posture between that of simply accepting the child we are given vs. a decision to engineer the genetic endowment of a child to replicate a desired genome or to select for personally desired or culturally valued characteristics. What will it mean to us, and to our children, if we embrace practices that make a child so decisively the project of its parents' will?

Certainly to seek such control involves abandoning a certain kind of reservation grounded in the fellow-humanity of our children, a respect based in religious awe for the child as a creature whose source and destiny are in God and who does not ultimately belong to us. It means shifting from a position in which we discover and foster the nature and flourishing of the children we receive, to one in which we determine the nature of the children whom we will accept. It is a kind of embodiment of all those corruptions of parenting in which the child is viewed primarily as the means of the parents' fulfillment and forcefully created in the image of their will.

There are, of course, many much more serious and compelling reasons to seek the power to intervene in the genetic makeup of human beings. About 2 percent of all live births are of children with genetic disorders, some of them imposing severe suffering and early death. To have the power to prevent such misery or to heal its effects is indeed a worthy goal, and an appropriate exercise of human powers to intervene. But it is not too soon to begin asking whether we can even hope to exercise so vast a power with the caution and deep self-scrutiny that wisdom would demand.

FOR DISCUSSION

1. "We don't know who is coming," Wheeler says, meaning by that something undeniable—every child has his or her own peculiar combination of genes, environment, and chance in self-formation, much of which parents cannot control. Will genetic manipulation do away with the need to accept our children, "simply because they are ours and we are theirs," as Wheeler phrases it?

2. One way to think about the ethics of a new technology is to ponder the ethics of existing ones in common use. We have ultrasound and amniocentesis, tools for assessing the condition of the unborn. Sometimes abnormalities are detected, which can result in abortion or in surgical procedures designed to correct the problem. What is your view of such technologies? How different are they from selecting an embryo based on genetic screening, done now in in-vitro fertilization? How different are they from germline manipulations, which may be common years from now?

3. Wheeler takes genetic enhancement as an "embodiment of all those corruptions of parenting in which the child is viewed primarily as the means of their parents' fulfillment and forcefully created in the image of their will" (paragraph 7). What might she have in mind by the phrase "all those corruptions of parenting"? Does the existence of such corruptions *prior to* our ability to alter children genetically indicate that our real concern should be the ethics of parenting rather than the ethics of a technology, which, like all technologies, can be used for good or ill?

4. Wheeler obviously has serious reservations about genetic manipulation, except to prevent or correct genetic disorders. If we permit, say, germ-line interventions for this reason, can we raise ethical objections to, for instance, interventions to reduce the likelihood of depression? to increase intelligence? Is there any place where the proverbial line in the sand can be drawn and the warning posted, "Do not cross"?

FOR INQUIRY

Wheeler says that "it is important to address what for Christians and Jews (at least) defines and limits the senses in which human beings may be said to belong to each other." Clearly "the senses in which human beings . . . belong to one another" are important for any religion and indeed for people who profess no religion. *It ought to be a fundamental ethical notion for everyone.* The problem is that, at best, most people observe it only in relation to family and friends—beyond the intimate circle it seems to have little force.

What role or roles might such an idea play in applications of genetic knowledge to human beings? Write an essay exploring the possibilities. What does it suggest for how and in what circumstances genetic engineering should be used?

The Tyranny of Happiness

CARL ELLIOTT

> Carl Elliott teaches philosophy and bioethics at the University of Minnesota. The
> following selection comes from the last chapter of his most recent book, *Better Than
> Well: American Medicine Meets the American Dream* (Norton, 2003).
>
> Elliott is concerned not with bioengineering as such but with the American passion
> for—some would say "compulsion toward"—enhancement of all kinds. He analyzes
> its motives and traces it to self-fulfillment as the goal of happiness. The problem is that
> such a notion of the good lacks social connection and eludes definition and assessment.
> How can we know what fulfills us? How can we know when we are fulfilled?

> *In America I have seen the freest and best educated of men in circumstances the
> happiest to be found in the world, yet it seemed to me that a cloud habitually hung
> on their brow, and they seemed serious and almost sad even in their pleasures.*
>
> —Alexis de Tocqueville

Thirty-five years ago, at the beginning of a twelve-year Senate inquiry into the drug
industry, Senator Gaylord Nelson opened the session on psychotropic drugs by
comparing them to the drugs in *Brave New World.* "When Aldous Huxley wrote his
fantasy concept of the world of the future in the now classic *Brave New World,* he
created an uncomfortable, emotionless culture of escapism dependent on tiny tablets of tranquility called soma."[1] Thirty-five years later, *Brave New World* is still
invoked, time and again, as a warning against the dangers that await us if we
embark on new enhancement technologies. News stories about psychotropic drugs,
stem cells, reproductive technologies, or genetic engineering inevitably appear with
headlines reading Brave New Medicine, Brave New Babies, Brave New Minds, or
Brave New People. It is as if we have no other metaphors for these technologies,
no competing visions of possible futures. Whatever the new technology of the
moment happens to be, we hear the same cautionary tale: it will lead us to a
totalitarian society where generic workers are slotted into castes and anesthetized
into bliss. The people in these totalitarian societies are not so much unhappy as
they are ignorant of what true happiness is, because they have been drugged and
engineered to want nothing more than that which their station allows them.

We keep returning to this story, I suspect, partly because we like stories of
individuals battling the forces of authority, and partly because it allows both teller
and listener to collude in the shared sense that we, unlike our neighbors and
coworkers and maybe even our family members, have figured out what is really
bad about a technology that looks so good. This story says, "Our neighbors may
have been sold a bill of goods, they may think that they have found happiness in
a Prozac tablet and a Botox injection, but you and I know it's a crock. You and I
are too smart to believe the cosmetic surgery Web sites, the drug companies ped-
dling Sarafem and Paxil, and the psychiatrists who tell us we have adult ADHD."
Yet as much as we like the *Brave New World* story, as many times as we read it and
repeat it and write high school essays about it, somehow it never seems to apply
to us. For men, the story of enhancement technologies is about the vanity of

women; for women, it is about the sexual gaze of men; for Europeans and Canadians, it is about shallowness of American values; for Americans, it is about "other" Americans—the ones who are either too crooked or deluded to acknowledge what 10 is really going on. If we blame anyone for the ill effects of enhancement technologies, it is either someone in power (the FDA, the media, Big Pharma, "the culture") or the poor suckers who have allowed themselves to be duped (Miss America contestants, neurotic New Yorkers, Michael Jackson). We imagine second-rate TV stars lining up for liposuction and anxious middle managers asking their family doctors for Paxil, and we just shake our heads and laugh. "Why can't they learn to accept themselves as they are?" we ask. Then we are asked to sing a solo in the church choir and can't sleep for a week, or our daughter starts getting teased at school for her buck teeth, and the joke doesn't seem so funny anymore.

We all like to moralize about enhancement technologies, except for the ones we use ourselves. Those technologies never seem quite so bad, because our view of them comes not from television or magazines but from personal experience, or the shared confidences of our troubled friends. There is often striking contrast between private conversation about enhancement technologies and the broader public discussion. In public, for example, everyone seems to be officially anti-Prozac. Feminists ask me why doctors prescribe Prozac more often for women than for men. Undergraduates worry that Prozac might give their classmates a competitive edge. Philosophy professors argue that Prozac would make people shallow and uncreative. Germans object that Prozac is not a natural substance. Americans say that Prozac is a crutch. Most people seem to feel that Prozac is creating some version of what historian David Rothman called, in a *New Republic* cover story, "shiny, happy people."

In private, though, people have started to seek me out and tell me their Prozac stories. They have tried Prozac and hated it; they have tried Prozac and it changed their life; they have tried Prozac and can't see what the big deal is. It has begun to seem as if everyone I know is on Prozac, has been on Prozac, or is considering taking Prozac, and all of them want to get my opinion. Most of all, they want me to try Prozac myself. "How can you write about it if you've never even tried it?" I can see their point. Still, it strikes me as a strange way to talk about a prescription drug. These people are oddly insistent. It was as if we were back in high school, and they were trying to get me to smoke a joint.

People who look at America from abroad often marvel at the enthusiasm with 5 which Americans use enhancement technologies. I can see why. It is a jolt to discover the rates at which Americans use Ritalin or Prozac or Botox. But "enthusiasm" is probably the wrong word to describe the way Americans feel about enhancement technologies. If this is enthusiasm, it is the enthusiasm of a diver on the high platform, who has to talk himself into taking the plunge. . . . I don't think Americans expect happiness in a handful of tablets. We take the tablets, but we brood about it. We try to hide the tablets from our friends. We worry that taking them is a sign of weakness. We try to convince our friends to take them too. We fret that if we don't take them, others will outshine us. We take the tablets, but they leave a bitter taste in our mouths.

Why? Perhaps because in those tablets is a mix of all the American wishes, lusts, and fears: the drive to self-improvement, the search for fulfillment, the desire to show that there are second acts in American lives; yet a mix diluted by nagging anxieties about social conformity, about getting too much too easily, about phoniness and self-deception and shallow pleasure. This is not a story from *Brave New World*. It is not even a story of enhancement. . . . It is less a story about trying to get ahead than about the terror of being left behind, and the humiliation of crossing the finish line dead last, while the crowd points at you and laughs. You can still refuse to use enhancement technologies, of course—you might be the last woman in America who does not dye her gray hair, the last man who refuses to work out at the gym—but even that publicly announces something to other Americans about who you are and what you value. This is all part of the logic of consumer culture. You cannot simply opt out of the system and expect nobody to notice how much you weigh.

Why here, why now? On one level, the answer seems obvious: because the technology has arrived. If you are anxious and lonely and a drug can fix it, why 15 stay anxious and lonely? If you are unhappy with your body and surgery can fix it, why stay unhappy? The market moves to fill a demand for happiness as efficiently as it moves to fill a demand for spark plugs or home computers. It is on a deeper level that the question of enhancement technologies becomes more puzzling. What has made the ground for these technologies so fertile? The sheer variety of technologies on display is remarkable. . . . Black folks rub themselves with cream to make their skin lighter, while white folks broil in tanning parlors to make their skin darker. Bashful men get ETS surgery to reduce blood flow above the neck, while elderly men take Viagra to increase blood flow below the belt. Each technology has its own rationale, its own cultural niche, a distinct population of users, and an appeal that often waxes or wanes with changes in fashion or the state of scientific knowledge. But do they have anything in common? Is there anything about the way we live now that helps explain their popularity?

The "self that struggles to realize itself," as philosopher Michael Walzer puts it, has become a familiar notion to most people living in the West today.[2] We tend to see ourselves as the managers of life projects that we map out, organize, make choices about, perhaps compare with other possible projects, and ultimately live out to completion. From late adolescence onward, we are expected to make important decisions about what to do for a living, where to live, whether to marry and have children, all with the sense that these decisions will contribute to the success or failure of our projects. Yet as Walzer points out, there is nothing natural or inevitable about this way of conceptualizing a life. Not everyone in the West today will think of their lives as planned projects, and most people at most times in history have probably thought of their lives differently. Marriages are arranged; educational choices are fixed; gods are tyrannical or absent. A life might be spontaneous, rather than planned; its shape might be given to us, rather than created. The shapes of lives can be determined not by the demands of personal values or self-fulfillment, but by those of God, family, social station, caste, or one's ancestors.

This notion of life as a project suggests both individual responsibility and moral uncertainty. If I am the planner and manager of my life, then I am at least partly responsible for its success or failure. Thus the lure of enhancement technologies: as tools to produce a better, more successful project. Yet if my life is a project, what exactly is the purpose of the project? How do I tell a successful project from a failure? Aristotle (for example) could write confidently about the good life for human beings because he was confident about what the purpose of being a human being was. Just as a knife has a purpose, so human beings have a purpose; just as the qualities that make for a good knife are those that help the knife slice, whittle, and chop, the qualities that make a human being better are those that help us better fulfill our purpose as human beings.

Our problem, of course, is that most of us don't have Aristotle's confidence 10 about the purpose of human life. Good knives cut, that much we can see, but what does a good human being do, and how will we know when we are doing it? Is there even such a thing as a single, universal human purpose? Not if we believe what we are told by the culture that surrounds us. From philosophy courses and therapy sessions to magazines and movies, we are told that questions of purpose vary from one person to the next; that, in fact, a large part of our life project is to discover our own individual purpose and develop it to its fullest. This leaves us with unanswered questions not just about what kinds of lives are better or worse, but also about the criteria by which such judgments are made. Is it better to be a successful bail bondsman or a second-rate novelist? On what yardstick do we compare the lives of Reform Jews, high-church Episcopalians, and California Wiccans? Where exactly should the choices we make about our lives be anchored?

Many people today believe that the success or failure of a life has something to do with the idea of self-fulfillment. We may not know exactly what a successful life is, but we have a pretty good suspicion that it has something to do with being fulfilled—or at the very least, that an unfulfilled life runs the risk of failure. In the name of fulfillment people quit their jobs in human resources and real estate to become poets and potters, leave their dermatology practices to do medical mission work in Bangladesh, even divorce their husbands or wives (the marriage was adequate, but it was not fulfilling). Women leave their children in day care because they believe that they will be more fulfilled with a career; they leave their jobs because they believe that it will be more fulfilling to stay home with the kids. Fulfillment has a strong moral strand to it—many people feel that they *ought* to pursue a career, that they *ought* to leave a loveless marriage—but its parameters are vague and indeterminate. How exactly do I know if I am fulfilled? Fulfillment looks a little like being in love, a little like a successful spiritual quest; it is a state centered largely on individual psychic well-being. If I am alienated, depressed, or anxious, I can't be completely fulfilled.

If I am not fulfilled, I am missing out on what life can offer. Life is a short, sweet ride, and I am spending it all in the station. The problem is that there is no great, overarching metric for self-fulfillment, no master schedule that we can look up at and say, "Yes, I've missed the train." So we look desperately to experts for instructions— counselors, psychiatrists, advice columnists, self-help writers, life coaches, even professional ethicists. We read the ads on the wall for cosmetic dentistry, and we look nervously at the people standing next to us in line. Does she know something that I don't? Is she more fulfilled? How does my psychic well-being compare to hers? . . .

In other times and places, success or failure in a life might have been determined by fixed and agreed-upon standards. You displeased the ancestors; you shamed your family; you did not accept Jesus Christ as your personal savior. You arrived late to the station, and the train left without you. But our situation today is different—not for everyone, of course, but for many of us. We have gotten on the train, but we don't know who is driving it, or where, some point off in the far distance, the tracks are leading. The other passengers are smiling, they look happy, yet underneath this facade of good cheer and philosophical certainty, a demon keeps whispering in our ears: "What if I have gotten it all wrong? What if I have boarded the wrong train?"

Tocqueville hinted at this worry over 150 years ago when he wrote about American "restlessness in the midst of abundance." Behind all the admirable energy of American life, Tocqueville saw a kind of grim relentlessness. We build houses to pass our old age, Tocqueville wrote, then sell them before the roof is on; we clear fields, then leave it to others to gather the harvest; we take up a profession, then leave it to take up another one or go into politics. Americans frantically pursue prosperity, and when we finally get it, we are tormented by the worry that we might have gotten it quicker. An American on vacation, Tocqueville marveled, "will travel five hundred miles in a few days as a distraction from his happiness."[3]

Tocqueville may well have been right about American restlessness, but it took   15
another Frenchman, surrealist painter Phillipe Soupault, to put his finger on the form that it has taken today. According to Soupault, Americans see the pursuit of happiness not just as a right, as the Declaration of Independence states, but as a strange sort of duty. In the United States, he wrote, "one is always in danger of entrapment by what appears on the surface to be a happy civilization. There is a sort of obligation to be happy." Humans are born to be happy, and if they are not, something has gone wrong. As Soupault puts it, "Whoever is unhappy is suspect."[4] Substitute self-fulfillment for happiness and you get something of the ethic that motivates the desire for enhancement technologies. Once self-fulfillment is hitched to the success of a human life, it comes perilously close to an obligation—not an obligation to God, country, or family, but an obligation to the self. We are compelled to pursue fulfillment through enhancement technologies not in order to get ahead of others, but to make sure that we have lived our lives to the fullest. The train has left the station and we don't know where it is going. The least we can do is be sure it is making good time.

NOTES

1. Mickey Smith, *A Social History of the Minor Tranquilizers: The Quest for Small Comfort in an Age of Anxiety* (New York: Praeger, 1989) 178.
2. Michael Walzer, *Thick and Thin: Moral Argument at Home and Abroad* (South Bend: Notre Dame UP, 1994) 23–24.
3. Alexis de Tocqueville, *Democracy in America,* trans. George Lawrence, ed. J. P. Mayer (New York: Harper and Row, 1988) 536.
4. Philippe Soupault, "Introduction to Mademoiselle Coeur Brise (Miss Lonely-hearts)," *Nathanael West: A Collection of Critical Essays,* ed. Jay Martin (Englewood Cliffs: Prentice-Hall, 1971) 112–13.

FOR DISCUSSION

1. According to Elliott, why do people appeal so often to Huxley's novel, *Brave New World,* when enhancement technologies, especially new ones, are discussed? Why does he consider the connection essentially misleading?

2. Elliott claims that American culture and values emphasize "life as a project"—hence, "the lure of enhancement technologies: as tools to produce a better, more successful project." Do you see this as the drive behind such popular TV shows as *Trading Spaces, What Not to Wear,* and *Extreme Makeover?*

3. "If I am alienated, depressed, or anxious, I can't be completely fulfilled," Elliott says, and the solution becomes a pill, plastic surgery, occupational change, divorce—something that will "fix" the problem. But are there circumstances when people ought to feel alienated, depressed, or anxious? Can such feelings be positive and productive rather than negative and counterproductive?

4. Elliott cites the French surrealist painter Phillipe Soupault, who claims that in the United States "there is a sort of obligation to be happy. . . . Whoever is unhappy is suspect." Thus, according to Elliott, the pursuit of happiness is not a right but rather "a strange sort of duty . . . an obligation to the self." Do you find this diagnosis persuasive? What, according to Elliott, makes such an understanding of the pursuit of happiness unsatisfying and ultimately self-defeating?

FOR PERSUASION

"Our problem," Elliott claims, "is that most of us don't have Aristotle's confidence about the purpose of human life. . . . [W]hat does a good human being do, and how will we know when we are doing it?"

Are we Americans so much in doubt about what we ought to be doing as Elliott claims? Write an essay arguing against his assertion of complete relativity where our notion of the good is concerned. Support it by referring to popular culture—to movies and TV dramas, for instance—which often reflect our values and sometimes expose them for reflection.

FOR FURTHER READING

Chapman, Audrey R., and Mark S. Frankel, eds., *Designing Our Descendants: The Promises and Perils of Genetic Engineering.* New York: Farrar, 2002.

Elliott, Carl. *Better Than Well: American Medicine Meets the American Dream.* New York: Norton, 2003.

Fukuyama, Francis. *Our Posthuman Future: Consequences of the Biotechnology Revolution.* New York: Farrar, 2002.

Gonick, Larry, and Mark Wheelis, *The Cartoon Guide to Genetics.* New York: Harper, 2005.

Gregory Stock, *Redesigning Humans: Our Inevitable Genetic Future.* Boston: Houghton, 2002.

A Short Guide to Editing and Proofreading

Editing and proofreading are the final steps in creating a finished piece of writing. Too often, however, these steps are rushed as writers race to meet a deadline. Ideally, you should distinguish between the acts of revising, editing, and proofreading. Because each step requires that you pay attention to something different, you cannot reasonably expect to do them well if you try to do them all at once.

Our suggestions for revising appear in each of Chapters 7–10 on the aims of argument. *Revising* means shaping and developing the whole argument with an eye to audience and purpose; when you revise, you are ensuring that you have accomplished your aim. *Editing*, on the other hand, means making smaller changes within paragraphs and sentences. When you edit, you are thinking about whether your prose will be a pleasure to read. Editing improves the sound and rhythm of your voice. It makes complicated ideas more accessible to readers and usually makes your writing more concise. Finally, *proofreading* means eliminating errors. When you proofread, you correct everything you find that will annoy readers, such as misspellings, punctuation mistakes, and faulty grammar.

In this appendix, we offer some basic advice on what to look for when editing and proofreading. For more detailed help, consult a handbook on grammar and punctuation and a good book on style, such as Joseph Williams's *Ten Lessons in Clarity and Grace* or Richard Lanham's *Revising Prose*. Both of these texts guided our thinking in the advice that follows.

www.mhhe.com/**crusius**

For a wealth of online editing resources, check out the tools grouped under:

Editing

EDITING

Most ideas can be phrased in a number of ways, each of which gives the idea a slightly distinctive twist. Consider the following examples:

In New York City, about 74,000 people die each year.

In New York City, death comes to one in a hundred people each year.

www.mhhe.com/**crusius**

To Take a diagnostic test covering editing skills, go to:

Editing > Diagnostic Test

> Death comes to one in a hundred New Yorkers each year.

To begin an article on what becomes of the unknown and unclaimed dead in New York, Edward Conlon wrote the final of these three sentences. We can only speculate about the possible variations he considered, but because openings are so crucial, he almost certainly cast these words quite deliberately.

For most writers, such deliberation over matters of style occurs during editing. In this late stage of the writing process, writers examine choices made earlier, perhaps unconsciously, while drafting and revising. They listen to how sentences sound, to patterns of rhythm both within and among sentences. Editing is like an art or craft; it can provide you the satisfaction of knowing you've said something gracefully and effectively. To focus on language this closely, you will need to set aside enough time following the revision step.

In this section, we discuss some things to look for when editing your own writing. Don't forget, though, that editing does not always mean looking for weaknesses. You should also recognize passages that work well just as you wrote them, that you can leave alone or play up more by editing passages that surround them.

Editing for Clarity and Conciseness

Even drafts revised several times may have wordy and awkward passages; these are often places where a writer struggled with uncertainty or felt less than confident about the point being made. Introductions often contain such passages. In editing, you have one more opportunity to clarify and sharpen your ideas.

Express Main Ideas Forcefully

Emphasize the main idea of a sentence by stating it as directly as possible, using the two key sentence parts (*subject* and *verb*) to convey the two key parts of the idea (*agent* and *act*).

As you edit, first look for sentences that state ideas indirectly rather than directly; such sentences may include (1) overuse of the verb *to be* in its various forms (*is, was, will have been,* and so forth), (2) the opening words "There is . . ." or "It is . . . ," (3) strings of prepositional phrases, or (4) many vague nouns. Then ask, "What is my true subject here, and what is that subject's action?" Here is an example of a weak, indirect sentence:

> It is a fact that the effects of pollution are more evident in lower-class neighborhoods than in middle-class ones.

The writer's subject is pollution. What is the pollution's action? Limply, the sentence tells us its "effects" are "evident." The following edited version makes pollution the agent that performs the action of a livelier verb, "fouls." The edited sentence is more specific—without being longer.

Pollution more frequently *fouls* the air, soil, and water of lower-class neighborhoods than of middle-class ones.

Editing Practice   The following passage about a plan for creating low-income housing contains two weak sentences. In this case, the weakness results from wordiness. (Note the overuse of vague nouns and prepositional phrases.) Decide what the true subject is for each sentence, and make that word the subject of the verb. Your edited version should be much shorter.

As in every program, there will be the presence of a few who abuse the system. However, as in other social programs, the numbers would not be sufficient to justify the rejection of the program on the basis that one person in a thousand will try to cheat.

Choose Carefully between Active and Passive Voice

Active voice and passive voice indicate different relationships between subjects and verbs. As we have noted, ideas are usually clearest when the writer's true subject is also the subject of the verb in the sentence—that is, when it is the agent of the action. In the passive voice, however, the agent of the action appears in the predicate or not at all. Rather than acting as agent, the subject of the sentence *receives* the action of the verb.

www.mhhe.com/**crusius**

For more coverage of voice, go to:

Editing > Verb and Voice Shifts

The following sentence is in the passive voice:

The air of poor neighborhoods is often fouled by pollution.

There is nothing incorrect about the use of the passive voice in this sentence, and in the context of a whole paragraph, passive voice can be the most emphatic way to make a point. (Here, for example, it allows the word *pollution* to fall at the end of the sentence, a strong position.) But, often, use of the passive voice is not a deliberate choice at all; rather, it's a vague and unspecific way of stating a point.

Consider the following sentences, in which the main verbs have no agents:

It *is believed* that dumping garbage at sea is not as harmful to the environment as *was* once *thought*.

Ronald Reagan *was considered* the "Great Communicator."

Who thinks such dumping is not so harmful? environmental scientists? industrial producers? Who considered former president Reagan a great communicator? speech professors? news commentators? Such sentences are clearer when they are written in the active voice:

Some environmentalists believe that dumping garbage at sea is not as harmful to the environment as they used to think.

Media commentators considered Ronald Reagan the "Great Communicator."

In editing for the passive voice, look over your verbs. Passive voice is easily recognized because it always contains (1) some form of *to be* as a helping verb and (2) the main verb in its past participle form (which ends in *-ed, -d, -t, -en,* or *-n,* or in some cases may be irregular: *drunk, sung, lain,* and so on).

When you find a sentence phrased in the passive voice, decide who or what is performing the action; the agent may appear after the verb or not at all. Then decide if changing the sentence to the active voice will improve the sentence as well as the surrounding passage.

Editing Practice

1. The following paragraph from a student's argument needs to be edited for emphasis. It is choking with excess nouns and forms of the verb *to be,* some as part of passive constructions. You need not eliminate all passive voice, but do look for wording that is vague and ineffective. Your edited version should be not only stronger but shorter as well.

   Although emergency shelters are needed in some cases (for example, a mother fleeing domestic violence), they are an inefficient means of dealing with the massive numbers of people they are bombarded with each day. The members of a homeless family are in need of a home, not a temporary shelter into which they and others like them are herded, only to be shuffled out when their thirty-day stay is over to make room for the next incoming herd. Emergency shelters would be sufficient if we did not have a low-income housing shortage, but what is needed most at present is an increase in availability of affordable housing for the poor.

2. Select a paragraph of your own writing to edit; focus on using strong verbs and subjects to carry the main idea of your sentences.

Editing for Emphasis

When you edit for emphasis, you make sure that your main ideas stand out so that your reader will take notice. Following are some suggestions to help.

Emphasize Main Ideas by Subordinating Less Important Ones

Subordination refers to distinctions in rank or order of importance. Think of the chain of command at an office: the boss is at the top of the ladder, the middle management is on a lower (subordinate) rung, the support staff is at an even lower rung, and so on.

In writing, subordination means placing less important ideas in less important positions in sentences in order to emphasize the main ideas that should stand out. Writing that lacks subordination treats all ideas equally; each idea may consist of a sentence of its own or may be joined to another idea by a coordinator (*and, but,* and *or*). Such a passage follows with its sentences numbered for reference purposes.

(1) It has been over a century since slavery was abolished and a few decades since lawful, systematic segregation came to an unwilling halt.

(2) Truly, blacks have come a long way from the darker days that lasted for more than three centuries. (3) Many blacks have entered the mainstream, and there is a proportionately large contingent of middle-class blacks. (4) Yet an even greater percentage of blacks are immersed in truly pathetic conditions. (5) The inner-city black poor are enmeshed in devastating socioeconomic problems. (6) Unemployment among inner-city black youths has become much worse than it was even five years ago.

Three main ideas are important here—that blacks have been free for some time, that some have made economic progress, and that others are trapped in poverty—and of these three, the last is probably intended to be the most important. Yet, as we read the passage, these key ideas do not stand out. In fact, each point receives equal emphasis and sounds about the same, with the repeated subject-verb-object syntax. The result seems monotonous, even apathetic, though the writer is probably truly disturbed about the subject. The following edited version, which subordinates some of the points, is more emphatic. We have italicized the main points.

> *Blacks have come a long way* in the century since slavery was abolished and in the decades since lawful, systematic segregation came to an unwilling halt. Yet, although many blacks have entered the mainstream and the middle class, *an even greater percentage is immersed in truly pathetic conditions*. To give just one example of these devastating socioeconomic problems, *unemployment among inner-city black youths is much worse now than it was even five years ago.*

Although different editing choices are possible, this version plays down sentences 1, 3, and 5 in the original so that sentences 2, 4, and 6 stand out.

As you edit, look for passages that sound wordy and flat because all the ideas are expressed with equal weight in the same subject-verb-object pattern. Then single out your most important points, and try out some options for subordinating the less important ones. The key is to put main ideas in main clauses and modifying ideas in modifying clauses or phrases.

Modifying Clauses Like simple sentences, modifying clauses contain a subject and verb. They are formed in two ways: (1) with relative pronouns and (2) with subordinating conjunctions.

Relative pronouns introduce clauses that modify nouns, with the relative pronoun relating the clause to the noun it modifies. There are five relative pronouns: *that, which, who, whose,* and *whom.* The following sentence contains a relative clause:

> Alcohol advertisers are trying to sell a product *that is by its very nature harmful to users.*
>
> —Jason Rath (student)

Relative pronouns may also be implied:

I have returned the library book [that] *you loaned me.*

Relative pronouns may also be preceded by prepositions, such as *on, in, to,* or *during:*

Drug hysteria has created an atmosphere *in which civil rights are disregarded.*

Subordinating conjunctions show relationships among ideas. It is impossible to provide a complete list of subordinating conjunctions in this short space, but here are the most common and the kinds of modifying roles they perform:

To show time: *after, as, before, since, until, when, while*

To show place: *where, wherever*

To show contrast: *although, though, whereas, while*

To show cause and effect: *because, since, so that*

To show condition: *if, unless, whether, provided that*

To show manner: *how, as though*

By introducing it with a subordinating conjunction, you can convert one sentence into a dependent clause that can modify another sentence. Consider the following two versions of the same idea:

Pain is a state of consciousness, a "mental event." It can never be directly observed.

Since pain is a state of consciousness, a "mental event," it can never be directly observed.

—Peter Singer, *"Animal Liberation"*

Modifying Phrases Unlike clauses, phrases do not have a subject and a verb. Prepositional phrases and infinitive phrases are most likely already in your repertoire of modifiers. (Consult a handbook if you need to review these.) Here, we remind you of two other useful types of phrases: (1) participial phrases and (2) appositives.

Participial phrases modify nouns. Participles are created from verbs, so it is not surprising that the two varieties represent two verb tenses. The first is present participles ending in *-ing:*

Hoping to eliminate harassment on campus, many universities have tried to institute codes for speech and behavior.

The desperate Haitians fled here in boats, *risking all.*

—Carmen Hazan-Cohen (student)

The second is past participles ending in *-ed, -en, -d, -t,* or *-n:*

> Women themselves became a resource, *acquired by men much as the land was acquired by men.*
>
> —Gerda Lerner

> *Linked more to the Third World and Asia than to the Europe of America's racial and cultural roots,* Los Angeles and Southern California will enter the 21st century as a multi-racial and multicultural society.
>
> —Ryszard Kapuscinski

Notice that modifying phrases should immediately precede the nouns they modify.

An *appositive* is a noun or noun phrase that restates another noun, usually in a more specific way. Appositives can be highly emphatic, but more often they are tucked into the middle of a sentence or added to the end, allowing a subordinate idea to be slipped in. When used like this, appositives are usually set off with commas:

> Rick Halperin, *a professor at Southern Methodist University,* noted that Ted Bundy's execution cost Florida taxpayers over six million dollars.
>
> —Diane Miller (student)

Editing Practice

1. Edit the following passage as needed for emphasis, clarity, and conciseness, using subordinate clauses, relative clauses, participial phrases, appositives, and any other options that occur to you. If some parts are effective as they are, leave them alone.

   The monetary implications of drug legalization are not the only reason it is worth consideration. There is reason to believe that the United States would be a safer place to live if drugs were legalized. A large amount of what the media has named "drug-related" violence is really prohibition-related violence. Included in this are random shootings and murders associated with black-market transactions. Estimates indicate that at least 40 percent of all property crime in the United States is committed by drug users so they can maintain their habits. That amounts to a total of 4 million crimes per year and $7.5 billion in stolen property. Legalizing drugs would be a step toward reducing this wave of crime.

2. Edit a paragraph of your own writing with an eye to subordinating less important ideas through the use of modifying phrases and clauses.

Vary Sentence Length and Pattern

Even when read silently, your writing has a sound. If your sentences are all about the same length (typically fifteen to twenty words) and all structured according to a subject-verb-object pattern, they will roll along with the monotonous rhythm of an assembly line. Obviously, one solution to this problem is to open some of your sentences with modifying phrases and clauses, as we discuss in the previous section. Here we offer some other strategies, all of which add emphasis by introducing something unexpected.

1. Use a short sentence after several long ones.

    [A] population's general mortality is affected by a great many factors over which doctors and hospitals have little influence. For those diseases and injuries for which modern medicine can affect the outcome, however, which country the patient lives in really matters. Life expectancy is not the same among developed countries for premature babies, for children born with spina bifida, or for people who have cancer, a brain tumor, heart disease, or chronic renal failure. *Their chances of survival are best in the United States.*

    —John Goodman

2. Interrupt a sentence.

    The position of women in that hippie counterculture was, *as a young black male leader preached succinctly,* "prone."

    —Betty Friedan

    Symbols and myths—*when emerging uncorrupted from human experience*—are precious. Then it is the poetic voice and vision that informs and infuses—*the poet-warrior's, the prophet-seer's, the dreamer's*—reassuring us that truth is as real as falsehood. And ultimately stronger.

    —Ossie Davis

3. Use an intentional sentence fragment. The concluding fragment in the previous passage by Ossie Davis is a good example.

4. Invert the order of subject-verb-object.

    Further complicating negotiations is the difficulty of obtaining relevant financial statements.

    —Regina Herzlinger

    This creature, with scarcely two thirds of man's cranial capacity, was a fire user. Of what it meant to him beyond warmth and shelter, we know nothing; with what rites, ghastly or benighted, it was struck or maintained, no word remains.

    —Loren Eiseley

Use Special Effects for Emphasis

Especially in persuasive argumentation, you will want to make some of your points in deliberately dramatic ways. Remember that just as the crescendos stand out in music because the surrounding passages are less intense, so the special effects work best in rhetoric when you use them sparingly.

Repetition   Deliberately repeating words, phrases, or sentence patterns has the effect of building up to a climactic point. In Chapter 9, we noted how Martin Luther King, Jr., in the emotional high point of his "Letter from Birmingham Jail," used repeated subordinate clauses beginning with the phrase "when you" to build up to his main point: " . . . then you will understand why we find it difficult to wait" (paragraph 14, pages 256–257). Here is another example, from the conclusion of an argument linking women's rights with environmental reforms:

> Environmental justice goes much further than environmental protection, a passive and paternalistic phrase. *Justice requires that* industrial nations pay back the environmental debt incurred in building their wealth by using less of nature's resources. *Justice prescribes that* governments stop siting hazardous waste facilities in cash-poor rural and urban neighborhoods and now in the developing world. *Justice insists that* the subordination of women and nature by men is not only a hazard; it is a crime. *Justice reminds us that* the Earth does not belong to us; even when we "own" a piece of it, we belong to the Earth.
>
> —H. Patricia Hynes

Paired Coordinators   Coordinators are conjunctions that pair words, word groups, and sentences in a way that gives them equal emphasis and that also shows a relationship between them, such as contrast, consequence, or addition. In grade school, you may have learned the coordinators through the mnemonic *FANBOYS,* standing for *for, and, nor, but, or, yet, so.*

Paired coordinators emphasize the relationship between coordinated elements; the first coordinator signals that a corresponding coordinator will follow. Some paired coordinators are:

both _____   and _____

not _____   but _____

not only _____   but also _____

either _____   or _____

neither _____   nor _____

The key to effective paired coordination is to keep the words that follow the marker words as grammatically similar as possible. Pair nouns with nouns, verbs with verbs, prepositional phrases with prepositional phrases, and whole sentences with whole sentences. (Think of paired coordination as a variation on repetition.) Here are some examples:

> Feminist anger, or any form of social outrage, is dismissed breezily—*not* because it lacks substance *but* because it lacks "style."
>
> —Susan Faludi

> Alcohol ads that emphasize "success" in the business and social worlds are useful examples *not only* of how advertisers appeal to people's envy *but also* of how ads perpetuate gender stereotypes.
>
> —Jason Rath (student)

Emphatic Appositives   While an appositive (a noun or noun phrase that restates another noun) can subordinate an idea, it can also emphasize an idea if it is placed at the beginning or the end of a sentence, where it will command attention. Here are some examples:

> *The poorest nation in the Western hemisphere,* Haiti is populated by six million people, many of whom cannot obtain adequate food, water, or shelter.
>
> —Sneed B. Collard III

> [Feminists] made a simple, though serious, ideological error when they applied the same political rhetoric to their own situation as women versus men: *too literal an analogy with class warfare, racial oppression.*
>
> —Betty Friedan

Note that at the end of a sentence, an appositive may be set off with a colon or a dash.

Emphatic Word Order   The opening and closing positions of a sentence are high-profile spots, not to be wasted on weak words. The following sentence, for example, begins weakly with the filler phrase "there are":

> *There are* several distinctions, all of them false, that are commonly made between rape and date rape.

A better version would read:

> My opponents make several distinctions between rape and date rape; all of these are false.

Even more important are the final words of every paragraph and the opening and closing of the entire argument.

Editing Practice

1. Select one or two paragraphs from a piece of published writing you have recently read and admired. Be ready to share it with the class, explaining how the writer has crafted the passage to make it work.

2. Take a paragraph or two from one of your previous essays, perhaps even an essay from another course, and edit it to improve clarity, conciseness, and emphasis.

Editing for Coherence

Coherence refers to what some people call the "flow" of writing; writing flows when the ideas connect smoothly, one to the next. In contrast, when writing is incoherent, the reader must work to see how ideas connect and must infer points that the writer, for whatever reason, has left unstated.

Incoherence is a particular problem with writing that contains an abundance of direct or indirect quotations. In using sources, be careful always to lead into the quotation with some words of your own, showing clearly how this new idea connects with what has come before.

Because finding incoherent passages in your own writing can be difficult, ask a friend to read your draft to look for gaps in the presentation of ideas. Here are some additional suggestions for improving coherence.

Move from Old Information to New Information

Coherent writing is easy to follow because the connections between old information and new information are clear. Sentences refer back to previously introduced information and set up reader expectations for new information to come. Notice how every sentence fulfills your expectations in the following excerpts from an argument on animal rights by Steven Zak.

> The credibility of the animal-rights viewpoint . . . need not stand or fall with the "marginal human beings" argument.

Next, you would expect to hear why animals do not have to be classed as "marginal human beings"—and you do:

> Lives don't have to be qualitatively the same to be worthy of equal respect.

At this point you might ask upon what else we should base our respect. Zak answers this question in the next sentence:

> One's perception that another life has value comes as much from an appreciation of its uniqueness as from the recognition that it has characteristics that are shared by one's own life.

Not only do these sentences fulfill reader expectations, but each also makes a clear connection by referring specifically to the key idea in the sentence before it, forming an unbroken chain of thought. We have italicized the words that accomplish this linkage and connected them with arrows.

> The credibility of the animal-rights viewpoint . . . need not stand or fall with the *"marginal human beings"* argument.
>
> Lives don't have to be *qualitatively the same* to be worthy of *equal respect.*
>
> One's perception that *another life has value* comes as much from an *appreciation of its uniqueness* as from the recognition that it has characteristics that are shared by one's own life.
>
> One can imagine that the lives of various kinds of animals *differ radically.* . . .

In the following paragraph, reader expectations are not so well fulfilled:

> We are presently witness to the greatest number of homeless families since the Great Depression of the 1930s. The cause of this phenomenon is a shortage of low-income housing. Mothers with children as young as two weeks are forced to live on the street because there is no room for them in homeless shelters.

Although these sentences are all on the subject of homelessness, the second leads us to expect that the third will take up the topic of shortages of low-income housing. Instead, it takes us back to the subject of the first sentence and offers a different cause—no room in the shelters.

Looking for ways to link old information with new information will help you find problems of coherence in your own writing.

Editing Practice

1. In the following paragraph, underline the words or phrases that make the connections back to the previous sentence and forward to the next, as we did earlier with the passage from Zak.

> The affluent, educated, liberated women of the First World, who can enjoy freedoms unavailable to any women ever before, do not feel as free as they want to. And they can no longer restrict to the subconscious their sense that this lack of freedom has something to do with—with apparently frivolous issues, things that really should not matter. Many are ashamed to admit that such trivial concerns—to do with physical appearance, bodies, faces, hair, clothes—matter so much. But in spite of shame, guilt, and denial, more and more women are wondering if it isn't that they are entirely neurotic alone but rather that something important is indeed at stake that has to do with the relationship between female liberation and female beauty.
>
> —Naomi Wolf

2. The following student paragraph lacks coherence. Read through it, and put a slash (/) between sentences expressing unconnected ideas. You may try to rewrite the paragraph, rearranging sentences and adding ideas to make the connections tighter.

Students may know what AIDS is and how it is transmitted, but most are not concerned about AIDS and do not perceive themselves to be at risk. But college-age heterosexuals are the number-one high-risk group for this disease (Gray and Sacarino 258). "Students already know about AIDS. Condom distribution, public or not, is not going to help. It just butts into my personal life," said one student surveyed. College is a time for exploration and that includes the discovery of sexual freedom. Students, away from home and free to make their own decisions for maybe the first time in their lives, have a "bigger than life" attitude. The thought of dying is the farthest from their minds. Yet at this point in their lives, they are most in need of this information.

Use Transitions to Show Relationships between Ideas

Coherence has to be built into a piece of writing; as we discussed earlier, the ideas between sentences must first cohere. However, sometimes readers need help in making the transition from one idea to the next, so you must provide signposts to help them see the connections more readily. For example, a transitional word like *however* can prepare readers for an idea in contrast to the one before it, as in the second sentence in this paragraph. Transitional words can also highlight the structure of an argument ("These data will show three things: first . . . , second . . . , and third . . ."), almost forming a verbal path for the reader to follow. Following are examples of transitional words and phrases and their purposes:

To show order: *first, second, next, then, last, finally*

To show contrast: *however, yet, but, nevertheless*

To show cause and effect: *therefore, consequently, as a result, then*

To show importance: *moreover, significantly*

To show an added point: *as well, also, too*

To show an example: *for example, for instance*

To show concession: *admittedly*

To show conclusion: *in sum, in conclusion*

The key to using transitional words is similar to the key to using special effects for emphasis: Don't overdo it. To avoid choking your writing with these words, anticipate where your reader will genuinely need them, and limit their use to these instances.

Editing Practice   Underline the transitional words and phrases in the following passage of published writing:

When people believe that their problems can be solved, they tend to get busy solving them.

On the other hand, when people believe that their problems are beyond solution, they tend to position themselves so as to avoid blame. Take the woeful inadequacy of education in the predominantly black central cities. Does the black leadership see the ascendancy of black teachers, school administrators, and politicians as an asset to be used in improving those dreadful schools? Rarely. You are more likely to hear charges of white abandonment, white resistance to integration, conspiracies to isolate black children, even when the schools are officially desegregated. In short, white people are accused of being responsible for the problem. But if the young- sters manage to survive those awful school systems and achieve success, leaders want to claim credit. They don't hesitate to attribute that success to the glorious Civil Rights movement.

—William Raspberry

PROOFREADING

www.mhhe.com/**crusius**

For some advice and practice related to spelling, go to:

Editing > Spelling

Proofreading is truly the final step in writing a paper. After proofreading, you ought to be able to print your paper out one more time; but if you do not have time, most instructors will be perfectly happy to see the necessary corrections done neatly in ink on the final draft.

Following are some suggestions for proofreading.

Spelling Errors

If you have used a word processor, you may have a program that will check your spelling. If not, you will have to check your spelling by reading through again carefully with a dictionary at hand. Consult the dictionary whenever you feel uncertain. You might consider devoting a special part of your writer's notebook to your habitual spelling errors: some students always misspell *athlete*, for example, whereas others leave the second *n* out of *environment*.

Omissions and Jumbled Passages

Read your paper out loud. Physically shaping your lips around the words can help locate missing words, typos (*saw* instead of *was*), or the remnants of some earlier version of a sentence that did not get fully deleted. Place a caret (∧) in the sentence and write the correction or addition above the line, or draw a line through unnecessary text.

Punctuation Problems

Apostrophes and commas give writers the most trouble. If you have habitual problems with these, you should record your errors in your writer's notebook.

Apostrophes

Apostrophe problems usually occur in forming possessives, not contractions, so here we discuss only the former. If you have problems with possessives, you may also want to consult a good handbook or seek a private tutorial with your instructor or your school's writing center.

Here are the basic principles to remember.

1. Possessive pronouns—*his, hers, yours, theirs, its*—never take an apostrophe.

2. Singular nouns become possessive by adding -*'s*.

   A single parent's life is hard.

   A society's values change.

   Do you like Mr. Voss's new car?

3. Plural nouns ending in -*s* become possessive by simply adding an apostrophe.

   Her parents' marriage is faltering.

   Many cities' air is badly polluted.

   The Joneses' house is up for sale.

4. Plural nouns that do not end in -*s* become possessive by adding -*'s*.

   Show me the women's (men's) room.

   The people's voice was heard.

If you err by using apostrophes where they don't belong in nonpossessive words ending in -*s*, remember that a possessive will always have a noun after it, not some other part of speech such as a verb or a preposition. You may even need to read each line of print with a ruler under it to help you focus more intently on each word.

www.mhhe.com/**crusius**

For some additional help using apostrophes, go to:

Editing > Apostrophes

Commas

Because commas indicate a pause, reading your paper aloud is a good way to decide where to add or delete them. A good handbook will elaborate on the following basic principles. The example sentences have been adapted from an argument by Mary Meehan, who opposes abortion.

1. Use a comma when you join two or more main clauses with a coordinating conjunction.

   Main clause, conjunction (and, but, or, nor, so, yet) *main clause.*

   Feminists want to have men participate more in the care of children, but abortion allows a man to shift total responsibility to the woman.

2. Use a comma after an introductory phrase or dependent clause.

   Introductory phrase or clause, main clause.

   To save the smallest children, the Left should speak out against abortion.

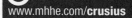

www.mhhe.com/**crusius**

For some additional coverage of comma use, go to:

Editing > Commas

3. Use commas around modifiers such as relative clauses and appositives unless they are essential to the noun's meaning. Be sure to put the comma at both ends of the modifier.

_____, *appositive,* _____

_____, *relative clause,* _____

One member of the 1972 Presidential commission on population growth was Graciela Olivarez, a Chicana who was active in civil rights and anti-poverty work. Olivarez, who later was named to head the Federal Government's Community Services Administration, had known poverty in her youth in the Southwest.

4. Use commas with a series.

____x____, ____y____, and ____z____,

The traditional mark of the Left has been its protection of the underdog, the weak, and the poor.

Semicolons

www.mhhe.com/**crusius**

For more coverage of semicolons, go to:

Editing > Semicolons

Think of a semicolon as a strong comma. It has two main uses.

1. Use a semicolon to join two main clauses when you choose not to use a conjunction. This works well when the two main clauses are closely related or parallel in structure.

Main clause; main clause.

Pro-life activists did not want abortion to be a class issue; they wanted to end abortion everywhere, for all classes.

As a variation, you may wish to add a transitional adverb to the second main clause. The adverb indicates the relationship between the main clauses, but it is not a conjunction, so a comma preceding it would not be correct.

Main clause; transitional adverb (however, therefore, thus, moreover, consequently), *main clause.*

When speaking with counselors at the abortion clinic, many women change their minds and decide against abortion; however, a woman who is accompanied by a husband or boyfriend often does not feel free to talk with the counselor.

2. Use semicolons between items in a series if any of the items themselves contain commas.

___,___ ; ___,___ ; ___,___

A few liberals who have spoken out against abortion are Jesse Jackson, a civil rights leader; Richard Neuhaus, a theologian; the comedian Dick Gregory; and politicians Mark Hatfield and Mary Rose Oakar.

Colons

The colon has two common uses.

1. Use a colon to introduce a quotation when both your own lead-in and the words quoted are complete sentences that can stand alone. (See the section in Chapter 5 entitled "Incorporating and Documenting Source Material" for more on introducing quotations.)

   Main clause in your words: "Quoted sentence(s)."

   Mary Meehan criticizes liberals who have been silent on abortion: "If much of the leadership of the pro-life movement is right-wing, that is due largely to the default of the Left."

2. Use a colon before an appositive that comes dramatically at the end of a sentence, especially if the appositive contains more than one item.

   Main clause: appositive, appositive, and appositive.

   Meehan argues that many pro-choice advocates see abortion as a way to hold down the population of certain minorities: blacks, Puerto Ricans, and other Latins.

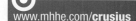

www.mhhe.com/**crusius**

For some additional help using colons, go to:

Editing > Colons

Grammatical Errors

Grammatical mistakes can be hard to find, but once again we suggest reading aloud as one method of proofing for them; grammatical errors tend not to "sound right" even if they look like good prose. Another suggestion is to recognize your habitual errors and then look for particular grammatical structures that lead you into error.

Introductory Participial Phrases

Constructions such as these often lead writers to create dangling modifiers. To avoid this pitfall, see the discussion of participial phrases earlier in this appendix. Remember that an introductory phrase dangles if it is not immediately followed by the noun it modifies.

   Incorrect: Using her conscience as a guide, our society has granted each woman the right to decide if a fetus is truly a "person" with rights equal to her own.

(Notice that the implied subject of the participial phrase is "each woman," when in fact the subject of the main clause is "our society"; thus, the participial phrase does not modify the subject.)

   Corrected: Using her conscience as a guide, each woman in our society has the right to decide if a fetus is truly a "person" with rights equal to her own.

Paired Coordinators

If the words that follow each of the coordinators are not of the same grammatical structure, then an error known as nonparallelism has occurred. To correct this error, line up the paired items one over the other. You will see that the correction often involves simply adding a word or two to, or deleting some words from, one side of the paired coordinators.

> not only _____ but also _____
>
> *Incorrect:* Legal abortion not only protects women's lives, but also their health.
>
> *Corrected:* Legal abortion protects not only women's lives but also their health.

Split Subjects and Verbs

www.mhhe.com/**crusius**

For additional coverage of agreement, go to:

Editing > Subject/Verb Agreement

If the subject of a sentence contains long modifying phrases or clauses, by the time you get to the verb you may make an error in agreement (using a plural verb, for example, when the subject is singular) or even in logic (for example, having a subject that is not capable of being the agent that performs the action of the verb). Following are some typical errors:

> The *goal* of the courses grouped under the rubric of "Encountering Non-Western Cultures" *are* . . .

Here the writer forgot that *goal,* the subject, is singular.

> During 1992, *the Refugee Act of 1980,* with the help of President Bush and Congress, *accepted* 114,000 immigrants into our nation.

The writer here should have realized that the agent doing the accepting would have to be the Bush administration, not the Refugee Act. A better version would read:

> During 1992, the Bush administration accepted 114,000 immigrants into our nation under the terms of the Refugee Act of 1980.

Proofreading Practice Proofread the following passage for errors of grammar and punctuation.

> The citizens of Zurich, Switzerland tired of problems associated with drug abuse, experimented with legalization. The plan was to open a central park, Platzspitz, where drugs and drug use would be permitted. Many European experts felt, that it was the illegal drug business rather than the actual use of drugs that had caused many of the cities problems. While the citizens had hoped to isolate the drug problem, foster rehabilitation, and curb the AIDS epidemic, the actual outcome of the Platzspitz experiment did not create the desired results. Instead, violence increased. Drug-related deaths doubled. And drug users were drawn from not only all over

Switzerland, but from all over Europe as well. With thousands of discarded syringe packets lying around, one can only speculate as to whether the spread of AIDS was curbed. The park itself was ruined and finally on February 10, 1992, it was barred up and closed. After studying the Swiss peoples' experience with Platzspitz, it is hard to believe that some advocates of drug legalization in the United States are urging us to participate in the same kind of experiment.

Fallacies—and Critical Thinking

Arguments, like [people], are often pretenders.

—Plato

Throughout this book we have stressed how to argue well, accentuating the positive rather than dwelling on the negative, poor reasoning and bad arguments. We'd rather say "do this" than "don't do that." We'd rather offer good arguments to emulate than bad arguments to avoid. In stressing the positive, however, we haven't paid enough attention to an undeniable fact. Too often unsound arguments convince too many people who should reject them. This appendix addresses a daily problem—arguments that succeed when they ought to fail.

Traditionally, logicians and philosophers have tried to solve this problem by exposing "fallacies," errors in reasoning. About 2,400 years ago, the great ancient Greek philosopher Aristotle was the first to do so in *Sophistical Refutations*. "Sophistry" means reasoning that *appears* to be sound. Aristotle showed that such reasoning only seems sound and therefore shouldn't pass critical scrutiny. He identified thirteen common errors in reasoning. Others have since isolated dozens more, over a hundred in some recent treatments.

We respect this ancient tradition and urge you to learn more about it. Irving M. Copi's classic textbook, *Introduction to Logic,* offers an excellent discussion. It's often used in beginning college philosophy courses. However, our concern is not philosophy but arguments about public issues, where a different notion of fallacy is more useful. Let's start, then, with how we define it.

WHAT IS A FALLACY?

Our concern is arguing well, both skillfully and ethically, and arguments have force through *appeals to an audience*. Therefore, we define *fallacy* as "the misuse of an otherwise common and legitimate form of appeal."

A good example is the appeal to authority, common in advancing evidence to defend reasons in an argument. If I'm writing about flu epidemics, for instance, I may cite a scientist studying them at the national Centers for Disease Control to support something I've said. As long as I report what he or she said accurately, fully, and without distortion, I've used the appeal to authority correctly. After all, I'm not a flu expert and this person is—it only makes sense to appeal to his or her authority.

But let's suppose that my authority's view does not represent what most experts believe—in fact most leading authorities reject it. Perhaps I just don't know enough to realize that my authority is not in the mainstream. Or perhaps I do know, but for reasons of my own I want my audience to think a minority view is the majority view. It doesn't matter whether I intend to deceive or not—if I present my authority in a misleading way, I have misused the appeal to authority. I have committed a fallacy in the meaning we're giving it here.

There are other ways of misusing the appeal to authority—for instance, citing someone as an authority on a subject unrelated to the person's field or citing an authority likely to be biased because of his or her affiliation. Stephen Hawking is a genuine expert on physics but probably not on American policy in the Middle East. Scientists employed by an oil company are suspect when they talk about global warming.

Here's the point of our definition of fallacy: There's nothing wrong with the appeal to authority itself. Everything depends on how it's used in a particular case. That's why fallacies must be linked with critical thinking. Studying fallacies can lead to mindless "fallacy hunts" and to labeling all instances of a kind of appeal as fallacious. Fallacies are common, but finding them requires *thinking through any appeal that strikes us as suspect for some reason*. We have to decide in each case whether to accept or reject the appeal—or more often, how much we should let it influence our thinking.

WHY ARE FALLACIES SO COMMON?

Fallacies are common because they are deeply rooted in human nature. We must not imagine that we can eliminate them. But we can understand some of their causes and motivations and, with that understanding, increase our critical alertness. The following account is far from complete; we offer it to stimulate your own thinking about why fallacies occur.

We've distinguished unintended fallacies from intentional ones. We think most fallacies are not meant to deceive, so let's deal with this bigger category first. Unintentional fallacies can result from not knowing enough about the subject, which we may not realize for a number of reasons:

- *Inaccurate reporting or insufficient knowledge.* Arguments always appeal to the facts connected with a controversial question. Again, as with the appeal to authority, there's nothing wrong with appealing to what's known about something. It's hard to imagine how we'd argue without doing so. But we have to get the facts right and present them in a context of other relevant information.

So, for example, experts think that about 300,000 undocumented, foreign-born people immigrate to the United States each year. Not 3,000 or 30,000, but 300,000, and not per month or decade, but annually. The first way we can misuse the appeal to facts is not to report the information accurately. Mistakes of this kind occur often. Even magazines and newspapers frequently acknowledge errors in their stories from previous issues.

If we cite the correct figure, 300,000 per year, to support a contention that the Border Patrol isn't doing its job, we'd be guilty of a fallacy if we didn't know that about half of these immigrants come legally, on visas, and simply stay. They are not the Border Patrol's problem. So, even if we cite information accurately, we can still misrepresent what it means or misinterpret it. Accuracy is important but not enough by itself to avoid fallacies. We have to double-check our facts and understand what the facts mean. Because many people don't, fallacies of fact are common.

- *Holding beliefs that aren't true.* If what we don't know can hurt us, what we think we know that's false does more damage. We pick up such beliefs from misinformation that gets repeated over and over in conversation and the media. For example, many Americans equate Islam with Arabs. But most Muslims aren't Arabs, and many Arabs aren't Muslims. The linkage is no more than a popular association. Furthermore, many terrorists are neither Arabs nor Muslims—we just don't hear about them much. Unfortunately, even when informed people point out the facts just mentioned, they tend not to register or be forgotten quickly. Such is the hold of incorrect beliefs on the minds of many people.

  We have to read deeply in good sources to overcome mistaken associations in our minds; we have to allow ourselves to be corrected when what we thought was true turns out to be false; and we have to be alert not to slip back into old habits of thought. Because this requires more intellectual discipline than many people are willing to exert, fallacies abound.

- *Stubbornly adhering to a belief despite massive counterevidence.* At one time most climate scientists resisted the notion that human activities could influence the weather, much less cause global warming. But as more and more evidence accumulated, the overwhelming majority eventually came to agree that carbon dioxide emissions, especially from vehicles and power-generating plants, are the major cause of global warming. But dissenters still exist, and not all of them are being paid by oil companies. Some may sincerely feel that natural variation in the Earth's climate is the real cause of global warming. Some may enjoy the role of outsider or maverick. Some may say that often the majority opinion turns out to be wrong, which is true enough, and somebody needs to play the skeptic.

Whatever the motivation may be, the dissenters are brushing aside an enormous amount of evidence. Their fallacious arguments have helped to convince too many Americans that we don't have a problem when we do. We cite this example to show that fallacies are not restricted to popular arguments. Scientists can be as stubborn as anyone. It's human nature, against which no degree of expertise can protect us.

- *Dodging issues we don't understand or that disturb or embarrass us.* The issues that immigration, both legal and illegal, raises, for example, are more often avoided or obscured than confronted. People talk about immigrants becoming "good Americans" and worry about whether the latest wave can or will "assimilate." But what is a "good American"? The question is rarely posed. Exactly what does "assimilate" involve? Again, few ask the question. Thus, arguments about this subject often dodge the important questions connected with it. In many cases those making these arguments do so while thinking they are confronting it.

  Just as often, we deliberately dodge issues that we understand very well. We know, for example, that most SUVs use more gas than cars, and because of their high center of gravity, they are more prone to flip over. Furthermore, we know that the United States uses too much gasoline and diesel and is therefore dependent on uncertain foreign supplies of crude oil. We also know that burning hydrocarbons releases massive amounts of greenhouse gases, especially carbon dioxide. Yet only high gasoline prices have reduced SUV sales, and people come up with all sorts of bad arguments designed to justify or excuse continuing to drive them. Perhaps a few people, because of large families or their work, really need SUVs, but most who drive them don't and they know this too. They just like them and dodge the issues connected with driving them.

If you recognize yourself and people you know in some or all of these causes and motivations that drive fallacious arguments, welcome to the club. We are all guilty. Without meaning to, we all get the facts wrong; we all pick up notions we take to be true that aren't; and we all are at times stubborn and evasive.

Fortunately, unintended fallacies usually have telltale signs we can learn to detect, such as these:

- the reported fact that seems unlikely or implausible

- the interpretation that reduces a complex problem to something too simple to trust

- the belief that doesn't fit what we know of the world and our own experience

- the argument that strains too hard to downplay or explain away data that would call it into question

- the argument that dances around issues rather than confronting them

The good news is that unintended fallacies are seldom skillful enough to fool us often or for long. They tend to give themselves away once we know what to look for and care enough to exercise our natural critical capacity.

The bad news is that arguments coldly calculated to deceive, although less common than arguments that mislead unintentionally, are often much harder to detect. What makes the problem especially tough is that deceit comes too often from people we want and even need to trust: people in authority, with power, people who are talented, intelligent, charming, sophisticated, connected, and well-educated. Why? Why do people sometimes set out to deceive others? We think the philosopher and brilliant fallacy hunter Jeremy Bentham had the best answer. He called the motivation "interest-begotten prejudice." What did he mean?

He meant that all human beings have interests they consider vital—status, money, and power they either have and seek to protect or strive to acquire. As a direct result of these interests, their outlook, thinking, and of course their arguments are shot through with prejudices, unexamined judgments about what is good, desirable, worthwhile, and so on. For example, through much of American history, Native Americans had something the American government wanted—land. When it didn't take it by force, it took it by treaty, by persuading Native Americans to make bad bargains that often the government never intended to keep anyway. The whole process rode on prejudices: Native Americans were savages or children in need of protection by the Great Father in Washington; besides that, they didn't "do anything" with the land they had. Because the deceit paid off handsomely for its perpetrators, it went on until there was little land remaining to take.

We'd like to tell you that deliberate deceit in argument doesn't work—that deceivers are exposed and discredited at least, if not punished for what they do. We'd like to endorse Abraham Lincoln's famous statement: "You can fool all of the people some of the time, and some of the people all the time, but you can't fool all of the people all of the time." Maybe so—many Native Americans and some independent-thinking white people weren't fooled by the false promises of the treaties. But the humorist James Thurber's less famous observation is probably closer to the truth: "You can fool too many of the people too much of the time." This is so because the interest-begotten prejudices of the powerful coincide with or cooperate with the prejudices of a large segment of the audience addressed. That's why Hitler and his propaganda machine was able to create the disastrous Third Reich and why Joseph Stalin, who murdered more Russians than Hitler did, remains a national hero for many Russians even now, after his brutal regime's actions have long been exposed.

So, what can be done about the fallacious arguments of deliberate deceivers, backed as they often are by the power of the state or other potent interests? The most important thing is to examine our own interest-begotten prejudices, because that's what the deceivers use to manipulate us. They won't be able to push our buttons so easily if we know what they are and realize we're being manipulated. Beyond that, we need to recognize the interests of others, who may be in the minority and largely powerless to resist when too many people are fooled too much of the time. We can call attention to the fallacies of deliberate deceivers, exposing their game for others to see. We can make counterarguments, defending enlightened stances with all our skill. There's no guarantee that what should prevail will, but at least we need not lend support to exploiters nor fall into silence when we ought to resist.

SOME COMMON FALLACIES

For reasons that should be clearer now, people often misuse legitimate forms of appeal. We've mentioned two examples already—the misuse of the appeal to authority and the misuse of the appeal to facts. All legitimate appeals can be misused, and because there are too many to discuss them all, we'll confine our attention to those most commonly turned into fallacies.

In Chapter 9, "Motivating Action: Arguing to Persuade," we described and illustrated all the forms of appeal at length (pages 266–272). In sum, we are persuaded by

- *ethos:* the character of the writer as we perceive him or her
- *pathos:* our emotions and attitudes as the argument arouses them
- *style:* how well something is said
- *logos:* our capacity for logic, by the force of reasons and evidence advanced for a thesis

You'll encounter people, including many professors, who hold that only *logos,* rational appeal, *should* persuade. Anything else from their point of view is irrelevant and probably fallacious. We say in response that, regardless of what should be the case, people *are* persuaded by all four kinds of appeal—that we always have been and always will be. It therefore doesn't help to call appeals to *ethos, pathos,* and style fallacious. It *can* help to understand how these legitimate forms of appeal can be misused or abused. That's what we're trying to do in pointing to common fallacies.

The Appeal to *Ethos*

We don't know many people well whose arguments we encounter in print or in cyberspace. Typically, we don't know them at all. Consequently, we ordinarily rely on their qualifications and reputation as well as our impression of their character from reading what they've written. If *ethos* isn't important or shouldn't matter, we wouldn't find statements about an author's identity and background attached to articles and books they've written. Speakers wouldn't be introduced by someone providing similar information. But *ethos* does matter; as Aristotle said long ago, it's probably the most potent form of appeal. If we don't trust the person we're hearing or reading, it's highly unlikely we'll be persuaded by anything said or written. If we do, we're inclined to assent to all of it. Consequently, appeals to ethos are often misused. Here are some of the common ways.

Personal Attack

There are people we ought never to trust—confidence men who bilk people out of their life savings, pathological liars, and so on. There's nothing wrong with exposing such people, destroying the *ethos* they often pretend very persuasively to have, thereby rendering their arguments unpersuasive.

But too often good arguments by good people are undermined with unjustified personal attacks. The most common is name-calling. Someone offers an argument opponents cannot see how to refute, so instead of addressing the argument, they call him or her "a liberal," a "neocon," or some other name the audience equates with "bad."

This fallacy is so common in politics that we now refer to it as "negative ads" or "negative campaigning." We ought not to dismiss it because experience and studies show that it often works. It works because once a label is attached to someone it's hard to shake.

Common Opinion

It's hard to find any argument that doesn't appeal to commonly accepted beliefs, many of which are accurate and reliable. Even scientific argument, which extols the value of skepticism, assumes that some knowledge is established beyond question and that some ways of doing things, like experimental design, are the right ways. When we indicate that we share the common opinions of our readers, thinking and behaving as they do, we establish or increase our *ethos*.

Used fallaciously, a writer passes off as commonly accepted either a belief that isn't held by many informed people or one that is held commonly but is false or highly doubtful. "Of course," the writer says, and then affirms something questionable as if it was beyond question. For example, "Everybody knows that AIDS is spread by promiscuous sexual behavior." Sometimes it is, but one sexual act with one person can transmit the virus, and infection need not be transmitted sexually at all—babies are born with it because their mothers have AIDS, and addicts sharing needles is another common way AIDS is spread. Furthermore, health care workers are at higher risk because they often are exposed to bodily fluids from infected people. The common opinion in this and many other instances is no more than a half-truth at best.

Tradition

Few can see the opening of the musical *Fiddler on the Roof* and not be at least temporarily warmed by the thought of tradition. Tradition preserves our sense of continuity, helps us maintain stability and identity amid the often overwhelming demands of rapid change. No wonder, then, that writers appeal to it frequently to enhance their *ethos* and often in ways that are not fallacious at all. It was hardly a fallacy after 9/11, for instance, to remind

Americans that part of the price we pay for liberty, our supreme traditional value, is greater relative vulnerability to terrorism. A closed, totalitarian society like North Korea can deal with terrorism much more "efficiently" than we can, but at the price of having no liberty.

Many of the abuses of tradition as a source of ethical appeal are so obvious as to need no discussion: politicians wrapping themselves in the flag (or at least red, white, and blue balloons), television preachers oozing piety to get donations. You can easily provide your own examples. Much more difficult to discern is invoking tradition not to dupe the naïve but to justify resisting constructive change. Tradition helped to delay women's right to vote in the United States, for example, and plays a major role in the high illiteracy rate for women in India and many other countries now.

Like all fallacious uses of legitimate appeals, ethical fallacies can be revealed by asking the right questions:

For *personal attack,* ask, "Are we dealing with a person whose views we should reject out of hand?" "Is the personal attack simply a means to dismiss an argument we ought to listen to?"

For *common opinion,* ask, "Is this belief really held by well-informed people?" If it is, ask, "Does the common belief hold only in some instances or in every case?"

For *tradition,* ask, "Have we always really done it that way?" If so, ask, "Have conditions changed enough so that the old way may need to be modified or replaced?"

The Appeal to *Pathos*

After people understand the indispensable role *ethos* plays in persuasion, few continue to view it only negatively, as merely a source of fallacies. *Pathos* is another matter. In Western culture, the heart is opposed to the head, feeling and emotion contrasted with logic and clear thinking. Furthermore, our typical attitudes toward *pathos* affect *ethos* as well: Emotional people can't be trusted. Their arguments betray a disorganized and unbalanced mind.

With cause, we are wary of the power of emotional appeal, especially when passionate orators unleash it in crowds. The result often enough has been public hysteria and sometimes riots, lynchings, and verbal or physical abuse of innocent people. We know its power. Should it, then, be avoided? Are emotional appeals always suspect?

Let's take a brief look at a few of them.

Fear

"We have nothing to fear but fear itself," Franklin Roosevelt declared, at a time when matters looked fearful indeed. The Great Depression was at its height; fascism was gaining ground in Europe. The new president sought to reduce the fear and despair that gripped the United States and much of the world at the time.

About a year later, in 1933, Hitler came to power, but the authorities in Britain, France, and other countries failed to realize the threat he represented soon enough, despite warnings from Winston Churchill and many others. As a result, the Allied powers in Europe fell to the Nazis, and Britain came to the brink of defeat. Fear can paralyze, as Roosevelt knew, but lack of it can result in complacency when genuine threats loom.

How can we tell the difference? With appeals to fear, as with all appeals to any emotion, this hard-to-answer question is the key: *Does reality justify the emotion a speaker or writer seeks to arouse or allay?* Recently, for instance, it's been easy to play on our fear of terrorists. But the odds of you or me dying in a terrorist plot are very low. The risk of death is greater just driving a car. Far more Americans will die prematurely from sedentary ways than Osama bin Laden and his associates are ever likely to kill. 9/11 has taught us yet again that "eternal vigilance is the price of liberty," but the sometimes nearly hysterical fear of terrorism isn't justified.

The appeal to fear is fallacious when fear is trumped up, manufactured to scare people into doing unwise things. But playing down fear when we should be afraid is also fallacious and can do just as much damage. We should be more afraid, for instance, of the effects of global warming than most Americans appear to be. The fallacy is not the appeal to fear but the lack of justification or evidence for the fear we're attempting to arouse or reduce.

Pity

Fear has its roots in the body, in the fight-or-flight rush of adrenaline that helps us to survive. Pity, the ability to feel sorry for people suffering unjustly, has social roots. Both are fundamental emotions, part of being human.

Like the appeal to fear, the appeal to pity can be used fallaciously, to mislead us into, for example, contributing to a seemingly worthy cause which is really just a front for con artists. A favorite human ploy is attempting to dodge the consequences for irresponsible behavior by appealing to pity. Children do this well, learning at an early age to avoid punishment by pulling at the heartstrings of their parents. And some adults are pity-addicts, always ready with a tale of woe, in extreme cases even faking illness or making themselves sick to get attention—it's called Munchausen syndrome.

But if pity can be used to manipulate us, we can also fail to respond when pity is warranted. Or we can substitute the emotion for action. The suffering in Darfur in recent years has been acute but the response of the rest of the world has usually been too little, too late. Like fear, then, we can fail to respond to appeals for pity when they are warranted.

Which is worse? To be conned sometimes or to be indifferent in the face of unjust suffering? Surely the latter. Because fear can lead to hysteria and violence, we should meet appeals to it skeptically. Because unjust suffering is so common, we should meet appeals to pity in a more receptive frame of mind. But with both emotions we require critical thinking. "I just feel what

I feel" is not good enough. We have to get past that to distinguish legitimate emotional appeals from fallacious ones.

Ridicule

We mention ridicule because student writers are often advised to avoid it. "Don't ridicule your opponents in an argument" is the standard advice, advice you'll find elsewhere in this book. So, is ridicule always fallacious, always a cheap shot, always a way to win points without earning them?

Well, not always. With most positions on most issues, we're dealing with points of view we may not agree with but must respect. But what if a position makes no sense, has little or no evidence to support its contentions, and yet people persist in holding it? What then? Is ridicule justified, at least sometimes?

If it isn't, then satire isn't justified, for satire holds up for scorn human behavior the satirist considers irrational and destructive. We all enjoy political cartoons, which thrive on ridicule of the absurd and the foolish. How many stand-up comedians would have far less material if ridicule was never justified?

Like pity, ridicule is a social emotion. It tries to bring individuals who have drifted too far away from social norms back into the fold. It allows us to discharge our frustration with stupid or dishonest positions through largely harmless laughter—far better than "let's beat some sense into old So-and-So." Ridicule, then, has its place and its functions.

But it also has its fallacies. Most commonly an intelligent, well-reasoned, and strongly supported position suffers ridicule simply because it is unpopular, because most people have difficulty getting their minds around it. Some arguments are ahead of their time and fly in the face of commonly held prejudices. Only a half century ago, the arguments against segregating blacks and whites in our schools were ridiculed. Now the quite cogent arguments for recognizing some gay relationships as legal unions are likewise ridiculed. Clearly, the fact that an argument has been dismissed as ridiculous or absurd doesn't mean that it is, and we must be especially careful when we unthinkingly join in the ridicule. Maybe we need to rethink our prejudices. In any case, we need to think through the argument that's been scorned or dismissed with laughter. We may find an intelligent, well-reasoned, and strongly supported position that challenges us to change our minds.

Like the fallacies related to *ethos*, pathetic fallacies can be revealed with the right questions:

1. Is the emotion appropriate to the situation, in proportion to what we know about what's going on in the world?

2. What are the consequences of buying into a particular emotional appeal? Where will it take us?

3. Does the emotional appeal *substitute* for reason, for a good argument, or does it reinforce it in justified ways?

4. What is the relation of the appeal to unexamined and possibly unjustified prejudice or bias? Are we being manipulated or led for good reasons to feel something?

The Appeal to Style

Most experienced and educated people are aware of the seductions of *ethos* and *pathos*. They know how easy it is to be misled by people they trust or manipulated by emotion into doing something they ordinarily wouldn't and shouldn't do. They've been fooled enough to be wary and therefore critical. However, even experienced and educated people often aren't alert to the power of style, to the great impact that something can have *just because it is stated well*. One of the great students of persuasion, the American critic Kenneth Burke, explained the impact of style. He said that when we like the *form* of something said or written, it's a small step to accepting the *content* of it as well. We move very easily from "Well said" to "I agree," or even "It must be true." It's almost as if we can't distrust at a deep level language that appeals to our sense of rhythm and sound.

Yet fallacies of style are a major industry. It's called advertising. People are paid handsomely to create slogans the public will remember and repeat. From some time ago, for instance, comes this one: "When guns are outlawed, only outlaws will have guns." Has a nice swing to it, doesn't it? The play on words is pleasing, hard to forget, and captures in a powerful formula the fears of the pro-gun lobby. Of course, in reality there's never been a serious movement to outlaw guns in the United States. In some states, gun owners must register their weapons. Other laws may restrict gun ownership under certain circumstances or forbid carrying a concealed weapon in certain places. But no one is going to take away your guns, so the slogan is nothing more than scaremongering at best.

Now compare this slogan with another memorable phrase: "Justice too long delayed is justice denied." Martin Luther King used it to characterize the situation of black Americans in 1963 in his classic essay "Letter from Birmingham Jail." He got the phrase from a Supreme Court justice, but its appeal has less to do with the source of the statement than with its formula-like feeling of truth. It stuck in King's mind so he used it in his situation, and once you read it, you won't forget it either. In other words, it works in much the same way that the fallacious slogan works. But King's use of it isn't at all fallacious. As a matter of undisputed fact, black Americans were denied their civil rights legally and illegally for more than a century after the Emancipation Proclamation.

The point, of course, is that the form of a statement says nothing about its truth value or whether it's being used to deceive. If form pushes us toward unthinking assent, then we must exert enough resistance to permit critical thought. Even "justice too long delayed is justice denied" may require some careful thought if it is applied to some other situation. Many people who favor the death penalty, for example, are outraged by the many years it usually takes to move a murderer from conviction to execution. They could well apply the phrase to this state of affairs. How much truth should it contain for someone who has no legal, moral, or religious objections to capital punishment? It's true that often the relatives of a victim must wait a decade or more for justice. It's true that sometimes, for one reason or another, the execution never happens. Is that justice denied? But it's also true that convicted felons on death row have been found innocent and released. Some innocent ones have been executed. Has justice been too long delayed or not? Would it be wise to shorten the process? These are serious questions critical thought must address.

The appeal of style goes well beyond slogans and formulas. We have not offered a list of common stylistic devices and how they may be misused because there are far too many of them. All can be used to express the truth; all can be used to package falsehood in appealing rhythm and sound. Separating ourselves from appeals of language long enough to think about what is being said is the only solution.

The Appeal to *Logos*

Before we present a short list of common errors in reasoning, the traditional focus of fallacy research, let's review a fundamental point about logic: An argument can be free of errors in reasoning, be logically compelling, and yet be false. Logic can tell us whether an argument makes sense but not whether it is true. For example, consider the following statements:

> Australia began as a penal colony, a place where criminals in England were sent.

> Modern Australians, therefore, are descendents of criminals.

There's nothing wrong with the logical relation of these two statements. But its truth value depends on the *historical accuracy* of the first statement. It depends also on the *actual origins* of all modern Australians. As a matter of fact, Australia was used by the English as a convenient place to send certain people the authorities considered undesirable, but they weren't all criminals. Furthermore, native Australians populated the country long before any European knew it existed. And most modern Australians immigrated long after the days of the penal colony. So the truth value of these perfectly logical statements is low. It's true enough for Australians to joke about sometimes, but it's not really true.

Here's a good rule of thumb: *The reality of things reasoned about is far more varied and complex than the best reasoning typically captures.* Sometimes errors in reasoning lead us to false conclusions. But false conclusions result much more often from statements not being adequate to what's known about reality. Furthermore, there's always a lot about reality we don't know yet, and things we think we know that in time prove false. We should care a great deal about the logic of an argument but not jump to the conclusion it's true just because it's logical.

With that in mind, let's look at a few fallacies of logical appeal.

False Cause

We've defined *fallacy* as the misuse of a legitimate form of appeal. There's nothing more common or reasonable than identifying the cause of something. We're not likely to repair a car without knowing what's causing that wobble in the steering, or treat a disease effectively, or come up with the right solution to almost any problem without knowing the cause.

The difficulty is that just because "a" follows "b," "b" didn't necessarily cause "a." Yet we tend to think so, especially if "a" always follows "b." Hence, the possibility of "false cause," reasoning that misleads by confusing sequence with cause. If we flip a light switch and the light doesn't go on, we immediately think, "The bulb's burned out." But if we then replace the bulb, and it still doesn't work, we think the problem must be the switch. We may tinker with that for a while before we realize that none of the lights are working: "Oh, the breaker's cut off." By a process of trial and error, we eliminate the false causes to find the real one.

But if we're reasoning about more complex problems, trial and error usually isn't an option. For example, a recent newspaper article attributed the decline in the wages of Americans despite increased productivity to the influx of illegal aliens, especially from Mexico. Because they are paid less than most American citizens are, attributing the cause of lower wages to them may seem plausible. But actually some groups of Americans have endured a steady decline for some time, as high-paying industrial jobs were lost and lower-paying service work took their place. Globalization has allowed companies to force wages down and reduce the power of labor unions by taking advantage of people in other countries who will work for much less. It's highly unlikely that depressed wages are caused by illegal aliens alone. But if we don't like them, it's especially tempting to blame them for a more complex problem with which they are only associated. That's called *scapegoating,* and false cause is how the reasoning works that justifies it.

As a rule of thumb, let's assume that complex problems have multiple causes, and let's be especially suspicious when common prejudices may motivate single-cause thinking.

Straw Man

Nothing's more common in argument than stating an opponent's position and then showing what's wrong with it. As long as we state our opponent's position fully and accurately and attack it intelligently, with good reasons and evidence, there's nothing fallacious about such an attack.

The temptation, however, is to seek advantage by attributing to our opponents a weak or indefensible position they don't hold but which resembles their position in some respects. We can then knock it down easily and make our opponents look dumb or silly in the process. That's called "creating a straw man," and it's a common ploy in politics especially. It works because most people aren't familiar enough with the position being distorted to realize that it's been misrepresented, and so they accept the straw man as if it was the real argument. Often people whose views have been caricatured fight an uphill battle, first to reestablish their genuine position and then to get it listened to after an audience has accepted the distorted one as genuine. Thus, many fallacies succeed because of ignorance and ill will on the part of both the fallacious reasoner and the audience.

It's all very well to say, "Be fair. Don't say somebody thinks something she or he doesn't." Indeed, we shouldn't. It's just sophisticated lying that lowers the quality of public discussion. But the real challenge is to be critical when someone misrepresents a person or a position we didn't like beforehand. Being fair despite our own prejudice is very difficult, more perhaps than we can expect from most people.

Slippery Slope

Human experience offers many examples of "one thing leading to another." We decide to have a baby, for instance, and one thing follows another from the first diaper change all the way to college graduation, with so much in between and beyond that a parent's life is altered forever and fundamentally. Furthermore, it's always prudent to ask about any decision we face, "If I do x, what consequent y am I likely to face? And if y happens, where will that lead me?" We also know that what we do often sets in motion actions on the part of other people, sometimes with unforeseen results. The Bush administration invaded Iraq to remove an apparently dangerous dictator, succeeded in doing that, but also unleashed the forces that may well result in civil war in that country.

The slippery-slope fallacy takes advantage of our commonsense notion that actions have consequences, that one thing leads to another. The difference between the truth and the fallacy is that the drastic consequences the arguer envisions could not or are not likely to happen. Those who opposed making the so-called morning-after pill available without a prescription sometimes warned of a wholesale decline in sexual morality, especially among young adults. That hasn't happened, and in any case, technology is one thing, morality another. What makes sex right or wrong has little to do with the method of contraception.

The slippery-slope fallacy plays on fear, indicating one of the many ways that one kind of appeal—in this case, to logic, or reasoning about consequences—connects with other kinds of appeal—in this case, to emotion. Working in tandem, such appeals can be powerfully persuasive. All the more reason, then, to stand back and analyze any slope an argument depicts critically. Is the predicted slide inevitable or even probable? In many cases, the answer will be no, and we can see through the appeal to what it often is: a scare tactic to head off doing something that makes good sense.

Hasty Generalization

We can't think and therefore can't argue without generalizing. Almost any generalization is vulnerable to the charge of being hasty. All that's required for what some logicians label as "hasty generalization" is to find a single exception to an otherwise true assertion. So "SUVs waste gas." But the new hybrid SUVs are relatively gas efficient. "Since 9/11 American Muslims have felt that their loyalty to the United States has been in doubt." Surely we can find individual Muslims who haven't felt insecure at all.

The problem with hasty generalization is not exceptions to statements that are by and large true. The problem, rather, is generalization based on what's called a biased (and hence unrepresentative) sample, which results in a generalization that is false. If you visit an institution for the criminally insane, you'll probably encounter some schizophrenics. You may conclude, as many people have, that schizophrenics are dangerous. Most of them, however, are not, and the relatively few who are don't pose a threat when they stay on their meds. The common fear of "schizo street people" results from a hasty generalization that can do real harm.

With hasty generalization, then, we face the problem we face with all fallacies—distinguishing the legitimate appeal from its illegitimate misuse. The best attitude we can take is to be open to correction. We will make hasty generalizations based on a too-limited range of experience. That's just human. The question is, Will we allow additional experience or the greater experience of others to revise the generalizations that are more often false than true? If not, our minds have closed down and learning has stopped. We will victimize ourselves and others with actions based on hasty generalizations.

Begging the Question

We end with this because it is especially tricky. Every argument makes assumptions that haven't been and in some cases can't be proven. We simply couldn't argue at all if we had to prove everything our position assumes. Hence virtually all arguments can be said to "beg the question," to assume as true that which hasn't been shown definitively as true. Furthermore, we can never tell when an assumption that almost no one doubts can turn out to be very doubtful as new information emerges. Assumptions we used to make routinely can become hot issues of controversy.

Not long ago, for example, medicine assumed that increased environmental pollutants caused the higher incidence of allergies among recent generations of people who otherwise enjoy generally better health than their ancestors did. But now a competing theory is getting a lot of attention—that our homes are too clean, not contaminated enough for our immune system to react appropriately when we encounter ordinary levels of pollen and other allergens. So now, older arguments about how to prevent and treat allergies seem to beg the question, and the cause of allergies, once considered settled, is now at issue again.

Consequently, we should confine "begging the question" to *taking as settled the very question that's currently at issue.* Someone is charged with a crime, and the press gives it much ink and air time. Inevitably, some people jump to the conclusion that the accused is guilty. This can be such a big problem that it's hard to impanel a jury that hasn't been hopelessly biased by all the coverage.

We beg the question whenever we assume something that can't be assumed because it's the very thing we must prove. Fallacies of this kind are usually no harder to spot than the juror who thinks the defendant is guilty simply because he or she has been charged with a crime. Pro-lifers, for example, argue in ways that depend on the fetus having the legal status of a person. Of course, if the fetus is a person, there is no controversy. Abortion would be what pro-lifers say it is, murder, and thus prohibited by law. The personhood of the fetus is *the* issue; assuming the fetus is a person is begging the question.

No doubt we'd all prefer a simpler world, where everything is either this or that, black or white, yes or no, where we could say, "This kind of appeal is always fallacious, but this kind you can always rely on." That's not how it is. Sorting out the good from the bad in reasoning requires critical thinking, the results of which may not be certain either.

The following exercise does not include what many such exercises offer—fallacies so obvious they would fool no one over the age of ten. You'll have to think them through, discuss them at length. In some cases, rather than flatly rejecting or accepting the arguments, you may want to give them "partial credit," a degree of acceptance. That's fine, part of learning to live with shades of gray.

EXERCISE

The following examples come from instances of persuasion that appeared in the fifth edition of this book. Some may not be fallacious in any way. Assess them carefully and be prepared to defend the judgment you make.

1. From an ad depicting the VW Beetle: "Hug it? Drive it? Hug it? Drive it?"

2. From a cartoon depicting a man holding a pro-life sign, above which appear two specimen jars, one containing "a dead abortion doctor," the other "a dead fetus." The man is pointing at the jar with the dead fetus. The caption reads "We object to this one."

3. From an essay called "The End of Life," James Rachels offers the following interpretation of the Biblical prohibition against taking human life: "The sixth commandment does not say, literally, 'Thou shalt not *kill*'—that is a bad translation. A better translation is, Thou shalt not commit *murder,* which is different, and which does not obviously prohibit mercy killing. Murder is by definition *wrongful killing*; so, if you do not think that a given kind of killing is wrong, you will not call it murder" [author's emphasis].

4. From a panel discussion in *Newsweek* about violence in the media: The moderator asks a representative of the movie industry why the rating NC-17 is not applied to "gratuitously violent movies." The response is "because the definition of 'gratuitous' is shrouded in subjectivity. . . . Creative people can shoot a violent scene a hundred

different ways. Sex and language are different, because there are only a few ways [you can depict them on screen]. . . . Violence is far more difficult to pin down."

5. From an essay critical of multiculturalism comes the following quotation from the political scientist Samuel B. Huntington, whose view the essay's author endorses: "Does it take an Osama bin Laden . . . to make us realize that we are Americans? If we do not experience recurrent destructive attacks, will we return to the fragmentation and eroded Americanism before September 11?"

6. From an essay advocating multiculturalism: "The attack on affirmative action isn't really about affirmative action. Essentially it is another tactic in today's war on the gains of the 1960's, a tactic rooted in Anglo resentment and fear. A major source of that fear: the fact that California will almost surely have a majority of people of color in 20 to 30 years at most, with the nation as a whole not far behind."

7. From an essay urging us to move beyond the multiculturalism debate, written by a naturalized American citizen who was born in India: "I take my American citizenship very seriously. I am a voluntary immigrant, and not a seeker of political asylum. I am an American by choice, and not by the simple accident of birth. I have made emotional, social, and political commitments to this country. I have earned the right to think of myself as an American."

8. From an article arguing that militant Islam and Islamic terrorism is like Nazism: "Once again, the world is faced with a transcendent conflict between those who love life and those who love death both for themselves and their enemies. Which is why we tremble."

9. From an article arguing that American foreign policy provokes terrorism and that the root of it all is "our rampant militarism": "Two of the most influential federal institutions are not in Washington but on the south side of the Potomac River: the Defense Department and the Central Intelligence Agency. Given their influence today, one must conclude that what the government outlined in the Constitution of 1787 no longer bears much relationship to the government that actually rules from Washington. Until that is corrected, we should probably stop talking about 'democracy' and 'human rights.'"

10. From an article that attempts to explain human mating in evolutionary terms: "Feelings and acts of love are not recent products of particular Western views. Love is universal. Thoughts, emotions, and actions of love are experienced by people in all cultures worldwide—from the Zulu in the southern tip of Africa to the Eskimos in the north of Alaska."

For additional examples of fallacies for analysis, see "Stalking the Wild Fallacy" <http://www.fallacyfiles.org/examples.html>.

allusion: Reference to a person, event, or text, usually not explained.

annotation: A brief critical commentary on a text or section of text.

apologia: An effort to explain and justify what one has done, or chosen not to do, in the face of condemnation or at least widespread disapproval or misunderstanding.

argument: Mature reasoning; a considered opinion backed by a reason or reasons.

bibliography: A list of works on a particular topic.

brief: Outline of a case, including thesis, reasons, and evidence.

case strategy: The moves a writer makes to shape a particular argument, including selecting reasons, ordering them, developing evidence, and linking the sections of the argument for maximum impact.

case structure: A flexible plan for making any argument to any audience; it consists of one or more theses, each of which is supported by one or more reasons, each of which is supported by evidence. See also *brief*.

claim: In argument, what the author wants the audience to believe or to do.

connotation: What a word implies or what we associate it with; see also *denotation*.

conviction: An earned opinion achieved through careful thought, research, and discussion.

convincing: One of the four aims of argument; to use reasoning to secure the assent of people who do not share the author's conviction.

critical reading: A close reading involving analyzing and evaluating a text.

denotation: A word's literal meaning; see also *connotation*.

dialectic: Dialogue or serious conversation; the ancient Greeks' term for argument as inquiry.

graphics: Visual supplements to a longer text such as an essay, article, or manual.

identification: A strong linking of the readers' interests and values with an image, which represents something desired or potentially desirable.

implied question: A question that is inherent in an argument but not explicitly stated; all statements of opinion are answers to questions, usually implied ones.

inquiry: One of the four aims of argument; to use reasoning to determine the best position on an issue.

issue: An aspect of a topic that presents a problem, the solution to which people disagree about.

mediation: One of the four aims of argument; using reason and understanding to bring about consensus among disagreeing parties or positions.

middle style: A style of persuasive writing that is neither stiff and formal nor chatty and familiar.

paraphrase: To restate someone else's writing or speech in one's own words.

persuasion: One of the four aims of argument; persuasion uses both rational and emotional appeals to influence not just thinking but also behavior.

plagiarism: The act of presenting someone else's words and/or ideas as one's own, without acknowledging the source.

position: An overall, summarizing attitude or judgment about some issue.

rhetoric: The art of argument as mature reasoning.

rhetorical context: The circumstances surrounding the text as an act of communication: the time and place in which it was written; its place of publication; its author and his or her values; the ongoing, historical debate to which it contributes.

rhetorical prospectus: A plan for proposed writing that includes a statement of the thesis, aim, audience, speaker's persona, subject matter, and organizational plan.

sampling: A fast, superficial, not necessarily sequential reading of a text, not to learn all that a text has to say but to get a feeling for the territory it covers.

thesis: In argumentation, a very specific position statement that is strategically designed to appeal to readers and to be consistent with available evidence.

topic: A subject or aspect of a subject; see also *issue.*

visual rhetoric: The use of images, sometimes coupled with sound or appeals to the other senses, to make an argument or persuade one's audience to act as the image-maker would have them act.

CREDITS

Text and Illustration Credits

THE AMERICAN HERITAGE DICTIONARY OF THE ENGLISH LANGUAGE, excerpts from definitions of "mature" and "critical." Copyright © 2006 by Houghton Mifflin Company. Reproduced by permission from *The American Heritage Dictionary of the English Language, Fourth Edition.*

TIM APPENZELLER, "The Coal Paradox," *National Geographic*, March 2006. Reprinted by permission of National Geographic Society.

DANIEL BENJAMIN AND STEVEN SIMON, "Jihad in the Age of Globalization," pp. 59–65 from *The Next Attack: The Failure of the War on Terror and a Strategy for Getting It Right* by Daniel Benjamin and Steven Simon. Copyright 2005 by Daniel Benjamin and Steven Simon. Reprinted by permission of Henry Holt and Company.

MIA BLOOM, "Mother. Daughter. Sister. Bomber," *Bulletin of the Atomic Scientists* (November/December 2005), pp. 54–62. Copyright © 2005 by *Bulletin of the Atomic Scientists*, Chicago, IL. Reproduced by permission of Bulletin of the Atomic Scientists.

SISSELA BOK, "Media Literacy" from *Mayhem: Violence as Public Entertainment* by Sissela Bok. Copyright © 1998 by Sissela Bok. Reprinted by permission of Da Capo Press, a member of Perseus Books Group.

LINDA CHAVEZ, "The Realities of Immigration," *Commentary*, July–August 2006, pp. 34–39. Reprinted by permission of *Commentary* Magazine.

ROSS DOUTHAT and JENNY WOODSON, "The Border," *The Atlantic Monthly*, January/February 2006, pp. 54–55. Copyright 2006 The Atlantic Monthly Group, as first published in *The Atlantic Monthly*. Distributed by Tribune Media Services. Chart: Data courtesy of U.S. Customs and Border Protection, Border Patrol, FY 2004.

TAMARA DRAUT, from *Strapped: Why America's 20- and 30-Somethings Can't Get Ahead* by Tamara Draut, copyright © 2005 by Tamara Draut. Used by permission of Doubleday, a division of Random House, Inc.

GREGG EASTERBROOK, "Some Convenient Truths," *The Atlantic Monthly*, September 2006, pp. 29–30. Copyright © 2006 by Gregg Easterbrook. Reprinted by permission of InkWell Management, LLC.

IVAN ELAND, "It's What We Do," *The American Prospect*, vol. 17, no. 1 (January 2006). Reprinted by permission of the author.

CARL ELLIOTT, "The Tyranny of Happiness," from *Better Than Well: American Medicine Meets the American Dream* by Carl Elliott. Copyright © 2003 by Carl Elliott. Used by permission of W. W. Norton & Company, Inc.

HELEN FISHER, adapted from "'That First Fine Careless Rapture': *Who We Choose*" and "Notes" from *Why We Love: The Nature and Chemistry of Romantic Love* by Helen Fisher. Copyright 2004 by Helen Fisher. Reprinted by permission of Henry Holt and Company.

JAMES FORMAN, JR., "Arrested Development: The Conservative Case against Racial Profiling." From *The New Republic*, September 10, 2001. Reprinted by permission of The New Republic. Copyright © 2001 The New Republic, L.L.C.

HELEN FREMONT, "First Person Plural" from *Why I'm Still Married: Women Write Their Hearts Out on Love, Loss, Sex, and Who Does the Dishes*, edited by Karen Propp and Jean Trounstine. Hudson Street Press, published by Penguin Group, 2006. Copyright © 2005 by Helen Fremont. All rights reserved. Reprinted by permission of the author.

FRANCIS FUKUYAMA, "In Defense of Nature, Human and Non-Human," *World Watch*, July–August 2002, pp. 30–32. The Worldwatch Institute, *World Watch Magazine*, www.worldwatch.org. Reprinted with permission.

JACK GRIMES, "Hook-Up Culture." Jack Grimes, *Tufts University Daily*, March 30, 2004. Reprinted with permission.

Club, San Francisco, California, June 28, 2006. © 2006 National Trust for Historic Preservation. Reprinted with permission.

BHARATI MUKHERJEE, "Beyond Multiculturalism: A Two-Way Transformation," in *Multi-America: Essays on Cultural Wars and Cultural Peace*, ed. Ishmael Reed. Viking, 1997. Copyright © 1997 by Bharati Mukherjee. Reprinted with permission of author.

MICHELLE NIJHUIS, from "Selling the Wind" by Michelle Nijhuis. First published in *Audubon* magazine, September–October 2006. © 2006 by the National Audubon Society. Reprinted by permission of *Audubon* magazine.

ROBERT A. PAPE, from *Dying to Win* by Robert A. Pape, copyright © 2005 by Robert A. Pape. Used by permission of Random House, Inc.

DON PECK and ROSS DOUTHAT, "Does Money Buy Happiness?" *The Atlantic Monthly*, January/February 2003, pp. 42–43. Copyright 2003 The Atlantic Monthly Group, as first published in *The Atlantic Monthly*. Distributed by Tribune Media Services.

VIRGINIA POSTREL, pages 4–9 from "The Aesthetic Imperative" from *The Substance of Style* by Virginia Postrel. Copyright © 2003 by Virginia Postrel. Reprinted by permission of HarperCollins Publishers.

ALISSA QUART, "X-Large and X-Small" from *Branded: The Buying and Selling of Teenagers* by Alissa Quart. Copyright © 2003 by Alissa Quart. Reprinted by permission of Basic Books, a member of Perseus Books Group.

RICHARD RHODES, "Hollow Claims about Fantasy Violence." From *New York Times*, September 17, 2000. Copyright © 2000 The New York Times. Reprinted by permission.

WILLIAM F. RUDDIMAN, "Consuming Earth's Gifts" from *Plows, Plagues, and Petroleum: How Humans Took Control of Climate* by William F. Ruddiman. Copyright © 2005 by Princeton University Press. Reprinted by permission of Princeton University Press.

JULIET B. SCHOR, "When Spending Becomes You" from *The Overspent American: Why We Want What We Don't Need* by Juliet B. Schor. Copyright © 1998 by Juliet B. Schor. Reprinted by permission of Basic Books, a member of Perseus Books Group.

JOHN F. SCHUMAKER, "The Happiness Conspiracy: What Does It Mean to Be Happy in a Modern Consumer Society?" *New Internationalist*, July 2006. Reprinted by kind permission of the New Internationalist. Copyright New Internationalist www.newint.org.

LESLIE MARMON SILKO, "The Border Patrol State." First published in *The Nation*, October 17, 1994. © 1994 by Leslie Marmon Silko, permission of The Wylie Agency.

LAUREN SLATER, "Love: The Chemical Reaction," *National Geographic*, February 2006. Reprinted by permission of National Geographic Society.

JESSICA STERN, "The Protean Enemy." Reprinted by permission of *Foreign Affairs*, vol. 82, no. 4 (July–August 2003). Copyright 2003 by the Council on Foreign Relations, Inc.

GARY STIX, "Climate Repair Manual," *Scientific American*, September 2006. Text: Reprinted with permission. Copyright © 2006 by Scientific American, Inc. All rights reserved. Illustrations: "Hockey stick graph" from *IPCC Synthesis Report 2001*, Figure 2-3. Reprinted by permission of the Intergovernmental Panel on Climate Change. "Greenhouse Effect" illustrations by Lucy Reading-Ikkanda for *Scientific American* magazine. Reprinted by permission of Lucy Reading-Ikkanda.

GREGORY STOCK, "Choosing Our Genes." Originally published in *The Futurist*, July-August 2002, pp. 17–23. Used with permission from The World Future Society, 7910 Woodmont Avenue, Suite 450, Bethesda, Maryland 20814. Telephone: 301-656-8274; www.wfs.org.

JAMES B. TWITCHELL, "Needing the Unnecessary," *Reason*, vol. 34, no. 4 (August/September 2002). The article in *Reason* was excerpted and adapted from *Living It Up: America's Love Affair with Luxury* by James B. Twitchell. Copyright © 2002 James B. Twitchell. Reprinted with permission of Columbia University Press.

JAMES B. TWITCHELL, "How I Bought My Red Miata" from *Lead Us Into Temptation: The Triumph of American Materialism* by James B. Twitchell. Copyright © 1999 James B. Twitchell. Reprinted with permission of Columbia University Press.

UNION OF CONCERNED SCIENTISTS, "Ten Personal Solutions." © 2006 Union of Concerned Scientists. Reprinted with permission.

NANCY WARTIK, "The Perils of Playing House," *Psychology Today*, July–August 2005. Reprinted with permission from *Psychology Today* Magazine, Copyright © 2005 Sussex Publishers, LLC.

ETHAN WATTERS, "In My Tribe." As appeared in *The New York Times Magazine*, October 14, 2001. Reprinted by permission of the author.

SONDRA WHEELER, "Making Babies? *Sojourners*, May 1999, p. 14. Reprinted with permission from Sojourners. 1 (800) 714-7474 www.sojo.net.

BARBARA DAFOE WHITEHEAD and DAVID POPENOE, "Who Wants to Marry a Soul Mate?" from *The State of Our Unions 2001: The Social Health of Marriage in America*. Piscataway, NJ: The National Marriage Project, Rutgers, June 2001, pp. 6–16. Copyright © 2001 David Popenoe and Barbara Dafoe Whitehead. All rights reserved. Reprinted with permission.

Photo Credits

Page 4: Fig. 1.1, The J. Paul Getty Museum, Villa Collection, Malibu, California; © The J. Paul Getty Museum; **6:** © The Art Archive/Corbis; **25:** © Bill Aron/Photo Edit; **39** (top & bottom), © Chris Rainer/Getty Images; **48:** © Reuters/Corbis; **Color Insert:** C-1 © Image courtesy of The Advertising Archives; C-2 © U.S. Postal Service/AP/Wide World Photos; C-3 Holzman & Kaplan Worldwide, Bret Wills, photographer; C-4 © Louis Vuitton; C-5 © Geek Squad/Best Buy Inc.; C-6 By permission of Leagas Delaney, Inc., for Adidas. Adidas has not authorized, sponsored, endorsed, or approved this publication and is not responsible for it's contents; C-7 © AP Photo/Seth Wenig; C-8 © Frances Fife/AFP/Getty Images; **68:** Courtesy of the Department of Defense; **69** (top): © Barbara Alper/Stock Boston; **69** (bottom): © Richard Pasley/Stock Boston; **70:** © Bruce Young/Reuters/Corbis; **72** (top): © Anthony Suau 2006; **72** (bottom): © Marco Di Lauro/Getty Images; **144, 145, and 149:** © Carolyn Channell; **162:** © John Engstead/Hulton Archive/Getty Images; **195:** © Tim Boyle/Getty Images; **213:** © Kathy Willens/AP/Wide World Photos; **245:** © Liz Mangelsdorf/San Francisco Chronicle/Corbis;

252: © Gene Herrick/AP/Wide World Photos; **253:** © Flip Schulke/Corbis; **287:** © Bettmann/Corbis; **327** (top & bottom), **328** (top & bottom): © Michael Maloney/San Francisco Chronicle/Corbis; **366:** Copyright (1990) Mazda Motor of America, Inc. Used by permission; **374:** © Keith Bedford/Reuters; **382** (left): © Ho New/Reuters; **382** (right): © Maria Jose Zubillaga/AP Wide World Photos; **383:** © Image courtesy of The Advertising Archives; **395:** © Image courtesy of The Advertising Archives; **422:** © Jodi Cobb/National Geographic Image Collection; **446:** © Antonio Canova/The Bridgeman Art Library/Getty Images; **447:** © Robert Doisneau/Hachette Photos Presse; **450** (top): © Camerique/American Stock Photography; **450** (bottom): © Everett Collection; **452:** © Jim Goldberg/Magnum Photos; **479:** © Kimberly White/Corbis; **492:** NASA; **496** (top): © Richard Michael Pruitt/Dallas Morning News; **492** (bottom): © McGraw-Hill Companies, Inc./ photographer, David C. Johnson; **499** (top): © AP Photo/McIntyre 1939, R. D. Karpilo 2005, Courtesy of the National Park Service; **499** (bottom): © AP Photo/McIntyre 1939, R. D. Karpilo 2005, Courtesy of the National Park Service; **515:** fuel cell bus, © Koichi Kamoshida/Getty Images; hybrid car, © David Paul Morris/Getty Images; solar panels, © Mark Segal/Getty Images RF; geothermal station, © Photodisc/Getty Images RF; Chicago rooftop, Courtesy of City of Chicago, Mark Farina; light-bulbs, © William Thomas Cain/Getty Images; fuel cell, © Joe Raedle/Getty Images; **534:** © Stockbyte/Punchstock; **548 and 549:** © Jean Twenge, San Diego State University; **562:** © Anthony Suau 2006; **561:** © PictureHistory; **566:** Courtesy www.printsofpropaganda.com. **596:** © Yuri Kozyrev; **599:** © Patrick Sison/AP/Wide World Photos; **600** (top): © Stan Honda/AFP/AP/Getty Images; **600** (bottom): © Cheryl Diaz Meyer/Dallas Morning Star; **601** (top): © Ali Haider/AP/WideWorld Photos; **601** (bottom left): © Cheryl Diaz Meyer/Dallas Morning Star; **601** (bottom right): © Ho/AFP/Getty Images; **602:** © Davor Kovacevic/AP/WideWorld Photos; **603** (top): © Adel Hana/AP Images; **603** (bottom): © Mohammed Adnan/AP Images; **622:** © Rodrigo Abd/AP Images; **643** (top): © Heidi Levine/SIPA; **643** (bottom left): © Getty Images; **643** (bottom right): © Newscom.com; **652:** © Peter Macdiarmid/Reuters/Corbis.

INDEX

Note: Pages on which a term is defined are in bold type.